Indigenous and Tribal Peoples and Cancer

Gail Garvey
Editor-in-Chief

Indigenous and Tribal Peoples and Cancer

with Linda Burhansstipanov, Lea Bill,
Nina Scott, and Lisa Whop

Editor-in-Chief
Gail Garvey
Brisbane, QLD, Australia

ISBN 978-3-031-56805-3 ISBN 978-3-031-56806-0 (eBook)
https://doi.org/10.1007/978-3-031-56806-0

Cover Credit to Craig Carson and Colleen Lourenco.

This Springer imprint is published by the registered company Springer Nature Switzerland AG
The registered company address is: Gewerbestrasse 11, 6330 Cham, Switzerland

Foreword: Too Tough for Our Own Good

Archie Roach in Conversation with Louis Irving (recorded in 2016)

Archie Roach AC (1956–2022) was a Gundtijmara and Bundjalung Elder, much-loved singer-songwriter, and Aboriginal activist who was diagnosed with lung cancer in 2011. His doctor, respiratory specialist Associate Professor Louis Irving spoke to Archie about his experiences with the health system at a plenary session of the inaugural World Indigenous Cancer Conference (Brisbane, Australia, 2016) (Fig. 1). Here, we include excerpts from their conversation to set the tone for the chapters that follow.

Lou — Lung cancer is … almost twice as common in Indigenous people in Australia, and the outcomes are worse. I wanted to use Archie's story to highlight that, but more importantly moving forward [to think] about how all of us deal with issues. Archie … are you OK talking about your own health issues?

Archie — … it's different to talking about your music and your songs and where you come from. … The biggest barrier [to addressing health issues] I think is that I'm an Aboriginal man. What I mean by that is we're too tough for our own good. It reminds me of the Monty Python film *The Holy Grail*. The black knight … he cuts off his arm and he says, "oh it's just a scratch." It's like that … when it comes to health, not just myself, most of my cousins, brothers, uncles, we suffer in silence and we don't want to talk about what we might be going through if there's any problems or issues.

Fig. 1 Uncle Archie Roach and Dr Louis Irving in conversation at the 2016 World Indigenous Cancer Conference

Archie I noticed that things weren't quite right, with my breathing in particular. I had troubles with my breathing and walking long distances. … I chose to ignore it. … It'll be right you know. Give it a few days or a week or so. It'll be sweet. I'll come good.

Lou Eventually you did get to see the doctor. You have a good local GP. … Has there always been trust or is that something you've had to develop over time?

Archie … I had to develop [trust] … there's always been a mistrust of doctors. Most people in society … health, law, whatever, you don't you tend [to trust] because of what's happened to us in the past. You tend to mistrust people. … It's something I had to develop through the years. Now I realize there are good people out there, especially good doctors … [who] have been educated and have worked with Aboriginal people and understand the … problems we have.

Lou Archie was found to have a lump in his lung and luckily it was localized. He was referred to a tertiary center in Melbourne. … I was asked to see Archie as to whether his lungs would be strong enough for surgery. … I distinctly remember our first meeting. Archie was sitting in a chair and there were a number of doctors in the room. There was an x-ray … a lot of talking … but Archie wasn't engaging and I was struck by the fact that there are parallel worlds. … It took a couple of weeks for me to understand there was more to Archie than a spot on his lung.

Archie It wasn't by my prompting that we first noticed the lump. … Jill Shelton my manager who went behind my back …

Archie [In that meeting] I was listening to all this medical talk about the lungs … whether it should be radiotherapy or an operation. … I remember just thinking, actually … maybe we'll just leave it and don't worry about it at all. That's what I actually thought. I don't know why. Because of things from the past. … I thought I went through a lot of trouble, and heartache and pain, being taken away as a kid, jails, institutions, homelessness, alcoholism, you know. And [I'd] come good. I got through that and dealt with it. Sobered up. Got my life together. Straightened out. I had a good couple of years of life. I'm grateful for those years that I had. And I just thought maybe it's time to go. That's what I actually thought.

Archie … your family is that important. It doesn't matter what you're going through personally in your life, physically or mentally. Your mind is constantly on your family and just making sure that they're all right. That's the way we are. So there was a responsibility to family and community. … what will happen if I go through with this?

Lou You were there because Jill had insisted you go through with the x-ray … and you were concerned about what was going to happen to the rest of the family if something happened to you. … And you also asked the question whether you'd be able to sing after the operation.

Archie That was most important to me, because if I couldn't sing anymore, it definitely wouldn't have been worth it. Whatever time I had left … [if] the cancer grew, at least I could go out singing, which I wanted to do. … I was worried about that because it was a lung – whether it would affect my singing.

Lou Archie had successful treatment, but has been left with a significant disability. … the size of your lungs is smaller. Has it been worth it?

Archie At first I didn't think so. … I still have problems and I carry oxygen with me. … [But] living with this is … better than the alternative. Today, I wouldn't be here … I've been incapacitated but I deal with it, I manage it as best I can. … The interesting thing about singing is that you utilize your lungs a lot more efficiently when you're singing and you're using different muscles. If I just walked around singing all the time I'd probably be OK. … But people would look at [me] oddly. Is that guy all right?

Lou What other techniques do you do to maintain meaning in life?

Archie [I've learned] to take some time for [myself] – some "me" time. … It's more than a cliché, it's true. You have to find time for yourself, and have that time and give yourself some space. … Music is always … an important part of my continual healing. Going back to Killarney, a place about 3 or 4 hours southwest Melbourne near the coast, a beautiful part of the world. Sitting outside there on the deck just looking at the birds. … Things like that. Nature, Country, [they] keep me.

Lou Archie is the only patient that I've met with cancer who hasn't asked me how long he's got. … You seem to live in the present.

Archie I don't like to project too much. Each moment is that important. If I don't take the time to live in that moment, you know, you just miss it. There's so many things you miss. …

Lou Last night [I was talking to someone] about the pressures on healthcare workers and the fact that we've got so little time to spend with our patients. I've come across the concept of the golden rule and the platinum rule. The golden rule is what we all grew up with as healthcare workers, to treat other people as we'd like to be treated ourselves. But the platinum rule is to treat people the way they'd like to be treated. But in order to practice the platinum rule, you need time to get to know the person and understand what their value systems are and what their belief systems are. And you need to do that before bad things happen, because when bad things happen it's very hard to start from the beginning and get to know the person. I mention this because I've spent a lot of time with Archie and I've learned a lot about the platinum rule. Different people have different views on life, and it's certainly enhanced my understanding. Archie, do you feel … empowered to be able to express what you believe, or do you believe there are pressures … to do what the system wants you to do?

Archie I feel quite free now to talk to health workers and anyone in the profession. … Sometimes I don't ask questions and I just leave it up to the professional and their opinion. But I feel that I can ask the questions and explain to people how I feel about things. It's not like it was years ago. It's a lot easier now to talk about my health. … … Sometimes I'm afforded the type of treatment I get because of my name. My countrymen are not afforded the same respect. And that makes me wild.

Preface

Indigenous and Tribal Peoples and Cancer aims to provide an overview of cancer and Indigenous and Tribal peoples—from prevention and diagnosis to treatment and cancer care. It considers cancer incidence, mortality, prevalence, survival, and inequities for Indigenous and Tribal peoples globally. Most importantly, it extends beyond issues and challenges, to offer an Indigenous-knowledges, strengths-based approach to successful health interventions, research projects, research translation, and living well—both with and beyond cancer. It incorporates contributions from 223 individual authors, whose knowledge spans a wide range of disciplines and experiences. Some of the contributions are highly personal, while others report on the latest science and issues for the future.

This book was the vision of Professor Gail Garvey AM, and the need for a book of this type was originally developed in discussions with Dr Brenda Elias at the 23rd World Cancer Congress (WCC) held in Melbourne, Australia, in 2014. This was apt, as the WCC supports the Union for International Cancer Control mission to "unite and support the cancer community to reduce the global cancer burden, to promote greater equity, and to ensure that cancer control continues to be a priority in the world health and development agenda" (see https://www.uicc.org/who-we-are/about-uicc). That mission captures the central purpose of this book, with a focus on Indigenous and Tribal peoples globally.

Originally, this book was seen as a vehicle for raising awareness, improving understanding, and stimulating international action about the impact of cancer and the social inequities facing Indigenous and Tribal peoples. The idea was further developed through discussions with colleagues across the globe. *Indigenous and Tribal Peoples and Cancer* began to take shape in early 2023. In May 2023, the co-editors met at the Hawai'i Cancer Center for a week-long workshop to refine the book's outline and issue an international call for contributions. We also made a key decision: that every chapter in this book must include collaboration with an Indigenous or Tribal author.[1] What followed was an overwhelming response from cancer researchers, health practitioners, policy makers, and individuals with lived experience of cancer who were keen to be part of this collection. The resulting collection will enhance global efforts to reduce the burden of cancer for Indigenous and Tribal communities across the world.

The book's foreword includes excerpts from a moving conversation in 2016 between the Late Uncle Archie Roach (a Gunditjmara and Bundjalung Elder, Australian singer-songwriter, and Aboriginal activist) and his clinician at that time Dr Louis Irving (Respiratory Physician). The conversation captures several key principles of patient-centered care, which prioritizes the individual needs, preferences, and values of patients, and emphasizes collaboration between healthcare providers and patients to make informed decisions. Patient-centered care and participant-centered research are foundational concepts for this book.

The introductory chapter provides an orientation for the discussion that follows. It addresses three main topics: who are Indigenous and Tribal peoples, key factors affecting the health and wellbeing of Indigenous and Tribal peoples, and data about cancer outcomes.

The 76 chapters that follow are clustered into seven parts:

[1]The editors accepted two personal stories from non-Indigenous health practitioners; 75 of the 77 chapters that follow include at least one Indigenous or Tribal author.

- Part I, *Partnerships and Collaborations*, highlights the importance of local community leadership to ensure programs are culturally appropriate. It discusses several successful interventions, including community–academic partnerships, patient navigation, culturally appropriate screening, and international networks to support the Indigenous health workforce.
- Part II, *Policies and Systems*, addresses key issues relevant to data collection and reporting, including cancer registries globally. It also describes the policy environment informing cancer control programs in some nations.
- Part III, *Communication and Resources*, includes examples of programs that provide accessible, high-quality, culturally responsive health information for optimal and equitable cancer care. It presents examples of research and programming that support clinicians to obtain knowledge about culturally responsive and appropriate programs and resources.
- Part IV, *Prevention and Early Detection*, provides key examples of prevention, early detection, and screening programs designed to improve outcomes for Indigenous and Tribal peoples.
- Part V, *Cancer Services and Cancer Care*, discusses important topics about holistic views of health and wellbeing, including the application of Indigenous and Tribal knowledges and the psychosocial aspects of cancer care. The chapters provide clear guidance and wisdom for improving cancer outcomes.
- Part VI, *Research*, discusses innovative approaches to improving cancer outcomes in Indigenous and Tribal communities, ranging from international collaborations to highly local, community-led interventions. A consistent theme across this section is the need for genuine co-design with the people most affected by the research or program being developed.
- Part VII, *Clinical Trials and Genomics*, addresses the challenges of increasing the participation of Indigenous and Tribal peoples in cancer clinical trials, and discusses concerns about data erasure, developments in genomics, and the emergence of personalized medicine.

Brisbane, QLD, Australia Gail Garvey

Our Cover Artwork

The illustration on the book's cover includes a dove, which represents hope, transformation, love, compassion, and kindness to people in times of difficult transition. The designs on the dove represent the many Indigenous peoples who collaborated to produce this book. The designs also show the flow of culture and peace, with resilience and strength displayed within the bird's wings. The dove carries a lavender ribbon in its beak, representing support for those living with all types of cancer. The illustration is inspired by artworks used by the Indigenous peoples of Australia, Aotearoa New Zealand, Canada, and the USA. Cover illustration by Craig Carson, Wakka Wakka, with graphic design support by Colleen Lourenco.

Acknowledgments

The outline and vision for this book were finalized at a week-long editorial meeting hosted by the Hawai'i Cancer Center in May 2023. Not only is Hawai'i a central place for editors from Australia, Aotearoa New Zealand, Canada, and the USA to meet, it is a welcoming and culturally affirming location to discuss issues relevant for Indigenous and Tribal peoples. In Hawai'i, we discussed our vision and issued a global call for contributions. We are deeply grateful to Professor Neal Palafox, Dr Marjorie K Leimomi Mala Mau, Dr Dee-Ann Carpenter, and their colleagues at the University of Hawai'i for the time they contributed to the project and the knowledge they shared with us. We also thank Mavis Nita for her tireless support during the long days of our meetings and Myra Ruka for her generous and thoughtful contributions.

Several individuals supported the production of this book. Dr Judy Gregory (The University of Queensland) provided exceptional support, project management, and copy editing. Colleen Lourenco (The University of Queensland) provided graphic design support. Craig Carson developed the design for our stunning cover. Key administrative support was provided by Alison Karsh (The University of Queensland), Tina Hamilton (Te Aka Whai Ora, Māori Health Authority), and Gina Rodriguez (Aberta First Nations Information Governance Centre).

The National Health and Medical Research Council Indigenous-led Centre of Research Excellence in Targeted Approaches to Improve Cancer Services for Aboriginal and Torres Strait Islander Australians (TACTICS) supported the editorial meetings and project staff.

We thank the 223 individuals who contributed to the content of this book. Thank you for sharing your knowledge, expertise, and wisdom.

We also acknowledge the organizations that supported Open Access publication of this book, including The University of Queensland, TACTICS, Te Aka Whai Ora (Māori Health Authority), and Hei Āhuru Mōwai (Māori Cancer Leadership Aotearoa).

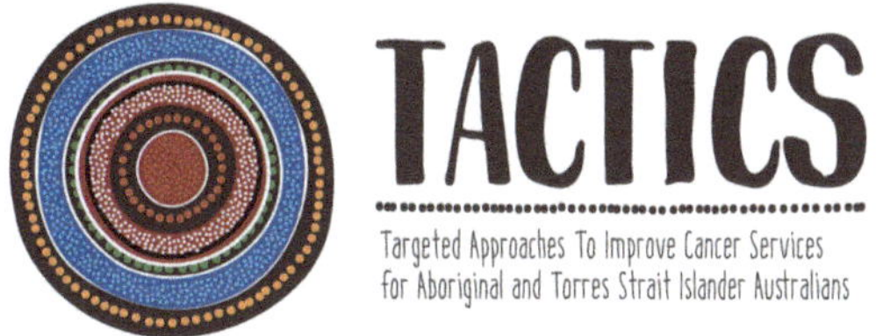

Contents

Part VII Clinical Trials and Genomics

About the Contributors

Anna Adcock (Māori—Ngāti Mutunga), is a researcher and doctoral student in Te Tātai Hauora o Hine National Centre for Women's Health Research Aotearoa, Victoria University of Wellington. Anna does Kaupapa Māori (by Māori, for Māori) research that centers the lived experiences and perspectives of whānau (Māori family collectives).

Sheikh Iqbal Ahamed is Founding Chair and Wehr Professor of Computer Science and director of Ubicomp lab at Marquette University, USA. He is a senior member of IEEE, ACM, and the IEEE Computer Society. His research interests include mHealth, security and privacy in pervasive computing, affective computing, and non-invasive computing.

Tira Albert Tribal affiliations—Te Whānau-A-Apanui, Ngāti-Rahiri me Te Waipounamu. Tira Albert has extensive experience in Māori health promotion, specializing in equity and providing Māori specific cancer support services. She was primary investigator for the first Indigenous cancer program for Aotearoa using Mātauranga Māori pūrakau (traditional Indigenous stories) Te Mauri.

Kate Anderson is a non-Indigenous Senior Research Fellow in the First Nations Cancer and Wellbeing Research Program at the University of Queensland who has worked in collaboration with Indigenous Australian researchers and communities for more than 15 years across the areas of cancer, kidney disease, and wellbeing.

Amanda Andrew is a white settler with mixed European ancestry. As a Research and Project Coordinator in the Department of Health at the Métis Nation of Alberta, she supports research development to enhance the cancer journey of Métis Albertans by centering their cancer care experiences and self-determined priorities.

J. Anitha is a PhD scholar at Meenakshi Academy of Higher Education and Research, Chennai, in India.

Te Hao Apaapa-Timu Tauranga Moana, Ngāti Pōrou, Ngāti Kahungunu currently works as a researcher in the Te Aka Whai Ora Māori Health Authority in Aotearoa. She is a public health and Kaupapa Māori researcher who is undertaking her PhD on Māori ethics in clinical research.

Sandra Avery has been with South Western Sydney LHD Cancer Services since 2002 and manages strategic planning and implementation, provides innovation and change management, and applies her experience to reducing clinical variation. She has contributed to the development and implementation of patient reported outcome measures.

Peter Baade is a cancer epidemiologist and biostatistician at Cancer Council Queensland, with two decades of experience leading a research program aiming to quantify the impact of cancer among the Australian population, in particular the inequalities by geographical location, cultural, and population subgroups.

Reagan Bartel is a proud Métis-settler woman and the Director of Health for the Métis Nation of Alberta (MNA). In her role, Reagan focuses on ensuring that Métis stories, experiences, and perceptions given to the MNA are incorporated into health advocacy, policy, programs, and services.

Siddhartha Baxi is a radiation oncologist with GenesisCare Gold Coast, with links to Griffith University and Menzies School of Health Research. He is an advocate of equity and access to quality radiation oncology in regional and remote Australia, and a clinical reference expert for a Human Research Ethics Committee.

Sewunet Admasu Belachew is a Postdoctoral Research Fellow in the First Nations Cancer and Wellbeing Research Program at The University of Queensland, and has diverse research interests encompassing cancer and antimicrobial research.

Ryan Benavente was born and raised in Honolulu, O'ahu. The son of a Filipino immigrant and a CHamoru native, he was inspired by his family's health experiences and aims to increase healthcare accessibility across the Pacific. He is currently a second-year medical student at Harvard Medical School.

Stéphane Bertani is a molecular biologist at the French National Research Institute for Sustainable Development (IRD), who has led programs on cancer in Andean-Amazonian Indigenous peoples and the anthropo-environmental risk factors associated with it. In 2022, he co-founded the International Joint Laboratory of Molecular Anthropological Oncology (LOAM) at Instituto Nacional de Enfermedades Meoplasicas (INEN) in Peru.

Lea Bill (Pelican Lake First Nation, Saskatchewan). Lea's maternal grandmother, a Cree midwife, instilled a life-long healing foundation, leading to a 35-year career as a registered nurse. Recognized as a leader in language-based cultural research methodologies and practice, Lea works with Knowledge Holders/Practitioners to guide Indigenous-led cancer research.

Habtamu Mellie Bizuayehu is a Postdoctoral Research Fellow in the First Nations Cancer and Wellbeing Research Program at The University of Queensland, working on cancer epidemiology and screening among Indigenous peoples. He has a broad range of research interests in cancer epidemiology.

Jenny Brands is an experienced implementation scientist whose expertise is in drawing together complex facets of context, evidence, and human behavior to identify feasible and effective ways to bring about improvements in Australian health systems/services and improve access to culturally appropriate quality healthcare for First Nations peoples.

Kathryn L. Braun served as Research Director and Co-PI of ʻImi Hale Native Hawaiian Cancer Network from 2000 to 2017. She is Professor and Barbara Cox Anthony Endowed Chair of Aging at the University of Hawaiʻi. Her current research focuses on documenting Native Hawaiian stories of struggle, resilience, and meaning.

Peter Brett is a Board-Certified Medical Oncologist. He did his oncology fellowship at the National Institutes of Health and practiced medical oncology in Northern California until 2019. Since 2019 he's lived and worked in the Commonwealth of the Northern Mariana Islands (CNMI) providing oncology care with an oncology team to the largely underserved population.

Tegan Brock is a fifth-generation Canadian with French, British, and Norwegian settler ancestry and raised in Tkaronto, Ontario. She is committed to health promotion and harm reduction within Métis and First Nation communities and populations. Tegan is the Senior Health Research Manager for the Métis Nation–Saskatchewan government.

Alex Brown is the Professor of Indigenous Genomics at Telethon Kids Institute and Australian National University. He is an internationally leading Aboriginal clinician/researcher (Yuin Nation) in Aboriginal health. His research aims to build Indigenous leadership in genomic and data sciences, precision health, and ethics.

Amanda Bruegl is a citizen of Oneida Nation and is Associate Director of the Education Core for the Northwest Native American Center of Excellence, Associate Professor and Vice Chair for Diversity, Equity and Inclusion in the Department of Obstetrics and Gynaecology at Oregon Health and Science University School of Medicine.

Victor and Sophie Bruno are a Nehiyaw (Cree) couple from the Samson Cree Nation #137, Maskwacis, Alberta, Canada. As cultural leaders, they work tirelessly to transfer ancestral knowledge systems within all settings to promote wellbeing and Pimatisiwin (Way of Life). They are dedicated to advancing First Nations cancer research.

Jessica Buck is a Kamilaroi woman and an early career postdoctoral researcher in the Brain Tumour Research team at the Telethon Kids Institute. Her research focuses on developing more effective and less toxic treatments for childhood brain cancer, and improving outcomes for Indigenous children with cancer.

Amy Budrikis is a wadjela (non-Indigenous) Research Adviser at Kurongkurl Katitjin, Edith Cowan University. She has a broad range of research interests from language revitalization and historical linguistics to public health and social change.

Meredith Burgess is a member of the First Nations Cancer and Wellbeing Research Program, the University of Queensland, and project manager for the Pathways to Healthy Hearts after Cancer for All (Healthy Hearts) project. Her research focus span broadly across areas of health equity.

Linda Burhansstipanov (Cherokee Nation) taught at California State University, Long Beach (CSULB) and University of California, Los Angeles (UCLA) full and part-time from 1971 to 1989. She worked for the National Cancer Institute (NCI) and the AMC Cancer Center and founded Native American Cancer Research Corporation, a community-based organization, and Native American Cancer Initiatives, Incorporated, a minority woman–owned business.

Tamara Butler is an Undumbi woman and a National Health and Medical Research Council Emerging Research Fellow in the First Nations Cancer and Wellbeing Research Program at the University of Queensland. Her research is focused on improving gynecological cancer outcomes for Indigenous Australians.

Tom Calma AO is an Aboriginal Elder from the Kungarakan tribal group and a member of the Iwaidja tribal group whose traditional lands are south west of Darwin and on the Cobourg Peninsula in the Northern Territory of Australia, respectively.

Jessica K. Cameron is a Research Fellow at Cancer Council Queensland, with adjunct positions at Queensland University of Technology and the University of Queensland. Her research has involved statistical modeling to reveal health inequalities and communicating the complex and nuanced results to diverse audiences.

Nadine R. Caron is a mother, daughter, sister, member of the Sagamok Anishnawbek First Nation, practicing surgeon, Professor (UBC), Senior Scientist (Canada's Michael Smith Genome Sciences Centre, BC Cancer), First Nations Health Authority Chair in Cancer/Wellness at UBC, and Director of UBC's Centre for Excellence in Indigenous Health.

Dee-Ann Leialoha Carpenter is Native Hawaiian Board-Certified Internal Medicine physician and Associate Professor at the University of Hawai'i, John A Burns School of Medicine (JABSOM), Department of Native Hawaiian Health and Office of Medical Education. She is an award-winning teacher and Robert Wood Johnson Foundation Clinical Scholar.

Sandro Casavilca-Zambrano is a pathologist specializing in oncology at the National Cancer Institute of Peru (INEN). He has established the National Cancer Research Biobank of Peru, a facility dedicated to collecting biological samples and data from Peruvian cancer patients, particularly those from the local Indigenous communities.

Andrea Casey is an Aboriginal woman with a strong family history of breast cancer and was diagnosed with breast cancer at 48 years of age.

Kevin Cassel is the Faculty Director of the Community Outreach and Engagement Office at the University of Hawai'i Cancer Center. He has conducted a number of intervention studies with Native Hawaiian and Pacific Islander populations that have addressed topics including colon cancer prevention, skin cancer prevention, and clinical trial participation.

Juan Pablo Cerapio is a molecular biologist and bioinformatician at the Cancer Research Center of Toulouse (CRCT). He conducted an integrative genomics study of the molecular subtype of liver cancer developed by Native Andean individuals. His research focuses on the transcriptomic and epigenetic aspects of virus-associated cancers.

Melissa Cernigoy is a Manager, Research and Innovation at the Canadian Partnership Against Cancer, and works with partners to advance First Nations, Inuit, and Métis–governed research and data systems.

Jessica Chan is a settler (Chinese heritage), radiation oncologist at BC Cancer Vancouver, and Clinical Assistant Professor in the Department of Surgery at UBC. Her research focuses on assessing and addressing cancer system inequities, particularly in high-income countries and in collaboration with Indigenous peoples.

Chitraa R. Chandran is a periodontist with 40 years' teaching and clinical experience. She spent more than 20 years as the Dean of a dentistry school. She has made numerous contributions to the dental community and has a stellar track record of enhancing the oral health of rural Indians.

Alwin Chong is a Wakamin man from Far North Queensland, and Director of Arney Chong Consulting. He has over 35 years' research experience in senior management roles. He is a member of the National Health and Medical Research Council (NHMRC) Australian Health Ethics Committee, The Principal Committee Indigenous Caucus, and the Australian Institute of Aboriginal and Torres Strait Islander Studies (AIATSIS) Human Research Ethics Committee.

Kristin Cina is a Lead Research Associate for Walking Forward and has worked for the program since 2004. She has been the Community Research Representative serving the American Indian population in Rapid City since 2011. Her roles have included community cancer educator and tobacco treatment specialist.

Justine R. Clark is an Adnyamathanha woman and early career postdoctoral researcher with the Indigenous Genomics Team at Telethon Kids Institute. Her research aims to utilize genomics-guided precision cancer medicine to alleviate the burden of cancer on Indigenous Australians, their families, and their communities.

Michele Connolly enrolled member of the Blackfeet Nation in Montana, worked as a mathematical statistician in federal agencies (e.g., Office of the Secretary, Department of Health and Human Services, US Government (DHHS), with White House assignments). She is Co-Chair, International Group for Indigenous Health Measurement; her research focuses on measurement/survey data and American Indians/Alaska Natives.

Mackenzie K. Connon is a fourth-generation Canadian settler who graduated from the University of Northern British Columbia (BHSc in Biomedical Studies, minoring in First Nations Studies). She is a University of British Columbia medical student of the Northern Medical Program in Prince George, British Columbia.

Ali Coomber is Samoan and was diagnosed with breast cancer in 2021 at the age of 60.

Felina Cordova-Marks is a member of the Hopi Tribe, and an Assistant Professor in the Department of Health Promotion Sciences at the University of Arizona's Zuckerman College of Public Health. Her professional research interests include American Indian health, cancer, caregiving, and resilience.

Danica Cossio has 25 years' experience managing cancer information; she is Acting Senior Director of the Cancer Alliance Queensland, whose goal is accelerating cancer control, and chair of the Australasian Association of Cancer Registries. Danica focuses on developing innovative applications that support collection of information to improve cancer care.

Gordon and Doris Courtoreille are a dedicated Nehiyaw (Cree) couple and Knowledge Holders/Practitioners from the Swan River Band, Alberta, Canada, who advance land-based learning for youth and families. Gordon acquired medical plant knowledge in his youth, which he later applied to overcome cancer; he remains a role model and mentor.

Susanna M. Cramb is an NHMRC Emerging Leader Fellow and Principal Research Fellow at the Centre for Healthcare Transformation, Queensland University of Technology. Leading the Health Equity Research with Outcomes (HERO) group, her research investigates location-based inequities for injuries and diseases in Queensland and across Australia.

Taylor James Cromarty is the Research Management Lead of the CAN*Help* Working Group at the University of Alberta. He facilitates research activities to address health concerns of communities engaged in partnerships with the research team. He has several years' experience supporting community-driven projects in Indigenous communities in Canada.

Joan Cunningham is a social epidemiologist and Senior Principal Research Fellow at the Menzies School of Health Research, Charles Darwin University. She is a member of the Centre of Research Excellence in Targeted Approaches to Improve Cancer Services for Aboriginal and Torres Strait Islander Australians (TACTICS CRE) executive committee and an award-winning mentor, supervisor, and researcher in Aboriginal and Torres Strait Islander health and wellbeing.

Paramita Dasgupta is a Research Fellow at Cancer Council Queensland. She has extensive experience in the analysis and reporting of cancer registry-based data, including using complex statistical models to look at geographical and spatial variations in cancer outcomes and quantifying survival differences across population groups.

May Rose Dela Cruz worked at ʻImi Hale Native Hawaiian Cancer Network (2012–2018) and is affiliated with the University of Hawaiʻi and the Hawaiʻi Public Health Institute. She incorporates community-based participatory research that focuses on health disparities in Hawaiʻi's Filipino community, vaccine-preventable cancers, and COVID-19 community outreach.

Wayne Denning is Birri and Guugu Yimidhirr man who seeks to make a real difference to the lives of First Nations Australians through storytelling and creativity. After more than a decade of working on Australian government policies in Native Title and Land Rights, Wayne launched Carbon Creative.

Haryana Dhillon co-leads the Survivorship Research Group at the University of Sydney. Haryana has more than 25 years' experience in cancer clinical research across a range of investigator-initiated cancer clinical trials. Haryana's research interests encompass cancer survivorship, health literacy, and interventions for survivorship, symptom management, and psycho-oncology.

Abbey Diaz is a non-Indigenous epidemiologist researcher and cancer research group lead of the First Nations Cancer and Wellbeing Research Program, the University of Queensland. Her research program focuses on health equity and the impact of comorbidity in cancer.

Mark B. Dignan is a Professor at the University of Kentucky. He has led and participated in cancer control research for over 30 years and has extensive experience with efforts to increase screening rates for breast, cervical, and lung cancer among American Indian and Alaska Native populations.

Joanne Doherty is a writer and researcher who belongs to Hei Āhuru Mōwai (Māori Cancer Leadership Board) and Te Mauri whānau, and is committed to equity-based cancer outcomes for whanau Māori. Joanne lives on Wellington Harbour, loves her 14 mokopuna, and belongs to Te Wakaiti in South Wairarapa.

Andrea (Andi) Dwyer is a Program Director at the University of Colorado and a co-investigator on grants focusing on health equity and sustainability strategies for cancer prevention. Andrea is on the board of the Alliance of Community Health Workers (CHWs), Patient Navigators (PNs) and Promotores De Salud (PdS), Academy of Oncology Nurse & Patient Navigators (AONN+) and Chair of the National Navigation Roundtable.

Ria Earp (Ngāti Pikiao, Ngāti Whakaue) was a long-time senior manager in the New Zealand public service, including a national focus on Māori Health. She was a Chief Executive at Mary Potter Hospice (Wellington) for over a decade before retiring. Ria is now working on governance and Māori Health Service advice roles.

Sonya Egert is a Noonuccal Goenpul woman, living and working on Yuggera Country in Inala, Queensland. She previously worked at the Southern Queensland Centre of Excellence in Aboriginal and Torres Strait Islander Primary Health Care and coordinated the Inala Community Jury. Sonya is now CEO at Inala Wangarra.

Elaina Elder-Robinson is a non-Indigenous research assistant in the First Nations Cancer and Wellbeing Research Program at the University of Queensland, and a Clinical Dietitian at the Institute for Urban Indigenous Health.

Vanessa Eldridge (Rongomaiwahine, Ngāti Kahungunu mai i te whānau Te Rito) has a background in nursing. She has developed programs relating to loss and grief and compassionate communities. She contributes to national strategy, resources, and frameworks. She is Director of Health Equity at Mary Potter Hospice, Wellington, Aotearoa.

Jaklin A. Eliott has extensive experience in designing and conducting qualitative research, particularly examining perceptions and experiences of serious illness, palliative care, and death and dying. Jaklin collaborates with diverse stakeholders across the healthcare spectrum, including psychology, public health, palliative care, qualitative research, sociology, bioethics, and clinical ethics.

Jacinta Elston is a cancer survivor and Aboriginal woman from Queensland with global experience in Indigenous health and expertise in higher education and leadership. She was the first Aboriginal person appointed to the Cancer Australia Advisory Board in 2011, and Chair of Cancer Australia's Leadership Group from 2015 to 2021.

Marc Emerson is an Assistant Professor in the Department of Epidemiology at Gillings School of Global Public Health, University of North Carolina at Chapel Hill. His research focuses on integrating biological and socioecological perspectives in addressing cancer care disparities and access. He is Diné (Navajo) and Jemez from the Navajo Nation.

Michelle Erai Originally from Whangārei, Aotearoa New Zealand, Michelle graduated from Victoria University, Wellington. After several years Michelle moved to the USA where she completed a PhD and wrote her award-winning book *Girl of New Zealand: Colonial Optics in Aotearoa* (2020). Michelle's tribal affiliations are *Ngāpuhi* and Ngāti Wh*ātua.*

Jennifer Erdrich is Assistant Professor in the Division of Surgical Oncology at the University of Arizona College of Medicine–Tucson. Her operative specialties are breast cancer, melanoma, and sarcoma surgery. Her tribal affiliation is Turtle Mountain Ojibwe. Her professional interests include AI/AN multidisciplinary cancer care.

Kristine Falzon is a Gummeah, WandiWandian, Wodi Wodi, Walbunja Balaang (woman) who lives with family on her Nabu's (Grandmother's) Ngura (Country) in the Shoalhaven. She is Executive Manager, Waminda South Coast Women's Health and Wellbeing Aboriginal Corporation, and embeds cultural ways of knowing, being, and doing throughout education, health, and wellbeing.

Sam Faulkner is a Torres Strait Islander and Aboriginal woman from the Wuthuthi and Yadhaigana peoples, Cape York Peninsula and Badu and Moa Islands, Torres Strait. She has over 20 years' experience in the Australian Public Service and is Director of Indigenous Health Advice at the National Health and Medical Research Council.

Anna Fitzgerald is the Communications Manager at Breast Cancer Trials.

Linda Fleisher Research Professor at Fox Chase Cancer Center, has over 35 years' experience leading the National Cancer Institute's Regional Cancer Information Service, founding a state-level navigation network and designing/implementing navigation and technology interventions addressing health disparities. She served with AONN+ Leadership and is Vice-Chair of the ACS's National Navigation Roundtable.

Claudio Flores is an epidemiologist with expertise in prevention and cancer control. Claudio is a Visiting Professor at Universidad Peruana Cayetano Heredia (UPCH), Peru.

Kwun M. Fong is a Thoracic and Sleep Physician at The Prince Charles Hospital. He is the hospital's Clinical Manager of the Pulmonary Malignancy Unit and Director of the University of Queensland's Thoracic Research Centre, which undertakes genomic and translational research in lung diseases.

Delfin Lovelina Francis is a dental public health professional, certified tobacco counselor, chair of the executive committee mass tobacco awareness program among Indigenous people, and 2018 Fellow Cancer Prevention Summer Curriculum Fellow, National Cancer Institute, USA. The Limca Book of Records recognized her efforts in the first Tribal tobacco program in India.

Barbara Frazer (Big River First Nations, Saskatchewan) is an Indigenous Knowledge Systems researcher, curriculum developer, and writer. In her role and responsibility as an Elder's helper in Maskihkiya (traditional medicine) ways of being, Barbara was taught to serve the Creator and the whole community—the Cree way of life.

Marg Friesen is Minister of Health & Finance, a governing member of the Provincial Métis Council, Métis Nation–Saskatchewan, and Chairperson for Métis Addictions Council Saskatchewan Inc. She is a Métis woman from the Qu'Appelle Valley, part of the historical Métis Homeland.

Alana Gall is a Pakana woman from the north-east coast of Lutruwita (Tasmania) and a Research Fellow in the National Centre for Naturopathic Medicine at Southern Cross University. Her research focuses on the protection, preservation, and access of Indigenous Traditional Medicines for Indigenous Australians.

Tendani Gaolathe is an Internal Medicine physician and lecturer at the University of Botswana. As a clinician, she has managed public health programs and conducted observational and clinical trials related to the HIV/AIDS epidemic in Botswana since 2001.

Darren Garvey is a Senior Research Fellow in the First Nations Cancer and Wellbeing Research Program at the University of Queensland with matrilineal connections to the Torres Strait. He has over 30 years' teaching and research experience in Indigenous Social and Emotional Wellbeing, psychology, and health workforce development.

Gail Garvey is a proud Kamilaroi woman, a National Health and Medical Research Council Research Leadership Fellow, and Professor of Indigenous Health Research at the University of Queensland. She leads the First Nations Cancer and Wellbeing Research Program at the University of Queensland, which focuses on cancer and wellbeing research for Indigenous Australians.

Leonie Garvey is a proud Kamilaroi woman who manages the Greater Aboriginal Health Unit, Hunter New England Local Health District (New South Wales, Australia). Leonie's team works with key stakeholders across the district, providing cancer yarn ups and supporting people through their cancer journeys.

Janis Geary was the Scientific Director of the CAN*Help* Working Group. She has over a decade of experience establishing research partnerships between academic and community groups, and her publication record focuses on data governance inclusive of underrepresented groups and respects Indigenous data sovereignty.

Darren Germaine has been a registered nurse for 25 years and a Clinical Research Coordinator (CRC) for 17. Darren worked at Menzies School of Health Research as a Clinical Trial Manager (INFERR study). He currently works as a CRC in the Oncology/Haematology Clinical Trial Unit at Royal Darwin Hospital.

Elder Elmer Ghostkeeper was born on the Paddle Prairie Metis Settlement, in Alberta, and, speaks fluent Bushland Cree, Michif, and English. He holds a Bachelor of Arts in Anthropology, Master of Arts in Cultural Anthropology, Civil Engineering Technology Diploma, and Doctorate of Laws.

Rosamond Gilden is a Senior Implementation and Evaluation Project Officer for the SA Aboriginal Chronic Disease Consortium and Aboriginal and Torres Strait Islander Diabetes-related Foot Complications Program at Wardliparingga at South Australian Health and Medic al Research Institute. With degrees in Biomedical Science, Orthoptics, and Public Health, she is the DR-NET Regional Coordinator, South Pacific Region.

Megan Gimmen is Yapese, of the Indigenous people of Wa'ab, and was born and raised in Guåhan. She previously studied patient perspectives on cancer screening and spearfishing physiology. Megan is now a medical student at Harvard Medical School and is passionate about sustainable solutions for Pacific Islander health.

Karen J. Goodman is a Professor in the University of Alberta Department of Medicine and School of Public Health. She leads the Canadian North *Helicobacter pylori* (CAN*Help*) Working Group, a collaboration of Indigenous community leaders, healthcare providers, and academic researchers who conduct community-driven research focused on cancer prevention.

Nils Graber is a health anthropologist at the University of Lausanne. His research relates to patients' experiences, interprofessional relations, and participatory methods in oncology. His fieldwork has mainly taken place in Cuba and Switzerland. Nils is currently conceiving a new research project on indigeneity and cancer in the Peruvian Andes.

Kalinda Griffiths is a Yawuru woman and cancer epidemiologist, Director of Poche SA+NT at Flinders University, and Research & Education Lead for Aboriginal and Torres Strait Islander Health at Victorian Comprehensive Cancer Centre Alliance. Her research focuses on population-level data, Indigenous data governance, and health and research capabilities.

Kate M. Gunn having lived and worked in rural Australia, leads a team at University of South Australia who works with rural people to understand their health and mental health-related issues and co-develop meaningful solutions. Kate has particular interest in psycho-oncology and improving outcomes for rural people affected by cancer.

Jason Gurney (Ngāpuhi) is an epidemiologist and Director of the Cancer and Chronic Conditions (C3) Research Group at the University of Otago, Wellington, Aotearoa New Zealand. Jason is currently leading multiple national-level projects on equity in health outcomes for Indigenous Māori, with a focus on cancer.

Georgia Halkett holds a Cancer Council of WA Research Fellowship and is based at Curtin University. She practiced as a radiation therapist before moving into research focusing on people's lived experiences of radiation therapy. She contributed to the initial development and testing of the Radiation Therapy Talking Book.

Marissa Haring is an enrolled member of the Seneca Nation of Indians (Wolf Clan). She works as a Community Patient Navigator at Roswell Park Comprehensive Cancer Center's Department of Indigenous Cancer Health. She has a master's degree in Native American Leadership and a bachelor's degree in Community Health.

Rodney C. Haring is an enrolled member of the Seneca Nation of Indians (Beaver Clan), Chair of the Department of Indigenous Cancer Health at Roswell Park Comprehensive Cancer Center, and a former delegate on the US Department of Health and Human Services, American Indian and Alaska Native, Health Research Advisory Council.

Lisa Harjo member of the Choctaw Nation of Oklahoma, is Native Patient Navigator and Executive Director of Native American Cancer Research Corporation. She received her BS in Native American Education/Child Development from the University of California and MEd in Elementary Curriculum and Instruction from the University of Colorado.

Muhammad Haroon is a PhD student at the Centre for Health Services Research, The University of Queensland. He has 9 years' experience working in the creative industries as a visual communication designer. He holds a master's degree in computer science (medical image analysis) and a bachelor's degree in design.

Diane Harper is an internationally recognized physician–scientist whose work has changed cervical cancer prevention. She has authored publications on HPV vaccine efficacy and immunogenicity, worked to evolve screening techniques for cervical cancer, and is currently at the University of Michigan testing cures for HPV infection among her patients.

Joanne Hedges is a Yamatji woman and Director of the Indigenous Oral Health Unit at University of Adelaide. For 12 years she has been involved in oral health studies such as Indigenous early childhood caries, oropharyngeal cancer, and end-stage kidney disease. Joanne is passionate about improving health in Aboriginal communities.

Suzanne Held is a Professor at Montana State University. She has worked since 1996 as a non-Indigenous partner with the Messengers for Health program. Her interests are to work in partnerships to establish trust, share power, foster co-learning, and address community-identified health issues using strengths- and community-based approaches.

Kimiora Henare (Te Aupōuri, Te Rarawa) is a research fellow based at the University of Auckland with intersecting research interests in the tumor microenvironment, cancer immunology, genomics, bioethics, and Māori health. Dr Henare is also a member of Hei Āhuru Mōwai and a co-convener of SING-Aotearoa.

Whitney Ann E. Henry Tuscarora Nation (Deer Clan), is a resident of the Tuscarora Nation. She received her Bachelor of Science in Child and Family Studies from Syracuse University. She is an Indigenous patient navigator coordinator with the Department of Indigenous Cancer Health at Roswell Park.

Nicole Hewlett is a proud Palawa woman in the First Nations Cancer and Research Wellbeing Program and Child Health Research Centre, The University of Queensland. Nic has extensive experience in translating culturally responsive frameworks, strengths-based approaches, and wellbeing models into practice to create equitable access for Aboriginal and Torres Strait Islander peoples.

Paula Higuchi has worked at the University of Hawai'i Cancer Center for 25 years. She is the Administrative Director of the Community Outreach and Engagement Office. Higuchi has a broad background in social work with a concentration in gerontology community-based participatory research, and strategies to address cancer health disparities.

Leema A. Hiri is a professional educationist with a Bachelor of Education Science in Biology and a Master of Education, Science Education degree. He joined the University of Botswana in 2006 as an outreach officer and currently works as center administrator at the San Research Centre.

Felicia Schanche Hodge a Wailaki Indian, is UCLA Professor/Researcher of Nursing and Public Health. She heads the Center for American Indian/Indigenous Research and Education. She was a member of the NIH-NINR National Advisory Council and NIH Library of Medicine. She received the Frank C Dukepoo Award for research.

James Hofschneider is a Board-Certified Internist, and a Chamorro Pacific Islander, born on the island of Tinian in the Commonwealth of the Northern Mariana Islands. He did his medical residency at UC San Francisco. He has worked as an internist in the CNMI for many years and recently focused on providing care to people with cancer.

Ernest Holburt a graduate of Wayne State Medical School and Harvard School of Public Health, worked as a physician on the San Carlos Apache reservation, where he developed a coherent practice among physicians, established an air ambulance service, and worked with the CDC on enteric disease outbreaks.

Claire K. Hughes is a public health professional and retired registered dietitian with years of experience working in communities. As an expert on Hawaiian culture, Dr Hughes has created components of interventions to improve the health of Native Hawaiians specifically using diet and physical activity in a culturally grounded manner.

Peter Hutchinson is a Métis researcher working as an Assistant Professor in Indigenous Studies at the University of British Columbia, Canada, focused on increasing Indigenous knowledge within the Canadian cancer care system. Peter also works in chronic disease surveillance, HIV/AIDS, commercial tobacco use, and engaging in cultural health-promoting activities.

Shafkat Jahan is a Research Fellow in the First Nations Cancer and Wellbeing Research Program at The University of Queensland, specializing in assessing public health outcomes and environmental impacts. She focuses on vulnerability risk assessment and explores the financial costs of cancer in First Nations communities using linked administrative data.

Ashton James is a white settler with mixed European ancestry, and the Senior Manager of Health at the MNA. Ashton works to incorporate the stories and worldviews of Métis Albertans in health research, policy, and programming decisions, and to advocate for self-determined opportunities to advance Métis health and wellbeing.

Lisa Jamieson is a NHMRC Senior Research Fellow and Director of the Australian Research Centre for Population Oral Health and founder of the Indigenous Oral Health Unit at University of Adelaide. Lisa is recognized as a leading researcher in Indigenous oral health.

Parameswari Jayaraman is an Assistant Professor in the Department of Psychology, Periyar University, Salem, Tamil Nadu. She is from the Nilgiri district of Tamil Nadu and specializes in parent-child mental health. She has published over 40 research articles in national and international journals.

Mi Hye Jeon is a Master of Philosophy candidate in the First Nations Cancer and Wellbeing Research Program at The University of Queensland, focused on understanding and reducing exposure to modifiable risk factors associated with cardiovascular complications of breast cancer treatments.

Katrina Johnson is a Gooreng Gooreng woman and breast cancer survivor. She is Managing Director of MARKAT Enterprises (USA), Co-Director of the Master of Indigenous Business Leadership at Monash University, Teaching Fellow at Harvard University, and Cultural Advisor and Expert Reference Group member for *Our Mob and Cancer*.

Rachel Joyce is a proud Koorie person of Wayilwan descent, and stem cell/cancer biologist who works to identify novel treatments for lung cancer on Wurundjeri Country. They hold a Peeneeyt Thanampool Aunty Joan Vickery and Aunty Angela Clarke Indigenous Post-doctoral Fellowship at the University of Melbourne and Walter and Eliza Hall Institute of Medical Research.

Joseph Keawe'aimoku Kaholokula a clinical health psychologist, is chair of the Department of Native Hawaiian Health at the John A Burns School of Medicine. He has provided clinical services in community health centers, studied discrimination, stress, and health status among Native Hawaiians, and conducted interventions on topics important for Native Hawaiians.

Martina Leialoha Kamaka FAACP, is a Board-Certified Native Hawaiian Family Physician and currently an Associate Professor in the Department of Native Hawaiian Health at the University of Hawai'i, John A Burns School of Medicine. She holds leadership positions locally, nationally, and internationally in organizations seeking health equity for Indigenous populations.

Giam Kar was Practice Manager and Chief Radiation Therapist at Alan Walker Cancer Care Centre in Darwin until early 2023. He is passionate about improving cancer outcomes for Aboriginal people through healthcare initiatives and cancer education. He is a Director of Cancer Council Northern Territory and the Medical Radiation Practitioners Board of Australia.

Malina C. Kaulukukui retired from the University of Hawai'i School of Social Work. She is a cultural practitioner of traditional, family-based ho'oponopono (conflict resolution) and respected kumu hula (hula teacher) whose teaching incorporates behavioral health and cultural programming. She is the 2023 Native Hawaiian Education Association (NHEA) Native Hawaiian Educator of the Year.

Judith Salmon Kaur (Choctaw and Cherokee from Oklahoma) is the second American Indian oncologist in the USA. She was the leader of the Native Circle and Sprit of Eagles projects and has over 100 peer-reviewed publications, of which half are focused on AI/AN cancer and health.

Dorothy Keefe is CEO of Cancer Australia, a distinguished medical oncologist, and a Professor of Cancer Medicine at the University of Adelaide. She focuses on supportive care in cancer and holds a Masters degree in Medical Leadership, actively advocating for patient-centered care and reducing disparities in cancer outcomes.

Brian Kelly is a psychiatrist within the School of Medicine and Public Health, University of Newcastle, Australia, and an Adjunct Professor, Division of Psychosocial Oncology Cumming School of Medicine, University of Calgary, Canada. He is Chair of the Psycho-oncology Cooperative Research Group (PoCoG).

Michelle Kennedy is a Wiradjuri woman who grew up on Worimi country. She is an NHMRC early-career researcher, partnering with Aboriginal communities to drive research to improve Aboriginal and Torres Strait Islander health.

June Kima is a passionate public health professional with over seven years' experience pursuing community-led and action-oriented research that responds to community priorities. Her work centers on disease prevention and health promotion to support communities to live healthy and achieve the highest quality of life possible.

Keith King is a Métis Two Spirit researcher living in Alberta, Canada, and a PhD candidate at the University of Alberta. Keith is currently a practicing Public Health Nurse and a traditional oskapiew (helper) working closely with the Métis Nations of Alberta and Ontario.

John Kingi Tribal Affiliations—Muaūpoko, Ngāti Porou ōku Iwi. Cultural identity, retention, and continuation of ancestral knowledge in all its forms is something that I have come to realize has been my life's work. Seeing our people express themselves as unique Whānau, Hapū, Iwi through the rich narratives of their ancestors is what I'm all about!

Anita Konczi Working with First Nations since her early years, Anita was educated in Québec and Ontario. She earned a DÉC (college diploma) in Health Sciences, a BSc in Zoology/Psychology, and an MA in Psychology. Anita has worked as a researcher and data analyst in both academia and in the private sector for 35+ years.

Linda U. Krebs is Associate Professor Emerita, University of Colorado, College of Nursing and Vice President, Native American Cancer Initiatives, Inc. She is a Fellow of the American Academy of Nursing and the American Association for Cancer Education and past national president of the Oncology Nursing Society.

Lynnette Tumwine Kyokunda is an Anatomical Pathologist with 21 years of experience (basic, immunologic and molecular pathology). She is an Associate Professor and Head of Pathology, Faculty of Medicine, University of Botswana since 2018.

Marg Lavery is Oncology and Haematology Clinical Trials Co-ordinator at Royal Darwin Hospital. She has worked as a registered nurse in the Northern Territory for over 30 years, with the last 14 years in oncology. She is passionate about patient-focused care and support, particularly in the clinical trial space.

Bev Lawton (ONZM) nō Ngāti Porou is founder/director of Te Tātai Hauora o Hine National Centre for Women's Health Research Aotearoa at Victoria University of Wellington. Professor Lawton's significant contribution to advancing equitable cervical cancer prevention is in her advocacy and research in HPV self-testing in Aotearoa New Zealand.

Sophie Lebel is a non-Indigenous clinical psychologist and Professor of Psychology at the University of Ottawa, Canada, which sits on the traditional, unceded territory of the Omamìwìnini Anishnàbeg First Nation. Her research program involves the design, empirical evaluation, and implementation of screening tools and psychosocial interventions to address Fear Of Cancer Recurrence (FCR).

Palama Lee is Director of Research and Evaluation at Lili'uokalani Trust. He has a Masters and PhD in Social Welfare. He serves on several initiatives to protect and promote Native Hawaiian community health for kāne (Kū Ola), the elderly, individuals experiencing behavioral health recovery, and keiki in foster care.

Angeline Letendre is a Cree Métis researcher at Alberta Health Services, working in collaboration with Indigenous communities to improve cancer prevention and screening outcomes. She is co-lead with Alberta First Nations' partnership with Australia to address the needs of Indigenous youth aging out of care.

Kevin J. Linn is of European ancestry and grew up in British Columbia, Canada. He worked at the First Nations Health Authority and as an advisor to the First Nations Health Authority (FNHA) Chair in Cancer and Wellness at University of British Columbia (UBC). He is currently completing a Doctor of Public Health degree at Harvard University.

Cheryl Louzado is the Lead, Diversity and Inclusion at the Canadian Partnership Against Cancer, and works within the organization and with partners to center health equity in the implementation of the Canadian Strategy for Cancer Control.

Raglan Maddox is from the Bagumani (Modewa) Clans in Papua New Guinea. Raglan's program of research has focused on developing and analyzing population-based Indigenous heath information systems using community-driven processes.

Maria Marama is an Indigenous researcher and evaluator whose philosophy is grounded in Kaupapa Māori (Māori ways of thinking and being). She advocates for Māori at all levels of the health system. Maria experienced first-hand the bureaucracies and barriers facing Māori across health and gives her voice to positive change.

Luis Mas is a medical oncologist at INEN in Peru, with interests in lung cancer, molecular oncology, and public health.

Carole Mayer is a Clinical Expert Advisor for Models of Care with the Canadian Partnership Against Cancer. She is an Affiliate Scientist with the Health Sciences North Research Institute in Sudbury, Ontario, and an Adjunct Associate Professor, Department of Oncology, Cumming School of Medicine with the University of Calgary.

Dan McAullay is the Dean of Kurongkurl Katitjin and Edith Cowan University's Director, Aboriginal Research. Dan is a Registered Nurse (BSc) with Australian Health Practitioner Regulation Agency (AHPRA) and has postgraduate qualifications in Epidemiology and Primary Health Care at Masters and Doctorate levels. He has considerable experience in Aboriginal health research, policy, and practice.

Alma McCormick is a member of the Crow Indian Nation and Executive Director of Messengers for Health, a nonprofit organization on the Crow Reservation with the mission of improving health and wellbeing of the Crow people. Alma has led community health programs and research amongst her people since 2001.

Des McGrady is a Kamilaroi man from the Darling Downs region in Australia and a cancer advocate who contributes much of his time to ensuring that Aboriginal and Torres Strait Islander people understand the signs and symptoms of cancer and know how to advocate for their rights.

Rob McNeill is a Senior Lecturer and health services researcher in the School of Population Health at the University of Auckland.

Elizabeth Meusburger is an Oncology Haematology Clinical Trials Registered Nurse and Cancer Services Safety and Quality Nurse with 9 years' experience working across Cancer Services at the Royal Darwin Hospital. Elizabeth is passionate about improving outcomes for First Nations and Non-English Speaking Background (NESB) Cancer Services patients in the Northern Territory.

Andrea Meza is a medical oncologist at Lamas Hospital, II-E, San Martin Peru, with interests in clinical oncology and public health.

Tess Moeke-Maxwell (Ngāi Tai ki Tāmaki, Ngāti Porou, Pākehā) is a Senior Research Fellow in the School of Nursing, University of Auckland. Co-director of Te Ārai Palliative Care and End of Life Research Group, Tess leads Kaupapa Māori end-of-life research on behalf of the Te Ārai Kāhui.

Renee Moore is a Gomeroi/Kamilaroi woman from Quirindi, a wife, mum, and health worker. Renee is currently an Aboriginal Health Worker in Palliative Care Tamworth, and was part of the working group for the "Into the Dreaming" booklet. She is passionate about making a positive change in people's health journeys.

Kim Morey is of Anmatyerre/Eastern Arrernte descent with family connections to Central Australia. Kim has over 28 years' experience in Aboriginal health and community management including 10 in Aboriginal health research. Kim leads the South Australian Aboriginal Chronic Disease Consortium, and co-leads the Wardliparingga Aboriginal Health Equity Theme at South Australian Health and Medical Research Institute.

Stacey Morrison is a New Zealand television and radio broadcaster.

Keneilwe Motlhatlhedi is a Family Physician and lecturer at the University of Botswana. She completed her undergraduate medical training at the University of Ghana and her postgraduate in Family Medicine from the University of Botswana. She has a Professional Diploma in Tropical Medicine and Hygiene (East African Partnerships).

Liela Murison is a Ku Yalangi/Takalaka, Djabugay, and Djiru woman and an Indigenous Health worker within the Townsville Cancer Centre, Townsville University Hospital. She has served in several local and national working groups to develop cancer-related guidelines and frameworks.

Rebecca Murray is a proud Kamilaroi woman, living on Dharawal Land. She is currently an Aboriginal Health Worker for Cancer Services in NSW. Bec is in her final year completing a bachelor's degree in organizational leadership and will be the first person in her family to have a tertiary qualification.

Jeannie Navarro is a public health specialist at INEN in Peru.

Andrew Ndlovu is a lecturer at the University of Botswana, School of Allied Health Professions, Faculty of Health Science. He holds a PhD from University of Cape Town and an MSc from University of the West of England (UWE). His research interest is in translational research for medical intervention (decoding the biological code for therapeutic purposes).

Caroline Nehill is Director, Aboriginal and Torres Strait Islander Cancer Control at Cancer Australia. Caroline has over 20 years' experience in cancer control including across government and not for profit. Caroline has a Masters in Public Health and is a Registered Nurse.

Patricia Nez Henderson is from Teesto, Arizona—a community in the Navajo Reservation. As a Diné scientist, Dr Nez Henderson is one of the leading authorities in tobacco control and prevention in American Indian communities.

Khwanruethai Ngampromwongse is a Wiradjuri and Ngemba-Wailwaan woman and Senior Research Administration Officer in the First Nations Cancer and Wellbeing Research Program at The University of Queensland. She is undertaking a PhD at The University of Queensland, focused on Aboriginal and Torres Strait Islander people's wellbeing and health sovereignty.

Tina Noutsos is a Haematologist at Royal Darwin Hospital with 20 years' experience serving Aboriginal and Torres Strait Islander peoples living with blood disorders. She co-chairs the Northern Territory (NT's) cancer clinical trials committee and is Senior Research Fellow/Head of Global and Tropical Health at Menzies School of Health Research.

Margaret O'Connor is a Community Research Representative, Community Navigator, and Educator for the Rosebud Reservation and the surrounding communities. Margaret is Inupiaq and an enrolled member of the Native Village of Unalakieet, Alaska.

Teresea Olsen Tribal affiliations—Te Aitanga a Hauiti. Teresea Olsen is General Manager, Tākiri-Mai-te-Ata Whānau Ora & Kōkiri Marae Health and Social Services. She received a Queen's Service Medal 2022 for services to Māori Health and Wellingtonian 2022 for overseeing a COVID-19 vaccination program in vulnerable communities of the Hutt Valley.

Ian N. Olver is a medical oncologist, cancer researcher, and bioethicist; he co-ordinates the Master of Bioethics, University of Notre Dame Australia, and is an Adjunct Professor, Faculty of Health and Medical Sciences, University of Adelaide. Previous roles include CEO, Cancer Council Australia, and Clinical Director, Royal Adelaide Hospital Cancer Centre.

Neal Palafox Born in Hawai'i, Neal A Palafox, MD, MPH, is a Professor at the University of Hawai'i John A Burns School of Medicine and University of Hawai'i Cancer Center. He is the co-founder of the US Pacific Regional Central Cancer Registry and the Cancer Council of the Pacific Islands.

Adel Panahi is passionate about community empowerment and Indigenous health and wellbeing. Adel worked for Métis Nation–Saskatchewan (2018–2023) as Director of Health and is committed to promoting health and wellbeing of Métis citizens in Saskatchewan. He is now the Director of Income Assistance Service Delivery for Northern Saskatchewan.

Michael Penniment is Director of Radiation Oncology at Royal Adelaide Hospital, Alan Walker Cancer Care Centre, and Australian Bragg Centre for Proton Therapy, and Senior Radiation Oncologist with Icon Cancer Centres. He has an interest in rural and remote radiation oncology services and helped establish Alan Walker Cancer Care Centre.

Daniel G. Petereit is a radiation oncologist in Rapid City, SD, and a Professor at the University of South Dakota Medical School. He developed and has been Principal Investigator of the Walking Forward Program since 2002. He has established expertise in cancer disparities, radiation oncology, brachytherapy, and clinical trials.

Talia Pfefferle is the Director, First Nations, Inuit and Métis Cancer Strategy with the Canadian Partnership Against Cancer and works across Canada with partners for improved outcomes, care closer to home and cultural safety in cancer care. Talia is a Métis citizen from Treaty 6 Territory and Homeland of the Métis.

Rena Phearsdorf is an enrolled member of the Seneca Nation of Indians (Deer Clan) raised on the Allegany Territory. She received her Bachelor of Science in Health Information Management from SUNY-Polytechnic Institute and Master of Legal Studies in Healthcare Law from the University of Oklahoma.

Pascal Pineau is a molecular biologist at the Institut Pasteur. As a leading expert in virology, he has made significant contributions to our understanding of the role hepatitis viruses play in liver cancer worldwide. Pascal has led research on the molecular peculiarities associated with liver cancer in Native Andean patients.

Pallav Pokhrel is Program Director for the Cancer Prevention in the Pacific Program at the University of Hawai'i Cancer Center. His research on tobacco use includes studies of marketing influences, peer crowds, motives for e-cigarette use, racial/ethnic differences, and long-term effects of the COVID-19 pandemic on stress and substance use.

Rami Rahal held several senior leadership roles at the Canadian Partnership Against Cancer and implemented a national cancer control strategy, before moving to Aotearoa New Zealand in 2023 as Tumuaki (Chief Executive) of the national cancer control agency, Te Aho o Te Kahu.

Rajkumar Rajamanickam is a research collaborator with the International Agency for Research on Cancer (World Health Organization) and Professor of Community Medicine at Meenakshi Medical College Hospital & Research Institute, Meenakshi Academy of Higher Education and Research (MAHER), Chennai, India.

Reena Ramsaroop is the Clinical Director of Surgical Pathology, Waitemata District Health Board.

Patricia S. Rantshabeng is Medical Laboratory Scientist at the University of Botswana. She obtained her training from the University of Botswana. Her research interest is understanding HIV and high-risk HPV dual infection carriage as drivers of cervical cancers in Botswana, a high HIV prevalent setting.

Saravanan Sampoornam Pape Reddy is a periodontist, vivacious clinical researcher, and classified expert in the Indian military services, with a strong commitment to promoting oral health worldwide. He is a member of the Indian Society of Periodontology, the British Society, the American Academy, and the Nepalese Society.

Chelsea Redeye is from the Cattaraugus Seneca Nation and an enrolled member of the Walker River Paiute Tribe. She studied Anthropology and Psychology at Syracuse University with a focus in Native American Studies. Chelsea is currently a patient navigator with Roswell Park, who works with Federally Qualified Health Centers.

Andrew Redfern is an Associate Professor of Medical Oncology at the University of Western Australia and Associate Director for Clinical Strategy at Harry Perkins Institute of Medical Research.

Rose Richardson is a Métis Knowledge Holder/Practitioner from Green Lake, Saskatchewan. Rose is a teacher and holds a Bachelor of Education degree. A renowned social health advocate, she works to decolonize cancer care and position traditional healing methodologies for those marginalized within Canadian society.

Ian Ring was previously Head of School of Public Health & Tropical Medicine (PHTM) at James Cook University (JCU), Principal Medical Epidemiologist at Queensland Health (QH), Foundation Director of the Queensland Cancer Registry, and Foundation Director Australian Primary Health Care Research Institute (APHCRI) at The Australian National University (ANU). He is an advisor to Close the Gap Steering Committee and various national statistical agencies.

Patricia Rioja is a medical oncologist at INEN. She holds a Masters degree in Medical Oncology (UPCH) and is a Professor of medical oncology at the Universidad San Martín de Porres (USMP). Her interests include genitourinary tumors, breast cancer, molecular oncology, and health services management.

Luke Roberto was raised in Sacramento, California. As a graduate of Santa Clara University, he has studied juvenile idiopathic scoliosis correction and paper-based microfluidic devices. His interest in Native Hawaiian and Pacific Islander (NHPI) culture started from a young age, as his CHamoru Grandfather frequently recounted vivid memories of life in Guåhan.

Julianne Rose is a proud Gamilaroi women from Awabakal Country, with a 30-year career in caring for community. Her research and leadership have shaped culturally safe models of care for her Aboriginal community, around a spirit of co-design and consultation. Julianne's knowledge influences policy development at a health-district level.

Marilyn A. Roubidoux is an enrolled member of the Iowa Tribe of Kansas and Nebraska, a 40-year member of the American Association of Indian Physicians, Professor of Radiology at the University of Michigan Medical School, and graduate of the University of Utah School of Medicine.

Eloy Ruiz is a surgeon specializing in gastroenterological oncology at the National Cancer Institute of Peru (INEN). A Native of the northern highlands of Peru, Eloy was the first person to describe in 2007 the early-age occurrence of liver cancer among Native Andean patients.

Sabe Sabesan is a senior medical oncologist and clinical dean at the Townsville University Hospital, North Queensland. He has designed and implemented several teleoncology models to provide cancer care closer to home for rural and Indigenous communities.

Isang Soso Saidoo is of the Nama Tribe and currently the Ward Councilor for Bere and Kacgae constituency in the Ghanzi District. He has a Trade C in Auto Mechanics from Gantsi Brigade (2006–2007). The need to improve livelihoods for Indigenous people in Kacgae motivated him to politics.

Louisa Salemi is the Scientific and International Engagements Specialist at the Canadian Partnership Against Cancer. She fosters collaboration with the scientific and international community to advance the Canadian Strategy for Cancer Control. She has a PhD in Biochemistry and is dedicated to advancing cancer research championing diversity and equity.

Jane Salisbury is the Director of Health Promotion and Communication at Cancer Australia. She leads a team of communications professionals to strengthen engagement and broaden communication channels, including co-design and development of Australia's first national website for Aboriginal and Torres Strait Islander people about cancer.

Michele Sargent RN, is a graduate of University of San Diego (USD) School of Nursing. She has worked for the Walking Forward Program since 2008, following years in pediatric nursing. She became Walking Forward Program Manager in 2013. Michele also serves as the Institutional Review Board coordinator on all projects.

Cate Scholte is a Research Assistant in the First Nations Cancer and Wellbeing Research Program at The University of Queensland. She is experienced in evaluating existing consumer information resources, including for lung cancer screening for Indigenous people.

Shawnda Schroeder is a Professor in the Department of Indigenous Health at University of North Dakota's School of Medicine and Health Sciences. She teaches PhD candidates in qualitative methods, mixed methods, and program evaluation. She is a non-Indigenous ally supporting Indigenous scholars working to promote health equity.

Nina Scott (Ngāpuhi, Ngāti Whātua and Waikato) is a public health physician who works to advance Māori health. She is Director of Rangahau Hauora Māori at Te Aka Whai Ora and Co-Chair of Hei Āhuru Mōwai, the national Māori cancer leadership group. She is passionate about Kaupapa Māori approaches to research.

Sneha Sethi is a postdoctoral researcher at the Indigenous Oral Health Unit at University of Adelaide. She is currently leading the Human Papillomavirus and Oropharyngeal cancer in Indigenous Australians cohort study, and is passionate about cancer disparities and oral health inequities in the Australian Indigenous health context.

Kirthana Sharma is a physician and public health researcher, with interests in addressing health inequities for vulnerable populations. She is Senior Research Manager at the Rutgers Global Health Institute, and Assistant Professor of Medicine at Robert Wood Johnson Medical School.

Joanne Shaw is Executive Director of the Psycho-Oncology Co-operative Research Group and Senior Research Fellow, School of Psychology, The University of Sydney. She is a research psychologist, and psycho-oncology and medical communication researcher with expertise in developing interventions for people affected by cancer.

Tania Slater is from Ngāpuhi and Ngati Kahu tribes in the North of Aotearoa New Zealand. Her PhD explored the role of community care for Māori with cancer. She is a senior research fellow at Te Tātai Hauora o Hine National Centre for Women's Health Research Aotearoa.

Ben Smith is a non-Indigenous Cancer Institute NSW Career Development Fellow leading the development of a culturally sensitive Fear Of Cancer Recurrence (FCR) clinical pathway. Ben works at the Daffodil Centre, The University of Sydney, and Cancer Council NSW, on the unceded lands of the Gadigal people of the Eora Nation.

Brianna Smith (Ngāti Kahungunu ki Wairoa me Ngāti Kahungunu ki Heretaunga, Te Aitanga a Māhaki) is a research assistant in the Te Ārai Palliative Care and End of Life Research Group in the School of Nursing, University of Auckland.

Sian Smith is a Research Associate at Aston University (UK) and consultant with the World Health Organization, Regional Office for Europe. She is a health psychologist with expertise in developing and testing interventions to support people affected by cancer. Sian obtained funding for the original Radiation Therapy Talking Book.

Jeanette Starlight is a grandmother and executive director of the Tsuu'tina Museum, Tsuu'tina Nation, Alberta, Canada. Jeanette mentors many in promoting culture and language retention including organizing local prevention and screening campaigns; she's a matriarchal voice for the fair and equitable treatment of Indigenous peoples within Oncology healthcare setting.

Kendall Stevenson nō Ngāti Awa, Ngāti Kurī, Ngāpuhi is a postdoctoral senior research fellow at Te Tātai Hauora o Hine at Victoria University of Wellington. Kendall has a major interest in Indigenous health including community involvement and ownership of health innovations with a focus on women and whānau wellbeing.

Lara Stoll is a research project coordinator with the First Nations Cancer and Wellbeing Research Program at The University of Queensland. Her background is in Public Health Nutrition, with a Master of Public Health. She worked for many years within regional and remote Aboriginal and Torres Strait Islander communities within the Northern Territory's top end.

Francesca Storey (non-Indigenous) is a Senior Research Fellow and Deputy Director of Te Tātai Hauora o Hine National Centre for Women's Health Research Aotearoa. Originally from England, with a background in neonatal nursing, Francesca works with iwi in women's and infant's health research to inform policy and practice for equitable outcomes.

Natalie Strobel is a Senior Research Fellow in the Maladjiny Research Centre within Kurongkurl Katitjin, Edith Cowan University. Her research focuses on improving evidence-based best practice within health services for primary prevention and early detection, particularly for Aboriginal and/or Torres Strait Islander infants, children, adolescents, and their families.

Veeraiah Surendran is Professor and Head, Department of Psycho-oncology and Resource Centre for Tobacco Control at Cancer Institute (WIA), Chennai, and has more than 20 years' experience in the field. He has been instrumental in initiating and conducting numerous education and training programs on psycho-oncology in India.

Rajaraman Swaminathan is an Associate Director of the Cancer Institute (WIA) in Chennai, and has more than 120 publications. He completed his post-doctoral research work in International Agency for Research on Cancer (IARC), France, and is a WHO consultant on Cancer registration and control.

Angela Sy has research expertise is health disparities among Asian and Pacific Islander communities, with NIH-funded projects in cancer prevention and community engaged research. She served as Co-Investigator for the Indigenous Samoan Partnership to Initiate Research Excellence (INSPIRE) program, assisting in training researchers, designing evaluation activities, and guiding overall study design.

Munirih R. Taafaki has an MS in Clinical and Translational Research. She is the graduate program administrator at the Department of Quantitative Health Sciences, John A Burns School of Medicine (JABSOM), University of Hawai'i at Mānoa teaching courses on cultural competency in biomedical research, clinical trials, bioethics, and regulatory knowledge.

Kekoa Taparra is a Native Hawaiian born and raised in Mililani, O'ahu. He is a physician-scientist at Stanford, with a PhD from Johns Hopkins and an MD from Mayo Clinic. He advocates for disaggregating AAPI health data with publications in journals like *JAMA*, *The Lancet*, and *NEJM*.

Rev Singaryan Thaddeus is Principal, Don Bosco College, Yelagiri Hills, and has worked extensively for the development of Malayali Tribes offering education, shelter, and employment opportunities. His primary emphasis is to translate the vision of the organization's founder, Fr Francis Guezou, into mission.

Romaine Tobacco is a Community Research Representative, Community Navigator, and educator for the Pine Ridge Reservation and the surrounding communities. She is an enrolled member of the Oglala Sioux Tribe.

Va'atausili Tofaeono is a Samoan researcher with 20 years' public health experience, a PhD student, and PI for Alzheimer's Disease and Related Dementias and artificial intelligence and machine learning for colorectal cancer studies in American Samoa. His interests include social determinants, health inequities, and cultural perspectives in health research.

Katherine Tong focuses on teaching nurses faithfully to provide compassionate and safe care. Her health literacy work on Samoans living in California for her dissertation was invaluable for the INSPIRE program, where she served as Co-Investigator and guided the S-TOFHLA assessment process, analysis, and validation.

Joan Torony has worked in research for 23 years across multiple therapeutic areas in private and public health organizations. Her passion in inclusivity of diverse populations in research and education. She holds a GradCert Clinical Trial Management, Dip Human Resources Management, AdvDip Business/Finance Management and Workplace Training.

JoAnn 'Umilani Tsark served as the Program Director of 'Imi Hale Native Hawaiian Cancer Network (U01CA86105, U01CA114630, U54CA153459) for 17 years, leading 'Imi Hale's team in operationalizing Community-Based Participatory Research (CBPR) principles to engage and serve Indigenous communities in Hawai'i in health programming and research. She is affiliated with the University of Hawai'i.

Billy Tsima is an Associate Professor of Family Medicine and Clinical Epidemiology at the University of Botswana. He obtained his medical training from the University of Newcastle, Australia. He has practiced medicine in Botswana since 2007 in various capacities including rural communities, district hospitals, and academic settings.

Claudette Tyson is a Kuku Yalanji woman born and raised in Inala and Acacia Ridge, Brisbane. She works at Southern Queensland Centre of Excellence in Aboriginal and Torres Strait Islander Primary Health Care (Inala Indigenous Health). Claudette's expertise in community engagement and training was crucial in leading Inala Community Jury.

Guillermo Valencia is a medical oncologist at INEN. Guillermo holds a Masters degree in Medical Oncology (UPCH) and is a professor of medical oncology at Universidad San Martín de Porres (USMP), with interests in breast cancer, melanoma, molecular oncology, and public health.

Jule Vásquez is a medical oncologist at INEN, with interests in hematology oncology, molecular oncology, and public health.

Tatiana Vidaurre is a medical oncologist, former director of INEN in Peru, and a Professor at the Universidad Peruana Cayetano Heredia (UPCH). She coordinated the first national cancer plan for Peru and founded "Club de la Mama," an advocacy program. Tatiana is a *Doctor honoris causa* of Toulouse University in France.

Andrew (Anaru) Waa (Ngāti Hine/Ngāpuhi) is a Research Fellow with the Department of Public Health, at the University of Otago. He is a trained social scientist with postgraduate degrees in Public Health.

Rose Wadwell is a Gomeroi/Kamilaroi women born in Quirindi, who has worked with the Hunter New England Local Health District for 34 years. Her current role is as Aboriginal Chronic Care program officer. Her passion is changing stories and being part of improving health outcomes for our people.

Nancy Washburn Mohawk, Six Nations of the Grand River (Turtle Clan), is an Indigenous navigator with the Department of Indigenous Cancer Health at Roswell Park Comprehensive Cancer Center. Nancy received her Bachelor of Science in Health Analytics and a minor in Management from D'Youville College.

Sasha Webb (Ngāti Kahu, Ngāpuhi, Pākehā) is the Tumutuarua Mana Taurite (Equity Director) at Te Aho o Te Kahu. Sasha has spent 20 years working with public, private, and not-for-profit organizations and has a background in communications and systems change. She joined Te Aho o Te Kahu in 2020.

David K. White is a partner with Dakota Radiology and is the lead radiologist for LD Lung Screening and PET/CT. Dr White and Dakota Radiology are committed to bringing the highest quality of radiologic imaging and support to the clinicians and patients they serve.

Margaret Whitson is a proud Kamilaroi woman and Aboriginal Liaison Officer at Calvary Mater Waratah, NSW. Her work involves supporting patients and their families through their cancer journeys.

Lisa Whop is a Gumulgal Wagadagam woman from Mabuiag Island in the Torres Strait. Trained as an epidemiologist, Lisa is a senior researcher and a leading authority on cervical cancer elimination and cancer control more broadly. She is the Chair of Cancer Australia's Leadership Group (2023–2026).

Thomas Wills is a health psychologist and faculty member with the Cancer Prevention in the Pacific Program at University of Hawai'i Cancer Center. His research has focused on risk and protective factors for adolescent cigarette smoking and e-cigarettes but is now on respiratory diseases that are predisposing factors for lung cancer.

Verena S. Wu is a non-Indigenous Research Associate and Conjoint Lecturer at the University of New South Wales (South West Sydney Clinical Campuses). Her research interests lie in using qualitative methods and community engagement to improve equity and equality in accessing care.

Introduction

1

Gail Garvey, Linda Burhansstipanov, Lea Bill, Nina Scott, and Lisa Whop

Key Points

- Indigenous and Tribal peoples account for most of the world's cultural diversity.
- For Indigenous and Tribal peoples, health and wellbeing are culturally bound concepts linked to physical, mental, emotional, and spiritual wellbeing.
- Globally, Indigenous and Tribal peoples experience poorer health outcomes than non-Indigenous peoples, including higher cancer incidence and higher mortality rates.
- Colonization has disrupted established societal structures, economies, and belief systems, and its devastating effects continue to be experienced by Indigenous and Tribal peoples globally.
- This book seeks to address the cancer inequities for Indigenous and Tribal peoples across the world by promoting discussion and including examples of targeted and tailored strategies designed to address them.

According to the United Nations (UN), more than 476 million Indigenous peoples live in more than 90 countries worldwide, constituting 6.2% of the world's population (Fig. 1.1). Even though globally Indigenous peoples are a numerical minority, we account for most of the world's cultural diversity, with as many as 5000 Indigenous cultures and over 7000 languages [1].

Given the diversity of Indigenous peoples and to respect the autonomy of Indigenous and Tribal communities, we do not attempt to provide a universal definition for "Indigenous." The UN Permanent Forum on Indigenous Issues emphasizes the significance of self-identification and the right to determine one's identity or membership in accordance with lore, customs, and traditions. This self-identification approach includes seven concepts [2]:

1. Self-identification as an Indigenous person at the individual level and accepted by the community as a member.
2. Historical continuity with pre-colonial and/or pre-settler societies.
3. Strong link to territories and surrounding natural resources.
4. Distinct social, economic, or political systems.
5. Distinct language, culture, and beliefs.
6. Form non-dominant groups of society.
7. Resolve to maintain and reproduce ancestral environments and systems as distinctive peoples and communities.

About 80% of the world's Indigenous peoples live in Africa, Asia, and Latin America. Gaining a precise statistical overview of Indigenous populations poses significant challenges. Under-reporting or misclassification of Indigenous populations occurs globally. In some countries, Indigenous and Tribal peoples are not identified in data collection or are not recognized; in others, the data are inadequate. Some countries lack the infrastructure to collect data for their populations. In addition, some Indigenous and Tribal communities inhabit regions that span contemporary national borders—for example, the Sámi in northern Europe, Samoans who live in Samoa (an independent country) as well as in American Samoa (just 140 miles from Samoa), and Pascua Yaqui who live in both the USA and Mexico [3]. In other countries, Indigenous peoples' right to be counted is met, with population-level data for Indigenous peoples available and reported.

A range of terms are used globally to describe Indigenous and Tribal peoples. Some countries categorize multiple distinct Indigenous groups under a single umbrella term, such as "Native American" in the USA and "Aboriginal" in Australia; in other countries, the preferred term is "Tribal." Some countries have many distinct groups of Indigenous peoples, including Bolivia (36 recognized Indigenous groups), Cambodia (up to 24 Indigenous groups), and Kenya (5 Indigenous groups) [3].

Indigenous peoples are diverse, both within and between countries, with distinctive languages and cultural traditions. We live in a wide variety of environments and circumstances.

G. Garvey (ed.), *Indigenous and Tribal Peoples and Cancer*, https://doi.org/10.1007/978-3-031-56806-0_1

Fig. 1.1 Overview of the world's Indigenous peoples. (Adapted from Indigenous World 2023 [3])

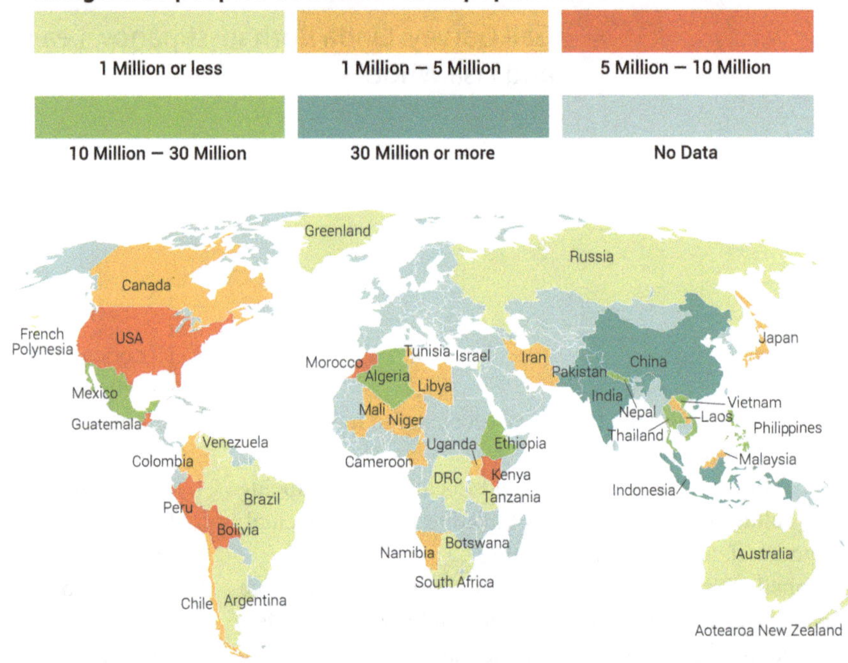

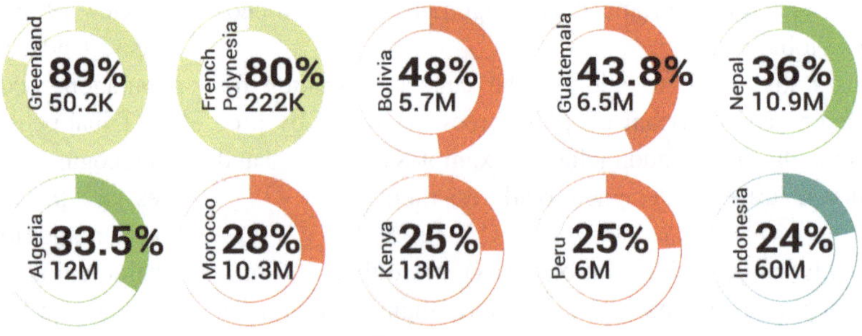

Many, in rich and poor countries alike, continue to face substantial economic, health, and social disadvantages as a result of an enduring legacy of colonization; ongoing marginalization and disempowerment; and the social, structural, and political arrangements of the countries in which we live [1].

Indigenous Knowledge Systems, Land, and Ways of Being

As the First Peoples of a country or region, Indigenous and Tribal peoples have distinct traditions, knowledge systems, and characteristics—spiritual, social, cultural, economic, and political. Many of these traditions stem from deep and familial relationships with ancestral lands, seas, and waterways [1]. Indigenous and Tribal peoples' understandings and systems of health are holistic; are woven into our relationships with land and place; are fundamentally important to our cultural, spiritual, and physical survival and wellbeing; and are characterized through various practices and responsibilities. Indigenous and Tribal peoples maintain and reproduce ancestral environments and systems in distinctive ways. The collective dimension of this relationship is significant, and the intergenerational aspect is crucial to Indigenous and Tribal peoples' identity, survival, and cultural viability.

The Cultural Context: What It Means to Be Indigenous

The content for this section emerged from a discussion at our editorial meeting in Hawai'i in May 2023, with Dr. Marjorie K Leimomi Mala Mau (Director, Center for Native and Pacific Health Disparities Research, University of Hawai'i). We thank Dr. Mau for her substantial contribution to this section.

While government and international entities (UN, WHO, etc.) have proposed definitions of "Indigenous people," the question remains: How do we, as Indigenous peoples, define ourselves? What does it mean to be "Indigenous?" Furthermore, how does understanding who we are interface with the concept of health and wellbeing that extends beyond the absence of disease? How do Indigenous peoples, with our various Indigenous ways of life, perceive health, illness, and the healthcare systems that have long ignored us—or, at best, been indifferent to our rights to health alongside non-Indigenous peoples?

The developing interest in defining what it means to be Indigenous is reflected in the growing number of citations in peer-reviewed literature on Indigenous knowledge, traditional ecological knowledge, and ancestral knowledge systems [4, 5]. What is clear is that further investigation on ancestral knowledge is needed, including the voices, stories, and experiences of Indigenous and Tribal peoples as well as interdisciplinary perspectives from sociologists, epidemiologists, anthropologists, psychologists, physicians, and so on.

Dr. Mau provides a useful perspective of this from a Native Hawaiian (NH) perspective. A deeper and evolving understanding of the NH culture, traditional values, and practices that existed prior to the overthrow of the Hawaiian Kingdom in 1893 has activated a growing appreciation of traditional culture. NH culture is recognized as a system of learned and shared beliefs, language, norms, values, and symbols used by members of the culture to identify themselves and provide a framework for life. Culture is seen as both traditional and dynamic: it adapts to other cultures and changing environments and to situations that impact the group.

Today, scores of NH and Pacific communities are revitalizing traditional culture and remaining steadfast in increasing knowledge, practice, and active participation of culture within a modern context. Practitioners of traditional healing, traditional dance (hula), NH language (olelo Hawai'i), and deep ocean voyaging and navigation are active throughout Oceania (Pacific region). The widespread use and frequent implementation of traditional culture has allowed Indigenous communities to experience a measurable and reproducible sense of holistic health [6]. For many NHs, the practice of culture has been transformational to their sense of health and wellbeing. A growing number of NH cultural practitioners strongly endorse the idea that culture IS health. This idea resonated for us as an editorial group.

Indigenous and Tribal peoples share the cultural context of "who we are" by knowing and practicing culture and teaching culture across generations. The essence of being Indigenous lies in an intergenerational bond with ancestors (including land and water), a commitment to preserving cultural heritage, and the pursuit of self-governance and rights within the framework of ancestral landscapes and responsibilities.

Indigenous Sovereignty and Self-Determination

In an Indigenous and Tribal context, sovereignty manifests as the inherent right to self-determination and governance over ancestral lands and lives. It embodies the autonomy to uphold cultural practices; maintain distinct social, economic, and political systems; and preserve and build the integrity of Indigenous communities [2]. The United Nations Declaration on the Rights of Indigenous Peoples (UNDRIP) is a powerful advocacy tool and a moral and political commitment by states to uphold the rights of Indigenous peoples [2]. UNDRIP is a landmark document that outlines the collective and individual rights of Indigenous peoples around the world. It was the result of more than two decades of negotiation and consultation with Indigenous peoples and states. Some key aspects of UNDRIP include:

- Self-determination rights, including the right to be actively involved in making decisions that affect them.
- Health rights, including rights to traditional medicines and health practices, and rights to access social and health services without discrimination.
- Cultural rights to maintain, control, protect, and develop cultural heritage, traditional knowledge, and traditional cultural expressions.
- Rights of Indigenous peoples to their lands, territories, and resources.
- Rights of non-discrimination, including prohibiting discrimination against Indigenous peoples.
- Language and education rights, including the right of Indigenous peoples to revitalize, use, develop, and transmit their languages, and including culturally appropriate education that reflects history and culture.
- Consultation and consent rights, including the importance of obtaining the free, prior, and informed consent of Indigenous peoples before adopting and implementing measures that may affect them.

Strength and Survival

Indigenous and Tribal peoples have survived and thrived for thousands of years, with worldviews that are grounded in traditions, culture, ceremonies, stories, language, songs, communities, and family. While there is much diversity between and within Indigenous and Tribal peoples globally, there are also notable commonalities such as [2]:

- Indigenous epistemologies of relationality and the interconnectedness of each other, the land and all it encompasses.
- Holistic and collectivist worldviews.
- A shared history of colonization, oppression, resistance, and survival experienced by many (though not all) Indigenous and Tribal peoples around the world.

Indigenous and Tribal communities have established laws and knowledge systems that provide trusted guidance passed on through the generations—including knowledge of medicines, environmental management, ecological and cultural systems, and spiritual knowledge [7]. We, the editors of this book, know and understand the power of learning from and caring for our Indigenous and Tribal Knowledge Holders and Elders. They protect and maintain a deep understanding of their community's approach to knowing, being, and doing. Indigenous and Tribal Knowledge Holders and Elders teach and guide the next generation their values, traditions, and beliefs through their languages, social practices, arts, music, ceremonies, and customs [3]. Many Indigenous communities are united in their respect for Knowledge Holders and Elders, honoring of history, and understanding that the community stands on the shoulders of ancestors.

Colonization disrupted established Indigenous societal structures, economies, food, health, and belief systems, and its devastating effects continue to be experienced by Indigenous and Tribal peoples globally [8]. For many, colonization brought policies purposefully designed to control the lives of the people. Across the world, traditional lands were confiscated and whole communities were relocated to less desirable places, often with multiple communities co-located on barren land on the outskirts of towns where traditional lifestyles were impossible to maintain. Whole communities became dependent on their colonizers. Many nations enacted deliberate efforts of cultural erasure through racist policies that included prohibition from speaking their native languages, forced separation of Indigenous children from their families (e.g., Stolen Generations in Australia, residential/boarding schools in Canada), and the destruction of kinship systems [2].

Colonization has a profound impact on the health and wellbeing of Indigenous and Tribal peoples globally. Colonizers brought and in some cases deliberately spread new infectious diseases, such as smallpox and measles, for which Indigenous and Tribal populations had no immunity [7]. At the same time, the disruption of traditional lifestyles had a negative impact, with reduced access to healthy food, the fracturing of traditional diets, and the introduction of addictive substances such as alcohol and commercial tobacco [7].

Today, Indigenous and Tribal peoples across the globe experience poorer health outcomes compared to their respective non-Indigenous populations, regardless of the country's economic and health status. The reasons for these poorer outcomes are complex and multifaceted, including poverty, racism, lower levels of education and employment rates, and difficulties accessing health services [8].

As Dr. Papaarangi Reid notes [9, p. 1]:

> … attempts to make sense of the health and well-being of Indigenous peoples is inadequate unless health providers engage critically with the history of their respective nations and any subsequent patterns of privilege or disadvantage. Understanding this history, within the framework of western *imperialism* and other similar colonial projects, allows us to make sense of international patterns of Indigenous health status.

The legacy of colonization cannot be ignored, and neither can ongoing colonization be accepted unchallenged as an unchangeable driver of health inequities and poorer outcomes for Indigenous peoples. In the face of the ongoing effects of repressive policies and discrimination, Indigenous and Tribal peoples demonstrate remarkable resistance, resilience, and strength. Increasingly, attention is turning to the strengths and knowledges of Indigenous and Tribal peoples, with an acceptance that there is much wisdom and deep understanding to be shared. Indigenous and Tribal peoples offer cultural values that provide strong bonds to family, community, and all that is around us (earth, air, water, sky) in a way that understands and respect "balance" in life.

Indigenous and Tribal Peoples' Understanding of Health and Wellbeing

For Indigenous and Tribal peoples, health and wellbeing are culturally bound concepts linked to physical, mental, emotional, and spiritual wellbeing. While the Western world frequently sees health as the absence of illness, for Indigenous and Tribal peoples the concept of health is broad and holistic [10].

Definitions of Indigenous health and wellbeing should be driven by Indigenous and Tribal peoples, and this is occurring in some countries [10]. For example, in Australia, the National Aboriginal Community Controlled Health Organisation describes Aboriginal health as [11]:

> "Aboriginal health" means not just the physical well-being of an individual but refers to the social, emotional and cultural well-being of the whole Community in which each individual is able to achieve their full potential as a human being thereby bringing about the total well-being of their Community. It is a whole of life view and includes the cyclical concept of life-death-life.

In addition, policies and practices for Indigenous and Tribal communities should reflect and arise from sovereignty and a comprehensive understanding of their holistic conceptions and determinants of health that extend to the collective (family and community), which Carrol et al. describe as "community-driven and Indigenous-nation based" in a way that moves beyond the standard framework of social determinants [10].

Several chapters in this book describe models of healthcare that embody Indigenous collectivist worldviews, enact relationality, and speak to Indigenous concepts of health and wellbeing. In some locations, health services designed by and for Indigenous and Tribal peoples now offer culturally appropriate, strengths-based, effective, and accessible healthcare services. In Australia, for example, Aboriginal Community Controlled Health Organisations deliver holistic, comprehensive, culturally appropriate primary healthcare [11]. These health services—designed by Indigenous peoples and offering services for Indigenous peoples—are an important act of Indigenous sovereignty.

Cancer and Indigenous and Tribal Peoples: A Global Perspective

Cancer remains a major global health issue, and cancer rates and deaths from cancer are increasing around the world. Globally, Indigenous and Tribal peoples experience higher cancer incidence and poorer cancer outcomes. Information about cancer for Indigenous and Tribal populations tends to be either lacking or of subpar quality. Even in countries that have published reports on cancer for Indigenous peoples, many are unable to report national-level data [12]. Aotearoa New Zealand is the only country in the world that can routinely report national-level cancer statistics for its Indigenous population.

Most published reports on cancer in Indigenous populations have originated from four countries: the United States, Canada, Australia, and Aotearoa New Zealand [12]. There are also reports from countries in Africa, in South America, and on Sámi populations in Norway, Sweden, and Finland [13–15]. Reports consistently reveal that Indigenous populations face notable disparities compared to non-Indigenous populations in terms of the prevalence of risk factors, incidence of cancer, access to prevention and screening services, stage of diagnosis, quality of care received, and ultimately disease outcomes [12]. While differences exist both between and within countries, Indigenous and Tribal peoples are more likely to have a higher prevalence of risk factors, poorer outcomes, and lower access to prevention and screening. They are also more likely to develop cancers that are largely preventable, detectable through screening, and/or associated with poorer prognoses, such as lung and liver cancers [12].

Despite the challenges posed by limited data, it is evident that cancer is a significant and growing health concern for Indigenous and Tribal populations globally. As presented in Fig. 1.2, Indigenous peoples experience higher death rates from many cancers compared to their non-Indigenous counterparts.

To eliminate inequities, it is crucial to understand and address their underlying causes. The practical consequences of colonization—including limited access to healthcare, geographical isolation, systemic inequalities, and mistrust of both governments and health systems—tend to result in delayed diagnoses and reduced treatment options. In addition, cultural disconnection can compound the difficulties experienced by Indigenous and Tribal peoples in terms of cancer prevention, treatment, and survivorship. Inequities are driven by unequal access to the determinants of health, with political power at a country level a peak driver of unfair distribution. This demonstrates the link with ongoing colonization through asymmetrical distribution of political power between the colonized and the colonizing, continuing to contribute to inequities. Efforts to improve cancer outcomes must acknowledge and address the structural legacies of colonization in order to foster strong, thriving, culturally safe approaches that empower communities to navigate the complexities of cancer.

The social determinants of health, including poverty and racism, are well-established drivers of health inequities and these contribute to the disparities in cancer outcomes for Indigenous and Tribal peoples [9]. Increased prevalence of other chronic health conditions—including type 2 diabetes, chronic renal failure, and/or respiratory conditions—exacerbates the burden of disease, morbidity, and mortality among Indigenous and Tribal peoples [20]. Cancer care services may not provide adequate treatment for people with comorbidities, which further drives the equity gap [20]. Cancer-causing infections such as *Helicobacter pylori* and hepatitis B virus, which are also related to poverty and overcrowding, tend to be higher in Indigenous and Tribal populations [20]. Cancer outcome disparities are compounded by health service factors, including limited access to culturally and clinically appropriate healthcare services due to a lack of partnership with Indigenous and Tribal communities and leaders, unresponsive service design and management, and services staffed by a largely non-Indigenous workforce [20].

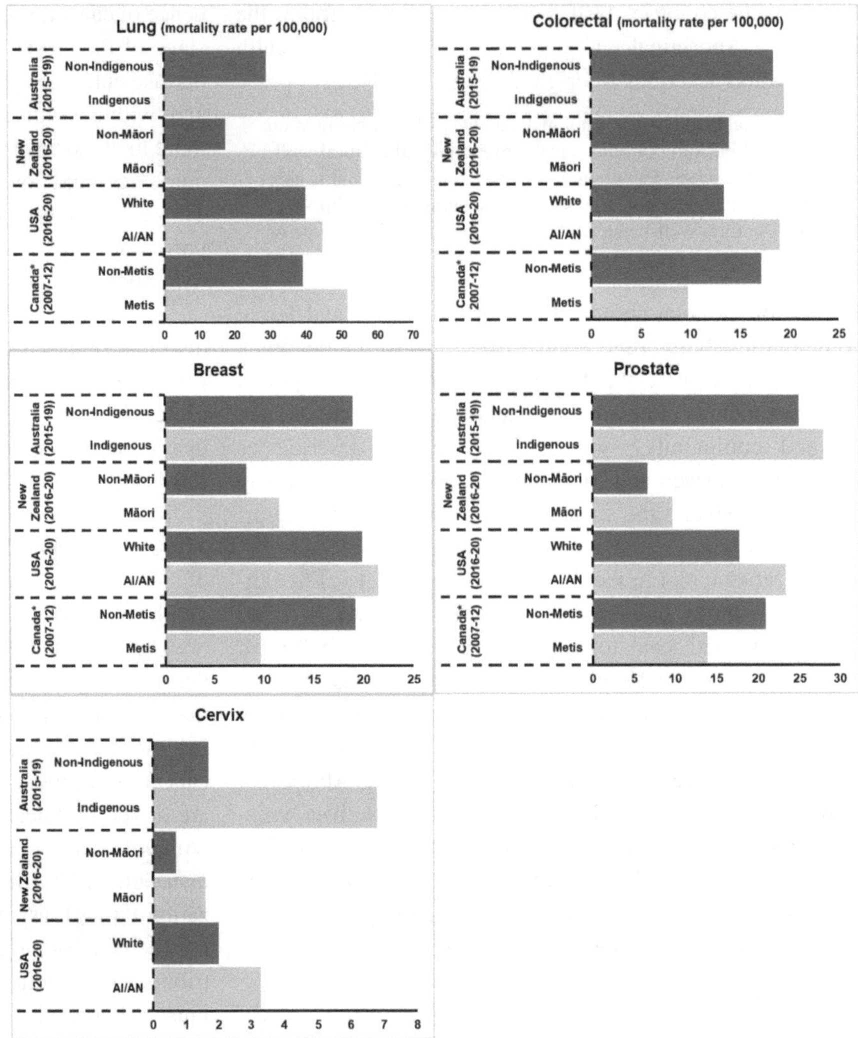

Fig. 1.2 Age-standardized cancer mortality rate (per 100,000) across countries by Indigenous status. (Sources: Australia: AIHW [16], Aotearoa New Zealand: Manatu Hauora [17], USA: Kratzer et al. [18], Canada: Sanches-Ramirez [19])*Figures are based on the estimates in Alberta. AI/AN: American Indian/Alaskan Native

In addition, cancer control quality assurance mechanisms to monitor and eliminate inequities between Indigenous and non-Indigenous peoples are poorly developed and adhered to at national and service levels in most countries.

Emerging International Leadership and Collaboration

This book is part of a growing international movement to address the cancer inequities experienced by Indigenous and Tribal peoples. In 2014, at the World Cancer Congress, Professor Gail Garvey began to develop an idea for an international forum on cancer among Indigenous peoples. While the World Cancer Congress was a general meeting open to all, Prof. Garvey wanted to create a space to gain a greater understanding of the burden of cancer among Indigenous peoples globally. She envisioned an opportunity to share research findings and cancer control activities related specifically to Indigenous peoples and communities, and identify international research priorities, enhance capacity, and build connections.

Prof. Garvey chaired the inaugural 2016 World Indigenous Cancer Conference (WICC) in Brisbane, Australia, with the theme "Connecting, Communicating, and Collaborating across the Globe." At the 2016 conference, there was a clear call for ongoing collaboration, leading to the establishment of the World Indigenous Cancer (WIC) Network—a group of people dedicated to improving cancer outcomes for Indigenous peoples around the world [21].

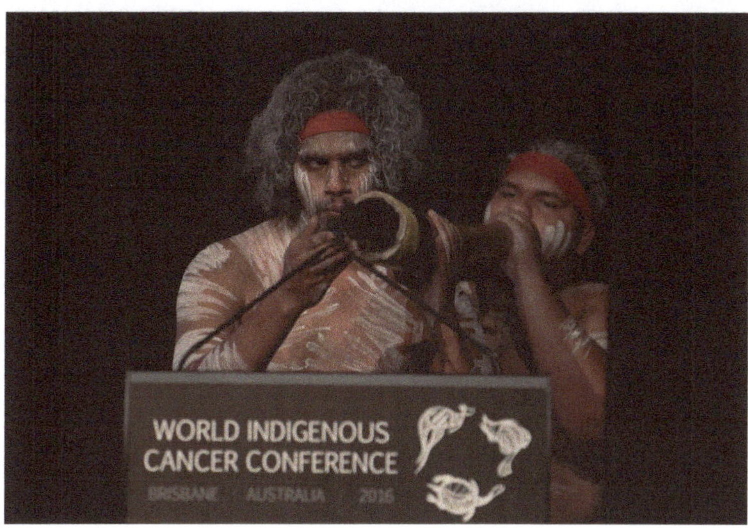

Fig. 1.3 Aboriginal dance group, Nunukul Yuggera, welcomed participants to the inaugural World Indigenous Cancer Conference, Brisbane, Australia, 2016. (Photo: Surge Media)

Prof. Garvey co-chaired the second WICC in 2019, in Alberta, Canada, with Dr. Angeline Letendre and Mrs. Lea Bill, on the theme "Respect, Reconciliation, and Reciprocity." The 2019 conference was attended by over 500 delegates, including leading cancer researchers, public health practitioners, clinicians, advocacy groups, Indigenous community leaders, and people living with cancer.

The third WICC occurred in March 2024, in Melbourne, Australia, chaired by Associate Professor Kalinda Griffiths, on the theme of "Process, Progress, Power." The 2024 conference included youth and Elder forums to support and guide the next generation of Indigenous leaders.

This book fits within this global effort to address the significant disparities in cancer outcomes and care for Indigenous and Tribal Peoples across the world by bringing people together, promoting discussion, and including examples of targeted and tailored strategies to overcome the myriad challenges to closing the cancer equity gap (Fig. 1.3).

References

1. United Nations. Indigenous Peoples: Respect NOT Dehumanization [Internet]. [cited 2023 Dec 15]. Available from: https://www.un.org/en/fight-racism/vulnerable-groups/indigenous-peoples
2. United Nations. *UN Declaration on the Rights of Indigenous Peoples*. 2007. Available from: https://www.un.org/development/desa/indigenouspeoples/wp-content/uploads/sites/19/2018/11/UNDRIP_E_web.pdf
3. The International Work Group for Indigenous Affairs. *The Indigenous World 2023* (37th edition). Copenhagen: IWGIA; 2023. Available from: https://www.iwgia.org/en/resources/indigenous-world
4. Sandoval CDM, Lagunas RM, Montelongo LT, Diaz MJ. Ancestral knowledge systems: A conceptual framework for decolonizing research in social science. *AlterNative*. 2016;12(1):2. https://doi.org/10.20507/AlterNative.2016.12.1.2
5. Finn S, Herne M, Castille D. The Value of Traditional Ecological Knowledge for the Environmental Health Sciences and Biomedical Research. *Environ Health Persp*. 2017;125(8). https://doi.org/10.1289/EHP858
6. Mau MKLM, Minami CM, Stotz SA, Albright CL, Kana'iaupuni SM, Guth HK. Qualitative study on voyaging and health: perspectives and insights from the medical officers during the Worldwide Voyage. *BMJ Open*. 2021;11:e048767. https://doi.org/10.1136/bmjopen-2021-048767
7. Joe J, Burhansstipanov L, Ullrich JS, Braun KL. Standing on the Shoulders of our Ancestors: History and Contemporary Health Status of Indigenous Peoples in the US. In: Burhansstipanov L, Braun KL, editors. *Indigenous Public Health: Improvement through Community-Engaged Interventions*. Lexington, KY: University Press of Kentucky; 2022. p. 21–54.
8. Griffiths K, Coleman C, Lee V. How colonization determines social justice and Indigenous health: A review of the literature. *J Population Res*. 2016;33(1):9–30. Available from: http://www.jstor.org/stable/43919985
9. Reid P, Cormack D, Paine S-J. Colonial histories, racism and health—The experience of Māori and Indigenous peoples. *Public Health*. 2019;172:119–24. https://doi.org/10.1016/j.puhe.2019.03.027
10. Carroll SR, Suina M, Jäger MB, Black J, Cornell S, Gonzales AA, et al. Reclaiming Indigenous Health in the US: Moving beyond the Social Determinants of Health. *Int J Environ Res Public Health*. 2022 Jun 18;19(12):7495. https://doi.org/10.3390/ijerph19127495
11. NACCHO. *Aboriginal Community Controlled Health Organisations* (ACCHOs) [Internet]. [cited 2023 Dec 20]. Available from: https://www.naccho.org.au/acchos/
12. Garvey G, Cunningham J. Social inequalities and cancer in Indigenous populations. In Vaccarella S, Lortet-Tieulent J, Saracci R, Fidler MM, Conway DI, Vilahur N, et al. Reducing Social Inequalities in Cancer: Setting Priorities for Research. *CA Cancer J Clin*. 2018;68(5):324–32. https://doi.org/10.3322/caac.21463
13. Parkin DM, Sitas F, Chirenje M, Stein L, Abratt R, Wabinga H. Part I: Cancer in Indigenous Africans—burden, distribution, and trends. *The Lancet Oncology*. 2008;9(7):683–92. https://doi.org/10.1016/S1470-2045(08)70175-X
14. Galukande M, Wabinga H, Mirembe F, Karamagi C, Asea A. Difference in risk factors for breast cancer by ER sta-

tus in an indigenous African population. *ISRN Oncol.* 2013; June;2013:463594. https://doi.org/10.1155/2013/463594
15. Hassler S, Soininen L, Sjölander P, Pukkala E. Cancer among the Sami—a review on the Norwegian, Swedish and Finnish Sami populations. *Int J Circumpolar Health.* 2008;67:5,421–32. https://doi.org/10.3402/ijch.v67i5.18351
16. Australian Institute of Health and Welfare. *Cancer in Australia 2021.* Cancer series no. 133. Cat. No. CAN 144. Canberra: AIHW; 2021.
17. Manatu Hauora, Ministry of Health New Zealand. Rates and numbers of cancer deaths by cancer type [Internet]. [cited 2023 Apr 27]. Available from: https://tewhatuora.shinyapps.io/cancer-web-tool/
18. Kratzer TV, Jemal A, Miller KD, Nash S, Wiggins C, Redwood D, et al. Cancer statistics for American Indian and Alaska Native individuals, 2022: Including increasing disparities in early onset colorectal cancer. *CA Cancer J Clin.* 2023;73(2):120–46. https://doi.org/10.3322/caac.21757
19. Sanches-Ramirez DC, Colquhoun A, Parker S, Randall J, Svenson LW, Voaklander D. Cancer incidence and mortality among the Metis population of Alberta, Canada, *Int J Circumpolar Health.* 2016;75:30059. https://doi.org/10.3402/ijch.v75.30059
20. Sarfati D, Robson B, Garvey G. Cancer in Indigenous populations Focusing on inequalities that are sometimes invisible. In Wild CP, Weiderpass E, Stewart BW, editors. *World Cancer Report: Cancer Research for Cancer Prevention.* Lyon, France: International Agency for Research on Cancer; 2020. Available from: http://publications.iarc.fr/586. Licence:
21. WIC Network. *World Indigenous Cancer Network* [Internet]. [cited 2023 Dec 20]. Available from: https://wicnetwork.net

Part I

Partnerships and Collaborations

Mana Wāhine: Empowered Women: A Cultural Response to Encouraging Cancer Screening

2

Tira Albert, Joanne Doherty, and Teresea Olsen

Key Points

- Mana Wāhine (Empowered Women) is funded to increase breast and cervical cancer screening among Māori, Pacific, Asian, under-screened, and never-screened peoples in Aotearoa New Zealand.
- We work in partnership with the woman and her family to ensure spiritual and cultural needs are acknowledged and that women are prepared, informed, and supported to access screening.
- Mana Wāhine brings together old knowledge and new knowledge, with a focus on relationships and culturally appropriate services. We normalize women's health and make it OK for women to talk about cervical and breast screening.

Mana Wāhine (Empowered Women) is a collective of five Indigenous health providers working across health districts in the greater Wellington region of Aotearoa New Zealand. All five providers are either Iwi (Tribal peoples), mana whenua (Tribal peoples who have the right to manage a particular area of land), or belong to a whānau ora collective (a culturally based, family-centered approach to wellbeing, focused on family groups).

Mana Wāhine is an independent service provider that held a direct contract with the National Screening Unit (NSU) Ministry of Health from 1990 to 2022. In 2023, the contract was transferred to Te Aka Whai Ora, the Māori Health Authority (TAW), following recent health reforms in Aotearoa New Zealand. We are funded to provide support to Māori, Pacific, Asian, under-screened, and never-screened peoples to participate in cancer screening programs.

Collectively, we have over 60 years' experience in providing culturally appropriate and accessible breast and cervical screening support services, alongside education and health promotion. All of our services are free, including our own cervical screening undertaken by five Māori nurses based across our collective organizations. All our collective organizations provide a range of other health and social services.

The most important and effective partnership focus is with the woman and her family. We meet women at their home, at the marae (Tribal meeting house), and at other community venues. The Kapu Tī Kōrero (a chat over a cup of tea) with the kaimahi (community health worker) at the beginning is an important pathway that leads to the clinician at the end. When the women are prepared, informed, and supported to access screening, their spiritual and cultural needs are acknowledged as well as their family. This makes a difference.

Waireti Walters, a pioneering Māori community health worker, was a powerful advocate for breast and cervical screening for Māori women. She was committed to wāhine ora (healthy women) and was a key driver and a supporter of our Mana Wāhine collective from the beginning. Waireti was famous for her quote "know my face before you know my cervix." Once relationships are established, the woman and her family may then be linked into multiple health and social services. We believe that any door is the right door.

In 2018, we launched a new kaupapa (Māori customary practice or principle) of Mana Wāhine called Te Mauri (Life Essence). Te Mauri supports families with cancer and is a significant community service, unique in Aotearoa New Zealand. Te Mauri is funded by our own collective, by local partnerships with a primary healthcare network Te Awakairangi and the Cancer Society (Wellington), and by the goodwill of others.

Mana Wāhine leadership is about strong Māori women in a network of Māori providers, including traditional healing of mirimiri (traditional massage), rongoā (traditional medicine), and karakia (traditional prayer). It brings together the old knowledge and the new knowledge. The focus is not on what we provide, but how we provide the service. This whānau ora (healthy holistic family) approach goes way beyond statistics and counting. Mana Wāhine normalizes women's health and makes it OK to talk about cervical and breast screening. As one of the old kuia (respected elderly

G. Garvey (ed.), *Indigenous and Tribal Peoples and Cancer*, https://doi.org/10.1007/978-3-031-56806-0_2

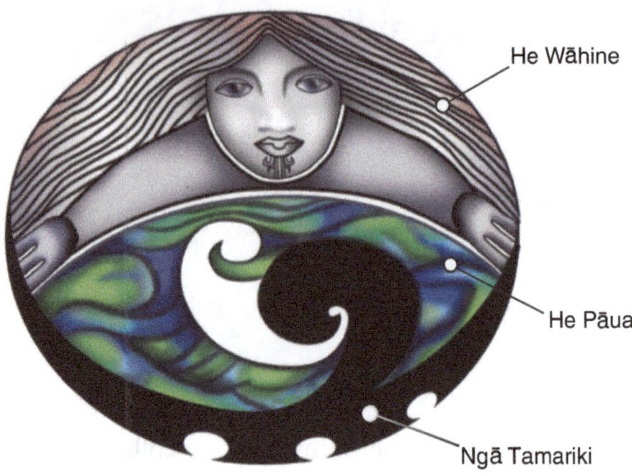

He Wāhine (Women) – who hold the taonga (treasure) of childbirth, mother, raising, guiding, teaching, believing in and, most of all, loving her tamariki (children).

He Pāua (Abalone) – symbolizes the many paths in life that can be chosen. Whether they are right or wrong paths, there are always lessons to be learned.

Ngā Tamariki (Children) – the most precious taonga of all. They are the key to the future and can hold the knowledge to build and create many great things for the next generation.

Fig. 2.1 Mana Wāhine logo and interpretation

women) said 30 years ago, "Do you realize you are sitting on a gold mine? You must look after it."

The overall vision and essence of Mana Wāhine is:

> *Mā te hauora o ngā whaea, ka piki te ora o te whānau o te hapū, me te iwi.* (Healthy mothers ensure healthy families.)

This is presented beautifully in our logo, created by Tracey Kane in 1996 (Fig. 2.1).

The partnerships we build are at multiple levels and focus on a collective approach of working together to achieve better outcomes for our wāhine Māori.

Part of the role of the current manager for Mana Wāhine is to continue to grow and develop these partnerships for the betterment of the wellbeing of all women. Membership on Hei Āhuru Mōwai (Māori Cancer Leadership Aotearoa) and Māori Monitoring Equity Group NSU ensures the community voice is heard at the table. The Mana Wāhine manager chairs the National Cervical Screening Programme Advisory and Action Group that oversees, through an equity lens, the human papillomavirus primary screening and self-testing project implemented from late September 2023. Mana Wāhine has significant partnerships with public health regional screening and sexual health services dedicated to health promotion and prevention.

Key challenges for Mana Wāhine have continued from the beginning. This includes short-term contracting and inadequate funding and the subsequent risk to staff retention of valuable clinical and nonclinical staff who can secure improved job security and higher wages elsewhere. The continuous restructuring of health services, and screening services in particular, results in staff turnover, a loss of organizational knowledge, and considerable time spent rebuilding relationships. When pilots and innovations are funded and succeed, there is no guarantee of them continuing in the future. The focus of the funder is on numbers and Māori providers sometimes have to compete with each other to be awarded a contract to deliver a service. There is still lip service paid to equity and the COVID-19 pandemic has seen significant delays identified for Māori women accessing screening. The inequity has increased.

The future direction for Mana Wāhine is co-designing the service with whānau at the center. Māori health providers need to stay strong and stay together.

Community–Academic Partnerships for Evidence-Based and Métis-Specific Cancer Prevention in Alberta

3

Taylor James Cromarty, Reagan Bartel, June Kima, Ashton James, Amanda Andrew, Janis Geary, and Karen J. Goodman

Key Points

- Community-driven research answers questions posed by those who bear the disease burden.
- Inclusion of Métis leaders in policy design, research, and cancer prevention strategies is crucial to ensure that appropriate interventions are implemented for Métis people.
- Métis people seeking cancer care face structural, distance, time, financial, cultural, and health challenges that contribute to late diagnosis and poor treatment outcomes and create inequities in cancer incidence.
- Supportive factors, including assistance with costs and accommodation, and providing a guidebook for patients and support persons, improve treatment outcomes and wellbeing.

Alongside Inuit and First Nations, the Métis are one of the three constitutionally recognized Indigenous peoples of Canada. The Métis are a post-contact Indigenous Nation descended from unions of European fur traders and First Nations women in the eighteenth century. A robust community with a unique identity, culture, way of life, and historic self-government, the development of distinct Métis communities within the Métis Nation Homeland predates the confederation of Canada. The Métis Nation Homeland includes modern-day Manitoba, Saskatchewan, Alberta, and parts of British Columbia, Ontario, the Northwest Territories, and the northern United States [1].

The Métis National Council defines *Métis* as "a person who self-identifies as Métis, is distinct from other Aboriginal [Indigenous] peoples, is of historic Métis Nation Ancestry, and who is accepted by the Métis Nation" [2]. Those who fulfill these requirements can apply to obtain citizenship in their province of residence. Canadian Census data from 2016 showed 587,545 Canadians who reported Indigenous ancestry identified as Métis; they represented 35% of the total Indigenous population and 1.6% of Canada's population [3]. The Métis Nation of Alberta (MNA) is the governing body for the Métis people in the province of Alberta, representing over 63,000 citizens. The MNA strives to advance the self-determined priorities of its citizens through socioeconomic, health, cultural, and educational development.

A history of colonial violence and ongoing racism and discrimination within the healthcare system has shaped the unique health experience of Métis people. Beginning in 1885, bureaucratic fraud, motivated by abusive Canadian government land policy, displaced Métis people from their Homeland—an injustice that was only legally recognized by the Government of Canada in 2017 [1, 4]. Despite growing recognition of the impacts of colonialism on Métis people in Canada, jurisdictional barriers to the equitable distribution of health resources persist. Although Alberta has an area of over 660,000 km^2, spanning hundreds of distinct municipalities, provincially operated health services are located primarily within the ~50,000 km^2 urban corridor between the cities of Edmonton and Calgary, Alberta's two major urban centers [5, 6]. To address the specific needs of Métis people in Alberta, the MNA established a Department of Health.

Structured around the core pillars of community wellness and health research advocacy, the MNA Department of Health integrates the needs, values, and beliefs of Métis Albertans into all aspects of health intervention. This community-driven approach to wellness ensures that health policy is driven by the self-determined priorities of Métis Albertans. Since 2010, the MNA Department of Health has collaborated with academic researchers and provincial data stewards to design cancer intervention initiatives in Métis communities.

This chapter weaves together Métis perspectives on cancer with findings from analysis of Métis-specific descriptive cancer data to highlight strengths-based approaches to cancer interventions. Our work serves as a guide for future community partnerships that promote evidence-based cancer prevention in Indigenous and Tribal Peoples.

G. Garvey (ed.), *Indigenous and Tribal Peoples and Cancer*, https://doi.org/10.1007/978-3-031-56806-0_3

What Is Known

Cancer is the leading cause of death in Canada by a large margin, accounting for 26.3% of all deaths in women and 26.8% in men [7, 8]. Results from a Canada-wide study conducted from 1991 to 2001 identified cancer as the leading cause of death among Métis women (33% of all deaths) and the second-leading cause of death among Métis men (23% of all deaths) [8–10]. While there is very little published data comparing Métis and non-Métis cancer patterns, a 2018 publication on cancer incidence and survival among Métis adults across Canada, using an analysis of census data from 1992 to 2009 and cancer data from the Canadian Cancer Registry, reported that, compared to non-Indigenous adults, Métis adults had excess prostate cancer mortality and higher incidence of female breast, lung, liver, larynx, gallbladder, and cervical cancers [11].

While Canadian Indigenous health studies are numerous, few differentiate the three distinct Indigenous peoples recognized in the Canadian Constitution when reporting health findings [8–11]. Métis people are dramatically underrepresented in health research relative to First Nations and Inuit populations, primarily due to an inability to identify Métis people within administrative health databases [8]. Thus, more studies characterizing the health of Métis people are necessary to identify priorities, develop relevant policy, and design and implement effective and culturally meaningful interventions responding to the needs of the Nation [8].

What Is Being Done

From 2010 to 2017, the MNA initiated partnerships with provincial health officials and academic researchers to address the dearth of Métis representation in health research, with the ultimate goal of investigating cancer epidemiology in the Métis population in Alberta. Among these partnerships was a collaboration with the Canadian North *Helicobacter pylori* (CAN*Help*) Working Group in the University of Alberta (UA) Department of Medicine. This group specializes in conducting collaborative research with community partners who currently lack the necessary resources to address community-identified health concerns. The CAN*Help* Working Group was established between 2006 and 2008 when residents of Indigenous communities and healthcare providers in the Northwest Territories (NWT) voiced concerns about cancer risks from *Helicobacter pylori* infection. In response, NWT health officials invited UA researchers to investigate the health burden resulting from *H. pylori* infection in the territory. Subsequent funding permitted the formation of the CAN*Help* Working Group, which links academic researchers with community leaders and healthcare providers. While initial community projects focused on *H. pylori* infection and related diseases, the specific goals of research projects are identified by stakeholders in each partnered community or Nation. The publication *Stewardship and Dissemination of Knowledge Generated Collaboratively in CAN*Help *Working Group Community Projects* outlines how community-driven research values should guide the collection, management, and use of data and specimens and dissemination of the resulting collaboratively generated knowledge [12].

In 2017, the CAN*Help* Working Group and the MNA established a research collaboration agreement to identify cancer prevention strategies to support Alberta Métis community goals. Collaborative activities included focus groups to illuminate the cancer journeys of Métis Albertans and the development of Métis-specific cancer journey resources. In 2021, in collaboration with provincial government epidemiologists and data stewards, the CAN*Help* Working Group and the MNA partnered to produce descriptive cancer incidence and mortality research to characterize the Métis-specific disease burden.

Between 2018 and 2019, the MNA held Annual Health Forums and regional engagement focus groups across Alberta to learn more about the unique cancer survival experience of Métis Albertans. Focus groups took the form of guided discussions in a culturally safe environment, where cancer patients, survivors, family members, and caregivers were invited to share any experiences of importance to their cancer journeys. A Métis Resource Worker—who assists MNA citizens in areas including education, housing, income assistance, employment, financial support, and medical services—was made available to all participants on-site. The goals of these sessions were to (1) inform the development of cancer resources in which Métis culture and experience were reflected, (2) generate better information about culturally appropriate cancer care and support for Métis Albertans, (3) inform future cancer care and support programs, (4) educate relevant stakeholders in the healthcare system, (5) advocate for culturally appropriate resources at the provincial level, and (6) inform the development of the Alberta Métis Cancer Strategy. The CAN*Help* Working Group conducted qualitative analysis of the focus group transcriptions and aided in developing evidence summary reports.

What Was Found

Analysis of the focus group data identified a number of barriers faced by Métis people seeking cancer care. While primary care experiences varied, several cancer survivors indicated that their healthcare providers did not take their concerns seriously, did not carry out adequate testing, or misdiagnosed their cancer. In addition, the process of receiving a cancer diagnosis was unduly long. Community members affirmed that self-advocacy was essential to overcome this structural violence. Once a cancer diagnosis was received, travel was a near-universal barrier to cancer care due to unbalanced health services across the province. Many participants had limited resources to drive themselves and, given the distance to treatment centers, often faced the burden of having to find their own accommodation. Healthcare practitioners were not usually aware of facilities where patients could stay during their treatment. Family caregivers and support persons were not consistently available as travel companions. When treatment required an extended stay far from home, Métis Albertans were sometimes isolated from their support network. In addition, many patients could not afford to leave their homes or take time off work for treatment.

Members of the Métis community reported feeling alienated by modern cancer intervention strategies. Métis Albertans often take a holistic approach to health and wellbeing, and some view Western medicine as having too many gaps and divergent agendas to meet their needs. The discussions revealed that the provincial healthcare system did not legitimize Métis approaches to wellness; several focus group participants indicated that spiritual aspects of care were ignored or disrespected by healthcare practitioners. Some community members reported that when Indigenous spiritual care was provided in-hospital, Métis-specific wellness practices were not included or were poorly understood. The health priorities of Métis Albertans and Western medicine were often perceived as incongruent; Métis participants reported that seniors received delayed, poorer-quality care relative to younger patients in the provincial healthcare system. These systemic inadequacies created barriers for Métis people seeking cancer care, leading to late diagnosis and poor treatment outcomes.

Despite these challenges, our work identified supportive factors that can be leveraged to improve treatment outcomes and wellbeing. To address regional gaps in health programs and services, the MNA launched the Compassionate Care Cancer Transportation Pilot Program in 2018 to provide financial assistance to Métis citizens for necessary travel to cancer-related appointments. The program provides reimbursement, within 30 days of travel, for travel costs for Métis citizens north of the Edmonton–Calgary urban corridor who must travel long distances (>145 km) to receive cancer care. Travel costs eligible for reimbursement include gas fees, accommodation, food, parking, and related expenses. Focus group feedback was overwhelmingly positive and revealed the program has significantly reduced financial strain and improved mental wellbeing throughout Métis Albertans' cancer journeys. Subsequently, with the support of Alberta Health, the Urban Programming of Indigenous Peoples program, and the Métis Housing Corporation, the MNA was able to provide safe, accessible, and free accommodation for medical travel to Edmonton, the northernmost Alberta city with tertiary healthcare facilities. With the support of these services, Métis Albertans affirmed that the time period from diagnosis to finishing the first round of treatment was reduced, with less than a month between diagnosis and therapy in most cases.

In addition, this collaboration led to the development of the *Miyooayaan* (Wellness) *Cancer Journey Guidebook*, a comprehensive guide for Métis wellness while living with cancer (Fig. 3.1). This guidebook provides recommendations for Métis Albertans covering four broad themes: (1) screening and diagnosis, (2) treatment, (3) caregiver experiences, and (4) posttreatment wellness. In addition to educational resources, it provides information on (1) self-advocacy and patient rights to ensure Métis Albertans can safely navigate available healthcare services, (2) tools to prevent burnout among caregivers, (3) posttreatment support resources, and (4) recommended questions to ask healthcare staff during screening and diagnosis, treatment, follow-up, and beyond. Finally, the guidebook outlines specific recommendations from Métis Albertans, including other MNA programs and services, cancer journey video supports, and external partners who provide culturally safe support.

Our epidemiologic analysis carried out in parallel with the focus group research identified inequities in cancer incidence among Métis people in Alberta, similar to findings reported previously for all Métis people across Canada. The most common cancers for Métis Albertans and non-Métis Albertans alike were breast, colorectal, prostate, bronchial, and lung cancers. Overall mortality estimates for most types of cancer were similar when comparing Métis and non-Métis people. However, Métis people tended to develop cancers at a younger age compared to non-Métis people: from 2013 to 2019, the proportion of new cancer cases diagnosed under the age of 44 was 35.8% in Métis people and 18.8% in the non-Métis population. As well, the lung cancer incidence rate in the Métis population was 1.3 times [95% confidence interval: 1.1–1.7] the lung cancer incidence rate in the non-Métis population. After stratifying by sex, Métis men had a similar incidence of lung cancer relative to non-Métis men, while Métis women had a lung cancer incidence rate 1.7 times [95% CI: 1.3–2.2] the rate of non-Métis women. While age-standardized incidence rates for all cancers combined decreased slightly between 2013 and 2019 for non-Métis people, these incidence rates either increased or returned to baseline during the same period among Métis people.

This research furthered understanding of the Métis community's needs and helped to identify the programs and services the MNA would advocate for. Ultimately, the analysis addressed gaps in the information available on cancer in Métis people, to be used by public health and health policy stakeholders to design and implement strategies directed at reducing cancer incidence and mortality. In the final report, *Cancer Incidence and Mortality Among the Métis Population Of Alberta*, Audrey Poitras, President of the MNA, wrote:

Fig. 3.1 Cover for *Miyooayaan: A Métis Guide for Wellness with Cancer* [13]

> Our community has felt the full force of this disease as it stole our elders, our family members, and our friends. This analysis is essential in understanding the cancer incidence and mortality among Métis Albertans, informing us of interventions we can likely adopt to alleviate the burden of cancer among Métis Albertans [8, p. 3].

Conclusions

This collaboration demonstrates that incorporating the perspectives of those who bear the burden of disease produces novel, high quality, cost-effective, and culturally appropriate research and health interventions. Including the MNA in policy design, research, and cancer prevention strategies was crucial to ensuring that appropriate interventions were implemented for Métis people. Finally, our community–academic partnership built capacity for research autonomy and wellness self-determination among the Métis people. These collaborations will continue for future cancer research and health status surveillance of Métis people. We hope this collaboration encourages future community–academic partnerships that promote evidence-based cancer prevention in Indigenous and Tribal peoples.

This collaboration was made possible through funding from the Canadian Partnership Against Cancer (CPAC) and Alberta Health ("Community–Academic Partnerships for Evidence-Based Cancer Prevention Strategies that Support Métis Community Goals," Grant #007548). The authors would like to acknowledge the Métis Albertans and their families who shared their cancer stories and experiences and the work of D.C. Sanchez-Ramirez, A. Colquhoun, S.H. Parker, J. Randall, L.W. Svenson, and D. Voaklander, who pioneered the Métis Cancer Incidence and Mortality report in a preceding community–academic partnership. They would also like to acknowledge the work of Li Huang, Senior Epidemiologist at Alberta Health, who conducted the statistical analysis of the updated Métis Cancer Incidence and Mortality report.

References

1. Métis Nation of Alberta. *Metis in Alberta: History* [Internet]. [cited 2023 Aug 7]. Available from: https://albertametis.com/metis-in-alberta/history/
2. Métis National Council. *Citizenship: Métis Registration Guide* [Internet]. [cited 2022 Jan 3]. Available from: https://www.metisnation.ca/about/citizenship
3. Statistics Canada. *Census Profile, 2016 Census* [Internet]. 2017 Nov 29 [cited 2022 Jan 3]. Available from: https://www12.statcan.gc.ca/census-recensement/2016/dp-pd/prof/details/page.cfm?Lang=E&Geo1=PR&Code1=01&Geo2=&Code2=&SearchText=Canada&SearchType=Begins&SearchPR=01&B1=All&TABID=1&type=0
4. Rupertsland Centre for Métis Research. Métis Scrip in Alberta. 2018 [cited 2023 Aug 7]. Available from: https://www.ualberta.ca/native-studies/media-library/rcmr/publications/rcmr-scrip-booklet-2018-final-150dpi.pdf
5. Government of Alberta. *Population Statistics* [Internet]. 2023 Jan 8 [cited 2023 Aug 7]. Available from: https://www.alberta.ca/population-statistics
6. Alberta Energy Regulator. *Regional Hydrology of the Edmonton-Calgary Corridor.* 2014 Feb [cited 2023 Aug 7]. Available from: https://static.ags.aer.ca/files/document/OFR/OFR_2014_02.pdf
7. Statistics Canada. Leading causes of death, total population (age standardization using 2011 population) [Internet]. 2023 Aug 28 [cited 2023 Aug 28]. Available from: https://www150.statcan.gc.ca/n1/en/subjects/indigenous_peoples
8. Sanchez-Ramirez DC, Colquhoun A, Parker S, Randall J, Svenson LW, Voaklander D. Cancer Incidence and Mortality Among the Métis Population of Alberta (2007–2012). 2016 [cited 2023 Aug 7]. Available from: https://albertametis.com/app/uploads/2018/03/Health-Report_Cancer-Report-Final.pdf
9. Statistics Canada. *Increase in mortality from 2020 to 2021 entirely attributable to deaths among males* [Internet]. 2023 Aug 23 [cited 2023 Aug 30]. Available from: https://www150.statcan.gc.ca/n1/daily-quotidien/230828/dq230828b-eng.htm
10. Tjepkema M, Wilkins R, Senécal S, Guimond E, Penney C. Mortality of Métis and registered Indian adults in Canada: an 11-year follow-up study. *Health Rep.* 2009 Dec;20(4):31–51.
11. Mazereeuw MV, Withrow DR, Nishri ED, Tjepkema M, Vides E, Marrett LD. Cancer incidence and survival among Métis adults in Canada: Results from the Canadian census follow-up cohort (1992-2009). *CMAJ.* 2018 Mar 19;190(11):E320–E326. https://doi.org/10.1503/cmaj.170272
12. CANHelp Working Group. *Collaborative Partnerships* [Internet]. 2013 [cited 2012 Aug 7]. Available from: http://www.canhelp-workinggroup.ca
13. Metis Nation of Alberta. *Cancer Research* [internet]. 2023. Available from: https://www.google.com/search?q=albertametis.com%2Fprograms-services%2Fhealth%2Fhealth-research-and-advocacy%2Fcancer-research%2F&sca_esv=b3263d4d2be9fb73&sca_upv=1&rlz=1C1GCEU_enIN1080IN1080&ei=ydxOZoO5GLWQseMPyoiQmAs&ved=0ahUKEwjDwcDDjaOGAxU1SGwGHUoEBLMQ4dUDCBE&uact=5&oq=albertametis.com%2Fprograms-services%2Fhealth%2Fhealth-research-and-advocacy%2Fcancer-research%2F&gs_lp=Egxnd3-Mtd2l6LXNlcnAiV2FsYmVydGFtZXRpcy5jb20vcHJvZ3JhbXMtc2VydmljZXMvaGVhbHRoL2hlYWx0aC1yZXNlYXJjaC1hbmQtYWR2b2NhY3kvY2FuY2VyLXJlc2VhcmNoL0iwFVCfEFifEHABeAGQAQCYAWOgAWOqAQExuAEDyAEA-AEC-AEBmAIBoAIJwgIKEAAYsAMY1gQYR8ICDRAAGIAEGLADGEMYigXCAg4QABiwAxjkAhjWBNgBAcICExAuGIAEGLADGEMYyAMYigXYAQKYAwCIBgGQBhO6BgYIARABGAm6BgYIAhABGAiSBwExoAeLAQ&sclient=gws-wiz-serp

4 Two-Row Wampum: Indigenous Cancer Patient Navigation

Whitney Ann E. Henry, Marissa Haring, Chelsea Redeye, Rena Phearsdorf, Nancy Washburn, and Rodney C. Haring

Key Points

- Cross collaboration between clinicians and community organizations is essential for cancer education and screening.
- Successful patient navigation includes working with sovereign Native Nations, not-for-profits serving the community, grassroots organizations, and human/health service providers adjacent to Native Nations.
- The Two-Row philosophy is a framework other Indigenous communities may benefit from.

Indigenous peoples experience higher cancer disparities and mortality rates due to a variety of preventable cancers [1, 2]. However, narratives of resilience are starting to emerge that balance out the cancer journey. This is exemplified by Indigenous women who have experienced cancer, who share strength stories by reflecting on their own personal growth in response to having cancer, and who assist others facing their own cancer journeys [3]. Cancer detection, services, and outcomes are influenced by geographic location, availability, proximity, and access to health centers and cancer health services. A cancer diagnosis is both life changing and intimidating [4, 5].

Indigenous patient navigators provide many unique services to community members undergoing cancer treatment. These include but are not limited to cancer education, cancer screening scheduling, appointment reminders, health literacy, and in-person appointment support. Patient navigator roles and training differ by site and program specifics. This level of complex relationship building requires a team that can provide comprehensive, quality cancer care and provide support that incorporates cultural norms and beliefs. It also requires collaborative efforts between healthcare systems that border reservations and urban areas to capture Indigenous populations on and off sovereign land.

The Two-Row framework respects different cultures while striving for the same goal of peace and harmony. It is reflected in the patient navigation program by having two arms or two vessels, Indigenous and rural communities, with the same goal of reducing the cancer burdens in these areas.

Patient navigators are an essential component of community-based cancer screening and of cancer patients' recovery, strength, and healing. Key components of successful navigation include trust in healthcare systems, community integration of navigation programs into current health systems on sovereign land, communication between Indigenous Nations and urban centers, and familiarity with Indigenous knowledge, traditional medicines, ceremonies, and cultural protocols through the cancer journey. Indigenous cancer- and health-focused patient navigators are an integral part of saving lives as they provide education, appointment reminders, support, resources, and a familiar face to those who may hesitate to attend cancer screenings, cancer education, or cancer treatment. They are resiliency leaders in cancer healthcare and are integral to preventive medicine [6].

Two-Row Wampum: A Parallel for Collaborating in Different Health Systems

The Two-Row Wampum Agreement was a 1613 agreement between the Haudenosaunee (Iroquois) and representatives of the Dutch government, in what is now New York State. The Wampum consists of two purple rows or lines representing two vessels traveling in parallel along the river of life. These two rows never intersect and are surrounded by white wampum shells, which represent the two parties to the agreement traveling in peace and friendship without mutual interference. The Two-Row Wampum framed a process of nation-to-nation governance, demonstrating how multiple nations can work side-by-side while respecting each other's governance and ways of life by avoiding navigating into the other's path. This wampum was a contract upon which a treaty was founded, and it served as guide to peaceful, respectful, and friendly collaboration. The agreement also showcased sovereignty and respect between cultures, ways of life, languages, and coexisting governance [7].

G. Garvey (ed.), *Indigenous and Tribal Peoples and Cancer*, https://doi.org/10.1007/978-3-031-56806-0_4

In a recent health initiative implemented in the Haudenosaunee landscapes throughout New York State and primarily in Western New York, the Two-Row philosophy was woven into a cancer-focused quality improvement project, "Two-Row Collaboration: Indian Health Service, Rural Partnerships, and the Cancer Care Continuum," that collaborated with health systems on Indigenous sovereign land, Indigenous community health programs, Indigenous not-for-profit organizations, grassroots organizations, and health organizations in neighboring Haudenosaunee territories. A collective review of successes and gaps in service related to the cancer-care continuum was formalized into a plan of action.

UN, US Treaty, and Trust Responsibilities: Indigenous Health Programs

Wampum agreements were interwoven with treaties [8], which are supreme laws of the land between Indigenous Nations and the US government. Many of the first wampum agreements and treaties were between the United States and the Haudenosaunee Nations. Part of Article VI of the 1794 Treaty of Canandaigua states, "Now that provision sets aside money to be used annually to purchase goods and to compensate artificers, who shall reside with or near them, and be employed for their benefit." Venables [9, 10] suggests that provision and obligation extend to Haudenosaunee education, social welfare, and health, notwithstanding any financial limitation. Furthermore, the United States acknowledges that its trust obligations toward American Indian governments and peoples extends to healthcare (e.g., health service evaluation, quality improvement) in both the *Snyder Act* (25 USC 13) [11] and the *Indian Health Care Improvement Act* (25 USC 1602) [12]. Combined, these form part of government-to-government responsibilities to Indigenous healthcare programming, including cancer-care programming and patient navigation. They coincide, at the international level, with the United Nations' positioning on the health rights of Indigenous peoples.

Quality Improvement, Service, and Bidirectional Modeling

The project "Two-Row Collaboration: Indian Health Service, Rural Partnerships, and the Cancer Care Continuum" conducted multiple roundtable discussions on sovereign Indigenous lands in New York State, Ontario and Quebec (Canada), and neighboring rural communities. Quality improvement findings documented ways of improving culturally driven cancer prevention and cancer screening services, with specific needs in patient navigation focused on all aspects of the cancer-care continuum. That includes education, screening, diagnosis, treatment, and survivorship. The results of this project are jointly informed by cancer health disparities specific to the Haudenosaunee confederacy, made up of ancestrally related Indigenous Nations. The project led to the creation of a multi-area Indigenous patient navigation program founded on the principles of the Two-Row Wampum. This includes respectfully implementing sovereign understanding across multiple health delivery systems and community organizations.

The emerging service paired patient navigators to practice in community-based settings on Indigenous territories and to geographically matched off-territory healthcare systems. These teams of Indigenous navigators and off-territory navigators provided in-person and on-site navigation with specific attention toward co-occurring conditions including cancer, obesity, and Type 2 diabetes. The navigation focused on prevention, screening, treatment, education, palliative care, and survivorship. Navigators were embedded in community spaces with rotations in a cancer center to cover in-hospital concerns. Navigators were also drawn from local Indigenous and rural communities to honor community knowledge and provide employment opportunities. Lastly, local and regional mobile screening efforts were coupled with virtual navigation to ensure robust integration.

Quality improvement initiatives to translate findings into service delivery lay the foundation for bidirectional networks to support navigation services and collective service programs working with and for Indigenous communities and adjacent safety-net providers across the cancer-care continuum. Bidirectional sharing between health systems identifies existing community resources and addresses gaps in care to streamline cancer screening, information, and treatment processes, making navigation a crucial and life-saving part of the process.

Health Sovereignty in Patient Navigation

Indigenous peoples have the right to self-determination, sovereignty, and treaty. According to the American Indian Law Alliance, a non-governmental organization with consultative status on the United Nations Economic and Social Council [13], many Indigenous Nations continue to operate under their own laws and traditional governance from the perspective or mindset of healthy generations. This right to self-determination is affirmed in Article 4 of the United Nations Declaration on the Rights of Indigenous Peoples.

In the realm of cancer care, Indigenous governments have the sovereign right to prioritize and implement health policies, including initiatives such as cancer patient navigation incorporating implementation, collaboration, medical billing, payment, and reimbursement structures [14].

Institutions that co-create strategic plans to work with Indigenous Nations in and around their geographic service area via affiliated offices and networks create sovereign frameworks for sustainable change [15]. Part of these responsibilities can be through service contracts or cancer-specific memorandums of understanding that honor sovereign leadership and direction. By doing so, cancer centers and cancer-care organizations can engage long-standing conversations and historical relationships through treaties or agreements such as the Two-Row Wampum, cognizant of nation-to-nation responsibilities toward Indigenous cancer healthcare [8, 11, 12]. Collectively, Indigenous cancer center teams led and facilitated by members of local and regional Indigenous Nations can work together toward action-focused and strategic quality improvement initiatives that shape future cancer-care services.

The goal for Indigenous navigation programs is partnership with community champions such as Indigenous health systems, community not-for-profit organizations, or grassroots organizations. Doing so helps to create the trust needed to proactively provide early screening and detection information and train eligible community members to provide cancer and cancer-screening education. Navigators can work closely with community-based teams to engage in warm handoffs from provider, social worker, or case worker to navigator and assist in proactive screening education sessions. Navigators can also work closely with primary care providers and clinical staff to initiate screening opportunities at federal cancer centers and/or other providers across the region. They can work with existing community-oriented resources to avoid duplicating effort while supporting existing teams. In the absence of resources, navigators work with community partners to build culturally appropriate cancer health resources [16]. Ultimately, cancer-focused patient navigators continue to help create and maintain trust of cancer screening within Indigenous communities and provide support across the cancer continuum, thus reducing overall healthcare costs, saving lives, and supporting wellness for future generations.

Conclusion

Cancer is a concern in many Indigenous communities. Programs that intersect cancer centers and urban, rural, territory, reservation, or reserve-based services are critical to improving screening, treatment, and survivor rates. Translational, structured, and sustainable quality improvement efforts to develop new practice models are essential in the ever-changing field of cancer service delivery. This includes the use of successful Indigenous-based models of cancer care-focused patient navigation and based on self-determination, Indigenous knowledge, and strengths-based models. Continued community-based quality improvement mechanisms of cancer care that move toward permanent integration of patient navigation programs are important for community programs to initiate, track, and evaluate ways to tackle the cancer incidence and improve cancer outcomes in Indigenous communities. In addition to quality improvement, there is a need for scientific research in cancer prevention, service, and treatment. These actions will contribute to the maintenance of sovereign health through ancestral ways of living that look forward through multiple generations toward continued resilience built on partnership, relationship, and sovereignty.

This research was supported by shared resources from the Roswell Park Comprehensive Cancer Center Support Grant, National Cancer Institute (P30CA016056), and the Bristol Myers Squibb Foundation.

References

1. Australian Institute of Health and Welfare. *The health and welfare of Australia's Aboriginal and Torres Strait Islander peoples: 2015, Table of contents—Australian Institute of Health and Welfare* [Internet]. Canberra: Australian Institute of Health and Welfare; 2015. Available from: https://www.aihw.gov.au/reports/indigenous-health-welfare/indigenous-health-welfare-2015/contents/table-of-contents
2. Haring RC, Jim MA, Erwin D, Kaur JS, Henry WA, Haring ML, Seneca DS. Health Disparities, Cancer among the Haudenosaunee, New York State. *Cancer Health Disparities*. 2018 Jul 29;2. https://doi.org/10.9777/chd.2018.10009
3. Burnette CE, Roh S, Liddell J, Lee YS. The resilience of Indigenous women of the US who experience cancer: Transcending adversity. *J Ethn Cult Divers Soc Work*. 2021 May 4;30(3):198–213. https://doi.org/10.1080/15313204.2019.1628680
4. O'Keefe VM, Maudrie TL, Cole AB, Ullrich JS, Fish J, Hill KX, et al. Conceptualizing Indigenous strengths-based health and wellness research using group concept mapping. *Arch Public Health*. 2023 Apr 26;81(1):71. https://doi.org/10.1186/s13690-023-01066-7
5. Kirmayer LJ, Dandeneau S, Marshall E, Phillips MK, Williamson KJ. Rethinking resilience from Indigenous perspectives. *Can Journal Psychiatry*. 2011 Feb;56(2):84–91. https://doi.org/10.1177/070674371105600203
6. Rankin A, Baumann A, Downey B, Valaitis R, Montour A, Mandy P. The role of the indigenous patient Navigator: a scoping review. *Can J Nurs Res*. 2022 Jun;54(2):199–210. https://doi.org/10.1177/08445621211066765
7. Hill Sr RW, Coleman D. The Two Row Wampum-covenant chain tradition as a guide for Indigenous-University Research Partnerships. *Cultural Studies↔ Critical Methodologies*. 2019 Oct;19(5):339–59. https://doi.org/10.1177/1532708618809138
8. United Nations. *United Nations Declaration on the Rights of Indigenous Peoples* [Internet]. United Nations; 2008 Mar. Available from: https://www.un.org/esa/socdev/unpfii/documents/DRIPS_en.pdf
9. Vernables, RW. *A brief analysis of the State of New York's Obligations* [Internet]. Onondaga Nation; 2021 Sep 12. Available from: https://www.onondaganation.org/history/2012/a-brief-analysis-of-the-state-of-new-yorks-obligations/

10. Venables, RW. Iroquois Environments and "We the People of the United States". In: Vecsey C, Venables, RW, editors. *American Indian Environments: Ecological Issues in Native American History*. Syracuse: Syracuse University Press; 1980. p. 81–127.
11. National Library of Medicine. *Congress funds American Indian health care—Timeline—Native Voices* [Internet]. Available from: https://www.nlm.nih.gov/nativevoices/timeline/427.html
12. *Indian Health Care Improvement Act* (25 USC 1602).
13. American Indian Law Alliance. *Sovereignty* [Internet]. American Indian Law Alliance. Available from: https://aila.ngo/issues/sovereignty/
14. Haring RC, McNaughton L, Seneca DS, Henry WA, Warne D. Post-pandemic, translational research, and indigenous communities. *Journal of Indigenous Research*. 2021;9(2021):5.
15. Toombs MR, Curtis C, Brolan CE. Supporting Indigenous health equity strategic planning: a Queensland perspective. *Med J Aust*. 2023 Jan;218(1):5. https://doi.org/10.5694/mja2.51794
16. Whop LJ, Valery PC, Beesley VL, Moore SP, Lokuge K, Jacka C, et al. Navigating the cancer journey: a review of patient navigator programs for Indigenous cancer patients. *Asia Pac J Clin Oncol*. 2012 Dec;8(4):e89–96. https://doi.org/10.1111/j.1743-7563.2012.01532.x

5 A Model for Health Screening Linked to a Native Hawaiian Cultural Event, Hoʻokuikahi i Puʻukoholā

Dee-Ann Leialoha Carpenter and Martina Leialoha Kamaka

Key Points

- The Association of Native Hawaiian Physicians has provided first aid and health screening at the Hoʻokuikahi i Puʻukoholā annual cultural gathering for many years.
- By engaging in the community's culture, the doctors have been able to open doors and establish trust.
- Kukākukā (talk story) sessions are a great tool for encouraging Native Hawaiians to do cancer screening.
- Bringing the tools of Western medicine to cultural activities and important gatherings of Indigenous people to improve health is something we believe can be done with other Indigenous groups.

Hoʻokuikahi i Puʻukoholā has been an annual cultural gathering on Hawaiʻi Island since 1972, where cultural activities and strict Native Hawaiian protocol are practiced. Ohua (groups) that attend are mainly Native Hawaiian men, who typically do not use Western medicine for their healthcare needs. It is a gathering where "living history" is perpetuated [1].

ʻAhahui o nā Kauka (the Association of Native Hawaiian Physicians or AONK) first attended Puʻukoholā (Hawaiʻi Island) during a cultural huakaʻi (trip) in 2004. Subsequently, AONK representatives were invited to the upcoming Hoʻokuikahi i Puʻukoholā, mainly to provide first aid during activities such as a "sham battle" (mock fighting with spears covered with padding). Having doctors there proved to be helpful, not only for the purposes of providing first aid but also for the general wellbeing of all participants. August is the hottest month of the year in Hawaiʻi, and participants follow strict Hawaiian protocol, including kapu (avoiding certain activities such as eating specific foods), often with many hours spent in ceremony. Medical problems ranged from simple injuries (such as cuts, bruises, and sprains/strains) to more urgent problems such as heat exhaustion and heat stroke. Per cultural protocol, males must be tended by male doctors, and females need to be tended by females. Since 2004, the AONK has provided both kane (male) and wahine (female) kauka (doctors). Over the years, AONK activities have expanded from first aid and urgent care to health screenings and educational talks. In return, AONK members have learned and participated in Native Hawaiian protocols and rituals, including the performance of oli (chants) used when entering the heiau (temple).

In recent years, the AONK health screening activities have become more prominent in response to the significant health disparities experienced by Native Hawaiians (NH), especially type 2 diabetes, cardiovascular disease (CVD), and cancer. NH typically experience disease at a younger age (such as with CVD, which presents 10 years earlier than in their Caucasian counterparts) [2]. Cancer is the second leading cause of death in Hawaiʻi, accounting for about 2500 deaths each year (124.1 deaths/100,000 age-adjusted population) [3, 4]. NHs have the highest rates of mortality for all cancers, including breast, lung, colorectal, and pancreatic cancers compared to any ethnic group in Hawaiʻi. In the second place, Japanese males have higher mortality rates of colorectal and pancreatic cancers with Filipino males leading the way with lung cancer, compared to other ethnicities in Hawaiʻi [3].

Trust from the Community: Health Screening

As AONK continued to provide first aid at Hoʻokuikahi i Puʻukoholā and discussed health issues with different ohua (groups), we learned that participants wanted information about how to improve their health. As the community started to feel comfortable having the AONK team around, they started to ask questions and lay the groundwork for our screening activities, which have now been embedded within the event. Because of the leaders' encouragement, young NH men, usually a hard-to-reach group, now actively participate in the screening.

G. Garvey (ed.), *Indigenous and Tribal Peoples and Cancer*, https://doi.org/10.1007/978-3-031-56806-0_5

Kauka reviewing health screening results with participants at Puʻukoholā

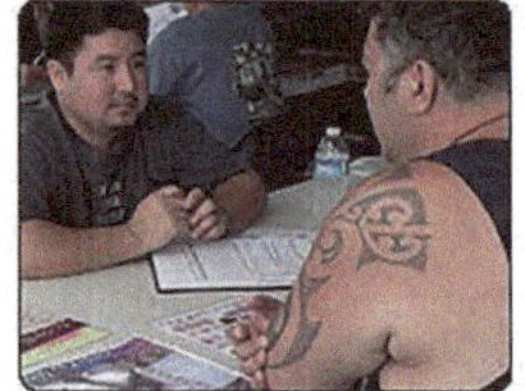
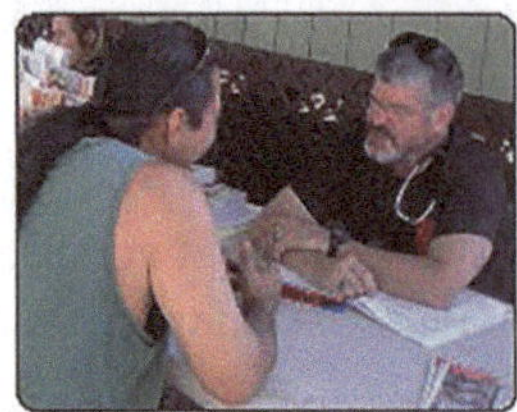

Fig. 5.1 The exit interview: clinic in the field. (Photos: M.A. Cardejon (top) and D. Carpenter (bottom row))

We offer a range of screening activities, including body mass index (BMI) measurement, blood pressure, cholesterol, blood sugar, and skin cancer screening. We found that many participants believe the brown skin of Native Hawaiians means they have little chance of developing skin cancer and therefore they don't need sunscreen. At the exit interview with the kauka (doctor), we discuss further cancer screening and the prevention of breast, cervical, prostate, and lung cancers. We provide participants with instructions for follow-up with their doctors or, if needed, provide assistance in finding a doctor. Figure 5.1 shows some of our field clinic experiences.

Over the years, AONK has worked with Papa Ola Lokahi (Native Hawaiian Health Care System) to bring in other groups of educators and healthcare providers, including the University of Hawaiʻi (UH) at Mānoa John A. Burns School of Medicine, Department of Native Hawaiian Health, Native Hawaiian Center of Excellence (NHCOE), Hui Mālama Ola Nā ʻŌiwi (NH Health Care System on Hawaiʻi Island), UH Hilo Daniel K. Inouye College of Pharmacy, Hawaiʻi Island Family Medicine Residency Program, and Chaminade University School of Nursing.

Kukākukā (Talk Story) Sessions

During Hoʻokuikahi i Puʻukoholā, we were asked to have some kukākukā (talk story) sessions with participants, with kauka wahine (female doctors) addressing women and kauka kane (male doctors) addressing men. In safe spaces, we talk about health disparities experienced by NH and the importance and impact of screening. We also provide time for questions and concerns. Participants share stories, some very personal, about their own or family members' bouts with cancer, fears of getting cancer, prevention, and what can be done to help them. A prominent topic for deep discussion is caring for oneself in order to care for others—which is a topic not previously discussed among these participants. These conversations provide a catalyst for many to accept the need for health screening. Each year, many participants return to report on their lifestyle changes and physician follow-up.

Lessons Learned and Implications

We are members and past presidents of the AONK and faculty at the John A. Burns School of Medicine who have been privileged to be part of Hoʻokuikahi i Puʻukoholā for almost 20 years. We continue to provide education and service and, through health screening and exit interviews, we help navigate participants through the healthcare system to prevent illnesses, including cancer. Over the years, we have diagnosed diabetes, hyperlipidemia, hypertension, and skin cancer.

We have learned these key lessons from Hoʻokuikahi i Puʻukoholā:

1. An invitation from the community and, in our case, the cultural groups that are stewards of Puʻukoholā was essential. With this we gained legitimacy and, with leadership encouragement, we were able to reach out to a population of NH that does not normally trust Western medicine.
2. Cultural orientation of all Western practitioners involved in health screening and first aid in the NH communities is

imperative. For NHs in this setting, this would include an attitude of respect, humility, and professionalism, as well as knowledge of culture and history, kapu (activities or foods being avoided), and NH protocol specific to Hoʻokuikahi i Puʻukoholā. Having our kauka (doctors) follow protocol helped to build trust.

3. The kukākukā (talk story) sessions are especially important. These sessions allow for safe spaces to share stories, provide information, and discuss the need for prevention, which is key to optimal health of our Indigenous people. We were encouraged to hear in subsequent years stories from the participants who shared what they learned with family and friends and had helped to change lives.

We believe that this model of bringing the tools of Western medicine to cultural activities and important gatherings of Indigenous people to improve health can be undertaken with other Indigenous groups. Especially when addressing scary topics such as cancer, it is critical to allow for safe spaces to share stories and make it easy to access screening and information. We believe similar programs can be successful with other Indigenous groups as we all try to improve the cancer health disparities impacting our communities.

We would like to thank all our partners, including those already mentioned as well as the National Park Service at Puʻukoholā, Na Aikane o Puʻukoholā, Na Papa Kanaka o Puʻukoholā, and Na Waʻa Lalani. Partial support came from funds from the Health Resources and Services Administration (HRSA), Department of Health and Human Services (DHHS), grant number D34HP16044 and title Native Hawaiian Center of Excellence. This information or content and conclusions are those of the authors and should not be construed as the official position or policy of, nor should any endorsements be inferred by the BHPr, HRSA, DHHS, or the US Government.

References

1. National Park Service. *Puʻukoholā Heiau: National Historic Site Hawaiʻi* [Internet]. [cited 2023 Jul 3]. Available from: https://www.nps.gov/puhe/index.htm
2. Aluli NE, Jones KL, Reyes PW, Brady SK, Tsark JU, Howard BV. Diabetes and cardiovascular risk factors in Native Hawaiians. *Hawaii Med J*. 2009 Aug;68(7):152–7.
3. Hawaiʻi Health Data Warehouse. *Health Topics: Cancer* [Internet]. [cited 2023 Jul 3]. Available from: https://hhdw.org/health-topics/cancer-2/
4. Hawaiʻi Health Matters. *Community Dashboard: Build a Custom Dashboard* [Internet]. [cited 2023 July 3]. Available from: https://www.hawaiihealthmatters.org/indicators/index/indicatorsearch?module=indicators&controller=index&action=indicatorsearch&doSearch=1&i=1232_180_2333_2417_181_2334&l=14&primaryTopicOnly=&b%5B%5D=100&subgrouping=1&card=0&handpicked=1&resultsPerPage=150&showComparisons=1&showOnlySelectedComparisons=&showOnlySelectedComparisons=1&includeArchivedIndicators=&includeArchivedIndicators=1&grouping=1&ordering=1&sortcomp=0&sortcompIncludeMissing=

6 The Indigenous Peoples Navigation Network (IPNN): An International Virtual Support Network

Linda Burhansstipanov

Key Points

- Indigenous navigation programs have been successfully implemented in many countries.
- Many resources exist to support patient navigators and sharing these resources has benefited local programs.
- Sharing lessons learned from local Indigenous programs can assist other Indigenous navigation programs.
- Globally, and despite historical and cultural differences, Indigenous programs share many commonalities.

Native American Cancer Research Corporation (NACR) has implemented patient navigation services since 1994 and conducted Native Patient Navigation training since the late 1990s. Patient navigators (PNs) who completed the training repeatedly expressed appreciation for the opportunity to talk, network, and collaborate with other PNs who work in Indigenous settings.

In response to this feedback, the Indigenous Peoples Navigation Network (IPNN, pronounced "I-pin") was initiated on September 21, 2021. The concept was first discussed in 2016, during the first World Indigenous Cancer Conference (Brisbane, Australia) while participants were sharing their histories and experiences. The idea came to fruition when the Academy of Oncology Nurse & Patient Navigators (AONN+)[1] introduced Local Navigation Networks. The IPNN is categorized as a "Local Navigation Network" within AONN+. However, this is a misnomer, as a global organization is clearly not "local."

The purpose of the IPNN is to provide a virtual support program to address the culturally and geographically unique challenges of Indigenous navigation programs and provide appropriate solutions to them. Many navigators work in isolation. The rationale and focus of the IPNN is to share stories of how navigation programs have overcome challenges in culturally respectful ways. Such stories may prompt PNs working in other regions or continents to try something new or to adapt a strategy that proved successful in another setting.

The IPNN is a voluntary organization for which there is no funding. It includes navigators from different countries who are interested in helping others avoid mistakes and enjoy successes. It presents four webinars each calendar year that average 90 min. Most involve speaker presentations. Participants suggest aspects of their work for which they would like help and, when feasible, identify speakers for those topics.

Participants include cancer PNs who work within Indigenous programs in the USA, Pacific Islands, Canada, Aotearoa New Zealand, and Australia. Most of these countries have similar historical backgrounds, typically involving (but not limited to) invasion and occupation by European and/or other countries, bio-colonialism, loss of lands, and attempts to eliminate local cultural languages and practices. The IPNN members include both Indigenous and non-Indigenous people who work (or want to work) respectfully with Indigenous people and programs. As of August 2023, the IPNN had 59 participants, mostly from the USA and Canada. Its membership in Aotearoa New Zealand and Australia continues to grow.

In 2022, the Professional Oncology Navigation Task Force (PONT) obtained consensus for consistent definitions and phrasing about patient navigation after receiving input from about 50 oncology navigation groups [1, 2]. These PONT definitions are:

- *Professional Navigator*: A trained individual who is employed and paid by a healthcare, advocacy, and/or community-based organization to fill the role of oncology navigator. Positions that fall under this category include:
  - *Oncology Patient Navigator*, who provides individualized assistance to patients and families affected by

[1]For information about AONN+, see https://aonnonline.org/about

G. Garvey (ed.), *Indigenous and Tribal Peoples and Cancer*, https://doi.org/10.1007/978-3-031-56806-0_6

cancer to improve access to healthcare services. The navigator may work at the point of screening, diagnosis, treatment, or survivorship or across the cancer care spectrum. An oncology patient navigator does not have or use clinical training (and is sometimes referred to as a "lay" or "community" navigator).

- *Clinical Navigator*:
  - *Oncology Nurse Navigator*, a professional RN with oncology-specific clinical knowledge who offers individual assistance to patients, families, and caregivers to help overcome healthcare system barriers. An oncology nurse navigator provides education and resources to facilitate informed decision-making and timely access to quality health and psychosocial care throughout all phases of the cancer continuum.
  - *Oncology Social Work Navigator*, a professional social worker with oncology-specific and clinical psychosocial knowledge who offers individual assistance to patients, families, and caregivers to help overcome healthcare system barriers. An oncology social work navigator provides education and resources to facilitate informed decision-making and timely access to quality health and psychosocial care throughout all phases of the cancer continuum.
- *Oncology Navigation*: Individualized assistance offered to patients, families, and caregivers to help overcome healthcare system barriers and facilitate timely access to quality health and psychosocial care from pre-diagnosis through all phases of the cancer experience.
- *Patient*: An individual screened for or diagnosed with cancer as well as their family and support systems.

In the USA, recommendations in July 2023 from the Centers for Medicare & Medicaid Services enabled reimbursement for some patient navigation services [3]. This is a substantial breakthrough for the sustainability of navigation services and professional recognition. PNs complete competency-based training under a variety of domains including professional issues, client and care team interaction, health knowledge, patient care, and communication [4].

The IPNN includes all types of PNs and community health workers. Most IPNN participants are community-based. Some work entirely alone with little or no access to relevant resources.

Many IPNN navigators focus on prevention (e.g., cessation of tobacco smoking, increased physical activity), some specifically on screening (e.g., breast, cervix, colon), and some on survivorship programs. Others address the full cancer continuum (outreach and education through to end of life). Most are involved in small programs, while many are start-ups comprising navigators who want to learn from others about effective and respectful ways to work with Indigenous peoples around the world.

The greatest challenge the IPNN encounters is the fact that its membership spans 24 time zones. Furthermore, many participants have internet issues, such as low bandwidth or lack of access, especially in rural regions. This is extremely problematic, given that all IPNN gatherings are virtual. Since March 2022, the IPNN's webinars have been recorded and posted on the IPNN website, to address this problem.[2]

Since September 2021, the IPNN has held nine webinars, which are summarized below.

1. An overview of patient navigation and international perspectives, with an informal discussion about how the IPNN could assist Indigenous PNs.
2. Community Action Boards and the Seasons of Care Study (to identify cultural modifications, which resulted an online resource[3]) and Roswell Park's Indigenous Cancer Program and their new Indigenous navigation program.
3. Patient navigation for Aboriginal and Torres Strait Islander people in Australia and the Indigenous Women's Cancer Action Group in South Australia.
4. The PONT definitions, issues specific to PN metrics, and strategies to integrate AONN+-recommended navigation metrics.
5. A focus on colorectal cancer incidence and mortality for Alaska Natives, including a discussion about strategies to increase Alaska Natives' participation in CRC screening.
6. The use of consistent terminology and umbrella terms and discussion about resources to help PNs with terminology related to genetic and precision medicine.
7. The American Indian Accelerating Colorectal Cancer Screening and Follow-up through Implementation Science (ACCSIS) projects, with a focus on barriers to screening and ways to improve cultural relevance of programs, and an overview of the success of the New Mexico American Indian ACCSIS CRC project.
8. A panel discussion about Walking Forward Community Research outcomes which identified culturally specific tailoring of low-dose computed tomography (LDCT) education materials for South Dakota healthcare providers and community members.
9. The Michigan Self-Sampling Home Health studies and how PNs can help people learn how to use home testing for human papillomavirus (HPV), and resources available from the AONN+ Cancer Advocacy & Patient Education initiative.

[2]The webinars are available at https://natamcancer.org/IPNN

[3]The online resource about health insurance and healthcare for Native American elders is available at https://nativeelderhealthguide.com/

References

1. Academy of Oncology Nurse & Patient Navigators. *Professional Oncology Navigation Task Force Releases Oncology Navigation Standards of Professional Practice* [Media Release]. 2022 Mar 29 [cited February 20, 2023]. Available from: https://aonnonline.org/press/4463-professional-oncology-navigation-task-force-releases-oncology-navigation-standards-of-professional-practice-2022
2. Franklin E, Burke S, Dean M, Johnston D, Nevidjon B, Simms Booth L. Oncology Navigation Standards of Professional Practice. *Clin J Oncol Nurs*. 2022 Jun;26(3):E14–25. https://doi.org/10.1188/22.CJON.E14-E25
3. American Cancer Society. *CMS Includes Reimbursement for Oncology Patient Navigation in CY24 Medicare physician Fee Schedule Proposal* [Internet]. 2023 Jul 14 [cited 2023 Aug 28]. Available from: https://www.fightcancer.org/releases/cms-includes-reimbursement-oncology-patient-navigation-cy24-medicare-physician-fee-schedule
4. American Cancer Society National Navigation Roundtable. *Patient Navigation Job Roles by Levels of Experience: Workforce Development Task Group, National Navigation Roundtable (ACS NNRT) 2023*. Available from: https://navigationroundtable.org/resource/https-navigationroundtable-org-wp-content-uploads-workforce-development-job-performance-behaviors-pdf

References

Part II

Policies and Systems

Cancer Care and Indigenous Peoples: One Canadian Perspective

7

Nadine R. Caron, Jessica Chan, and Mackenzie K. Connon

Key Points

- Cultural safety, legislation, and Indigenous collaboration lead to quality care.
- Cultural safety must be embedded throughout the cancer-care journey.
- Equity in research can drive improved access, care, and outcomes.

There are multiple avenues for approaching the goal of improving the cancer-care journey of an Indigenous person and their family. This care should be culturally safe, multidisciplinary, and equitably delivered, allowing optimal access to the full spectrum of diagnostic tools, procedures, and treatments. It should be adapted to innovative research findings specific to Indigenous cancer care, with increasing numbers of Indigenous researchers, healthcare providers, and leaders in these spaces. These principles are relevant on a global scale, including within Canada.

Culturally Safe Cancer Care: From Aspiration to Legislation

While cancer prevention and screening are critical, once diagnosed there is a need to focus on culturally safe and equitable cancer care specific to Indigenous individuals and families on this path. This dialogue has expanded over the years—from these concepts being seen as aspirational and compassionate to being expected and vital. In Canada, this recognition includes obligations documented in *Truth and Reconciliation Calls to Action* [1], and the province of British Columbia's (BC) *In Plain Sight Report on Indigenous-Specific Racism and Discrimination in BC Health Care* [2]. Challenges faced by Indigenous peoples in healthcare and witnessed across the cancer-care spectrum are not unique to Canada, as efforts to enshrine the right to "the highest attainable standard of physical and mental health" are well documented in the *United Nations Declaration on the Rights of Indigenous Peoples* (UNDRIP) [3]. Notable is the subsequent legislation of these UNDRIP promises in the BC DRIP Act [4], enabling ongoing implementation of BC's inaugural Indigenous-specific cancer strategy [5] and the expected increased scope and impact of subsequent strategies and growing partnerships. Partnerships with Indigenous communities, leadership, and healthcare organizations are necessary for creating tools and legislation to optimize cancer care for Indigenous individuals. This includes sharing experiences internationally to demonstrate how Indigenous self-determination, data governance, access to care, and the research driving it all contribute to the goal of improved outcomes and wellness on one's cancer journey.

The Cancer-Care Spectrum: Equity and Optimizing the Journey

The cancer-care journey can be smooth and predictable, but for many it can be frightening and sub-optimal. Unfortunately, as in most healthcare cases, the experiences of Indigenous people tend to fall into the latter category [2]. Policies implemented through colonization and Western biomedical models have led to systemic anti-Indigenous stereotyping and racism within healthcare. This has created culturally unsafe environments along the entire cancer-care spectrum, from prevention and screening, diagnosis and treatment, to palliative care and survivorship.

Cancer is complex, and optimal care requires a multidisciplinary approach to treatment. Cancer surgeons are often the first specialists that patients meet, either upon symptom presentation, during a diagnostic biopsy, or for surgical resection for treatment and staging. Surgeons may disclose a cancer diagnosis to patients and families, but healthcare professionals (HCPs) often lack the training to do so in a culturally safe and appropriate manner. Following surgery, a patient may see a medical oncologist for systemic drug treat-

G. Garvey (ed.), *Indigenous and Tribal Peoples and Cancer*, https://doi.org/10.1007/978-3-031-56806-0_7

ments (e.g., chemotherapy) and/or a radiation oncologist for radiation treatment. Medical oncologists increasingly rely on genomic testing to guide treatment decisions. Unfortunately, such testing may be less relevant to Indigenous peoples who were excluded from the study populations used to derive treatment options or guidelines. Radiation treatment has a unique challenge of geographic accessibility, as radiotherapy centers are typically situated in larger cities, given the infrastructure and human resources required [6], meaning patients often travel long distances to access a center. Discussions around end of life, including the decision to stop treatment, are critical to ensure patients' wishes are respected and to preserve quality of life and dignity. These discussions must be in culturally safe environments with supportive resources, but both are often absent.

Across all healthcare professions, there is a significant lack of Indigenous HCPs. Despite this challenge, every point of care is an opportunity for cancer HCPs to embed humility and cultural safety into their practice. Healthcare delivery is supported and led by a wide range of HCPs, including nurses, social workers, dieticians, pharmacists, and Indigenous patient navigators. This interdisciplinary space optimizes care, especially when the full range of perspectives, expertise, and resources are available and discussed with patients and their advocates. In Canada, there are programs and initiatives that aim to increase the presence of Indigenous trainees, researchers, and faculty in healthcare programs and Indigenous leadership in post-secondary institutions, research funding agencies, and cancer-care centers. In addition to having Indigenous peoples in these roles, all HCPs must learn how to provide culturally safe healthcare and commit to doing so in concert with other professional competencies. The University of BC has mandatory cultural safety and humility training for most first-year HCP students, including those studying medicine [7].

Knowledge Development Via Research and Capacity

Evidence-based cancer care in Canada is not based on research conducted with Indigenous communities. Cancer research is typically conducted in metropolitan regions affiliated with postsecondary academic institutions and tertiary cancer-care centers (clustered along the southern border in BC and Canada). Given the Canadian population demographics, Indigenous peoples are often based in rural, remote, and/or northern populations—that is, those least likely to have access to tertiary cancer care or research opportunities. This is especially true regarding clinical trials and oncogenomic research towards precision medicine. Without Indigenous participation, the challenges of generalizing research results to Indigenous individuals seeking cancer care continue to grow, including the expanding "genomic divide" when care is not taken to address inequities in access to genomic research as it evolves [8, 9]. Indigenous-led construction and governance of population-specific entities such as biobanks as research platforms [9] and background-variant libraries [10] as diagnostic tools are two examples emerging in Canada. While contemporary health and healthcare delivery are increasingly indexed to predictive, preventive, and participatory models, these require a shift towards considering the physical, emotional, mental, spiritual, and social facets of healthcare and wellbeing through culturally safe healing approaches [11, 12].

Just as cancer treatment inequities must be addressed, inequities in access to—and inclusion in—research that increases cancer knowledge must also be considered. While global examples show that Indigenous leadership in biobanks can lead to increased access to oncogenomic research, similar efforts must focus on participation and options in clinical trials, health-services research, and health-policy development and evaluation. Once again, with increased Indigenous expertise in these arenas and the contribution of passionate Indigenous individuals to determining solutions, this can be addressed nationally and internationally. Capacity building within healthcare and research must continue as a focus to provide potential solutions and optimize current (or create alternative) models of cancer-care delivery. These efforts must be led by Indigenous peoples, for Indigenous peoples—now a common, well-understood expectation.

Moving Forward

With official published reports, strategies, legislation, and policy developments, we are deepening our understanding of where we are at and where we must go regarding cancer care and Indigenous peoples in Canada. Cancer care is improving, and the provision of culturally safe care is an acknowledged goal in many facets of our healthcare system. Cancer research lags, but it is moving in a similar direction, with national and provincial research funding bodies, postsecondary institutions, and publishers recognizing the need to address inequities in their own fields. Access to culturally relevant, respectful, and safe cancer research and care involves increasing the number of Indigenous scholars, physicians, and leaders across all fields, allowing evidence-based care, providing precision medicine when possible, and considering innovative solutions to improve the cancer-care journey and ultimate outcomes for Indigenous peoples.

References

1. Truth and Reconciliation Commission of Canada. *Truth and Reconciliation Commission of Canada: Calls to Action.* 2012. Available from: https://www2.gov.bc.ca/assets/gov/british-columbians-our-governments/indigenous-people/aboriginal-peoples-documents/calls_to_action_english2.pdf
2. Turpel-Lafond ME. *In Plain Sight.* 2020 November. Available from: https://engage.gov.bc.ca/addressingracism/
3. UN General Assembly. *United Nations Declaration on the Rights of Indigenous Peoples* [Resolution adopted by the General Assembly]. 2007 October 7. Available from: https://www.un.org/development/desa/indigenouspeoples/wp-content/uploads/sites/19/2018/11/UNDRIP_E_web.pdf
4. *Declaration On The Rights Of Indigenous Peoples Act 2019* [British Columbia].
5. First Nations Health Authority, Métis Nation BC, the BC Association of Aboriginal Friendship Centres & BC Cancer. *Improving Indigenous Cancer Journeys in BC: A Road Map.* 2017. Available from: https://www.fnha.ca/WellnessSite/WellnessDocuments/improving-indigenous-cancer-journeys-in-bc.pdf
6. Chan J, Griffiths K, Turner A, Tobias J, Clarmont W, Delaney G, et al. Radiation Therapy and Indigenous Peoples in Canada and Australia: Building Paths Toward Reconciliation in Cancer Care Delivery. *Int J Radiat Oncol Biol Phys.* 2023 June 1; 116(2): 421–429
7. The University of British Columbia. *UBC 23 24–Indigenous Cultural Safety Program* [Internet]. Available from: https://health.indigenous.ubc.ca/home-page/programs/ubc-23-24/
8. Hudson M, Garrison NA, Sterling R, Caron NR, Fox K, Yracheta J, et al. Rights, interests and expectations: Indigenous Perspectives on unrestricted access to Genomic Data. *Nature Reviews Genetics.* 2020;21(6):377–84. https://doi.org/10.1038/s41576-020-0228-x
9. Caron NR, Adam W, Anderson K, Boswell BT, Chongo M, Deineko V, et al. Partnering with First Nations in Northern British Columbia Canada to Reduce Inequity in Access to Genomic Research. *Int J Environ Res Public Health.* 2023;20:5783–813.
10. BC Children's Hospital. *Silent genomes project* [Internet]. Updated 2022 [cited 2023 July 30]. Available from: https://www.bcchr.ca/silent-genomes-project
11. Provincial Health Services Authority. *Culturally Connected* [Internet]. 2021. Available from: https://www.culturallyconnected.ca/
12. BC Cancer. *Spiritual Health: Supporting person-centred care* [Internet]. 2019. Available from: http://www.bccancer.bc.ca/coping-and-support-site/Documents/BCCancer_SpiritualHealth_Brochure.pdf

8 Advancing First Nations Principles of OCAP®

Anita E. Konczi and Lea Bill

Key Points

- The OCAP® principles of ownership, control, access, and possession assert that First Nations peoples have control over data collection processes in their communities and that they own and control how information can be stored, interpreted, used, or shared.
- OCAP® received registered trademark status by the Canadian Intellectual Property Office in August 2015. The First Nations Information Governance Centre is responsible for upholding the trademark.
- OCAP® provides principles for interpretation by each First Nation or community in a way that supports their core values and belief systems.
- With the full implementation of OCAP®, First Nations can no longer be treated as a mere source of data with no consideration for their unique worldviews and cultural systems.

OCAP®[1] (Ownership, Control, Access, Possession) asserts that First Nations have control over data collection processes in their communities and that they own and control how information can be stored, interpreted, used, or shared. OCAP® is not intended as a pan-Indigenous set of principles; rather, it is a set of First Nations principles that encompasses First Nations practices and values regarding applying ancestral ways and sharing of knowledge systems. The oral tradition is a highly sacred process and is the mechanism by which knowledge is transferred. The guiding principle and value of how data are collected and treated within this system is centered in respect and data sovereignty by First Nations.

The History of OCAP®

The concepts that underlie OCAP® are neither new nor unique; however, the acronym and terminology were not formalized until 1998 at a First Nations and Inuit Regional Longitudinal Health Survey (the precursor to the Regional Health Survey) National Steering Committee (NSC) meeting in Canada. During a brainstorming session, Cathryn George, the representative from the Association of Iroquois and Allied Indians, suggested the acronym OCA (ownership, control, access). As First Nations' possession of their own data is of equal importance, the steering committee soon added the letter P, giving the current name of OCAP® (Fig. 8.1).

In 2000, NSC became the First Nations Information Governance Committee. In 2009, National Chiefs in Assembly mandated the NSC to become a stand-alone, non-partisan, apolitical, non-profit organization, subsequently named the First Nations Information Governance Centre (FNIGC), which was formed and incorporated in April 2010 [1].

The concept and formalized term OCAP® faced challenges from the beginning, due to universities and other organizations misinterpreting, misapplying, and misusing the principles. Due, in part, to these difficulties, the FNIGC Board of Directors undertook the process of trademarking OCAP® (PCAP® in French)—first as a trademarked acronym and logo (OCAP™/PCAP™).

Alberta First Nations leadership passed the OCAP™ Resolution 30-03-2010-03R during the Assembly of Treaty Chiefs (AOTC) on March 30, 2010. The resolution is intended to promote, protect, and advance the First Nations principles of OCAP™ and the First Nations' inherent rights to self-determination and jurisdiction over research and information management.

FNIGC was granted registered trademark status by the Canadian Intellectual Property Office in August 2015. The FNIGC and its regional satellite organizations (10 in total, 1 being the Alberta FNIGC) are now responsible for upholding and "defending the integrity" [2] of the name, logo, and principles of OCAP® for First Nations as a whole.

[1] OCAP® is a registered trademark of Canada's First Nations Information Governance Centre (FNIGC); additional information can be found on their website: https://fnigc.ca/ocap-training/

G. Garvey (ed.), *Indigenous and Tribal Peoples and Cancer*, https://doi.org/10.1007/978-3-031-56806-0_8

Fig. 8.1 OCAP/PCAP logo. (© FNICG)

The Principles of OCAP®

Ownership Ownership refers to the relationship of a First Nations community to its cultural knowledge, data, and information. It is distinct from stewardship, which is discussed in more detail below, under the principle of possession. In the same way an individual owns their own personal information, so too a community or group collectively owns its information. This includes intellectual property rights that arise from First Nations information. Where First Nations people do not have stewardship (possession) of their own data, their ownership of the information can still be recognized in data-sharing agreements and other legally binding documents.

Control First Nations, their communities, and representative bodies must have jurisdiction and oversight over how information about them is collected, used, and disclosed. "This principle extends to all aspects of information management, from collection of data to the use, disclosure, and ultimate destruction of data" [3].

Access First Nations are entitled to and must be given access to data and information being held about their individuals and communities regardless of which individual or organization has possession of the data. This "principle also refers to the right of First Nations communities and organizations to manage and make decisions regarding access to their collective information" [3].

Possession Possession is distinct from ownership in that it speaks to the stewardship (physical location or state) of data and information and is a "mechanism to assert control over First Nations data" [4]. Data that are under the stewardship of a nation or a First Nations entity entrusted with this responsibility enable nations to assert the OCAP® principles of access and control, which do not fully exist when data are in the possession of a government or organization not managed by First Nations.

Interpretation of OCAP®

As stated previously, the concepts behind OCAP® are neither new nor unique. However, the interpretation of OCAP® *is* unique to each First Nations community or region. Since OCAP® is a set of principles rather than a doctrine, it can, and must, be interpreted by each First Nation or community in a way that supports their community core values and belief systems. OCAP® represents each First Nation's jurisdiction over its own information—be it cultural knowledge, scientific data, oral teachings, or any other form of data.

Despite the principles themselves being defined, implementation of those principles is dependent on each nation, each cultural/language group, each region, or even each project a nation chooses to become involved in. It is not a one-size-fits-all concept, but a set of guidelines to apply based on a nation's unique worldview. The principles can, therefore, be adapted for the over 600 distinct First Nation communities in Canada.

Why Is OCAP® So Important?

First and foremost, OCAP® seeks to "use and share information in a way that brings benefits to the community while minimizing harm" [4]. Research and data collection about First Nations people has often taken place without benefit to First Nations communities or their members. The topics of research have been of either personal or academic interest to researchers and/or of potential value to society as a whole. At best, these studies have neglected to address the needs or interests of the communities involved. At worst, they have caused considerable harm to the individual participants and/or their nations.

Previously, researchers have cited community *collaboration,* but this has largely consisted of presenting a completed research design to the community for approval, rather than soliciting meaningful community involvement from the project inception. Researchers were also disinterested in First Nations research priorities. Data and other information gathered were analyzed and presented without a First Nations lens or worldview resulting in deficit-based interpretations that caused harm to First Nations communities.

The principles of OCAP®, when implemented by an individual First Nation or First Nations group, ensures that research begins with meaningful community involvement, and this should extend throughout the project and beyond the completion of the project to approving the final outcomes prior to dissemination. First Nations people must be able to provide insight and background (contexts) to *their* stories. This avoids deficit-based reporting and negative interpretation and addresses the priorities of the First Nation(s) rather than solely that of the researchers.

OCAP® seeks to prevent the appropriation, distortion, and commodification of First Nations information using specifically tailored data-sharing agreements between the nation and any researchers or organizations. Because of this, some researchers have claimed that OCAP® is a barrier to conducting research. On the contrary, data-sharing agreements based on the principles of OCAP® ensure an equitable partnership that provides benefits and protection for both parties.

OCAP® and First Nations Sovereignty

Data sovereignty is an important component of First Nations' inherent constitutional and Treaty rights to self-government and self-determination. It is only through the exercise of First Nations laws and the principles of OCAP® that the governments' unilateral decision-making can be changed to include First Nations in a multilateral approach to decision-making with protocols, processes, and worldviews inherent in each First Nation's culture [5].

Governments have long collected administrative and other forms of data with neither First Nations knowledge nor consent. Not only is more information collected than is needed to administer programs and services, First Nations have had no say in how that information is used or disclosed.

With the full implementation of OCAP®, First Nations can no longer be treated as a mere source of data with no consideration for their unique worldviews and cultural systems.

References

1. First Nations Information Governance Centre. *Our History* [Internet]. 2023 [cited 2023 Nov 3]. Available from: https://fnigc.ca/about-fnigc/our-history/
2. First Nations Information Governance Centre. *The First Nations Principles of OCAP ®* [brochure]. Ottawa: FNIGC; 2019.
3. First Nations Information Governance Centre. *Ownership, Control, Access and Possession (OCAP™): The Path to First Nations Information Governance*. Ottawa: FNIGC; 2014 May 23. Available from: https://fnigc.ca/wp-content/uploads/2020/09/5776c4ee9387f966e6771aa93a04f389_ocap_path_to_fn_information_governance_en_final.pdf
4. Algonquin College of Applied Arts and Technology. *Fundamentals of OCAP®*. eLearning course presented 2018, May 24 and 25, notes developed 2015.
5. First Nations Information Governance Centre. *Exploration of the Impact of Canada's Information Management Regime on First Nations Data Sovereignty*. Ottawa: FNIGC; 2022 Aug. Available from: https://fnigc.ca/wp-content/uploads/2022/09/FNIGC_Discussion_Paper_IM_Regime_Data_Sovereignty_EN.pdf

9 Considerations in Operationalizing Indigenous Data Sovereignty in Cancer Reporting

Kalinda Griffiths

Key Points

- To enact Indigenous Data Sovereignty in cancer reporting, it is imperative that data collection systems recognize the rights of Indigenous peoples to collect, use, and manage their own data.
- The emergence of an Indigenous Data Sovereignty framework and principles empowers Indigenous peoples to control, protect, and develop data, ensuring that it reflects their experiences, values, and understandings.
- Implementing Indigenous governance processes and achieving Indigenous leadership in cancer reporting underscore the ongoing work needed to support Indigenous Data Sovereignty.

Discussions on the development of data and information concerning Indigenous peoples have been occurring since the 1950s. The initial issues related to Indigenous data were recognized and addressed internationally through the United Nations International Labour Organization Conventions No.107 (1957) and No.169 (1989) [1, 2]. The 2007 United Nations Declaration on the Rights of Indigenous Peoples (UNDRIP) underscores the rights of Indigenous peoples to live in dignity; maintain and strengthen their institutions, cultures, and traditions; and pursue self-determined development based on Indigenous needs and aspirations [3]. This includes ensuring the quality and usability of Indigenous data to best serve the needs and aspirations of Indigenous peoples.

The concept of Indigenous Data Sovereignty (ID-SOV) has emerged as a way to ensure the UNDRIP rights are met, describing the right to control, maintain, protect, develop, and use data as it relates to Aboriginal and Torres Strait Islander peoples and their communities [3]. Essentially, ID-SOV describes how the rights of Indigenous peoples and the information that pertains to them and their experiences, including their cultural knowledge, values, and understandings, are developed and reflected in the data [4]. There are developing processes regarding how Indigenous peoples globally assert their rights in the collection, use, and management of data, including the operationalization of these rights across cancer data.

ID-SOV can provide a principle-based framework to operationalize how cancer data are collected and used to report on the care and outcomes of those affected by cancer. This chapter describes the Australian cancer data reporting landscape and proposes practical strategies for operationalizing ID-SOV. By examining the Australian context, the chapter aims to contribute some insights that can inform similar initiatives globally.

Indigenous Data Sovereignty Principles

ID-SOV provides guiding principles that articulate the rights of Indigenous peoples over their data and information. These principles emphasize the autonomy, control, and self-determination of Indigenous communities in the collection, management, and use of data that pertain to them.

In Australia, the Maiam nayri Wingara Indigenous Data Sovereignty Collective has developed ID-SOV principles [5]. These principles are designed to counter historical practices of data colonialism, where external entities often collected, controlled, and used data from Indigenous communities without meaningful consent or benefit, often to the detriment of individuals and communities. ID-SOV principles provide a framework to guide ethical, equitable, and culturally sensitive approaches to data management and research involving Indigenous peoples. They aim to empower Indigenous communities, foster trust, and ensure data are used in ways that align with the self-determined priorities of Indigenous peoples.

G. Garvey (ed.), *Indigenous and Tribal Peoples and Cancer*, https://doi.org/10.1007/978-3-031-56806-0_9

International Data Guidelines to Support Indigenous Data Sovereignty

Supporting the operationalization of ID-SOV in official population-level reporting of health and wellbeing data requires understanding the legal and regulatory systems in which data are collected and used. Data governance is "… managing information in a way that is consistent with the laws, practices and customs of the nation-state in which it is located" [6]. Data governance creates tensions when it comes to ensuring the inherent and inalienable rights of Indigenous peoples are met by being the custodians of their knowledges and the information that pertains to them.

There are some general international guidelines and frameworks relevant to data used for official reporting and data reuse, including the principles found across the General Data Protection Regulation (GDPR) [7], the FAIR and CARE principles [8, 9], and the Five Safes principles [10] (Table 9.1). This is by no means a comprehensive list; however, together they do capture a range of key principles about population-level data used for health measurement and reporting. Furthermore, they provide international standards for data management and sharing.

Specifically, GDPR principles focus on the legal and ethical processing of personal data, emphasizing transparency, purpose limitation, and accountability. FAIR principles advocate for findable, accessible, interoperable, and reusable data, promoting a standardized approach to data management. The CARE Principles for Indigenous Data Governance define collective benefit, authority to control, responsibility, and ethics in relation to the engagement with and secondary use of Indigenous data. In Australia, the FAIR and CARE principles are currently being incorporated across organizations that collect, access, and use Aboriginal and Torres Strait Islander population-level data. The Five Safes principles ensure safe research access to data by addressing data confidentiality, project approval, researcher training, secure settings, and screened outputs. In Australia, the Five Safes are used within the regulatory bodies for national data collection, including by the Australian Bureau of Statistics.

Table 9.1 Four international guidelines in Indigenous data

GDPR (legislation)	FAIR (guidelines)	CARE (guidelines)	Five Safes (guidelines)
Lawfulness, fairness, and transparency	Findable	Collective benefit	Safe data
Purpose limitation	Accessibility	Authority to control	Safe projects
Data minimization	Interoperability	Responsibility	Safe people
Accuracy	Reusable	Ethical	Safe settings
Storage			Safe outputs
Integrity and confidentiality			
Accountability			

Sources: Council of the European Union [7], Wilkinson et al. [8], Carroll et al. [9], Richie [10]

The CARE principles are important to enacting ID-SOV because they prioritize Indigenous self-determination, equity, and ethics in data governance. They empower Indigenous peoples to reclaim control over their data, promote local development, and ensure that data ecosystems are designed to benefit Indigenous communities [11]. By integrating these principles into policies and practices, institutions can build trust, respect Tribal sovereignty, and foster meaningful relationships with Indigenous communities.

Understanding Indigenous Data Sovereignty in Practice

Operationalizing ID-SOV in practice requires identifying the factors that influence the way it is conceptualized. This is described in Figs. 9.1 and 9.2, with Fig. 9.1 showing the multiple levels that ID-SOV can be actioned [12, 13], and Fig. 9.2 showing a range of components that can be considered when working towards developing ID-SOV into practice [13].

Levels of Action to Operationalize Indigenous Data Sovereignty

International considerations highlight the importance of aligning data practices with legal standards, adopting interoperable data standards, and following ethical frameworks to ensure responsible and equitable data management on a global scale. Nationally, legislation can provide a legal framework, while ethics and data policies provide the necessary guidelines for responsible and ethical conduct in research and data management. In a place-based context, institutional policies and localized governance mechanisms are essential for tailoring data practices to the specific needs and values of a community or organization. At the individual level, considerations such as self-identification within the data, data literacy, and informed dynamic consent highlight the importance of respecting individuals' rights, promoting transparency, and empowering them to make informed decisions about their data.

Indigenous Perspectives on Cancer Data and Reporting

Accurate and appropriate cancer data are required to support routine reporting and important research. These data are also required to provide policy assessment. Cancer data exist

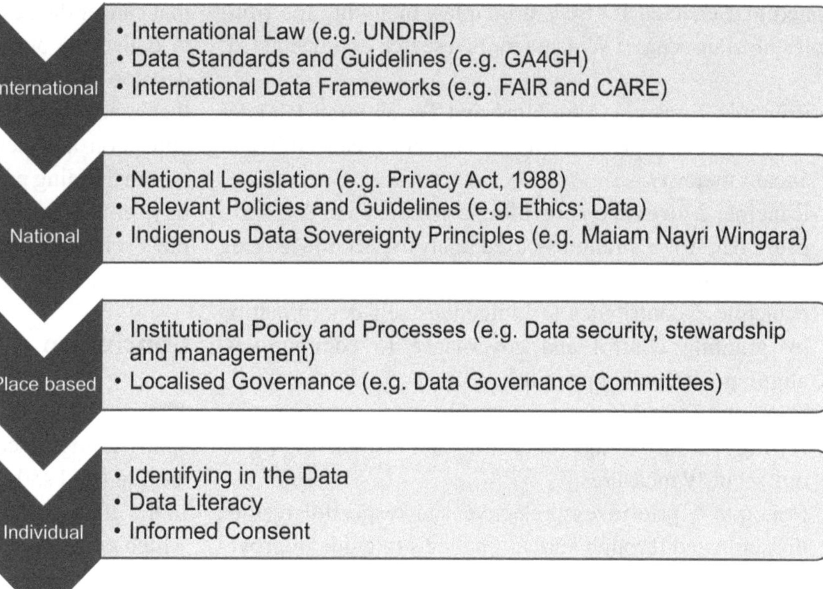

International
• International Law (e.g. UNDRIP)
• Data Standards and Guidelines (e.g. GA4GH)
• International Data Frameworks (e.g. FAIR and CARE)
National
• National Legislation (e.g. Privacy Act, 1988)
• Relevant Policies and Guidelines (e.g. Ethics; Data)
• Indigenous Data Sovereignty Principles (e.g. Maiam Nayri Wingara)
Place based
• Institutional Policy and Processes (e.g. Data security, stewardship and management)
• Localised Governance (e.g. Data Governance Committees)
Individual
• Identifying in the Data
• Data Literacy
• Informed Consent

Fig. 9.1 Levels to consider in understanding Indigenous Data Sovereignty in practice. (Sources: Trudgett et al. [12] and Griffiths et al. [13])

Fig. 9.2 Components to consider in operationalizing Indigenous Data Sovereignty. (Source: Griffiths et al. [14])

across a range of fields of research and systems, including data collected and used for research and reporting, data collected for administrative processes (e.g., hospital data, registry data, and primary healthcare data), and data used to address specific questions about people affected by cancer (e.g., clinical trials data, survey data, genomics data). Cancer reporting for Indigenous people consists of two components: (1) cancer measures, which include epidemiological measures such as incidence and survival, measures that center those affected by cancer and their experiences, and measures that assess service function and quality, and (2) cancer data, which are collected to provide information on the measures that are routinely reported upon and that have been or may yet be developed.

An Australian Case Study: The Kulay Kalingka National Cohort Study

The Kulay Kalingka national cohort study of the cancer experiences of Aboriginal and Torres Strait Islander peoples utilizes focus groups, interviews, workshops, and presentations to identify cancer-related measures that are meaningful to the study cohort [15]. Importantly, this study has demonstrated and enacted ID-SOV principles, including the principles of Maiam nayri Wingara in its research approach [15]:

- Principle 1 ensures Aboriginal and Torres Strait Islander control over the project, led by Indigenous leadership and a team majority.
- Principle 2 focuses on providing contextual and disaggregated data for a strengths-based analysis, acknowledging cultural diversity and historical impacts.
- Principle 3 contributes to Indigenous self-determination by granting control and governance to communities, aligning with policy priorities.
- Principle 4 establishes accountable data structures, following specific storage procedures and maintaining rigorous security measures.
- Principle 5 prioritizes protective and respectful results, disseminated through various channels to guide improvements in cancer experiences for Indigenous populations.

Australian Cancer Policy

In Australia, several national cancer-related documents have been developed through the leadership of Aboriginal and/or Torres Strait Islander individuals and groups. As an example, the National Cancer Control Indicators were developed to include a range of indicators that report against the National Aboriginal and Torres Strait Islander Cancer Framework [16]. These indicators are the result of mechanisms that provided space for the voices of Indigenous people to be heard within the current colonial systems, such as the Leadership Group on Aboriginal and Torres Strait Islander Cancer Control within Cancer Australia, the Australian Government's cancer authority. This Leadership Group provides an advocacy platform for the inclusion, collection, and reporting of measures and indicators that matter to Indigenous people in cancer care and control.

Challenges and Opportunities for Operationalizing Indigenous Data Sovereignty in Cancer Reporting

Enacting the principles of ID-SOV requires those working in cancer to address the research–practice–policy links that can enable this to occur. There has been limited research exploring the implementation processes of Indigenous governance that can support mediating pathways and enable Indigenous leadership and voices across the levels described in Fig. 9.1.

While there has been a growing movement addressing the ways Indigenous people engage within and lead research, normalcy in supporting ID-SOV is developing slowly. Furthermore, there has been varied engagement by the fields that cancer data exist within in the ways that Indigenous data is collected, owned, and used. There are opportunities to develop and strengthen national and international legislation that recognizes and protects ID-SOV. Further, investing in education and developing capabilities in data that support nation building provides opportunities to ensure that technology, infrastructure, and systems align with Indigenous people's priorities and needs when it comes to cancer data.

Conclusion

The discourse on Indigenous data and information rights spans several decades, with international recognition beginning in the 1950s through UN Conventions and culminating in the 2007 UNDRIP. The emergence of ID-SOV principles, which emphasize control, relevance, and protection, offers a framework to operationalize the rights of Indigenous and Tribal peoples. Applying ID-SOV in the context of cancer data is critical, considering the multiple levels involved in accurate reporting for Indigenous populations. Australia, particularly the Kulay Kalingka Study, has demonstrated commitment to these principles, ensuring Indigenous control, contextual data, self-determination, and accountable structures. However, challenges persist in aligning research–practice–policy links and mediating pathways, necessitating further exploration of Indigenous governance implementation processes. While progress has been made, ongoing efforts are required to normalize and enhance ID-SOV in the collection, use, and management of data across various fields, including cancer reporting.

References

1. International Labour Organization. *Indigenous and Tribal Peoples Convention (No.107)*. Geneva, Switzerland: ILO; 1957.
2. International Labour Organization. *Indigenous and Tribal Peoples Convention (No.169)*. Geneva, Switzerland: ILO; 1989.
3. The United Nations General Assembly. *United Nations Declaration on the Rights of Indigenous Peoples*. New York: UN General Assembly; 2007.
4. Kukutai T, Taylor J. Data sovereignty for Indigenous peoples: Current practices and future needs. In: Kukutai T, Taylor J, editors. *Indigenous data sovereignty: Toward an Agenda*. Canberra: Australian National University Press; 2016. p. 1–22.
5. Walter M, Lovett R, Bodkin Andrews G, Lee V. *Indigenous Data Sovereignty Briefing Paper 1*. Miaim nayri Wingara Data Sovereignty Group and the Australian Indigenous Governance Institute; 2018. Available from: https://static1.squarespace.com/static/5b3043afb40b9d20411f3512/t/5b70e7742b6a28f3a0e14683/1534125946810/Indigenous+Data+Sovereignty+Summit+June+2018+Briefing+Paper.pdf
6. Snipp M. What does data sovereignty imply: What does it look like? In Kukutai T, Taylor J, editors. *Indigenous data sovereignty: Toward an agenda*. Canberra: Australian National University Press; 2016. p. 39–55.

7. Council of the European Union. *General Data Protection Regulation. L119.* European Union; 2016 May 4. p. 1–8.
8. Wilkinson MD, Dumontier M, Aalbersberg IJ, Appleton G, Axton M, Baak A, et al. The FAIR Guiding Principles for scientific data management and stewardship. *Sci Data.* 2016;3:160018. https://doi.org/10.1038/sdata.2016.18
9. Carroll S, Garba I, Figueroa-Rodriguez OL, Holbrook J, Lovett R, Materechera S, et al. The CARE Principles for Indigenous Data Governance. *Data Sci J.* 2020;19:43. https://doi.org/10.5334/dsj-2020-043
10. Ritchie F. The 'Five Safes': a framework for planning, designing and evaluating data access solutions. *Data for Policy.* 2017 Sept. https://doi.org/10.5281/zenodo.897820
11. Carroll SR, Garba I, Plevel R, Small-Rodriguez D, Hiratsuka VY, Hudson M, et al. Using Indigenous Standards to Implement the CARE Principles: Setting Expectations through Tribal Research Codes. *Front Genet.* 2022;13:823309. https://doi.org/10.3389/fgene.2022.823309
12. Trudgett S, Griffiths K, Farnbach S, Shakeshaft A. A framework for operationalising Aboriginal and Torres Strait Islander data sovereignty in Australia: Results of a systematic literature review of published studies. *EClinicalMedicine.* 2022;45:101302. https://doi.org/10.1016/j.eclinm.2022.101302
13. Griffiths KE, Blain J, Vajdic CM, Jorm L. Indigenous and Tribal Peoples Data Governance in Health Research: A Systematic Review. *Int J Enrivon Res Public Health.* 2021;18(19):10318. https://doi.org/10.3390/ijerph181910318
14. Griffiths KE, Johnston M, Bowman-Derrick S. *Indigenous Data Sovereignty: Readiness Assessment and Evaluation Toolkit.* Melbourne: Lowitja Institute; 2021. Available from: https://www.lowitja.org.au/page/services/tools/indigenous-data-sovereignty-readiness-assessment-and-evaluation-toolkit
15. Wells S, Brinckley M, Thurber KA, Banks E, Whop LJ, Maddox R, et al. Kulay Kalingka, a national cohort study of Aboriginal and Torres Strait Islander peoples' cancer experiences: a study protocol. *BMJ Open.* 2023;13:e072045. https://doi.org/10.1136/bmjopen-2023-072045
16. Cancer Australia. National Aboriginal and Torres Strait Islander Cancer Framework. Surry Hills, NSW: Cancer Australia; 2015. Available from: https://www.canceraustralia.gov.au/affected-cancer/indigenous/national-aboriginal-and-torres-strait-islander-cancer-framework

Providing Leadership in Developing National Cancer Control Policy in Australia

10

Jacinta Elston, Lisa Whop, Caroline Nehill, and Dorothy Keefe

Key Points

- A governance group of Aboriginal and Torres Strait Islander leaders is essential for providing strategic advice, guidance, and credibility to national Aboriginal and Torres Strait Islander cancer policy.
- Cancer Australia established the Leadership Group on Aboriginal and Torres Strait Islander Cancer Control to assist in achieving equity in overall cancer outcomes.
- The Leadership Group has provided guidance on key national policies, including the development of the Australian Cancer Plan, National Lung Cancer Screening Program, and the Optimal Care Pathway for Aboriginal and Torres Strait Islander people with cancer.

Despite Australia having some of the best cancer outcomes in the world, Aboriginal and Torres Strait Islander people have higher rates of cancer diagnosis and are approximately 40% more likely to die from cancer than non-Indigenous Australians [1]. To improve outcomes for Aboriginal and Torres Strait Islander people with cancer, leadership by and accountability to Aboriginal and Torres Strait Islander people are critical. Historically, government agencies have notoriously failed to ensure Indigenous voices are heard. However, increasing efforts are being made globally to ensure that Indigenous voices are at the center of policymaking to improve cancer outcomes.

Cancer Australia, the Australian Government's national cancer control agency, aims to reduce the impact of all cancers and improve outcomes and experiences for all people affected by cancer. Cancer Australia was established in 2006 to provide leadership and vision, support to consumers and health professionals, and make recommendations to the government about cancer policy and priorities. In July 2011, Cancer Australia amalgamated with the National Breast and Ovarian Cancer Centre (NBOCC) to form a single national agency. NBOCC had previously developed a strong agenda focused on Aboriginal and Torres Strait Islander women impacted by breast cancer. The amalgamation resulted in Cancer Australia's first appointment of an Aboriginal person to its Advisory Council. In 2015, Cancer Australia established its Leadership Group on Aboriginal and Torres Strait Islander Cancer Control (the Leadership Group).

The Leadership Group advises on policy initiatives relevant to achieving equity in cancer outcomes for Aboriginal and Torres Strait Islander people affected by cancer. It brings together leaders in Aboriginal and Torres Strait Islander health, research, and policy, as well as people with a lived experience of cancer. Multiple stakeholder groups including the National Aboriginal Community Controlled Health Organisation and the National Association of Aboriginal and Torres Strait Islander Health Workers and Practitioners are represented on the Leadership Group. The group champions cross-sector collaboration and leads a shared agenda to improve cancer outcomes at system, service, and community levels. Since its inception, the Leadership Group has helped to develop the national conversation about cancer, informed the sector about the increasing cancer burden experienced by Aboriginal and Torres Strait Islander peoples and communities, and guided system change.

In this chapter, we outline key policy areas the Leadership Group has contributed to. Past and current members of the Leadership Group are included at the end of this chapter.

Key Principles and Best Practices for Co-design

The Leadership Group recommended that Cancer Australia should establish a co-design approach to develop programs and policies that impact Aboriginal and Torres Strait Islander peoples. The co-design approach is collaborative and iterative, with active engagement of stakeholders, including end users, from idea synthesis to policy implementation. Stakeholders are active partners who interact with policymakers to define problems and generate and/or modify solutions through iterative testing and refinement.

G. Garvey (ed.), *Indigenous and Tribal Peoples and Cancer*, https://doi.org/10.1007/978-3-031-56806-0_10

The Leadership Group advised on the co-design approach used by Cancer Australia. Co-design has become an essential way of highlighting equal power in decision-making and showing respect for the knowledge and diversity of Aboriginal and Torres Strait Islander people. For example, the new Lung Cancer Screening Program is informed by co-design principles and practices identified and defined by Aboriginal and Torres Strait Islander people.

Following the Leadership Group's advice, Cancer Australia partnered with the First Nations Cancer and Wellbeing Research Program at The University of Queensland, led by Professor Gail Garvey, to identify key principles and best practice approaches to co-design with Aboriginal and Torres Strait Islander peoples in the cancer control context in Australia [2, 3]. This work identified six key principles for co-design, which informed early scoping of a Lung Cancer Screening Program and now informs all future work at Cancer Australia:

1. First Nations leadership.
2. Culturally grounded approach.
3. Respect.
4. Benefit to community.
5. Inclusive partnerships.
6. Transparency and evaluation.

These principles provide a valuable starting point for the future development of guidelines, toolkits, reporting standards, and evaluation criteria to guide co-design with First Nations Australians. Insight from the Leadership Group informed this critical and foundational piece of work for Cancer Australia.

Aboriginal and Torres Strait Islander–Led Co-design Approach to the Development of the Australian Cancer Plan

The Australian Cancer Plan [4] (the Plan), published in November 2023, sets a national agenda to accelerate world-class cancer outcomes and improve the lives of all Australians affected by cancer. It provides a 10-year national strategic framework, including integrated actions to improve outcomes for Aboriginal and Torres Strait Islander people, which were identified and led by Aboriginal and Torres Strait Islander people. Achieving equity for Aboriginal and Torres Strait Islander people is the most significant ambition for the future of cancer care in Australia.

The Plan was developed through collaborative partnerships and engagement with Aboriginal and Torres Strait Islander people and under the guidance of the Leadership Group and Cancer Australia's Advisor on Aboriginal and Torres Strait Islander Cancer Control. It identifies six strategic objectives that require national, coordinated leadership and concerted effort across the sector for the next decade to deliver world-class cancer outcomes and experiences for all Australians (Fig. 10.1). Each strategic objective contains a 10-year ambition and 2- and 5-year goals with associated actions.

The strategic objective *Achieving Equity in Cancer Outcomes for Aboriginal and Torres Strait Islander People* complements the ambitions, goals, and actions identified for the other five strategic objectives. Of the 46 actions in the Plan, all are relevant to Aboriginal and Torres Strait Islander cancer control and one-third are specific to Aboriginal and Torres Strait Islander peoples.

All actions in the Plan were developed through a co-design approach with Aboriginal and Torres Strait Islander leaders, including the Leadership Group; the National Aboriginal Community Controlled Health Organisation; leaders in Aboriginal and Torres Strait Islander health, research, and policy; jurisdictional Aboriginal and Torres Strait Islander health policy representatives; and people affected by cancer. Aboriginal and Torres Strait Islander representatives actively participated in key engagement activities; contributed to drafting and refining the ambitions, goals, and actions; and reviewed draft Plan content. In addition, a stakeholder engagement strategy was undertaken to encourage input to the Plan from Aboriginal and Torres Strait Islander people, including 35 national stakeholder engagement visits with representatives of cancer services and Aboriginal and Torres Strait Islander health organizations across all states and territories.

Development of the Aboriginal and Torres Strait Islander Cancer Framework

In 2015, Cancer Australia worked with Professor Gail Garvey and her team from the Menzies School of Health Research to develop an evidence-based, nationally agreed strategic framework to guide future Aboriginal and Torres Strait Islander cancer control efforts [5]. The project was overseen by the Leadership Group and a steering group with a majority of Aboriginal and Torres Strait Islander members.

The Framework provides high-level guidance and direction to improve cancer outcomes for Aboriginal and Torres Strait Islander people. It complements and enhances national, jurisdictional, regional, and local efforts to improve Aboriginal and Torres Strait Islander cancer outcomes, such as cancer plans and related policies, frameworks, and action plans. It determines priority areas for action, while providing flexibility for adaptation to local contexts and needs. It encompasses the full continuum of cancer control, including prevention, screening and early detection, diagnosis and

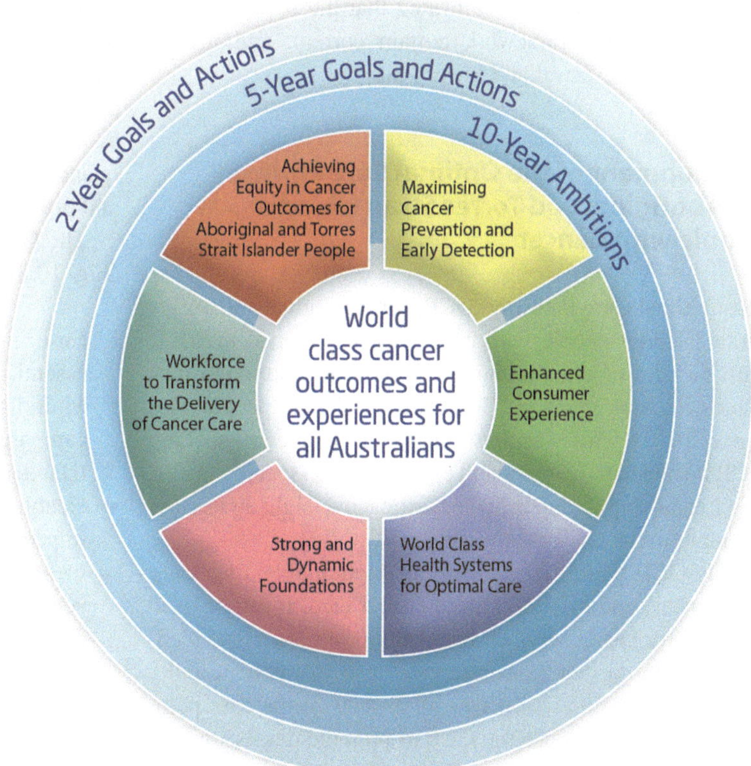

Fig. 10.1 Six strategic objectives encompass the Plan's vision [4]

treatment, palliative care, and survivorship. It also addresses the policies and research that surround these service areas.

The Framework was developed through a systematic literature review that examined the issues, gaps, and priorities for improving cancer outcomes in Aboriginal and Torres Strait Islander people. The review provided an evidence base to inform stakeholder consultations. A range of consultative approaches were used to reach stakeholders across Australia, including six face-to-face forums, a widely circulated online survey, and online discussion boards. Key stakeholder groups included:

- Aboriginal and Torres Strait Islander people affected by cancer, their families and support people, community leaders, and advocates within communities.
- Health professionals and service providers who work with Aboriginal and Torres Strait Islander people in cancer control, prevention, diagnosis and treatment, including the community-controlled health sector.
- Peak professional bodies and associations.
- Non-government organizations, researchers, state and territory governments, and Commonwealth departments.

Several hundred people provided input into the Framework via these consultations. A high proportion of participants were Aboriginal and Torres Strait Islander people, including many directly affected by cancer, their families, and/or carers. The Leadership Group informed the development of this foundational piece of policy, which has underpinned Cancer Australia's work to improve outcomes for Aboriginal and Torres Strait Islander people since 2015.

The Framework identified seven priorities that would have the greatest impact on disparities in cancer outcomes:

1. Improve knowledge, attitudes, and understanding of cancer by individuals, families, carers, and community members (across the continuum).
2. Focus prevention activities to address specific barriers and enablers to minimize cancer risk for Aboriginal and Torres Strait Islander peoples.
3. Increase access to and participation in cancer screening and immunization for the prevention and early detection of cancers.
4. Ensure early diagnosis of symptomatic cancers.
5. Ensure Aboriginal and Torres Strait Islander people affected by cancer receive optimal and culturally appropriate treatment, services, and supportive and palliative care.
6. Ensure families and carers of Aboriginal and Torres Strait Islander people with cancer are involved, informed, supported, and enabled throughout the cancer experience.
7. Strengthen the capacity of cancer-related services and systems to deliver good quality, integrated services that meet the needs of Aboriginal and Torres Strait Islander people.

In 2020, stakeholders reaffirmed that the seven original priorities of the Framework remain current, and this is reflected in the Australian Cancer Plan.

Development of the Optimal Care Pathway for Aboriginal and Torres Strait Islander People with Cancer

The Optimal Care Pathway (OCP) for Aboriginal and Torres Strait Islander people with cancer was developed in 2018, with the aim of eliminating disparities and improving outcomes for Aboriginal and Torres Strait Islander people with cancer [6, 7]. This was Australia's first population-specific OCP, designed to complement existing tumor-specific OCPs. The Leadership Group provided critical oversight and strategic input to the OCP's development.

The OCP guides the delivery of high-quality, culturally appropriate, and evidence-based cancer care. It can be used as a tool for health services and health professionals to identify gaps in current cancer services and to inform quality improvement initiatives across all aspects of the care pathway. Clinicians can use the OCP to promote discussion and collaboration between health professionals and people affected by cancer.

The OCP was developed through an iterative methodology over a 2-year period, in collaboration with the Leadership Group and more than 70 organizations and individuals. The process included a national review of care experiences and national consultation with the Aboriginal and Torres Strait Islander health sector and community, health professionals, and professional colleges.

The OCP identifies three areas that require prioritization (Fig. 10.2):

- Ensuring culturally safe and accessible health services is essential to support early presentation and diagnosis.
- Multidisciplinary treatment planning and patient-centered care are required for all Aboriginal and Torres Strait Islander people, irrespective of location.
- Health planners and governments acknowledge the imperative for change and have expressed strong commitment to work with Indigenous Australians to improve the accessibility, cultural appropriateness, and quality of cancer care.

The Leadership Group informed the OCP's development, including its key themes and appropriate messaging, and confirmed the importance of measuring the OCP's impact.

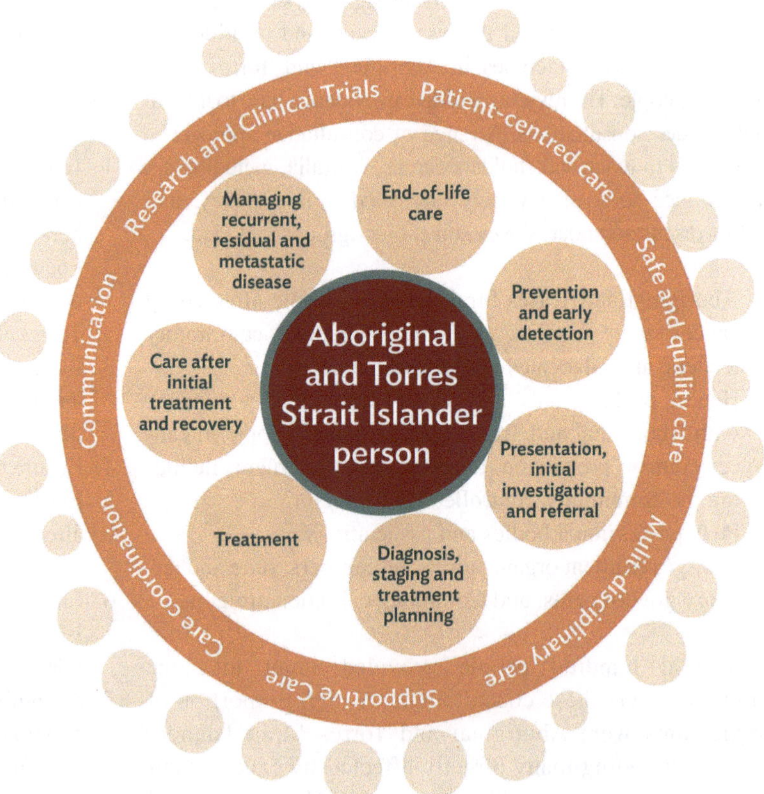

Fig. 10.2 Optimal Care Pathway (OCP) principles and steps [6, p. 26]

The Leadership Group provided input on supporting resources:

- A quick reference guide for health professionals.
- Consumer guides for Aboriginal and Torres Strait Islander people undergoing tests for suspected cancer and for those who have received a cancer diagnosis.

Reflections

The Leadership Group marks a significant step towards addressing cancer disparities. This group of leaders brings together diverse expertise and perspectives and fosters a strategic and focused approach to tackling the complex challenges surrounding cancer outcomes for Indigenous people. The policy advice of respected Aboriginal and Torres Strait Islander leaders and academics brought credibility to the process, strengthening engagement and supporting buy-in to national policy.

Increasing advocacy and leadership around the need for a national focus on cancer for Aboriginal and Torres Strait Islander people has enabled Cancer Australia to shape and lead discussions across health services alongside the recognition that cancer has become the leading cause of death for Aboriginal and Torres Strait Islander people.

Since 2015, Cancer Australia has placed increasing attention on the needs of the Aboriginal and Torres Strait Islander community. The ongoing advocacy and leadership of the National Aboriginal Community Controlled Health Organisation continues to provide partnership and alliance for Cancer Australia.

While the Leadership Group is one crucial step forward, it's just one part of the comprehensive effort needed to address cancer outcomes for Indigenous communities. Achieving sustainable change requires broader systemic shifts, increased funding, and long-term commitment from governments and institutions. The Leadership Group has made important and meaningful contributions to strategic policy. To truly make a lasting impact, the group's recommendations must be integrated into national policies, healthcare systems, and community initiatives, with ongoing consultation and collaboration with Indigenous communities at every stage.

Leadership Group Membership 2015–2023

Professor Jacinta Elston	2016–2022
Professor Gail Garvey	2016–current
Associate Professor Lisa Whop	2016–current
Ms. Tanya McGregor	2016–current
Associate Professor Phillip Carson	2017–2023
Ms. Sandra Miller	2017–2019
Professor Tom Calma AO	2018–current
Dr. Dawn Casey PSM	2018–current
Ms. Marilyn Morgan	2019–2023
Ms. Leanne Bird	2019–2023
Mr. Peter Bucksin	2019–2022
Mr. Karl Briscoe	2020–current
Associate Professor John Gilroy	2020–2023
Ms. Kristine Falzon	2023–current
Mr. Rob McPhee	2023–current
Mr. Trevor Pearce	2023–current
Ms. Leanne Pilkington	2023–current
Ms. Kate Thomann	2023–current
Ms. Kelly Trudgen	2023–current

Acknowledgments We acknowledge the traditional owners of country throughout Australia and their continuing connection to land, sea, and community. We pay our respects to them and their cultures and to Elders both past and present. We thank Aboriginal and Torres Strait Islander people for their contributions, without which these projects would not be possible. In addition, we thank all past and present members of the Leadership Group on Cancer Control for their valuable insights, expertise, strategic advice, and ongoing commitment to improving the cancer outcomes and experiences of Aboriginal and Torres Strait Islander peoples.

References

1. Australian Institute of Health and Welfare. *Cancer in Aboriginal & Torres Strait Islander people of Australia*. Canberra: AIHW; 2018.
2. Butler T, Gall A, Garvey G, Ngampromwongse K, Hector D, Turnbull S, et al. A Comprehensive Review of Optimal Approaches to Co-Design in Health with First Nations Australians. *Int J Environ Res Public Health*. 2022;19(23):16166. https://doi.org/10.3390/ijerph192316166
3. Anderson K, Gall A, Butler T, Ngampromwongse K, Hector D, Turnbull S, et al. Development of Key Principles and Best Practices for Co-Design in Health with First Nations Australians. *Int J Environ Res Public Health*. 2023;20(1). https://doi.org/10.3390/ijerph20010147
4. Cancer Australia. *Australian Cancer Plan 2023* [Internet]. Available from: https://www.australiancancerplan.gov.au/
5. Cancer Australia. *National Aboriginal and Torres Strait Islander Cancer Framework*. Surry Hills, NSW, Australia: Cancer Australia; 2015. p. 32.
6. Cancer Australia. *Optimal care pathway for Aboriginal and Torres Strait Islander people with cancer*. Cancer Australia; 2018.
7. Chynoweth J, McCambridge MM, Zorbas HM, Elston JK, Thomas RJS, Glasson WJH, et al. Optimal Cancer Care for Aboriginal and Torres Strait Islander People: A Shared Approach to System Level Change. *JCO Glob Oncol*. 2020;6:108–14. https://doi.org/10.1200/JGO.19.00076

BY NC ND

11 Cancer Control Agencies in Australia, Aotearoa New Zealand, and Canada

Sasha Webb, Rami Rahal, Louisa Salemi, Melissa Cernigoy, Talia Pfefferle, Cheryl Louzado, Gail Garvey, Jacinta Elston, and Dorothy Keefe

Key Points

- Cancer control agencies in Australia, Aotearoa New Zealand, and Canada play critical roles in driving national cancer strategies, policies, and approaches to eliminate inequities in cancer control that disproportionately impact Indigenous peoples.
- There is still much to do to achieve equitable cancer outcomes and experiences. Ensuring that government agencies work in partnership with Indigenous peoples, governments, organizations, and communities for the governance, design, delivery, and monitoring of health services for Indigenous peoples is key to eliminating inequities and meeting health and human rights.
- UNDRIP declares that Indigenous people have the right to participate in decision-making in matters that affect them, and aligned with the fundamental importance of the right to self-determination, cancer control agencies are committed to consult and collaborate with Indigenous peoples.
- Only with contributions, leadership, and direction from Indigenous peoples will services and programs truly address what is important to address disparities experienced by Indigenous peoples.

Cancer control agencies drive national cancer strategies, policies, and approaches to improve cancer outcomes for people affected by cancer, their families, and carers. These agencies are in positions to facilitate system-level opportunities that, through collaboration and coordination, will enable countries to eliminate cancer control inequities, which disproportionately impact Indigenous peoples.

Cancer control agencies worldwide have roles and responsibilities under the United Nations Declaration on the Rights of Indigenous Peoples (UNDRIP), which establishes a universal framework for reconciliation, healing, and peace. We are accountable to support and create spaces for ethical engagement based on the principles of justice and respect for human rights and equity for all [1, 2]. Cancer Australia, Te Aho o Te Kahu (the Aotearoa New Zealand Cancer Control Agency), and the Canadian Partnership Against Cancer each recognize that:

- Indigenous people have experienced, and continue to experience, significant injustices, discrimination, and ongoing effects of colonization that have negatively influenced their health outcomes and prevented them from fully exercising their rights.

We explore how Cancer Australia, Te Aho o Te Kahu (the Aotearoa New Zealand Cancer Control Agency), and the Canadian Partnership Against Cancer lead efforts to deliver better cancer outcomes for Indigenous peoples in Australia, Aotearoa New Zealand, and Canada. We acknowledge this work must be undertaken in partnership with Indigenous partners and we commit to creating spaces to support collaborative approaches to culturally appropriate care. We are stewards of this work, and our role is that of a supporter when and if identified by Indigenous partners. Our partners lead this work, our partners guide our priorities, and our partners continue to teach us how we can better create a cancer system that is equitable, accessible, and kind to all.

Cancer Australia

Cancer Australia provides national leadership in cancer control across all cancers and across the continuum of care, with a focus on populations who experience poorer health outcomes, including Aboriginal and Torres Strait Islander peoples.

Australia has one of the highest cancer survival rates in the world; however, this is not experienced uniformly. As cancer incidence and mortality have decreased for non-Indigenous Australians, they have increased for Indigenous Australians [3]. Cancer is now the leading cause of mortality

G. Garvey (ed.), *Indigenous and Tribal Peoples and Cancer*, https://doi.org/10.1007/978-3-031-56806-0_11

for Aboriginal and Torres Strait Islander peoples [4]. Disadvantage across a range of socioeconomic and health indicators, poorer access to health services, systemic discrimination, communication barriers, lower health literacy, and a lack of culturally appropriate care all contribute to this widening gap [5, 6].

The Australian Government invested $238.5 million (AUD) in the 2023–2024 budget to ensure mainstream cancer care services are culturally safe, respectful, and accessible to Aboriginal and Torres Strait Islander people and to build the capacity and capability of the Aboriginal Community Controlled Health Services (ACCHS) sector to support cancer care needs on the ground. Professor Jacinta Elston, Advisor to Cancer Australia, Aboriginal and Torres Strait Islander Cancer Control, and previous Chair of the Leadership Group on Aboriginal and Torres Strait Islander Cancer Control commented [personal communication, September 26, 2023]:

> Ten years ago, there was nothing much happening nationally for Aboriginal and Torres Strait Islander people around cancer. Over the past decade, I have seen that Cancer Australia has driven a change in the narrative that cancer is a priority for Aboriginal and Torres Strait Islander health. … Since 2022 Cancer Australia has engaged me as an Advisor on Aboriginal and Torres Strait Islander Cancer Control … and I, along with the Leadership Group, have helped their development of the Aboriginal and Torres Strait Islander elements of Australia's first national cancer plan.

Cancer Australia encourages and supports the cancer care system to provide optimal care that embeds Aboriginal and Torres Strait Islander voice, culture, strength, and knowledge. The agency collaborates with and seeks guidance from representative Aboriginal and Torres Strait Islander health organizations.

National Strategies, Policies, and Approaches in Relation to Aboriginal and Torres Strait Islander Peoples

The National Agreement on Closing the Gap (the Agreement) [7] is a commitment from all Australian governments and the Coalition of Aboriginal and Torres Strait Islander Peak Organisations to a new way of developing and implementing policies and programs that affect the lives of Aboriginal and Torres Strait Islander people. The four priority reforms in the Agreement are (1) formal partnerships and shared decision-making, (2) building the community-controlled sector, (3) transforming government organizations, and (4) shared access to data and information, to enable Aboriginal and Torres Strait Islander communities to make informed decisions. Cancer Australia recognizes that structural change in the way we work with Aboriginal and Torres Strait Islander people is needed to close the gap in cancer outcomes and is working in a new way that prioritizes partnership and shared decision-making between Aboriginal and Torres Islander people and governments.

The Australian Cancer Plan aims to deliver world-class outcomes and experiences for all Australians. It has a 10-year horizon, with 2-, 5-, and 10-year priorities and goals for its 6 strategic objectives. Its implementation will accelerate action to address system-level opportunities that involve partnerships between government and all elements of the health sector including ACCHS. Cancer Australia adopted an Aboriginal and Torres Strait Islander–led co-design approach to develop the components of the Plan specific to Aboriginal and Torres Strait Islander people and to provide advice across all strategic objectives [8].

Professor Tom Calma AO, member of the Leadership Group on Aboriginal and Torres Strait Islander Cancer Control, commented [personal communication, September 26, 2023]:

> As a member of the Leadership Group on Aboriginal and Torres Strait Islander Cancer Control, I have been significantly engaged in the development of the Australian Cancer Plan. The Leadership Group has brought diverse views and input on the Australian Cancer Plan from members with cancer expertise, public policy, and lived experience with cancer. I was involved in directly engaging community-controlled health organizations to discuss the plan and local approaches to support Aboriginal and Torres Strait Islander people with cancer and noted the keen interest of all stakeholders to learn more about cancers, treatment, and coordinated and integrated service provision. They particularly welcomed the opportunity to be engaged and heard.

The Plan has a specific strategic objective to achieve equity in cancer outcomes for Aboriginal and Torres Strait Islander people, and 15 of the Plan's 46 actions are Indigenous-specific (across all strategic objectives). The Plan acknowledges that Aboriginal and Torres Strait Islander health belongs in Aboriginal and Torres Strait Islander hands and gives priority to closing the gap in cancer outcomes by addressing individual and institutional racism and discrimination across cancer services. The Plan emphasizes the need to co-design services, deliver place-based care, and partner with Aboriginal and Torres Strait Islander people to deliver culturally safe and appropriate care across the cancer continuum.

Te Aho o Te Kahu, Aotearoa New Zealand Cancer Control Agency

Like other Indigenous peoples around the world, the Māori people of Aotearoa New Zealand experience significant inequities across many parts of the cancer continuum. Māori are 20% more likely to be diagnosed with cancer than non-Māori; and once diagnosed, are twice as likely to die from cancer [9]. Māori people are also less likely to access cancer screening [10] and less likely to access best practice treatment for their stage of disease [11–13]. As in other jurisdictions, these disparities reflect systemic disparities in access to the social determinants of good health, including cancer prevention and best practice care [14].

In 2019, in response to public advocacy, the Aotearoa New Zealand Government created the country's first national Cancer Control Agency, reporting directly to the Minister of Health. The agency provides strong central leadership, oversees cancer control, and leads and unites efforts to improve cancer outcomes for Aotearoa New Zealand.

The whakapapa (genealogy) and māoritanga (meaning) of the agency's Māori name reflects its commitment to working with Māori. The new Cancer Control Agency established a partnership with Hei Āhuru Mōwai, an independent organization of Māori cancer experts. The members of Hei Āhuru Mōwai worked alongside the agency's leaders and others to develop the agency's vision and values (see Fig. 11.1).

As part of this process, Hei Āhuru Mōwai gifted the name Te Aho o Te Kahu to the agency. This translates as the central or binding thread (te aho) of the cloak (te kahu). The central thread symbolizes the agency, whereas the strands (whenu) symbolize all the organizations, services, stakeholder groups, and individuals across Aotearoa New Zealand's cancer continuum. The kahu (cloak) metaphorically provides wrap-around care, protection, and support for patients and their whānau (families) as they navigate the cancer control system. The agency is envisioned as a unifying connector that enables and drives the equitable provision of cancer control across the country [14].

The agency's creation and operating model reflected a renewed government commitment to deliver on the principles and aspirations of Te Tiriti o Waitangi (Treaty of Waitangi), the founding agreement between Māori and the British Government. Initially ignored in many ways by successive governments, all public sector organizations now must give effect to Te Tiriti o Waitangi. In the health context, this has resulted in five principles to drive the future delivery of healthcare in Aotearoa New Zealand [15].

Te Aho o Te Kahu was created as the country prepared to undergo once-in-a-generation reforms to the health system. This created two new health entities to drive future decision-making and the commissioning of health services in Aotearoa New Zealand. Their first joint strategic plan [16] and the passing of legislation focused on the health sector reforms [17] have created the foundations for change.

Te Aho o Te Kahu vision:

- Fewer cancers
- Better survival
- Equity for all

Te Aho o Te Kahu values:

- Equity-led
- Knowledge-driven
- Outcomes-focused
- Person and whānau (family)–centered

Fig. 11.1 Vision and values of Te Aho o Te Kahu

Working with Māori: What This Looks Like in Practice

This environment has created many opportunities for Te Aho o Te Kahu to embed system-level change, including:

- A formal partnership with Hei Āhuru Mōwai including reporting on how the mana (prestige and status) of the name is upheld.
- The creation of two advisory groups (a Clinical Assembly and a Consumer Advisory Group), with 50% membership reserved for Māori.
- Incorporating equity and Te Tiriti o Waitangi analysis into business and project management processes.
- Involving Māori cancer professionals and patients in work to deliver options for the future delivery of cancer treatment services [18].
- Partnering with iwi (Tribal groups) and local organizations to deliver the largest Māori cancer engagement process undertaken in this country. The resulting report series [19] is influencing Te Aho o Te Kahu work programs and those of the wider health system.
- Measuring and reporting information about Māori on most cancer indicators, including a comprehensive summary of the cancer sector [9] and ongoing quality improvement reports [20].

While the agency is proud of its work to date and its partnership with Hei Āhuru Mōwai, there is still much to do to achieve equitable cancer outcomes and experiences, particularly for Māori. In this context, the agency is driven by a whakatauāki (proverb) from renowned kaumātua (respected Elder), the late Sir James Henare, which roughly translates as follows: you've come too far not to go further and you've done too much not to do more.

Canadian Partnership Against Cancer

The Canadian Partnership Against Cancer (the Partnership) is the steward of the Canadian Strategy for Cancer Control. The Partnership facilitates efforts and supports partners across the country to advance the Strategy's pan-Canadian priorities and actions. Together, the Partnership strives to ensure:

- Fewer people in Canada develop cancer.
- More people in Canada survive cancer.
- People in Canada affected by cancer have a better quality of life.
- All people in Canada have equitable access to high-quality cancer care, no matter who they are or where they live.
- Three peoples–specific priorities identified by First Nations, Inuit, and Métis [21].
- Culturally appropriate care closer to home: peoples-specific, self-determined care.
- First Nations, Inuit, and Métis–governed research and data systems [21].

Partnership is at the heart of this work, which supports cancer agencies and programs, health system partners, and communities across provinces and territories with funding, skills, resources, and evidence to develop sustainable solutions, take action, and improve cancer outcomes. While not delivering patient care, the Partnership works alongside partners to advance pan-Canadian cancer priorities and implement initiatives to ensure equity of access, experience, and outcomes in cancer care for everyone in Canada within a sustainable healthcare system.

The Partnership's approach is strengths-based, evidence-led, and inclusive. It builds on the unique and diverse strengths of partners and draws from the latest research and knowledge. The Partnership champions the needs of equity-denied populations and advancing equity is a key focus of work with partners [22].

We continue to hear from First Nations, Inuit, and Métis partners that, to create change, representation must be included in spaces of policy development, priority setting, strategic planning, and program implementation. Trust in the healthcare system was broken due to colonial policies and practices that continue to exist and will take many years, if not generations, to mend. Representation matters when First Nations, Inuit, and Métis patients see themselves reflected in the care they receive. Representation also matters where long-term changes are being made, such as representation in leadership roles with the ability to impact the development of cancer care policies and standards of practice. Inclusion of cultural practices led and owned by First Nations, Inuit, and Métis peoples would eliminate mistrust in the cancer care system and reflect reconciliation in practice. Cultural knowledge from lived experience must be a contributing factor to recruitment and be weighted at a level that impacts staffing outcomes. Furthermore, First Nations, Inuit, and Métis staff must be recruited, hired, and retained in roles that impact [23].

National Strategies, Policies, and Approaches in Relation to First Nations, Inuit, and Métis People

The Partnership acknowledges that colonial practices and policies continue to impact the wellbeing of First Nations, Inuit, and Métis. First Nations, Inuit, and Métis governments, organizations, and communities are leading the work that will result in improved wellbeing with the development and implementation of peoples-specific, self-determined solutions. The Partnership is providing funds to almost 30 partners, who are collectively working with over 130 First Nations, Inuit, and Métis governments, organizations, and community partners to develop and implement peoples-specific cancer strategies [24]. Supporting this work is key to sustainable system change and to closing the gaps in cancer care and outcomes between First Nations, Inuit, Métis, and other people in Canada.

The Partnership is committed to working in a reconciliatory way with First Nations, Inuit, and Métis to improve the cancer system by:

- Implementing the Truth and Reconciliation Commission's Calls to Action [23].
- Supporting self-determined, regional, and peoples-specific priorities in the Canadian Strategy for Cancer Control [22].
- Supporting partners in their efforts to improve the quality of life, access, experience, and health outcomes of all First Nations, Inuit, and Métis patients and families [25].
- Encouraging an organization-wide approach to implementing the Canadian Strategy for Cancer Control guided by First Nations, Inuit, and Métis governments, organizations, advisors, and partners, supported by ongoing, mandatory cultural competency training for Partnership staff.

The Partnership's Reconciliation Pathway is a living record and summary of the Partnership's journey towards reconciliation. The intent of this pathway is to support the organization by highlighting the importance of engagement, relationships, and meaningful partnership—and the work it takes to do these in a respectful way.

References

1. United Nations. *United Nations Declaration on the Rights of Indigenous Peoples*. United Nations; 2007. Available from: https://www.un.org/development/desa/indigenouspeoples/wp-content/uploads/sites/19/2018/11/UNDRIP_E_web.pdf
2. *United Nations Declaration on the Rights of Indigenous Peoples Act 2021* (Canada).
3. Australian Institute of Health and Welfare. *Cancer in Aboriginal & Torres Strait Islander people of Australia*. 2018 Mar 15. Available from: https://www.aihw.gov.au/reports/cancer/cancer-in-indigenous-australians/contents/summary

4. Aboriginal and Torres Strait Islander Health Performance Framework, *1.23 Leading causes of mortality* [Internet]. Australian Institute of Health and Welfare; 2023. Available from: https://www.indigenoushpf.gov.au/measures/1-23-leading-causes-mortality#:~:text=The%20leading%20causes%20of%20death,endocrine%2C%20nutritional%20and%20metabolic%20diseases.
5. Dasgupta P, Harris VM, Garvey G, Aitken JF, Baade PD. Factors associated with cancer survival disparities among Aboriginal and Torres Strait Islander peoples compared with other Australians: A systematic review. *Front Oncol.* 2022;12:968400. https://doi.org/10.3389/fonc.2022.968400
6. Whop LJ, Bernardes CM, Kondalsamy-Chennakesavan S, Darshan D, Chetty N, Moore SP, et al. Indigenous Australians with non-small cell lung cancer or cervical cancer receive suboptimal treatment. *Asia Pac J Clin Oncol.* 2017;13(5):e224–e31. https://doi.org/10.1111/ajco.12463
7. Coalition of Aboriginal and Torres Strait Islander Peak Organisations, Australian Governments. *National Agreement on Closing the Gap.* 2020. Available from: https://www.closingthegap.gov.au/national-agreement
8. Anderson K, Gall A, Butler T, Ngampromwongse K, Hector D, Turnbull S, et al. Development of Key Principles and Best Practices for Co-Design in Health with First Nations Australians. *Int J Environ Res Public Health.* 2023; 20(1). https://doi.org/10.3390/ijerph20010147
9. Te Aho o Te Kahu. *He Pūrongo Mate Pukupuku o Aotearoa 2020, The State of Cancer in New Zealand 2020.* Te Aho o Te Kahu; 2021. Available from: https://teaho.govt.nz/reports/cancer-state
10. Robson B, Stanley J. *BreastScreen Aotearoa Programme Monitoring Report: For Maori. Pacific and Total women screened during the two or four years to June 2016.* National Screening Unit, Ministry of Health; 2016. Available from: https://www.nsu.govt.nz/system/files/page/bsa_monitoring_report_for_women_screened_to_june_2016.pdf
11. Hill S, Sarfati D, Blakely T, Robson B, Purdie G, Dennett E, et al. Ethnicity and management of colon cancer in New Zealand: do indigenous patients get a worse deal? *Cancer.* 2010;116(13):3205–14. https://doi.org/10.1002/cncr.25127
12. Signal V, Sarfati D, Cunningham R, Gurney J, Koea J, Ellison-Loschmann L. Indigenous inequities in the presentation and management of stomach cancer in New Zealand: a country with universal health care coverage. *Gastric Cancer.* 2015;18(3):571–9. https://doi.org/10.1007/s10120-014-0410-y
13. Lawrenson R, Lao C, Campbell I, Harvey V, Brown C, Seneviratne S, et al. The use of trastuzumab in New Zealand women with breast cancer. *Asia Pac J Clin Oncol.* 2018;14(2):e152–e60. https://doi.org/10.1111/ajco.12766
14. Mako M, Gurney J, Goza M, Ruka M, Scott N, Thompson G, et al. Te Aho o Te Kahu: weaving equity into national-level cancer control. *Lancet Oncol.* 2022;23(9):e427–e34. https://doi.org/10.1016/S1470-2045(22)00279-0
15. Ministry of Health. *Whakamaua: Māori Health Action Plan 2020–2025.* 2020. p. 16. Available from: https://www.health.govt.nz/publication/whakamaua-maori-health-action-plan-2020-2025
16. Te Aka Whai Ora – Māori Health Authority, Te Whatu Ora – Health New Zealand. *Te Pae Tata Interim New Zealand Health Plan 2022.* 2022. Available from: https://www.tewhatuora.govt.nz/whats-happening/what-to-expect/nz-health-plan/
17. *Pae Ora (Healthy Futures) Act 2022* (New Zealand).
18. Te Aho o Te Kahu. *He Mahere Ratonga Mate Pukupuku. Cancer Services Planning: A vision for cancer treatment in the reformed health system.* 2022. Available from: https://teaho.govt.nz/publications/cancer-services-planning
19. Te Aho o Te Kahu. *Rongohia Te Reo, Whatua He Oranga: The voices of whānau Māori affected by cancer.* 2023. Available from: https://teaho.govt.nz/publications/hui-reports
20. Te Aho o Te Kahu. *Cancer Quality Performance Indicator Programme.* 2023. Available from: https://teaho.govt.nz/reports/qpi
21. Canadian Partnership Against Cancer. *Priority 8: First Nations-, Inuit- and Métis-governed research and data systems.* 2023. Available from: https://www.partnershipagainstcancer.ca/cancer-strategy/strategic-priorities/priority-8-first-nations-inuit-metis-governed-research-data-systems/
22. Canadian Partnership Against Cancer. *Cancer Strategy 2019.* Available from: https://www.partnershipagainstcancer.ca/cancer-strategy/
23. Truth and Reconciliation Commission of Canada. *Truth and Reconciliation Commission of Canada: Calls to Action.* 2015 Available from: https://ehprnh2mwo3.exactdn.com/wp-content/uploads/2021/01/Calls_to_Action_English2.pdf
24. Canadian Partnership Against Cancer. *First Nations, Inuit and Métis—Current work.* 2023. Available from: https://www.partnershipagainstcancer.ca/about-us/who-we-are/first-nations-inuit-metis/current-work/
25. Canadian Partnership Against Cancer. *Developing the Peoples-specific, self-determined priorities and indicators.* Available from: https://www.partnershipagainstcancer.ca/cancer-strategy/strategic-priorities/co-development-peoples-specific-self-determined-priorities-indicators/

Barriers and Enablers to Collecting Indigenous Identification Information by Cancer Registries

12

Abbey Diaz, Shafkat Jahan, Neal A. Palafox, Ian Ring, Lisa Whop, Danica Cossio, Kalinda Griffiths, and Gail Garvey

Key Points

- Cancer registries are an important element of population cancer control.
- An estimated one-third of population-based cancer registries in countries or regions with an Indigenous population do not collect information on patients' Indigenous identity and more do not report Indigenous cancer statistics.
- Barriers and solutions at the data, person, service/information system, and sociopolitical levels are identified and described in this chapter.

Population-based cancer registries (PBCRs) are data information systems that systematically collect, record, and manage data of cancer patients within a defined population [1]. They play a valuable role in cancer surveillance within a given population, identifying changes in cancer incidence over time, across regions, and among diverse population groups, and, when linked to death registration data, enable the analysis of survival patterns [2]. These data are critical for assessing the need for and effectiveness of national cancer control programs, identifying possible cancer causes, and assisting patients and their healthcare professionals to make informed care decisions [3].

PBCRs collate secondary data, primarily from hospital, laboratory, and death registry records. At a minimum, PBCRs collect information on some clinical features of cancer (e.g., cancer diagnosis date, type, and diagnosis basis) and individual demographics (e.g., date of birth/age and place of residence) [3]. While race/ethnicity data are considered a basic element [3], the extent to which Indigenous identification is captured remains unclear. PBCRs that collect this information derive it from multiple administrative sources. Therefore, the quality of Indigenous identification in PBCRs is only as good as in the original sources.

The United Nations recognizes the right of Indigenous peoples to be counted in population and health data collections [4]. Due to the persistent inequalities in cancer outcomes, efforts to improve the measurement of Indigenous peoples' health data, including in cancer registries, have increased [5, 6]. A 2019 assessment evaluated the collection, recording, and reporting practices of Indigenous identification information by global PBCRs [7]. PBCRs in countries or regions with an Indigenous population, per the 2018 and 2019 Indigenous World yearbooks [8, 9], were invited to participate. Key barriers, strategies, and progress related to collecting and reporting of Indigenous data from PBCRs are summarized here.

Barriers and Strategies Related to PBCR's Collection and Reporting of Indigenous Data

Of the 371 eligible registries invited from 54 countries, 83 PBCRs from 25 countries participated in the 2019 assessment [7]. In brief, 12% were national registries and 78% were subnational (i.e., state, provincial, or district-based). Two-thirds (66%) of PBCRs collected Indigenous identification information of new registrations: 100% in the Pacific/Oceania region, 78% in North America, 61% in Asia, 44% in Central/South America, and 33% each in the Arctic Circle and Africa. Just over two-thirds had published Indigenous-specific statistics using registry data. Twenty-eight (34%) PBCRs did not collect Indigenous identity information and a further 18 (28%) that did contain Indigenous identity data did not use it to report cancer statistics specific to Indigenous peoples.

The key barriers to PBCR's collecting and/or reporting Indigenous people's data identified in the 2019 report were predominately relating to health services, information systems, and sociopolitical environments [7]:

1. Lack of routine and/or standardized data collection at point of care by healthcare staff—most frequently reported by PBCRs in Asia, Central/South America, and North America.

G. Garvey (ed.), *Indigenous and Tribal Peoples and Cancer*, https://doi.org/10.1007/978-3-031-56806-0_12

2. Not all PBCR information systems allow transfer of Indigenous identification data from point of care to the cancer registries.
3. Perception by some PBCR respondents that Indigenous identification was not a clinically relevant variable and Indigenous peoples' cancer statistics had no bearing on clinical decision-making.
4. Legislation prohibiting the collection of Indigenous identification data—most frequently reported by Asian and North American PBCRs.
5. Lack of legal and social recognition of Indigenous peoples.
6. Lack of interest from national health authorities to produce cancer statistics for Indigenous peoples.
7. Perception that collecting such information was a form of discrimination against non-Indigenous peoples.
8. Perception that collecting such data had potential to cause discrimination against Indigenous peoples or infringe on individuals' privacy.

The report also identified potential strategies to improve the collection and use of Indigenous data, at various levels of influence [7]. These included:

1. Strategies to influence sociopolitical barriers:
   (a) Raise public awareness of Indigenous peoples and the importance of Indigenous-specific cancer statistics.
   (b) Engage and consult with local Indigenous and Tribal groups to understand definitions of Indigeneity and how these groups wish to be identified.
   (c) Lobby for legislation change to allow and mandate that health service staff and health professionals ask about Indigenous identity at point of care, not only to enable accurate collection of Indigenous identification data but to support culturally safe and responsive care.
2. Strategies to influence health system/service barriers:
   (a) Develop and implement guidelines to standardize the collection and reporting of Indigenous identification information.
   (b) Develop and implement systems capable of capturing and transferring Indigenous identification through the information pathway, including ensuring referral and other forms contain a field to support the collection of these data.
   (c) Develop and implement best practice guidelines to assess completeness and accuracy of these data and guide the conduct of data linkage to enable reporting of Indigenous peoples' cancer statistics.
   (d) Collaborate with Indigenous communities to guide systems and service improvements that support collecting, recording, categorizing, and reporting Indigenous information.
3. Strategies to influence health professional barriers:
   (a) Design/re-design and deliver education for health-care professionals and administrative staff to improve primary data collection and raise awareness of the importance of asking about identity.
   (b) Improve the cultural safety of health services and facilities to support patients to provide accurate information about their identity.
4. Strategies to influence data systems and patient behavior:
   (a) Provide information/education to patients and families explaining the importance of PBCRs and the inclusion of Indigenous identification data, what the information will be used for, and that they have the right to not disclose their Indigeneity.
   (b) Where small population size prohibits typical approaches to reporting cancer statistics, aggregation of multiple years or jurisdictions should be explored to enable the reporting of Indigenous cancer statistics.

Notably, the importance of community engagement in addressing this issue was identified.

Progress Towards Routine Collection and Reporting of Indigenous Cancer Information

Here we will discuss progress regarding three key barriers to the collection of Indigenous identification information in various countries or regions.

Legislation Regarding the Definition and Collection of Indigenous Data in Selected Asian Countries

Several countries in Southern/Southeast Asia face significant issues in realizing the right of Indigenous peoples to health due to the lack of birth registration, citizenship, or legal status. This limits their access to essential healthcare services and inclusion in official health data collection [10]. For some countries, defining Indigenous identity is complex due to the region's ethnic diversity and government efforts to integrate these groups into the broader national identity. This complexity is exacerbated by the presence of various laws and policies aimed at assimilating Indigenous peoples into mainstream society [11]. For instance, India's government resists defining Tribal populations (referred to as "Scheduled

Tribes" or "Adivasi") as Indigenous because it deems it impractical after centuries of migration, absorption, and differentiation [11, 12]. This resistance is primarily driven by the aim of assimilation, as acknowledging Indigeneity could be perceived as supporting territorial separation from the Indian state [13]. The absence of clear definitions and limited policies for collecting Indigenous status data restricts the ability of cancer registries to accurately estimate cancer incidence in these countries.

Historical, political, and social influences on legislative definitions of Indigeneity may result in an under-estimation of Indigenous status in cancer registries. While some countries (e.g., Malaysia, the Philippines, Nepal, Myanmar, Taiwan, and Japan) have officially recognized the term "Indigenous peoples" to identify those with distinct cultural traditions and histories following international declarations (UNDRIP and ILO Convention 169) [14], definitions are disputed in other countries like China, India, and Bangladesh, which subsequently resist Indigenous recognition. In the spirit of the UN Sustainable Development Goal to leave no one behind [15], it is imperative that governments support cancer control in Indigenous populations through legislative requirements and increased societal recognition and representation in political decision-making.

Improving Point-of-Care Data Collection in Australia

The Australian Government's definition of Indigeneity is based on three components: descent, self-identification, and community acceptance [16]. Operationally, the definition is typically based on self-identification. A Standard Indigenous Question was developed in 1996 by the Australian Bureau of Statistics to enable systematic collection of self-reported identification at the point of contact and routine recording of these data in a wide range of government collections [16]. The Australian Institute of Health and Welfare (AIHW) has developed training and education resources for health service staff to assist healthcare services to ask all patients about Indigenous identity [17]. This initiative has paralleled advances in health services information technologies, which enable the assertation, recording, and transfer of Indigenous identification information [18]. Additionally, best practice approaches to data linkage to enhance the completeness and consistency of Indigenous identification information in health datasets, including Australian cancer registries, have been established [19].

Hospital admission records are the primary source of Indigenous identification data for Australian cancer registries. The quality of Indigenous identification in public hospital admissions records was assessed in 2011–2012 by the AIHW [20]. This report estimated that 88% of Indigenous patients were correctly identified in these records. Correction factors were derived to adjust national statistics for Aboriginal and Torres Strait Islander people to account for incomplete and inaccurate records. In Queensland, cancer registry data are currently housed within the Queensland Cancer Alliance and are continually linked to multiple administrative datasets, which inform the Indigenous identification variable. Consequently, the rate of unknown Indigenous identification for Queenslanders with cancer has reduced from 5% in 2011 census [21] to 0.4% in 2021 [22].

Coding Race/Ethnicity Data in the Pacific Regional Central Cancer Registry

The Pacific Regional Central Cancer Registry (PRCCR) was established in 2005 and sits within the governance of the North American Association of Central Cancer Registries. The PRCCR includes numerous US-affiliated Pacific Islanders, including Guam, the Commonwealth of Northern Marianas, America Samoa, the Federated States of Micronesia, the Republic of Palau, and the Republic of Marshall Islands, and it works closely with the Hawai'i Tumor Registry. The coding of race data in the PRCCR was designed to align with the specifications of the US Surveillance, Epidemiology, and End Results (SEER) Cancer Registry [23], which uses categories created during the 2000 US census. Due to the lack of granularity, they do not meet the needs of Pacific Island Nations/Territories.

The PRCCR derives race from two key data sources, patient hospital records and death registrations/certificates, and if provided it is coded by the cancer registrars. The existing race variable includes the following categories relevant to the US-affiliated Pacific Islander nations/territories: Hawaiian, Micronesian not otherwise specified (NOS), Chamorro/Chamoru, Guamanian NOS, Polynesian NOS, Pacific Islander NOS, and "other." To overcome the lack of granularity, a second *"full"* race variable has been added to the PRCCR to help identify patients' specific racial identification.

A persistent challenge is streamlining the coding for cases that are shared with the PRCCR from other US registries, which include the SEER race variable but not the PRCCR *"full"* race variable. In this event, the *"full"* race variable is left blank (missing). The purpose of collecting the PRCCR *"full"* race variable is to enable an in-depth understanding of the demographics and distribution of cancer across racial groups in Pacific Islander Nations/Territories to inform local cancer control strategies. This level of data is not reported to the Centers for Disease Control and Prevention nor back to the SEER register.

Conclusion

Cancer registry data can and should be used by governments, non-government organizations, communities, and researchers to identify changes in cancer trends, investigate cancer etiology, evaluate the need for and effectiveness of policy or population-level programs, and measure and monitor inequities. Increasingly, cancer registries are being linked to other datasets to enable analyses to address complex questions about a population's health [24, 25]. In turn, cancer trends and statistics play a crucial role in policy setting, resource allocation, and service delivery—and consequently, reduced cancer incidence, morbidity, and mortality.

The findings from the 2019 survey suggest that up to one-third of PBCRs in countries or regions with an Indigenous population are not collecting Indigenous identity information. More may not be reporting or enabling the reporting of Indigenous cancer statistics. This chapter sheds light on the significant challenges PBCRs face in collecting and reporting Indigenous identity information. The barriers, and therefore the solutions, vary across countries, highlighting the need for a global strategy that has local flexibility to tackle the issues that matter most.

References

1. National Cancer Institute: Surveillance, Epidemiology, and End Results Program. *What is a Cancer Registry?* [Internet]. US: NIH; 2023. Available from: https://seer.cancer.gov/registries/cancer_registry/
2. Johnson CJ, Weir HK, Fink AK, German RR, Finch JL, Rycroft RK, et al. The impact of National Death Index linkages on population-based cancer survival rates in the United States. *Cancer Epidemiol.* 2013;37(1):20–28. https://doi.org/https://doi.org/10.1016/j.canep.2012.08.007
3. Bray F, Znaor A, Cueva P, Korir A, Swaminathan R, Ullrich A, et al. *Planning and Developing Population-Based Cancer Registration in Low- or Middle-Income Settings.* Lyon (FR): IARC; 2014.
4. United Nations Department of Economic and Social Affairs. *State of the World's Indigenous Peoples.* New York: United Nations; 2015. Available from: https://www.un.org/development/desa/indigenous-peoples/publications/state-of-the-worlds-indigenous-peoples.html
5. Chino M, Ring IT, Pluver LJ, Waldon JA, King M. Improving health data for indigenous populations: The international group for indigenous health measurement. *Stat J IAOS.* 2019;35(1):15–21. https://doi.org/10.3233/SJI-180479
6. Griffiths K, Coleman C, Al-Yaman F, Cunningham J, Garvey G, Jackson L, et al. The identification of Aboriginal and Torres Strait Islander people in official statistics and other data: Critical issues of international significance. *Stat J IAOS.* 2019:35(1):91–106. https://doi.org/10.3233/SJI-180491
7. Diaz A, Soerjomataram I, Moore S, Whop LJ, Bray F, Hoberg H, et al. Collection and Reporting of Indigenous Status Information in Cancer Registries Around the World. *JCO Glob Oncol.* 2020 Feb;6:133–142. https://doi.org/10.1200/JGO.19.00119
8. Berger DN. *The Indigenous World 2019.* Copenhagen (Denmark): IWGIA; 2019. Available from: https://www.iwgia.org/images/documents/indigenous-world/IndigenousWorld2019_UK.pdf
9. Jacquelin-Andersen P. *The Indigenous World 2018.* Copenhagen (Denmark): IWGIA; 2018. Available from: https://www.iwgia.org/images/documents/indigenous-world/indigenous-world-2018.pdf
10. Asia Indigenous Peoples Pact. *Situation of the right to health of indigenous peoples in Asia* [Internet]. Chiang Mai (Thailand): AIPP; 2016. Available from: https://aippnet.org/situation-of-the-right-to-health-of-indigenous-peoples-in-asia/
11. Bhagabati DS. How to Be Indigenous in India? *Law Crit.* 2023 Apr 18. https://doi.org/10.1007/s10978-023-09343-8
12. United Nations: Office of the High Commissioner for Human Rights. *Submission to the Special Rapporteur on Freedom of Religion or Belief on Indigenous Peoples: Mapping lived experiences of Indigenous Peoples.* OHCHR; 2023. Available from: https://www.ohchr.org/sites/default/files/documents/issues/indigenouspeoples/sr/cfis/indigenous-freedom-religion/subm-indigenous-freedom-religion-cso-survival.pdf
13. Subramanian SV, Smith GD, Subramanyam M. Indigenous health and socioeconomic status in India. *PLoS Medicine.* 2006;3.10:e421. https://doi.org/10.1371/journal.pmed.0030421
14. Candelaria SM. *Comparative Analysis on the ILO Indigenous and Tribal Peoples Convention No. 169, UN Declaration on the Rights of Indigenous Peoples (UNDRIP), and the Indigenous Peoples' Rights Act (IPRA) of the Philippines.* Geneva (Switzerland): ILO; 2012. Available from: https://www.ilo.org/wcmsp5/groups/public/%2D%2D-asia/%2D%2D-ro-bangkok/%2D%2D-ilo-manila/documents/publication/wcms_171406.pdf
15. United Nations Sustainable Development Group. *Leave No One Behind* [Internet]. UNSDG; 2023. Available from: https://unsdg.un.org/2030-agenda/universal-values/leave-no-one-behind
16. Australian Bureau of Statistics. *Indigenous Status Standard* [Internet]. Canberra (AU): ABS; 2014. Available from: https://www.abs.gov.au/statistics/standards/indigenous-status-standard/latest-release
17. Australian Institute of Health and Welfare. *First Nations people* [Internet]. Canberra (AU): AIHW; 2023. Available from: https://www.aihw.gov.au/reports-data/population-groups/indigenous-australians/indigenous-identification
18. Australian Institute of Health and Welfare. *Taking the next steps: identification of Aboriginal and Torres Strait Islander status in general practice* [Internet]. Canberra (AU): AIHW; 2013. Available from: https://www.aihw.gov.au/reports/indigenous-australians/taking-the-next-steps-in-general-practice/summary
19. Australian Institute of Health and Welfare. *National best practice guidelines for data linkage activities relating to Aboriginal and Torres Strait Islander people: 2012* [Internet]. Canberra (AU): AIHW; 2012. Available from: https://www.aihw.gov.au/reports/indigenous-australians/national-best-practice-guidelines-for-data-linkage/summary
20. Australian Institute of Health and Welfare. *Indigenous identification in hospital separations data* [Internet]. Canberra (AU): AIHW; 2013. Available from: https://www.aihw.gov.au/getmedia/adcaf32e-d2d1-4df0-b306-c8db7c63022e/13630.pdf?v=20230605181102&inline=true
21. Australian Bureau of Statistics. *2077.0—Census of Population and Housing: Understanding the Increase in Aboriginal and Torres Strait Islander Counts, 2006-2011* [Internet]. Canberra (AU): ABS; 2013. Available from: https://www.abs.gov.au/ausstats/abs@.nsf/Lookup/2077.0main+features42006-2011
22. Cancer Alliance Queensland. *Queensland Health: Cancer Data Explorer* [Internet]. Brisbane (AU): Queensland Cancer Control

Analysis Team; 2023. Available from: https://cancerallianceqld.health.qld.gov.au/cancerdataexplorer/

23. North American Association of Central Cancer Registries. *Data Standards and Data Dictionary: Version 22 Data Item #160: Race 1* [Internet]. Available from: https://apps.naaccr.org/data-dictionary/data-dictionary/version=22/data-item-view/item-number=160/
24. Harron K. Data linkage in medical research. *BMJ Medicine*. 2022;1(e000087). https://doi.org/10.1136/bmjmed-2021-000087
25. Public Health Research Network. *Using data linkage to battle cancer* [Internet]. Australia: PHRN; 2021. Available from: https://www.phrn.org.au/media/82138/impact-story_using-data-linkage-to-battle-cancer_final.pdf

Issues in Reporting Cancer Statistics for Indigenous and Tribal Peoples

13

Kalinda Griffiths and Michele Connolly

Key Points

- Cancer statistics are required to support public health decisions, healthcare planning, research, and policy development.
- There are flaws in the accuracy and completeness of Indigenous peoples' cancer data, resulting in under-reporting.
- Both relative and absolute measures are required when reporting Indigenous peoples' cancer statistics.
- There are numerous considerations in the collection and use of Indigenous peoples' data for cancer surveillance and reporting.

Conventional cancer indicators, such as incidence, survival, and mortality rates, serve as critical metrics for understanding the impact of cancer on populations at large. However, when assessing the impact upon Indigenous and Tribal communities, issues with these conventional indicators and the comprehensiveness of the reporting become apparent. Indigenous and Tribal communities often face unique challenges, including limited access to healthcare, cultural and language barriers within healthcare systems, and socioeconomic factors, which can significantly influence the accuracy and relevance of standard cancer data.

Incidences of cancer in Indigenous and Tribal communities have been documented since the early 1920s, but not widely until the mid-1950s [1]. It is widely recognized that there are gaps in the accuracy and availability of the cancer data pertaining to Indigenous peoples, limiting routine reporting around the globe. This highlights an imperative to ensure the quality and availability of Indigenous peoples' cancer data and to provide measures that reflect the impact of cancer on Indigenous peoples.

This chapter aims to provide an overview of cancer statistics in Indigenous and Tribal communities globally, with a focus on Australia, Aotearoa New Zealand, Canada, and the United States.

An Overview of Cancer Surveillance and Systems in Indigenous and Tribal Communities

Australia Efforts have been made to improve cancer surveillance among Aboriginal and Torres Strait Islander peoples in Australia. This has included recognition of data gaps and collective efforts to improve cancer reporting across state and territory jurisdictions through Aboriginal and Torres Strait Islander leadership in collaboration with governments.

In Australia, Aboriginal and Torres Strait Islander standard cancer reporting on incidence, treatment, and outcomes is still only possible at a semi-national level due to limitations in data collection systems and processes.

Cancer Australia has developed a range of Aboriginal and Torres Strait Islander Cancer Control Indicators that reflect priority areas of (1) cancer awareness and beliefs, (2) prevention, (3) screening and immunization, (4) diagnosis, (5) treatment and support, (6) families and carers, and (7) services and systems [2]. While these are appropriate measures, there is limited or no data to report against these indicators. This highlights the ongoing need to ensure routine reporting of Aboriginal and Torres Strait Islander-prioritized cancer indicators in Australia.

Aotearoa New Zealand The Aotearoa New Zealand Cancer Registry has implemented initiatives to improve data collection and reporting for Māori populations, acknowledging the importance of comprehensive national reporting and addressing government obligations under Te Trirti o Waitangi (Treaty of Waitangi) to support Māori health and wellbeing aspirations. Aotearoa New Zealand is the only country in the world that has the ability to routinely report national Indigenous cancer statistics.

Canada Indigenous communities, including First Nations, Inuit, and Métis peoples, experience unique challenges

G. Garvey (ed.), *Indigenous and Tribal Peoples and Cancer*, https://doi.org/10.1007/978-3-031-56806-0_13

related to cancer measurement. The First Nations Cancer Surveillance Program, as part of the Canadian Partnership Against Cancer, as well as Statistics Canada [3] provide valuable data on cancer incidence, mortality, and survival rates within these populations. Culturally appropriate data collection strategies, community engagement, and collaboration with Indigenous organizations are essential components of measuring cancer in Canada's Indigenous communities.

United States The National Program of Cancer Registries of the Centers for Disease Control and/or the Surveillance, Epidemiology, and End Results (SEER) Program in the National Cancer Institute's Division of Cancer Control and Population Sciences provides data on cancer incidence and mortality among Indigenous populations in the United States.

Other Nations Many nations, such as Brazil, Mexico, and India, have implemented initiatives to collect cancer data specific to Indigenous populations. However, significant gaps remain in terms of comprehensive data collection, comparability, and access to healthcare services.

Global Perspective On a global scale, efforts have been made to address the disparities in cancer measurement among Indigenous and Tribal communities. The International Agency for Research on Cancer (IARC) and the World Health Organization (WHO) play crucial roles in coordinating data collection, providing technical support, and promoting research collaborations. There are also opportunities for global data collections to incorporate cancer reporting on Indigenous peoples and/or support existing measurement systems that enable and ensure routine reporting where Indigenous peoples' data are currently collected, but not reported on. However, challenges remain in terms of data standardization and quality, as well as governance that ensures Indigenous peoples' leadership and oversight of their data.

Considerations When Collecting and Analyzing Indigenous Peoples' Cancer Data

Cancer registries allow for the collection, storage, and analysis of information on people diagnosed with cancer. This information is used to monitor cancer rates, trends over time, patterns across regions and populations, and the outcomes of treatment and cancer care. Historically, developments in collecting and reporting cancer data have provided enormous benefits for the general population. However, major efforts are still required today to collect data and information regarding Indigenous and Tribal peoples to better support equitable outcomes.

There are several considerations that require our attention to ensure the appropriate collection, storage, and use of Indigenous and Tribal peoples' cancer data. The operational considerations outlined below are also important when it comes to cancer data. Specific operational considerations regarding Indigenous peoples' data include (1) recognition and identification, (2) systems and processes, (3) priority setting, and (4) monitoring.

Recognition and Identification

The identification of Indigenous peoples in official data can only be fully realized if there is recognition within the nation states in which they live [4]. The identification of Indigenous peoples within data ensures visibility in reporting, which is critical in assessing progress in cancer and service delivery. Furthermore, data and the information collected about Indigenous peoples that reflect both standard cancer measures (incidence, survival, mortality, etc.) and Indigenous-specific measures (wellbeing, wellness, experiences of cancer care, etc.) are required to support appropriate, reflective cancer reporting. For Indigenous peoples to have quality and accurate cancer reporting, they must be represented in the data and their realities and needs must be accurately reflected.

Recommendations from the 2007 United Nations Declaration on the Rights of Indigenous Peoples that are relevant to supporting recognition and identification across national data collections include Article 8, which aims to:

> … provide effective mechanisms for prevention of, and redress for … any action which has the aim or effect of depriving them of their integrity as distinct peoples or ethnic identities, or of their cultural values [5].

Furthermore, Article 15 states:

> Indigenous Peoples have the right to the dignity and diversity of their cultures, traditions, histories and aspirations which shall be appropriately reflected in education and public information [5].

Systems and Processes

Systems and processes include the infrastructure and associated procedures surrounding the collection, storage, and use of cancer data. Indigenous peoples' engagement with data systems and processes is embedded within the historical positionality of their communities within those nations. Ensuring the rights of Indigenous peoples are met, and building systems and processes that enable accurate and appropriate health and disease reporting, requires resourcing, governance, and policy that reflect values, understandings, and aspirations of Indigenous peoples within their

Table 13.1 Care principles for indigenous data governance

Principles	Description
Collective benefit	Data ecosystems shall be designed and function in ways that enable Indigenous peoples to derive benefit from the data
Authority to control	Indigenous peoples' rights and interests in Indigenous data must be recognized and their authority to control such data be empowered. Indigenous data governance enables Indigenous peoples and governing bodies to determine how Indigenous peoples, as well as Indigenous lands, territories, resources, knowledges, and geographical indicators, are represented and identified within data
Responsibility	Those working with Indigenous data have a responsibility to share how those data are used to support Indigenous peoples' self-determination and collective benefit. Accountability requires meaningful and openly available evidence of these efforts and their benefits to Indigenous peoples
Ethics	Indigenous peoples' rights and wellbeing should be the primary concern at all stages of the data life cycle and across the data ecosystem

Adapted from Carroll et al. [7]

respective nations. Global developments in Indigenous data sovereignty provide a charter to build data systems that work for Indigenous peoples.

Indigenous data sovereignty has been defined by Kukutai and Taylor as the inherent and inalienable rights and interests of Indigenous peoples relating to the collection, ownership, and application of data and information about their people, ways of life, and territories [6]. Internationally, the CARE Principles for Indigenous Data Governance (Table 13.1) have been developed to support the governance of Indigenous peoples' data [7].

Indigenizing cancer systems and processes that support the rights of Indigenous people is only possible with government support and collective agreements that work to enact resourcing, governance, and policy. However, this cannot be achieved without recognition of Indigenous peoples that is reflected in the cancer data and resulting reporting.

Priority Setting

Priority setting considers how and by whom decisions are made. Supporting mechanisms that ensure the voices of communities and Indigenous leaders are a requirement within colonial systems. Without these mechanisms, priority setting may not appropriately recognize the needs and aspirations of Indigenous peoples. It is important to understand that there are varying levels of power by which these priorities can be set. For example, there are opportunities for reference and advisory individuals and/or groups as well as boards to support priority setting. However, some of these groups and committees may lack the structural power required to formalize decision-making.

Regarding data and statistics, priority setting is necessary across measurement development as well as an understanding of variables and monitoring. In Australia, for example, a number of National Cancer Control Indicators have been developed to report against the National Aboriginal and Torres Strait Islander Cancer Framework and align with the Optimal Cancer Care Pathways for Aboriginal and Torres Strait Islander people [2]. These indicators were developed through the existing Aboriginal and Torres Strait Islander Leadership Group within Cancer Australia, the nation's government body for cancer control.

Monitoring

Cancer is a notifiable disease as a function of public health legislation within most nations. The point of this is to enable statistical reporting to governments that they may better understand the public health needs of their citizens. The same logic is applied to providing statistics for subpopulations. Governments are responsible for their citizens and must recognize that some populations have different impacts and needs. Understanding and addressing the impact of cancer upon Indigenous peoples in their respective nations requires ongoing monitoring that accurately and appropriately reflects such needs.

Measuring Risk Factors and Cancer Prevention

Understanding the social, cultural, and commercial determinants of cancer requires further efforts in measuring risk factors and the effectiveness of prevention strategies within Indigenous communities. There are structural and intermediary determinants that impact service provision and cancer risk factors, respectively. Structural determinants include governance, macroeconomic and social policies, as well as cultural and social positionality and values. Intermediary determinants can include housing, work environment, social support, and stress, as well as behavioral factors that can be affected through commercial entities. Cultural determinants, including traditional practices, beliefs, and spirituality, should be acknowledged and incorporated into prevention efforts. Identifying the commercial determinants, such as the impact of tobacco, alcohol, mining, and unhealthy food marketing on Indigenous and Tribal communities, should be measured and assessed to address the combined effects of these and other determinants on cancer outcomes.

Measuring risk factors, such as tobacco and alcohol use, obesity, and exposure to environmental toxins, provides valuable insights into the potential impact of cancer among Indigenous and Tribal populations. Understanding the unique risk profiles within these communities allows for targeted interventions, policy development, and resource allocation. Collecting data on risk factors also helps monitor the effectiveness of prevention programs and identify areas requiring further attention.

Future Directions and Recommendations

Strengthening Data Collection Systems Investing in robust data collection systems that recognize and identify Indigenous peoples is essential. Building culturally reflective datasets that adequately assess impact and need, as well as ensuring participatory mechanisms, will enable accurate and appropriate statistical reporting.

Enhancing Collaboration and Partnerships Strong partnerships between governments, researchers, healthcare providers, Indigenous organizations, and Indigenous communities are crucial. Collaboration should be fostered at all stages. Joint decision-making, knowledge exchange, and capacity-building initiatives that ensure culturally safe and competent environments will contribute to more meaningful and impactful outcomes.

Improving Data Quality and Accessibility Efforts should be made to improve the quality and comparability of cancer data among Indigenous populations. Standardized protocols, data validation processes, and quality assurance measures should be implemented. Additionally, relevant data should be made accessible to Indigenous communities, policymakers, and healthcare providers through user-friendly platforms and culturally relevant reporting formats.

Addressing Structural Barriers Structural barriers, such as systemic racism, colonization, and social inequities, contribute to cancer disparities among Indigenous communities. Addressing these barriers requires structural changes, in terms of policy reforms, increased funding for healthcare services, and enabling Indigenous self-determination in health governance. Accordingly, the inclusion of Indigenous perspectives and voices in policy-making processes is essential.

Conclusions

Statistical reporting of cancer in Indigenous and Tribal communities is essential for addressing existing disparities and improving health outcomes. Efforts to collect, analyze, and interpret cancer data should be culturally relevant and Indigenous led. By considering the challenges, risk factors, and cultural determinants faced by Indigenous and Tribal populations, we can develop targeted prevention strategies, reduce cancer burden, and improve survival rates. Through relevant and appropriate reporting that enables Indigenous visibility, supports collective rights and Indigenous voices, and enacts data sovereignty, we can make significant progress towards achieving health equity for Indigenous and Tribal communities globally.

References

1. Warwick OH, Phillips AJ. Cancer among Canadian Indians. *Br J Cancer.* 1954 Jun;8(2):223–30. https://doi.org/10.1038/bjc.1954.22
2. Cancer Australia. *Aboriginal and Torres Strait Islander National Cancer Control Indicators* [Internet]. [cited 2023 Aug]. Available from: https://ncci.canceraustralia.gov.au/aboriginal-and-torres-strait-islander-cancer-control-indicators
3. Jamal S, Jones C, Walker J, Mazereeuw M, Sheppard AJ, Henry D, Marrett LD. *Cancer in First Nations people in Ontario, Canada: Incidence and mortality, 1991 to 2010.* Statistics Canada; 2021 June 16. https://doi.org/10.25318/82-003-x202100600002-eng
4. Griffiths K, Coleman C, Al-Yaman F, Cunningham J, Garvey G, Whop L, et al. The Identification of Aboriginal and Torres Strait Islander People in Official Statistics and Other Data: Critical Issues of International Significance. *Stat J IAOS.* 2019;35(1):91–106. https://doi.org/10.3233/SJI-180491
5. United Nations General Assembly. *Declaration on the Rights of Indigenous Peoples.* 2007. Available from: https://www.un.org/development/desa/indigenouspeoples/wp-content/uploads/sites/19/2018/11/UNDRIP_E_web.pdf
6. Kukutai T, Taylor J, editors. *Indigenous Data Sovereignty: Towards an Agenda.* Canberra: Australian National University Press; 2016.
7. Carroll SR, Garba I, Figueroa-Rodríguez OL, Holbrook J, Lovett R, Materechera S, et al. The CARE Principles for Indigenous Data Governance. *Data Sci J.* 2020;19(1):43. https://doi.org/10.5334/dsj-2020-043

Indigenous Data Aggregation Perpetuates Structural Racism

14

Megan Gimmen, Ryan Benavente, Luke Roberto, and Kekoa Taparra

Key Points

- Aggregating Indigenous Native Hawaiian and Other Pacific Islander (NHPI) populations with Asian populations masks key NHPI disparities.
- NHPI patients have a higher comorbidity burden and worse survival rates compared to Asian patients.
- Indigenous erasure stifles NHPI research, funding, and public health initiatives.
- Medical researchers should adopt best research practices for NHPI health data collection.

In the United States (USA), the term "Asian Americans and Pacific Islanders" (AAPI) permeates both everyday conversation and mainstream media [1]. Initially established to foster solidarity between two distinct marginalized groups, the term "AAPI" has been widely scrutinized in recent decades [1, 2]. Critics argue that aggregation of the majority Asian American group, which itself is heterogenous, overshadows crucial health outcomes of the frequently excluded Native Hawaiian or Other Pacific Islander (NHPI) population, the Indigenous peoples of the Pacific Islands [2]. While Asian Americans trace their ancestry to over 30 countries across South, East, and Southeast Asia, Pacific Islanders share an Oceanic wayfinding heritage across over 20 island nations and territories in Melanesia, Micronesia, and Polynesia.

In this chapter, we explore the ways that data aggregation negatively impacts Indigenous Pacific Islander communities in the USA and discuss how this form of Indigenous erasure perpetuates structural racism, with a specific emphasis on cancer data. First, we review Indigenous Pacific Islander history in the context of US colonial and imperial ties (Fig. 14.1).

In the 1830s, White businessmen arrived in the Kingdom of Hawai'i to establish profitable plantations [3]. Economic interests pushed these businessmen to seize power from Indigenous rulers and urged the US government to do the same [3]. By 1893, Queen Lili'uokalani was forced to abdicate her throne, a direct violation of international humanitarian law [3]. In the coming decades, the Native Hawaiian monarchy was dismantled, the region annexed, and the territory given its statehood [3]. For generations, the Indigenous Native Hawaiian identity was suppressed. US colonialism and imperialism occurred in a similar vein throughout Oceania, in Palau, the Marshall Islands, the Northern Mariåna Islands, Guåhan, the Federated States of Micronesia, and American Samoa [4]. Today, some of these islands, particularly the US Pacific territories, are still under direct colonial rule [4]. These relationships of colonialism, imperialism, and militarization have widely suppressed Indigenous sovereignty across the Pacific.

In the USA, the term "Asian American" likely originated in the midst of the Black Power and American Indian movements of the 1960s [1]. Emma Gee and Yuji Ichioka at the University of California, Berkeley, are credited with creating the term by naming their group the Asian American Political Alliance (AAPA) [1]. The AAPA aimed to create unity by cultivating a pan-Asian identity [1]. Pacific Islanders initially aligned themselves with this movement, but struggled to commit to this racial identity given cultural and historical differences [1]. Nearly a decade later, the US government sought to address the long-standing use of broad, non-standardized race and ethnic categories used in federal data collection [5]. In 1977, the USA created four federally defined US racial categories: American Indian and Alaska Native (AI/AN), Asian and Pacific Islander (API), Black, and White [5]. The aggregated API racial category was first used in the US Census in the 1980s [1].

On July 9, 1997, a Federal Register Notice was issued with racial category recommendations from the Federal Interagency Committee. These included retaining the API category as an aggregated group [6]. The Native Hawaiian congressional delegation, 7000 postcard signees, and the Hawai'i legislature all opposed this recommendation. Native Hawaiian advocates wished to combine the Native Hawaiian group with the AI/AN category, expressing solidarity as fellow US-occupied Indigenous populations [6]. However, American Indian Tribal governments disagreed, arguing that aggregation would hinder informative data collection and

G. Garvey (ed.), *Indigenous and Tribal Peoples and Cancer*, https://doi.org/10.1007/978-3-031-56806-0_14

Fig. 14.1 Historical timeline of the NHPI community in the USA, with key time points informing how Indigenous NHPI race terminology came into existence and advocacy efforts for data disaggregation. (Abbreviations: *AI/AN* American Indian and Alaska Native, *API* Asian and Pacific Islander, *NH* Native Hawaiian, *NHPI* Native Hawaiian or Other Pacific Islander)

1830s	US businessmen arrive to the Kingdom of Hawai'i to build plantations.
1893	US businessmen overthrow Queen Lili'uokalani.
1898	Hawai'i is annexed.
	The US takes control of Guåhan, the Marshall Islands, the Northern Mariåna Islands, Palau, other Micronesian Islands, American Samoa, and more. Over time, political relationships evolve.
1959	The US makes Hawai'i a state.
1960	The Asian American Political Alliance is created, credited with the beginning of the pan-Asian identity in the US.
	Pacific Islanders align with the Asian American movement.
1977	The US creates 4 federally defined racial categories: AI/AN, API, Black, and White.
1980	The Census first utilizes the aggregated API category.
1997	NH advocates request removal from the API category and placement with the AI/AN category, united by Indigeneity.
	AI/AN leaders disagree citing concerns for AI/AN data collection and program administration.
	Likewise, NH leaders cite difficulties with NHPI data collection and monitoring as a result of the API category.
	The Office of Management and Budget agrees to disaggregate the API category.
	The US establishes 5 federally defined racial categories: AI/AN, Asian, NHPI, Black or African American, and White.
2000	The Census first utilizes the disaggregated Asian and NHPI categories.
2003	Deadline for federal programs to comply with these 5 racial categories.
2023	The NHPI category is still not honored in government, research, and academia which fuels the erasure of Indigenous Pacific Islanders

program administration for AI/AN communities [6]. Native Hawaiian advocates similarly argued that the aggregated API category inhibited data collection and monitoring of NHPI communities [6]. On October 30, 1997, the federal government reported that, while Native Hawaiian advocates initially wished to stand in solidarity with AI/AN, creating a new racial category was a viable option [6]. Thus, the federal government scrapped the API category and created separate Asian and NHPI categories [6]. This established the five federally defined racial categories used in the US today: AI/AN, Asian, Black or African American, NHPI, and White [6]. The disaggregated Asian and NHPI categories were first used in the 2000 Census [1]. Federal programs were expected to comply with these five revised racial categories by 2003 [6].

Unfortunately, widespread awareness has yet to be achieved. Government officials, medical experts, and researchers continue to aggregate NHPI and Asian populations [2, 7]. Advocates argue that NHPI aggregation is structural racism, defined as society's promotion of racial discrimination through institutions, ideas, and processes [2]. Specifically, data aggregation hides and perpetuates NHPI health issues [2, 7].

Data Disaggregation Hinders Research, Public Health Action, and Funding

The aggregation of NHPI data with those of unrelated non-Indigenous groups perpetuates structural barriers that hinder NHPI health equity. This section explores barriers in research, public health, and funding. Through four case studies, we explore ways in which Indigenous erasure contributes to structurally racist practices.

Data Aggregation and the Impact on Cancer Research

Recent advances in cancer research have come about due to the tireless work of NHPI champions advocating for NHPI data inclusion [7–9]. Here, we review two studies that report clinically important differences between Asian and NHPI patients with cancer.

Data Disaggregation in Cancer Research: Case Study 1

In research published in 2023, Taparra et al. investigated predictors of radiation therapy refusal among patients with the top 10 cancers in the USA who were recommended for radiation therapy treatment by an oncologist [8]. Specifically, their analysis stratified the results by race. Earlier studies identified that radiation therapy refusal when recommended by an oncologist was associated with a doubled likelihood of cancer mortality. However, none of these studies had included all five federally defined races including the NHPI population, exemplifying the practice of Indigenous erasure. This Indigenous knowledge gap among NHPI patients with cancer is significant given the high rates of cancer among this population.

The authors compared the rate at which patients refused radiation therapy from 2004 to 2016 by race in a national sample of patients across the country. Compared to all racial groups, NHPI patients with cancer had the highest rates of refusing oncologist-recommended radiation therapy and the largest increase of refusal over the course of the study. Indigenous NHPI and AI/AN patients were significantly more likely to refuse radiation therapy when compared to non-Hispanic White patients. No significant difference in treatment refusal rates was found among Asian patients compared to White patients. In addition, greater comorbidity burden was associated with increased radiation therapy refusal likelihood in NHPI, White, Asian, and Black patients.

While it is important that disparities are reported, they must also be contextualized by Indigenous scholars. While those outside the NHPI community may blame "lack of education" for radiation therapy refusal, the authors of this study underscore the impact of possible multigenerational historical trauma on NHPI radiation refusal. They propose that the history of atomic bomb detonations in the Pacific Islands may contribute to NHPI attitudes. During the Cold War, the US military test-detonated the equivalent of 7200 Hiroshima-sized bombs in the Marshall Islands. These events exposed Indigenous Marshallese communities to dangerous amounts of radiation and forced them to evacuate, all in violation of their human rights. This highlights how historical human rights violations might impact current NHPI cancer treatments. Moreover, it underscores the importance of Indigenous narratives to contextualizing health data.

In a follow-up study disaggregating Asian and NHPI patients, the same authors found that Japanese patients with cancer were not any more or less likely to refuse radiation therapy compared to other East Asian patients, suggesting that this history of atomic bomb detonation may be more specific to the experiences of the NHPI community [9]. Together, these studies provide an example of how cancer treatment decision-making by NHPI patients may differ from that of Asian patients, including Japanese patients whose country experienced the effects of atomic bomb use. Importantly, the authors provide historical context that may contribute to understanding of radiation therapy refusal.

Data Disaggregation in Cancer Research: Case Study 2

In a 2022 study, Taparra et al. reported disparities in survival and comorbidity burden between disaggregated Asian and NHPI patients with cancer [7]. They examined almost 6 million patients with nine of the most common cancers in the USA, with data disaggregated into East Asian, South Asian, Southeast Asian, NHPI, and non-Hispanic White patients.

The authors evaluated comorbidity burden (Charlson-Deyo comorbidity index) and survival outcomes for each of the disaggregated categories and subcategories. All previous studies of this nature had aggregated or omitted the Indigenous NHPI population. However, Taparra et al. found that NHPI patients with cancer have the highest comorbidity burden of all racial groups, with the comorbidity burden statistically higher than that of White and Asian patients. East Asian patients had significantly lower comorbidity burden. For most of the included cancers, Asian patients had improved overall survival outcomes compared to White patients, while NHPI patients had significantly worse overall survival outcomes for the majority of included cancers. Even after controlling for the significantly higher comorbidity burden among the NHPI population, NHPI patients still had significantly worse survival outcomes, suggesting multifactorial genetic and social influences.

These stark findings indicate that current aggregation practices give physicians, policy makers, and patients the false and damaging impression that NHPI patients with cancer have lower comorbidities and more positive outcomes than is the case. Many oncology clinical trials, including those supported by pharmaceutical companies, include strict performance status or comorbidity burden inclusion criteria. The authors suggest that comorbidity burden may play a role in the disproportionate exclusion of NHPI patients from oncology clinical trials.

Data Aggregation and the Impact on Public Health

There is an unmet need for cancer-related public health efforts that focus on the NHPI community. In this section, we review a relevant and contemporary example from the COVID-19 pandemic.

Leveraging Public Health Data: Case Study 3

Kamaka et al. describe how the NHPI data disaggregation movement informed public health efforts during the COVID-19 pandemic [10]. The first case of COVID-19 was reported in the USA in January 2020. By March of that year, the USA was in a state of national emergency. In April, the Centers for Disease Control and Prevention (CDC) excluded the federally recognized NHPI racial category from COVID-19 data reports stratified by race. However, by May 2020, NHPI patients had the highest case rates of COVID-19 compared to other races in 8 out of the 10 states with disaggregated data.

In May 2020, the Hawaiʻi NHPI COVID-19 Response, Recovery, Resiliency (3R) Team was formed. Within a year, the 3R Team successfully collaborated with the Hawaiʻi State Department of Health (HSDH) to address barriers to state-level data disaggregation through a public health lens. With these changes, the HSDH showed that high case rates were largely driven by other Pacific Islander communities, and not necessarily Native Hawaiian communities alone. Overall, COVID-19 remains a key example of a public health effort that has identified Indigenous populations in need.

Data Aggregation and the Impact on Federal Funding

Federal agencies can only fund solutions to identified problems. Since much NHPI health data is aggregated, issues of NHPI health are more likely to persist. Policy makers must decide between funding projects with convincing data or NHPI proposals that lack the same level of quality data. Thus, the realities of Indigenous NHPI people are overlooked and underfunded. Here, we review an example of long-term federal under-investment in the NHPI community.

Examining Federal Funding Trends: Case Study 4

A growing spotlight on the importance of NHPI research prompted scientists to investigate National Institutes of Health (NIH) budget allocation to Asian and NHPI population research [11]. Đoàn et al. examined NIH-funded extramural projects from 1992 to 2018 and found that only 0.17% of the total NIH budget was allocated to studies that focused on Asian American (AA) and NHPI health [11]. At first glance, a significant increase in total budget allocation pre- and post-2000 appeared promising. However, deeper analysis shows that the 0.12% pre-2000 allocation increased to just 0.18% post-2000. Indeed, the increased total NIH budget over this time was not associated with increases in AA and NHPI budget allocation. This demonstrates the NIH's lack of prioritization of Asian and NHPI communities, despite overall federal health budget increases.

Notably, the authors found that while Asian clinical trial participation increased from 2011 to 2016, NHPI participation decreased. When disaggregated from Asian participant data, almost no NHPI participants were included in the grants the authors examined. In the uphill battle for NHPI data disaggregation, support from the research community is imperative. Đoàn et al. exemplify this allyship with their awareness, inclusivity, and caring tone.

Conclusions and Best Practices

Indigenous erasure via NHPI data omission is harmful and masks health disparities. Researchers should critically evaluate current data reporting methods and adopt best practices to collect, disaggregate, and report NHPI data (Fig. 14.2). Clinical researchers should consider data oversampling to enable valid analysis that reflects the state of NHPI health [12]. Community collaboration is critical to building trust, facilitating participation, and honoring context for the communities the research intends to highlight [8, 10, 12]. Increased language translation would expand accessibility for those more comfortable communicating in Indigenous languages [12]. Demographic survey questions should include the option to specify multiple races given that most NHPI people identify as having multiple racial backgrounds [12].

Researchers should use the critical framework of Indigeneity during study design, including taking key steps such as the formation of robust community advisory boards [12]. Results should be socially and culturally contextualized to better capture the nuance of NHPI health outcomes [8]. Importantly, colonialism, imperialism, and globalization throughout Oceania should be factors included in the evaluation of NHPI inequities [2, 12]. It is broadly recommended that researchers reflect on their position relative to the communities they study [12]. Finally, scientists and institutions should empower Indigenous researchers and their sustainability through meaningful allyship [10, 12].

In embracing these inclusive and culturally sensitive data practices, researchers hold the power to illuminate the path toward a brighter future for our Indigenous NHPI communities, where health disparities are recognized and addressed,

Oversampling
To draw meaningful, statistically valid conclusions
Community collaboration
To honor cultural insight, gain context, and build trust
Language translation
To alleviate participation barriers
Multi-race reporting
To increase visibility of multi-racial NHPI participants
Indigenous framework
To provide critical context
Reflect on positionality
To identify areas of improvement
Empower NHPI researchers
To improve equity, representation, and sustanability

Fig. 14.2 Recommended NHPI patient data reporting practices

where research is guided by community-rooted collaboration, and where Indigenous voices are uplifted, fostering hope and resilience for generations to come.

The authors acknowledge that KT was supported by the Stanford Cancer Institute, an NCI-designated Comprehensive Cancer Center. KT was funded by a Stanford Cancer Institute Women's Cancer Center Innovation Award and the Stanford Cancer Institute Fellowship Award. KT was also funded by the American Society for Clinical Oncology Dr. Judith and Alan Kaur Endowed Young Investigator Award.

References

1. National Endowment for the Humanities. *Asian American and Pacific Islander Heritage and History in the U.S.* [Internet]. [cited 2023 Jul 28]. Available from: https://edsitement.neh.gov/teachers-guides/asian-american-and-pacific-islander-heritage-and-history-us
2. Morey BN, Chang RC, Thomas KB, Tulua A, Penaia C, Tran VD, et al. No Equity without Data Equity: Data Reporting Gaps for Native Hawaiians and Pacific Islanders as Structural Racism. *J Health Polit Policy Law*. 2022 Apr;47(2):159–200.
3. National Archives. *The 1897 Petition Against the Annexation of Hawaii* [Internet]. 2016 [cited 2023 Jul 28]. Available from: https://www.archives.gov/education/lessons/hawaii-petition
4. Office of the Law Revision Counsel United States Code. *48 USC Ch. 14: Trust Territory of the Pacific Islands* [Internet]. [cited 2023 Jul 28]. Available from: https://uscode.house.gov/view.xhtml?path=/prelim@title48/chapter14&edition=prelim
5. The White House. *Standards for the Classification of Federal Data on Race and Ethnicity* [Internet]. 1995 August 28 [cited 2023 Jul 28]. Available from: https://obamawhitehouse.archives.gov/omb/fedreg_race-ethnicity
6. The White House. *Revisions to the Standards for the Classification of Federal Data on Race and Ethnicity* [Internet]. 1997 October 30 [cited 2023 Jul 28]. Available from: https://obamawhitehouse.archives.gov/omb/fedreg_1997standards
7. Taparra K, Qu V, Pollom E. Disparities in Survival and Comorbidity Burden Between Asian and Native Hawaiian and Other Pacific Islander Patients With Cancer. *JAMA Netw Open*. 2022;5(8):e2226327. https://doi.org/10.1001/jamanetworkopen.2022.26327
8. Taparra K, Qu V, Lau B, Pollom E. A National Cancer Disparities Analysis of Predictors for Radiation Therapy Refusal by Race. *Int J Radiat Oncol Biol Phys*. 2023;116(1):96–102. https://doi.org/10.1016/j.ijrobp.2023.01.033
9. Lau B, Tominez P, Shing JZ, Vo JB, Pollom E, Taparra K. Racial Disparities among Asian American, Native Hawaiian, and Other Pacific Islander Patients with Cancer Who Refuse Recommended Radiation Therapy or Surgery. *Cancers (Basel)*. 2023 Jun 26;15(13):3358. https://doi.org/10.3390/cancers15133358
10. Kamaka ML, Watkins-Victorino L, Lee A, Freitas SM, Ramsey KW, Quint J, et al. Addressing Native Hawaiian and Pacific Islander Data Deficiencies Through a Community-based Collaborative Response to the COVID-19 Pandemic. *Hawaii J Health Soc Welf*. 2021 Oct;80(10 Suppl 2):36–45.
11. Đoàn LN, Takata Y, Sakuma K-LK, Irvin VL. Trends in Clinical Research Including Asian American, Native Hawaiian, and Pacific Islander Participants Funded by the US National Institutes of Health, 1992 to 2018. *JAMA Netw Open*. 2019;2(7):e197432. https://doi.org/10.1001/jamanetworkopen.2019.7432
12. Sasa SM, Yellow Horse AJ. Just data representation for Native Hawaiians and Pacific Islanders: A critical review of systemic Indigenous erasure in census and recommendations for psychologists. *Am J Community Psychol*. 2022;69(3–4):343–54.

15 From Insufficient Data to New Models of Healthcare in the USA

Judith Salmon Kaur and Linda Burhansstipanov

Key Points

- Accurate statistical data are necessary to develop and sustain culturally appropriate American Indian/Alaska Native (AI/AN) cancer programs that address the full cancer continuum.
- Due to cultural and statistically significant geographical variation in cancer incidence, mortality, and survival, AI/AN healthcare data cannot be aggregated.
- Early detection and screening support needs to expand to all AI/AN communities, inclusive of all types of screenable cancers. Partnerships are essential for long-term, proactive, and productive community-based programs and research.
- A new generation of AI/AN medical and public health professionals are leading research into cancer and cancer care among AI/AN people.

This chapter is dedicated to James W Hampton, MD (Chickasaw and Choctaw Nation) (September 15, 1931–October 1, 2022), the first American Indian medical oncologist in the USA.

The purposes of this chapter are to (1) briefly explain the transition from having no useable American Indian/Alaska Native (AI/AN) data (in the late 1980s) to NUKA, a successful, culturally based healthcare system in Alaska (1996), and (2) highlight efforts to increase the number of Indigenous professionals in the public health and medical fields.

Accurate Indigenous Statistics Are Necessary for Effective Programs to Evolve

In the 1950s, Dr. James Hampton raised the issue of inaccurate and under-reported AI/AN health data. However, it was not until 1980 that the US Congress Office of Technology Assessment released *Indian Health Care* [1], which reported the poor health of AI/AN populations. Congress directed federal agencies, including the Indian Health Service (IHS), Centers for Disease Control and Prevention (CDC), and National Institutes of Health (NIH), to address these reported substandard levels of health.

Insufficient and lack of AI/AN cancer data were raised as issues that contributed to substandard levels of health. To address data issues, in the late 1980s AI/AN health and cancer professionals, IHS, National Cancer Institute (NCI), and Tribal and urban Indian health program experts convened and discussed the dearth of and/or inaccuracies in AI/AN data that contributed to widespread misinformation and lack of Indigenous cancer care programs. In 1989, Dr. Ken Chu of the NCI Special Populations Studies Branch delineated and released AI/AN cancer mortality data (the first time AI/ANs were separated from the "other" group that combined all smaller populations). In the same year, the NCI established the Network for Cancer Control Research among American Indian and Alaska Native Populations, comprising 18 individuals from diverse regions. Among the key outcomes of this Network was the 1992 *National Strategic Plan for Cancer Prevention and Control to Benefit the Overall Health of American Indians and Alaska Natives* [2]. Two recommendations and associated outcomes from this Strategic Plan report follow [2, Ch. 12, p. 15]:

> *Recommendation A.* … the underreported mortality from cancer and other inaccurate cancer data on American Indians and Alaska Natives be recognized by federal agencies. The process of data collection should be corrected to prevent misleading conclusions.
>
> *Outcomes*: (1) Federal agencies will contract with an unbiased independent agency to assess the magnitude of racial misclassification in all federal databases …. (2) Federal agencies will organize training workshops for professionals and organizations involved with collecting cancer statistics.
>
> *Recommendation B.* … the overall quality of cancer data be objectively scrutinized and improved. The process of collecting American Indian and Alaska Native cancer statistics should be reviewed to reduce racial misclassification, diagnostic, and/or other errors.
>
> *Outcomes*: Federal agencies will develop an initiative to improve the cancer database by training tumor registrars/medical records staff …. To improve the reporting of cancer staging, federal agencies will encourage hospitals … to develop American College of Surgeons-approved cancer programs.

G. Garvey (ed.), *Indigenous and Tribal Peoples and Cancer*, https://doi.org/10.1007/978-3-031-56806-0_15

The strategic plan helped raise awareness about data insufficiencies affecting AI/ANs, programs, resources, and research. In 1993, the NCI Surveillance, Epidemiology, and End Results (SEER) and the CDC began to recognize the existence of statistically significant geographic differences among Tribal Nations. SEER leadership (Drs. Brenda Edwards and Judith Swan) allocated resources to improve racial misclassification of data and to support biannual meetings of the network (1996–2003). The CDC, NCI, IHS, National Cancer Registries, and others collaborated to improve AI/AN data collection and reporting. Currently, the CDC supports interactive websites that tailor AI/AN data to the user's needs.

These major improvements mean that most states now have databases linked with the IHS. However, some states with significant AI/AN populations have yet to create these links. Overall, state and local cancer data continue to be under-reported and inaccurate, and improvements are needed. In addition, with greater understanding has come the realization that different questions need to be asked, for example: why do some AI/AN cancer patients experience severe side effects leading to their withdrawal from cancer clinical trials, and are there unique genetic markers affecting AI/AN populations? Longitudinal tracking of AI/AN cancer survivors is required to understand the excessive chronic/long-term and late effects of cancer and/or cancer treatments among these populations [3–7]. In addition, data are almost entirely lacking on cancer diagnosis for AI/AN children, adolescents, and young adults. These data gaps need to be addressed so that research, support services, and interventions can be identified.

NUKA: A Model of Culturally and Medically Effective Indigenous Healthcare

The NUKA System of Care is an excellent model of care, relevant for selected regions of Indian Country [8]. Southcentral Foundation in Alaska created this relationship-based, customer-owned approach to transforming healthcare, improving outcomes, and reducing costs. Under this model, Alaska Natives are "customers" and "owners" and not patients; the 12 Alaska Native corporations are at the will of the people whose healthcare needs they serve. In contrast, most US healthcare is based around insurance payments, rather than patient needs. NUKA emphasizes being culturally respectful and finding ways by which the culture can support health, and preventative health in particular. Rather than repeatedly highlighting negative issues in Indigenous cultures, NUKA builds on Alaska Native strengths and responds to the wants and needs of customers and owners. This contrasts to a government approach that assumes it knows best what AI/AN people need or want. NUKA has made significant changes, including in palliative care, and it has improved patient outcomes. NUKA has evolved through grant support, including from the Robert Wood Johnson Foundation in 2020, illustrating the role of research and funding as Tribes seek resources to support their desire for improved cancer and healthcare outcomes. In the case of NUKA, customers/owners direct when, where, and how care systems function, leading to improved patterns of care and increased patient and staff satisfaction.

IHS, Tribal, and Urban Indian Partnerships

Partnerships exist between Tribes, urban Indian clinics, research institutions, and academic institutions. These partnerships must be honest and equal if significant improvements are to occur. For example, the partnership between Judith Salmon Kaur, MD (Choctaw), and Marilyn Roubidoux, MD (Iowa Tribe of Kansas and Nebraska), began in 1995 when the two met at an Association of American Indian Physicians (AAIP) meeting, at which Dr. Kaur spoke about her attempts to address cervical and breast cancers among AI/AN women. Later, Dr. Roubidoux approached Dr. Kaur and suggested that, given the shortage of Native patients at the University of Michigan where Dr. Roubidoux worked, the two should work together to improve mammography services. This led to a 40-year partnership.

The New Generation of AI/AN Researchers

There currently are several Native leaders engaged in academic research (Fig. 15.1), including:

- Donald Warne, MD, MPH (Oglala Lakota tribe from Pine Ridge, South Dakota), co-director of the Center for Indigenous Health and full professor and Provost Fellow for Indigenous Health Policy at Johns Hopkins University.[1]
- Rodney C. Haring, PhD, MSW (Seneca Nation), Associate Professor of Oncology at the Office of Community Outreach and Engagement, Department of Cancer Prevention & Control, and Director at the Center for Indigenous Cancer Research at the Roswell Cancer Center.[2]

[1]Biography at: https://cff.hms.harvard.edu/fellows/fellows-bios/donald-warne-md-mph#:~:text=Donald%20Warne%2C%20MD%2C%20MPH%2C,Fellow%20for%20Indigenous%20Health%20Policy

[2]Biography at: https://www.roswellpark.org/rodney-haring

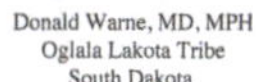

Fig. 15.1 Five Native American faculty and researchers: (from left) Donald Warne, Rodney Haring, Francine Gachupin, Jani Ingram, and Dorothy Rhoades. (Photos provided by each researcher)

- Francine C. Gachupin, PhD, MPH (Pueblo of Jemez), co-director of Native American Cancer Prevention, University of Arizona.[3]
- Jani Ingram, PhD (Navajo), co-director of Native American Cancer Prevention, Northern Arizona University.[4]

Investments in the next generation of AI/AN researchers will lead to many more similar positions, creating opportunities for Indigenous-led community cancer intervention partnerships.

Other program leaders, such as Dorothy Rhoades, MD, MPH (Kiowa Nation), at the Oklahoma University College of Medicine and Stephenson Cancer Center[5] have initiated patient navigation programs that have significantly increased the number of AI/ANs enrolled in cancer clinical trials, with health, wellness, and disease prevention programs spanning Alaska through to Florida.

The health of Indigenous people should be valued. Cross-cultural programs that include complementary and alternative medicine and programs based on the integral strengths of local Indigenous cultures will remain the most successful over the long term. At its annual conference, the Association of American Indian Physicians offers and leads cross-cultural workshops that encourage respect for traditional ways of healing. It also sponsors intermittent spiritual events to assist emerging American Indian physicians. Similarly, the National Alaska Native American Indian Nurses Association and the American Indian, Alaska Native, and Native Hawaiian Caucus of the American Public Health Association provide mentoring to new and emerging healthcare professionals and public health students.

Under the auspices of the Center to Reduce Cancer Health Disparities program of the NCI, Mayo Clinic's Spirit of EAGLES program initiated the Hampton Faculty Fellows, a mentorship program to train and promote the career development of qualified health disparities researchers. Hampton Faculty Fellows were chosen competitively from 2010 to 2015. This national program brought together researchers from various academic and clinical practices to increase research capacity through one-on-one mentoring, course training, and the development of research collaborations with and for native communities. Given this cadre of scholars, many communities can now confidently design and participate in ethical research. AI/AN communities increasingly see the value of research and no longer need to mistrust the intentions or motives or researchers.

[3]Biography at: https://medicine.arizona.edu/person/francine-c-gachupin-phd-mph

[4]Biography at: https://nau.edu/bridges/jani-ingram/

[5]Biography at: https://medicine.ouhsc.edu/academic-departments/internal-medicine/sections/general-internal-medicine/dorothy-rhoades-md-mph

References

1. Government Accounting Office, *Indian Health Care.* Washington, DC: Congress of the US; 1986. Office of Technology Assessment Publication OTA-H-290.
2. Burhansstipanov L, Dresser CM. *Documentation of the Cancer Research Needs of American Indians and Alaska Natives.* Native American Monograph Series No. 1. NIH Pub. No. 93-3603. National Cancer Institute; 1993.
3. Bastian TD, Burhansstipanov L. Sharing Wisdom, Sharing Hope: Strategies Used by Native American Cancer Survivors to Restore Quality of Life. *J Glob Oncol.* 2020 Jan;6:161–166. https://doi.org/10.1200/JGO.19.00215
4. Goodwin EA, Burhansstipanov L, Dignan MB, Jones, KL, Kaur JS. The Experience of Treatment Barriers and Their Influence on Quality of Life in American Indian/Alaska Native Breast Cancer Survivors. *Cancer*, 2017 Mar;123:861–68. https://doi.org/10.1002/cncr.30406
5. Kaur JS, Coe K, Rowland J, Braun KL, Conde FA, Burhansstipanov L, et al. Enhancing life after cancer in diverse communities. *Cancer*: 2012; Nov:118(21):5366–73. https://doi.org/10.1002/cncr.27491
6. Burhansstipanov L, Dignan, MB, Jones KL, Krebs LU, Marchionda P, Kaur JS. A comparison of Quality of Life between Native and Non-Native Cancer Survivors. *J Cancer Educ.* 2012 Apr; 27(Suppl 1):S106–S11. https://doi.org/10.1007/s13187-012-0318-3
7. Burhansstipanov L, Krebs LU, Seals BF, Bradley AA, Kaur JS, Iron P, et al. Native American Breast Cancer Survivors' Physical Conditions and Quality of Life. *Cancer.* 2010 Mar;116(6):1560–71. https://doi.org/10.1002/cncr.24924
8. Southcentral Foundation. NUKA System of Care [Internet]. [Cited 2023 Sept 7). Available from: https://www.southcentralfoundation.com/nuka-system-of-care

BY NC ND

Part III

Communication and Resources

Cancer-Related Information Resources for Aboriginal and Torres Strait Islander People

16

Abbey Diaz, Meredith Burgess, Cate Scholte, Tamara Butler, Joanne Shaw, Brian Kelly, and Gail Garvey

Key Points

- Accessible, high-quality, and culturally responsive health information is essential to optimal and equitable cancer care.
- There is a lack of health information specifically for Aboriginal and Torres Strait Islander people across the cancer care continuum.
- A new measure of the cultural responsiveness of health information was developed and used to assess health information in cardiovascular health and cancer, lung cancer screening, and gynecological cancers.

Accessible information for people affected by cancer is a fundamental element of optimal cancer care [1]. Information about cancer and the availability of preventive and treatment services may increase engagement with services, reduce anxiety, and improve outcomes [2]. A recent survey of adult cancer patients in Western Australia identified that the greatest informational needs relate to treatment options and side effects, cancer types and diagnoses, and prognosis and survivorship [3]. Among Aboriginal and Torres Strait Islander people, the most common unmet informational need relates to the purpose of diagnostic tests and the effects of cancer treatment [4].

Health literacy refers to the cognitive and social skills required to access, read, understand, and action health information [5]. Low levels of health literacy are associated with reduced engagement with and uptake of health services and poorer health outcomes [5]. Developing accessible, readable, understandable, and actionable resources for all segments of the population is vital.

It is estimated that approximately 80% of Australians seek health information online [6]. In Australia, it is recommended that print resources are written at a Grade 8 reading level or lower [7], to help ensure equitable access to information across cultural, language, and socioeconomic backgrounds [8]. However, Australian health information is typically written above a Grade 10 level [9] and most of this information lacks actionable advice [10]. Good health information should be relevant and respectful to populations with the greatest need [11]. Given that cancer care and outcomes are worse for Aboriginal and Torres Strait Islander people than other Australians [12], the co-design of culturally responsive and high-quality cancer information resources addressing the unique needs of Aboriginal and Torres Strait Islander people is needed.

Several existing health literacy tools assess the quality of health information resources, including readability (e.g., the Flesch Reading Ease (FRE) [13] and Simple Measure of Gobbledygook (SMOG) [13]) and understandability and actionability (e.g., Patient Education Materials Assessment Tool (PEMAT) [14]). However, a validated tool to assess the cultural responsiveness of consumer information resources for Aboriginal and Torres Strait Islander people is lacking, and, to our knowledge no such tool exists for any Indigenous or Tribal population internationally. Here, we outline three case studies of cancer information resource evaluation and/or development for Aboriginal and Torres Strait Islander people affected by cancer.

Case Study 1: Assessment Tool for the Cultural Responsiveness of Cardiotoxicity Information Resources

There is growing evidence that chemotherapy, radiation therapy, and targeted systemic therapies can adversely affect cardiovascular structure and function [15]. Cancer patients with preexisting cardiovascular disease are at increased risk of treatment-related cardiotoxicity [16]. Aboriginal and Torres Strait Islander people are more likely to have preexisting cardiovascular disease at the time of cancer diagnosis [16].

An advisory group for cardio-oncology convened by the First Nations Cancer and Wellbeing Research

G. Garvey (ed.), *Indigenous and Tribal Peoples and Cancer*, https://doi.org/10.1007/978-3-031-56806-0_16

(FNCWR) Program at the University of Queensland (UQ) identified a critical lack of information for Aboriginal and Torres Strait Islander patients and their families. In response, we conducted a comprehensive gray literature search [11] and identified 17 print-based, cancer treatment-related cardiotoxicity resources published by Australian health authorities. Most resources contained limited information on this topic and only one [17] was assessed as readable (Grade 8 reading level and/or lower using SMOG and standard/average or easier using FRE) and understandable and actionable (by scoring ≥70 and ≥ 50, respectively, on these measures using the PEMAT), highlighting the critical need for useful information for all Australians.

None of the 17 resources was designed by or for Aboriginal and Torres Strait Islander people. In the absence of a validated or co-designed measure, Indigenous and non-Indigenous members of the UQ FNCWR Program, with input from the advisory group, devised a guide using seven criteria to assess the cultural responsiveness of information resources (Fig. 16.1). To ensure its validity, the group recommended that at least two Aboriginal and/or Torres Strait Islander people conduct and discuss the assessments. In this evaluation, Aboriginal and/or Torres Strait Islander (n = 3) and non-Indigenous (n = 1) staff independently assessed the 17 resources. They found only 1 of the 7 criteria present (i.e., weblink or contact details for a translation service) and this criterion was identified in only 7 of the 17 resources; however, it was unclear whether the translation services included Indigenous languages.

This assessment guide provided a starting point to systematically assess the cultural responsiveness of information resources. However, working with Aboriginal and Torres Strait Islander people to co-design and validate a tool to guide development of culturally responsive resources is still urgently needed.

Case Study 2: Lung Cancer Screening

Lung cancer is the leading cause of cancer-related deaths worldwide and, in 2022, accounted for 7% of Australia's total cancer-related deaths [18]. Aboriginal and Torres Strait Islander people are approximately two times as likely to be diagnosed with and die from lung cancer than other Australians [12]. Lung cancer screening programs aim to detect lung cancer early to improve outcomes. Nine countries have already implemented national or regional lung cancer screening programs (Canada, China, Croatia, Czech Republic, Poland, South Korea, Taiwan, United Arab Emirates, and the USA) [19], and, in May 2023, the Australian Government announced plans to introduce a national lung cancer screening program by mid-2025 [20].

To address persistent inequalities, the design of Australia's new lung cancer screening program must meet the needs of Aboriginal and Torres Strait Islander peoples. This includes developing culturally responsive screening information and education resources. To learn from other countries, the UQ FNCWR Program conducted a comprehensive gray literature search of consumer-focused resources from countries with existing programs. Of the 86 resources identified, four (4.7%) were designed for Indigenous peoples. These four varied in format and health literacy quality, and only one (Fig. 16.2) met readability, understandability and actionability criteria (Table 16.1).

Key Design Findings

All four resources were reviewed by a panel of six Aboriginal and Torres Strait Islander staff from UQ to identify elements for consideration in the design of a new draft resource for Aboriginal and Torres Strait Islander people. The panel was asked to share its perspectives regarding the look and feel (font, spacing, colors, visuals, and design) and content and scope (topics, depth, length, and word choice and structure) of the resources.

Fig. 16.1 Assessment guide to culturally responsive information resources for Aboriginal and Torres Strait Islander people

Assessing the cultural responsiveness of information resources

1. Does the resource include visual representation of Aboriginal and Torres Strait Islander people?
2. Does the resource include relevant data (e.g., statistics) about Aboriginal and Torres Strait Islander people?
3. Does the resource include Aboriginal and/or Torres Strait Islander design/artwork?
4. Does the resource provide evidence of Aboriginal and Torres Strait Islander leadership or governance?
5. Is the resource available in Aboriginal and Torres Strait Islander languages or is a translation service offered?
6. Is the language used strengths-based and respectful of culture?
7. Are users directed to further culturally safe support/information?

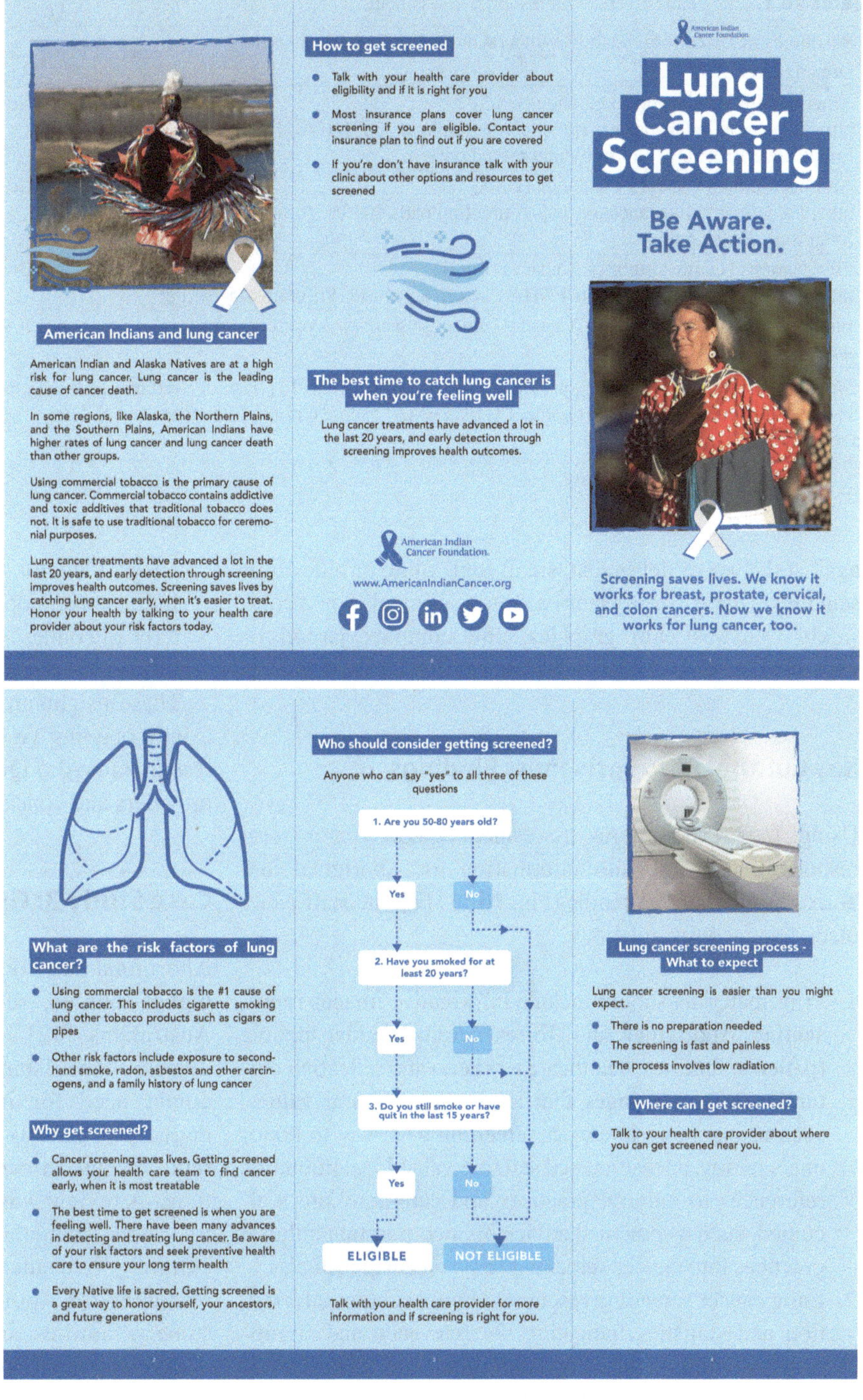

Fig. 16.2 American Indian Cancer Foundation double-sided flyer on lung cancer screening for American Indian and Alaska Native peoples, which met criteria for readability, understandability, and actionability

The staff panel preferred informative resources that reflected cultural values. For example, an Indigenous Elder pictured alone was seen to undermine culturally safe healthcare. Similarly, while a picture of an Indigenous family was appreciated, it failed to capture the importance of multigenerational family and Elders. Panel members also highlighted the value of relatable, empowering, and actionable plain language that connects cancer screening to cultural values (e.g., honor and family).

The staff panel advised that easy-to-read text, use of white space and cultural designs, natural and earth colors (e.g., green), and culturally relevant images enhanced the look and feel of information resources. In terms of content and scope, the panel suggested that resources that were comprehensive in scope but simple in delivery included affirming messaging (e.g., "be aware, take action"), and those that used plain, empowering, actionable, and culturally respectful language were most useful. The staff warned

Table 16.1 Lung cancer screening resource assessment

Resources assessed for readability, understandability, and actionability			
Organization	Readability[a]	Understandability[b]	Actionability[b]
American Indian Cancer Foundation (USA) https://americanindiancancer.org/wp-content/uploads/2021/10/051121_LungCancerBrochure_NoLogo-compressed.pdf	Grade 7	80 acceptable	80 acceptable
American Indian Cancer Foundation (USA) https://americanindiancancer.org/wp-content/uploads/2019/07/Lung-Caner-Signs-Symptoms-Blank.png	Grade 11	63 unacceptable	20 unacceptable
First Nations Health Authority (Canada) (flyer) https://www.fnha.ca/Documents/FNHA-Cancer-Screening-Programs-in-BC.pdf	Grade 8	75 acceptable	40 unacceptable
First Nations Health Authority (Canada) (video) https://www.youtube.com/watch?v=baTr1Qm8Ge0	NA	88 acceptable	67 unacceptable

[a]Simple Measure of Gobbledygook (SMOG) readability scores [13] were derived using an online calculator (https://readabilityformulas.com)
[b]Patient Education Materials Assessment Tool (PEMAT) score cutoff of ≥70 was used to determine acceptable levels of both understandability and actionability [14]

against the use of dense text, small font, white or blue color schemes (these were seen as "too clinical" or "cold, sickly"), mainstream graphics, and complex jargon or vague language.

Key Cultural Responsiveness Findings

Using the seven-criteria assessment guide for cultural responsiveness of health information for Aboriginal and Torres Strait Islander people (Fig. 16.1) [13], the staff panel made five recommendations:

1. Print materials should include informative images representing Aboriginal and Torres Strait Islander people (patients, families, healthcare workers) and reflecting cultural values. Messages that align with cultural values, such as engaging in cancer screening as a way to honor one's family, ancestors, and self, are valued. Additionally, references to cultural practices and ceremony are welcomed, such as practical advice on incorporating cultural practices into cancer screening (e.g., cleansing rituals).
2. Lung cancer screening resources should contain information and statistics indicating the relevance and significance of lung cancer for Aboriginal and Torres Strait Islander people and communities.
3. The authentic and thoughtful use of Indigenous art and visual elements is recommended. It is essential that this art is created by an Indigenous person to represent the intended audience and the knowledge being shared. It is also good practice to name the artist and their country, and tell the story of the art, to avoid tokenistic practices of Indigenous involvement and to ensure acceptability.
4. Respectful, strengths-based language is essential. Words should be carefully chosen to avoid overly complex language ("doctor talk") while avoiding talking down to Indigenous people and repeating healthcare system patterns of condescension.

These insights are contributing to the UQ FNCWR Program team's ongoing co-design of a new lung cancer screening resource for Aboriginal and Torres Strait Islander healthcare providers and consumers across Queensland.

Case Study 3: Gynecological Cancers

Aboriginal and Torres Strait Islander people experience a higher burden of gynecological cancers than other Australians [12]. Additionally, female Aboriginal and Torres Strait Islander cancer patients report a higher unmet need for information and communication than males [4]. This is particularly important in the face of rapid change in cervical cancer prevention recommendations. A review was conducted to determine the availability, understandability, actionability, readability, and cultural relevance of gynecological cancer-related resources for Aboriginal and Torres Strait Islander consumers, families, and caregivers [21].

A comprehensive Google search and targeted website search of leading gynecological cancer organizations identified 16 resources, including a flip chart, posters, webpages, videos, brochures, and information sheets. Resources were assessed for understandability and actionability using PEMAT [14], for readability using SMOG [13], and for cultural responsiveness using the seven-criteria assessment guide (Fig. 16.1) [11]. The latter assessment was conducted independently by four Aboriginal staff (all women) in the UQ FNCWR Program. Through discussion, the assessors determined a final consensus rating for each item. Resources relating to cervical cancer were also checked to ensure that screening and human papillomavirus (HPV) vaccination recommendations were consistent with current clinical recommendations.

Most resources were assessed to be understandable and actionable, and almost all print resources (n = 11/13) met reading level recommendations of Grade 8 or lower [21]. Most resources (n = 14) focused on cervical cancer prevention through screening and HPV vaccination. Only three resources conveyed information relating to diagnosis, treatment, or survivorship of a gynecological cancer and these resources related to cervical, uterine, and ovarian cancers. Cervical cancer prevention resources aligned with current clinical guidelines for screening and vaccination. However, older, outdated versions of four of the resources were still easily accessible.

All resources met at least one criterion for cultural responsiveness, although none met all criteria. Three resources met six of the seven criteria. The most frequently met criterion was for the use of strengths-based and respectful language. Few resources provided translation into Aboriginal and Torres Strait Islander languages or provided evidence of the involvement of Aboriginal and Torres Strait Islander people in resource development leadership, governance, or design. Additionally, most resources did not include an Aboriginal and Torres Strait Islander–specific contact for further information or support.

Although the resources were generally understandable, actionable, readable, and moderately culturally relevant, the findings highlighted a dearth of resources relating to non-cervical gynecological cancers and information relating to diagnosis, treatment, and survivorship. Furthermore, none of the resources presented gynecological cancers as a cancer group. A resource containing signs, symptoms, prevention, and diagnosis information shared by gynecological cancers would benefit community members.

The findings indicate a need for high-quality, accessible gynecological cancer information developed by and for Aboriginal and Torres Strait Islander people relating to all aspects of the cancer continuum and including all gynecological cancer types.

Conclusion

Accessible, high-quality, and culturally relevant health information is an important aspect of optimal and equitable cancer care. Two of the three evaluations presented in this chapter highlight a lack of resources designed specifically for Aboriginal and Torres Strait Islander people; the exception was the case of HPV vaccination and cervical screening information.

An assessment guide designed by the authors evaluates the cultural responsiveness of existing and new health information resources for Aboriginal and Torres Strait Islander people. The guide has been used to evaluate existing resources (case studies 1 and 3) and to qualitatively inform the co-design of a new resource (case study 2). These steps support researchers and health services in the design of more culturally responsive cancer information resources for Aboriginal and Torres Strait Islander people, thus contributing to improved health literacy and health outcomes. This guide may be applied to initiatives internationally to improve cancer outcomes for other Indigenous peoples.

References

1. Chua G, Tan H, Gandhi M. What information do cancer patients want and how well are their needs being met? *Ecancermedicalscience*. 2018;12:873. https://doi.org/10.3332/ecancer.2018.873
2. Husson O, Mols F, van de Poll-Franse LV. The relation between information provision and health-related quality of life, anxiety and depression among cancer survivors: a systematic review. *Ann Oncol*. 2011;22(4):761–72. https://doi.org/10.1093/annonc/mdq413
3. Ives A, Sengsourinho S, Millar L, Do T. *Understanding Consumers' Needs for Cancer Information*. [Internet] Western Australia (AU): The Cancer and Palliative Care Research and Evaluation Unit; 2022. Available: https://www.health.wa.gov.au/~/media/Corp/Documents/Health-for/Health-Networks/Cancer/Cancer-fellowships/Understanding-Consumers-Needs-for-Cancer-Information-report.pdf
4. Bernardes CM, Diaz A, Valery PC, Sabesan S, Baxi S, Aoun S, et al. Unmet supportive care needs among Indigenous cancer patients across Australia. *Rural Remote Health*. 2019;19(3):4660. https://doi.org/10.22605/RRH4660
5. Australian Institute of Health and Welfare. *Health literacy*. Canberra (AU): AIHW; 2022.
6. National Digital Health Agency. *Australia's National Digital Health Summary*. Australian Government; 2016. Available: https://www.digitalhealth.gov.au/sites/default/files/2020-11/Australia%27s%20National%20Digital%20Health%20Strategy%20-%20Safe%2C%20seamless%20and%20secure.pdf
7. South Australia Health. *Engaging with Consumers, Carers and the Community: Guide and Resources*. Adelaide (AU): SA Health; 2021. Available: https://www.sahealth.sa.gov.au/wps/wcm/connect/6dead9da-d1c2-4cbf-9568-74d2131df162/EngagingwithConsumersCarersandCommunityGuide%2526Resources_Apr+2021+%25281%2529.pdf?MOD=AJPERES&CACHEID=ROOTWORKSPACE-6dead9da-d1c2-4cbf-9568-74d2131df162-nKMnNqM
8. Murfet G, Lin S, Ridd J, Cremer G, Davidson S, Muscat DM. Shifts in Diabetes Health Literacy Policy and Practice in Australia—Promoting Organisational Health Literacy. *Int J Environ Res Public Health*. 2023;20(10):5778. https://doi.org/10.3390/ijerph20105778
9. Cheng C, Dunn M. Health literacy and the Internet: a study on the readability of Australian online health information. *Aust N Z J Public Health*. 2015;39(4):309–14. https://doi.org/10.1111/1753-6405.12341
10. Ayre J, Bonner C, Gonzalez J, Vaccaro T, Cousins M, McCaffery K, et al. Integrating consumer perspectives into a large-scale health literacy audit of health information materials: learn-

ings and next steps. 2023;23:416. https://doi.org/10.1186/s12913-023-09434-3
11. Diaz A, McErlane J, Jeon MH, Cunningham J, Sullivan V, Garvey G. Patient Information Resources on Cardiovascular Health After Cancer Treatment: An Audit of Australian Resources. *JCO Glob Oncol*. 2023;9:e2200361. https://doi.org/10.1200/go.22.00361
12. Australian Institute of Health and Welfare. *Cancer in Australia 2021*. Canberra: AIHW; 2021. Available: https://www.aihw.gov.au/reports/cancer/cancer-in-australia-2021/summary
13. El-Haddad N, Spooner C, Faruqi N, Denney-Wilson E, Harris M. Readability and content analysis of lifestyle education resources for weight management in Australian general practice. *BMC Obes*. 2016;3(1):16. https://doi.org/10.1186/S40608-016-0097-1
14. Shoemaker SJ, Wolf MS, Brach C. Development of the Patient Education Materials Assessment Tool (PEMAT): A new measure of understandability and actionability for print and audiovisual patient information. *Patient Educ Couns*. 2014;96(3):395–403. https://doi.org/10.1016/j.pec.2014.05.027
15. Lenihan DJ, Cardinale DM. Late cardiac effects of cancer treatment. *J Clin Oncol*. 2012;30(30):3657–64. https://doi.org/10.1200/jco.2012.45.2938
16. Diaz A, Sverdlov AL, Kelly B, Ngo DTM, Bates N, Garvey G. Nexus of Cancer and Cardiovascular Disease for Australia's First Peoples. *JCO Glob Oncol*. 2020 Feb;6:115–119. https://doi.org/10.1200/JGO.19.00088
17. Cancer Council. *Understanding Chemotherapy: A guide for people with cancer, their families and friends*. Cancer Council; 2022. Available: https://www.cancer.org.au/assets/pdf/understanding-chemotherapy-booklet
18. Cancer Australia. *Lung Cancer in Australia Statistics*. Cancer Australia; 2022. Available from: https://www.canceraustralia.gov.au/cancer-types/lung-cancer/statistics
19. Lung Cancer Policy Network. *Interactive Map of Lung Cancer Screening* (2nd ed). 2023. Available: https://www.lungcancerpolicynetwork.com/interactive-map-of-lung-cancer-screening/
20. Cancer Australia. *Lung Cancer Screening*. 2023. Available: https://www.canceraustralia.gov.au/about-us/lung-cancer-screening
21. Kinghorn M, Garvey G, Butler TL. Gynaecological cancer resources for Aboriginal and Torres Strait Islander women: A resource audit. *Health Promot J Austr*. 2023 Oct 26. https://doi.org/10.1002/hpja.822

17 Online Learning for Clinicians and Researchers Who Work with Cancer-Affected First Nations People

Joan Cunningham, Brian Kelly, Joanne Shaw, Lara Stoll, and Gail Garvey

Key Points

- Online learning modules can be a useful part of ongoing clinician education, filling a gap in professional development.
- There was high uptake of the modules, indicating strong interest from researchers and clinicians for knowledge and skills in this field.
- Building knowledge and skills in culturally appropriate healthcare and research practice is key to improving psychosocial outcomes for First Nations people with cancer.

Strengthening the capacity of health services to deliver high-quality, culturally appropriate care for Aboriginal and Torres Strait Islander people affected by cancer is a key priority to improve cancer outcomes [1]. However, appropriate educational resources are lacking. To help address this shortfall, an e-learning package was developed to increase the knowledge, skills, and confidence of health professionals who work with Aboriginal and Torres Strait Islander people affected by cancer.

Who Was Involved

The e-learning package was created through a partnership between the Psycho-oncology Co-operative Research Group (PoCoG) and the Centre of Research Excellence in Targeted Approaches to Improve Cancer Services for Aboriginal and Torres Strait Islander Australians (TACTICS CRE).

PoCoG was established in 2005 as 1 of 14 Cancer Clinical Trials Groups funded by Cancer Australia, the national government's cancer control agency. It brings together researchers, clinicians, and people with personal experience of cancer [2]. PoCoG's multidisciplinary membership includes Australian researchers and clinicians with an interest in psycho-oncology and supportive care research. PoCoG's goals focus on promoting research and health-system improvements in the provision of psychosocial aspects of cancer across all stages, from cancer prevention, treatment, recovery, and survivorship through to end-of-life care and bereavement. PoCoG's work to promote the psychosocial aspects of cancer care reflects broader national priorities in cancer, including specific efforts to reduce inequities in cancer outcomes for Aboriginal and Torres Strait Islander people.

The TACTICS CRE is an Aboriginal-led consortium of researchers from institutions across Australia. This 5-year program, funded by Australia's National Health and Medical Research Council (NHMRC), is focused on improving cancer outcomes for First Nations people through applied research on (1) increasing prevention and early detection through immunization and screening, (2) improving diagnosis through health-service innovation, and (3) providing appropriate care to enhance the psychosocial wellbeing of cancer survivors, their partners, and carers [3]. Key aspects of the CRE include a focus on translating research knowledge into policy and practice, training and developing future research leaders, and building community awareness and understanding of cancer.

Members of the TACTICS CRE have been instrumental in guiding the work undertaken by PoCoG to identify research priorities and develop research programs that directly address the psychosocial needs of Aboriginal and Torres Strait Islander people affected by cancer. Through this collaboration, a need was identified to build greater capability and cultural understanding among clinicians, researchers, and healthcare providers. This was seen as critical to promoting inclusive care that improved access to cancer screening and early access to treatment and promoting participation in clinical trials—through building a greater understanding of the health and wellbeing of Aboriginal and Torres Strait Islander people and their experiences with cancer. This included the need to promote understanding of the evidence

G. Garvey (ed.), *Indigenous and Tribal Peoples and Cancer*, https://doi.org/10.1007/978-3-031-56806-0_17

regarding cancer outcomes and the contributing factors to disparities in outcomes, along with supporting and guiding clinicians on ways they can better engage, support, and communicate effectively with Aboriginal and Torres Strait Islander patients, their families, and carers. Promoting such capability is key to improving experiences of cancer care for Aboriginal and Torres Strait Islander people, and it is fundamental to minimizing, identifying, and responding to psychosocial needs at all stages of cancer.

Action Taken

Online learning modules were developed to increase knowledge in three specific areas: (1) Aboriginal and Torres Strait Islander health and current disparities in cancer outcomes, (2) culturally inclusive communication with patients and carers, and (3) strategies to address the under-representation of Aboriginal and Torres Strait Islander people in clinical trials.

The content for the series was developed by TACTICS CRE members from the Menzies School of Health Research and The University of Queensland in collaboration with PoCoG members from the University of Sydney and the University of Newcastle. Module development was guided by adult-learning principles.

Three modules were produced and released and are freely available on the PoCoG YouTube channel [4].

Each module was designed to be self-contained but complementary, with clear learning outcomes (Figs. 17.1, 17.2, and 17.3). There is a common look and feel across the modules, and all three are narrated by the same First Nations actor. Each module begins with an Acknowledgement of Country (recognition of traditional custodians of the land) and a statement of respect for First Nations Elders.

Module 1: Cancer Overview and Factors Impacting Health Inequalities

Module 1 provides an overview of cancer among Aboriginal and Torres Strait Islander peoples and explores the factors that impact on the current health inequalities affecting

Module 1: Cancer overview and factors impacting health inequalities

This learning module was developed by Menzies School of Health Research, under the auspices of the NHMRC-funded Centre of Research Excellence *Targeted Approaches to Improve Cancer Services* (TACTICS) for Aboriginal and Torres Strait Islander people, in collaboration with the Psycho-Oncology Co-operative Research Group (PoCoG)

Learning outcomes

After completing this module you will have a greater understanding of:

-Aboriginal and Torres Strait Islander people's health and the factors that contribute to the health inequality gap

-The cancer indicators and trends for Aboriginal and Torres Strait Islander people

-Some of the factors that impact cancer outcomes for Aboriginal and Torres Strait Islander people

Fig. 17.1 Module 1 title slide and learning outcomes

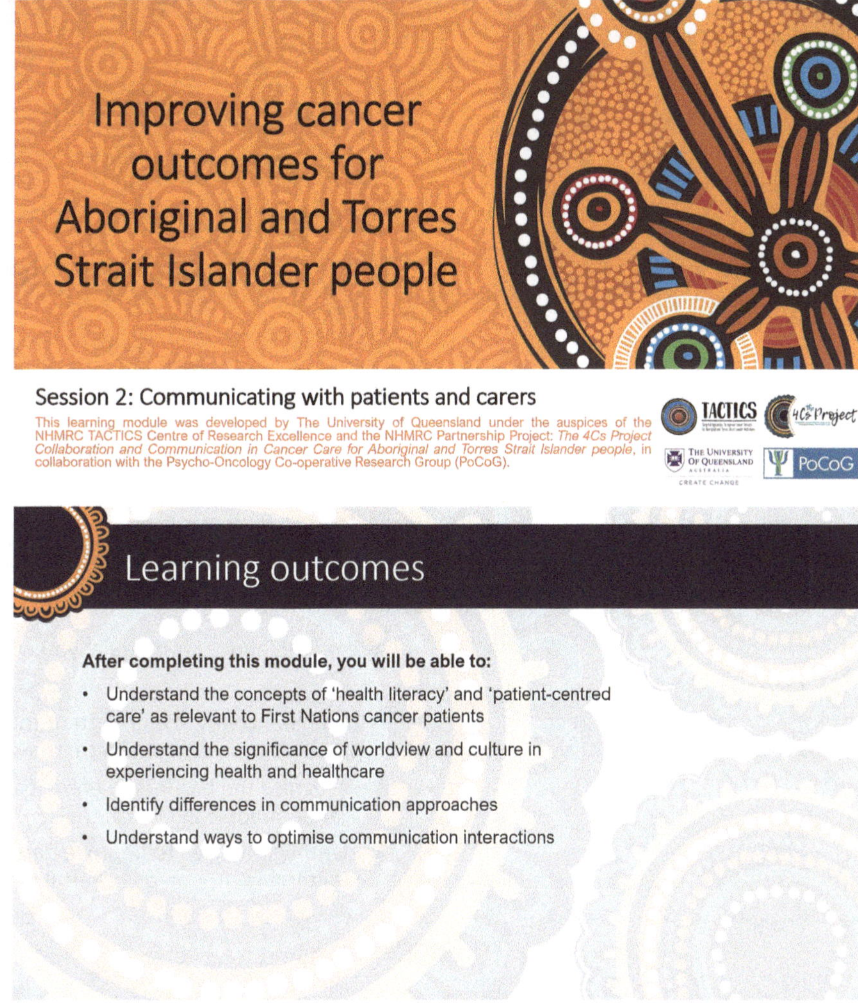

Fig. 17.2 Module 2 title slide and learning outcomes

First Nations Australians (Fig. 17.1). It covers various aspects that clinicians and researchers need to know regarding the context in which Aboriginal and Torres Strait Islander people live, and the burden of cancer for this group, including the most common types of cancer. It provides details of inequities across the cancer continuum, using Australia's National Cancer Control Indicators as a framework. Individual-, service-, and system-level factors that impact on outcomes are discussed, as well as enablers of improved outcomes, including cultural safety, communication, and appropriate, evidence-based resources and tools. References and links are provided. The module also includes a First Nations cancer survivor talking about his experiences of diagnosis, treatment, and survivorship. The module, which runs for just under 24 minutes, was released in March 2021.

Module 2: Communicating with Patients and Carers

Module 2 aims to build effective and culturally appropriate communication skills among clinicians and researchers working with First Nations peoples (Fig. 17.2). Safe, effective, and culturally inclusive communication is an important aspect of high-quality, patient-centered care. The module begins by discussing what health literacy is and the factors that influence it before offering a range of practical strategies that clinicians and researchers can use to improve communication with First Nations patients and their carers. These strategies include understanding your impact, considering culture and cultural complexities, seeking support from people who can help, building rapport and creating a safe environment, thinking about how you communicate,

Fig. 17.3 Module 3 title slide and learning outcomes

and using other forms of communication. Module 2, which is just under 21 min long, was originally developed as part of an NHMRC-funded project (the 4Cs Project—Coordination and Collaboration in Cancer Care) undertaken under the auspices of the TACTICS CRE. It was modified for a more general audience and released as part of the e-learning series ahead of World Cancer Day in February 2023.

Module 3: Aboriginal and Torres Strait Islander People's Participation in Clinical Trials

Module 3 focuses on understanding and improving Aboriginal and Torres Strait Islander people's access to and participation in clinical trials (Fig. 17.3). The module begins by addressing why clinical trials are important and why it is important to include Aboriginal and Torres Strait Islander people in trials, as well as what is known about current levels of participation. The module outlines key barriers and facilitators and highlights important resources—including the new National Clinical Trials Governance Framework, which explicitly addresses the inclusion of Aboriginal and Torres Strait Islander people in clinical trials [5]. Module 3 is approximately 24 min long and was released in April 2023.

Impact of the Modules

The modules were promoted through cancer-professional networks and clinical-trials groups to their memberships. As of October 9, 2023, the three modules had been viewed approximately 2250 times. Some 220 participants registered to attend a webinar held in July 2023 to build on the information and resources shared in the series and to provide practical examples of implementation.

Modules 1 and 2 were utilized as part of the 4Cs Project. A pre–/post-evaluation looked at changes in the confidence, skills, and knowledge of those who completed the modules, as well as health professionals' feedback on the modules themselves. Although the sample size for the project was small ($n = 21$), everyone who completed the training rated the modules as good to excellent, with most or all indicating that the modules' content was relevant (100%), easy to follow (95%), and useful in the context of their work (100%).

While no formal evaluation has been conducted beyond what was done in the 4Cs project, the number of views does indicate interest and willingness among many health professionals to engage in activities aimed at improving their skills, knowledge, and understanding of what is needed to ensure high-quality, culturally appropriate care for Aboriginal and Torres Strait Islander people with cancer.

We gratefully acknowledge the contributions of all those involved in the development of the modules. The TACTICS CRE is funded by the National Health and Medical Research Council (GNT#1153027). PoCoG is funded by Cancer Australia Cancer Support for Cancer Clinical Trials Program. The artwork in the online modules was created by Casey Coolwell-Fisher from Chaboo.

References

1. Cancer Australia. *National Aboriginal and Torres Strait Islander Cancer Framework.* 2015. Available from: https://www.canceraustralia.gov.au/publications-and-resources/cancer-australia-publications/national-aboriginal-and-torres-strait-islander-cancer-framework
2. The University of Sydney. *Psycho-Oncology Co-operative Research Group (PoCoG)* [Internet]. [cited 2023 August 25]. Available from: https://www.pocog.org.au/
3. TACTICS CRE. Centre of Research Excellence in Targeted Approaches To Improve Cancer Services for Aboriginal and Torres Strait Islander Australians (TACTICS CRE) [Internet]. [cited 2023 August 25]. Available from: https://www.tactics-cre.com/
4. Psycho-Oncology Co-operative Research Group, PoCoG YouTube Channel Playlist. [cited 2023 August 25]. Available from: https://www.youtube.com/@psycho-oncologyco-operativ7909/playlists
5. Australian Commission on Safety and Quality in Health Care. *The National Clinical Trials Governance Framework and user guide for health service organisations conducting clinical trials.* Sydney: ACSQHC; 2022. Available from: https://www.safetyandquality.gov.au/sites/default/files/2022-05/final_design_-_national_clinical_trials_governance_framework_and_user_guide_-_30_may_2022.pdf

Métis-Specific Cancer Patient Resources

18

Marg Friesen, Adel Panahi, and Tegan Brock

Key Points

- Métis Nation–Saskatchewan identified a need for culturally relevant information about cancer.
- *Your Guide to Help You Understand Cancer & Heal* includes culturally responsive information about cancer, treatment, and living with cancer.
- *A Journal and Planner for Métis Cancer Patients* provides opportunities for patients and their carers to track medical information and notes from appointments and record experiences.

During community engagement sessions and interviews with Métis cancer patients, survivors, and caregivers, the Métis Nation–Saskatchewan (MN–S) Department of Health identified a need for better and more culturally relevant information about the cancer journey and for information to help Métis citizens navigate the cancer system.

The Department developed two Métis-specific cancer patient resources (see Fig. 18.1):

1. *Toon Liivr chi Nishitoohtamun li Kaansayr (Your Guide to Help You Understand Cancer & Heal)* [1].
2. *Aen Ooshipayhaamihk aen Pchi Liivr pi aen Kalaandriyii poor aniki kaa Aahkooshichik avik li Kaansayr (A Journal and Planner for Métis Cancer Patients)* [2].

These two resources support Métis cancer patients in Saskatchewan by providing culturally relevant and accessible information about cancer and the cancer experience to Métis citizens in one place for easy reference. The educational guide begins with a written opening prayer by Elder Norman Fleury and includes Métis stories and culturally responsive information about cancer, treatment, living with cancer, and available programs and services. Examples of culturally responsive information include sharing traditional medicines and options for healing, changing language to say "wanting to leave this world sooner" instead of "wanting to die sooner," and referring to "cancer in your body" rather than "your cancer." The journal and planner provide space for people to record their medical information; take notes during appointments; track their medicines, treatment plans, and side effects; and record their experiences throughout their cancer journey. It also contains Métis art, poetry, stories, and humor to offer comfort and laughter to patients while they wait during their medical appointments.

Both resources include quotes from Métis citizens that come from one-on-one interviews with Métis cancer patients, survivors, and caregivers. Citizens gave consent for their comments to be included. The two resources were designed to be complementary, but also to stand alone.

These booklets are available in print at Saskatchewan Cancer Centres and MN–S Regional Offices. They are also available online through the MN–S website (https://metisnationsk.com/).

These quotes are examples of those included in the resources:

> My grandma and others were doctors in our culture, in our own way. … The medicines are land-based. They were life-giving and involved lifelong learning. Today, there's Western medicine and there's Traditional medicine so how do we infuse them? I think that's what we're trying to do here. (Michif Elder Norman Fleury) [1, p. 38]

> Stay positive, ask questions if you don't understand. Don't just say "yes." If you don't understand, ask questions. Have a support person with you to help you decipher that conversation afterwards, and just stay positive. There's lots of help, lots of things out there. You're not the only person going through it. And we're a strong group of people. (Anita N Smith, Métis cancer patient) [1, p. 44–45]

> If you can try to have a strong mind and think that you're gonna beat it or gonna tackle it, your frame of mind kinda changes. He had the idea he was gonna beat it and he was gonna be cured. But as he went into the hospital he said, "Well, we're in this together and we'll come through. I'm gonna sing again." And three weeks later he was at Batoche. He wasn't a real good singer, but he sang two or three songs. (Lorna Arcand, Métis caregiver) [1, p. 71]

G. Garvey (ed.), *Indigenous and Tribal Peoples and Cancer*, https://doi.org/10.1007/978-3-031-56806-0_18

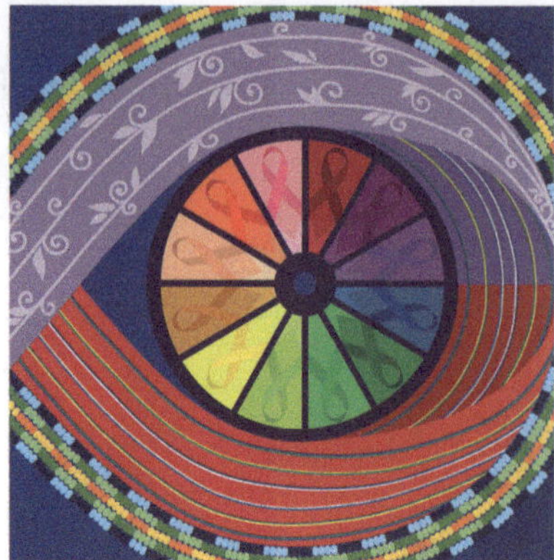

Fig. 18.1 Covers of the two cancer patient resources. (Cover illustrations by Victoria Beahm)

References

1. Métis Nation–Saskatchewan. *Your Guide to Help You Understand Cancer & Heal (Toon Liivr chi Nishitoohtamun li Kaansayr)*. 2023. Available from: https://metisnationsk.com/wp-content/uploads/2023/03/MNS_CCGuidebook_web2023.pdf
2. Métis Nation–Saskatchewan. *Journal and Planner for Métis Cancer Patients (Aen Ooshipayhaamihk aen Pchi Liivr pi aen Kalaandriyii poor aniki kaa Aahkooshichik avik li Kaansayr)*. 2023. Available from: https://metisnationsk.com/wp-content/uploads/2023/03/MNS_CCJournal_web2023.pdf

Adapting a Medical Education Cultural Competency Curriculum for Clinical Researchers

19

Martina Leialoha Kamaka, Dee-Ann Leialoha Carpenter, Munirih R. Taafaki, and C. Malina Kaulukukui

Key Points

- Training in cultural competency can improve clinical researchers' skills in interacting with study participants.
- A culturally competent workforce has the tools to address barriers in the recruitment and retention of clinical trial participants from health disparate populations.
- Existing cultural awareness training designed for health-care providers can be adapted to meet the needs of clinical researchers.

Minority groups experience significant health disparities in the USA, including disparities in cancer [1–4]. Cancer disparities in some smaller populations, such as Native Hawaiians and Pacific Islanders (NHPI), may be masked by being aggregated with larger groups—such as grouping NHPI with Asians (AANHPI or API) [2]. Fortunately, detailed disaggregated NHPI cancer incidence and mortality data can be found in academic and government data sets from the US State of Hawai'i. These data indicate Native Hawaiians suffer from the highest cancer mortality rates compared to the other four major racial groups in Hawai'i: Chinese, Filipino, Japanese, and Whites [4].

New innovations in cancer therapy depend on clinical trials for ascertaining effectiveness. However, clinical trials targeting minority groups face challenges in recruitment [5, 6]. Native Hawaiians, who experience large cancer disparities, have been reluctant to engage in clinical trials [5–7]. The reasons for this may likely be similar to those experienced by other Indigenous communities, such as a lack of trust and cultural differences in communication styles [8, 9]. Cultural competency training is important for the clinical research team, especially because it can address differing communication styles and trust issues. Training the clinical research team to gain a greater understanding of social–cultural factors, barriers to the involvement of minority populations in clinical trials, and the role of community-based facilitators could enhance recruitment of Indigenous peoples in clinical trials and research [10].

Background for Training Curriculum

The University of Hawai'i Cancer Center (UHCC) Minority Underserved NCORP (National Cancer Institute's Community Oncology Research Program) had funding to provide cultural competency (CC) training to nurses, clinical research coordinators, and other research staff. In 2017, the UHCC approached the Department of Native Hawaiian Health (DNHH) at the John A. Burns School of Medicine (JABSOM) to assist with this training. The Department's interdisciplinary C3 (cultural competency curriculum development) team, consisting mostly of Native Hawaiians, has been designing CC curricula for medical students and medical residents since 2006 [11]. CC training is defined as "a set of congruent behaviors, attitudes, and policies that come together in a system, agency, or among professionals" that enables effective work in cross-cultural situations [12]. JABSOM C3 team training is broader and tries to focus on core elements needed to improve Native Hawaiian health and patient care. Examples include being able to respectfully interact with, understand, and advocate for people from cultures different from their own; becoming self-aware (how personal values and biases influence care); and being aware of the impacts of power differentials, racism and bias, and social and cultural determinants of health, as well as history including trauma and colonization. Finally, learners need some basic mastery of communication skills to help with the work of respecting each patient while striving to gain trust and address needs.

The initial aim was to develop CC training to help increase recruitment of Native Hawaiians into clinical trials, and later other groups, such as Pacific Islanders and Filipinos. The target audiences for the half-day training workshop were

G. Garvey (ed.), *Indigenous and Tribal Peoples and Cancer*, https://doi.org/10.1007/978-3-031-56806-0_19

community physicians, investigators, nurses, coordinators, and other staff involved in clinical research. While the main focus was to develop CC training to help improve the researcher–study participant relationship, we were also interested in whether the training designed for medical students could be adapted for clinical researchers or those in other health-related professions.

Our existing CC training for JABSOM medical students is delivered throughout their first and second years of study and includes a series of workshops, lectures, an elective, a standardized patient exercise, and problem-based learning cases. A major challenge, therefore, was deciding what components of the medical student curriculum to include in the proposed workshop. We decided that several foundational components were needed to give a better understanding of the target population—including information on history, social determinants of health, health disparities, values and beliefs, communication skills, and the impacts of racism and bias.

Native Hawaiian populations were the initial focus of the workshop; therefore, the program included a historical overview on the impacts of colonization including cultural conflicts, the loss of language, culture, sovereignty, racism, and cultural historical trauma. It was important to highlight the impact of trauma as a significant contributor to the health disparities, including chronic disease and cancer, experienced by Native Hawaiians [9, 13].

Bias and racism influence interactions, whether implicitly or explicitly, personally or structurally. For this reason, workshop time was allocated for participants to explore in personal ways the concept that understanding bias starts with understanding their own personal values and beliefs and how these color perspectives and judgments. The self-awareness exercises encouraged storytelling, which allowed people to engage with each other on a more emotional or intuitive level, and were rooted in Indigenous ways of understanding oneself and one's place in the world. These exercises were built around our understanding of a Native Hawaiian "sense of place" and genealogy and aimed to develop participants' capacity to connect and foster trust with others.

While all cultures have some shared values and beliefs, there is also a lot of heterogeneity. Communication skills and understanding rely on being familiar with, and knowing how to negotiate within, cultures and values. Therefore, communication preferences for certain groups, as well as basic communication skills, were included in the workshop.

To attract a larger audience for the training, an educational workshop was offered through the Society of Clinical Research Associates (SOCRA) Hawai'i Chapter, an educational membership organization that provides educational credits to certified clinical research professionals (CCRP).

The Training Curriculum

The 4.5-hour workshop was presented by Native Hawaiian faculty (see Fig. 19.1). Native Hawaiian welcoming protocols opened the meeting. The workshop included four modules:

1. NH protocols, NH health disparities, and the need for cultural competency.
2. Self-awareness exercises.
3. NH history and the impact of cultural historical trauma.
4. The study participant–researcher interaction and communication skills.

The modules included a mix of lectures and small-group work.

Participants' Responses to the Training

A total of 22 participants attended the workshop; most were female (77%). Almost all (82%) were associated with the UH cancer center, with 48% working at clinical sites and 43% working directly with study participants. Participants came from a variety of specializations and geographic origins: 32% were from Hawai'i, 50% from the US continent, and 19% from other countries.

There was a 91% completion rate for the workshop evaluation, which consisted of post-curricular Likert-scale quantitative and qualitative open-ended questions. All participants (100%) agreed that the workshop achieved its stated objective of utilizing cultural competency training to improve study participant–researcher relationships. For Modules 1, 3, and 4, 100% agreed that module objectives were met; for Module 2, 95% agreed that objectives were met (5% neutral).

Initial questions revealed that, prior to the workshop, 50% were unsure or disagreed that they could form effective, trusting relationships with NH research participants. At the end of the workshop, all agreed or strongly agreed that they had learned skills to improve relationships with NH study participants. See Fig. 19.2 for the quantitative evaluation results.

Participants' responses to the qualitative open-ended questions revolved around the applicability and practicality of lessons and activities, and growth in individual self-awareness. They valued the lessons about Hawaiian history (and its impact on health) and recognized the importance of building rapport and trust with patients and research participants. Figure 19.3 summarizes the qualitative responses to the workshop.

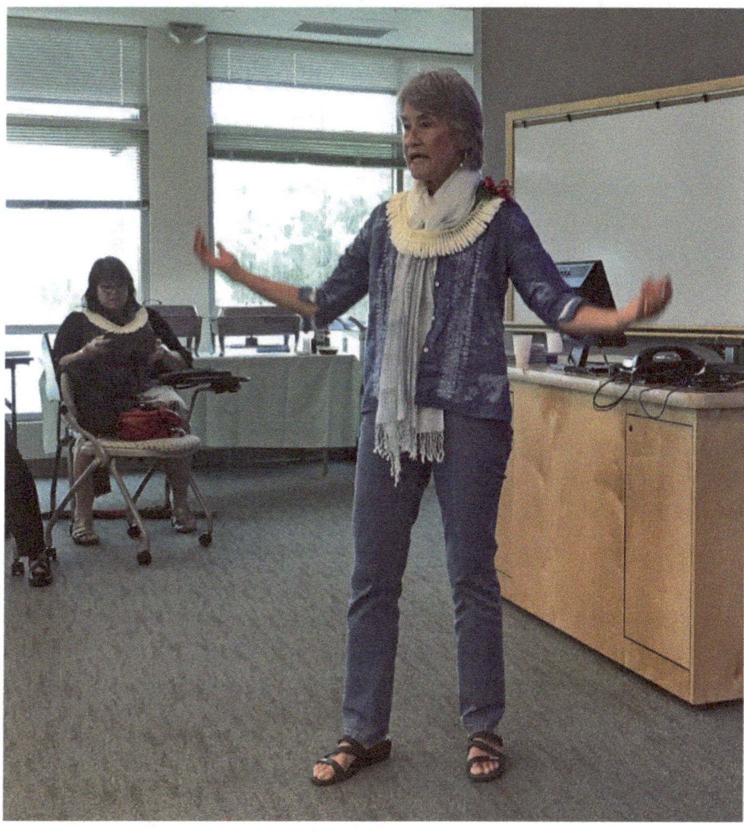

Fig. 19.1 Malina Kaulukukui leading a training session. (Photo: M Taafaki)

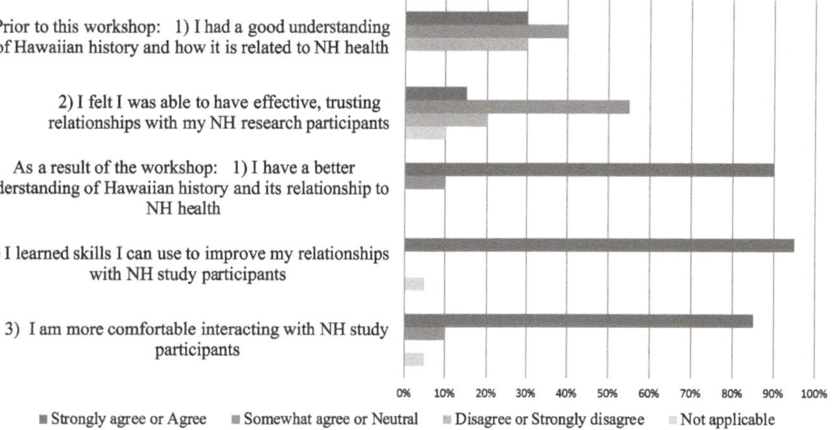
Prior to this workshop: 1) I had a good understanding of Hawaiian history and how it is related to NH health
2) I felt I was able to have effective, trusting relationships with my NH research participants
As a result of the workshop: 1) I have a better understanding of Hawaiian history and its relationship to NH health
2) I learned skills I can use to improve my relationships with NH study participants
3) I am more comfortable interacting with NH study participants
0% 10% 20% 30% 40% 50% 60% 70% 80% 90% 100%
Strongly agree or Agree
Somewhat agree or Neutral
Disagree or Strongly disagree
Not applicable

Fig. 19.2 Participants' responses to the post-workshop evaluation

Participants' feedback was overwhelmingly positive. We found that the CC training used with JABSOM medical students was easily adaptable to this set of learners. The modified CC curriculum yielded encouraging responses from our attendees, many of whom will be working with Native Hawaiian study participants. Organizers were encouraged to continue this type of workshop for other health disparate minority groups involved in clinical trials.

Conclusions

To achieve success, this type of workshop needs to be strongly supported by organizational leaders, such as the head of the research center. Since researchers and their staff may not come from Indigenous or minority backgrounds nor from other health disparate groups, training should include

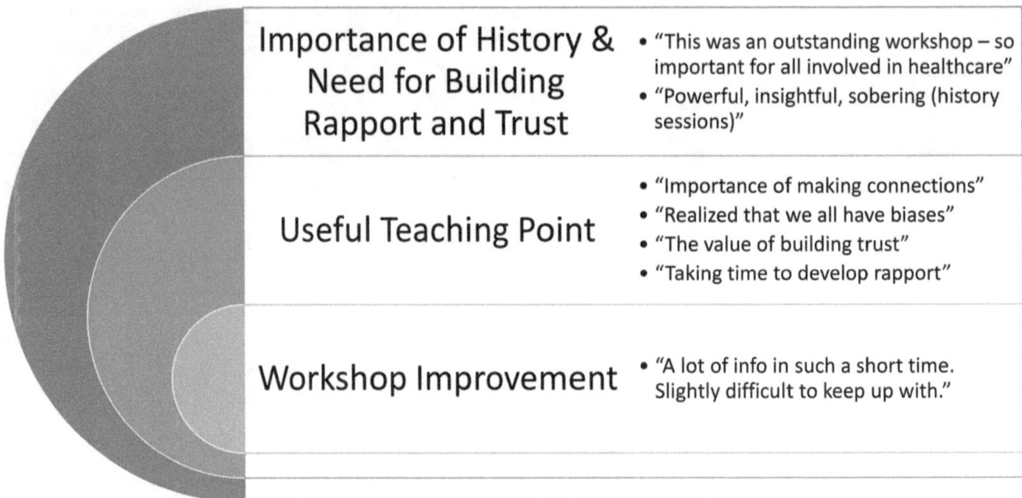

Importance of History & Need for Building Rapport and Trust
• "This was an outstanding workshop – so important for all involved in healthcare"
• "Powerful, insightful, sobering (history sessions)"
Useful Teaching Point
• "Importance of making connections"
• "Realized that we all have biases"
• "The value of building trust"
• "Taking time to develop rapport"
Workshop Improvement
• "A lot of info in such a short time. Slightly difficult to keep up with."

Fig. 19.3 Qualitative results of post-workshop assessment

not only research staff and clinical trial recruiters but also the researchers themselves. We believe that conducting training like this can help attendees to develop cultural humility through authentic self-reflections, increase knowledge and awareness of communities and their values, and learn communication skills. These would be important initial steps toward strengthening effective relationships with study participants. Addressing recruitment and retention issues in Indigenous and minority populations through training may help to empower patients, ultimately contributing to making them full partners in the challenges around cancer treatment, including the decision to participate in clinical trials. The ultimate goal of cancer research is to eliminate cancer inequities, and, to do that, we need patients from the hardest-hit communities to be our partners in this crusade.

Next Steps

We believe this type of training can be helpful and impactful. We also believe that certain changes might create even more successful training. More time should be allocated, as it is difficult to limit CC training to a half-day workshop. More time would allow for deeper exploration of topics or other useful content such as patient panels. To fully understand the impact of the training, long-term assessments might be helpful, including follow-up surveys of trainees to ascertain behavior change, surveys of clinical study sites to see if recruitment and retention have changed, and focus groups of past participants to ascertain long-term impact or training gaps.

For cancer, it is critical to have the populations most impacted participate in clinical trials, and we offer this example of a way to help with known recruitment and retention issues with Indigenous and other health disparate groups.

The project described was supported by grant number U54GM138062 from the National Institute of General Medical Sciences (NIGMS), National Institutes of Health (NIH). Its contents are solely the responsibility of the authors and do not necessarily represent the official view of NIGMS or NIH, who provided faculty used to help design the training, as well as NCORP, who provided faculty, support for speakers, and access to trainees.

References

1. Chen Jr MS, Lara PN, Dang JHT, Paterniti DA, Kelly K. Twenty years post-NIH Revitalization Act: Enhancing minority participation in clinical trials (EMPaCT): Laying the groundwork for improving minority clinical trial accrual. *Cancer.* 2014;120:1091–1096. https://doi.org/10.1002/cncr.28575
2. Cronin KA, Scott S, Firth A, Sung H, Henley SJ, Sherman RL, et al. Annual report to the nation on the status of cancer, part 1: National cancer statistics. *Cancer*. 2022;128:4251–4284. https://doi.org/10.1002/cncr.34479
3. US Dept of Health and Human Services, National Institute of Health, National Cancer Institute. *Cancer Stat Facts: Cancer Disparities* [Internet]. National Cancer Institute Surveillance, Epidemiology, and End Results Program. Available from: https://seer.cancer.gov/statfacts/html/disparities.html
4. Hawai'i Tumor Registry. *Cancer at a Glance 2014-2018.* Honolulu: University of Hawai'i Cancer Center; 2022.
5. Ford JG, Howerton MW, Lai G, Gary TL, Bolen S, Gibbon MC, et al. Barriers to recruiting underrepresented populations to cancer clinical trials: A systematic review. *Cancer*. 2008;112(2):228–242. https://doi.org/10.1002/cncr.23157
6. George S, Duran N, Norris K. A Systematic Review of Barriers and Facilitators to Minority Research Participation Among African Americans, Latinos, Asian Americans, and Pacific Islanders. *Am J Pub Health*. 2014;104 (2):e16–e31. https://doi.org/10.2105/AJPH.2013.301706

7. Harrigan R, Perez MH, Beaudry S, Johnson C, Sil P, Mead K, Apau-Ludlum N. Recruitment and retention of under-represented groups with health disparities into clinical trials: a formative approach. *J Immigr Minor Health.* 2014;16(5):898–903. https://doi.org/10.1007/s10903-013-9786-8
8. Pacheco CM, Daley SM, Brown T, Filippi M, Greiner KA, Daley CM. Moving forward: Breaking the cycle of mistrust between American Indians and researchers. *Am J Pub Health.* 2013;103(12):2152–2159. https://doi.org/10.2105/AJPH.2013.301480
9. Blaisdell RK. Culture and Cancer in Kanaka Maoli (Native Hawaiians) Abstract. *Asian Am Pac Isl J Health.* 1998;6(2):400.
10. Salman A, Nguyen C, Lee, YH, Cooksey-James T. A Review of Barriers to Minorities' Participation in Cancer Clinical Trials: Implications for Future Cancer Research. *J Immigr Minor Health.* 2016;18:447–453. https://doi.org/10.1007/s10903-015-0198-9
11. Carpenter D, Kamaka M, Kaulukukui M. An Innovative Approach to Developing a Cultural Competency Curriculum: Efforts at the John A. Burns School of Medicine, Department of Native Hawaiian Health. *Hawaii Med J.* 2011;70s:15–19.
12. Cross TL, Bazron BJ, Dennis KW, Isaacs MR. Towards a Culturally Competent System of Care: A Monograph on Effective Services for Minority Children Who Are Severely Emotionally Disturbed, Vol. 1. Washington, DC: Georgetown University Child Development Center. 1989, p.13. https://ia800204.us.archive.org/35/items/towardsculturall00un/towardsculturall00un_bw.pdf. (accessed June 10, 2024)
13. Anderson I, Crengle S, Kamaka M, Chen T, Palafox N, Jackson-Pulver L. Indigenous Health: Australia, New Zealand and the Pacific. *The Lancet.* 2006; 367:1775–1785. https://doi.org/10.1016/S0140-6736(06)68773-4

20 Yarn for Life: Improving Cancer Outcomes Through a National Communication Campaign

Wayne Denning, Caroline Nehill, Jacinta Elston, and Dorothy Keefe

Key Points

- Yarn for Life is the first national cancer awareness campaign developed by and for Aboriginal and Torres Strait Islander people. It aims to reduce the impact of cancer within Aboriginal and Torres Strait Islander communities by encouraging conversations about cancer.
- An evaluation of Yarn for Life with the target audience showed that the campaign messaging is engaging and easy to understand, and encourages people to talk about cancer with their family and communities.
- As the Yarn for Life campaign builds, it must innovate to expand its reach among Aboriginal and Torres Strait Islander peoples.

While Australia's cancer survival rates are among the best in the world, Aboriginal and Torres Strait Islander people experience significant disparities in cancer outcomes.

Evidence review and consultation with Aboriginal and Torres Strait Islander people during the development of the National Aboriginal and Torres Strait Islander Cancer Framework (the Framework) confirmed that a widespread lack of knowledge about cancer is a significant barrier to improving cancer outcomes for Aboriginal and Torres Strait Islander people [1]. This informed Priority 1 of the Framework: "Improve knowledge, attitudes, and understanding of cancer by individuals, families, carers, and community members (across the continuum)." Enablers of this priority include:

- Using evidence-based public-awareness programs and health-promotion strategies that specifically address the concerns and needs of Aboriginal and Torres Strait Islander people.
- Ensuring that information is available and accessible to Aboriginal and Torres Strait Islander people across the cancer continuum, in formats and language(s) that are culturally appropriate.
- Ensuring community involvement throughout the development of public-awareness and health-promotion campaigns.
- Enhancing community capacity and engaging and supporting key community members to promote cancer literacy [1].

What Was Done

Developing the Campaign

As the national cancer control agency, Cancer Australia developed a communication campaign in line with the Framework to reduce the impact of cancer within Aboriginal and Torres Strait Islander communities. An Indigenous-owned and Indigenous-operated creative agency (Carbon Creative) was engaged to develop and implement culturally appropriate communications through a multichannel strategy.

To successfully define and articulate key messages, an evidence-based campaign schema was developed based on three content pillars that guided campaign development:

- Myth busting and education.
- Fatalism.
- Facing fears.

The campaign aims to address the shame and stigma associated with cancer by changing how Aboriginal and Torres Strait Islander people think about cancer. Key objectives of the campaign, identified by Cancer Australia and Carbon Creative, include:

- Increasing awareness and understanding of cancer among Aboriginal and Torres Strait Islander people.
- Normalizing conversations about cancer.
- Emphasizing the importance of early detection.

G. Garvey (ed.), *Indigenous and Tribal Peoples and Cancer*, https://doi.org/10.1007/978-3-031-56806-0_20

As part of the creative concept development, preliminary qualitative research was conducted to determine how the campaign would be received by the target audience. A survey of Aboriginal and Torres Strait Islander people was conducted to determine the target audience's views on the creative aspects of the campaign, including its proposed look and feel, its slogan "Yarn for Life," the call to action "There's no shame in cancer," and its imagery. Learnings from this research informed the final creative concept. The creative concept was well received, and recommendations to amend the tagline to "It's OK to talk about cancer" were accepted and progressed.

Yarn for Life

Yarn for Life is the first national cancer awareness campaign developed by and for Aboriginal and Torres Strait Islander people [2]. It aims to reduce the impact of cancer within Aboriginal and Torres Strait Islander communities by encouraging and normalizing conversations about cancer and promoting the importance of early detection and timely referral (Fig. 20.1).

Yarn for Life delivers the central message "It's OK to talk about cancer" by sharing personal stories of courage and survivorship from Aboriginal and Torres Strait Islander people. The stories are provided by three people and their respective loved ones sharing their cancer journeys. Two prominent Indigenous leaders, Leila Gurruwiwi and Charlie King, also speak to the key messages of the campaign with a call to action for the audience. These stories are shared through a suite of resources including videos, animations, audio grabs, and posters.

Implementation was completed using a multichannel communication strategy, including a website landing page, paid social media, radio, Spotify, YouTube, and television. Videos played on rotation across the National Aboriginal Health Television network, which is shown in the waiting rooms of Aboriginal Medical Services (AMSs). Key messages were translated and shared on radio as well as on the Yarn for Life website. The communication strategy is implemented annually for six to 12 weeks. Since commencing in 2019, the Yarn for Life campaign has had five rounds of implementation (Fig. 20.2).

The Yarn for Life campaign is intended for all Aboriginal and Torres Strait Islander communities; however, the campaign resources have been delivered at higher volumes in areas with high Aboriginal and Torres Strait Islander populations, particularly those areas most related to the origins of the people featured in the campaign's resources (greater metropolitan Sydney, South Australia, Queensland, and the Northern Territory).

Outcomes

In December 2020, approximately one year into the campaign, qualitative research was undertaken to explore attitudes, knowledge, and understanding around cancer in communities from remote locations of Australia. Phone and text surveys were undertaken with representatives from the target audience, and positive feedback was received from participants on the messaging and campaign strategy. Key insights included that many remote communities receive their health information from their local AMSs. Accordingly, a key recommendation was to engage remote AMSs through the Australian Aboriginal Health Television network, which delivers culturally relevant health and wellbeing messages via more than 300 screens across AMSs nationally. This was incorporated into further iterations of the campaign.

Fig. 20.1 Yarn for Life website landing page

Fig. 20.2 Yarn for Life posters featuring Indigenous leaders Charlie King (left) and Leila Gurruwiwi (right)

A comprehensive evaluation of Yarn for Life was undertaken in June 2021. Cancer Australia engaged an external Indigenous consultant for the evaluation. Ethical approval was granted by the Australian Institute of Aboriginal and Torres Strait Islander Studies (AIATSIS) Research Ethics Committee in March 2021. The evaluation used pre-campaign and post-campaign online surveys to measure changes in awareness, attitudes, intentions, and behaviors. A post-campaign face-to-face survey was also used, providing perspectives from Aboriginal and Torres Strait Islander people in regional and remote Australia. The subject sampling for the evaluation included an Australia-wide opt-in recruitment round through social media for the online survey, and three convenience samples in Darwin, Alice Springs, and the Torres Strait Islands for the face-to-face survey.

The evaluation results showed that the majority of respondents found the content of the campaign "easy to understand" (97–100%) and endorsed its key messages. The most prevalent message respondents took from the campaign was "it's OK to talk/yarn about cancer." Another highly positive result was that around 8 in 10 (67–87%) respondents agreed that the campaign resources prompted them to think about talking to family and friends about cancer. Further, survey results suggested the campaign improved respondents' knowledge about who to speak to about cancer, with 83% of those who had seen the campaign indicating they knew where to go, compared to 69% of those who had not seen the campaign.

Reasonable levels of campaign awareness were recorded, with one in four (26%) online respondents and one in five (19%) face-to-face respondents recognizing de-branded campaign resources. Radio advertisements had higher levels of prompted recognition compared to other communication channels in metropolitan areas, while recognition in regional and remote areas was mainly driven by television and video advertisements. One barrier to radio advertisement recall in remote areas was the audio not being in an Indigenous language. Resources featuring prominent Indigenous leaders were deemed to be the most effective of the campaign.

Learnings

The Yarn for Life campaign is competing against many cancer-related advertisements targeting a similar audience. This was evident in the evaluation, with very few survey respondents agreeing the campaign "told you something new." This highlighted the need to focus on audience engagement through refreshing campaign resources and communication strategies.

Communication should be tailored for different audience members. For example, audio grabs have now been recorded in 14 different languages for in-language radio advertisements. In the future, content with prominent Indigenous leaders could be expanded and new local champions could be engaged to increase the reach of the campaign.

Yarn for Life demonstrates the value and necessity of Indigenous people leading and partnering in designing and implementing communication campaigns that are for them. As the campaign builds, innovation is needed to expand the reach of the campaign and ensure its longevity. This will only be achieved through leadership from and partnership with Aboriginal and Torres Strait Islander people.

References

1. Cancer Australia. *National Aboriginal and Torres Strait Islander Cancer Framework.* Surry Hills, NSW: Cancer Australia; 2015.
2. Cancer Australia. *Yarn for Life* [Internet]. Cancer Australia; 2019. Available from: https://yarnforlife.com.au/

21 Our Mob and Cancer

Kristine Falzon, Katrina Johnson, Jane Salisbury, and Dorothy Keefe

Key Points

- *Our Mob and Cancer* is a national website designed to provide a central hub of culturally appropriate, evidence- and strengths-based information about cancer for Aboriginal and Torres Strait Islander people and their health professionals.
- Developed by and for Aboriginal and Torres Strait Islander people, *Our Mob and Cancer* is a first-of-its-kind, culturally safe space for Aboriginal and Torres Strait Islander people affected by cancer, their communities, and their health professionals.
- To guide and design the project from inception, Cancer Australia incorporated the voices and experiences of Aboriginal and Torres Strait Islander people impacted by cancer, their communities, the Aboriginal and Torres Strait Islander Expert Reference Group, and Cancer Australia's Leadership Group on Aboriginal and Torres Strait Islander Cancer Control.

Although Australia's cancer survival rates are among the best in the world, cancer is the leading cause of death for Aboriginal and Torres Strait Islander people, and the gap in cancer mortality rates between Aboriginal and Torres Strait Islander and non-Indigenous Australians is widening [1]. Cancer places a heavy burden not only on those diagnosed with the disease but also on their families, carers, Elders, and community. The impact of a cancer diagnosis and death can have specific cultural and spiritual implications.

The National Aboriginal and Torres Strait Islander Cancer Framework 2015 (the Framework) notes that "… a widespread lack of knowledge about cancer, its causes and symptoms, treatments and likely survivability is a significant barrier to improving the cancer outcomes of Aboriginal and Torres Strait Islander people" [2]. We identified that *improving knowledge, attitudes, and understanding of cancer by individuals, families, carers, and community members (across the continuum)* was a key priority of the Framework. Enablers of this priority include:

- Ensure that information is available and accessible to Aboriginal and Torres Strait Islander people across the cancer continuum, in formats and languages that are culturally appropriate.
- Recognize that gender-specific strategies may be needed, depending on local context [2].

Why We Need a Dedicated Website About Cancer for Aboriginal and Torres Strait Islander People

As Australia's national cancer control agency, Cancer Australia aims to reduce the impact of cancer, address disparities, and improve cancer outcomes for all Australians. From a review of the existing website and online information hubs dedicated to cancer in Aboriginal and Torres Strait Islander people (state-based and national), we identified a need for a national website that provides a central source of current information about cancer that is relevant to and resonates with Aboriginal and Torres Strait Islander people with cancer and their health professionals.

To fill this important gap in culturally appropriate information, Cancer Australia embarked on the development of a new, national, co-designed website that would provide a central hub of culturally informed, evidence- and strengths-based information about cancer for Aboriginal and Torres Strait Islander people and their health professionals. The dedicated cancer information hub would need to provide a wide range of culturally respectful and safe information for Aboriginal and Torres Strait Islander people; be culturally appropriate in look, feel, and imagery; and incorporate the voices and experiences of Aboriginal and Torres Strait Islander people affected by cancer and their communities.

G. Garvey (ed.), *Indigenous and Tribal Peoples and Cancer*, https://doi.org/10.1007/978-3-031-56806-0_21

Co-designing the Website

An end-to-end, co-design approach was undertaken by establishing and collaborating with an Aboriginal and Torres Strait Islander Expert Reference Group, Cancer Australia's Leadership Group on Aboriginal and Torres Strait Islander Cancer Control, stakeholders, and advisors, with input and feedback from Aboriginal and Torres Strait Islander community members. This ensured that grassroots community voices were heard and embedded across all levels of development and design. Diverse representations from communities located across the country were included while always privileging Aboriginal and Torres Strait Islander people's ways of knowing, being, and doing.

Expert Guidance and Advice

To support the website co-design from its earliest development, Cancer Australia brought together an Aboriginal and Torres Strait Islander Expert Reference Group with national representation. The membership included Aboriginal and Torres Strait Islander cancer survivors and communications professionals, clinicians working in Aboriginal healthcare, representatives from Aboriginal Community Controlled Health Organisations, and Aboriginal and Torres Strait Islander Health Research Groups. The group met on five occasions between 2020 and 2022.

Cancer Australia's Leadership Group on Aboriginal and Torres Strait Islander Cancer Control provided strategic overview and monitored the website's development.

Suppliers

As agreed by the Expert Reference Group, all contractors engaged to develop, design, build, and write content for the dedicated website were certified and registered Indigenous Australian-owned and Indigenous Australian-operated businesses from Supply Nation [3] to ensure the website was culturally appropriate and safe, strengths-based, respectful, engaging, and consumer-friendly for Aboriginal and Torres Strait Islander people affected by cancer and their communities and people with cancer.

Audience Testing

Website development was guided by multiple rounds of user experience and focus-group testing nationally with members of Aboriginal and Torres Strait communities. All content was culturally reviewed and focus-group tested during website development and prior to its launch.

Artwork

To ensure the design of the website was culturally welcoming, visually engaging, and positive, Indigenous artist and graphic designer Riki Salam (Mualgal, Yalanji, Ngai Tahu) created the website artwork *Hope and Healing for Country* (Fig. 21.1). The design aims to allow Aboriginal and Torres Strait Islander people to feel connected and experience a sense of safety, belonging, hope, and healing throughout the website.

Fig. 21.1 Hope and Healing for Country. (Artist: Riki Salam—Mualgal, Yalanji, Ngai Tahu)

Launching the *Our Mob and Cancer* Website

Our Mob and Cancer, which was launched in October 2022, is Australia's first national comprehensive cancer website developed by and for Aboriginal and Torres Strait Islander people [4].

Our Mob and Cancer contains critical information about how cancer affects Aboriginal and Torres Strait Islander people, ways to protect against cancer, types of cancer diagnosis, treatment, living with cancer, how cancer spreads, and where to get help and support. The website also includes information about the culturally sensitive topics of Sorry Business,[1] Men's[2] and Women's Business,[3] and Shame,[4] and how these relate to cancer and associated health outcomes.

Following Aboriginal and Torres Strait Islander stakeholder recommendations and audience research, we produced a suite of videos featuring cancer survivors, Elders, and health professionals covering themes of early detection and screening, diagnosis and treatment, and Shame and Sorry Business. These were embedded throughout the website.

The *Health Professionals* section of the website includes guidance for health professionals on providing culturally appropriate optimal cancer care for Aboriginal and Torres Strait Islander cancer patients and explains the importance of this in supporting the best cancer outcomes possible.

Other user features of the website include:

- A clickable body map that illustrates the organ or body part concerned and links to common cancer-type information, designed to be culturally appropriate with respect to Men's and Women's Business.
- A glossary of technical terms called *What does this word mean?*
- Culturally relevant lifestyle and technical illustrations to provide cultural context and support medical information.
- Improved intuitive navigation, including accordion dropdowns for denser areas of text and easy access to key information.
- Read speaker functionality, allowing the text on the website to be read aloud for accessibility.
- Helpful links on where to find further help, support, and services.
- Print-friendly format, providing users with the ability to print and/or save the content as a PDF document.

Cancer Australia extends sincere thanks and recognition to the Aboriginal and Torres Strait Islander Expert Reference Group and Cancer Australia's Leadership Group on Aboriginal and Torres Strait Islander Cancer Control, which provided expert advice and guidance to *Our Mob and Cancer*, and to Riki Salam who created the *Our Mob and Cancer* artwork. We also thank the Aboriginal and Torres Strait Islander people affected by cancer and communities across Australia who contributed to *Our Mob and Cancer*.

References

1. Australian Institute of Health and Welfare 2018. Cancer in Aboriginal & Torres Strait Islander people of Australia. Cat. no. CAN 109, Accessed: September 2023; https://www.aihw.gov.au/reports/cancer/cancer-in-indigenous-australians
2. Cancer Australia. *National Aboriginal and Torres Strait Islander Cancer Framework*. Surry Hills, NSW: Cancer Australia; 2015.
3. Supply Nation. *Indigenous Business Direct* [Internet]. Supply Nation; 2023 [cited 2023 July]. Available from: https://supplynation.org.au/
4. Cancer Australia. *Our Mob and Cancer* [Internet]. Cancer Australia; 2022. Available from: https://www.ourmobandcancer.gov.au

[1] https://www.ourmobandcancer.gov.au/sorry-business

[2] https://www.ourmobandcancer.gov.au/mens-business

[3] https://www.ourmobandcancer.gov.au/womens-business

[4] https://www.ourmobandcancer.gov.au/why-cancer-is-no-shame-job

Developing an Indigenous Radiation Therapy Talking Book for Cancer Patients

22

Gail Garvey, Lara Stoll, Haryana Dhillon, Giam Kar, Joan Cunningham, Michael Penniment, Joanne Shaw, Georgia Halkett, Sid Baxi, Sabe Sabesan, and Sian Smith

Key Points

- Radiation therapy talking books are potentially useful education resources for people with lower health literacy; however, these resources need to be culturally adapted to appropriately meet the needs of Aboriginal and Torres Strait Islander cancer patients and their families.
- Consultation with Aboriginal and Torres Strait Islander people to ensure cultural acceptability of educational health resources is essential.
- Effective health communication between clinicians and Aboriginal and Torres Strait Islander cancer patients and their families is critical to improving health outcomes.

Health literacy is strongly linked with reduced engagement with and uptake of health services and poorer health outcomes. In Australia, little is known about health literacy levels among Aboriginal and Torres Strait Islander cancer patients. Accessible and culturally responsive health information is an important aspect of optimal and equitable cancer care. Health information and resources are most likely to be successful with Indigenous Australians if they are developed, planned, and evaluated with community members, and if they adopt culturally appropriate communication methods (such as artwork and storytelling) [1, 2].

This case study describes the development of an Indigenous radiation therapy talking book for Aboriginal and Torres Strait Islander cancer patients, their carers, and health professionals.

Radiation therapy is recommended for approximately 50% of Australian cancer patients [3]. However, few resources exist that provide radiation therapy information to individuals with lower health literacy or that are specifically for Aboriginal and Torres Strait Islander peoples. Researchers in Australia have previously developed and piloted a radiation therapy talking book (RTB) to provide information for cancer patients with lower levels of health literacy [4], building on research that demonstrated the effectiveness of talking books in reducing anxiety and improving information recall in dementia and diabetes settings [5]. When trialed, the RTB significantly improved cancer patients' knowledge and decreased their anxiety and concerns [6]. Nearly half of participants reported using the book during appointments, with many reporting it helped them to communicate with health professionals.

Developing an Indigenous Radiation Therapy Book (IRTB)

The original RTB was adapted by our team into a culturally appropriate printed booklet and an e-book for Aboriginal and Torres Strait Islander cancer patients and their carers.

Consultations were conducted with Indigenous people affected by cancer, including those who had previously received radiation therapy and Indigenous health professionals from three cancer centers. The consultations utilized Indigenous research methods such as Yarning Circles to gather stories, feedback, and ideas on an Indigenous RTB. The outcome of these consultations resulted in the original RTB booklet being adapted to (Fig. 22.1):

- Add color, artwork, and more images of Indigenous Australians.
- Reduce the amount of text and include more diagrams and illustrations.
- Reorder the pages to support a storytelling approach.
- Rearrange the information so it is more patient-centered.
- Move information about patient and family support nearer to the start.
- Add information about traditional medicines, healing, and natural therapies.

G. Garvey (ed.), *Indigenous and Tribal Peoples and Cancer*, https://doi.org/10.1007/978-3-031-56806-0_22

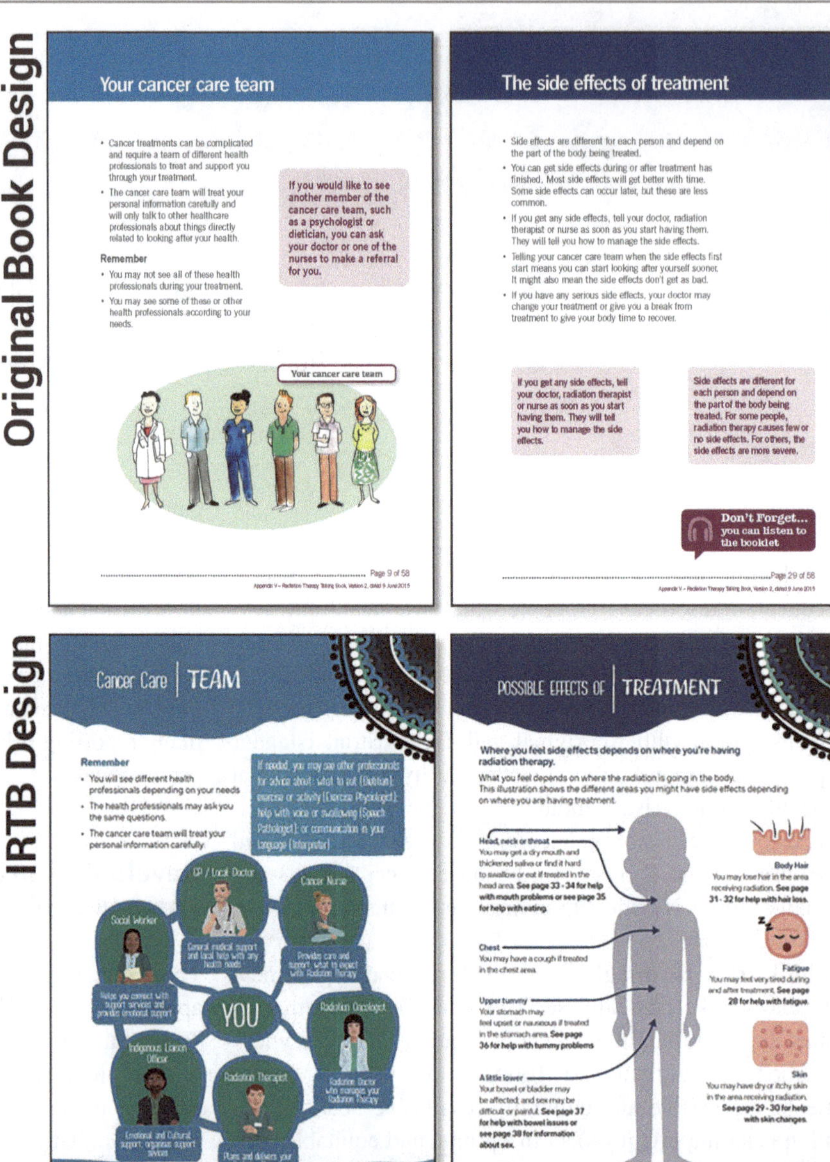

Fig. 22.1 Snapshot of the original RTB and revised IRTB content and design

Once our consultation groups approved the revised printed booklet, we converted it into an e-book IRTB.

The importance of hearing an Indigenous voice in the IRTB was highlighted through the Yarning Circles. As a result, local Indigenous voice actors were engaged to provide the voiceover. With support from an Australian online education specialist/designer, the audio and graphics for the IRTB were combined into an e-book with the graphics and audio matched page by page. The e-book was tested and revised to enable animations and text to appear with timing matched to the audio, and as each page was turned. This supported a storytelling approach, preferred by participants in our Yarning Circles.

Our IRTB e-book is best described as a tablet-based adaptation of traditional print-plus-audio talking books. It is an electronic flip book, with accompanying audio, allowing participants to read while they listen [7]. We developed a simple English-language version and a version in Yolngu Matha, a language used in north-east Arnhem Land in the Northern Territory (NT) of Australia and relevant for one of our study trial sites.

Training for Health Professionals

Our IRTB is designed specifically for Aboriginal and Torres Strait Islander cancer patients and their families/carers. The IRTB can also be used by radiation oncologists and therapists in discussions with patients about treatment options and during patient education sessions.

Radiation therapy requires conveying complex technical details to patients who might not be familiar with the terminology. Radiation therapists are pivotal in offering information and emotional support to patients. When information is communicated clearly, avoids excessive technical terms, and is presented in a way that is tailored to the patient's level of understanding, patients are less likely to feel anxious or emotionally distressed [8].

To support health professionals' use of the IRTB, we developed three short, Indigenous-specific, online communication skills training modules, including one about how to use the IRTB in clinics. Health professionals seeking to use the IRTB must complete all the training modules [9].

Implementation of the IRTB

Our Australian-specific e-book IRTB has been finalized and is currently being trialed and evaluated in three large cancer services: two regional cities in Queensland and one regional site in the Northern Territory. Indigenous cancer patients who are newly diagnosed and referred to radiation therapy will receive both a printed booklet, in which they can make notes, and the e-book IRTB. The project is due to be completed and evaluated in 2024.

The research is being conducted by the First Nations and Cancer Wellbeing Research Program at The University of Queensland, in partnership with the Royal Australian and New Zealand College of Radiologists, the Alan Walker Cancer Care Centre in Darwin, Townsville Cancer Centre, and the Radiation Oncology Centre in Cairns, and is funded by an NHMRC Partnership Grant (#1152653). We thank all of those involved in developing the radiation therapy talking book, particularly Dr. Lorraine Bell.

References

1. Davis B, McGrath N, Knight S, Davis S, Norval M, Greelander G, et al. Aminina Nud Mulumuluna ("You Gotta Look After Yourself"): Evaluation of the use of traditional art in health promotion for Aboriginal people in the Kimberley region of Western Australia. *Aust Psychol.* 2004;39(2):107–13. https://doi.org/10.1080/00050060410001701816
2. Schoen D, Balchin D, Thompson S. Health Promotion Resources for Aboriginal People: Lessons Learned from Consultation and Evaluation of Diabetes Foot Care Resources. *Health Promot J Austr.* 2010;21(1):64–9. https://doi.org/10.1071/he10064
3. Australian Institute of Health & Welfare. *Radiotherapy in Australia: report on the second year of a pilot collection 2014–15.* Cat. no. HSE 181. Canberra: AIHW; 2016.
4. Smith SK, Cabrera-Aguas M, Shaw J, Shepherd H, Naehrig D, Meiser B, et al. A low literacy targeted talking book about radiation therapy for cancer: development and acceptability. *Support Care Cancer.* 2019;27:2057–67. https://doi.org/10.1007/s00520-018-4446-0
5. Goeman D, Michael J, King J, Luu H, Emmanuel C, Koch K. Partnering with consumers to develop and evaluate a Vietnamese Dementia Talking-Book to support low health literacy: a qualitative study incorporating codesign and participatory action research. *BMJ Open.* 2016;6(9):e011451. https://doi.org/10.1136/bmjopen-2016-011451
6. Smith-Lickess SK, Stefanic N, Shaw J, Shepherd H, Naehrig D, Turner RM, et al. What is the effect of a low literacy talking book on patient knowledge, anxiety and communication before radiation therapy starts? A pilot study. *Med Radiat Sci.* 2022;69:463–72. https://doi.org/10.1002/jmrs.606
7. Smith SK, Cabrera Aguas M, Shaw J, Shepherd H, Halkett G, Dhillon HM. *Development and acceptability of a radiation therapy talking book for people with low health literacy.* COSA Annual Scientific Meeting. Hobart; 2015.
8. Halkett GK, Kristjanson LJ, Lobb EA. 'If we get too close to your bones they'll go brittle': women's initial fears about radiotherapy for early breast cancer. *Psychooncology.* 2008;17(9):877–84. https://doi.org/10.1002/pon.1298
9. Durey A, Halkett G, Berg M, Lester L, Kickett M. Does one workshop on respecting cultural differences increase health professionals' confidence to improve the care of Australian Aboriginal patients with cancer? An evaluation. *BMC Health Serv Res.* 2017;17(1):660. https://doi.org/10.1186/s12913-017-2599-z

23 Expression of My Mana Motuhake (Self-Agency) to Guide Breast Cancer Recovery

Maria Marama

Key Points

Four dimensions of holistic wellbeing:

1. Hinengaro (mental health)—the power of knowledge and positive thinking.
2. Tinana (physical health)—integration of traditional and complementary treatments.
3. Wairua (spiritual health)—faith and trust in phenomena (tangible and intangible).
4. Whānau (family)—the importance of close relationships.

The Māori world is rich in metaphor where deep understanding of one phenomenon or concept can be usefully applied to make meaning of many things that seem inexplicable. Developed by Sir Mason Durie in 1984, Te Whare Tapa Whā (the four-sided house) is a traditional Māori model of holistic wellness [1]. The model is premised on a wharenui (meeting house) structure, requiring all four sides to be of equal dimension and strength in order to stand strong. This model is applied ubiquitously throughout Aotearoa New Zealand, and it was this model that I turned to following my diagnosis of cancer to make meaning of the inexplicable: the news that I have breast cancer. As frightening a prospect as that was, I knew that if I was going to survive, I needed to draw on the knowledge, resilience, and fortitude of my tūpuna (ancestors) and my mana motuhake (self-agency) to have rangatiratanga (self-determination) over my own healing journey.

Hinengaro: Knowledge Is Power

A critical component of my journey has been learning. In my roles as a mother, advocate, and research evaluator, I critically understood the value of arming myself with as much information as I could to inform my thinking and decision-making. I found that our people, like other Indigenous people, do not fare well within the Western cancer-care system [2]. I was not prepared to wager my life on one treatment pathway. In reviewing the use of complementary medicine (CM) and traditional medicine (TM), I discovered that systemic racism and discrimination impacted levels of access to medical treatment to CM and TM for Indigenous peoples [3]. I grew a heightened awareness about the potential of Te Ao Māori (the Māori world) for my healing journey. I met with tohunga (Māori experts) to access mātauranga Māori (traditional knowledge), rongoā Māori (traditional medicines), and tikanga (traditional practice). I immersed myself in research and participated in alternative treatments including vitamin C and mineral infusions, cannabis oil, Chinese medicines, and kinesthesiology.

Tinana: The Capacity for Physical Healing and Wellbeing

Exercising mana motuhake (self-agency) over my breast cancer was literally a contest of my mind over matter. While I was fortunate to have private medical insurance, the Western treatment pathway was nothing short of intensively grueling. It included a mastectomy, chemotherapy, radiotherapy, Herceptin, heart checks, weekly blood tests, and meetings with the surgeon and oncologist. Despite the physical toll, my research led me to lifestyle changes, including rongoā maori (Māori medicines), eating a wholesome diet, decreasing stress levels, and making natural products for my body and home. I continued to work and coach netball teams, and I completed an adult teaching diploma. These activities kept me physically connected to life and I made a conscious decision not to simply give up but to be an active participant in my own recovery.

G. Garvey (ed.), *Indigenous and Tribal Peoples and Cancer*, https://doi.org/10.1007/978-3-031-56806-0_23

Wairua: The Capacity for Faith and Wider Communication

I connected with my cultural spirituality through the guidance of tohunga (Māori experts), friends and whānau (family), and embracing the holistic approaches to wellness of my tupuna (ancestors). This spiritual journey enriched my soul and reinforced my resolve to overcome the physical challenges. I never lost faith that I would survive and move beyond breast cancer to a place of sustained health and wellbeing. Reaching a place of "tau" or being settled and calm was important for my wairua (spiritual health).

Whanaungatanga: The Importance of Support Networks

Whanaungatanga (family connection) is foundational to the centrality of being Māori. As a collective culture, our identity is inextricably linked to our kin—past, present, and future. So, it was natural that my diagnosis saw me immediately drawing on these links as my primary support system. From providing meals, being chauffeured to appointments and advocating for my needs, to gifting encouraging words that uplifted my spirit, the support of my whānau (family) and friends was essential to my healing. Their physical and practical support was something I couldn't have done without, and their unwavering presence gave me the courage to face each day with resilience and hope.

Conclusion

My journey through breast cancer has been one of challenges and triumphs. I am conscious of the toll taken on my whānau—my partner and our tamariki (children)—and my relatives and friends and the impact my breast cancer diagnosis had on their own "Te Whare Tapa Whā" (dimensions of wellbeing). We must be cognizant that their lives are affected as much as ours, and, as they watch and observe our struggles, they are struggling too. My experience has taught me that drawing on collective support, traditional healing practices, and our Indigenous knowledge, medicines, and stories of resilience and determination can overcome most challenges. It is my hope that sharing my story inspires others to exercise their mana motuhake (self-agency), trust in their own Indigeneity, and find their own healing pathway. Further, I hope that we, as Indigenous peoples, can collectively challenge Western-centric cancer-care approaches and improve access for our people to holistic, culturally responsive, cancer treatment options.

References

1. Durie M. Te Whare Tapa Whā: A Māori model of a unified theory of health. In: Meijl H, editor. *Proceedings of the National Māori Graduates of Nursing Conference.* Victoria University of Wellington; 1984.
2. Seneviratne S, Campbell I, Scott N, Coles C, Lawrenson R. Treatment delay for Māori women with breast cancer in New Zealand. *Ethn Health.* 2015;20(2):178–193. https://doi.org/10.1080/13557858.2014.895976
3. Gall A, Leske S, Adams J, Matthews V, Anderson K, Lawler S, Garvey G. Traditional and complementary medicine use among Indigenous cancer patients in Australia, Canada, New Zealand, and the United States: A systematic review. *Integr Cancer Ther.* 2018;17(3):568–581. https://doi.org/10.1177/1534735418775821

Cancer Survivors' Circles of Support 24

Lisa Harjo

Key Points

- American Indian and Alaska Native cancer survivors need integrated and expanded services, such as support circles.
- Denver American Indian Cancer Survivors Circle was founded in 2001. It weaves traditional knowledge, complementary medicine, and modern/Western medicine together to enable and support a better quality of life. Members receive companionship, conversation, information, referrals, and links or pathways to a better life.
- Members of the support circle are more likely to have formal plans for their own future healthcare, improved access to check-ups and regular cancer screening, increased adherence to treatment protocols, and improved quality of life.

In 1987, Mary P. Lovato (Santo Domingo Pueblo, passed February 2008) was diagnosed with bone cancer. At the time, culturally relevant cancer education did not exist in Indian Country. In 1994, Santo Domino Pueblo leadership allowed Mary to create cancer education and support within her community. She developed a program based on her own experiences, the People Living Through Cancer organization curricula, and support from Indian Health Service (IHS) Cancer Program staff. The result was a weeklong education program, "A Gathering of Cancer Support." From 1995, the IHS provided financial support including resources to promote the training, educational materials for training and for individual and group support, and travel support to defray the cost of participation. The Native American Cancer Research Corporation conducted an external review and evaluation of the program's first decade (1995–2005). More than 164 people completed Mary's training and almost all started support circles in their communities. Participants reported that, rather than circles run by hospitals in clinical settings, they wanted the circles facilitated by trained Native American people. Participants also noted that circles are both difficult to initiate and to sustain. Ms. Lovato changed her world through persistence, passion, and tenacity. This case study is dedicated to her memory and to the program she created.

Traditional Knowledge

Indigenous cultures throughout the world continue to use and rely on their traditional knowledge. This knowledge is passed on to each new generation through oral traditions, practical applications, and real-time experience. Traditional knowledge is the essential knowledge that protects people and guides them through life. It includes oral tradition and culture and has been shared through many lifetimes to guide generations to make their lives better. It is used by the people to heal their sick, take care of their young and old, find food and shelter, practice culture, make good decisions, and learn about the natural world. Essential knowledge includes knowledge of traditional foods, where to find them, how to prepare them, and how to eat them. It values good health and wellbeing. It teaches about family, clans, bands, and other groups and societies that exist in traditional American Indian and Alaska Native (AI/AN) cultures and how each works to teach, protect, and guide people every day and when they face challenges. Traditional values teach adherence to protocols, good self-care, respect for the rigor of ceremonies, and caring for others.

As the number of AI/AN cancer survivors increases daily, there is a growing need for integrated and expanded services and support to enable survivors to live healthy, happy lives. Indigenous peoples turn to traditional knowledge, health practices, and support circles to heal themselves. Many Indigenous support circles have been formed to meet the need to care, teach, and support each other through life, families, children, illnesses, seasons, famine, drought, and bounty. The commitment to live and work together is part of the commitment of the support circle.

G. Garvey (ed.), *Indigenous and Tribal Peoples and Cancer*, https://doi.org/10.1007/978-3-031-56806-0_24

Denver American Indian Cancer Survivors Circle

An example of an American Indian cultural cancer support circle is the Denver American Indian Cancer Survivors Circle founded in Denver, Colorado, in 2001. It was established and facilitated by a Native patient navigator, who had been trained by Mary Lovato and had worked alongside her to educate AI/AN Tribal members about cancer, early detection, screening, and survivorship in the early 2000s. This support circle has filled the gap that exists for American Indian cancer patients in Denver, who need someone to talk to and share their story with—someone who understands their experience and can provide support and shelter both physically and culturally, spiritually, and emotionally, when fighting a significant foe—in this case, cancer. Native American Cancer Research Corporation shared printed information about how to start and retain a local cancer survivorship circle on their website [1].

AI/AN members of this cancer support circle have found a way to weave traditional knowledge, complementary medicine, and modern/Western medicine together to enable and support a better quality of life. The support circle has met monthly for over 22 years, with only brief breaks for summer events, due to illness, and during the COVID-19 pandemic. It provides each member with companionship, conversation, information, referrals, and links or pathways to a better life. It is open to cancer survivors and their families. The support has been invaluable for participants, some of whom have been members for over a decade, and others who have more recently joined following diagnosis. In some cases, family members have joined alongside relatives who have been diagnosed with cancer. At times, when the person with cancer no longer attends the group, relatives, including children and grandchildren, continue to participate.

Many AI/AN cancer survivors do not return to their primary care provider after their cancer experience, perceiving their oncologist to now be their physician. To address this, members of the Denver support circle identified primary care providers and initiated annual check-ups for cancer survivors. As part of this process, group members learned to continue to document changes in their bodies and keep track of all cancer screenings, annual exams, and medications. They learned that each cancer survivor has unique medical outcomes from their diagnosis and treatment that must be managed as part of their wellness habits. The circle members have become each other's advocates, learning from each other and helping each other, including sharing traditional herbal remedies and teas from their unique heritages. They continue to meet monthly to exchange ideas, support each other, and learn from and uplift each other.

AI/AN cancer survivors throughout Indian Country and here in the Denver American Indian Cancer Survivors Circle have a commitment to their Elders' and ancestors' ways of life. They share the oral traditions of their Tribes with younger generations. They practice days-long ceremonies throughout the year at prescribed dates and times to keep the Earth in balance and to keep themselves in harmony. This translates to AI/AN people who, with support, meet their screening and treatment appointments and complete long-term treatments.

Improved outcomes of this AI/AN cancer survivor support circle in Denver include more AI/AN survivors who have (1) formal plans for their own future healthcare, (2) improved access to annual check-ups and regular cancer screening, (3) increased adherence to treatment protocols, (4) regular social opportunities to share with friends and relatives at the support group, and (5) improved quality of life and wellness. At meetings once a month, they share their activities and their progress toward meeting their goals. They share meals and traditional knowledge to help other members with their challenges. They regard each other as family. They also hold an annual event, usually in conjunction with a PowWow, to honor patients and their families. The American Indian PowWow, as referenced here, is a social gathering of members of various American Indian tribes who share their music, songs, dance, arts, and foods while interacting with each other around cultural traditions that have evolved for thousands of years.

Reference

1. Native American Cancer Research. Cancer Support Circles in Indian Country [presentation]. Available from: https://natamcancer.org/userfiles/2021/Repository/NACR-Curricula/RESOURCES_CURRICULA_Survivor_Support_Circle_Training_10-2004_handout.pdf

"Into the Dreaming": A Guide for First Nations People as They Approach "Sorry Business"

25

Leonie Garvey, Rose Wadwell, Margaret Whitson, and Renee Moore

Key Points

- *Supportive Care: "Into the Dreaming"—A guide for Aboriginal and Torres Islander people through "Sorry Business"* supports respectful conversations about the end-of-life journey.
- The booklet was produced by the Hunter New England Local Health District in Australia following a 12-month community consultation process.
- It includes artwork, stories, and clear information about planning for the end of life and supports Aboriginal health workers in yarning with patients and their families during their cancer journey.

For health workers, starting conversations about end-of-life planning can be difficult—particularly in situations where patients or family members feel alienated or distrustful of the healthcare system.

Some years ago, health workers in Australia's Hunter New England region realized that the local health district had no suitable resources to support end-of-life planning conversations with people from an Aboriginal and/or Torres Strait Islander background. A small group of health workers decided that needed to change. The result is a beautiful booklet: *Supportive Care: "Into the Dreaming"—A guide for Aboriginal and Torres Islander people through "Sorry Business"* (Fig. 25.1).

The booklet is designed to support sensitive, respectful, responsive, and appropriate ways of communicating with Aboriginal and Torres Strait Islander people about their end-of-life journey and Sorry Business. It aims to provide comfort to patients and their loved ones during a time of difficulty. It also aims to improve communication between Aboriginal and Torres Strait Islander patients, their families and carers, and their clinicians and health services.

Our Part of Australia

We are from the Hunter New England Local Health District—an area that covers 23 local government areas in New South Wales. Our district includes the large mining city of Newcastle, several large regional towns, and rural and remote communities. We have 27 hospitals, 43 community health clinics, and 12 palliative care facilities to serve a population of just under one million.

Our health district is on the traditional lands of the Kamilaroi, Gomilaroi, Gomeroi, Geawegal, Bahtabah, Thungutti, Awabakal, Aniawan, Biripi, Worimi, Nganyaywana, Wonnarua, Wanaruah, Banbai, Ngoorabul, Bundjalung, Yallaroi, and Darkinjung Nations. Around 7.5% of our population identify as Aboriginal and/or Torres Strait Islander (compared to the New South Wales state average of 2.9%). The health disparities experienced by the Aboriginal and Torres Strait Islander people living in our communities are similar to those experienced in other parts of Australia.

Why We Needed a Specific Resource

As health workers, we understood that our Aboriginal and Torres Strait Islander patients were not well prepared for their end-of-life journey. We noticed that our patients and their families had difficulty discussing their wishes. Many thought they didn't need any end-of-life planning—often because they felt that things like wills and enduring power of attorney documents were only relevant for people who had property or wealth. They didn't realize that end-of-life planning is about expressing their wishes and taking control of the final stages of life.

We were also aware that many Aboriginal and Torres Strait Islander people feel unsafe in the healthcare environment.

G. Garvey (ed.), *Indigenous and Tribal Peoples and Cancer*, https://doi.org/10.1007/978-3-031-56806-0_25

Fig. 25.1 *Supportive Care: "Into the Dreaming"* booklet

Aboriginal people typically believe that hospital—and particularly palliative care—is where they go to die. They avoid going to hospital until they're very unwell, because they don't expect to ever leave. It's a scary time for people, and as health workers we had no resources to help them navigate their journey.

Many Aboriginal people have no words to describe palliative care, and palliative care is not something they're comfortable speaking about. It's not a concept they understand, and they often don't realize that good palliative care can make a huge difference to the quality of life they experience in their end-of-life journey. We wanted to encourage people to think more carefully about how palliative care could help them.

We also know that many of our people are not aware that they can make their own choices about healthcare. Some of our patients are members of the Stolen Generation: they were removed from their families when they were young, and grew up in an environment where they had no capacity to make choices. With that history, they don't trust the health system and they don't know that it's OK to express their personal wishes—or that their wishes will be respected.

Consulting and Yarning to Get It Right

A team of health workers from our district developed *Supportive Care: "Into the Dreaming"* through a 12-month process of community yarning. Nearly 500 people participated in the community yarns. The team used yarning to learn from the community and to raise awareness about cancer, chronic disease, and palliative care. They spent time with people, giving them opportunities to ask questions and learn about the things that mattered to them.

When the team was finally ready to launch the booklet, they took it back to the communities and thanked them for their work. The communities own this information. As health workers, we're the guardians of it and we share it with everyone, but the communities own it. The booklet reflects the things that are important to the people who helped to develop it. To us, it's a community resource that we have the privilege of sharing.

The Resource

Supportive Care: "Into the Dreaming" is a 24-page booklet full of artwork, stories, and clear information about planning ahead. It's a culturally safe, respectful resource that demonstrates an understanding of Aboriginal people's values and beliefs and focuses on the things that are important to people during their cancer journey into the dreaming. We usually give it to patients as a hard-copy booklet, but we've also made it available online.[1]

The development team invited local Aboriginal people to contribute their artworks and stories about Sorry Business, and they included nine of these in the booklet. The artworks and stories are ways of talking about the end of life. They express who we are as Indigenous people. By including them in the booklet, readers have something they can connect with and think about. The stories also help to explain how health workers can support people to live as well as possible for as long as they have left in their life journey.

The booklet provides information about how to plan for the future, including writing a will, advance care planning, enduring guardianship, and power of attorney. It explains why these things matter and provides simple steps for getting them done.

The center pages include an advance care planning form that patients can use to record their wishes. At the back, it provides the details of local organizations that provide support and help. It also has a pocket at the back so that patients and health workers can add extra information.

How We Use the Booklet

We're aware that talking about Sorry Business can be confronting. Sometimes people don't realize they're approaching the end of their journey. When that happens, we can't just give them the booklet. We need to get to know them first, then introduce the topic when the time is right.

We like to sit with people and yarn with them about what the booklet says (Fig. 25.2). Often we'll leave it with them so they can think about the content and decide for themselves about what's important. When they're ready, we can help them to complete the advance care plan, if that's what they want. Sometimes we'll do multiple copies of the patient's plan—enough so they can give one to all their family members whenever they're ready.

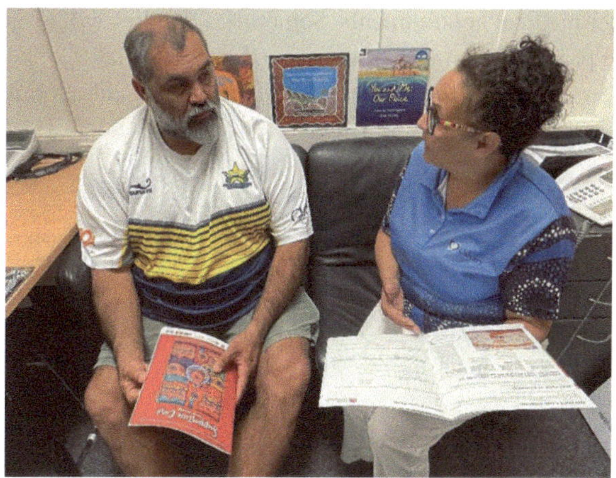

Fig. 25.2 Margaret Whitson and a patient yarning about the cancer journey. (Photo: L Garvey)

We're aware that many Aboriginal people don't want to talk about dying. This booklet helps us to focus on preparing for the future. It embraces the idea that eventually everyone will pass on, and we need to prepare. It helps people to think about why they need to prepare culturally, and how they can have control. For many Aboriginal people, entering the dreaming is about preparing to meet our ancestors and meet our loved ones. The booklet helps to introduce a positive aspect into it, because we can plan our own dreaming.

The booklet is a way of helping people to think through their wishes and identify anything they're really frightened about. It helps to open up conversations about something that many people find very difficult to discuss. They can put these things down in writing so that everyone understands their wishes. Having it in writing means they don't need to keep saying it. And it means that when they can't talk for themselves any more, their wishes are already recorded. It helps people to take care of themselves and feel more confident about what lies ahead.

In our communities, it's usually important for Men's Business and Women's Business to be addressed separately. Our female health workers often can't talk about Men's Business. But we don't have many male palliative care workers, and that can create difficulties. This booklet helps to bridge that gap. We can introduce the things that need to be discussed, then leave the resource with people for them to think about.

For some of our patients, the booklet becomes a precious thing. They carry it with them when they go to hospitals or

[1] You can access the booklet online at: https://www.hnehealth.nsw.gov.au/__data/assets/pdf_file/0004/400693/201920palliative20care20booklet.pdf

other medical appointments. Sometimes families will keep it as a precious reminder of their loved one's wishes.

Supportive Care: "Into the Dreaming" is a collaborative project produced by the Hunter New England Local Health District, Calvary Mater Newcastle, and MyNetCare. Thanks to the artists who shared their personal and traditional journeys and stories and the communities that participated in the cancer yarn ups.

Breast Cancer in American Indian and Alaska Native Women

26

Marilyn A. Roubidoux

Key Points

- While breast cancer mortality rates have improved among US Black, White, and Hispanic populations, no improvements have occurred among American Indian and Alaska Native (AI/AN) women.
- Unlike all other ethnic groups, breast cancer incidence rates among AI/AN women vary dramatically by geographic location; this disparity remains unexplained.
- AI/AN women face much longer travel times to breast imaging services and lower access to breast conservation as a breast cancer treatment relative to other ethnic groups.
- Strategies for overcoming the barriers to breast cancer screening for AI/AN are discussed, such as wider implementation of mobile mammography and enabling transportation to breast cancer specialists for state-of-the-art treatment with radiation therapy and lumpectomy.

Breast cancer is the second most common cancer in women and features may vary by age, risk factors, geographic location, and ethnicity. Breast cancer screening has established benefits, including the earlier detection of tumors; however, disparate messages remain—such as varying screening intervals and the age to begin screening. Other gaps may relate to irregular screening and delays in follow-up imaging after an abnormal screening result. Similar screening gap problems exist in other cancer tests, including for lung cancer, colon cancer, and Pap tests.

Screening is a helpful but imperfect way to detect cancer [1], and consistent compliance with screening is needed to be effective. Patients often do not receive breast cancer screening or follow-up care due to lack of provider recommendation, noncompliance with annual or biannual screening, lack of knowledge of guidelines, difficulties accessing healthcare systems, and other constraints, such as transportation, time, or personal issues. Furthermore, health disparity research in the American Indian and Alaska Native (AI/AN) population is hampered by regional differences and because AI/AN data are often aggregated or mixed with other ethnic groups. Additionally, racial misclassification has occurred in AI/AN medical records [2, 3].

Breast Cancer Rates Among AI/AN Women

Breast cancer incidence rates among AI/ANs in the USA vary persistently by geographic location. For example, incidence rates among Southern Plains and Alaskan AI/AN women are twice those of AI/AN women in the Southwest. The reasons for regional differences in breast cancer incidence among AI/AN women remain unknown [4].

Data indicate that 30% of breast cancers in AI/AN women occur before the age of 50, compared to 19% for non-Hispanic White (NHW) women. Furthermore, 73% of breast cancer cases in AI/AN women occur before 65 years, compared to 60% for NHW women [5]. Fewer cancers are diagnosed at early stage (localized disease without regional or distant metastases) for AI/AN women compared to NHW women [6], and the risk of invasive breast cancer among AI/AN women under 50 years is 1.46 times that of NHW women. AI/AN women also have higher ratios of invasive breast cancer (that has spread to adjacent breast tissues) and advanced breast cancer (metastatic disease is cancer that has spread to other sites beyond the breast) as compared to NHW women [7]. Furthermore, compared with NHW women, AI/AN women have an 8% higher mortality rate and a higher mortality to incidence (MIR) ratio across all age groups and geographic regions [8]. This indicates that, despite lower incidence rates, prognosis is worse in AI/AN women [9].

Although breast cancer mortality rates have decreased nationally by 40% among NHW and Black/African American women in the last several years, mortality rates among AI/AN women are unchanged since the 1990s [10]. AI/AN women have a worse prognosis post-diagnosis than other ethnic groups. These disparities may be due to the unequal distribution of mammography screening among AI/AN women nationally. It is not surprising, therefore, that breast cancer mortality rates have not decreased for AI/AN women.

G. Garvey (ed.), *Indigenous and Tribal Peoples and Cancer*, https://doi.org/10.1007/978-3-031-56806-0_26

Breast cancers are more prevalent among Native American women under the age of 50 compared to NHW women. Additionally, breast cancers are diagnosed at an early stage in Native American women as compared to White women [6].

Barriers to Early Detection

The 2018 National Health Interview Survey revealed that only 66% of AI/AN women aged 50–74 years underwent mammographic screening within 2 years prior to the survey, making this the lowest screening rate of all ethnic groups [10]. In addition, adherence to breast cancer screening varies among AI/AN women in different regions of the country.

The most commonly reported barriers to mammogram screening in this population are economic and geographic constraints (including cost, lack of insurance, location of screening, and transportation problems), cultural differences, mistrust of the American healthcare system, and deficiencies in the Indian Health Service (IHS) [11]. Access to screening mammography can be inconsistent, difficult, or limited, meaning that AI/AN women may not benefit from early detection of breast cancer.

Up to 40% of AI/ANs live on reservations and/or in rural locations, where access to mammography screening is limited. The IHS does not employ oncologists, and cancer care must be purchased and/or referred. Referrals to oncologists depend on funding from Congress. Although this disparity has been well-documented, there are few programs in place to address it [4]. In the absence of local mammography services, mammograms are frequently contracted to private facilities. However, if funding for external care is depleted or if patients do not meet eligibility criteria, then the cost of mammography screening becomes a barrier.

AI/AN women have reported 2–3 times longer travel to obtain mammography, which is the longest of any racial group. Among the new and more accurate breast imaging technologies, tomosynthesis and MRI are less often found in rural areas, further worsening screening disparities [12, 13]. In the absence of fixed mammography facilities in rural areas and small towns, mobile mammography screening can service under-represented populations in both rural and urban settings. However, few mobile units currently specifically serve AI/AN populations.

Socioeconomic and structural barriers impede access to mammography for AI women who commonly do not or cannot prioritize their non-urgent medical care or preventive care over family care priorities. Screening mammography is only the first step in early breast cancer detection. Approximately five additional appointments are required to complete diagnosis and treatment. Therefore, variations in access can substantially affect treatment decisions [14].

Limited Treatment Choices

AI/AN women are more likely to undergo mastectomy than lumpectomy, even in early stage disease, despite the decreased complications, decreased recovery time, and improved quality of life associated with lumpectomy [14]. One reason for this is the distances that AI/AN women have to travel for radiation therapy following lumpectomy.

Post-diagnosis, AI/AN women in some regions experience disparities in surgical treatment and are more likely to undergo mastectomy [14]. AI/AN women in the Northern Plains and Alaska are less likely to obtain surgical care concordant with guidelines, adjuvant therapy, chemotherapy, or post-therapy surveillance. In addition, they are likely to face more delays to their treatment and less surveillance [14]. Northern Plains and Alaska AI/AN women are more likely to have mastectomy compared to NHW women in the same region, suggesting that travel times may not be the determining factor in these choices. However, radiation therapy, an essential part of breast conservation with lumpectomy, requires multiple visits over several weeks, which can be a substantial barrier to patients living on rural Tribal lands. In North Dakota, for instance, breast cancer is associated with higher likelihood of mastectomy and lower likelihood of radiation therapy. In addition, across all AI/AN groups, post-treatment surveillance imaging and follow-up treatment are more limited [15].

Transportation, time off work for extended travel, or lower incomes limit access to breast conservation as well as follow-up screening or diagnostic mammography. Treatment with adjuvant endocrine therapy also may be compromised by travel times.

Overcoming Barriers to Timely Cancer Diagnosis and Treatment Choices

Access to breast cancer screening and other preventive care actions is a multidimensional issue, with input and actions from providers and the population needed to be successful. Equitable cancer screening ought to be a public health priority, especially among medically underserved populations that have higher risk of death and lower likelihood of follow-up care.

In order to improve access to breast cancer trials for AI/AN women, collaboration between academic centers, Tribes, mobile screening units, telemedicine, patient navigators, and providers of radiation therapy is needed [14].

Efforts to overcome cultural barriers to diagnosis and treatment have already been improved through the use of patient navigators who assist AI/AN women through detection, diagnosis, and treatment [16]. Patient navigators help to improve patient compliance and provide assistance with care in complex medical systems. Since 1995, the Native American Cancer Research Corporation has employed and trained patient navigators who have guided over 1000 cancer patients through breast cancer continuum [16]. The consistent use of community health navigators remains a challenge, with wide variability in training, roles and responsibilities, patient load, supervision, and credentials [16]. Standardized and appropriate training and credentialing should be put in place to ensure that the patient navigators and/or community health workers employed by or contracted to healthcare organizations are trained in culturally sensitive communication.

Patient education plays an important role in breast cancer screening adherence and follow-up. A study among Navajo women found that a home-based mammography intervention with culturally sensitive cancer education materials provided hope that steps can be taken to prevent and treat cancer. Results of this study suggest that women's perceptions may have changed concerning the prevention and treatability of breast cancer [17].

To lower geographic access barriers, deploying imaging centers at convenient locations or launching and staffing mobile mammography units should be considered. Programs to encourage cancer screening, navigation, access to screening, and access to treatment are vital. Services such as the Great Plains Indian Health Service mammography program [18] or the Hopi Cancer Support Service (a Tribal health program that promotes cancer screening among Hopi patients) [19] are model cancer prevention programs that should be expanded.

Healthcare providers should support and improve breast cancer screening and recommend additional screening for women at high risk. Access to genetic testing should also be expanded. Guidelines should be advertised and widely promoted to all communities and populations.

Interactions with land and territory are important and unique aspects of AI/AN cultures. Ideally, healthcare would move away from something that is done to AI/AN communities to something that is generated within these communities.

To address ongoing disparities in breast cancer detection and treatment among AI/AN women, community-based efforts are the best hope. Such efforts could be provided via reservations, municipalities, or virtually. Greater support for mobile mammography to reliably bring screening to underserved and rural communities is urgently needed.

References

1. Cotes C, Morozova A, Pourhassan S, Aran S, Singh H. Community Outreach in Breast Imaging: What Radiologists Can Do to Close the Gap for the Uninsured Population. *RadioGraphics*. 2023;43(10). https://doi.org/10.1148/rg.230011
2. Richman I, Tessier-Sherman B, Galusha D, Oladele CR, Wang K. Breast Cancer Screening during the COVID-19 Pandemic: Moving from Disparities to Health Equity. *JNCI*. 2023 Feb;115(2):139–145. https://doi.org/10.1093/jnci/djac172
3. Roubidoux MA, Richards B, Honey NE, Begay JA. Adherence to Screening Among American Indian Women Accessing a Mobile Mammography Unit. *Acad Radiol*. 2021 Jul;28(7):944–949. https://doi.org/10.1016/j.acra.2021.03.014
4. Giaquinto AN, Sung H, Miller KD, Kramer JL, Newman LA, Minihan A, et al. Breast Cancer Statistics, 2022. *CA Cancer J Clin*. 2022 Nov;72(6):524–541. https://doi.org/10.3322/caac.21754
5. Longacre CF, Neprash, Hannah T, Shippee, Nathan D, Tuttle, et al. Travel, Treatment Choice and Survival Among Breast Cancer Patients: A Population-Based Analysis. Women's Health Reports. 2021 Mar;2(1):1–10.
6. American Cancer Society. *Cancer Facts & Figures 2022: Special Section: Cancer in the American Indian and Alaska Native Population*. 2022 [cited 2023 Jun 26]. Available from: https://www.cancer.org/content/dam/cancer-org/research/cancer-facts-and-statistics/annual-cancer-facts-and-figures/2022/2022-special-section-aian.pdf
7. Hendrick RE, Monticciolo DL, Biggs KW, Malak SF. Age distributions of breast cancer diagnosis and mortality by race and ethnicity in US women. *Cancer*. 2021 Dec;127(23):4384–4392. https://doi.org/10.1002/cncr.33846
8. Kratzer TB, Jemal A, Miller KD, Nash S, Wiggins C, Redwood D, et al. Cancer statistics for American Indian and Alaska Native individuals, 2022: Including increasing disparities in early onset colorectal cancer. *CA Cancer J Clin*. 2023 Mar;73(2):120–146. https://doi.org/10.3322/caac.21757
9. White A, Richardson LC, Li C, Ekwueme DU, Kaur JS. Breast cancer mortality among American Indian and Alaska Native women, 1990–2009. *Am J Public Health*. 2014 Jun;104 Suppl 3:S432–8. https://doi.org/10.2105/AJPH.2013.301720
10. American Cancer Society. *Breast Cancer Facts and Figures 2019-2020*. 2019. Available from: https://www.cancer.org/content/dam/cancer-org/research/cancer-facts-and-statistics/breast-cancer-facts-and-figures/breast-cancer-facts-and-figures-2019-2020.pdf
11. Miller BC, Bowers JM, Payne JB, Moyer A. Barriers to mammography screening among racial and ethnic minority women. *Soc Sci Med*. 2019 Oct;239:112494. https://doi.org/10.1016/j.socscimed.2019.112494
12. Onega T, Alford-Teaster J, Leggett C, Loehrer A, Weiss, JE, Moen EL, et al. The interaction of rurality and rare cancers for travel time to cancer care. *J Rural Health*. 2023 Mar;39(2):426–433. https://doi.org/10.1111/jrh.12693
13. Jerome-D'Emilia B. A systematic review of barriers and facilitators to mammography in Hispanic women. *J Transcult Nurs*. 2015 Jan;26(1):73–82. https://doi.org/10.1177/1043659614530761
14. Erdrich J, Cordova-Marks F, Monetathchi AR, Wu M, White A, Melkonian S. Disparities in Breast-Conserving Therapy for Non-Hispanic American Indian/Alaska Native Women Compared with Non-Hispanic White Women. *Ann Surg Oncol*. 2022 Feb;29(2):1019–1030. https://doi.org/10.1245/s10434-021-10730-7
15. Emerson MA, Achacoso NS, Benefield HC, Troester MA, Habel LA. Initiation and adherence to adjuvant endocrine therapy among urban, insured American Indian/Alaska Native breast cancer survivors. *Cancer*. 2021 Jun;127(11):1847–1856. https://doi.org/10.1002/cncr.33423
16. Burhansstipanov L, Harjo L, Krebs LU, Marshall A, Lindstrom D. Cultural roles of native patient navigators for American Indian cancer patients. *Front Oncol*. 2015;5:79. https://doi.org/10.3389/fonc.2015.00079

17. Sinicrope PS, Bauer MC, Patten CA, Austin-Garrison M, Garcia L, Hughes CA, et al. Development and Evaluation of a Cancer Literacy Intervention to Promote Mammography Screening Among Navajo Women: A Pilot Study. *Am J Health Promot.* 2020 Jul;34(6):681–685. https://doi.org/10.1177/0890117119900592
18. Roubidoux MA, Richards B, Honey NE, Begay JA. Adherence to Screening Among American Indian Women Accessing a Mobile Mammography Unit. *Acad Radiol.* 2021 Jul;28(7):944–949. https://doi.org/10.1016/j.acra.2021.03.014
19. Batai K, Sanderson PR, Hsu C-H, Joshweseoma L, Russel D, Joshweseoma L, et al. Factors Associated with Cancer Screening Among Hopi Men. *J Cancer Educ.* 2022 Aug; 37(4):915–923. https://doi.org/10.1007/s13187-020-01900-4

Breast Cancer Screening in British Columbia, Canada: Opportunities to Increase Uptake

27

Nadine R. Caron, Kevin J. Linn, and Mackenzie K. Connon

Key Points

- Lack of access to primary care providers (PCPs) causes decreased access to screening services for First Nations women in British Columbia (BC).
- Mobile screening mammography (SM) is a key part of breast cancer screening in rural and remote communities in BC.
- The Virtual Doctor-of-the-Day program may help to overcome screening barriers, including issues associated with attachment[1] to PCP that is required for access to SM.

British Columbia (BC) is the most westerly of Canada's provinces. It has a population of more than 5.3 million people distributed over 944,735 km^2 [1]. Most non-surgical cancer care services are organized provincially, with interdisciplinary care provided at six BC Cancer (BCC) regional centers. The province's population-based breast, colorectal, cervical, and lung cancer screening programs are overseen by BCC and incorporate a partnership framework with primary care providers identifying eligible patients for screening, and regional health authorities and community (private) imaging clinics and laboratories delivering screening tests. Depending on the screening program, primary care providers (PCPs) are key to informing, referring, and/or performing screening tests and follow-up.

The breast cancer screening mammography (SM) program, known as the BCC Breast Screening Program (BSP), was established in 1988 and is publicly funded (free of charge). The BSP operates 36 fixed SM sites across BC in hospitals or clinics with trained staff and permanent technology. In addition, it operates 3 mobile units across the province, which transport mammogram machines and technicians by van to 170 rural and remote communities, including over 40 First Nations communities [2]. Women who are eligible for SM can self-refer to access the BSP; however, attachment to a PCP is required. Eligibility for BSP has varied over the years. The current criteria are shown in Table 27.1. SM in BC is only available via the BSP. Fixed SM sites provide follow-up for patients with abnormal mammograms, including recommendations for diagnostic mammograms and/or ultrasounds, biopsy, and/or in some locations, breast MRI.

[1]In British Columbia, being "attached" to a physician typically refers to a patient having an established and ongoing relationship with a specific PCP.

Screening Barriers

Barriers to screening for First Nations women in BC may be similar to those found for Indigenous peoples in other Canadian regions. These include jurisdictional ambiguity, suboptimal program design, geographic distance and lack of transport, low levels of health literacy often linked to lack of PCPs, and lack of cultural safety [3]. First Nations women in BC are less likely to be attached to a PCP, which is a requirement to access SM in the province [4]. PCP attachment is required to ensure that the responsible PCP receives the SM results for patient records and coordinates and supports next steps if the SM is abnormal. The PCP's role is critical, as SM is only the first step in a continuum of care for breast cancer that spans from prevention to treatment. It is unknown whether PCP attachment is associated with differences in SM uptake, but, given that being attached to a PCP is required for booking SM, this question should be explored to increase accessibility and utilization of the BSP program among First Nations people in BC.

G. Garvey (ed.), *Indigenous and Tribal Peoples and Cancer*, https://doi.org/10.1007/978-3-031-56806-0_27

Table 27.1 SM eligibility recommendations for average-risk women

Age range	Recommendation for average risk
Average risk, ages 40–49	Healthcare providers are encouraged to discuss the risks and benefits of screening mammography with asymptomatic women in this age group. If screening mammography is chosen, patients will be recalled every 2 years. A healthcare provider's referral is not required but is recommended
Average risk, ages 50–74	Routine screening mammograms are recommended every 2 years for asymptomatic women at average risk of developing breast cancer. Patients will be recalled every 2 years. A healthcare provider's referral is not required
Average risk, ages 75+	Healthcare providers are encouraged to discuss the benefits and limitations of screening mammography with asymptomatic women in this age group. Healthcare providers should discuss stopping screening when there are comorbidities associated with limited life expectancy or physical limitations for mammography that prevent proper positioning. If screening mammography is chosen, it is available every 2–3 years. Patients will not be recalled by the BSP. A healthcare provider's referral is not required but is recommended

Source: BC Cancer [12]

Mobile Services: Bringing Resources to Communities

A number of practices show promise for increasing cancer screening among BC's First Nations communities [5]. Mobile screening services have led to an increase in screening uptake among both Indigenous and non-Indigenous communities [6]. BC's mobile mammography service, which began in 1990, has expanded to include approximately 40 of over 200 First Nations communities per year. This suggests the need for further expansion of this service.

Many BC First Nations communities are rural, remote, and/or northern, which can make it challenging for mobile vans to access them, especially during winter months. This reality highlights the need for creative solutions to address challenges related to weather and location. Multisector collaboration is needed to address the logistical challenges in delivering BSP services to rural and remote First Nations communities, in addition to challenges to access SM services outside of First Nations communities (for both fixed sites and mobile units). The adoption of digital mammography may have been useful, given the limited number of accredited SM radiologists in much of BC. In other jurisdictions, digital SM has been shown effective, enabling accredited radiologists distant from the SM site to interpret images [7].

Mobile SM units could increase uptake and impact by (1) increasing the number of participating communities, and (2) adding additional mobile resources for communities that already have access. For example, mobile units could also provide access to fecal occult blood testing for colorectal cancer screening and access to cervical cancer screening opportunities. Culturally relevant resources can be presented or provided to improve health literacy regarding all cancer screening programs along with cancer prevention education and assistance (e.g., smoking cessation). Resource development should be specific to community-identified needs and requests from First Nations communities as these programs expand in scale and scope under their leadership (Fig. 27.1).

Supporting Individual Travel to the Screening Program

The First Nations Health Authority (FNHA) [11] Health Benefits Program provides transportation support to increase accessibility for "Status First Nations peoples" (i.e., those recognized as First Nations by federal government legislation) who require medically necessary services unavailable in their communities of residence. A transportation subsidy supports travel to publicly funded diagnostic tests and preventive screening services, including SM [8]. Promotional campaigns co-produced by FNHA and BCC aim to increase understanding of program benefits and partnership development with SM services to address barriers to participation [9]. The extent to which financial support impacts uptake of out-of-community SM compared to mobile SM by those living in rural and remote locations is unknown. However, it is hypothesized that in-community, "closer-to-home" services would have greater influence.

Opportunities to Increase Screening: Virtual Doctor of the Day

Cultural safety is the foundation of access to healthcare services. In the absence of cultural safety, even if resources are accessible, they will not be used and benefits will go unfulfilled. A major operational barrier is the requirement to be registered with a PCP in order to self-refer for BSP. In April 2020, the FNHA launched the Virtual Doctor-of-the-Day program for Indigenous individuals in BC to increase access to PCPs via remote virtual consultation, with five telephone lines currently in use [10]. This is a unique service for First Nations peoples in BC and their family members, even if those family members are not Indigenous. The program strives to include doctors of Indigenous ancestry and all doctors are trained to follow the principles and practices of cultural safety and humility. The program provides health services for people who require episodic and ongoing care. This resource has been discussed as an opportunity to increase access to SM by overcoming PCP attachment barriers. During the appointment, the PCP and the patient can discuss SM and the role of screening and, when indicated, enable the individual to sign up for a SM.

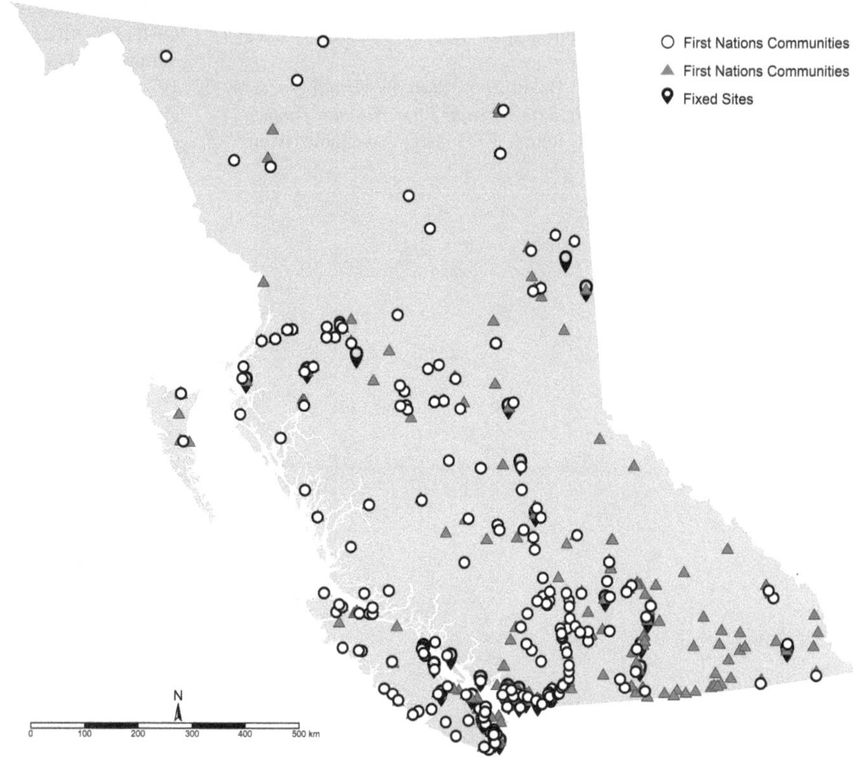

Fig. 27.1 Map of British Columbia First Nations communities, fixed SM sites, and participating mobile SM units. (Map: N Raveinthiranathan)

This "Doctor of the Day" would then be the contact for mammogram results and program physicians can support the individual on the next steps.

Conclusion

The SBP aims to prevent or diagnose malignancies at an earlier stage. First Nations women in BC and in other Indigenous communities across Canada have lower rates of uptake of breast cancer screening. To address this, we must demand culturally safe services, improve understanding of the role and impact of cancer screening, increase accessibility (including, but not limited to, increasing the scope and scale of the mobile SM units that bring resources to communities), and break down barriers to SM that are embedded in BSP policies, such as issues related to the requirement for PCP attachment. There is much to be done to address the well-documented priority of screening and prevention in the BC Indigenous cancer strategy.

References

1. Government of British Columbia. *British Columbia Official Website* [Internet]. 2023 [cited 2023 Aug 9]. Available from: https://www2.gov.bc.ca/gov/content/home
2. BC Cancer Screening. *Breast* [Internet]. [cited 2023 Aug 9]. Available from: http://www.bccancer.bc.ca/screening/breast
3. Tobias J, Tinmouth J, Senese L, Jumah N, Llovet D, Kewayosh A, et al. Health policy as a barrier to First Nations peoples' access to cancer screening. *Health Policy*. 2020;15(3):28–46. https://doi.org/10.12927/hcpol.2020.26132
4. Turpel-Lafond DME. *In Plain Sight: Addressing Indigenous-specific Racism and Discrimination in BC Health Care*. Health Care Data Report; 2020 Nov. p.104. Available from: https://www.bcchr.ca/sites/default/files/group-opsei/in-plain-sight-full-report.pdf
5. Bryant J, Patterson K, Vaska M, Chiang B, Letendre A, Bill L, et al. Cancer screening interventions in indigenous populations: A rapid review. *Curr Oncol*. 2021;28(3):1728–43. https://doi.org/10.3390/curroncol28030161
6. Mema SC, Yang H, Elnitsky S, Jiang Z, Vaska M, Xu L. Enhancing access to cervical and colorectal cancer screening for women in rural and remote Northern Alberta: A pilot study. *CMAJ Open*. 2017;5(4). https://doi.org/10.9778/cmajo.20170055
7. Johnston K, Smith D, Preston R, Evans R, Carlisle K, Lengren J, et al. "From the technology came the idea": Safe implementation and operation of a high quality teleradiology model increasing access to timely breast cancer assessment services for women in rural Australia. *BMC Health Serv Res*. 2020;20(1):1103. https://doi.org/10.1186/s12913-020-05922-y
8. First Nations Health Authority, Métis Nation BC, the BC Association of Aboriginal Friendship Centres and BC Cancer. *Improving Indigenous Cancer Journeys in BC: A Road Map*. 2017. Available from: https://www.fnha.ca/WellnessSite/WellnessDocuments/improving-indigenous-cancer-journeys-in-bc.pdf
9. First Nations Health Authority. *Health Benefits Guide*. 2019 September [cited 2023 Aug 9]. Available from: https://www.fnha.ca/Documents/FNHA-Health-Benefits-Guide.pdf

10. First Nations Health Authority. *Screening* [Internet]. [cited 2023 Aug 9]. Available from: https://www.fnha.ca/what-we-do/healthy-living/cancer/screening
11. British Columbia Ministry of Health. *First Nations Virtual Doctor of the Day Brings Culturally Safe Care to First Nations Peoples Across B.C.*[Internet]. 2021 [cited 2023 Aug]. Available from: https://www2.gov.bc.ca/assets/gov/health/about-bc-s-health-care-system/heath-care-partners/health-newsletter/first-nation-doctor-summer-2021.pdf
12. BC Cancer. *Screening/Early Detection* [Internet]. 2015 August. Available from: http://www.bccancer.bc.ca/books/breast/screening-early-detection

28 Cancer Management Among American Indians: In Their Own Voices

Felicia Schanche Hodge, Michele Connolly, and Ernest Holburt

Key Points

- Community is a source of strength for American Indian families and individuals diagnosed with cancer.
- American Indians do not view disease, disability, or death in the same way as those in Western society. A cultural strength is the acknowledgement and acceptance that life processes of birth and death are normal.
- American Indian culture, worldview, and circumstances influence how cancer is perceived, addressed, and managed.
- American Indian cancer survivors describe their experiences in managing cancer symptoms and the way cancer influenced their identity.

Cancer incidence rates among American Indians appear to be on the rise, while similar rates for US population are decreasing slightly [1]. In this chapter, we discuss how American Indian culture, worldview, and circumstances influence how cancer is perceived, addressed, and managed. We present the everyday experience of American Indians with cancer residing in a Southwestern state, in their own voices. These cancer survivors share how they managed cancer symptoms and the changing identity and roles that often accompany treatment.

American Indians and Alaska Natives (AI/ANs) have survived and thrived for thousands of years through their traditions, culture, ceremonies, stories, songs, communities, and family. Their cultures have survived despite genocide, loss of lands, forced migration, assimilation, prejudice, and deliberate efforts at cultural erasure, including boarding schools. Thus, while culture improves the lives of Indigenous peoples in every aspect, including cancer management, certain circumstances undermine their cultural strengths.

The 574 federally recognized Tribes in the USA [2] represent a vast diversity of cultures, histories, and traditions, but there are many similarities between them. Culture and community remain as important as ever and are key to adapting and living through adverse conditions—ranging from climate change to cancer diagnoses and treatment. Indigenous healthcare extends beyond physical health considerations as it encompasses emotional, mental, and spiritual healing.

American Indians may live on remote reservations and Tribal lands where healthcare services are provided by the Indian Health Service (IHS) and administered by the federal government. The IHS facilities range from small single-purpose clinics, such as prenatal clinics, to mid-size hospitals. Although there are some urban IHS facilities, those outside of Phoenix, Albuquerque, Gallup, and Anchorage tend to be small and not adequately resourced for cancer care. American Indians living far from their reservations typically rely on the same kinds of care and health insurance coverage available to non-AI/ANs.

Voices of Study Participants

Study participants were American Indians from the Southwestern United States residing in Arizona. The cancer survivors interviewed for this chapter were a part of a large randomized clinical trial on cancer-symptom management [3]. Many study participants were interviewed at a large Indian hospital in Arizona, where they told of their cancer journey from diagnosis to treatment and their physical and cognitive concerns.

Indigenous Outlook on Health

AI/ANs do not view disease, disability, or death in the same way as those in Western society. Nevertheless, medical provision, caregiving, and protocols are designed for non-Indigenous Americans. This is especially evident for a disease as serious as cancer. Western perceptions of wellness and illness are built around a fear of death and disability. Life insurance salesmen in the United States typically talk about "… if you die."

American Indians are much more realistic in their outlook on life and the disease process. A cultural strength among

G. Garvey (ed.), *Indigenous and Tribal Peoples and Cancer*, https://doi.org/10.1007/978-3-031-56806-0_28

these communities is the acknowledgment and acceptance that life processes of birth and death are normal. This means that bodily losses, disabilities, and aging are also accepted and viewed as an ordinary part of life. The opposite is true in Western society, where elders are not strongly valued and are often rendered invisible. Older Americans are essentially disregarded once their working life is over, and they are seen as being engaged in the uncomfortable processes of aging and dying. People with disabilities and/or those with physical marks are often kept from the eyes of general society in hospitals, in housing complexes, or in homes.

Conversely, AI/ANs hold great respect for their elders because they have the wisdom of their lifetime experiences. All Tribal members are accepted, and illness and death are respected as part of the process of living. Loss of physical function due to surgery is not hidden but is accepted as a part of the healing process. American Indians with cancer have an advantage over non-Indigenous cancer patients who experience the stigma of cancer and the attendant loss of function, body parts, or their lives. In the USA, cancer patients and survivors are seen as "fighting" cancer. They may experience guilt in contracting cancer in the first place (e.g., by smoking), or, if they die, their legacy can be tarnished for "losing their fight" or "not fighting hard enough." American Indians view cancer as part of their journey through life, during which both foreseen and unforeseen events occur.

Healthcare and Cancer

Healthcare providers and educators are primarily coordinated through the IHS, a federal agency charged with raising the health status of AI/AN. Because of the remoteness of many Indigenous communities, many individuals with cancer undergo screening and treatment in cities far from the strengths and support of their communities. Screening, diagnosis, and treatment are not shared with their communities—and often not with their families—as cancer patients are guided away from home.

Western healthcare providers bring the patient into a clinic room for screening and diagnosis; thus, AI/ANs are forced into Western models of the nuclear family and environment. American Indian community strengths are not known or recognized by wider society. In fact, a national poll sponsored by the Native Truth Research Project found that 40% of Americans were unaware that American Indians still exist, and a majority admitted that they do not know any AI/ANs. The "invisibility and the dominant narratives that limit Native opportunities, access to justice, health and self-determination" [4] will counter community strengths in terms of culture, perception of illness and wellness, as well as the process of healing though ceremonies and social/family support and care.

Once diagnosed, cancer treatment and care are all too often managed within the Western model. For pain management, over-the-counter pain medicine may be replaced by strong pharmacolites. These drugs can dull the senses and may bring about periods of confusion and extended sleep. While American Indians perform interventions such as healing ceremonies, they do not reject the need for oncologists for those with cancer. Healing ceremonies bring together families and loved ones to provide support, help plan for the needs of the cancer patient/survivor, and stand beside the patient during their journey with cancer. Thus, while AI/ANs are aware of Western models of cancer care, the opposite is not true. Western medicine seems to lack knowledge regarding the strengths of Indigenous communities that provide a network of support and surveillance, as well as mental care through activities such as mediation and relaxation sessions.

Adverse Effects

Adverse effects associated with diagnostic and treatment procedures present myriad problems. These include issues of cancer-symptom management, loss of physical and cognitive abilities, and loss of personal identity.

Managing Cancer-Related Pain, Fatigue, and Loss

Cancer symptoms include pain, depression, fatigue, and loss of function. Of these, pain is a significant problem. Cancer-related pain is managed in several ways by the patient/survivor. Attempts to bear or ignore pain eventually give way to accepting the need for pain control. However, prescribed pain medication is often avoided for fear of addiction [3]. Massage and heating pads have been effectively employed to ease pain. In one study, several American Indian cancer patients drew pictures of their pain in an attempt to share an understanding of how they both "see" and "experience" cancer pain [5]. Furthermore, differing views, beliefs, and communication styles between the care provider and the patient [6] highlight the importance of culture in patient communications and provider perceptions of patient pain and other adverse symptoms [7, 8].

Loss of Physical Ability

Loss of limbs, sight, and organs can be traumatic, not only due to the resultant mobility limitations, but also to limitations in communication and bodily functions. Physical losses can also have significant impacts on the role of cancer survivors within their families and communities. The role of provider may need to be relinquished to another family member who is not a cancer survivor. The role of parent may be transferred to siblings or to grandparents, and the role of community leader, healer, teacher, or participant in song or dance ceremonies may need to be ceded to another. However, new roles may emerge, such as that of cancer educator for families and communities. Accordingly, cancer survivors can continue to serve as valued members of their communities, where the experiences and knowledge gathered during their cancer journey are valued.

Changing Identities

Tribal members share commonalities in terms of identity that are displayed in song, body markings, regalia, and even hairstyles. One Tribal member shared his experience of losing his long "Indian hair" following cancer treatment. Wearing a baseball hat, he met the research interviewer in a private room, insisting on privacy as he did not want to be seen by others. He removed his hat to show his bald head, stating "this is what they did to me." During the initiation of chemotherapy, he was not advised of possible adverse effects such as nausea, fatigue, and hair loss. He told of a morning shower where handfuls of his hair were dropping from his head. He did not know what was happening nor what to do. He refused to be seen in public as his "Indian hair" was gone—his identity as an Indian male was destroyed. He had no idea if it would grow back, only that this was a worse horror than the cancer diagnosis itself. He was hiding, as his "Indian male" identity was lost.

Interaction with Medical Providers

The process of cancer diagnosis and treatment requires a good relationship with medical providers. Cancer survivors have reported a range of experiences, from positive interactions with doctors and nurses to confusion regarding diagnosis and treatment. One elderly Navajo woman in our study agreed to be interviewed while in the cancer infusion room. With a needle in her arm, she was asked if she knew what was being put in her arm. "I don't know," she replied, "they did not tell me." She then asked the nearby nurse who said, "Oh, she has breast cancer—here, I will give her a brochure." A practicing physician at the San Carlos Apache Reservation stated, "it was also common for the elderly to pretend they understood English, when they did not. It was important to bring an Indian nurse into the exam room at that point" [personal communication with E Holburt, 2023 September 13]. The relationship between the cancer patient/survivor is of utmost importance and must be one that allows for mutual exchange of information, dialogue, and respect. Assuming that a patient would not want to know about or be able to understand a diagnosis and treatment is unconscionable and patronizing. Healing begins with good communication, and each party needs to fully participate in the process.

Conclusions

Communities share words of wisdom and hope, just as they have for thousands of years. Cancer is not new, and it has been found in the ancient bones of American Indians. It is an illness that in the past the Apache called "Ka," which describes an illness, "Cho'I," which describes an evil, and "Do na tsdzihi," which states that it does not heal. The Navajo do not have a specific word for cancer, but use the phrase "Lood doo na'ziihii," which translates to the "sore (or wound) that does not heal." These words have slowly fallen from use as more educational programs have been provided that bring knowledge of the need for screening, treatment, and healing. Community outlook on wellness and illness has expanded over the years to include new definitions, understanding, and responses to unfamiliar illnesses such as cancer, type 2 diabetes, and tuberculosis.

New roles and healing trajectories are being developed. Understanding of cancer diagnoses and treatments—along with their process and adverse effects—is being expanded. A cultural advantage of the Indigenous outlook on life and health is its holistic approach. While Western medicine focuses on physical health for diseases like cancer, AI/AN cultures view physical, mental, emotional, and spiritual health as necessary for healing. This outlook will have positive effects as communities work to heal their members. They work with clinic nurses, educators, and outreach workers to spread awareness of successful treatments, diets, lifestyle choices, and new therapeutic technologies. It is important to note that educational efforts must not only be focused on AI/AN individuals, their families, and their communities; they should also inform healthcare providers in the IHS as "providers literally had no orientation on American Indian culture in general or Apache culture in particular" (participant comment). Cultural orientation needs to be provided at other facilities as well so that their members can better understand the unique worldview and lives of AI/ANs. Finally, prevention should always be addressed in dialogue with communities and their providers. Early diagnosis means better hope.

References

1. U.S. Cancer Statistics. U.S. *Cancer Statistics Data Visualizations Tool, based on 2022 submission data (1999-2020)* [Internet]. U.S. Department of Health and Human Services, Centers for Disease Control and Prevention and the National Cancer Institute; June 2023 [cited 2023 Sep 16]. Available from: https://www.cdc.gov/cancer/uscs/dataviz/index.htm

2. Indian Affairs Bureau. Indian Entities Recognized by and Eligible to Receive Services From the United States Bureau of Indian Affairs. *Federal Register*. 2023 Jan 12;88: 2112–16.
3. Hodge FS, Line-Itty T, Arbing RHA. Cancer-Related Symptom Management Intervention for Southwest American Indians. *Cancers*. 2022;14:4771. https://doi.org/10.3390/cancers14194771
4. Nagle MK. *Reclaiming Native Truth: A Project to Dispel America's Myths and Misconceptions*. Reclaiming Native Truth Project. Available from: https://www.ncai.org/4._draft_NCAI_midyear_RNT_final_findings.pdf
5. Hodge FS, Line-Itty T, Arbing RHA, Samuel-Nakamura C. A Window into Pain: American Indian Cancer Survivors' Drawings. *Front Pain Res*. 2022 Oct;3:1031347. https://doi.org/10.3389/fpain.2022.1031347
6. Miner, J, Biros MH, Trainor A, Hubbard D, Beltram M. Patient and physician perceptions as risk factors for oligoanalgesia: a prospective observational study of the relief of pain in the emergency department. *Aced Emerg Med*. 2006;13(2):140–6. https://doi.org/10.1197/j.aem.2005.08.008
7. Calvillo ER, Flaskerud JH. Review of literature on culture and pain of adults with focus on Mexican-Americans. *J Transcult Nurs*. 1991;2(2):16–23. https://doi.org/10.1177/104365969100200203
8. Pachter LM. Culture and clinical care. Folk illness beliefs and behaviors and their implications for health care delivery. *JAMA*. 1994;271(9):690–4. https://doi.org/10.1001/jama.1994.03510330068036

Part IV

Prevention and Early Detection

India's Tribal Populations and Cancer

29

Veeraiah Surendran, Parameswari Jayaraman, Rajkumar Rajamanickam, and Rajaraman Swaminathan

Key Points

- India's Tribal populations are likely to be at increased risk of poor cancer outcomes due to poverty, poor general health, low health literacy, and poor access to healthcare.
- Oral cancers are common among India's Tribal population, with very high use of tobacco (smoking and smokeless forms). In some areas, 90% of youth use tobacco.
- Cervical cancer is the second-most common cancer among Tribal women, but many women have little knowledge about prevention and early detection.
- India's Tribal communities need improved access to cancer screening and prevention information.
- Establishing specific cohorts of Tribal populations and linking them with cancer registries would improve understanding about cancer incidence and outcomes in India.

India is a diverse country with multiple ethnic groups and the world's second-largest Tribal population, following Africa [1]. India is home to around 635 different Tribes, comprising 8.9% of the total population; 73 of these considered to be ancient [2]. Despite this significant proportion, India's Tribal population has limited access to healthcare, and factors such as poverty, low literacy, and poor living conditions are linked to failure to diagnose or delayed diagnosis and increased mortality due to cancer. In addition, Tribal communities experience higher rates of noncommunicable diseases such as diabetes, hypertension, and cardiovascular disease. While rates of diseases such as diabetes and high blood pressure are reported in India and are known to be high in Tribal populations, the cancer incidence in these groups is not reported [3]. No population-based studies accurately describe the incidence of cancer across all Tribal communities in India.

Tribal populations in India are likely to be at increased risk of poor cancer outcomes, due to factors such as malnutrition, poor general health, poverty, and low health literacy. Research suggests that 72% of Tribal peoples use tobacco and more than 50% consume alcohol [4]. In addition, Tribal people typically have limited access to healthcare facilities and health information.

Available Data About Cancer in Tribal Populations

While a few states document cancer incidence through population-based cancer registries, research publications, and hospital registries, available data indicate that states in the northeast, including Mizoram, Manipur, and Arunachal Pradesh, have the highest cancer incidence, especially among men [5].

Oral cancer is the most prevalent cancer among India's Tribal population, accounting for around 30% of all cancers [6]. While treatment and survival for oral cancer have improved, prevention and early diagnosis remain an ongoing challenge. It is likely that poor access to healthcare and high levels of tobacco use (both smoking and smokeless) are key contributors to oral cancer for the Tribal population.

Overall, in the northeast region where the proportion of Tribal populations is higher, the most common cancers include nasopharynx, hypopharynx, esophagus, stomach, liver, gallbladder, larynx, lung, breast, and cervix uteri. While Manipur and Mizoram report the highest numbers of lung cancer, the East Khasi Hills district of Meghalaya reports the highest proportion of tobacco-related cancer. Beyond the northeast, the most prevalent malignancies among Tribal men are nasopharynx, throat, esophagus, stomach, and lung. The Tamil Nadu Cancer Registry Project (TNCRP), which is a joint population-based cancer surveillance study by the Cancer Institute (WIA) and department of health and family welfare, government of Tamil Nadu, reveals a variable cancer incidence pattern in Nilgiris district, which has a sizeable Tribal population; here cancer of the esophagus was the most common among men, unlike in the rest of the state [7].

Some research has examined tobacco use among the Tribal population. In Madhya Pradesh, for example, nearly

G. Garvey (ed.), *Indigenous and Tribal Peoples and Cancer*, https://doi.org/10.1007/978-3-031-56806-0_29

37% of Tribal women and 34% of Tribal men chew tobacco [8], with the smokeless tobacco products supari, gutka, and naswar the most commonly used. Tobacco smoking is more widespread than tobacco chewing, with nearly 80% of India's Tribal population found to smoke tobacco, often beginning at around age 10 years [9]. Tobacco use in Madhya Pradesh is initiated as a form of tooth cleansing and is more common among women [9]. Similarly in South India, nearly 65% of the Narikurava population use tobacco, with 29% smoking tobacco, 63% using smokeless tobacco, and nearly 8% using both. In this population, tobacco use is particularly high among youth, with approximately 90% using some form of tobacco. There are calls to educate the young Tribal community on the harmful effects of tobacco and to offer cessation services to quit [9].

In the southern state of Andhra Pradesh, researchers examined knowledge and attitudes toward cervical cancer screening. Cervical cancer is the second-most common cancer among Tribal women, but many women have little knowledge about prevention and early detection. The Government of India has introduced cervical cancer screening programs and awareness campaigns. In the general Indian population, major barriers to cervical cancer screening include modesty, anxiety about screening procedures, stigma, and fear of being judged. Among Tribal women, barriers also include the unavailability of regular cervical cancer screening programs, lack of awareness, and low interest in being screened [10]. A study among the Koraga, Malekudiya, and Marathi Naika Tribes of the Udupi district in Karnataka reported that Tribal women were unaware of cancer risk factors but had a positive attitude toward cancer screening. In a study of breast cancer screening among Tribal women in the Nilgiris district, Tamil Nadu, researchers found that most women had heard of breast cancer, but only half were aware of the symptoms. The research suggests that knowledge about early detection and screening is yet to benefit the community [11, 12]. In another study, only 16% of Tribal people were found to be aware of the risk of oral cancers and that they are preventable with lifestyle modification [13].

Education about cancer for India's Tribal populations is increasing. A randomized controlled trial in Kerala tested the efficacy of small-group education, reinforcement sessions, telephone reminders, navigation, guidance about Pap smear tests, and a follow-up visit for improving awareness of cancer and increasing take-up of screening [14]. The study found that community-based intervention was effective in improving screening among Tribal women. Ongoing education through motivation and regular reinforcement were reported as effective strategies [14]. However, barriers to screening remain, including the paucity of health facilities, out-of-pocket costs, misconceptions about screening, trust in traditional healers, and low priority given to health issues [15].

Conclusions

Financial burden remains a major barrier to cancer screening in India, including for Tribal populations. A report by the Indian Ministry of Health and Family Welfare found that nearly 50% of outpatient visits for the Tribal population are to public centers. The same report highlighted a 40% shortfall in primary health centers and 31% shortfall in community health centers in Tribal communities [2].

India's Tribal population urgently needs improved cancer control initiatives through the establishment of a convenient, appropriate, and reliable system that gives them access to cancer screening and information about prevention. Interventions must be tailored to communities' cultural norms and languages, and local healthcare workers need training to better identify cancer symptoms and improve community education. Mobile health services could address some of the geographic barriers, and media information could improve awareness. In addition, establishing specific cohorts of Tribal populations and linking with cancer registries are essential to fully understand cancer incidence and outcomes among India's Tribal populations.

References

1. Sathiyanarayanan S, Muthunarayanan L, Devaparthasarathy TA. Changing Perspectives in Tribal Health: Rising Prevalence of Lifestyle Diseases among Tribal Population in India. *Indian J Community Med.* 2019 Oct–Dec;44(4):342–6. https://doi.org/10.4103/ijcm.IJCM_40_19
2. Ministry of Health and Family Welfare & Ministry of Tribal Affairs. *Report of the Expert Committee on Tribal Health: Tribal Health in India, Executive Summary and Recommendations.* 2018 [cited 2019 Nov 20]. Available from: http://tribalhealthreport.in/executive-summary/
3. Sable MN, Mishra T. Cancer surveillance of the indigenous population in India: Much needed. *Indian J Cancer.* 2019 Apr–Jun;56(2):182–3. https://doi.org/10.4103/ijc.IJC_480_18
4. Jah DN. Lifestyle diseases among top killers in tribal districts: ICMR. *The Times of India.* 2022 Nov 24. Available from: https://timesofindia.indiatimes.com/india/lifestyle-diseases-among-top-killers-in-tribal-districts-icmr/articleshow/95724990.cms
5. Sarkar S, Datta D, Debbarma S, Majumdar G, Mandal SS. Patterns of Cancer Incidence and Mortality in North-Eastern India: The First Report from the Population Based Cancer Registry of Tripura. *Asian Pac J Cancer Prev.* 2020 Sep;21(9):2493–9. https://doi.org/10.31557/APJCP.2020.21.9.2493
6. Muthanandam S, Babu BV, Muthu J, Rajaram S, Sundharam BS, Kishore M. Burden of oral precancer and cancer among an indigenous tribal population of South India—An evaluative study. *Indian J Dent Res.* 2022;33(3):253–7. https://doi.org/10.4103/ijdr.ijdr_552_21
7. Swaminathan R, Shanta V on behalf of the TNCRP study group. *Cancer incidence and mortality (year 2016), incidence trend (2012–2016) and estimates (2017-2020) for Tamil Nadu state.* Chennai: Tamil Nadu Cancer Registry Project (TNCRP), Cancer Institute (WIA); 2020. p. 79–82.

8. Tomar SP, Kasar P, Tiwari R, Rajpoot S, Nayak S. Study of tobacco chewing and smoking pattern and its socio-demographic determinants in a Tribal Village in Mandla District, Madhya Pradesh. *National Journal of Community Medicine.* 2016;7(3):204–7.
9. Zahiruddin QS, Gaidhane A, Bawankule S, Nazli K, Zodpey S. Prevalence and pattern of tobacco use among tribal adolescents: Are tobacco prevention messages reaching the tribal people in India. *Ann Trop Med Public Health.* 2011;4(2):74–80. https://doi.org/10.4103/jfmpc.jfmpc_1344_20
10. Ghosh S, Mallya SD, Shetty RS, Pattanshetty SM, Pandey D, Kabekkodu SP, et al. Knowledge, attitude, and practices towards cervical cancer and its screening among women from tribal population: A community-based study from southern India. *J Racial Ethn Health Disparities.* 2021;8(1):88–93. https://doi.org/10.1007/s40615-020-00760-4
11. Shaista A, Madhavi M, Pradeep S, Reena B, Pandurang T, Rajesh G. A Study to Assess Knowledge, Attitude of Breast Cancer & Practice Of Breast Self Examination In Females of Help Groups (SHGs) in Tribal Area of Raigad District. *Int J Current Medical Applied Sciences.* 2016;11(2):86–93.
12. Santhiya, J. (2016). Awareness of Breast Cancer among Tribal Women in the Nilgiris District. *Int J Res Soc Sciences*, *6*(11), 449–55.
13. Muthanandam S, Babu BV, Muthu J, Suganya R, Vezhavendhan N, Kishore M. Assessment of knowledge, awareness and attitude towards oral precancer and cancer among Narikuravar population in Pondicherry state. *South Asian J Cancer.* 2021;10(4):225–9. https://doi.org/10.1055/s-0041-1733316
14. George TJ, Batra K. Effect of a community-based multicomponent intervention on cervical cancer behavior among women—A randomized controlled trial. *J Educ Health Promot* 2022;11:329. https://doi.org/10.4103/jehp.jehp_1742_21
15. Birje S, Patil AD, Munne KR, Chavan V, Joshi BN, Akula A, et al. Enablers & challenges of tribal women & health system for implementation of screening of non-communicable diseases & common cancers: A mixed-methods study in Palghar district of Maharashtra, India. *Indian J Med Res.* 2022 Aug;156(2):319–29. https://doi.org/10.4103/ijmr.ijmr_3240_21

Kū Ola: Cancer Prevention with Native Hawaiians

30

Claire K. Hughes, Paula Higuchi, Kevin Cassel, and Pālama Lee

Key Points

- Culturally grounded cancer prevention projects can be effective for men and women.
- Dialogue between project participants can inform project enhancement.
- Grounding projects in local communities can support project sustainability.

Native Hawaiians have populated the Hawaiian Islands since about 300 CE [1]. They descend from an ancient oceanic people, whose migration from northwestern Malaysia to Hawai'i began as early as 1600 BCE, taking a southern course from Malaysia through parts of the south Pacific before taking a northerly course to the Hawaiian Islands [1]. From the original colony, Hawaiians established approximately 18 settlements over several centuries, populating eight major islands in the archipelago. For almost a millennium and a half, Native Hawaiians remained isolated by the Pacific Ocean, situated many miles north of established voyaging routes. When British Sea Captain James Cook, the first recorded Western visitor, arrived at Waimea Bay on the island of Kaua'i in 1778 [2], he estimated the Native Hawaiian population numbered almost one million [3]. According to the 2000 US Census, full- and part-blooded Hawaiians comprise 19.25% of Hawai'i's total population of 1,244,898 [4].

Exposure to Western contagious illnesses, lifestyles, and foods has caused higher mortality among Native Hawaiians from cancer, type 2 diabetes, heart disease, and other chronic conditions, and Native Hawaiians have the shortest life expectancy among Hawai'i's major ethnic groups [5]. These conditions are attributed to certain barriers to seeking healthcare identified in the 1985 E Ola Mau study, which persist today—including challenges to accessing primary and specialty care, lack of availability of services including traditional healing, and the ways Native Hawaiians are treated by healthcare providers and systems [6].

In 1995, with a grant from the US Department of Health and Human Services as part of its 1990 Health Goals for the Nation, the American Cancer Society (ACS) assembled the Native Hawaiian Breast Cancer Sub-Committee. The committee, comprised of community health advocates representing a number of community agencies and individual Native Hawaiian women, facilitated efforts to increase awareness of the benefits of early detection of breast cancer.

Native Hawaiian women continue to have higher breast cancer incidence and mortality rates than any of Hawai'i's four other major ethnic populations (Caucasian, Japanese, Filipino, and Chinese). In addition, they have the third highest breast cancer mortality rate in the USA [7].

Developing Culturally Appropriate Health Settings

The ACS Native Hawaiian Sub-Committee conducted three focus groups with Native Hawaiian women and key informants to identify healthcare-seeking behaviors, perceived and real barriers, healthcare concerns, and possible solutions to improve health services. The results revealed barriers to care that included insensitive and inappropriate communication, lack of privacy, and poor healthcare environments. Concerns and potential solutions were organized into short-, mid-, and long-term projects, funded by the Office of Hawaiian Affairs, Longs Drug Stores, and the R.E. Black Foundation.

The short-term project involved creating medical chart reminders that read "Mammograms Due," printed on sticky label notepads, to cue physicians to tell patients, "Your mammogram is due. Please see the nurse to schedule an appointment."

The medium-term project consisted of four public service announcements featuring Native Hawaiian cancer survivors and using material culture (e.g., the pahu (drum)) to increase awareness of the importance of annual mammograms and early breast cancer detection.

G. Garvey (ed.), *Indigenous and Tribal Peoples and Cancer*, https://doi.org/10.1007/978-3-031-56806-0_30

In 2000, only 5.5% of physicians in Hawai'i and 7% of nurses were of Native Hawaiian ancestry [4]. This suggests that healthcare might not be sensitive to the cultural customs and needs of Native Hawaiians. Therefore, the long-term project consisted of developing training for health professionals to positively influence attitudes, communication styles, and the clinic environment, to foster cultural awareness and understanding among medical professionals providing healthcare to Native Hawaiian women. The training included:

- A 20-minute video, *Caring for Native Hawaiian Women: Understanding Cultural Values in the Treatment of Breast Health*, explaining aspects of Native Hawaiian spirituality, perceptions, customs, traditions, and values.
- A manual, *Ka Lōkahi Wāhine: The Healthy Balance of Women*, including sections on (1) interpersonal communication, (2) creating a healing environment, (3) guidelines for simplifying communication, and (4) a glossary of Hawaiian words and phrases.

By March 2004, over 300 health professionals, including physicians, nurses, health educators, homecare therapists, and providers had received training. Native Hawaiian women involved in this effort frequently reminded the group that Hawaiian men also needed health attention. Native Hawaiian men have the highest mortality rates for lung bronchus and colorectal cancers among the five major ethnic groups of Hawai'i. The ACS Native Hawaiian Sub-Committee, therefore, broadened its focus and negotiated a name change to the Native Hawaiian Cancer Committee (NHCC) of the ACS. With the limited funding ($5000) remaining from various grants, the committee turned its attention to the health of Native Hawaiian kāne (man/men). Since then, a group of dedicated individuals and organizations, including community physicians, the University of Hawai'i Cancer Center, the Department of Health, Ke Ola Mamo (Oahu's Native Hawaiian Health Care System), and the ACS, have worked to improve the health and wellbeing of Native Hawaiian kāne.

Many of the chronic health challenges facing Native Hawaiian men, such as type 2 diabetes, cardiovascular disease, and certain cancers, result from systemic inequalities that prevent doctor visits and deprioritize healthcare. High rates of chronic illnesses and behaviors result in higher risk of death for Native Hawaiians, particularly for Native Hawaiian men. For instance, while Native Hawaiian men have the lowest incidence of prostate cancer in Hawai'i compared to non-Hawaiians, they have the second highest mortality rate. Currently, Native Hawaiian men have the second-highest number of cases of diagnosed advanced-stage prostate cancer compared to the general male population of Hawai'i [8]. This suggests the need for education to promote overall health, identify cancer in its early stages, and reduce disproportionate rates of mortality among Native Hawaiian men.

Statewide Discussion Groups for Men

To understand the attitudes, beliefs, and health-seeking behaviors of Native Hawaiian men, the NHCC conducted a first round of research from October 2002 to August 2003. This involved focus groups in four geographic areas on O'ahu, Hawai'i, consisting of 54 Native Hawaiian male participants, ranging in age from 22 to 75. The participants discussed their attitudes and beliefs about overall health, their provider and care-type preferences when seeking healthcare, and perceived barriers to engaging in healthcare services and programs. They also expressed the critical importance of Native Hawaiian cultural values and practices to their access and acceptance of healthcare [9]. The findings highlighted the importance of creating culturally appropriate methods to protect and promote the health of Native Hawaiian men. As it considered actionable insights from the study, the NHCC transitioned from the ACS to Ke Ola Mamo, the Native Hawaiian Health Care System for the island of O'ahu and renamed the project No Ke Ola Pono o Nā Kāne (for the good health of men), or the Kāne Project.

Developing Resources for Men

The Kāne Project developed health education resources for Native Hawaiian men based on the study findings. The NHCC was aware that Native Hawaiian men (and probably men in general) are hesitant to share personal and family concerns in group settings, especially when women are present. The NHCC was also aware that, except in limited situations, contemporary society does not support men-only talking groups. However, there are abundant examples in Hawaiian history, traditions, and culture to inform culturally tailored interventions. The concept of the Hale Mua or kāne meeting house provided an overarching framework of how to advance men's health dialogue. Traditionally, the Hale Mua was a significant institution in Hawaiian society where men's educational, leadership, and spiritual and religious roles and responsibilities were learned, reinforced, and passed on to future generations [10, 11]. It was also a place where kāne discussed their role in community governance and health.

In 2005, the Kāne Project created and pilot-tested its first health education module on overall Native Hawaiian male health in a series of kāne-only hui kūkākūkā (focused group dialogue sessions) patterned after the Hale Mua. The module included a video recording of Dr. Richard Kekuni Blaisdell, one of the founders of the project and an advocate for Native Hawaiian health and wellbeing. At the end of the module, kāne were asked to write down and commit to one actionable behavior they would change in the subsequent 3 months to improve their health. These commitments were collected, and, after 3 months, an NHCC team of Native Hawaiian kauka (physicians) checked in with participants about their behavioral commitments.

To adhere to the fidelity of the module and to aid in data collection across multiple sites, a large, durable flip chart was designed by NHCC male cultural advisors. As a tool to promote health education among men, the front of the flip-chart contained information, questions, and cultural images viewable by participants, while the back was viewable only to the alaka'i (facilitator) and included a script to follow. Each session also had a kōkua (assistant to the alaka'i) and a notetaker and audio recorder.

Building Out and Scaling the Educational Model

During the pilot test and preliminary data collection, the NHCC discussed what they were learning from men during discussion sessions. Rapid feedback loops helped to evaluate the focus group process and provided a touchpoint on how well the intervention was received. Overwhelmingly, men shared their health concerns and offered each other solutions. While health dialogue was a mark of success, the NHCC knew that subsequent modules needed to include a Native Hawaiian kauka (physician) to provide an immediate response to the men's health questions. Based on the pilot study, the NHCC scaled out the model by developing subsequent cancer-specific modules to address the high incidence and prevalence of cancer among Native Hawaiian men.

Dissemination of the Project

In 2010, the NHCC secured modest funding from the Office of Hawaiian Affairs (OHA) to develop subsequent cancer modules and a statewide dissemination plan. Informed by the pilot testing, the NHCC adopted a peer-led implementation model. Community kāne were recruited as volunteers to deliver cancer prevention interventions using a "train-the-trainer" approach. The trainers in this case were committee members from the 2008 project, who trained other Native Hawaiian men from different communities to deliver sessions. Additionally, kauka were enlisted to provide the medical expertise needed during the sessions.

In 2016, additional funding from the Hawai'i Medical Service Association (HMSA), Hawai'i's Blue Cross Blue Shield insurance provider, and the Hawai'i Department of Health's Comprehensive Cancer Control Program facilitated extension to the islands of Lāna'i, Moloka'i, Kaua'i, Hawai'i, Maui, Ni'ihau, and rural areas of O'ahu. The first set of modules included topics on overall health, lung cancer, colorectal cancer, and oro–/nasopharyngeal cancer. The colorectal module also included the distribution of fecal immunochemical tests (FIT) to participants aged 50 years and older, with a small financial incentive to complete the test. Over the following 3 years, the project reached ~400 Native Hawaiian men who attended 1 of 43 educational sessions, with 79% of the 149 kāne over age 50 reporting they were up to date with colon cancer screening recommendations. The impacts of efforts to increase cancer prevention and early detection and improve the overall health of Native Hawaiian men continue [12].

Discussion-Informed Project Enhancement

As part of our cancer prevention educational activities, kāne-only hui kūkākūkā (focused group dialogue sessions) informed iterative improvement of the project's design and delivery. Discussion topics included knowledge, attitudes, and behaviors surrounding emergent risk for illness among men and identified non-health topics of concern. During the sessions, kāne expressed the need to identify, compile, and share dwindling traditional knowledge and cultural practices. Major themes included consistent and robust dialogue about the role of kāne in the modern Hawaiian family, including building capacities as men and family leaders to transmit cultural and traditional knowledge to younger generations. Other discussions emphasized the importance of protecting the 'āina (land) and the importance of kalo (taro) in Hawaiian culture, centered on the Hawaiian value of mālama 'āina (to love and respect the land) and claiming stewardship. Participants viewed the loss of land stewardship as a result of Western influences, specifically the overthrow of the Hawaiian Kingdom, which prevented Native Hawaiians from growing culturally important crops such as kalo, a dietary staple. The participants discussed specific activities, such as meal preparation and healthy foods, which served to build the robust physiques of Hawaiians in former times, and the importance of maintaining balance between physical, mental, and spiritual health as a part of traditional Hawaiian culture.

Cultural Modules Added

These discussions highlighted the importance of incorporating topics of concern into the existing project. The NHCC and project staff developed cultural modules to address these emergent issues, including (1) a session on modernizing the preparation of healthy traditional Hawaiian food, or ʻai pono (eating well), (2) a module on the traditional practice of kaula (cordage binding) to preserve knowledge of methods that were historically important in building robust infrastructure in the absence of metal, (3) a module on loko iʻa (fish ponds) that demonstrated historical sustainable eco-friendly fish farming, and (4) a module on pule (prayer) and the importance of maintaining a balance between physical, mental, and spiritual health. These new modules were contextually grounded in the theme of maintaining good health and delivered via video recordings by renowned Hawaiian cultural practitioners, capturing this cultural heritage for posterity.

Next Steps and Sustainability

In 2021, the project was renamed Kū Ola (upright and purposeful living) with guidance and support from the NHCC. With funding from the Hawai'i Community Foundation, the scope of this new project expanded, seeking to build the capacity of *all* Native Hawaiians to learn, incorporate, and disseminate key cultural concepts and practices as part of overall health and wellbeing. We continue to enlist new community partners and have begun expanding capacity at the community level. We intend to build a lasting example of how Native Hawaiian communities can continue to thrive. Our long-term goal is to establish and build upon relevant science, link scientific discovery with pragmatic engagement and health promotion in the Native Hawaiian community, and build the capacity of communities to support and extend the purposeful and joyful lives of Native Hawaiians.

References

1. Abbott I. A. *La'au Hawaii: Traditional Hawaiian Uses of Plants.* Honolulu Hawaii: Bishop Museum Press; 1992.
2. National Park Service. *Cook Landing Site, HI* [Internet]. 2022. Available from: https://www.nps.gov/places/cook-landing-site.htm
3. Stannard D. *Before the Horror: The Population of Hawaii on the Eve of Western Contact.* Honolulu Hawaii: The University of Hawaii Press; 1998.
4. Hawaiʻi Department of Business Economic Development and Tourism. *Non-English Speaking Population in Hawaii.* 2016 Apr. Available from: https://files.hawaii.gov/dbedt/economic/data_reports/Non_English_Speaking_Population_in_Hawaii_April_2016.pdf
5. Nguyen DH, Salvail FR. *The Hawaii Behavioral Risk Factor Surveillance System 2014 Results.* Honolulu Hawaii: State of Hawaii Department of Health. 2014. Available from: http://health.hawaii.gov/brfss/files/2015/08/HBRFSS_2014_results.pdf
6. Mental Health Task Force. *Native Hawaiian health needs study: Report of E Ola Mau task force on health needs of Native Hawaiians—Medical Task Force Report.* Honolulu Hawaii: Mental Health Task Force. 1985 Dec. Available from: https://papaolalokahi.org/wp-content/uploads/pol-pdf/91985-E-Ola-Mau-The-Native-Hawaiian-Health-Needs-Study-Mental-Health-Task-Force-Report.pdf
7. Palafox NA. Cancer in the US Associated Pacific Islands (UASPI): History and participatory development. *Pac Health Dialog.* 2004;11(2):8–13.
8. Hawai'i Tumor Registry. *Hawaii Cancer At a Glance 2014–2018* Honolulu Hawaii: University of Hawaii Cancer Center; 2022. Available from: https://www.uhcancercenter.org/pdf/htr/Cancer%20at%20a%20Glance%202014-2018.pdf
9. Hughes CK, Higuchi P. Ka Lōkahi Wahine: a culturally based training for health professionals. *Pac Health Dialog.* 2004;11(2):166–9.
10. Handy ES, Handy EG, Pukui MK. Native Planters in Old Hawaii: Their Life, Lore, and Environment. Honolulu: Bernice P. Bishop Museum Bulletin Press; 1892.
11. Malo D. Hawaiian antiquities (Moolelo Hawaii). Honolulu: Hawaiian Gazette Co., Ltd.; 1903.
12. Cassel KD, Hughes CK, Higuchi P, Lee P, Fagan P, Lono J, et al. No Ke Ola Pono o Na Kane: A Culturally Grounded Approach to Promote Health Improvement in Native Hawaiian Men. *Am J Mens Health.* 2020;14(1):1557988319893886. https://doi.org/10.1177/1557988319893886

31 Te Mauri, Te Tohu: A Māori Case Study

Tira Albert, Michelle Erai, and John Kingi

Key Points

- The Te Mauri program supports Māori families living with cancer based upon Māori principles, including making, seeing, and bringing to life meaningful images.
- The tohu (symbol) of Te Mauri is an example of deep engagement with an image as a component in developing and maintaining a Māori approach to living with cancer.
- Used as a symbol on all promotional material and resources, the tohu is a daily reminder, or iteration, of the values of Te Mauri.

Te Mauri is an Indigenous support program for Māori living with cancer that has become key to creating positive change and better health outcomes in Aotearoa New Zealand. This case study presents some of the theoretical, philosophical, and spiritual underpinnings within the Te Mauri framework and in the initial design of the tohu (symbol). The tohu is an example of how a Māori approach to living with cancer may represent a different paradigm for ensuring Māori wellbeing. The healing involved in this deeper understanding of whanau (family), based on social justice work, reveals priorities and measures likely to align with other Indigenous, poor, and people-of-color communities internationally.

Te Mauri seeks to address the critical gaps in cancer care for Māori in Aotearoa New Zealand. At every stage of an individual's process with cancer, the attention, diagnoses, and treatment that Māori receive are mediated by their status as tangata whenua (people of the land), including in the ways that ethnicity intersects with gender, sexuality, levels of disability, geographical location, class status, and spirituality.

Te Mauri is offered by three Indigenous health providers in the greater Wellington area. In 2017, the Mana Wāhine collective identified three Māori health providers (MHPs) with expertise in kaupapa Māori (knowledge) and working with cancer patients. The three MHPs are Whaiora, a Masterton-based service established in 2000 that provides comprehensive health and social services within the Wairarapa catchment area; Hora Te Pai Health Services (Hora Te Pai), established in 1990 in Paraparaumu on the Kapiti Coast north of Wellington; and Kōkiri Marae Health and Social Services (Kōkiri), a service based in Seaview, Wellington, with over 30 years' experience as an urban marae-based education, health, and social service provider, committed to the holistic wellbeing of whanau (families), hapū (subtribes), and iwi (tribes).

Our communities said they wanted a "by Māori for Māori" kaupapa (program) that spoke of traditional values and belief systems and of knowledge handed down to us by our ancestors. Based on this goal, mātauranga Māori (knowledge) concepts were chosen to guide the Te Mauri framework. These choices also reveal how European-centered structures and health systems typically fail and further damage Māori communities.

The Te Mauri Framework

The Te Mauri framework is epitomized by the image created during the kaupapa (program) development. The image represents the overlaps between the three different sites; it simultaneously demonstrates the collaborative nature of this work while retaining the local strengths of each site. It also is an invitation to Māori whānau being affected by cancer to remember a way of moving through periods of taimaha/taumaha (difficult times) using Māori concepts to sustain our mauri (flourishing).

A Māori worldview is deeply embedded in the way Te Mauri is structured—with, for example, biweekly meetings, transportation to and from the meetings, the use of a marae (traditional communal space), karakia (invocations), the singing of waiata (songs), speaking circles that involve passing a meaningful object, the inclusion of elders and youth, a welcome to family members, the provision of nourishing homemade food, the sharing of Tribal and genealogical affiliations, and visits from community speakers from hospice, cancer hospitals, and traditional wellbeing practitioners. The program seeks to whakamana te whakapapa (strengthen

G. Garvey (ed.), *Indigenous and Tribal Peoples and Cancer*, https://doi.org/10.1007/978-3-031-56806-0_31

ancestral connections) of each person and whānau participating.

Fundamental to the Te Mauri service is the belief that living with cancer is a wairua (spiritual) journey. The program creates a space for healing to occur, it provides a connection and relationship to the Atua (Divine); it moves beyond providing information and scheduling support to creating an opportunity to assist whānau to prepare for Mātangireia (a secular heaven). We take the position that a transformation from Te Pō i te Ao (the darkness into the light) is necessary to achieve mauri ora (wellbeing) for the whānau navigating the treatment of cancer. The intent is to aki aki te ti o te tangata (nurture the ineffable light of a person).

Early in the development of Te Mauri, artist John Kingi (coauthor JK) theorized a tohu that represented a Māori epistemology, or a way of thinking, for those affected by a cancer diagnosis:

> The name of the rōpū (group) "Te Mauri" is interesting in itself. All things created have a mauri (flourishing), from animals to trees, people, stones, and dirt. It takes all forms and is present in both living and inanimate objects. Therefore it is continuous and a part of the unbroken cycle of existence. We exist, we pass away, we continue to exist on another plane. We are connected via this whākaaro (understanding) to the world around us.

John explained the origins of the tohu as follows:

> The overall design is a representation of the journey each person must take in the physical world and in the spiritual world. Time does not dictate the life and death of an individual, it is immaterial. What matters, and is reflected in the many histories, whakatauki (sayings) and waiata (songs) of our people is the importance of striving to achieve excellence in life.

Contemporary in its design, the Te Mauri tohu references aspects of different types of Māori design using traditional symbols to convey messages and meaning and an exhortation to attain knowledge (through the step-like design in the lower half of the two sides). The sacred teachings of aligning with the flow of the essence or mauri of spirituality are held within the image (Fig. 31.1).

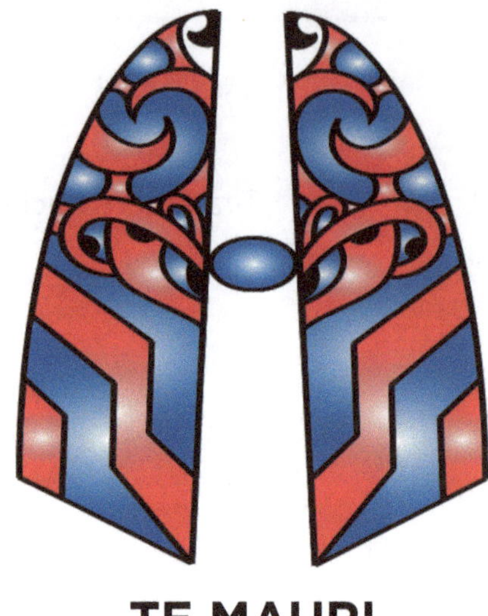

Fig. 31.1 The Te Mauri tohu created by John Kingi

Components of the Te Mauri Tohu

The tohu includes a number of components that communicate its message:

- Waka (canoe): the overall design is in the shape of the hiwi (hull) of a waka. Imagine looking up at the underside of a waka while it glides through the water: this is a significant symbol for Māori. The waka is used to move people in this world and to send—both literally and figuratively—people into the spirit world.
- Poutama (pattern) and kaitiaki (guardian figures): the lower half of the design, the poutama, is a step-like pattern that represents the "journey of life" and lifelong learning. The design represents the possibility from which we value each day we have been given, to live it with the grace inherent in each of us.
- The two kaitiaki at the top of the tohu are wheku (carved depictions of a human face with slanting eyes). At each side at the top of the tohu, these figures represent Māreikura (an order of female supernatural beings) and Whatukura (an order of male supernatural beings). They are the guardians of the uppermost heavens and a gateway to the most sacred and sought-after knowledge. John Kingi commented: "I have used these elements here to symbolize the importance of valuing each day we have, and striving to achieve our greatest potential in our time."
- Ngā Tae (the colors): the blue represents the color of mauri (life force); the red represents toto (blood), whakapapa (genealogy), and rangatiratanga (sovereignty); and the white represents dreaming as part of the eternal slumber.
- Ira Atua (supernatural life): the space between the two kaitiaki represents the next stage in our journey and an eternity of, among other things, a dream time. It is the threshold that separates the spirit world and the world of light.
- The kākano (circle or seed) suspended in between the two sides symbolizes the unbroken continuous line between both worlds. John Kingi commented:

> Once we cross this threshold, we are reconnected with Ngā Atua (the Gods) who are the source of all creation. The only way to access this realm is for each of us to take "the eternal sleep" and when we sleep we also DREAM. Therefore we must lose our physical essence to be able to experience not only the eternal slumber, but also an eternity of "DREAM TIME" among other things.

Conclusion

The tohu captures one aspect of the multifaceted Te Mauri approach. It is part of a dynamic framework that is deeply embedded within a broader program that supports Māori individuals and whānau who are on a cancer journey. We draw upon traditional principles to understand the stages that may be involved in living with cancer. The process for Te Mauri members is less about the demands of a struggling medical administration; instead, we focus more on the inherent divinity in each individual, supporting their movement through challenges in living with cancer with dignity, integrity, and sovereignty. The tohu designed for Te Mauri is a visual and epistemological icon that demonstrates an Indigenous paradigm for healing in a way that exceeds the goals of inadequate health administration and focuses instead on the flourishing of Māori who are living with cancer.

Conclusion

Metis Science and Perspectives on Cancer in the Context of HPV and HPV Vaccine Uptake

32

Angeline Letendre, Keith King, Peter Hutchinson, and Elder Elmer Ghostkeeper

Key Points

- Métis-specific concepts provide a foundation for demonstrating the resilience and healing powers of Métis science and knowledge.
- A broader recognition of the essentials of culturally relevant cancer care provision must include an understanding of the omnipresent interconnections and interactions between Métis patients and families.
- Métis conceptualizations of wahkohtowin (natural kinship laws) and keeoukaywin (visiting as a means of constructing Métis knowledge) promise to generate new knowledge grounded in our worldviews and ways of knowing and being that is useful to our people, communities, and nation.
- Research grounded in Métis science and knowledge is required to support increased uptake of human papillomavirus (HPV) vaccines across Métis communities.

This chapter introduces new understandings of the ways Métis people traverse health systems to seek out the support required to meet their health- and cancer-care needs. Findings from HPV/HPV vaccine research among Métis people in Alberta, Canada, are discussed with the intention to give voice to Métis, including Métis Elder, perspectives. We describe important concepts for health as a foundation for demonstrating the resilience and healing powers of Métis-specific knowledge and science. Addressing challenges in cancer and cancer prevention among Métis people, the chapter refers to political, social, and cultural inequities that impact the health and wellbeing of Métis people.

Métis People in Canada

Within Canada, there are three distinct groups of Indigenous people—First Nations, Inuit, and Métis [1]. Métis peoples originated with European settlers entering Canada and adopting First Nations' customs, including conjugal arrangements with women [2]. In this way, settlers learned the skills to survive in the Canadian wilderness and to pursue economic wealth and power in Canada's far north.

More than 127,000 Métis reside in Alberta, the only province to have land-based agreements with Métis settlements. There are eight such settlements, home to approximately 5600 people, who are provided health coverage by the province [3]. Métis people across Canada do not have the same treaty rights as First Nations peoples, contributing to limited programming dollars, insufficient health infrastructure, a lack of care providers and health programs, and barriers to care.

Health and Wellness in Métis Contexts

Canada's political landscape and its relationship with Métis people are complex and often serve to undermine their overall health and wellbeing. Unique to Alberta, Métis settlement communities have land-based agreements with the province and view themselves as independent self-governing entities. However, until recently, most communities have not received funding to develop Métis-specific health programs or services. Forced to rely on project funding, this lack of equity contributes to and perpetuates poor health despite needs and challenges similar to First Nations and Inuit populations.

In the past, dialogue with Métis Elders [4] has identified the many losses that impact Métis health: the loss of identity, traditional teachings, access to land, hunting, fishing, and trapping. Also, experiences of relocation, residential schooling, and influences from colonization and religion were noted. A recent gathering with First Nations and Métis Elders confirms that these factors persist with additional factors, including homelessness, human trafficking, substance abuse, and premature deaths from poison, including drug overdoses, affecting Métis youth [5].

G. Garvey (ed.), *Indigenous and Tribal Peoples and Cancer*, https://doi.org/10.1007/978-3-031-56806-0_32

Métis Identity and Language

Métis identity, as referred to by Bartlett, is grounded in the historical, cultural, and political experiences of Métis people [6]. These experiences or influences on the daily lives of Métis people are determinants of Métis health, which Cooper et al. describe as "structured around eight key wellness areas—nature, identity, development, relationships, supports, networks, environment, and governance" [7, p. 212]. Similarly, the values depicted below in the work of Métis artist and author Leah Dorion, based on extensive engagement with Métis Elders, are shown to mirror or be in parallel with what constitutes wellness in the context of Métis people (Fig. 32.1) [8].

Language and language loss affect Métis health in distinct ways. Michif, a language spoken only by Métis, is a mix of Nehiyawewin (Cree), Annishinabewewin (Annishinabek), and French and is inherent to Métis in northern parts of Canada's prairie provinces of Manitoba, Saskatchewan, and Alberta. Michif is significant to health and wellbeing as many of the cultural concepts that envelop and describe Métis health are best understood in that language. Métis Elder Tom McCallum says that Michif:

> … shows love, compassion, caring and dedication…. [Language is] one of your greatest identities, because the Creator gives you a language when he put you on this earth. He gives you language to describe who you are and what you are about. Your connection to the whole universe comes through that language. It is much more than the spoken word; it's not only the spoken word. It is a whole state of being and a way of viewing things [4, p. 88].

Métis Traditional Knowledge and Science

Indigenous Elders are the keepers and transmitters of traditional knowledge (TK) and science, including community histories, societal norms, beliefs and philosophies, traditional teachings, and healing methods. Such knowledge is

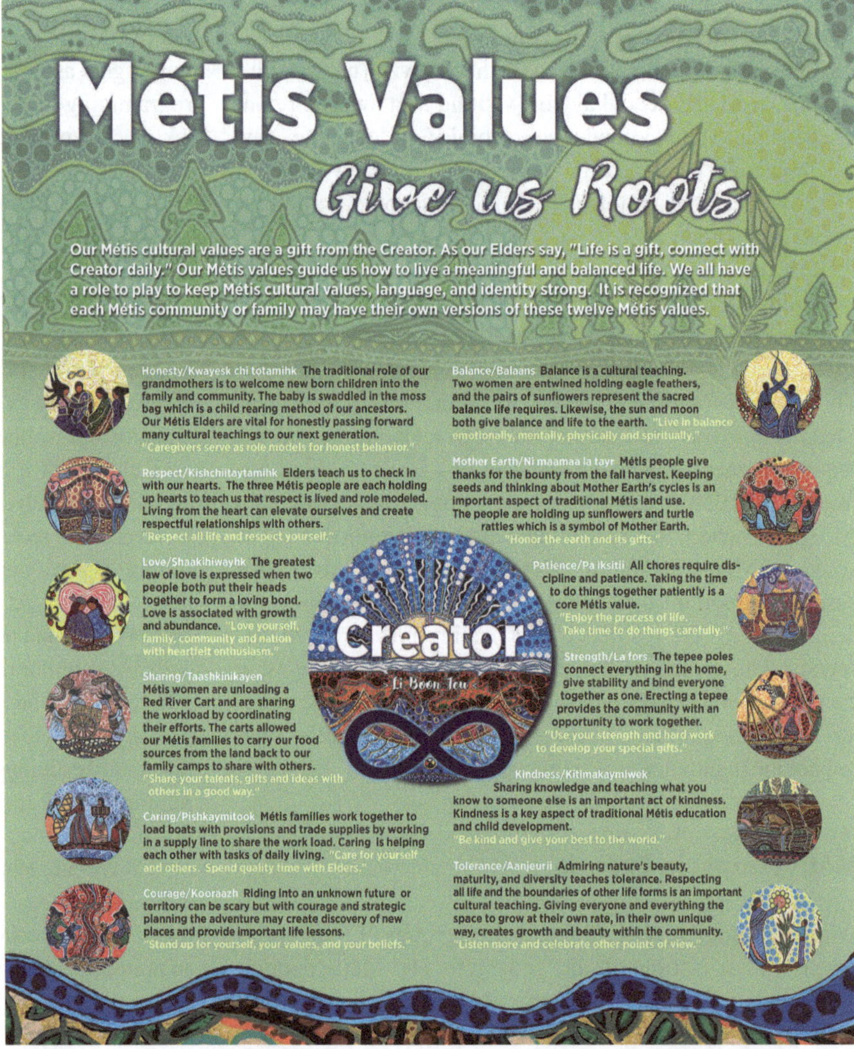

Fig. 32.1 Identified in both English and Michif, the 12 cultural values represent important ways of being and knowing and are intended to inform expectations for daily living from within Métis contexts. [8, p. 32]

maintained and transmitted through ceremonies and medicines. Moreover, Elders translate TK through oral means, rooted in ancestral stories and histories perceived to be relevant to the maintenance of Métis culture and critical to the health and wellbeing of Métis people. Likewise, Métis Elders are "rights-holders" and scientists of Métis TK, with information originating from a specific community or region often transmitted in Michif. It is important to note that Elders speak about TK as "not something of the past, but something that should be considered in a contemporary context" [4, p. 83]. For instance, although knowledge of land, climate, and water is traditional knowledge, it is by no means knowledge of the past [2].

Collective Ties to Land, Language, and Culture

The impacts of colonialism, including the loss of land, language, and culture, are generally understood to impact the health and wellbeing of Indigenous peoples globally [5]. Métis people in Canada are no exception, and until recently, they were often unseen or they represented a forgotten people, with the broader Canadian population offering limited or no acknowledgment of their place in the country's historical, economic, and sociopolitical landscape. This is evidenced by the lack of health research articulating or even recognizing the existence of Métis cultures, knowledge, and science to any degree of depth [7].

The following sections present two examples of Métis-led research that has taken place within Alberta Métis communities. These reflect the significance of grounding research with Métis people, in Métis science and concepts of health and wellness, and in connecting these concepts to provide culturally appropriate cancer prevention and care.

Metis People and HPV

Human papillomavirus (HPV) is a sexually transmitted infection that most sexually active people will contract at least once in their lifetime. Most infections resolve on their own, but those that do not can lead to cancers in the mouth, throat, anus, or genital areas of both men and women. HPV infection causes nearly all cases of cervical cancer [8]. Disproportionately impacted by HPV, Indigenous women in Canada experience higher rates of HPV infection [9], higher incidence of cervical cancer [10], and more cervical-cancer-related deaths [11] than the general population. Research recognizes that these differences may be a result of historical trauma from residential schooling and the Sixties Scoop (in which Indigenous children were adopted by non-Indigenous families, became Crown wards, or were placed in permanent care) experiences, the imposition of government policies, and marginalization due to poverty and racism [12–14]. Such very recent historical circumstances contribute to mistrust by Canada's Indigenous people of the healthcare system and care providers [15, 16].

HPV and Métis Nation of Alberta Project

A population-based descriptive epidemiological study has identified cervical, anal, and head and neck cancer incidence among the Métis. Due to comparatively small case numbers in comparison to the general population, the research has been unable to draw statistical comparisons [17]. Additional research is underway in collaboration with the Métis Nation Alberta to explore Métis vaccine coverage, attitudes and beliefs about HPV vaccines, and experiences regarding cancer screening and HPV vaccines.

Early vaccine coverage findings for a cohort of Métis children aged 17 in 2019 reveal that vaccination coverage among Métis children assigned female at birth had higher rates of complete vaccination for HPV at age 17 (82.6%) than the general Alberta population (81.0%). However, the same cohort of Métis children aged 17 in 2019 assigned male at birth had lower coverage (66.2%) than their general population counterparts (70.7%) in the same birth cohort. For children aged 13 in this cohort, Métis children's coverage in those assigned male (73%) and female (71.4%) at birth was higher than their counterparts in the general population (m = 69.6%, f = 69.1%). Additional phases of this research will include survey data on Métis parents' attitudes and beliefs about HPV-related cancer prevention and qualitative visits exploring their experiences.

This research is grounded in Michif traditional ways of gathering, expanding, and sharing knowledge among Métis people and scholars. The methodology used is referred to as keeoukaywin (the visiting way). Keeoukaywin is a decolonizing process that involves hospitality and teaching with the reciprocal exchange of knowledge and ideas, in connection with land and kin. Grounded firmly in the Michif kinship law system of wahkohtowin, it engages the shared responsibility to kinship relations, both human and nonhuman [18]. Métis Elder Maria Campbell speaks to the reciprocal relationship and responsibility embedded in life teachings:

> At one time, from our place it [wahkohtowin] meant the whole of creation. And our teachings taught us that all of creation is related and inter-connected to all things within it. *Wahkotowin* meant honoring and respecting those relationships. [It was] our stories, songs, ceremonies, and dances that taught us from birth to death our responsibilities and reciprocal obligations to each other. Human to human, human to plants, human to animals, to the water and especially to the earth. And in turn all of creation had responsibilities and reciprocal obligations to us [19].

From this perspective, every living thing is a keeper of wahkohtowin and for these reasons, keeoukaywin holds great promise as it aspires to bring all the pieces back together and lead us back to what is right—relational obligation and spiritual responsibility. By visiting with the information, knowledge and stories of our Métis kin, the research promises to generate new knowledge that is grounded in our worldviews, ways of knowing and being, and that is useful to our people, communities and nation.

HPV and Alberta Métis Settlements Project

Research to address the Action Plan for the Elimination of Cervical Cancer in Canada, 2020–2030 [20], included a qualitative study led by Alberta Health Services (AHS) to explore HPV immunization programming in Alberta Métis settlements. Designed to engage key stakeholders, the purposes of the study were to identify barriers and facilitators to HPV vaccine uptake among school-aged youth and to identify the information needs of care providers delivering HPV immunization services.

Utilizing survey outcomes, information from care professionals providing immunization services on settlements informed dialogue with AHS regional program leads and health managers. Community gatherings were held with five of the eight settlements to determine knowledge and awareness of HPV, identify barriers and facilitators to HPV immunization uptake, and learn about community-based solutions for increased uptake of the vaccine. A focus group with AHS health managers concluded the research activities to gain insights into potential improvements in vaccine uptake on settlements.

Community participants overwhelmingly spoke to the need for trust building with communities, including having culturally informed care providers, engaging with family and youth, and knowing the community through increased knowledge of Métis people and cultures. During the focus group, Elder Elmer Ghostkeeper conveyed how critical it is for care providers administering the HPV vaccine to build trust within communities to increase acceptance and uptake: "The community has to accept you. If you don't get to that first base, you're not going to develop a relationship, [you] might as well go home" [21, p. 10].

Elders, viewed as primary support in receiving reliable information about health and wellbeing, are trusted community members who are often asked to provide mediation with the healthcare system and care professionals. They do this, variously, through ceremony, knowledge transfer to health systems about the specific cultural needs of their communities, and community-driven solutions grounded from within the knowledge and values of the people. A key outcome from the gatherings emphasized the need for healthcare providers to "know the community." Elder Julia Auger speaks to the importance of multilevel "knowing" when working with Métis Settlements:

> …[it's] really crucial to look at your community and develop a type of community profile. What does the community look like? How many people are there and what are the characteristics of the population? Once you start to look at your community as a whole, you're going to be able to create a very culturally appropriate approach—that whole cultural piece has to be strong in terms of how you're going to develop your strategy [21, p. 11].

The research clearly revealed that many community members lack a good understanding of HPV and the role of the vaccine in preventing its spread and, in the long-term, preventing HPV-related cancers. These outcomes suggest that further research grounded in Métis science and knowledge is required to support increased screening and uptake of HPV vaccines across Métis communities.

Connections Impacting Métis Cancer Experience

Diverse in nature, Métis communities, knowledge, and culture are considered living, dynamic entities. Manifested through connections to land, community, and family, these connections are viewed as sacred and as immeasurable as the connection between the air and the wind or water and the wet.

Connections to the land, as our first teacher, come through harvesting foods and medicines, and we attribute significance to learning from the land that continuously provides us with lessons on how to heal and care for one another. Connection to family is also inextricably linked to Métis wellbeing as commonalities allow people to share health information in familiar settings through familiar language and mannerisms. These oral connections enable collective knowledge to be shared in stories from personal experiences to support Métis wellbeing.

These connections are essential to Métis health. The removal of any one of these is likely to delay healing as the balance between each connection erodes and becomes lost. Removing the connection to community, for instance, reduces the likelihood of sharing medicinal knowledge; removing the Elder removes the ceremony; and removing the land removes the teacher. When any of these elements are missing, essential cancer prevention, healing, and end-of-life care may be interrupted, avoided, or lost.

A broader recognition of what is essential to providing culturally relevant cancer care must include an understanding of these omnipresent interconnections in the interactions with Métis patients and families. These connections must be considered prior to, during, and after care to support healing and achieve optimal wellness. Families spread information through communities. By bringing the information to the family, the connections within and between families and across the community can adequately prepare patients, their families, and the entire community for informed decision-making when presented with new health information.

References

1. *1982 Canada Constitution Act.* Available from: https://caid.ca/ConstAct010208.pdf
2. Anderson DR, Anderson AM. *The Metis people of Canada: A history.* Toronto: Gage Publishing Ltd; 1978.
3. Government of Alberta. *Métis Relations* [Internet]. [cited 2023 Nov 11]. Available from: https://www.alberta.ca/metis-relations.aspx
4. Métis Centre, National Aboriginal Health Organization. *In The Words of Our Ancestors: Métis Health and Healing.* Ottawa: National Aboriginal Health Organization; 2008.
5. Allan B, Smylie J. *First peoples, second class treatment: The role of racism in the health and well-being of indigenous peoples in Canada.* Toronto: Wellesley Institute; 2015.
6. Bartlett JG. *Considerations in the life and health of Metis in Canada, and the social determinants of health.* Proceedings of the Canadian Medical Association Leaders Forum: Leaders Developing Leaders. Ottawa: Canadian Medical Association; 2007 May.
7. Cooper E, Sanguins J, Menec V, Chartrand A, Carter S, Driedger, S. Culturally Responsive Supports for Metis Elders and Metis Family Caregivers. *Can J Aging.* 2020;39(2):206–219. https://doi.org/10.1017/S0714980819000321
8. Métis Provincial Council of British Columbia. *Aansaambaenkikayhtaamuk Métis Early Years Professional Learning Resources for Educators.* Surrey, BC: Métis Provincial Council of British Columbia; 2023. p. 32
9. Canadian Cancer Society. *What do I need to know about HPV?* [Internet]. [cited 2023 Nov 13]. Available from: https://cancer.ca/en/cancer-information/reduce-your-risk/get-vaccinated/human-papillomavirus-hpv
10. Tricco AC, Ng CH, Gilca V, Anonychuk A, Pham B, Berliner S. Canadian oncogenic human papillomavirus cervical infection prevalence: systematic review and meta-analysis. *BMC Infect Dis* 2011;11:1–15. https://doi.org/10.1186/1471-2334-11-235
11. Mazereeuw MV, Withrow DR, Nishri ED, et al. Cancer incidence and survival among Métis adults in Canada: results from the Canadian census follow-up cohort (1992–2009). *CMAJ.* 2018;190(11):E320–E326. https://doi.org/10.1503/cmaj.170272
12. Health Canada. *First Nations Health Status Report.* 2013. Available from: https://publications.gc.ca/collections/collection_2013/sc-hc/H26-4-2012-eng.pdf
13. Truth and Reconciliation Commission of Canada. *Truth and Reconciliation Commission of Canada: Calls to Action.* 2015. Available from: https://www2.gov.bc.ca/assets/gov/british-columbians-our-governments/indigenous-people/aboriginal-peoples-documents/calls_to_action_english2.pdf
14. Public Health Agency of Canada. *Key Health Inequalities in Canada: A National Portrait.* 2018. Available from: https://www.canada.ca/content/dam/phac-aspc/documents/services/publications/science-research/key-health-inequalities-canada-national-portrait-executive-summary/hir-full-report-eng.pdf
15. Reading C, Wien F. *Health inequalities and social determinants of Aboriginal peoples' health.* 2009. Available from: https://www.ccnsa-nccah.ca/docs/determinants/RPT-HealthInequalities-Reading-Wien-EN.pdf
16. Health Council of Canada. Empathy, dignity, and respect: Creating cultural safety for Aboriginal people in urban health care. 2012. Available from: https://learningcircle.ubc.ca/files/2014/05/Empathy-dignity-and-respect-Creating-cultural-safety-for-Aboriginal-people-in-urban-health-care.pdf
17. Sanchez-Ramirez DC, Colquhoun A, Parker S, Randall J, Svenson LW, Voaklander D. Cancer incidence and mortality among the Métis population of Alberta, Canada. *Int J Circumpolar Health.* 2016 Feb 1;75: https://doi.org/10.3402/ijch.v75.30059.
18. Gaudet JC. Keeoukaywin: The Visiting Way—Fostering an Indigenous Research Methodology. *Aboriginal Policy Studies* 2018;7(2). https://doi.org/10.5663/apx.v7i2.29336
19. Campbell, M. We need to return to the principles of Wahkotowin. *Eagle Feather News.* 2008 Nov;10(11). Available from: https://www.eaglefeathernews.com/quadrant/media//pastIssues/November_2007.pdf
20. Canadian Partnership Against Cancer. *Action plan for the elimination of cervical cancer in Canada, 2020–2030.* Available from: Canadian Partnership Against Cancer. https://www.partnershipagainstcancer.ca/topics/elimination-cervical-cancer-action-plan/
21. Malkin J, Baxter T, Letendre A. *Solutions to Increase Youth Human Papillomavirus Immunization in Canada Youth Human Papillomavirus Immunization in Alberta Métis Settlements: A Final Project Report.* Alberta Health Services; 2023. 21.

A Study on Community Engagement in Cervical Cancer Screening in Botswana

33

Patricia S. Rantshabeng, Billy Tsima, Keneilwe Motlhatlhedi, Tendani Gaolathe, Kirthana Sharma, Leema A. Hiri, Isang Soso Saidoo, Andrew Ndlovu, and Lynnette Tumwine Kyokunda

Key Points

- Cervical cancer screening uptake in Botswana's Indigenous communities remains low.
- Our research explored culturally appropriate ways to improve cervical cancer screening uptake in western Botswana.
- Community leaders and healthcare workers were consulted to develop collaborative, inclusive screening. Locally trained female community healthcare assistants were engaged to support participant recruitment and healthcare talks in the community.
- Adopting culturally accepting and gender-choice-flexible services that overcome intimacy reticence may improve cervical cancer screening uptake in Indigenous and marginalized communities.

Botswana is a landlocked country with a population exceeding two million people and a national adult literacy rate of 87%. Cervical cancer and HIV are important public health concerns in Botswana [1], which was one of the southern African countries hardest hit by the HIV/AIDS pandemic and has an estimated 20.8% of adults living with HIV infection (corresponding to 390,000 adults) [2]. However, great progress has been made in the control of HIV/AIDS infection countrywide owing to the government's effective antiretroviral therapy (ART) program [3, 4].

Recent data show that the incidence of cervical cancer in Botswana stands at 34.4 per 100,000 people, with a mortality rate of 20 per 100,000 [5]. However, cervical cancer is preventable with organized screening, treatment, and follow-up.

Botswana's primary prevention strategy involves quadrivalent HPV vaccination, which was introduced in 2015 and is currently reaching almost 100% coverage of the target group of girls aged 9–13 years [6]. This is aligned with the World Health Organization (WHO) country cooperation strategy of reducing vaccine-preventable diseases [10]. Secondary prevention includes screening with Pap smears and its alternative, "See and Treat," which combines screening and treatment in single visits [7].

Despite the widespread availability of services, cervical cancer screening uptake in Indigenous communities remains very low, as evidenced by recent studies reporting uptake of 7–9% [5, 6, 8, 9]. The WHO expects that by 2030, 90% of girls by 15 years of age should be fully vaccinated with the HPV vaccine, 70% of women screened with high-performance tests, and 90% of women who are identified with cervical cancer should receive treatment and care [10]. In order to achieve the WHO targets, much wider coverage of the population needs to be achieved. The primary aim of this community-based study was to enroll women from marginalized or Indigenous communities of western Botswana and determine their risk factors, burden of cervical lesions, and barriers to cervical cancer screening uptake.

Study Sites

The study sites included Kacgae, Bere, and D'Kar settlements in the Ghanzi district, which are serviced through health posts, and Lokgwabe and Ncojane villages in the Kgalagadi district, which are serviced through a health post and a clinic, respectively (Fig. 33.1). The lack of radio coverage in these settlements presents a communication challenge in terms of spreading accurate healthcare screening information and creating awareness. Therefore, word of mouth, primarily through community leaders, was a critical tool.

Study Population

According to the Botswana 2022 census, the settlements and villages chosen for the study had the following populations: Kacgae—746, Bere—874, D'Kar—2814, Lokgwabe—1792, and Ncojane—2242 people. The majority of Kacgae and

G. Garvey (ed.), *Indigenous and Tribal Peoples and Cancer*, https://doi.org/10.1007/978-3-031-56806-0_33

Fig. 33.1 Map of Botswana with the study sites indicated in the Ghanzi and Kgalagadi districts. (Map: P Rantshabeng)

Bere residents identify as Basarwa, belonging to the !Xoo Tribe. D'Kar residents also identify as Basarwa, belonging to the Naro Tribe. Ncojane and Lokgwabe residents identify as a collective of Bakgalagadi Tribes, including Bangologa, Batlhware, and Barolong as the majority. In total, 171 women enrolled in the study, the majority of whom spoke and understood Setswana well.

Study Methods

Community Consultations and Engagement

Community-leader consultations were undertaken before the study commenced, guided by the understanding that Indigenous communities are held together by centuries-long traditions of having chiefs as the community glue. These consultations were used to engage community leaders at the initial stages of participant recruitment, seek access permission, explain the study aims, and discuss the procedures. We focused on the need to provide a place for culturally appropriate, safe conversations, as advised by the University of Botswana's San Research Center. The conservative nature of Indigenous communities was emphasized, which made the engagement of community leaders prior to the study recruitment a critical exercise. Consultations involved settlement/village chiefs, political leaders (councilors), village development committee chairs and their deputies, local health-post nurses, and social welfare officers. We noted that in the Indigenous communities, chiefs and their appointed leaders became vital mouthpieces for researchers.

In Kacgae, several community–leader consultations took place at the kgotla, the Chief's official premises, while some consultations involving community Elders took place around the fire in the evening. These consultations helped the researchers assimilate into the environment and better appreciate the settlement's history, cultural aspects, and anticipated barriers to screening. The consultations were conducted in the native language, Setswana, noting that the majority of people in Botswana speak and understand this language. A multilingual translator service was used only in Bere. In each community, information was shared about the proposed health screening and consent procedures, and they were provided with assurances about ethical recruitment practices. These engagements enabled a better understanding of local community needs with regard to public health, helped manage the expectations of both the researchers and the community, established mutual respect, and ensured confidence in the health screening procedures.

Participant Recruitment and Barriers to Cervical Cancer Screening

Recruitment started on the first day with fewer participants than expected in Kacgae and none at all in Bere. In Ncojane, Lokgwabe, and Dekar, enrollments began well. It is noteworthy that cervical cancer screening registers in Kagcae and Dekar indicated low uptake for previous years. Preliminary investigations indicated personal barriers such as fear, intimacy reticence, and general privacy concerns. In addition, health system barriers such as long turnaround times were cited by those with prior screening experience. Understanding that scientific concepts can be intimidating, we consulted with community leaders and healthcare workers to develop strategies for a more collaborative and inclusive screening exercise. They advised engaging trusted, locally trained female community healthcare assistants (HEAs) for the recruitment exercise. These HEAs went house to house, introducing the researchers and creating awareness.

In addition, researchers proposed holding healthcare talks in private spaces where women felt safe to talk about sexual and reproductive health issues. Community halls were used to hold these health talks, and through learning models and educational videos to demonstrate sample collection procedures, participants' fears about the proposed screening and possible treatment procedures were allayed. Differences between the proposed Pap smear and the cervical cancer screening modality commonly used in the region (See and Treat) were also discussed. We found that awareness and previous experience with See and Treat initially contributed to participation anxiety because some women who had experienced lesion excision on their first screening visit had spread news that cervical cancer screening was painful. Therefore, potential participants were fearful of cervical cancer screening and stayed away from the research sites at the initial stages of the screening process. T-shirts featuring messages about cervical cancer screening from the researcher-affiliated institution were distributed to participants postscreening. Banners were also mounted to spread the message about cervical screening awareness and increase service visibility in the study sites.

Key Findings

The participant interviews revealed that the majority of the women residing in the settlements had barely graduated from primary education, and therefore a lack of healthcare knowledge constituted a significant barrier to screening uptake. Additionally, intimacy reticence was cited as a barrier to cervical cancer screening and treatment uptake, especially in facilities dominated by male healthcare workers. To overcome this hurdle, a women-only researcher team was deployed for data collection. These strategies greatly improved knowledge and understanding among potential participants, leading to higher attendance at the screening sites in the follow-up visits—from the planned 171 enrollees to 228 women.

Community-leader-driven conversations at the initial stages of the study improved our understanding of critical cultural challenges and personal barriers to participating in the proposed healthcare screening exercises. Continuous community consultations highlighted the need for linguistically and culturally tailored healthcare talks to help understand and overcome cultural and personal barriers that could prevent these women from participating in health screening.

Conclusion

Botswana has seen great improvements in terms of access to cervical cancer screening countrywide. However, screening uptake among Indigenous populations faces additional challenges. Our research highlights some important lessons and underscores the importance of effective community engagement in the planning stages of health screening exercises where participation is core and results could impact policy. Women from Indigenous groups are seldom heard, and they are underrepresented in matters affecting their personal health. This can lead to decisions that may not serve them well. However, given a chance to lead discussions regarding their health and in their native language, positive interventions are possible. Adopting culturally tolerant and gender-choice-flexible service provision to overcome intimacy reticence may harmonize and improve screening participation in Indigenous and marginalized communities.

The researchers would like to acknowledge generous funding from the University of Botswana Office of Research and Development. We also acknowledge the assistance of Mr. Kesalopa from the National Health Laboratory, Mr. Nichodimus Cooper from the Nama Heritage in Lokgwabe, and the various community leaders from Kacgae, Bere, and Dekar settlements and Lokgwabe and Ncojane villages. Lastly, we would like to acknowledge the participants who made this work possible.

References

1. Statistics Botswana. *Population and Housing census report* [Internet]. 2022. Available from: www.statsbots.org.bw/census-2022
2. Statistics Botswana. *Fifth Botswana AIDS Impact Survey 2021 (BAIS V)*. National AIDS & Health Promotion Agency, Government of Botswana; 2023.
3. Grover S, Raesima M, Bvochora-Nsingo M, Chiyapo SP, Balang D, Tapela N, et al. Cervical cancer in Botswana: Current state and future steps for screening and treatment programs. *Front Oncol.* 2015;5:239. https://doi.org/10.3389/fonc.2015.00239

4. Gaolathe T, Wirth KE, Holme MP, Makhema J, Moyo S, Chakalisa U, et al. Botswana's progress toward achieving the 2020 UNAIDS 90-90-90 antiretroviral therapy and virological suppression goals: A population-based survey. *Lancet HIV*. 2016;3(5):e221–e230. https://doi.org/10.1016/S2352-3018(16)00037-0
5. Sung H, Ferlay J, Siegel RL, Laversanne M, Soerjomataram I, Jemal A, Bray F. Global Cancer Statistics 2020: GLOBOCAN estimates of incidence and mortality worldwide for 36 cancers in 185 countries. *CA Cancer J Clin*. 2021;71(3):209–49. https://doi.org/10.3322/caac.21660
6. Ministry of Health, Botswana Government. *Child and Adolescent Immunisation report* (2023). Unpublished.
7. Ministry of Health, Botswana Government. *Botswana National Cervical Cancer Prevention 2012–2016 Strategy*. Unpublished.
8. Ezem BU. Awareness and uptake of cervical cancer screening in Owerri, South-Eastern Nigeria. *Ann Afr Med*. 2007;6(3):94. https://doi.org/10.4103/1596-3519.55727
9. Young TK, Kliewer E, Blanchard J, Mayer T. Monitoring disease burden and preventive behavior with data linkage: cervical cancer among aboriginal people in Manitoba, Canada. *Am J Public Health*. 2000;90(9):1466. https://doi.org/10.2105/ajph.90.9.1466
10. World Health Organization. *WHO guideline for screening and treatment of precancerous lesions for cervical cancer prevention*. Geneva: World Health Organization; 2013.

Cervical Screening by HPV Self-Testing: A Game Changer for Māori

34

Bev Lawton, Anna Adcock, Kendall Stevenson, Tania Slater, and Francesca Storey

Key Points

- Cervical cancer is now preventable.
- Human papillomavirus (HPV) causes most cervical cancers, and screening for HPV prevents cervical cancer.
- HPV self-testing is a game changer because "it is empowering."
- Indigenous peoples demand "No Elimination Without Us!"

Few diseases reflect global and within-country inequities as much as cervical cancer, despite it now being largely preventable through vaccination, cervical screening, and the treatment of precancerous cell changes. In Australia, Canada, Aotearoa New Zealand, and the United States, Indigenous women (and people with cervices) have a markedly higher risk of cervical cancer incidence and mortality than non-Indigenous women [1]. Once screened, achieving timely diagnosis, treatment of abnormalities, and/or subsequent follow-up all support cervical health. Most cervical cancers occur in those who either have not or have less frequently been screened [2]. Barriers to screening, diagnosis, and treatment, including differences in access to and quality of care impacted by institutionalized racism and health system structure, result in unacceptable cervical cancer inequities across many countries. We can do much better.

Human Papillomavirus and Cervical Cancer

Human papillomavirus (HPV) causes cervical cancer. For most people, this virus is naturally eliminated, preventing abnormalities of cervical cells and cancer. Almost everyone comes into contact with HPV, and most people with HPV detected on the cervix do not develop cancer. However, for some, persistent infection by certain types of HPV can cause cervical cancer. The majority of precancerous lesions (cervical dysplasia) and cervical cancers are caused by HPV types 16 and 18 [3].

Compared with cervical cytology (the "cervical smear" involving a speculum examination by a trained provider), HPV-based screening is a more sensitive method for detecting cervical changes that may lead to cancer, providing 60–70% greater protection [4]. This better test enables greater detection of precancerous diseases compared to cytology. The negative HPV test provides protection that cancer will not occur in the next 5 years, supporting a longer interval between screens (e.g., 5 years).

HPV Self-Testing: An Equity Tool for Cervical Cancer Prevention

HPV self-testing using a vaginal swab is a game changer, providing sensitivity and specificity comparable with clinical testing [5] and reducing deaths by cervical cancer. For Indigenous peoples in high-income settler-colonial nation-states, HPV self-testing is more likely to be taken up compared with cervical cytology [6, 7].

Women appreciate the privacy and noninvasiveness and call it positive and empowering for them to be able to do it themselves. Women described it as taking the whakamā (reticence) out of the process: "I really actually enjoyed the process … less intrusive, that's what I liked, not having someone else to look at your bits to do it, and that whole whakamā [reticence] around it, and just something I could do with no concerns or no difficulties" [8].

Described as an empowering method, people report that, as a descriptive term, "self-testing" is, in itself, empowering [9].

When offered in a culturally responsive way, high uptake of HPV self-testing increases opportunities for people to successfully engage in follow-up diagnosis/treatment if required, substantially reducing inequities.

G. Garvey (ed.), *Indigenous and Tribal Peoples and Cancer*, https://doi.org/10.1007/978-3-031-56806-0_34

No Elimination Without Us!

The World Health Organization (WHO) recommends that all countries offer HPV testing as the primary method for cervical screening [10]. In May 2018, the WHO Director General announced a global call for action to eliminate cervical cancer, and in August 2020, the World Health Assembly adopted the global strategy for cervical cancer elimination (incidence rate of below four per 100,000 women). To achieve elimination in the next century, each country is called to meet the 90-70-90 targets by 2030:

- 90% of girls fully vaccinated with the HPV vaccine by the age of 15.
- 70% of women screened with a high-performance test by 35 and again by 45 years of age (scaling up to 95% in 2045).
- 90% of women identified with precancer treated and 90% of women with invasive cancer managed.

The WHO targets seek to address the unjust differential burden of cervical cancer between low-, middle-, and high-income countries, but they fail to address the rights of Indigenous peoples to be counted within the elimination targets. In this way, within-country inequities remain hidden. No country should be allowed to declare elimination without Indigenous peoples also reaching the target: *No Elimination Without Us!*

International Alliances

Concerned by the inequitable burden of HPV disease for Indigenous peoples globally and the lack of meaningful action to improve Indigenous cervical health, an international collaboration of Indigenous and non-Indigenous researchers, clinicians, and stakeholders published a call to action [11]. The International Indigenous HPV Alliance (IIHpvA), supported by the International Papillomavirus Society (IPVS), outlined fundamental principles to guide an equity-driven approach involving partnerships with Indigenous peoples and communities, with Indigenous leadership. To reduce Indigenous HPV-related health burden, recommendations for action included addressing and improving Indigenous data quality and ensuring that HPV-related issues affecting Indigenous peoples are presented at relevant forums. The IIHpvA continues to work to ensure that the call-to-action "No Elimination Without Us" is shared with a wide range of audiences (including media) and offers Indigenous-led appropriate and sustainable solutions to inform equitable elimination action strategies.

Cervical Cancer Prevention in Aotearoa

The National Cervical Screening Program (NCSP) in Aotearoa New Zealand was established in 1991. Prior to this, opportunistic screening was conducted in many general practices and family planning clinics, but there was no organized program nor national standards. Until 2023, those eligible for screening (since November 2019 between the ages of 25 and 69; previously between the ages of 20 and 69) were recalled three-yearly for cervical cytology, with recall administered firstly through primary care/general practice and back-up by a central register. While this led to a reduction in cervical cancer incidence by 50%, this screening method has never reached Māori equitably—it has failed Māori. The latest screening coverage data published by the National Screening Unit indicates that 41% of wāhine Māori (Māori women) are underscreened or never screened, compared with 21% of European/other women. These inequities are unacceptable. We need more Māori voices informing the NCSP! We need Māori-led solutions!

He Tapu Te Whare Tangata (The Sacred House/s of Humanity)

He Tapu Te Whare Tangata (The Sacred House/s of Humanity) is the name of a Kaupapa Māori (by, with, and for Māori) body of research, with the goal to eliminate cervical cancer among wāhine Māori through improved screening. He Tapu Te Whare Tangata reflects the veneration of wāhine Māori and people with cervices as whare tangata (the house where human life grows) and the sacredness of the womb from a Māori worldview. The cervix is the neck of the womb, and its health impacts the ability of the womb to fulfill its role as the whare tangata and the ability of wāhine Māori to lead long and healthy lives [8].

The Kaupapa Māori (by, with, and for Māori) research lens of He Tapu Te Whare Tangata values and privileges Māori experiences. Kaupapa Māori research paradigms see being Māori as normal and draw on principles such as Tino rangatiratanga (self-determination), He taonga tuku iho (cultural aspirations), Ako (culturally preferred pedagogy), Kia piki ake i ngā raruraru o te kainga (socioeconomic mediation), Whānau (extended family structure), and Kaupapa (collective philosophy) [12]. These principles drive Kaupapa Māori research projects that challenge inequitable systems to transform and ensure the best health outcomes and wellness for Māori, as Māori [13].

Through the research projects of He Tapu Te Whare Tangata, starting in 2016, HPV self-testing was made possible in selected regions and communities with high Māori populations. This was led by Māori and overseen by kaumātua (Māori elders and knowledge holders). Māori and non-Māori researchers, clinicians, and kaiāwhina (nonclinical community health workers) worked collaboratively in a strength-based, Māori-centered approach, guided by iwi (Tribal) partnerships (including with the Ngāti Pāhauwera Development Trust and Ngāti Porou Oranga) and reflecting tikanga Māori (Māori customs) [14]. Throughout, strong Māori community voices were featured alongside general practice, colposcopy services, and support-to-screen services, with key learnings and findings shared regularly with stakeholders and the National Screening Unit responsible for the NCSP (see Fig. 34.1 showing HPV self-testing promotional material).

Studies of He Tapu Te Whare Tangata (including qualitative interviewing, clinical implementation, and randomized controlled trials) have shown HPV self-testing to be highly acceptable. For underscreened wāhine Māori, the offer of an HPV self-test was almost three times more likely to result in a cervical screen [15]. Wāhine Māori >10 years from their last screen were almost five times as likely to be screened when offered HPV self-testing compared with the control group (cervical cytology with a speculum).

Wāhine Māori and their whānau have highlighted the importance of culturally safe and empathetic care through the cervical screening pathway—from self-testing to diagnosis and treatment [16]. Care must be taken in the delivery of HPV-positive self-test and colposcopy results to ensure understanding and mitigate any trauma.

Research as Activism

Offering the new and better cervical screening test through He Tapu Te Whare Tangata in communities with predominantly Māori populations was an intentional equity action—research as activism! Māori-driven research, privileging whānau Māori voices and experiences, has challenged the inequitable cervical screening system, highlighted system failings and barriers, and introduced possible solutions. As stated by influential Māori health champion the late Dr. Paratene Ngata, "If you get it right for Māori, you get it right for all."

Working overall toward global Indigenous wellbeing, together we can share research evidence, call for the improvement of safe Indigenous data collection, and build and grow alliances and collaborations that challenge colonialized systems to achieve equity for Indigenous peoples as a fundamental right [17].

Campaigning and Advocacy

In the absence of meaningful government action, we have used research to support Indigenous peoples in determining their own transformative change. The work of He Tapu Te Whare Tangata informed wider activism, including the establishment of a nationwide campaign committee of champions, which led to a submission to the Māori Health Select Committee in 2019 to persuade the Ministry of Health and

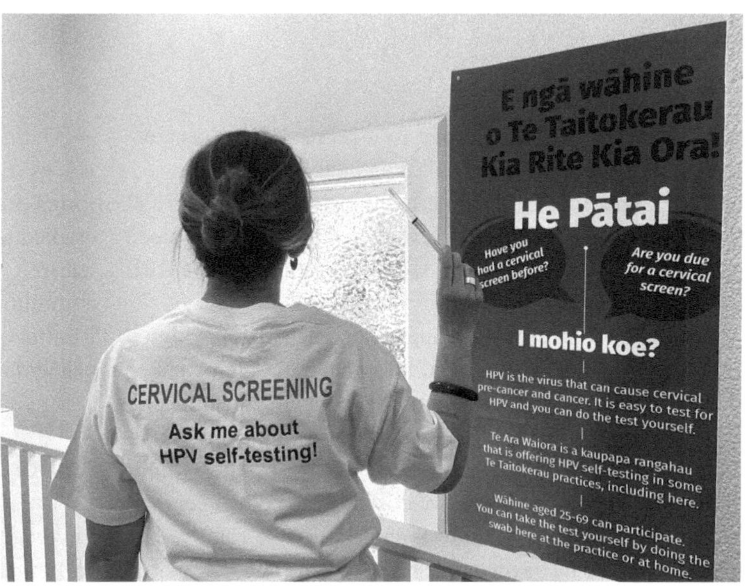

Fig. 34.1 Promoting HPV self-testing as a cervical screen for a research project in Te Tai Tokerau (Northland Aotearoa). (Photo: F Storey)

Fig. 34.2 Submission to the Māori Health Select Committee (pictured left to right: kaumātua Matthew Bennett, Lady Tureiti Moxon, Professor Bev Lawton, and Dame Silvia Cartwright). (Photo: NZ House of Representatives collection)

Fig. 34.3 Online petition host and campaigners calling for the HPV self-test to be introduced in a new National Cervical Screening Program (pictured left to right: Tracey Mackay, Kim Chappel, Jordanna Hermens, and Natalia Repia). (Photo: F Storey)

government to fund the change to a primary HPV cervical screening program (see Fig. 34.2) and public lobbying.

Campaigns included online petitions: "Prevent Cervical Cancer! Introduce HPV Self-Testing to Aotearoa—We Need it NOW" in 2021 (see Fig. 34.3) and "Urgent Call for FREE Cervical Screening" in 2023.

Through public crowdfunding, a documentary was filmed at "Shear-4-a-Cause"—a rural farming community sheep shearing fundraiser where a mobile cervical screening unit was piloted (see Fig. 34.4). In the film, shearers, wool handlers, whānau, health practitioners, and researchers highlighted the continuing barrier of cost and the unique cervical screening challenges faced by wāhine who live rurally. The film was published by an online news website and was shared widely through social media.

These campaigns featured strong Māori community voices and provided easily accessible and shareable platforms for individuals and organizations to champion the eradication of cervical cancer and a change to the NCSP. This led to a call from the champions for a cross-political party commitment to free cervical screening for all and an Aotearoa Elimination Action Strategy setting 2035 as the year cervical cancer is eliminated in Aotearoa New Zealand.

Equity Levers

Leveraging for change required a collective of individuals and organizations working together. The wide range of support, encouragement, and campaigning from kaumātua, Māori health providers, iwi organizations, communities

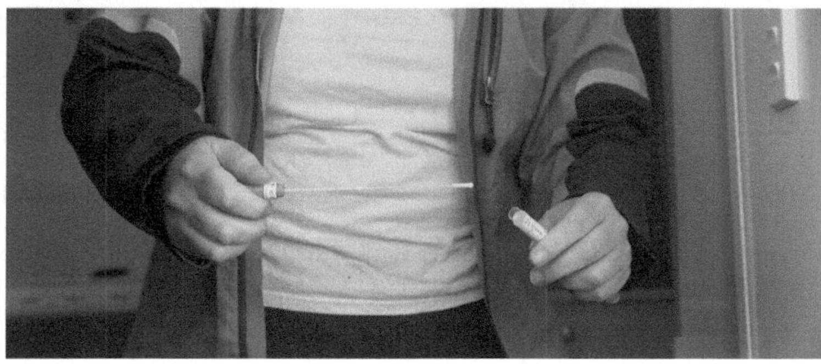

Fig. 34.4 The offer of HPV self-testing at "Shear-4-a-Cause" shown in the film "Cervical Screening in Rural Aotearoa: Preventing the Preventable." (Visit www.hpvselftest.nz to watch the documentary on YouTube)

associated with He Tapu Te Whare Tangata, medical and practitioner colleges, petition signers, Hei Āhuru Mōwai Māori Cancer Leadership Aotearoa, members of the IIHpvA, and others together contributed to seeing a more just and equitable program finally actioned. Whether the new NCSP responds adequately to the evidence provided by He Tapu Te Whare Tangata in regard to access, equity, and sustainability remains to be seen.

Policy Impact

In May 2021, funding to change the NCSP was announced, five years after the Minister of Health had declared that Aotearoa New Zealand would move to primary HPV screening. The Health (National Cervical Screening Program) Amendment Bill was passed in June 2021, during which the work of He Tapu Te Whare Tangata and its impact was acknowledged, and researchers received parliamentary thanks. In September 2023, after years of campaigning, challenging, and championing, Aotearoa New Zealand became the first high-income country to switch straight to HPV self-testing as the primary screening method for their cervical cancer prevention program. However, further lobbying was—and continues to be—required to ensure the new program is equitable. This included persuading the NCSP that participants presenting with HPV types 16 or 18 are to be referred directly to colposcopy [18]. Only as a result of extensive feedback and lobbying from key groups and organizations (including findings and recommendations from He Tapu Te Whare Tangata) and arguments that an additional cytology option could lead to increased inequities did the NCSP change the drafted pathway.

Separate from this, the collective of individuals and organizations working together have campaigned for cervical screening to be fully funded. While this led the government to commit limited funding to make cervical screening free for Māori and other populations at higher risk of cervical cancer for one year only, this is not enough. The call for the NSCP to be fully funded for all remains to bring Aotearoa New Zealand closer to our goal of cervical cancer elimination and to save lives.

While associated research activism in Aotearoa New Zealand has contributed to informing a new (albeit overdue) program, engaging in a high level of advocacy to ensure it was informed by Kaupapa Māori research findings, whānau voices, champions, and an equity-driven approach was not without its challenges. Whānau, researchers, and others engaging in such "positive disruption" benefited from support from other Indigenous peoples and non-Indigenous allies around the world, together influencing transformational changes and working toward Indigenous wellbeing. No one should die of this preventable cancer!

We first and foremost acknowledge the whānau who have generously participated in He Tapu Te Whare Tangata, with thanks to the practice groups involved—Queen Street Practice, Ngāti Porou Oranga, and the communities of Te Tai Tokerau. Special thanks to Te Tātai Hauora o Hine Kāhui Kaumātua (Council of Elders) for their guidance and vision—Matthew Bennett, Charlie Lambert, Wendy Dallas Katoa, and Dame Areta Koopu. We acknowledge our fellow researchers and the champions who have contributed and mobilized support to bring about change, including the Cancer Society of New Zealand, He Hono Wāhine, RANZCOG, Smear Your Mea, RNZCGP, Mana Wāhine, Mahitahi Hauora PHE, and Hei Āhuru Mōwai Cancer Leadership Aotearoa—ngā mihi (thank you). We pay our respects to all whānau who have been impacted by cervical cancer—me aro kī te hā o Hine–ahu-one (pay heed to the dignity of women).

References

1. Vasilevska M, Ross SA, Gesink D, Fisman DN. Relative risk of cervical cancer in indigenous women in Australia, Canada, New Zealand, and the United States: a systematic review and meta-analysis. *J Public Health Policy*. 2012;33(2):148–64. https://doi.org/10.1057/jphp.2012.8
2. Sykes P, Williman J, Innes C, Hider P. *Review of Cervical Cancer Occurrences in Relation to Screening History in New Zealand for the Years 2013–2017*. Christchurch: University of Otago Department of Obstetrics & Gynaecology; 2019. Available from: chrome-extension://efaidnbmnnnibpcajpcglclefindmkaj/https://www.nsu.govt.nz/system/files/resources/cancer-case-review-2013-2017-final-report-29-august-2019.pdf

3. Rerucha CM, Caro RJ, Wheeler VL. Cervical cancer screening. *Am Fam Physician*. 2018;97(7):441–8.
4. Ronco G, Giorgi-Rossi P, Carozzi F, Confortini M, Dalla Palma P, Del Mistro A, et al. Efficacy of human papillomavirus testing for the detection of invasive cervical cancers and cervical intraepithelial neoplasia: a randomised controlled trial. *Lancet Oncol*. 2010;11(3):249–57. https://doi.org/10.1016/S1470-2045(09)70360-2
5. Arbyn M, Smith SB, Temin S, Sultana F, Castle P. Detecting cervical precancer and reaching underscreened women by using HPV testing on self samples: updated meta-analyses. *BMJ*. 2018;363. https://doi.org/10.1136/bmj.k4823
6. Winer RL, Gonzales AA, Noonan CJ, Cherne SL, Buchwald DS, Assessing acceptability of self-sampling kits, prevalence, and risk factors for human papillomavirus infection in American Indian women. *J Community Health*. 2016;41(5):1049–61. https://doi.org/10.1007/s10900-016-0189-3
7. Cerigo H, Macdonald ME, Franco EL, Brassard P. HPV detection by self-sampling in Nunavik, Quebec: Inuit women's sampling method preferences. *Int J Indig Health*. 2012;8(1):29–39. https://doi.org/10.18357/ijih81201212386
8. Adcock A, Stevenson K, Cram F, MacDonald EJ, Geller S, Hermens J, et al. He Tapu Te Whare Tangata (sacred house of humanity): Under-screened Māori women talk about HPV self-testing cervical screening clinical pathways. *Int J Gynecol Obstet*. 2021;155(2):275–81. https://doi.org/10.1002/ijgo.13873
9. Whop LJ, Smith MA, Butler TL, Adcock A, Bartholomew K, Goodman MT, et al. Achieving cervical cancer elimination among Indigenous women. *Prev Med*. 2021;144:106314. https://doi.org/10.1016/j.ypmed.2020.106314
10. World Health Organization. *Global Strategy to Accelerate the Elimination of Cervical Cancer as a Public Health Problem*. Geneva; 2020. Available from: https://www.who.int/publications/i/item/9789240014107
11. Lawton B, Heffernan M, Wurtak G, Steben M, Lhaki P, Cram F, et al. IPVS Policy Statement addressing the burden of HPV disease for Indigenous peoples. *Papillomavirus Res*. 2020;9:100191. https://doi.org/10.1016/j.pvr.2019.100191
12. Smith GH. *The development of Kaupapa Maori: Theory and praxis* [PhD Thesis]. Auckland, University of Auckland; 1997.
13. Cram F. Kaupapa Māori health research. In: Liamputtong P, editor. *Handbook of research methods in health and social sciences*. Switzerland: Springer International Publishing; 2017. p. 1–18.
14. Lawton B, MacDonald EJ, Storey F, Stanton J, Adcock A, Gibson M, et al. A Model for Empowering Rural Solutions for Cervical Cancer Prevention (He Tapu Te Whare Tangata): Protocol for a Cluster Randomized Crossover Trial. *JMIR Res Protoc*. 2023;12(1):12e51643. https://doi.org/10.2196/51643
15. MacDonald EJ, Geller S, Sibanda N, Stevenson K, Denmead L, Adcock A, et al. Reaching under-screened/never-screened indigenous peoples with human papilloma virus self-testing: A community-based cluster randomised controlled trial. *Aust N Z J Obstet Gynaecol*. 2021;61(1):135–41. https://doi.org/10.1111/ajo.13285
16. Adcock A, Cram F, Lawton B, Geller S, Hibma M, Sykes P, et al. Acceptability of self-taken vaginal HPV sample for cervical screening among an under-screened Indigenous population. *Aust N A J Obstet Gynaecol*. 2019;59(2):301–7. https://doi.org/10.1111/ajo.12933
17. Hickey S, Roe Y, Ireland S, Kildea S, Haora P, Gao Y, et al. A call for action that cannot go to voicemail: Research activism to urgently improve Indigenous perinatal health and wellbeing. Women and Birth. 2021 Jul 1;34(4):303–5. https://doi.org/10.1016/j.wombi.2021.03.011
18. Bartholomew K, Lawton B, Sherman S, Bromhead C, Grant, J, McPherson G., et al. Recommendations for implementing HPV self-testing in Aotearoa. *N Z Med J*. 2021;134(1535):11–16.

Overcoming Barriers to Bowel Screening for First Nations Australians

35

Jenny Brands and Gail Garvey

Key Points

- A one-size-fits-all cancer screening program is unlikely to address logistical and cultural barriers that may discourage First Nations people from participating.
- Co-designing access to cancer screening programs to meet the needs and preferences of First Nations Australians can be an effective way to increase participation.
- A key enabler to increasing First Nations people's participation in bowel cancer screening is the involvement of a trained and trusted health professional to explain why bowel screening is important and to demonstrate how to do the test.

Bowel cancer kills more than one million people globally each year. It has few distinctive symptoms until it has reached an advanced stage, by which time survival rates are low. However, if diagnosed early, more than 90% of cases can be successfully treated [1].

Australia's National Bowel Cancer Screening Program (NBCSP) aims to reduce deaths from bowel cancer by detecting early signs of the disease. Drawing on Australian Government data, eligible Australians aged 50–74 are mailed a free test every two years, to be completed at home [2]. Like many bowel cancer screening programs around the world, the Australian program uses an immunochemical fecal occult blood test (iFOBT). In 2016, participation in this program was 41% nationally but was considerably lower among some population groups, particularly those in very remote locations (28%) and First Nations Australians (23%) [2].

Here, we describe a model of an alternative access pathway for the NBCSP, which we piloted at primary healthcare centers across Australia. Our work demonstrates that an alternative access pathway can achieve participation by First Nations people at similar rates to non-Indigenous Australians [3]. An adapted version of the alternative access model has since been incorporated as a permanent component of the NBCSP and is accessible to all Australians [4].

The development of the alternative access pathway was informed by the Promoting Action on Research Implementation in Health Services (PARiHS) framework [5]. This framework is based on the simple concept that effective implementation depends on understanding the evidence-based innovation to be implemented and the context in which it is to be implemented and facilitating the bridging of gaps between the two. In this case, the PARiHS framework was applied to understand how gaps between the evidence-based innovation (the NBCSP) and the context (how it fits the needs and preferences of First Nations people) might be improved. The project was led by a senior Aboriginal researcher, and its governance included First Nations advisors throughout the project. We consulted key stakeholder groups, including the Indigenous primary healthcare sector; Indigenous and non-Indigenous healthcare professionals; First Nations people eligible for bowel screening; individuals, families, and carers of First Nations people affected by bowel cancer; cancer councils; and relevant government departments. Our research involved four phases: (1) initial research to understand barriers and enablers to screening, (2) development of training and promotional resources to support the delivery of an alternative access pathway, (3) large-scale piloting of an alternative access model, and (4) evaluation of the model.

Barriers That Discourage First Nations People from Screening

Our research identified several key barriers to participation in the NBCSP. Most stemmed from a poor fit between the design features of the screening program and the diverse geographic, economic, and social contexts of First Nations communities.

- The NBCSP uses data from Medicare, Australia's universal healthcare system, to identify potential NBCSP participants. Some First Nations Australians are not enrolled

G. Garvey (ed.), *Indigenous and Tribal Peoples and Cancer*, https://doi.org/10.1007/978-3-031-56806-0_35

in Medicare, or may not have their contact details up to date, and thus will not receive a bowel screening kit.

- Some of those who receive kits may throw them away unopened, for reasons including the lack of understanding of what they contain, feeling alienated by the appearance, or distrust of the materials sent by the government.
- Some participants may have difficulty reading test instructions that are text heavy and written in small print.
- There is a distaste for the test itself. Many people are put off by the idea of storing samples in the fridge and imagine the test involves the direct handling of feces.
- Some people feel "shame" (embarrassment, shyness, discomfort, disrespect) about being seen carrying a bowel screening kit.

The Alternative Access Model

The alternative approach involved providing NBCSP kits to local primary healthcare centers, where health professionals have trusted relationships with eligible participants and can hand them kits directly. The appearance of the kit was improved by covering the front of the envelope with a large, brightly colored sticker featuring a First Nations design (Fig. 35.1). Healthcare professionals were actively engaged in their patients' bowel screening journey, discussing the kit with participants, explaining how to use it, and following up with patients who received positive test results.

What Did We Do?

We conducted a cluster-randomized controlled trial, with randomization of eligible health centers to receive either low-intensity or high-intensity support to implement the alternative approach. All centers received access to an online training module for health professionals, an implementation manual for the alternative approach, telephone help desk support, and promotion and information resources (e.g., posters, postcards, a flip chart, fact sheets, and colorful stickers to cover the front of the standard iFOBT kit). Health centers in the high-intensity group were also offered face-to-face training as part of a site visit by members of the research team. Thirty-six primary healthcare centers took part in the trial over 12 months.

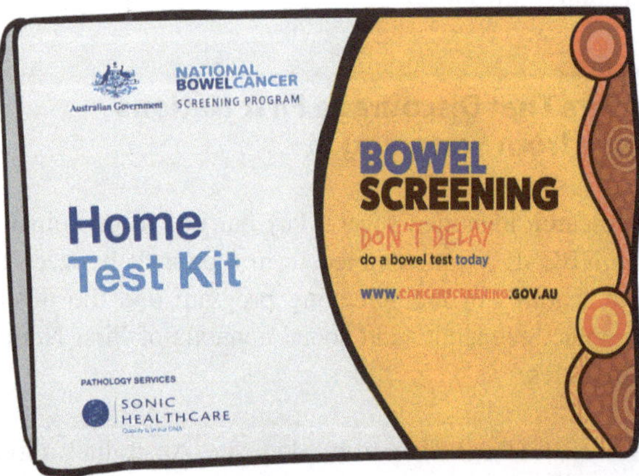

Fig. 35.1 Culturally relevant sticker attached to NBCSP kits

The trial resulted in a significantly higher participation rate for First Nations people (39.8%) compared to the usual pathway (23.3%), a rate more closely matching that of non-Indigenous Australians (40.6%). Screening rates were comparable across urban (47%), regional (45%), and remote (38%) locations. Of note, a 47% screening rate was achieved by those from the lowest socioeconomic group, compared with 37% for all Australians for the usual pathway.

Screening participation rates showed no significant difference between health centers that were in either the low-intensity or high-intensity support groups. Staff from both groups experienced a significant increase in confidence in discussing bowel screening with First Nations patients. The high-intensity group (which received face-to-face training) also improved their perceptions of their roles in relation to bowel screening.

Factors for Success

Several factors were identified that encouraged First Nations people to participate in the NBCSP:

- *Verbal and visual communication from a trusted health professional:* having a trusted health professional discuss the test with patients, explain its importance, and demonstrate how to do it was key. Doctors referred to the kit as a "game changer" and said that being able to handle the kit, show how to use it, and give it to the patient dissolved many previous barriers. Many health professionals reported that when they demonstrated how to take samples, patients responded: "Is that all it is?"
- *Education for healthcare professionals to overcome barriers to action:* prior to the trial, primary healthcare professionals only typically became involved in the NBCSP if a patient returned a positive test result. Some health professionals felt uneasy about raising the issue of bowel screening with First Nations patients for fear of causing offense. Aboriginal Health Workers expressed a desire to know more about bowel cancer and cancer care in order to increase their confidence in providing information to individuals, families, and the broader community. All health professionals had access to training that included information about the national program, bowel cancer, cancer care, the trial, and evidence-based techniques for commu-

nicating with First Nations patients about bowel screening.

- *Key messages and a starter set of health promotion materials:* health professionals were provided with a small set of evidence-based key messages, supported by a range of visually appealing materials. These materials were used largely as conversation starters, with patients receiving key messages through conversation.
- *Addressing the needs and preferences of patients:* health centers were encouraged to consider and address specific barriers to screening experienced by their patient cohort. For example, some health centers offered to store patient test samples at the clinic and mail them on behalf of the patient; others had the community bus driver collect test samples from the patient's home in a small cool box.
- *Getting the messages right:* the culturally appropriate key messages and materials used in the trial were developed and tested through many iterations, by and with First Nations consumers, educators, and health professionals. Some of the most powerful key messages came from community-developed music videos. An experienced facilitator and music production team worked with each of four First Nations communities to make a five-minute music video to encourage people to carry out the bowel screening test.

Patient Perspectives

The COVID-19 pandemic limited follow-up with participants. A small number of patients ($n = 5$) who completed the NBCSP test after receiving it from their local health center provided some feedback about the trial.

These patients perceived their health centers as trusted, credible, culturally safe places, which improved their receptiveness to screening. The health center's supportive approach provided important encouragement and support, features that were absent when the kit was received in the mail.

One patient said, "The Aboriginal Health Worker contacted me and we had that little yarn [talk about bowel screening] … He's very respectful and diligent and thorough and a good bit of sense of humor you know … He explained it all to me … rather than just having the package arrive."

Another said, "They both came [Aboriginal Health Workers] and dropped it off [at home] … went through a bit of an explanation and so I found it quite simple … but I think, to me, I probably wouldn't have bothered for a few more years unless they came and chased me up."

Staff's persistence in asking patients if they had taken the test also encouraged completion: "I think [when it comes through the post], people don't want to know about it and will probably … forget about it, but if you come in here and you've got [health professionals] on your case, well you get it done."

Participants reported on the impact of seeing First Nations people talk about bowel cancer on the health center's TV in the waiting room: "Yeah, they have a TV [medical information channel] … I saw one lady talking about her dad and she wished that he had done it, that he'd sought out help a lot earlier and he wouldn't have died on her … Because of the similarities in his life and my life … I was thinking, 'Oh well, that might happen to me [so I] better have a check-up.'"

A participant who received a positive test result became a passionate advocate for doing the test: "After … that first time … I was actually telling my mates down the pub and everywhere, you know, about doing the test and, you know, because you never know, it can grab you any time, bowel cancer."

Conclusions

Our team demonstrated that improvements in Indigenous health, in this case, cancer screening, are more likely to be achieved if Indigenous people are involved throughout the entire project. In addition, contextualizing projects or practices with input from Indigenous people and other key stakeholders is more likely to result in policies, programs, services, and projects that are appropriate, feasible, effective, and sustainable.

Following the successful trial, the Australian Government has developed a modified version of the alternative pathway model as an ongoing option in the NBCSP. Recent data suggest that First Nations participation in the NBCSP has increased from 23% in 2016 to 31% in 2023 [6]. The 2023 participation rate for all Australians (41%) remains unchanged from 2016.

Acknowledgments The National Indigenous Bowel Screening Pilot was funded by the Cancer Screening Section of the Australian Government Department of Health and Aged Care. We also acknowledge the generous contributions of participating health centers, health professionals, state and territory government cancer screening units, and the Menzies School of Health Research staff who made up the project team.

References

1. Morgan E, Arnold M, Gini A, Lorenzoni V, Cabasag CJ, Laversanne M, et al. Global burden of colorectal cancer in 2020 and 2040: incidence and mortality estimates from GLOBOCAN. *Gut*. 2023;(72): 338–344. https://doi.org/10.1136/gutjnl-2022-327736
2. Australian Institute of Health and Welfare. *National Bowel Cancer Screening Program: monitoring report 2016*. Canberra: Australian Institute of Health and Welfare; 2016.

3. Menzies School of Health Research, Australian Government Department of Health and Aged Care. *Final report on the National Indigenous Bowel Screening Pilot.* 2020 [cited 2023 September 12]. Available from: https://www.health.gov.au/resources/publications/final-report-on-the-national-indigenous-bowel-screening-pilot?language=en
4. Australian Government Department of Health and Ageing. *For health professionals with Indigenous patients.* [Internet]. [cited 2023 September 18]. Available from: https://www.health.gov.au/our-work/national-bowel-cancer-screening-program/indigenous/health-professionals#alternative-access-to-kits
5. Harvey G, Kitson A. PARIHS revisited: from heuristic to integrated framework for the successful implementation of knowledge into practice. *Implement Sci.* 2016;11:33. https://doi.org/10.1186/s13012-016-0398-2
6. Australian Institute of Health and Welfare. *National Bowel Cancer Screening Program monitoring report 2023.* 2023 Jun [cited 2023 September 15]. Available from: https://www.aihw.gov.au/reports/cancer-screening/nbcsp-monitoring-2023/summary

36 Commercial Tobacco and Cancer

Raglan Maddox, Andrew Waa, Patricia Nez Henderson, Tom Calma, and Michelle Kennedy

Key Points

- "Commercial tobacco" is a harmful product made and distributed by the tobacco industry. Commercial tobacco does not include "traditional," "ceremonial," or "sacred tobacco" used by Indigenous peoples and communities for ceremonial and cultural purposes.
- Commercial tobacco, addiction, and dependence on nicotine products are closely linked to colonization for many Indigenous peoples.
- Commercial tobacco and its derivatives, including derived products and associated toxicant(s), impact physical, social, emotional, and spiritual wellbeing.
- Commercial tobacco is the leading cause of preventable lung cancer and contributes to a significant portion of global cancer deaths.
- Despite colonization and active targeting by the tobacco industry and affiliates, there has been progress in reducing smoking prevalence in Indigenous communities. To help accelerate and eliminate reductions in tobacco-related disease and death and improve the health and wellbeing of Indigenous peoples and future generations, Indigenous-led programs and policies, along with structural reforms, are essential.

Indigenous peoples encompass a diversity of nations, practices, languages, knowledge systems, experiences, and relationships that bring vibrant diversity to the world. Indigenous peoples across the world have unique practices and relationships, particularly in relation to the natural environment and its flora and fauna [1]. It is important to recognize this diversity, including diversity and relationships with tobacco. Accordingly, it is important not to conflate commercial tobacco with ceremonial tobacco [1].

The word "tobacco" has roots in Taíno, a language of the Arawakan people of the Caribbean, but it was appropriated by the Spanish in 1550 [1]. The claiming of words from languages was a mechanism of colonization. European settlers continued colonial practices by modifying and industrializing tobacco production as a plantation crop, leading to the mass production of adulterated tobacco, which became cheap, widely available, and easily accessible [1]. To further lower costs and increase availability, the tobacco industry and its affiliates carefully and purposefully increased the nicotine content and addictive properties of tobacco, using additives to mask its smells, make it more palatable, reduce production expenses, and make products more easily accessible. Today, the mass production, promotion, and distribution of adulterated tobacco pose a direct threat to the sacred nature of tobacco for many Indigenous peoples [1].

The production, promotion, and distribution of commercial tobacco globally and the resultant addiction among Indigenous peoples and communities have been described as a form of modern colonization and subjugation [1, 2]. Indigenous knowledges and practices, such as ceremonial tobacco use, have been suppressed [2]. For example, across Turtle Island (North America), the Code of Indian Offenses in 1883, the Indian Act of 1885, and associated amendments prohibited ceremonial practices involving tobacco but allowed commercial tobacco use [1]. The suppression of ceremonial practices led to the systematic embedding of commercial tobacco into ceremonial practices, acutely undermining the connection of Indigenous communities with the native tobacco plant [1].

The machinery of colonization is often implicated as a "fundamental cause" that leads to the unequal distribution of the social and economic determinants of health and wellbeing. The unequal distribution of the social and economic determinants of health drives commercial tobacco use, such as socioeconomic status (SES) [3], alongside issues such as the forced removal and relocation of Indigenous peoples from their land, the removal of children, exclusion from education systems, and exclusion from the cash economy [3, 4]. In Australia, commercial tobacco was used as a form of payment and rationing of food in lieu of wages until the late 1960s, actively embedding and valuing commercial tobacco use from an early age [4]. As a result of colonial machinery, Indigenous populations have tended to report

G. Garvey (ed.), *Indigenous and Tribal Peoples and Cancer*, https://doi.org/10.1007/978-3-031-56806-0_36

Fig. 36.1 Changes in lung health depicted using flora native to Australia. (Photo: Claudine Thornton Creative)

lower socioeconomic status, which is a risk factor for commercial tobacco use, impacting individual and collective agency to stay nicotine free. Low SES among Indigenous populations is a common consequence of colonization that has persisted across generations, eroding power and influence, social structures, and community resources. While the drivers of commercial tobacco use are similar for Indigenous and non-Indigenous peoples, Indigenous peoples are disproportionately exposed to them.

Commercial Tobacco-Related Mortality

The World Health Organization (WHO) Framework Convention on Tobacco Control (FCTC) recognizes the disproportionate harm caused to Indigenous peoples by commercial tobacco use and promotes the participation of Indigenous peoples and communities in developing, implementing, and evaluating tobacco control programs and policies [5]. The tobacco industry and its affiliates continue to fuel the tobacco epidemic, with commercial tobacco smoking being one of the single largest causes of preventable disease and death, including cancer. More than eight million people die as a result of commercial tobacco use each year, including 1.3 million people whose deaths are due to secondhand smoke [6]. A large proportion of these deaths are from early heart attacks, chronic lung diseases, and cancers.

Commercial Tobacco and Cancer

The landmark 1964 Surgeon General's report *Smoking and Health* concluded that commercial tobacco smoking was a cause of lung cancer [7]. Since then, researchers have continued to advance their understanding of the mechanisms of tobacco-related diseases, including cancer [8]. This has reaffirmed the notion that there is no safe cigarette [9]. When individuals inhale commercial tobacco smoke, whether directly or passively, they are exposed to over 7000 chemicals, with hundreds of these being hazardous and at least 69 recognized as carcinogens [8, 10]. Further, the carefully and purposefully modified and enhanced addictive properties of commercial tobacco make it more difficult to abstain from and lead to greater exposure to toxicants, both for the person who smokes and for others around them. These chemicals are rapidly assimilated by cells within the body, leading to cellular alterations that give rise to diseases [8]. Polyaromatic hydrocarbons (PAH), *N*-nitrosamines, aromatic amines, 1,3-butadiene, benzene, aldehydes, and ethylene oxide are among the most important carcinogens in commercial tobacco because of their potencies and levels in commercial tobacco smoke. The major mechanisms through which commercial tobacco smoking causes cancer include:

- Exposure to cancer-causing substances (carcinogens).
- Formation of DNA adducts by linking these carcinogens to DNA.
- Accumulation of lasting genetic mutations [8].

Commercial tobacco use causes at least 12 different types of cancer, accounts for 25% of all cancer deaths globally, and is the biggest cause of lung cancer—causing at least 80% of global lung cancer incidence [8, 10]. Commercial tobacco use has a well-established causal relationship with head and neck, pancreatic, liver, and colorectal cancers [8, 10] and is responsible for over 60% of cancers in the larynx, oral cavity, and esophagus [10]. Figure 36.1 uses flowers to demonstrate how smoking affects lung health.

People who smoke commercial tobacco are at increased risk of death. Two-thirds of all people who smoke commercial tobacco long-term will die from smoking-related diseases [9]. Eliminating commercial tobacco would save approximately 22,000 lives per day worldwide, equating to over 900 lives every hour [6]. In Australia, this includes 37% of all Indigenous Australian deaths, and 50% of deaths of Indigenous Australians aged over 45 [11]. In Aotearoa New Zealand, approximately 13.4% of deaths between 2013 and 2015 were linked to smoking, including 22.6% of deaths among Māori and 13.8% of deaths among Pacific peoples. Smoking contributed 2.1 years to the life expectancy gap in Māori men, 2.3 years in Māori women, 1.4 years in Pacific men, and 0.3 years in Pacific women [12]. Thus, the impact of commercial tobacco use—on Indigenous and non-Indigenous peoples and communities—is catastrophic [3, 6] (Fig. 36.2).

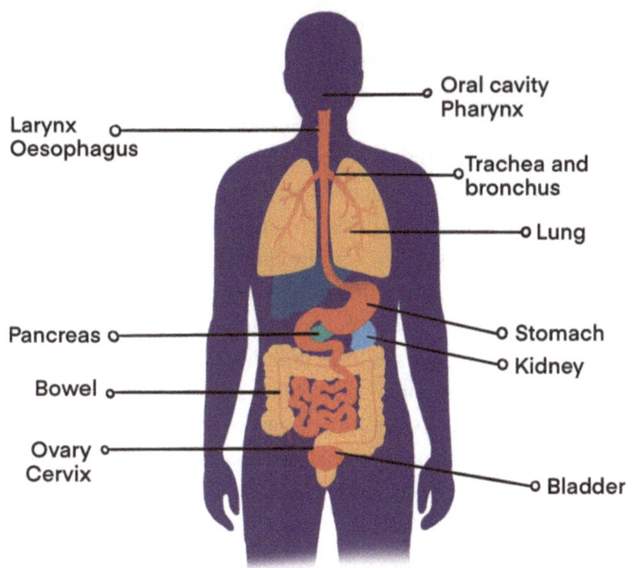

Fig. 36.2 Cancers related to commercial tobacco use. (Design: M Morton Ninomiya)

For people who smoke, quitting is beneficial for their health and wellbeing [8–10]. The quantity and duration of commercial tobacco use have a significant impact on an individual's susceptibility to cancer, with a dose-response relationship. In other words, the risk of cancer increases linearly with commercial tobacco smoke exposure. Reducing the amount of commercial tobacco consumed, ultimately to the point of complete cessation, is a vital step toward better health and wellbeing.

Commercial Tobacco Use: A Public Health Crisis

The substantial harm of commercial tobacco use has been understood since at least the 1950s. When commercial tobacco is used as "directed," it kills [7, 8]. Despite this understanding and the WHO FCTC, commercial tobacco use continues to be an international public health crisis [5]. Furthermore, it has a disproportionate impact on the health, economic, and cultural wellbeing of Indigenous peoples due to the disproportionately high drivers of commercial tobacco use experienced by Indigenous peoples [3].

Monitoring the drivers of commercial tobacco use and prevalence can assist in developing, implementing, and evaluating tobacco control programs and policies, including measures to reduce supply and demand [5]. Approximately 50% of the world's population is regularly surveyed regarding commercial tobacco use, including adolescents and adults [5]. In Australia, data suggest that there was a significant decline in smoking prevalence among Indigenous Australians from 2004 to 2018 (52% to 43%). This reflects the focus, efforts, and leadership in prioritizing smoke-free norms for Aboriginal and Torres Strait Islander communities [4]. In Canada, commercial tobacco prevalence is 40% among First Nations people, 49% among Inuit, and 37% among Métis [3]. In Aotearoa New Zealand, 21% of Māori people smoke, while in the USA, 32% of Indigenous American and Alaska Native populations smoke [11]. These figures are a stark contrast to smoking prevalence among the general populations in these countries, which vary from 12% (Aotearoa New Zealand) to 18% (Canada) [3, 11].

Commercial Tobacco Control Programs and Policies

The WHO FCTC recognizes the critical importance of engaging Indigenous peoples in developing, implementing, and evaluating tobacco control programs and policies. Self-determination is crucial for the health and wellbeing of Indigenous peoples, and communities should be actively involved in commercial tobacco control decision-making processes. Successful programs and policies for Indigenous peoples should consider [4]:

- *Cultural safety:* programs and policies should respect and align with the cultural values, beliefs, and practices of Indigenous communities to ensure acceptance and relevance.
- *Holistic approaches to health and wellbeing:* programs and policies should take into account the overall wellbeing of individuals and communities, recognizing that health and wellbeing are interconnected with various aspects of life, including social, spiritual, mental, and physical wellbeing.
- *Multifaceted approaches:* programs and policies should employ a variety of strategies and support, recognizing that there is no one-size-fits-all solution to addressing commercial tobacco use for any single Indigenous person or community.
- *Indigenous ways of knowing, being, and doing:* policies and programs should incorporate Indigenous worldviews and address the social determinants of health and wellbeing.
- *Self-determination:* Indigenous peoples need to be at all decision-making tables when programs and policies about commercial tobacco are discussed.

An example from Australia is the Tackling Indigenous Smoking program [13], which incorporates self-determination and opportunities for collaboration and coordination with different sectors. Programs like this help ensure that Indigenous peoples are decision-makers and foster smoke-free norms, ultimately preventing uptake and generating a supportive environment to quit and stay quit [4].

Indigenous Excellence: Accelerating Reductions in Commercial Tobacco Use

In Aotearoa New Zealand, after decades of Indigenous leadership, research, advocacy, and calls from communities, significant structural changes are expected through the Smokefree Aotearoa 2025 Action Plan [14]. This plan was designed to eliminate smoking in Aotearoa New Zealand by 2025 and help mitigate the structural drivers of commercial tobacco use that has disproportionately impacted Indigenous peoples. It had four key components:

- Making commercial tobacco less addictive by making the only commercially available cigarettes with very low nicotine [13].
- Reducing access to commercial tobacco through retail outlets [12].
- Preventing younger people and future generations from taking up smoking by implementing a "smoke-free generation" (ending the sale of tobacco to anyone born after 31 December 2008) [14].
- Ensuring key populations, including Indigenous peoples, are actively involved in driving programs and evaluation in a way that is consistent with Te Tiriti o Waitangi (Treaty of Waitangi) obligations and the FCTC [5, 14].

Around the world, Indigenous peoples continue to call for commercial tobacco control measures that will fundamentally change the nature and supply of commercial tobacco to ultimately eliminate its harm and the associated racialized health inequities [14, 15].

Bringing tobacco control into the twenty-first century requires ongoing resourcing and substantial funds for commercial tobacco control reforms. For Indigenous peoples, in particular, reducing smoking rates will have a critically important impact on health and wellbeing. The commitment required to ultimately eradicate commercial-tobacco-related cancers and other health impacts for future generations cannot be overstated. Any steps in the right direction will bring a monumental change for generations to come [14].

Relationality

This chapter was guided by the priorities, practices, and rights of Indigenous communities, aligned with the UN Declaration on the Rights of Indigenous Peoples (UNDRIP), the WHO FCTC, and principles of ethical conduct. It was conceptualized with Indigenous leadership, including (but not limited to) our own Indigenous lived experience.

Recognizing the significance of relationality and acknowledging our roles, responsibilities, and obligations to our communities, who we are, and where we come from are fundamentally important. This involves understanding our connections, recognizing our biases, and being aware of our worldviews [16].

Relationality is a distinct Indigenous social research presupposition that supports knowledge generation within specific contexts, times, places, and lands. The importance of valuing and respecting the distinctive ways in which individuals and communities acquire and generate knowledge is critical [16]. By valuing and adhering to our unique ways of understanding and acquiring knowledge, we gain insights into the relationships we have and those who recognize and relate to us in that context. This is a matter of ontology and epistemological consideration. Our being and how relationality informs Indigenous social research paradigms are critical to this chapter.

References

1. Nez Henderson PN, Lee JP, Soto C, O'Leary R, Rutan E, D'Silva J, et al. Decolonization of tobacco in Indigenous communities of turtle Island (North America). *Nicotine Tob Res.* 2022;24(2):289–91. https://doi.org/10.1093/ntr/ntab180
2. Waa A, Robson B, Gifford H, Smylie J, Reading J, Henderson JA, et al. Foundation for a smoke-free world and healthy Indigenous futures: an oxymoron? *Tob Control.* 2020;29(2):237–40. https://doi.org/10.1136/tobaccocontrol-2018-054792
3. Maddox R, Waa A, Lee K, Henderson PN, Blais G, Reading J, et al. Commercial tobacco and indigenous peoples: a stock take on Framework Convention on Tobacco Control progress. *Tob Control.* 2019;28(5):574–81. https://doi.org/10.1136/tobaccocontrol-2018-054508
4. Colonna E, Maddox R, Cohen R, Marmor A, Doery K, Thurber K, et al. Review of tobacco use among Aboriginal and Torres Strait Islander peoples. *HealthBulletin Journal.* 2020;20(2).
5. World Health Organization. *World Health Organization Framework Convention on Tobacco Control.* Geneva, Switzerland: World Health Organization; 2003. Available from: https://fctc.who.int/who-fctc/overview
6. Institute of Health Metrics. *Global Burden of Disease.* Washington DC: IHM; 2019. Available from: https://www.healthdata.org/research-analysis/gbd
7. United States Public Health Service. *Smoking and Health: Report of the Advisory Committee to the Surgeon General of the Public Health Service.* Washington, DC: US Department of Health, Education, and Welfare; 1964.
8. United States Department of Health Human Services. *The health consequences of smoking—50 years of progress: a report of the Surgeon General.* Atlanta, GA: US Department of Health and Human Services, Centers for Disease; 2014.
9. Banks E, Joshy G, Weber MF, Liu B, Grenfell R, Egger S, et al. Tobacco smoking and all-cause mortality in a large Australian cohort study: findings from a mature epidemic with current low smoking prevalence. *BMC Med.* 2015;13(1):38. https://doi.org/10.1186/s12916-015-0281-z
10. Te Aho O Te Kahu. *He Pūrongo Mate Pukupuku o Aotearoa 2020: The State of Cancer in New Zealand 2020.* Wellington: Te Aho O Te Kahu; 2021. Available from: https://teaho.govt.nz/reports/cancer-state
11. Edwards R, Ball J, Hoek K, Waa A. Key findings in the 2021/22 NZ Health Survey: Continued rapid falls in smoking prevalence

and increases in vaping [Blog post]. Public Health Expert Briefing. 2022 Dec. Available from: https://www.phcc.org.nz/briefing/key-findings-202122-nz-health-survey-continued-rapid-falls-smoking-prevalence-and
12. Walsh M, Wright K. Ethnic inequities in life expectancy attributable to smoking. *N Z Med J.* 2020;133(1509):28–4.
13. Thurber KA, Banks E, Joshy G, Soga K, Marmor A, Benton G, et al. Tobacco smoking and mortality among Aboriginal and Torres Strait Islander adults in Australia. *Int J Epidemiol.* 2021;50(3):942–54. https://doi.org/10.1093/ije/dyaa274
14. Maddox R, Kennedy M, Drummond A, Waa A, Bradbrook S, Tautolo E-S, et al. 'Dispelling the smoke to reflect the mirror': the time is now to eliminate tobacco related harms. *Aust N Z J Public Health.* 2022;46(6):727–9. https://doi.org/10.1111/1753-6405.13313
15. Ouakrim DA, Wilson T, Waa A, Maddox R, Andrabi H, Mishra SR, et al. Tobacco endgame intervention impacts on health gains and Māori:non-Māori health inequity: a simulation study of the Aotearoa/New Zealand Tobacco Action Plan. *Tob Control.* 2023 Jan 10. https://doi.org/10.1136/tc-2022-057655
16. Moreton-Robinson A. Relationality: A key presupposition of an Indigenous social research paradigm. In Andersen C, O'Brien JM, editors. *Sources and methods in Indigenous studies.* New York: Routledge; 2017. p. 69–77.

Tobacco Cessation and Oral Cancer Prevention in a South Indian Indigenous Tribal Population

37

Delfin Lovelina Francis, Saravanan Sampoornam Pape Reddy, Singaryan Thaddeus, and Chitraa R. Chandran

Key Points

- Tribal populations in India are at risk of oral health issues related to tobacco use, and their treatment requirements are growing.
- In this study, 45.4% of participants used tobacco in smoking or smokeless form daily.
- Over the eight years of this study, tobacco use was reduced due to consistent messages about the importance of oral healthcare and the hazards of tobacco use.
- Deep-rooted dental beliefs and treatment hesitancy were reasons for poor oral health among this population.

Adivasis (literally "original people of the forest"), or Scheduled Tribes, comprise a substantial Indigenous minority of the population of India. According to the 2011 census, Tribal people constitute 8.6% of India's population (over 67.8 million people) [1]. After African countries, India has one of the world's biggest Tribal populations with approximately half of the world's Indigenous peoples, making it home to many Tribes with diverse origins, customs, and social practices. The Imperial Gazetteer of India describes a Tribe as a "collection of families bearing a common name, speaking a common dialect, occupying or professing to occupy a common territory and is not usually endogamous though it may have been so originally " [2]. The Indian Government identifies 645 Tribal communities based on their preagricultural level of technology, low level of literacy, and small or diminishing population. They are generally considered the land's Indigenous inhabitants [3]. Despite significant advancements in preventative and curative medicine, the healthcare delivery system among Indigenous populations remains deficient and needs strengthening to achieve the national objective of universal healthcare access.

Scheduled tribes make up the majority of the population in the hills of Tamil Nadu—including the Yelagiri and Kalrayan hills of Tirupathur district (formerly Vellore district); the Jawadhu hills in Thiruvannamalai; the Pachamalai, Kollimalai, and Yercaud in Salem district; the Anaimalai of Coimbatore district; and the Sitteri and Palani hills of Dharmapuri and Madurai districts. Yelagiri, located midway between Chennai and Bangalore (920 m above sea level), is a jumble of 14 small settlements spread across four hills (Fig. 37.1). The area is still relatively remote and secluded. The local inhabitants of the region are the Malayali Tribal people, who are involved in economic activities such as agriculture, horticulture, and forestry. The name Malayali is derived from the combination of the terms malai (hills) and alu (person).

Despite the rapid global development in diagnostic, therapeutic, and preventive medicine, many Tribal communities live remotely in natural surroundings and maintain their traditional values, traditions, beliefs, and myths (Fig. 37.2). However, they are also confronted with the imminent threat of environmental degradation. The health problems of each community are influenced by a variety of social, economic, and political factors. Beliefs, customs, and practices are also significant determinants of health outcomes [4]. Health attitudes, knowledge about healthcare, and learned social and cultural definitions of health and illness influence individual willingness to pursue healthcare [5]. Ethnic beliefs and values may promote or limit the utilization of health services, and research indicates that individuals from low socioeconomic backgrounds and ethnic minorities are less likely to utilize healthcare [6].

Oral health is critical to overall health because it influences a person's ability to eat, communicate, and socialize in the absence of disease, discomfort, or embarrassment [7]. It also adds to general wellbeing. However, the oral health of Tribal populations in India is characterized by a lack of access to community-based preventative oral health services such as water fluoridation, fluoridated toothpaste, and sugar-free beverages [8]. The health of the Malayali population has been the subject of several anthropological investigations [9]. However, there is no information in the existing literature about their oral health. In light of this, in 2010, the primary author conducted a doorstep survey to assess the oral health of 660 inhabitants of Yelagiri Hills.

G. Garvey (ed.), *Indigenous and Tribal Peoples and Cancer*, https://doi.org/10.1007/978-3-031-56806-0_37

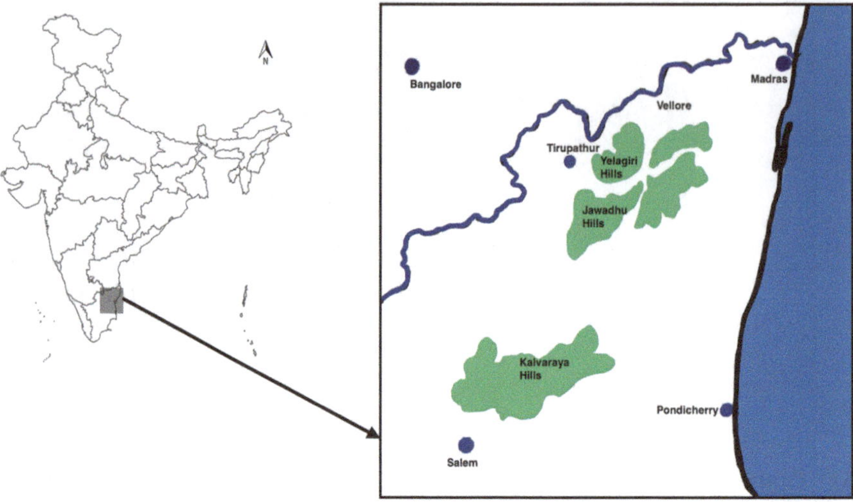

Fig. 37.1 Yelagiri Hills, Tamil Nadu, India. (Map: Saravanan SP)

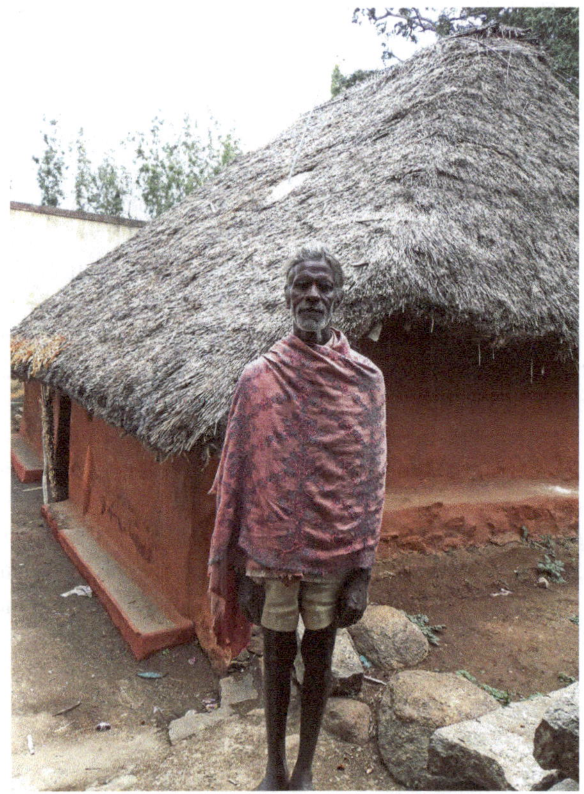

Fig. 37.2 Traditional thatched house of the Malayali tribe. (Photo: DL Francis)

The primary author has a high level of proficiency in the local language, Tamil, but does not have affiliations with the Malayali people and has not been involved in a Tribal advisory group. From 2010, she was engaged as a health educator and oral health program facilitator for this population. She observed that the prevalence of tobacco use among this Tribal population was much higher than the national average of 35%.

From 2010 to 2018, the primary author conducted an education program for the Malayali population in the Yelagiri Hills. The program involved regular oral health assessment and group health education sessions, designed to raise awareness within the community about the detrimental consequences of tobacco use and to disseminate information on effective strategies for tobacco cessation.

Methods

Ethical clearance and permissions were obtained from the village administrative officer, village panchayat leaders, and school authorities. A mass awareness program was then conducted through a cross-sectional household survey in the 14 villages. All age categories, including children, adolescents, adults, and the elderly were invited to participate; however, only residents consenting to do so were included. A school-based awareness program for children was implemented, with the permission of the school authorities. The program included health education, a tooth-brushing demonstration, and posters and videos illustrating the dangers of tobacco use. Adult study participants received an explanation of the study's purpose and gave their written consent before participating (which could be a thumb impression given in the presence of a legally authorized representative). Prior to the clinical examination, a pretested questionnaire was used to obtain information about demographics, tobacco use, utilization of dental care services, and beliefs and practices about oral hygiene and dental treatment. Type III clinical examination (using mouth mirror, explorer, and adequate illumination) was performed by a single calibrated examiner with the assistance of a recording assistant, in accordance with World Health Organization (WHO) standards. After the clinical examination, all tobacco users were given tobacco cessation counseling and nonusers were given health education counseling on the hazards of tobacco. Statistical Package for the Social Sciences (SPSS) (V.21) was used to compare and analyze the collected data.

Results

The 2010 study had 660 participants. It revealed that approximately 60% of the community had not completed formal schooling and that 64.5% of females and 50.3% of males had no formal educational qualifications (a significant statistical disparity in relation to gender and education ($p < 0.001$)).

In response to questions about oral health, 62% stated they brushed their teeth with charcoal or brick powder, 9.5% used toothpaste and a toothbrush, 4.1% used toothpowder and a toothbrush, 15.8% used toothpowder and their fingers, and 1.8% used a neem stick. There is a statistically significant difference in brushing materials (Chi-square test = 18.567; $p < 0.005$). Participants gave varied explanations for not visiting a dentist: 24.2% had never had a dental problem, 4.7% were not interested in consulting a dentist, 50% said they used traditional medicines for dental ailments, 0.6% believed dental treatment was prohibitively costly, and 13% said that there was no dentist nearby. The population exhibited a prevalence of calculus (62.6%), periodontitis (26.5%) (mean attachment loss of 4–5 mm), gingival bleeding (18.6%), and dental caries (79.5%). Figure 37.3 illustrates the decayed, missing due to caries, and filled teeth (DMFT) among males and females.

Nearly half of the participants (45.4%) reported regular tobacco use (either in smoking or smokeless form); however, only men and a small percentage of older women smoked tobacco. Only 10.9% used beedi, 16.0% used cigarettes, and 38.0% used cheroots (a locally produced form of smoking tobacco). Smokeless tobacco (SLT) use was more common than smoking: 9.85% chewed raw tobacco (5.42% of males, 13.87% of females), 2.73% chewed Hans (4.78% of males, 8.7% of females), 10.2% chewed Gukta, and 14% combined smoking and SLT. Among the elderly, 32% used snuff and betel leaves with areca nut powder. Statistical tests revealed a substantial relationship between tobacco use and gender, with much higher use by men than women ($p < 0.004$).

Out of the smokers, only 14.6% had been smoking for 10 years or more and 11% had been smoking for 6–9 years. In terms of tobacco consumption among smokers, 12.4% consumed tobacco more than ten times daily, 26% consumed tobacco four to nine times daily, and 14% consumed tobacco three times daily. There was a statistically significant difference between the duration and frequency of tobacco smoking, suggesting that a longer duration of tobacco use in years leads to a higher frequency of its use. The oral examination determined that the majority of the population (65.45%) did not have an abnormal condition of the oral mucosa. However, there was a prevalence of leukoplakia (19.09%), oral ulcers (3.94%), and leukoplakia with ulcers (15%). There were 5% malignancies affecting the oral cavity and 7.6% other abnormalities.

In 2018 at the 8-year follow-up, the awareness program (oral health and tobacco cessation education held at 3-monthly intervals), had 4456 participants, including 2271 school-aged children (aged 5–17) and 2185 adults (aged 18–85). Of the adults, 1195 (55.70%) were males and 990 (45.30%) were females; 75% used toothbrushes with toothpaste or toothpowder; and 52% had visited dental clinics in the nearby towns for tooth extraction, filling, and oral hygiene maintenance (calculus 45.3% and reduction in mean attachment loss). Reported tobacco use was 32.8%, and oral examination revealed leukoplakia and other oral abnormal conditions among 28.6%.

At follow-up, participants held firm beliefs about oral health and dental treatment, which were framed by religious and traditional belief systems: 69.1% believed spacing in the front teeth brings good luck, 67.3% believed cleaning with salt whitens teeth, 86.5% believed using clove kills germs, 94.5% believed burying milk teeth helps permanent teeth to grow correctly, 65% believed the extraction of an upper tooth leads to blindness, 81.1% stated they would not undergo dental treatment in the evening, and 71.2% believed the extraction of a single tooth loosens other teeth as well.

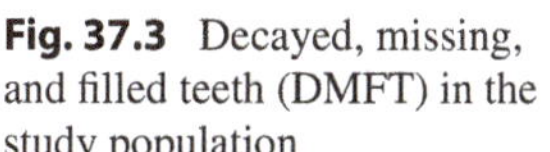

Fig. 37.3 Decayed, missing, and filled teeth (DMFT) in the study population

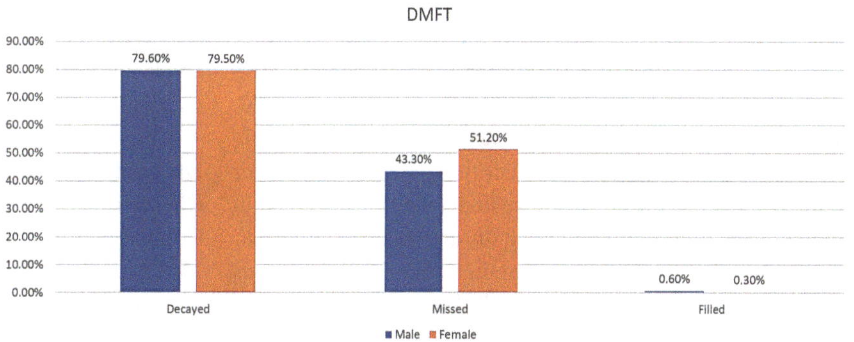

Discussion

The Malayali tribes of the Yelagiri Hills in Tamil Nadu present unique characteristics compared with other populations. Until recently, the group withstood acculturation. Living in isolation, the Malayalis had limited knowledge of oral health, and access to oral healthcare was primarily limited to the treatment of dental infections. No members of the Tribe had ever received preventive treatments such as oral prophylaxis or therapeutic services like root canal treatment. Acculturation and education have been pervasive in recent decades, resulting in a spectrum of diametrically opposed socioeconomic circumstances. The socioeconomic status of Tribal populations remains lower than that of other population groups, and due to their geographical, socioeconomic, and cultural characteristics, they endure a wide range of health problems. Differences between the oral health of Tribal communities and the general population are evident [10]. This study of the Malayali Tribe demonstrates characteristics consistent with this finding. The susceptibility to dental caries tends to increase with acculturation, particularly due to dietary modifications that increase the consumption of food containing sugar. As this study shows, dietary change may occur without substantial advancements in oral hygiene habits.

Oral hygiene is essential for preventing dental problems and achieving optimal dental health. In this study, the majority of participants reported using traditional methods to clean their teeth, while the use of dentifrice (toothpaste or powder) was low. The findings of this study are consistent with other studies of Indigenous populations, suggesting that Indigenous and Tribal people may not prioritize maintaining oral health [11–13]. The prevalence of dental caries in this study may be attributable to inadequate oral hygiene, alongside deep-rooted beliefs, the preservation of natural dentition, a lack of education, the preservation of traditional values, and a lack of awareness. In a similar study on the Bhil tribes of Rajasthan (India), Kumar et al. revealed that the Tribal population believed that the extraction of decayed teeth causes blindness [14].

A previous study by Janakiram et al. revealed that a significant proportion (73.8%) of the Tribal populations in Kerala (India) used tobacco in various forms [15]. The current study reveals a comparatively lower prevalence of tobacco usage (32.8%), similar to the prevalence found by Bhat et al. in a study of Kadukuruba tribes, where 38.50% used smokeless tobacco and 33.2% smoked tobacco [16]. According to the Global Adult Tobacco Survey (2016–2017) India report, on average, 33% of adults routinely used one or more types of SLT. Our data revealed a substantial connection between poor oral hygiene status and tobacco use, similar to the findings of Agarwal et al. in a study of Baiga tribes [17]. In India, the prevalence of SLT use is more than twice that of smoking. SLT use is associated with potentially malignant oral disorders (PMODs), such as leukoplakia, erythroplakia, erythroleukoplakia, and oral submucous fibrosis. In addition, SLT has been linked to physical health issues such as myocardial infarction, chronic obstructive pulmonary disease, infertility, and malignancies of numerous organs, including the pharynx, esophagus, and pancreas [18].

Our research found that Indigenous populations report an elevated sense of wellbeing through their consumption of tobacco, which they associate with resisting cold temperatures, alleviating pain, reducing stress and fatigue, and suppressing hunger. Adolescent females also used SLT to alleviate menstrual discomfort. Our follow-up study revealed that some participants opted to cease tobacco consumption following the continuous reinforcement of oral health education, with a reduction in tobacco use from 45.4% in 2010 to 32.8% in 2018. A prominent justification for consuming tobacco is social acceptance, which leads to addiction. The reduction in consumption that our study revealed may be due to consistent message reinforcement over eight years and heightened awareness about the hazards of tobacco use. This research demonstrates that reinforcement and motivation play a key role in tobacco cessation strategies.

Conclusion

The Malayali Tribes experience oral health challenges marked by a notable prevalence rate, substantial treatment needs, and limited availability of dental care resources. This study indicates that the community urgently needs healthcare assistance. Establishing healthcare programs for Indigenous populations can pose significant challenges due to low literacy rates, low socioeconomic status, and geographical remoteness. The lack of readily available medical and dental care services may contribute to the elevated prevalence of oral disorders within this community. WHO recommends using oral health surveys to gather data on a population's oral disease, oral health status, and treatment requirements. These surveys serve as valuable tools in the strategic planning of dental services. There is an ongoing need to conduct data analysis pertaining to the incidence and severity of diseases, as well as the population's treatment requirements. This is crucial to monitor fluctuations in the levels and patterns of these variables over time and to effectively allocate scarce resources to oral health.

The lead author sincerely thanks Dr. M. Dinesh Dhamodhar, reader, SRM Dental College and Hospital, Chennai; Dr. Kumara Raja MDS, reader, Ragas Dental College and Hospital, Chennai; Dr. Manojkumar M., tutor; Mr. Anantha Krishnan, camp organizing officer, Dental Interns (2013–2018), Tagore Dental College and Hospital,

Chennai; and the management, staff, and students of Don Bosco College Yelagiri Hills, who actively supported the program. Special mention goes to all the participants, without whom the program would not be a success.

References

1. Ganesh B, Rajakumar T, Acharya SK, Vasumathy S, Sowmya S, Kaur H. Particularly vulnerable Tribal groups of Tamil Nadu, India: A sociocultural anthropological review. *Indian J Public Health.* 2021;65(4):403–409. https://doi.org/10.4103/ijph.IJPH_2_21
2. Government of India. *Scheduled Tribes, Scheduled Areas and Tribal Areas in India.* Ministry of Social Justice and Empowerment (Tribal Division); 1998.
3. Ministry of Tribal Affairs. *Report of the High-level Committee on Socio-Economic, Health and Educational Status of the Tribals of India.* 2014 May [cited 2023 Jun 8]. Available from: https://ruralindiaonline.org/en/library/resource/report-of-the-high-level-committee-on-socio-economic-health-and-educational-status-of-the-tribals-of-india/
4. Andersen R, Lewis SZ, Giachello AL, Aday LA, Chiu G. Access to medical care among the Hispanic population of the southwestern United States. *J Health Soc Behav.* 1981;22(1):78–89. https://doi.org/10.2307/2136370
5. Suchman EA. Sociomedical variation among ethnic groups. *Am J Sociol.* 1964;70(3):319–331.
6. Acharaya SS, Srivastava HC. Distribution and growth of the Bhil population in India. In: Ahmad A, Noin D, Sharma HN, editors. *Demographic Transition: The Third World scenario.* Jaipur, India: Rawat Publications; 1997. p. 162–80.
7. Yewe-Dyer M. The definition of oral health. *Br Dent J.* 1993;174(7):224–225. https://doi.org/10.1038/sj.bdj.4808131
8. Kakodkar P. Oral health promotion for the Indigenous population in India. *The NEHU Journal.* 2020;8(2):13–20.
9. Ramanadhaswamy C, Naidu TS. *Healthcare practices and socio-cultural changes of Malayali Tribes in Tamil Nadu.* Kalapet, India: Department of Anthropology, Pondicherry University; 2009.
10. Valsan I, Joseph J, Janakiram C, Mohamed S. Oral Health Status and Treatment Needs of Paniya Tribes in Kerala. *J Clin Diagn Res.* 2016 Oct;10(10):ZC12–5. https://doi.org/10.7860/JCDR/2016/21535.8631
11. Hobdell M, Petersen PE, Clarkson J, Johnson N. Global goals for oral health 2020. *Int Dent J.* 2003;53:285–288.
12. Kumar G, Tripathi RM, Dileep CL, Trehan M, Malhotra S, Singh P. Assessment of oral health status and treatment needs of Santhal Tribes of Dhanbad District, Jharkhand. *J Int Soc Prev Community Dent.* 2016;6(4):338–43. https://doi.org/10.4103/2231-0762.186798
13. Raju PK, Vasanti D, Kumar JR, Niranjani K, Kumar MSS. Oral Hygiene Levels in Children of Tribal Population of Eastern Ghats: An Epidemiological Study. *J Int Oral Health.* 2015 Jul;7(7):108–10.
14. Kumar TS, Dagli RJ, Mathur A, et al. Oral health status and practices of dentate Bhil adult Tribes of southern Rajasthan, India, *Int Dent J.* 2009 Jun; 59(3):133–140.
15. Janakiram C, Joseph J, Vasudevan S, Taha F, Deepan Kumar CV, Venkitachalam R et al. Prevalence and dependency of tobacco use in an Indigenous population of Kerala, India, *J Oral Hyg Health.* 2016;4:1–4. https://doi.org/10.4172/2332-0702.1000198
16. Bhat M. Oral health status and treatment needs of a rural Indian fishing community. *West Indian Med J.* 2008; 57(4):414–417.
17. Agrawal R, Ghosal S, Murmu J, Sinha A, Kaur H, Kanungo S, Pati S. Smokeless tobacco utilization among Tribal communities in India: A population-based cross-sectional analysis of the Global Adult Tobacco Survey, 2016–2017. *Front Public Health.* 2023 Mar;11:1135–1143. https://doi.org/10.3389/fpubh.2023.1135143
18. Ramasamy J, Sivapathasundharam B. A study on oral mucosal changes among tobacco users. *J Oral Maxillofac Pathol.* 2021;25(3):470–477. https://doi.org/10.4103/jomfp.jomfp_105_21

The Landscape of Lung Cancer Screening Among Indigenous Peoples Worldwide

38

Habtamu Mellie Bizuayehu, Sewunet Admasu Belachew, Abbey Diaz, Shafkat Jahan, Kwun M. Fong, and Gail Garvey

Key Points

- Limited evidence addresses barriers to lung cancer screening (LCS) among Indigenous peoples.
- Barriers to LCS include limited awareness, communication difficulties, low health insurance coverage, financial concerns, mistrust of health services, time constraints, insufficient capacity of LCS programs, distance to LCS, inaccessible buildings, and lack of culturally informed guidelines.
- Evidence related to enablers for LCS among Indigenous peoples is important but remains underinvestigated.
- Strategies to improve LCS include increasing program awareness, expanding program capacity and access, scaling up health insurance coverage, understanding Indigenous peoples' communication preferences, offering training for health professionals, using co-design principles and practices, funding, and promoting inclusive research efforts.

Lung cancer is the most common cancer and the leading cause of death worldwide. Indigenous peoples are more likely to be diagnosed and die from lung cancer than their non-Indigenous counterparts [1]. Lung cancer screening (LCS) is a core strategy to enhance early lung cancer detection, which has the potential to reduce disparities in lung cancer outcomes [2]. A key advancement in the early detection of lung cancer is the use of low-dose computed tomography (LDCT). Several countries have initiated national or regional LCS programs using LDCT, with other countries expected to follow. Australia has committed to a national LCS program, which is due to commence in July 2025 [3].

Due to the elevated risk of lung cancer among Indigenous peoples, LCS programs should be designed and implemented in ways that enable equity of access and participation. For this reason, potential barriers and methods to support Indigenous peoples' participation need to be identified during LCS program development. Here, we describe the limited international literature regarding LCS participation, barriers, and potential strategies to improve LCS uptake among Indigenous and Tribal peoples worldwide.

The LCS participation rate among Indigenous peoples worldwide is underreported, with limited evidence from the United States and Canada [4–6]. In 2023, 4.7% of American Indian or Alaska Native veterans participated in LCS [4]. Of all individuals reported to have screened at Ontario Health LCS sites, 5.5% (174/3178) were Indigenous Canadians [6]. Given that Indigenous Canadians constitute 2.9% of the Ontario population, this finding may be cautiously and optimistically interpreted.

Barriers to Lung Cancer Screening Participation

Multiple barriers to LCS participation have been extensively described for general populations [7]. These include lack of health insurance, other financial concerns, low awareness of LCS, limited access to LCS information, low educational attainment, fear of cancer, time constraints, communication barriers, low screening facility capacity, and limited accessibility (due to transportation issues and distance to LCS services, especially in remote and rural areas). Factors shown to enable LCS include mobile screening initiatives, referrals by healthcare providers, relevant LCS advertising (e.g., mailing), community acceptance, positive peer pressure for screening, availability of educational materials, and patient navigator assistance [7].

For Indigenous and Tribal populations, however, evidence of enabling factors is lacking, and limited evidence addresses the barriers and potential strategies to improving LCS participation [7–9]. Critically, none of the randomized controlled trials used to develop LCS guidelines in the United States reported the effectiveness of LCS by Indigenous status; thus, such data were not available to inform US LCS programs and guidelines [10].

Barriers identified by Indigenous people include a lack of health insurance awareness and coverage, as well as other

G. Garvey (ed.), *Indigenous and Tribal Peoples and Cancer*, https://doi.org/10.1007/978-3-031-56806-0_38

financial challenges, including transportation costs and loss of earnings associated with attending screening [10]. Likewise, the distance to LCS services challenges timely access and may contribute to reduced participation [7–9].

Additional barriers identified as relevant for healthcare providers or screening programs in the United States include inadequate LCS service workforce and program resources, low levels of awareness of LCS among health professionals, poor communication between health professionals and patients, and insufficient time allocated to LCS appointments [9]. Patients may also experience challenges in navigating the health system. Cancer screening programs, which typically involve multiple touch points (including assessing eligibility, screening, result notification, and follow-up) may be particularly complex and cause confusion. Additionally, patients may have difficulty navigating physical buildings, if unfamiliar with the city and hospital grounds where screening typically occurs [7, 9].

At an individual level, a lack of awareness of lung cancer or LCS and time constraints may prohibit making and attending LCS appointments [7–9]. This may be exacerbated by a lack of LCS information in Indigenous languages. One study reported that only 3% (7/257) of websites containing LCS information gave options for non-English language resources [8].

Psychological factors (e.g., fear of cancer diagnosis and distress associated with undergoing the screening test and attending follow-up appointments) and concerns regarding LCS effectiveness have been reported by Indigenous patients [9]. Designers of LCS programs should also recognize the mistrust of sociopolitical institutions, including healthcare systems, felt by many Indigenous peoples as a result of colonization, systemic and interpersonal racism, and cultural insensitivities [9, 11]. Barriers and possible strategies to enhance LCS participation relevant for Indigenous peoples are summarized in Fig. 38.1 [7, 9, 12].

Barriers to LCS	Potential strategies for LCS
• Limited awareness • Financial concerns • Mistrust of health services • Communication barriers • Lack of inclusive guidelines • Limited capacity and/or access to LCS programs • Limited information sources	• Increase awareness • Expand LCS program capacity and access • Expand health insurance coverage and reduce financial concerns • Implement co-design principles and practices • Include research and evaluation • Understand Indigenous peoples' communication preferences

Fig. 38.1 Summary of barriers to lung cancer screening and strategies to improve screening uptake

Opportunities to Increase LCS Participation Rates

Ensuring optimal levels of LCS participation among Indigenous peoples is possible [7, 9, 12]. Health systems need to consider their capacity for supporting Indigenous LCS participation. As shown in Fig. 38.1, key strategies may include increasing individual awareness via LCS awareness campaigns, co-designing tailored and inclusive health education resources, advancing healthcare providers' LCS knowledge, improving identification and referral for the screening of eligible individuals, improving staff communication skills, and providing culturally safe practices in LCS. Services must also ensure that physical LCS facilities are accessible to all and that program staff and health professionals are culturally competent and have built trusting relationships with Indigenous people, families, and communities in their service area. This may be achieved through implementing a service provision model that includes recruiting Indigenous health professionals, expanding health insurance coverage and options, and encouraging and funding further research to enhance monitoring and evaluation.

It is crucial to strengthen awareness-raising campaigns for the general public by including relevant information on the benefits of LCS, what to expect from the screening program, where to find a local LCS service, and cost and insurance options [7, 9]. Additionally, improving communication through multilingual interpreters and multiple language information and education resources could further boost LCS participation. Advocating for adequate resources for health service managers and health professionals ensures sufficient time and appropriate staff availability to support optimal LCS for Indigenous patients [7, 9].

Successful implementation of an LCS program requires education and training resources for health professionals both in general practice and LCS-specific services. This should include cultural competency training to improve the understanding of Indigenous peoples' cultural values and perspectives and how these relate to LCS testing and care. In particular, training is required to ensure the determination of patient eligibility for LCS programs and the communication of outcomes to patients. Indigenous peoples' communication preferences need to be considered by LCS services; for instance, Indigenous peoples in the United States often prefer written notification of screening results [7, 9].

To ensure that the most marginalized in society participate in LCS, governments need to identify and implement sustainable funding schemes to cover costs associated with LCS participation. Such costs may include travel and parking costs, loss of income incurred while attending screening, and childcare. Likewise, existing health insurance schemes that cover LCS need to be identified and communicated to the general population [7, 9].

Expanding LCS programs by providing mobile outreach screening programs may help overcome distance barriers experienced in more rural and remote areas [7, 12]. Moreover, placing LCS facilities in community health services (e.g., Aboriginal Community Controlled Health Services in Australia) may help overcome barriers relating to system and service mistrust as patients typically are more familiar with and trust these services and their staff [12].

Increasing the capacity of LCS facilities to provide information, education, and psychosocial support can help enhance LCS participation [7, 13]. This may be achieved through increased staffing, developing education information and educational resources, and using technological support during referral and follow-up appointments (e.g., embedding an automatic reminder system into the LCS program). In the United States, LCS programs with these resources had higher monthly screening rates (17.7 per 1000 eligible persons) than those without (0.3 per 1000 eligible persons) [13].

Another strategy to enhance the effectiveness and efficiency of LCS programs could involve research. Strengthening cancer screening registries, which are an important element of screening programs, can be achieved by establishing data collection at the point of service. Indeed, most existing LCS screening participation studies from the United States and Canada used administrative databases, such as LCS registers, as the primary sources of data [5, 6]. However, the availability and usability of such data sources could be affected by factors including limited infrastructure to collect and maintain data (particularly in low- and middle-income countries) [14], as well as variations of data release policies for research across countries [15]. Moreover, for such data to be reliable, Indigenous identification information must be collected completely and accurately recorded [5, 6]. Administrative databases are not primarily collected for research purposes. As a result, they cannot provide comprehensive data on individual, provider, or system-level factors related to LCS. Therefore, strengthening ongoing initiatives to commence, maintain, and further expand Indigenous-focused clinical trials and prospective cohort studies can support the implementation, monitoring, and evaluation of LCS services.

Conclusion

LCS programs must be designed to be relevant for those with the greatest need if they are to work for the broader society. To do so, Indigenous communities must be engaged in the design and implementation of LCS programs, guided by principles of co-design [11]. By embracing from the outset the insights and cultural backgrounds of stakeholders, and Indigenous community members in particular, culturally responsive LCS programs may be developed to overcome LCS barriers. Notably, in Australia, a trial is underway to investigate the feasibility of an LCS program for Indigenous Australians, which can inform the new Australian program due to launch in 2025 [16].

References

1. Moore SP, Antoni S, Colquhoun A, Healy B, Ellison-Loschmann L, Potter JD, et al. Cancer incidence in indigenous people in Australia, New Zealand, Canada, and the USA: a comparative population-based study. *Lancet Oncol.* 2015;16(15):1483–92. https://doi.org/10.1016/S1470-2045(15)00232-6
2. National Lung Screening Trial Research Team. Reduced lung-cancer mortality with low-dose computed tomographic screening. *N Engl J Med.* 2011;365(5):395–409. https://doi.org/10.1056/NEJMoa1102873
3. Lung Cancer Policy Network. *Interactive map of lung cancer screening (second edition)* [Internet]. 2023 Jun. Available from: www.lungcancerpolicynetwork.com/interactive-map/
4. Rustagi AS, Byers AL, Brown JK, Purcell N, Slatore CG, Keyhani S. Lung Cancer Screening Among U.S. Military Veterans by Health Status and Race and Ethnicity, 2017–2020: A Cross-Sectional Population-Based Study. *AJPM Focus.* 2023;2(2). https://doi.org/10.1016/j.focus.2023.100084
5. Gould MK, Sakoda LC, Ritzwoller DP, Simoff M, Neslund-Dudas C, Kushi LH, et al. Monitoring Lung Cancer Screening Use and Outcomes at Four Cancer Research Network Sites. *Ann Am Thorac Soc.* 2017;14(12):1827–35. https://doi.org/10.1513/AnnalsATS.201703-237OC
6. Walker MJ, Meggetto O, Gao J, Espino-Hernández G, Jembere N, Bravo CA, et al. Measuring the impact of the COVID-19 pandemic on organized cancer screening and diagnostic follow-up care in Ontario, Canada: A provincial, population-based study. *Prev Med.* 2021;151:106586. https://doi.org/10.1016/j.ypmed.2021.106586
7. Lin YA, Hong YT, Lin XJ, Lin JL, Xiao HM, Huang FF. Barriers and facilitators to uptake of lung cancer screening: A mixed methods systematic review. *Lung Cancer.* 2022;172:9–18. https://doi.org/10.1016/j.lungcan.2022.01.022
8. Little BP, Gagne SM, Fintelmann FJ, McDermott S, Mendoza DP, Petranovic M, et al. United States lung cancer screening program websites: radiology representation, multimedia and multilingual content. *Clin Imaging.* 2022;86:83–8. https://doi.org/10.1016/j.clinimag.2022.03.007
9. Anderson MD, Pickner WJ, Begnaud A. Determinants of Lung Cancer Screening in a Minnesota Urban Indigenous Community: A Community-Based, Participatory, Action-Oriented Study. *Cancer Prev Res (Phila).* 2023;16(4):239–45. https://doi.org/10.1158/1940-6207.CAPR-22-0314
10. Perez NP, Baez YA, Stapleton SM, Muniappan A, Oseni TS, Goldstone RN, et al. Racially Conscious Cancer Screening Guidelines: A Path Towards Culturally Competent Science. *Ann Surg.* 2022;275(2):259–70. https://doi.org/10.1097/SLA.0000000000003983
11. Anderson K, Gall A, Butler T, Ngampromwongse K, Hector D, Turnbull S, et al. Development of Key Principles and Best Practices for Codesign in Health with First Nations Australians. *Int J Environ Res Public Health.* 2022;20(1):147. https://doi.org/10.3390/ijerph20010147
12. Bryant J, Patterson K, Vaska M, Chiang B, Letendre A, Bill L, et al. Cancer Screening Interventions in Indigenous Populations: A Rapid Review. *Curr Oncol.* 2021;28(3):1728–43. https://doi.org/10.3390/curroncol28030161

13. Lewis JA, Samuels LR, Denton J, Matheny ME, Maiga A, Slatore CG, et al. The Association of Health Care System Resources With Lung Cancer Screening Implementation: A Cohort Study. *Chest.* 2022;162(3):701–11. https://doi.org/10.1016/j.chest.2022.03.050
14. International Agency for Research on Cancer (IARC). Cancer Registries: A Worldwide Endeavour. [cited 2022 Dec 21]. Available from: https://publications.iarc.fr/_publications/media/download/4137/7b292cfee56b39a1a67f0b744e559f24aa21cb8b.pdf
15. Ramsey I, Corsini N, Hutchinson A, Marker J, Eckert M. Challenges and opportunities for using population health data to investigate cancer survivors' quality of life in Australia. *Qual Life Res.* 2022;31(10):2977–83. https://doi.org/10.1007/s11136-022-03112-3
16. Cancer Australia. Exploring the feasibility of a potential Lung Cancer Screening Program—Summary Report. Surry Hills, NSW: Cancer Australia; 2023 May. Available from: https://www.canceraustralia.gov.au/publications-and-resources/cancer-australia-publications/exploring-feasibility-potential-lung-cancer-screening-program-summary-report

Lung Cancer Among American Indians and Alaska Natives

39

Marilyn A. Roubidoux

Key Points

- American Indians and Alaska Natives (AI/AN) face unique regional differences in lung cancer incidence and mortality rates compared to US White populations.
- AI/AN have the highest prevalence of smoking of all US ethnic groups.
- The majority of AI/AN populations live geographically distant from lung cancer screening access, with a mean distance of 43.6–48.9 miles to screening.

Cancer of the lung and bronchus is the most common cancer among the American Indian and Alaska Native (AI/AN) population of the United States [1]. The incidence of lung cancer varies dramatically by region. For example, lung cancer rates for AI/AN in the Southwest are approximately 16/100,000, seven times lower than in the Northern Plains (109.3/100,000) [1]. In contrast, among White populations in the United States, there is little regional difference in lung cancer prevalence. The regional differences in lung cancer incidence among AI/AN correspond to regional differences in tobacco use [1]. Also, unique to AI/AN is the similar or higher incidence of lung cancer in women compared to men in some locations. This is particularly evident along the Pacific Coast, on the Northern Plain, and in the East [1].

Lung cancer incidence rates and rates of late-stage disease are up to 1.5 times higher among AI/AN. This is especially evident among Northern Plains, Alaska, Southern Plains, and Pacific Coast populations, where lung cancer rates are, in some places, up to 70% higher among AI/AN patients than White patients in the same region [1, 2]. Among all major groups in the United States, AI/AN have the highest prevalence of smoking and the lowest rates of smoking cessation and make fewer attempts to cease tobacco use. Smoking prevalence in AI/AN populations is 1.5–8 times higher than among other ethnic groups in the United States [3].

Mortality

Lung cancer mortality rates are 12% higher overall in AI/AN populations compared to White populations. This difference may be partly related to later tumor stage at the time of detection [1]. Just as AI/AN lung cancer incidence rates vary by region, lung cancer mortality rates also demonstrate large regional differences. This is unique to the AI/AN population, with White populations having minimal geographic differences in lung cancer mortality rates.

The stage of lung cancer at diagnosis correlates to a history of smoking and delays in detection. Between 61.6% and 71.8% of AI/AN women diagnosed with lung cancer present with later-stage cancer, compared to 58.6–67.3% among White women. The death rate among AI/AN women is up to 50% higher than the national average, and has been slow to improve [4].

Reasons for Disparities

Lung cancer survival is related to less-timely or lower-quality medical care, inadequate or delayed detection, and/or treatment gaps. A significant barrier is the difficult and confusing access to cancer screening centers, influenced by a complex combination of factors, including geographic distance, cost, health insurance coverage, rurality, level of social vulnerability, language, race, household problems, and transportation. Access is especially compromised by longer travel distances to lung cancer screening centers and treatment centers, resulting in disparities in services among AI/AN populations [5]. In the absence of screening, the early detection of cancer is far less likely, thus compromising survival owing to the later stage of disease at detection. Lung cancer screening, which requires regular computed tomography (CT) scans of the lungs, needs to be of high quality and should be easily accessible to save the lives of those who use tobacco.

G. Garvey (ed.), *Indigenous and Tribal Peoples and Cancer*, https://doi.org/10.1007/978-3-031-56806-0_39

Culturally informed, community-based interventions also are needed to reduce exposure to tobacco, promote smoking cessation, and enable recommended screening for lung cancer [5]. The cultural significance of traditional tobacco use complicates messaging, compounded by reduced access to medical care and smoking cessation programs. Of more significance is the greater amount of tobacco marketing targeted at AI/AN populations.

Screening for Lung Cancer

The early detection of lung cancer is possible with CT scans and is proven to reduce lung cancer mortality among smokers [6]. Without improved screening, improved efforts to prevent smoking, and increased smoking cessation, lung cancer outcomes cannot improve. Furthermore, lung cancer screening is not universally accessible. Barriers to screening are particularly evident among low-income, rural, and Tribal communities and across state lines. Among all AI/AN populations, 76.4% (454 of 594) report lung cancer screening centers within a distance of 200 miles, with a mean distance of 43.6–48.9 miles. Among those lung cancer screening centers located within 200 miles of AI/AN communities, only 26.9% (122 of 454) are accredited by the American College of Radiology, and quality or outcomes may not be assured [6]. Programs are needed to increase equity in screening across AI/AN communities [6].

There has been limited research on lung cancer screening in AI/AN communities, with outcomes or implementation understudied and underreported. Limitations to lung cancer screening are related to costs, which for many AI/AN healthcare systems depend on congressional appropriation. In addition, other barriers persist—for example, an urban Minnesota community clinic serving Tribal populations found that barriers to lung cancer screening included provider knowledge, patient trust, and patient fear of screening [5].

AI/AN Tribes may experience cancer screening "deserts," similar to other deserts described in the medical and sociological literature. These deserts are defined as geographic areas with a lack of access to nearby services or resources. Across all US states, there is a more than 26-fold variation in mean distance from an AI/AN community to the nearest lung cancer screening center. An increase in access to accredited cancer screening centers is imperative to improve early cancer detection rates and advance equity in cancer-related outcomes. Recent advancements in telehealth may help address the significant geographic barriers that AI/AN populations continue to face [6].

Following lung cancer diagnosis, treatment typically includes radiation therapy. Studies of AI/AN access to radiation therapy are limited, and more research is needed [7]. In South Dakota, the Walking Forward navigation program, in which patient navigators provide patients with services during their cancer care, has resulted in fewer days of interrupted radiotherapy for cancer patients [8, 9]. Improving access to care, making screening services available (e.g., mobile lung cancer screening units), and increasing efforts to reach underserved groups could increase screening uptake.

Lung cancer screening is lifesaving. While the overall lung cancer survival rate is 20% at 5 years, the disease is curable if detected early. Culturally tailored, community-centered approaches have greater success and increase motivation and support for screening and smoking cessation [10]. One example of community efforts is the Caring Ambassadors Lung Cancer Program, which supports screening and treatment for AI/AN communities. More programs are needed in which patient navigators enable patients to comply with screening protocols and engage in treatment and follow-up care when lung cancer is detected [11].

Raising awareness about the statistics, barriers, and opportunities for screening for lung cancer is essential. The American Indian Cancer Foundation is a national organization that provides educational resources, such as culturally tailored infographics, toolkits, and webinars for smoking cessation and for lung cancer screening guidance. These resources enable patient education and outreach activities. The foundation engages in multiple activities, including community cancer prevention education and outreach, early detection, encouraging positive health behaviors, providing system support for cancer screening and tracking systems, and assisting community-based research [12].

References

1. Kratzer TB, Jemal A, Miller KD, Nash S, Wiggins C, Redwood D, et al. Cancer statistics for American Indian and Alaska Native individuals, 2022: Including increasing disparities in early onset colorectal cancer. *CA Cancer J Clin.* 2023 Mar;73(2):120–146. https://doi.org/10.3322/caac.21757
2. Roubidoux MA, Kaur JS, Rhoades DA. Health Disparities in Cancer Among American Indians and Alaska Natives. *Acad Radiol.* 2022 Jul;29(7):1013–1021. https://doi.org/10.1016/j.acra.2021.10.011
3. Bandi P, Minihan AK, Siegel RL, Islami F, Nargis N, Jemal A, et al. Updated Review of Major Cancer Risk Factors and Screening Test Use in the United States in 2018 and 2019, with a Focus on Smoking Cessation. *Cancer Epidemiol Biomarkers Prev.* 2021 Jul;30(7):1287–1299. https://doi.org/10.1158/1055-9965.EPI-20-1754
4. Espey DK, Jim MA, Cobb N, Bartholomew M, Becker T, Haverkamp K, et al. Leading causes of death and all-cause mortality in American Indians and Alaska Natives. *Am J Public Health.* 2014 Jun;104 Suppl 3(Suppl 3):S303–11. https://doi.org/10.2105/AJPH.2013.301798
5. Melkonian SC, Chen L, Jim MA, Haverkamp D, King JB. Disparities in incidence and trends of colorectal, lung, female breast, and cervical cancers among non-Hispanic American Indian and

Alaska Native people, 1999-2018. *Cancer Causes Control.* 2023 Aug;34(8):657–670. https://doi.org/10.1007/s10552-023-01705-y
6. Pena MA, Sudarshan A, Muns CM, Narayan AK, Gonzalez C, Neil J, et al. Analysis of Geographic Accessibility of Breast, Lung, and Colorectal Cancer Screening Centers Among American Indian and Alaskan Native Tribes. *J Am Coll Radiol.* 2023 Jul;20(7):642–651. https://doi.org/10.1016/j.jacr.2023.04.007
7. McClelland S 3rd, Leberknight J, Guadagnolo BA, Coleman CN, Petereit DG. The pervasive crisis of diminishing radiation therapy access for vulnerable populations in the United States, part 2: American Indian patients. *Adv Radiat Oncol.* 2018 Jan–Mar;3(1):3–7. https://doi.org/10.1016/j.adro.2017.08.010
8. Dignan MB, Jones K, Burhansstipanov L, Ahamed AI, Krebs LU, Williams D, et al. A randomized trial to reduce smoking among American Indians in South Dakota: The walking forward study. *Contemp Clin Trials.* 2019 Jun;81:28–33. https://doi.org/10.1016/j.cct.2019.04.007
9. Pena MA, Sudarshan A, Muns CM, Narayan AK, Gonzalez C, Neil J, et al. Analysis of Geographic Accessibility of Breast, Lung, and Colorectal Cancer Screening Centers Among American Indian and Alaska Native Tribes. *J Am Coll Radiol.* 2023 Jul;20(7):P642–51. https://doi.org/10.1016/j.jacr.2023.04.007
10. Anderson MD, Pickner WJ, Begnaud A. Determinants of Lung Cancer Screening in a Minnesota Urban Indigenous Community: A Community-Based, Participatory, Action-Oriented Study, *Cancer Prev Res (Phila).* 2023 Apr 3;16(4):239–245. https://doi.org/10.1158/1940-6207.CAPR-22-0314
11. Dwyer AJ, Wender RC, Staples ES, Dean MS, Sharpe K, Fleisher L, et al. Collective pursuit for equity in cancer care: The National Navigation Roundtable. *Cancer.* 2022 Jul;128(S13):2561–2567. https://doi.org/10.1002/cncr.34162
12. American Indian Cancer Foundation. *AICAF Resources* [Internet]. [cited 2023 Jun 27]. Available from: https://americanindiancancer.org/resources/12.

Risk and Protection for Lung Cancer Among Native Hawaiians and Pacific Islanders

40

Thomas A. Wills, Joseph Keawe'aimoku Kaholokula, Pallav Pokhrel, and Kevin Cassel

Key Points

- Native Hawaiians and Pacific Islanders have elevated rates of asthma, chronic obstructive pulmonary disease (COPD), and lung cancer compared with other ethnic groups.
- These differentials in respiratory disease are attributable in part to risk factors that are also elevated in Pacific populations, including tobacco use, stress, and obesity, and which may be offset by protective factors such as family support.
- Promising screening and intervention approaches have been developed for Native Hawaiians and Pacific Islanders, which need to be more widely tested and disseminated in the Pacific region.

Lung cancer is the most common source of cancer mortality among Native Hawaiian and Pacific Islander (NHPI) men and the second most common among NHPI women. Moreover, compared with other ethnic groups, Native Hawaiians (NH) suffer worse cancer outcomes at a given level of cigarette smoking. To better understand the origins of these differentials, we focus on behavioral research conducted with NH in Hawai'i, along with data from Indigenous people in Guam and the US-Affiliated Pacific Islands (USAPI). We also present research on risk and protective factors for respiratory disease and on screening and intervention approaches that have been shown to be effective in NHPI communities.

The Hawaiian Islands are relatively isolated geographically and did not experience Western contact until 1778. NH were noted by observers in the initial contacts to be robust and healthy people, but after continued Western contacts, the Indigenous population was decimated by introduced diseases and suffered economically and culturally from the loss of their native lands, religion, and language [1]. Hawai'i was originally an independent nation until its monarch was deposed by a US-supported coup, and it was then annexed as a US territory in 1898 under protest by NH. In 1959, it received American statehood. From the mid-1800s, plantation owners imported agricultural laborers from China, Portugal, Japan, and the Philippines, who eventually became part of the local economy, and over the years, the Hawai'i population became multiethnic, with no ethnic majority. However, despite economic development for the population as a whole, significant economic and health disparities remain for NH. A somewhat similar situation occurred in the southern Pacific Islands, which were more accessible to Western exploration and, in many cases, became British, Dutch, French, or Spanish colonies. Some eventually became independent states or US-affiliated territories; however, many remained underdeveloped economically, and at present, some do not have a level of health infrastructure comparable with the continental United States [2].

Prevalence of Respiratory Disease

Cancer registries have now been established in Hawai'i and the USAPI (i.e., Federated States of Micronesia, Republic of the Marshall Islands, Republic of Palau, Guam, Northern Mariana Islands, and American Samoa). Lung cancer incidence and mortality data for Hawai'i (Table 40.1a) show marked elevation in NH (both genders) compared with other ethnicities in Hawai'i.

Data for the territory of Guam (Table 40.1b) show that the overall rate of lung cancer is particularly elevated for Chamorros, the Indigenous people of that region. Lung cancer is also elevated for Micronesians who have immigrated to Guam from other USAPI. Lung cancer accounts for 28% of all cancer deaths in Guam and is the leading cause of cancer-related mortality. These elevated rates can be linked to the fact that Guam is largely urban (95%) and its military installations may expose residents to air pollution, particularly diesel exhaust.

Separate tabulations for three states within the Federated States of Micronesia (Table 40.1c) show that lung cancer rates are relatively low for Chuuk and Pohnpei but are

G. Garvey (ed.), *Indigenous and Tribal Peoples and Cancer*, https://doi.org/10.1007/978-3-031-56806-0_40

Table 40.1a Lung cancer incidence and mortality (per 100,000 per annum) in Hawai'i adults by ethnicity and gender, 2014–2018 [3]

	Incidence					Mortality				
	Japanese	Chinese	White	Filipino	NH	Japanese	Chinese	White	Filipino	NH
Males	45.2	57.0	46.6	68.0	71.7	31.9	38.8	30.0	44.2	50.6
Females	22.6	38.4	39.3	30.9	52.6	14.7	21.5	26.0	19.3	36.6

Table 40.1b Lung cancer incidence and mortality (per 100,000 per annum) in Guam adults by ethnicity, 2013–2017 (Micro = Micronesian) [4]

Incidence					Mortality				
Asian	Filipino	White	Chamorro	Micro	Asian	Filipino	White	Chamorro	Micro
38.3	29.6	63.1	69.4	78.6	22.0	30.8	55.2	66.2	86.3

elevated in Yap, which has been suggested as being linked to a higher rate of cigarette smoking on the island.

Importantly, NH also have elevated rates for other respiratory diseases. Data from the Behavioral Risk Factor Surveillance System (BRFSS) in Hawai'i [6] show NH particularly elevated for the prevalence of asthma and COPD compared with Asian Americans (Japanese and Chinese), Filipinos, and Whites. This differential is relevant for lung cancer because longitudinal studies have shown asthma to predict the development of COPD, and ~1% of COPD patients develop lung cancer annually [7]. Thus, ethnic differentials in the prevalence of asthma and COPD may be significant for understanding differentials in lung cancer.

Risk Factors

Several behavioral factors are related to the risk of lung cancer. Cigarette smoking is a major pathway, and other factors can produce risk or protection independent of smoking. Ethnic differences in levels of these risk and protective factors may help account for differentials in the rates of lung disease.

Cigarette Smoking and Other Primary Carcinogens Cigarette smoking is a major risk factor for lung cancer. Secondhand smoke exposure (at home or worksite), asbestos, air pollution, genetic mutations, and radiation from either manufactured or natural sources (e.g., radon) are also established risk factors. These factors represent a more direct disease process because they involve exposure to primary carcinogens.

Social Determinants The probability of exposure to one or more cancer-risk factors can be derived in part from social determinants. Specifically, the rates of onset and progression for various diseases are related to lower socioeconomic status (SES) (i.e., income, education, and occupational status), job and food insecurity, and social isolation. SES differentials have been documented across a variety of Western and Asian countries [8], and similar findings have been demonstrated in USAPI populations [2]. Social determinants are presumed to represent a more indirect risk process because they influence the likelihood of exposure to primary carcinogens.

Pleasants et al. reported that the likelihood of developing COPD is related to several SES indices, being ~14 times higher for the lowest socioeconomic groups than for the highest [8]. Notably, these effects occur within a matrix of exposures because lower-SES populations are more likely to live in poverty, smoke, be exposed to secondhand smoke and air pollution, and have less access to healthcare. Our own research in Hawai'i has demonstrated that NH are more likely to smoke and be exposed to secondhand smoke, both factors elevating their risk for respiratory disease [9].

Life Stress A long-standing body of research has linked stress from negative life events to adverse health outcomes. Considering the particular circumstances of Native Hawaiians, researchers have studied the effects on NH of historical trauma derived from historical events including the loss of native lands, religion, and language. Though occurring in the past, these can have an impact in the present through discrimination and false or reconstructed narratives, communicated across generations. Research has shown the salience of historical trauma for cigarette smoking among NH students [10]. Stress also derives from insecurity regarding current life circumstances, such as financial insecurity from low income and unstable employment, which has been related to risk for respiratory disease among NH [9]. Food insecurity is a specific source of stress for NH. Whether stress contributes to lung cancer risk indirectly, by affecting the likelihood of cigarette smoking, or directly, by influencing rates of cancer progression, is not settled at this time, but recent reviews provide support for both possibilities.

Obesity Obesity has been linked to respiratory disorders among Hawai'i adolescents and adults. Recent data show that NH (compared to Asians) have a higher rate of overweight status, and this is related to both asthma and COPD [9]. The link between obesity and lung cancer has been debated among epidemiologists, but recent analyses have linked lung cancer specifically to central adiposity (i.e., stomach fat). Because obesity is more prevalent among lower-SES persons (at least in higher-income countries), this establishes obesity within the matrix of social determinants of health for this Indigenous population.

Protective Factors and Interventions

Social Support Emotional support (e.g., confiding and acceptance) and/or instrumental support from family members (e.g., assistance with finances or household tasks) is a well-established protective factor across a range of health conditions. Data from Hawai'i school studies indicate that NH youths who report a high level of support from parents show reduced health-risk behaviors, including cigarette smoking [11]. Moreover, family support helps buffer (i.e., reduce) the effect of life stress on health-risk behavior. For example, our data from a study of Hawai'i high-school students show that the impact of life stress on smoking and other substance use is reduced among teens with a higher level of parental support [11]. In the long run, reducing cigarette smoking will have a significant impact on the likelihood of being afflicted with lung cancer.

Cancer Screening Cancer screening programs are often problematic for Pacific Island populations, where access to medical personnel and sophisticated diagnostic equipment can be limited [2]. Accordingly, alternative approaches that address logistical and cultural barriers to screening have been developed. For example, a study conducted in Yap showed that urine self-sampling for cervical cancer screening is more feasible than clinician-collected cytology sampling [12]. Computed tomography (CT) screening allows lung cancer to be diagnosed early, addressing a particular issue in Pacific Island populations where cancer is often diagnosed in its later stages. While CT screening is less available in many of the USAPI, BRFSS data from Hawai'i adult smokers revealed that the proportion of NH receiving CT scans as a screening procedure ranged from 10.2% (2019) to 18.3% (2021), higher than the screening rates for Japanese and White adult smokers (9–12%) [6]. This positive disparity has been attributed to outreach efforts conducted in Native Hawaiian communities.

Table 40.1c Lung cancer prevalence (per 100,000 per annum) for Central Pacific adults, by state, 2007–2020. Data are for adjusted prevalence, standardized to the US population (Rep = republic; RMI = Republic of the Marshall Islands; FSM = Federated States of Micronesia) [5]

Guam	RMI	Rep Palau	FSM –Yap	FSM –Chuuk	FSM –Pohnpei
54.0	30.0	31.8	37.8	14.5	22.6

Interventions

Although there are limited data on lung cancer screening interventions in Hawai'i and Guam, several studies have illustrated effective approaches for various types of interventions in Pacific populations. Guiding principles for these interventions are that they must be culturally appropriate, utilize a broad-reaching public health model, and, where possible, be conducted by trained Indigenous personnel. We present three examples of such interventions.

Culturally Appropriate Physical Exercise

Cardiometabolic disease is an issue for NH, and physical exercise can help counter the risks derived from obesity and high blood pressure. Kaholokula et al. conducted an intervention for NH at risk from high systolic blood pressure; this involved recruiting adults from community settings and providing training in hula, which has long been a popular and important part of Hawaiian culture [13]. An intervention group received basic medical education and then participated in a 12-week series of lessons taught by a kumu hula (cultural practitioner). A wait-list control group initially received the educational component only. After all assessments were complete, participants in the control group were then invited to receive hula sessions.

The intervention group showed a significant decrease in risk for heart disease, while the control group showed some decrease in risk status (probably due to the educational component) but less than the intervention group. This study demonstrated the effectiveness of a culturally appropriate exercise intervention for NH, providing an empirically validated model that can be used by other populations.

Smoking Prevention in Guam Adolescents

Pallav Pokhrel and colleagues developed a culturally grounded, school-based curriculum to prevent cigarette smoking and betel nut chewing. The curriculum was developed through formative research conducted to understand the high rates of tobacco product and betel nut use observed among Guam adolescents [14]. The curriculum was implemented with middle-school students and focused on teaching students about the health risks of cigarette smoking and betel nut chewing; importantly, the intervention included training adolescents to resist the social influences that encourage the use of these products. Videos helped adolescents formulate and practice realistic and culturally appropriate strategies for resisting pressures to smoke or use betel nuts. A randomized controlled trial of the curriculum was recently completed in eight public middle schools in Guam, four of which received the curriculum and four served as controls. Evaluation data showed that at three-month follow-up, those who received the curriculum were likely to be less open to using e-cigarettes in the future.

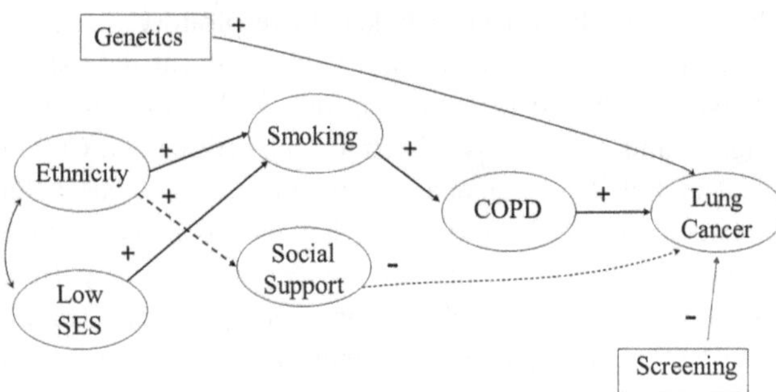

Fig. 40.1 Conceptual model of direct and indirect links between ethnicity and lung cancer. (+ indicates positive association; – indicates inverse association; solid lines indicate indirect pathways from ethnicity to lung cancer through cigarette smoking and COPD; dotted lines indicate indirect pathways from ethnicity to lung cancer through social support. Genetics and CT screening are hypothesized to have direct effects (in opposite directions) to the likelihood of lung cancer)

Increasing Pacific Islander Participation in Clinical Trials

Kevin Cassel and colleagues used their experience with building research infrastructure for colon cancer screening in American Samoa to design an intervention to increase participation by Pacific Islander women in the Tomographic Mammographic Imaging Screening Trial. Their approach utilized health educators from Micronesian backgrounds, who were trained to provide educational sessions with Pacific Islander women in community health centers. Across-time comparisons showed that the intervention increased clinical trial participation by Pacific Islander women from 2% at baseline to 20% at follow-up, exceeding the targeted effect [15].

Conclusions

In this chapter, we have outlined data on the prevalence of lung cancer among Pacific populations, identified cancer risk factors and protective factors, and discussed cancer screening approaches that can be useful among NHPI populations. Risk factors for lung cancer tend to occur within a matrix of social factors under the rubric of SES, and SES may have effects independent of ethnicity. Based on our research with NH, we have proposed a conceptual model of the direct and indirect links between ethnicity and lung cancer (Fig. 40.1). The model recognizes that while ethnicity carries risk, the risk is partly transmitted through intermediate behavioral factors such as a higher rate of cigarette smoking. The model also recognizes that ethnicity may have protective effects (e.g., through stronger family support).

We have also emphasized that while genetic factors may be relevant, lung cancer is related to respiratory diseases such as asthma and COPD, which begin earlier than the typical onset of cancer. The overall implication is that while screening for lung cancer can reduce cancer mortality among adult smokers, lung cancer prevention requires comprehensive efforts, which include smoking prevention programs in schools and screening for early signs of respiratory disease (e.g., chronic bronchitis) in young adulthood.

Acknowledgments The authors wish to thank Brenda Hernandez for her comments on a draft of this chapter.

References

1. Kaholokula JK, Miyamoto RES, Hermosura AH, Inada M. Prejudice, stigma, and oppression in the behavioral health of Native Hawaiians and Pacific Islanders. In: Benuto L, Duckworth M, Masuda A, O'Donohue W, editors. *Prejudice, Stigma, Privilege, and Oppression: A Behavioral Health Handbook*. New York: Springer; 2020. p. 107–34.
2. Rehuher D, Hishinuma ES, Goebert DA, Palafox NA. A historical and contemporary review of the contextualization and social determinants of health of Micronesian migrants in the United States. *Hawaii J Health Soc Welfare*. 2021 Sep;80(9 Suppl 1): 80–101.
3. University of Hawai'i Cancer Center, Hawai'i Tumor Registry. *Hawai'i Cancer at a Glance 2014–2018*. 2022. Available from: https://www.uhcancercenter.org/pdf/htr/Cancer%20at%20a%20Glance%202014-2018.pdf
4. University of Guam Cancer Research Center, Pacific Island Partnership for Cancer Health Equity. *Guam Cancer Facts & Figures 2007–2017*. 2022. Available from: https://www.uog.edu/_resources/files/research/gcr/reports/2013-2017GuamCancerFactsFigures.pdf
5. Pacific Regional Cancer Registry, Cancer Council of the Pacific Islands. *Cancer in the US Affiliated Pacific Islands 2007–2020*. 2023 March. Available from: https://pacificcancer.org/wp-content/uploads/sites/50/2023/04/PIJ-Cancer-Facts-Figures-2007-2020-Final-to-share_smallfile.pdf
6. Hawaii Health Data Warehouse. *Behavioral Risk Factor Surveillance System (BRFSS)* [Internet]. Available from: https://hhdw.org/data-sources/behavioral-risk-factor-surveillance-system/

7. Parris BA, O'Farrell HE, Fong KM, Yang IA. COPD and lung cancer: Common pathways for pathogenesis. *J Thoracic Dis.* 2019;11(Suppl 17):S2155–S2172. https://doi.org/10.21037/jtd.2019.10.54
8. Pleasants RA, Riley IL, Mannno DM. Defining and targeting health disparities in chronic obstructive pulmonary disease. *Int J Chron Obstruct Pulmon Dis.* 2016;11:2475–2496. https://doi.org/10.2147/COPD.S79077
9. Wills TA, Kaholokula JK, Pokhrel P, Pagano I. Ethnic differences in respiratory disease for Native Hawaiians and Pacific Islanders: Analysis of mediation processes in two community samples. *PLOS One.* 2023 Aug;18(8):e0290764. https://doi.org/10.1371/journal.pone.0290794
10. Pokhrel P, Herzog T. Historical trauma and substance use among Native Hawaiian college students. *Am J Health Behav.* 2014;38(3):420–429. https://doi.org/10.5993/AJHB.38.3.11
11. Wills TA, Okamoto SK, Knight R. Parental support, parent-adolescent conflict, and substance use of Native Hawaiian and Other Pacific Islander youth: Ethnic differences in stress-buffering and vulnerability effects. *Asian Am J Psychol.* 2019;10(3):218–226. https://doi.org/10.1037/aap0000139
12. Hernandez BY, Tareg AC, Reichardt M. Randomized controlled trial evaluating the utility of urine HPV DNA for cervical cancer screening in a Pacific Island population. *J Global Health Rep.* 2018;2:e2018016. https://doi.org/10.29392/joghr.2.e2018016
13. Kaholokula JK, Look M, Mabellos T, Ahn HJ, Choi SY, Sinclair KA, et al. A cultural dance program improves hypertension control and cardiovascular disease risk in Native Hawaiians: A randomized, controlled trial. *Annals Behav Med.* 2021;55(10):1005–1018. https://doi.org/10.1093/abm/kaaa127
14. Pokhrel P, Dalisay F, Pagano I, Buente W, Guerrero E, Herzog TA. Adolescent tobacco and betel nut use in the US-affiliated Pacific Islands: Evidence from Guam. *Am J Health Promotion.* 2019;33(7):1058–1062. https://doi.org/10.1177/0890117119847868
15. Wakuk S, Berenberg J, Capps E, Morris P, Cheng S, Bryant-Greenwood K, Cassel K. A multilevel intervention increased accrual of Native Hawaiians and other Pacific Islanders to a national breast cancer screening trial. *J Clin Oncol.* 2022;40:16(Suppl):6547. https://doi.org/10.1200/JCO.2022.40.16_suppl.6547

41 Low-Dose Computed Tomography Lung Cancer Screening for Northern Plains American Indians

Mark B. Dignan, Linda Burhansstipanov, Kristin Cina, Michele Sargent, Margaret O'Connor, Romaine Tobacco, Sheikh Iqbal Ahamed, David K. White, and Daniel G. Petereit

Key Points

- Lung cancer is a leading cause of cancer death among Northern Plains American Indians.
- Lung cancer can be detected through screening using low-dose computed tomography (LDCT).
- Participation in LDCT is low. An intervention for American Indian (AI) communities, healthcare providers, and clinic staff was implemented in four regions with high AI populations in South Dakota.

The US Census documented 74,975 American Indians (AIs) living in South Dakota, USA [1]. Monument Health Rapid City Hospital (formerly known as Rapid City Regional Hospital), South Dakota, is the secondary and tertiary oncology care provider to 60,000 adult AIs in western South Dakota, including Pine Ridge Oglala Sioux, Cheyenne River Sioux, Rosebud Sioux, and AIs from various Tribes living in Rapid City. According to the Index of Medical Underservice [2], the entire population of western South Dakota is medically underserved [3].

In 2002, the Walking Forward Program (WFP) was established to address high cancer incidence and mortality rates among Northern Plains AIs. The program, emphasizing comprehensive navigation in the community and the clinic, community cancer education, increased access to cancer screening and early detection, and enrollment in clinical trials, led to multiple projects spanning two decades. The projects were developed from meetings between Dr. Daniel Petereit, a non-Hispanic White (NHW) radiation oncologist, and Tribal council leaders.

Starting in 2000, Dr. Petereit drove to local reservations multiple times each year, over distances averaging a 280-mile roundtrip, to present his concerns about excessive and late-stage cancer at the time of diagnosis among the AI community to the respective Tribal health leaders (e.g., multiple separate sessions with both Pine Ridge Tribal Health Council and Rosebud Tribal Health Council).

Dr. Petereit and the Tribal leaders discussed the problems of low participation in cancer screening programs and the barriers many AI patients experienced in accessing quality and timely cancer care. The partnership between Dr. Petereit and the Tribal leaders was expanded to include community leaders and Indian Health Service (IHS) physicians. During those visits, Dr. Petereit demonstrated commitment to and respect for community leaders and physicians, while the long commute to reservations provided him with an understanding of the significant distance and financial barriers that patients face.

Collaboration between Tribal leaders, IHS, community leaders, and Dr. Petereit resulted in a 2003 awarded study that was culturally respectful and designed to increase early detection breast cancer screening at Pine Ridge, Cheyenne River, and Rosebud Reservations and among AIs living in Rapid City. After years of establishing a strong foundation, patient recruitment began [4].

In an outreach program that began in 2003, community research representatives (CRRs) (referred to as patient navigators in other settings) reached out to community members who were eligible for breast health screening. From 2003 to 2023, there were statistically significant results: (1) an increase in breast cancer screening rates, (2) earlier-stage determination of breast cancer at the time of diagnosis, (3) improved breast cancer survivorship and quality of life, and (4) lower breast cancer mortality in Pine Ridge and Rosebud Reservations in particular.

There are complex reasons for low participation in cancer screening and higher rates of late-stage cancer diagnosis among AI populations. These include systemic social determinants or drivers of health—such as geographic location, poverty, inequities in resources and opportunities, inadequate health insurance, culturally unresponsive healthcare, colonization, cultural genocide, historical trauma, systemic racism, decreased access to timely screening, and decreased access to high-quality primary and specialty treatment [5]. Since 2003, the WFP has screened over 2700 AIs in South Dakota

G. Garvey (ed.), *Indigenous and Tribal Peoples and Cancer*, https://doi.org/10.1007/978-3-031-56806-0_41

for breast cancer, enrolled over 5000 individuals in cancer research studies and clinical trials, and addressed multiple local issues, including the rollout of tobacco cessation programs and conducting genetic studies to understand how and why AIs experience more side effects from external beam radiation than other racial groups [6]. Between 2009 and 2012, the WFP also supplemented the care of more than 1900 cancer patients and survivors through patient navigation services provided by CRRs [7].

Lung Cancer in the Northern Plains AI Population

Over the years, the WFP study team has closely tracked both national and local data for specific cancers. Lung cancer has been a priority due to the high incidence of smoking among AIs and cancer data that indicate substantial differences from the general US population and statistically significant differences by geographic region. AIs living in the Northern Plains (North Dakota, South Dakota, and Nebraska) continue to have excessive incidence of lung cancer [8]. Lung cancer incidence among adult male and female AIs living in the Northern Plains is elevated relative to both Whites living in that region and AIs living in other regions. Over half of all Northern Plains AI lung cancers are diagnosed at later stages [8, 9]. The lung cancer incidence is 23% higher among AI men than women [9]. AI men in the Northern Plains have a lung cancer incidence rate of 109.3 per 100,000, compared to 66.9 per 100,000 among White men living in the Northern Plains [9], while the rate for AI women is 102 per 100,000, compared to 53.3 per 100,000 for White women living in the same area. The relative risk rates are 1.63 and 1.92 for AI men and women, respectively [9].

Between 2000 and 2009, AIs had the highest lung cancer mortality rates in the country (95.0/100,000, compared to 55.3/100,000 for Whites) [10]. Data collected between 2009 and 2015 at the Monument Health Cancer Care Institute in Rapid City revealed the same trends for non-small cell lung cancer [11]. Both Whites and AIs in South Dakota are more likely to present with stage IV diseases than earlier stages, although the incidence of late-stage presentation is higher for AIs. Smoking is the leading cause of lung cancer. The average rate of smoking among adults across the United States is 12.5%, while in South Dakota, 15.3% of the adult population of the state smoke, and 42.3% of South Dakota AI adults smoke [12, 13].

National Lung Cancer Screening Trial Low Dose Computed Tomography (LDCT) tests have been recommended as the standard for lung cancer screening by the US Preventive Task Force [14]. However, LDCT screening is underutilized, and screening rates are low for all eligible adults living in South Dakota. Only a few IHS clinics even own the equipment, or they do not have the staff to conduct LDCT. There are multiple reasons for low LDCT participation among eligible adults, including limited awareness of screening eligibility and the value of LDCTs, geographic distance to LDCT imaging centers, underlying systemic racism, lower likelihood of LDCT recommendation by primary care providers, and lower likelihood of screening among high-risk individuals owing to barriers and mistrust. Additionally, the AI community has limited and fragmented access to medical care; among those few with private health insurance, most do not know how to use it because their care has been provided by IHS (but IHS is not insurance).

The WFP LDCT Study

In 2018, the WFP initiated a study designed to increase lung cancer screening for eligible participants (see Table 41.1 for LDCT eligibility requirements) [14]. The study explored whether provider and/or individual intervention would increase LDCT lung cancer screening among high-risk smokers living in western South Dakota. The study was approved by Institutional Review Boards (IRBs) at Avera Health Systems and by the AI Tribal populations involved in the study (e.g., Pine Ridge IRB, Rosebud IRB).

WFP staff created two interventions: one for healthcare providers and clinic staff (provider intervention group) and the other for high-risk current or past smokers (community intervention group). Program evaluation for both used survey data and LDCT screening data. LDCT screening was tracked across four frontier study regions—three interventions and one control, all with high proportions of AI residents. Each region received a distinct intervention: Black Hills and Rapid City received provider intervention, residents of the Pine Ridge region received community intervention, those in the Rosebud region received both provider and community interventions, and those in the Cheyenne River were treated as observation only and received no intervention.

The provider intervention consisted of a 45- to 60-minute prerecorded PowerPoint presentation on LDCT screening, eligibility, treatment, and billing and coding and was facili-

Table 41.1 Eligibility for LDCT screening

Eligibility requirements for LDCT screening
Age: 50–77 years
Asymptomatic (no signs or symptoms of lung cancer)
Tobacco smoking history of at least 20 pack-years (1 pack-year = smoking 1 pack per day for 1 year; 1 pack = 20 cigarettes)
Current smoker or one who has quit smoking within the last 15 years
Receive an order for lung cancer screening with LDCT
Receive counseling and shared decision-making session

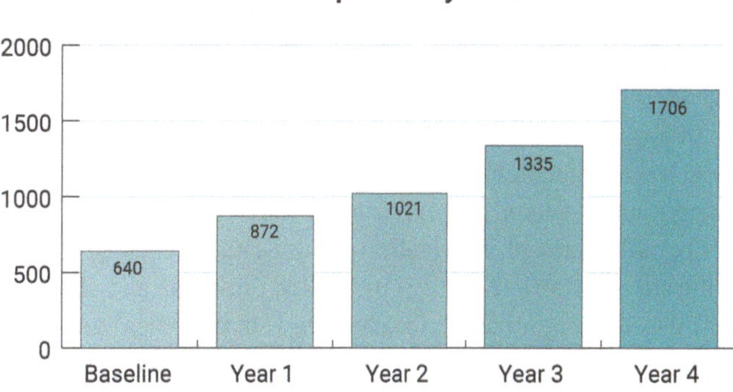

Fig. 41.1 LDCTs completed by study year

tated by a WFP CRR. It was narrated by a fellowship-trained radiologist with additional LDCT training (coauthor DKW). Healthcare providers received certified education credits upon completing the intervention. Participants completed a pre-education survey, and 6 months later, they were mailed/emailed a follow-up survey to document posteducation LDCT referrals.

The community intervention used a PowerPoint presentation developed and presented by WFP CRRs either one-on-one or in small groups. The presentation included content on lung health, smoking cessation, an introduction to an online resource, patient navigation, LDCT eligibility, and treatment of lung cancer. Refreshments and $20 stipends were provided for participants' time and travel. The CRRs provided lung cancer navigation, including travel assistance to help overcome geographical and logistical barriers to obtaining screening.

WFP collaborated with imaging centers to track quarterly LDCT completion numbers. Patients were asked to complete an intake survey when they arrived for their LDCT. The survey included anonymous demographic data and reasons for obtaining an LDCT.

A total of 21 provider education intervention workshops were conducted between June 2018 and June 2021 in three intervention sites. Table 41.2 describes the screenings undertaken at each site. A total of 131 participants (nurses, social workers, medical assistants, and billing and coding staff) completed the sessions. Workshop size ranged from three to 26, and providers' experience ranged from zero to 60 years (average 14.7 years). During the six-month follow-up survey, 47 providers recalled attending the LDCT workshop, and of those, 31 (63%) referred at least one patient for LDCT ($p < 0.05$, Fisher exact test). Of those making referrals, 18 (51%) reported referring between one and five patients, ten (28.6%) referred six to ten patients, two (5.7%) referred 11–15 patients, and one provider reported making over 16 referrals.

Out of the 306 community education intervention session attendees surveyed at the six-month follow-up, 124 (39.6%) reported having a medical appointment for something other than lung cancer screening since attending the education workshop. At that appointment, 40 (32.3%) reported that their provider recommended LDCT, and of those, 30 (75%) reported getting an LDCT ($p < 0.05$, $Z = 4.75$). Participants provided a variety of reasons for *not* getting an LDCT, including the lack of provider recommendation, not feeling at risk for lung cancer, distance to screening facility, travel cost, and fear of what the screening might reveal. Additionally, 69 participants reported contacting their provider and asking about LDCT lung cancer screening. In response to these requests, eight (2.6%) received a referral for LDCT and two (0.7%) reported completing the LDCT. When surveyed at the beginning of the community education sessions, 2.4% of community participants already had an LDCT; at the six-month follow-up assessment, this increased to 9.6%.

Table 41.2 LDCT screenings by intervention group

Number (percent) of LDCT screenings completed by intervention group	
Study site	*N* (%)
Cheyenne River (observation only)	24 (1%)
Rapid City and Black Hills (provider education only)	2279 (90.6%)
Pine ridge (community workshop only)	63 (3%)
Rosebud (provider education and community workshop)	149 (6%)
Total	2515 (100%)
Missing data on location	314

Between July 2018 and June 2022, 2829 AI patients completed LDCTs at screening centers participating in this investigation (see Fig. 41.1), with an increase of 1066 LDCTs in year 4 of the study compared to the 2017 baseline (i.e., a 90.9% increase). The majority of LDCTs were taken by residents of the Rapid City and Black Hills region, where LDCT screening was accessible (see Table 41.2). These findings underscore the importance of distance as a barrier to LDCT screening, with 22% reporting having to travel between 100- and 400-mile roundtrips to and from a screening center. The cancer burden among AI populations is exacerbated by personal and social factors, such as lower socioeconomic status, inadequate health coverage, decreased prevention and screening, and mistrust of the healthcare system [15–17]. Provider recommendation was the most common reason given for obtaining an LDCT. Other reasons included personal recommendations, information from the program's educational sessions, and exposure to mass media.

Overall, a lack of information about LDCT presented in a culturally appropriate manner by trusted providers and clinic staff was the major barrier to screening. On the other hand, a facilitator of screening was the WFP and clinic staff who are local residents. The presence of AI staff living in the communities they serve significantly increased the likelihood of LDCT screening uptake. The investigating team has two decades of experience establishing trusting relationships both within the community and with the IHS. An ongoing challenge is that IHS does not cover the costs of LDCTs conducted off-reservations, and most IHS facilities do not offer them. With supplemental foundation funding, in the WFP study, it was possible to pay for off-reservation LDCTs and provide participants with a stipend to cover travel costs.

Recommendations for future programs include the following:

- Increasing education on and awareness of the need and benefits of LDCT and processes to improve billing for LDCT for healthcare providers.
- Improving culturally appropriate education about LDCT throughout AI communities.
- Building relationships of trust.
- Finding alternative funding to support LDCT conducted off-reservation.
- Increasing travel support for personnel.

References

1. United States Census Bureau. *American Community Survey 5-Year Data (2009–2021).* 2023 Jun 15. Available from: https://www.census.gov/data/developers/data-sets/acs-5year.html
2. HRSA Health Workforce. *Reviewing shortage designation applications* [Internet]. 2022 Aug [cited 2018 Oct 4]. Available from: https://bhw.hrsa.gov/shortage-designation/muap-process
3. Burhansstipanov L, Braun KL, Blanchard J, Petereit D, Olson AK, Sanderson PR, et al. Cancer and Survivorship in American Indians and Alaska Natives. In: Burhansstipanov L, Braun KL, editors. *Indigenous Public Health: Improvement through Community-Engaged Interventions.* Lexington, KY: University Press of Kentucky; 2022.
4. Petereit DG, Burhansstipanov L. Establishing Trusting partnerships for successful recruitment of American Indians to clinical trials. *Cancer Control.* 2008;15:260–268. https://doi.org/10.1177/107327480801500310
5. Melkonian SC, Crowder J, Adam EE, White MC, Peipins LA. Social Determinants of Cancer Risk Among American Indian and Alaska Native Populations: An Evidence Review and Map. *Health Equity.* 2022 Sep 21;6(1)717–728. https://doi.org/10.1089/heq.2022.0097
6. Petereit DG, Rogers D, Govern F, Coleman N, Osburn CH, Howard SP, et al. Increasing access to clinical cancer trials and emerging technologies for minority populations: The Native American project. *J Clin Oncol.* 2004 Nov 15;22(22):4452–4455. https://doi.org/10.1200/JCO.2004.01.119
7. Petereit DG, Guadagnolo BA, Wong R, Coleman CN. Addressing cancer disparities among American Indians through innovative technologies and patient navigation: The Walking Forward experience. *Front Oncol.* 2011 Jun;1:11. https://doi.org/10.3389/fonc.2011.00011
8. Melkonian SC, Chen L, Jim MA, Haverkamp D, King JB. Correction: Disparities in incidence and trends of colorectal, lung, female breast, and cervical cancers among non-Hispanic American Indian and Alaska Native people, 1999–2018. *Cancer Causes Control.* 2023 Aug;34(8):671–672. https://doi.org/10.1007/s10552-023-01715-w
9. Melkonian SC, Weir HK, Jim MA, Preikschat B, Haverkamp D, White MC. Incidence of and Trends in the Leading Cancers With Elevated Incidence Among American Indian and Alaska Native Populations, 2012–2016. *Am J Epidemiol.* 2021 Apr 6;190(4):528–538. https://doi.org/10.1093/aje/kwaa222
10. Plescia, M, Henley, S J, Pate, A, Underwood, J M, Rhodes, K. Lung Cancer Deaths Among American Indians and Alaska Natives, 1990-2009. *Am J Public Health.* 2014;104:S388–S395. https://doi.org/10.2105/AJPH.2013.301609
11. Campaign for Tobacco-Free Kids. The Toll of Tobacco in South Dakota [Internet]. [cited 2023 Mar 6]. Available from: https://www.tobaccofreekids.org/problem/toll-us/south_dakota/
12. Be Tobacco Free South Dakota. Priority Population: *American Indians* [Internet]. [cited 2023 Mar 6]. Available from: https://befreesd.com/about-us/priority-population/american-indians/
13. National Lung Screening Trial Research Team; Aberle DR, Adams AM, Berg CD, Black WC, Clapp JD, Fagerstrom RM, et al. Reduced lung-cancer mortality with low-dose computed tomographic screening. *N Engl J Med.* 2011 Aug 4;365(5):395–409. https://doi.org/10.1056/NEJMoa1102873
14. American College of Radiology. *Lung Cancer Screening Resources* [Internet]. [cited 2023 Jul 25]. Available from: https://www.acr.org/Clinical-Resources/Lung-Cancer-Screening-Resources
15. Iglehart JK. The Challenging Quest to Improve Rural Health Care. *N Engl J Med.* 2018 Feb 1;378(5):473–479. https://doi.org/10.1056/NEJMhpr1707176
16. Levit L A, Byatt, L, Lyss AP, Paskett ED, Levit K, Kirkwood K, et al. Closing the Rural Cancer Care Gap: Three Institutional Approaches. *JCO Oncol Pract.* 2020;16:7;422–430. https://doi.org/10.1200/OP.20.00174
17. Patel MI, Lopez AM, Blackstock W, Reeder-Hayes K, Moushey EA, Phillips J, et al. Cancer Disparities and Health Equity: A Policy Statement From the American Society of Clinical Oncology. *J Clin Oncol.* 2020 Oct 10;38(29):3439–3448. https://doi.org/10.1200/JCO.20.00642

42 Cervical Cancer Prevention Among American Indian and Alaska Native Peoples

Diane M. Harper and Marilyn A. Roubidoux

Key Points

- The high-risk genotype for human papillomavirus (HPV), which causes cervical cancer, is higher among American Indian/Alaska Native (AI/AN) women than non-Hispanic White (NHW) women.
- The uptake of HPV screening among AI/AN women is below the US national average.
- The incidence of cervical cancer is subject to Tribal variation and is higher among some groups of AI/AN women.
- Cervical cancer mortality is higher among AI/AN women than NHW women.
- Self-sampling for HPV testing offers advantages and is preferred by women. Primary HPV testing is likely to be presented for approval in the USA, allowing this method to become available to AI/AN women.

The United States is home to over 570 federally recognized Tribes who speak about 150 Tribal languages. The majority (54%) of the American Indian/Alaska Native (AI/AN) population live in rural and small-town areas, while 30% live in suburban and exurban areas and 16% in urban areas [1]. Approximately 68% of the AI/AN population live on or near reservations or Tribal lands. In the context of AI/AN healthcare access, purchased/referred care delivery areas (PRCDAs) are counties that contain federally recognized Tribal lands or are adjacent to Tribal lands and to the Indian Health Service. Figure 42.1 shows the geographic distribution of PRCDAs [2]. A great deal of AI/AN healthcare is centered in community and Tribal centers, with a focus on healthy food and water sources and on creating local health awareness for disease prevention [3].

Primary Prevention of Cervical Cancer: HPV Vaccination

Cervical cancer prevention begins with human papillomavirus (HPV) vaccination uptake. A Cherokee Nation Health Services survey indicates that 71% of adolescents in the PRCDA have received at least one dose of the HPV vaccine [4]. However, the predominant high-risk HPV genotype across two separate AI communities was HPV 51, which is not included in the current HPV vaccine [5]. Likewise, prevalent HPV infection rates for women over 30 years old are higher among Great Plains Native American Tribal women than the general US population, with 35% of the Great Plains population testing positive for at least one high-risk HPV type [6]. In 2011, South Dakota AI/AN were reported to have a 42% HPV prevalent infection rate, with 32% of the HPV infections not vaccine-preventable types. This is significantly higher than the non-Hispanic White (NHW) comparison population [7]. The risk of cervical cancer may or may not be inherently higher for AI women as the HPV vaccination does not protect them from their most common forms of HPV infection. As such, AIs rely on screening as the next step in early detection and treatment.

HPV in the general population does not reflect HPV genotype distribution in the cervical cancer population [8]. Many common infections do not progress to the cancer stage. While HPV 16, 18, and 31 are relatively uncommon in general infections, they are the dominant types in cancers. HPV genotypes taken from the cervical cancer population among AN women between 1980 and 2007 (prevaccination) indicated the presence of HPV 16, 18, 31, 33, 39, 45, 58, 59, 73, and 82 with no HPV detected in 8% (5/62) of specimens [9]. This set of cervical cancers did not detect HPV 51.

G. Garvey (ed.), *Indigenous and Tribal Peoples and Cancer*, https://doi.org/10.1007/978-3-031-56806-0_42

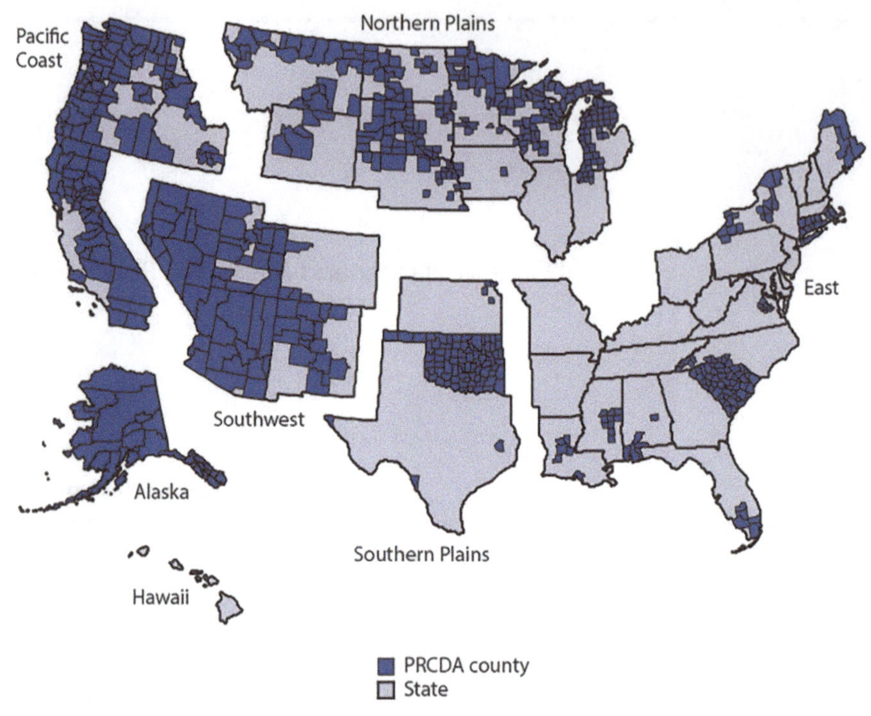

Fig. 42.1 Indian Health Service Purchased/Referred Care Delivery Area counties, by region—United States 2013–2017 [2]

Secondary Prevention: Historical Cytology Screening Results

In the past, cervical cancer screening was cytology dominated, with only recent advances that base the risk of cervical intraepithelial neoplasia grade 3 or worse (CIN 3+) on persistent high-risk HPV infection. Cytologic changes visually represent biochemical changes within the host, and viral DNA post-HPV infection and are necessarily subjective. Screening studies, to date, are based predominantly on women attending screening events and do not report the distribution of cytologic abnormalities for the AI/AN population.

The National Breast and Cervical Cancer Early Detection Program (NBCCEDP) was formally extended to AI/AN in 1993 [10, 11], with funding for 11 Tribal programs. In the 20 years between 1991 and 2012, almost 160,000 AI/AN women were screened with cytology, resulting in 2301 cases of CIN 2+ (1.4% of screened women) and 98 invasive cancers (0.06% of screened women). Between 1991 and 2012, cytology was used as the primary screen, using HPV triage for women with a cytology result of atypical squamous cells of undetermined significance (ASCUS). In the NBCCEDP between 2009 and 2011, AI/AN women with an ASCUS cytology result had the highest rate (56%) of HPV-positive ASCUS results of any race, 15 points higher than other races/ethnicities. Most importantly, 25% did not return for any follow-up, which was almost double the rate of no-follow-up for other races/ethnicities [12]. The lack of follow-up among AI/AN women was 14% when the level of cytologic abnormality extended to low-grade squamous intraepithelial lesions (LSIL), with a higher attendance at colposcopy [13].

Uptake of Screening Remains Low

Screening rates, including HPV testing in some programs, from 2011 to 2019 for Pacific Northwest AI/AN women reveal a nonimproving rate of between 57% and 62%, which is below the US national average of 73.5%. In addition, AI/AN women aged 50–64 years have the lowest cervical cancer screening rate [14]. Tribal variations show the lowest screening rates among AI/AN women in the Northern Plains (46%), followed by the Pacific Coast (49%) and the Southwest (52%) [15]. Screening result data are not available.

Cervical Cancer Incidence Remains High

PRCDA county data from over 10 years of cytology-based screening from 1999 to 2009 revealed a 1.5-fold increase in the incidence of cervical cancer (11/100,000 among AI/AN vs. 7.1/100,000 among NHW), with Tribal variation: women from the Northern Plains have the highest increased relative incidence (1.97) compared to NHW, followed by AN women from Alaska (1.94) and from Southern Plains (1.64), Southwest (1.19), and Pacific Northwest (1.36) Tribes [16, 17]. No cervical cancer incidence inequities were found among East Coast Tribes. Between 2001 and

2008, a similar proportion of AI/AN (22%) and NHW (21%) women on Medicaid were diagnosed with late-stage cervical cancer [18].

From 2014 to 2018, the incidence of cervical cancer worsened to 11.5 vs. 7.4/100,000, with AI/AN women having a 56% higher rate of cervical cancer incidence in PRCDA counties than NHW women [15]. Specifically, AI/AN women 35–49 years had a 1.5-fold increase in cervical cancer incidence over NHW women, and AI/AN women 50–64 years had a 1.8-fold increase in incidence rate [19]. AI/AN Tribal disparities continue, with Northern Plains and Pacific Tribes having nearly twice the rate of cervical cancer incidence as Alaska and Southern Plains AI/AN and 1.6-fold higher incidence as NHW [20].

Between 1999 and 2018, at 3.7/100,000, cervical cancer was the third most common cancer among adolescent and young adult (AYA) AI/AN females aged 15–29 years, after thyroid cancer and lymphoma [21]. Among 30- to 39-year-old AI/AN women, cervical cancer incidence is 18.1/100,000, which is significantly higher than the general US population rate of 7.1/100,000. In contrast, among this same demographic of AI/AN women, breast cancer incidence is 40.2/100,000 and thyroid cancer is 23.7/100,000 [21]. Cervical cancer incidence rates per 100,000 AYA AI/AN women vary by Tribal affiliation, with Southern Plains women having the highest incidence (14.7), followed by Alaska (13.2), Northern Plains (10.6), Pacific Coast (10.6), East Coast (7.8), and Southwest (5.3). Incidence trends did not change over this 20-year period.

By 2018, the incidence of cervical cancer among AI/AN women had increased by 0.6%, at a rate higher than all cancers combined among the AI/AN population [15]. In addition, AI/AN women present with later-stage cervical cancer than NHW women, with a 1.8-fold increase at the regional stage and a 2.4 increase in the distant stage at diagnosis compared to NHW women [15, 19]. Urban Indian Health Organizations (UIHO) data from 2008 to 2017 reveal that AI/AN women living in UIHO service areas had a 1.5-fold increase in the risk of cervical cancer compared to NWH urban counterparts, with Tribal inequities showing Alaskan AI/AN women at the greatest relative risk over NHW (2.0), followed by AI/AN women in the Northern Plains (1.8), Pacific Coast (1.6), Southern Plains (1.5), and Southwest (1.3) [22]. The significantly elevated relative risk of cervical cancer among AI/AN in urban areas (1.7-fold higher than urban NHW) was lower than in four Tribal regions, where the relative risk in Tribe-specific urban AI/AN women vs. NHW urban women is Pacific Coast (2.2), Northern Plains (2.1), Alaska (1.7), and Southern Plains (1.7) [23]. Only the East and Southwest Tribes had lower incidence.

Cervical Cancer Mortality Remains High

In parallel, cervical cancer mortality from 1999 to 2009 was twice as high among AI/AN as NHW (4.2/100,000 vs. US national rate 2.1/100,000), with AI/AN women aged 65–84 years having a 10/100,000 mortality rate (2.8-fold higher than NHW). Those older than 84 had a 23.7/100,000 mortality rate (6.1-fold higher than NHW) [17]. Again, rates varied between Tribal communities, with the highest relative mortality rate in the Northern Plains (4.2), Southwest (2.1), and Southern Plains (1.6), compared to NHW women, while relative rates of cervical cancer among the Eastern and Pacific Northwest Tribes, and Alaska Natives did not differ to those of the NHW population [17]. Up to 2019, mortality from cervical cancer remained 64% higher among AI/AN than NHW women and 2.9-fold higher for AI/AN women aged 50–64 years than for NHW women in the same age category [15, 19].

Screening Now Relies on More Accurate HPV Biomarkers

HPV detection is now a fundamental necessity in cervical cancer screening. The HPV genotypes requiring immediate referral to colposcopy are HPV 16, 18, and 31 [24]. Among AI/AN studies, the most common HPV genotypes, in descending order, are HPV 51, 58, 18, 52, 31, 66, 16, 56, 68, 59, 45, 39, 35, and 33 [6, 25]. The three highest-risk HPV types are present among AI/AN women. Other than prevalent epidemiologic studies on high-risk HPV genotypes in AI/AN populations, there are no data describing the results of a cervical cancer screening process based on HPV testing in the AI/AN population [26].

The Last Mile Initiative is a US-based National Cancer Institute (NCI)-sponsored trial to bring self-screening with primary HPV testing to women, regardless of race/ethnicity, to remove the barriers of the speculum exam and physician appointments. Piloted work carried out among several underserved populations reveals specific narratives for both the lack of screening uptake and the advantages of self-screening.

Primary themes from women involved in the pilot include the ease of collecting a vaginal sample, preference for HPV self-testing over the speculum exam, and positive recommendations to friends/relatives to use self-sampling for cervical cancer screening [25]. Nine countries (Albania, Kenya, Guatemala, Honduras, Malaysia, Netherlands, Peru, Rwanda, and Uganda) have introduced self-screening with primary HPV testing for all women, while eight countries (Argentina, Australia, Denmark, Ecuador, Finland, France,

Myanmar, and Sweden) have introduced self-screening with primary HPV testing for underscreened populations, in addition to an option for well-screened populations [27].

Within a short time, self-sampling for primary HPV testing is likely to be presented to the Food and Drug Administration (FDA) for approval in the United States, allowing this most popular method of cervical cancer screening to be available to AI/AN women.

References

1. Dewees S, Marks B. *Research Note #2: Twice Invisible: Understanding Rural Native America.* First Nations Development Institute; 2017 Apr [cited 2023 Nov 1]. Available from: https://www.usetinc.org/wp-content/uploads/bvenuti/WWS/2017/May%20 2017/May%208/Twice%20Invisible%20-%20Research%20Note.pdf
2. Melkonian SC, Henley SJ, Senkomago V, Thomas CC, Jim MA, Apostolou A, et al. Cancers Associated with Human Papillomavirus in American Indian and Alaska Native Populations – United States, 2013–2017. *MMWR Morb Mortal Wkly Rep.* 2020;69(37):1283-7. https://doi.org/10.15585/mmwr.mm6937a2
3. First Nations Development Institute. *2021 Annual Report: Moving Forward.* 2021 [cited 2023 Nov 1]. Available from: https://www.firstnations.org/wp-content/uploads/2022/11/FN-Annual-Report-2021-low-res.pdf
4. Gopalani SV, Janitz AE, Burkhart M, Campbell JE, Chen S, Martinez SA, et al. HPV vaccination coverage and factors among American Indians in Cherokee Nation. *Cancer Causes Control.* 2023;34(3):267-75. https://doi.org/10.1007/s10552-022-01662-y
5. Morales CG, Jimenez NR, Herbst-Kralovetz MM, Lee NR. Novel Vaccine Strategies and Factors to Consider in Addressing Health Disparities of HPV Infection and Cervical Cancer Development among Native American Women. *Med Sci (Basel).* 2022;10(3). https://doi.org/10.3390/medsci10030052
6. Lee NR, Winer RL, Cherne S, Noonan CJ, Nelson L, Gonzales AA, et al. Human Papillomavirus Prevalence Among American Indian Women of the Great Plains. *J Infect Dis.* 2019;219(6):908-15. https://doi.org/10.1093/infdis/jiy600
7. Schmidt-Grimminger DC, Bell MC, Muller CJ, Maher DM, Chauhan SC, Buchwald DS. HPV infection among rural American Indian women and urban white women in South Dakota: an HPV prevalence study. *BMC Infect Dis.* 2011;11:252. https://doi.org/10.1186/1471-2334-11-252
8. Leinonen MK, Anttila A, Malila N, Dillner J, Forslund O, Nieminen P. Type- and age-specific distribution of human papillomavirus in women attending cervical cancer screening in Finland. *Br J Cancer.* 2013;109(11):2941-50. https://doi.org/10.1038/bjc.2013.647
9. Kelly JJ, Unger ER, Dunne EF, Murphy NJ, Tiesinga J, Koller KR, et al. HPV genotypes detected in cervical cancers from Alaska Native women, 1980-2007. *Int J Circumpolar Health.* 2013;72. https://doi.org/10.3402/ijch.v72i0.21115
10. Espey D, Castro G, Flagg T, Landis K, Henderson JA, Benard VB, et al. Strengthening breast and cervical cancer control through partnerships: American Indian and Alaska Native Women and the National Breast and Cervical Cancer Early Detection Program. *Cancer.* 2014;120 Suppl 16:2557-65. https://doi.org/10.1002/cncr.28824
11. Lee NC, Wong FL, Jamison PM, Jones SF, Galaska L, Brady KT, et al. Implementation of the National Breast and Cervical Cancer Early Detection Program: the beginning. *Cancer.* 2014;120 Suppl 16(0 16):2540-8. https://doi.org/10.1002/cncr.28820
12. Watson M, Benard V, Lin L, Rockwell T, Royalty J. Provider management of equivocal cervical cancer screening results among underserved women, 2009-2011: follow-up of atypical squamous cells of undetermined significance. *Cancer Causes Control.* 2015;26(5):759-64. https://doi.org/10.1007/s10552-015-0549-9
13. Benard VB, Lawson HW, Eheman CR, Anderson C, Helsel W. Adherence to guidelines for follow-up of low-grade cytologic abnormalities among medically underserved women. *Obstet Gynecol.* 2005;105(6):1323-8. https://doi.org/10.1097/01.AOG.0000159549.56601.75
14. Bruegl AS, Emerson J, Tirumala K. Persistent disparities of cervical cancer among American Indians/Alaska natives: Are we maximizing prevention tools? *Gynecol Oncol.* 2023;168:56-61. https://doi.org/10.1016/j.ygyno.2022.11.007
15. Kratzer TB, Jemal A, Miller KD, Nash S, Wiggins C, Redwood D, et al. Cancer statistics for American Indian and Alaska Native individuals, 2022: Including increasing disparities in early onset colorectal cancer. *CA Cancer J Clin.* 2023;73(2):120-46. https://doi.org/10.3322/caac.21757
16. Gopalani SV, Janitz AE, Campbell JE. Trends in cervical cancer incidence and mortality in Oklahoma and the United States, 1999-2013. *Cancer Epidemiol.* 2018;56:140-5. https://doi.org/10.1016/j.canep.2018.08.008
17. Watson M, Benard V, Thomas C, Brayboy A, Paisano R, Becker T. Cervical cancer incidence and mortality among American Indian and Alaska Native women, 1999-2009. *Am J Public Health.* 2014;104:S415-22. https://doi.org/10.2105/AJPH.2013.301681
18. Adams SV, Burnett-Hartman AN, Karnopp A, Bansal A, Cohen SA, Warren-Mears V, et al. Cancer Stage in American Indians and Alaska Natives Enrolled in Medicaid. *Am J Prev Med.* 2016;51(3):368-72. https://doi.org/10.1016/j.amepre.2016.02.016
19. Bruegl AS, Joshi S, Batman S, Weisenberger M, Munro E, Becker T. Gynecologic cancer incidence and mortality among American Indian/Alaska Native women in the Pacific Northwest, 1996-2016. *Gynecol Oncol.* 2020;157(3):686-92. https://doi.org/10.1016/j.ygyno.2020.03.033
20. Melkonian SC, Weir HK, Jim MA, Preikschat B, Haverkamp D, White MC. Incidence of and Trends in the Leading Cancers With Elevated Incidence Among American Indian and Alaska Native Populations, 2012-2016. *Am J Epidemiol.* 2021;190(4):528-38. https://doi.org/10.1093/aje/kwaa222
21. Melkonian SC, Chen L, Jim MA, Haverkamp D, King JB. Disparities in incidence and trends of colorectal, lung, female breast, and cervical cancers among non-Hispanic American Indian and Alaska Native people, 1999-2018. *Cancer Causes Control.* 2023;34(8):657-70. https://doi.org/10.1007/s10552-023-01705-y
22. Melkonian SC, Jim MA, Pete D, Poel A, Dominguez AE, Echo-Hawk A, et al. Cancer disparities among non-Hispanic urban American Indian and Alaska Native populations in the United States, 1999-2017. *Cancer.* 2022;128(8):1626-36. https://doi.org/10.1002/cncr.34122
23. Melkonian SC, Jim MA, Haverkamp D, Wiggins CL, McCollum J, White MC, et al. Disparities in Cancer Incidence and Trends among American Indians and Alaska Natives in the United States, 2010-2015. *Cancer Epidemiol Biomarkers Prev.* 2019;28(10):1604-11. https://doi.org/10.1158/1055-9965.EPI-19-0288
24. Bonde JH, Sandri MT, Gary DS, Andrews JC. Clinical Utility of Human Papillomavirus Genotyping in Cervical Cancer Screening: A Systematic Review. *J Low Genit Tract Dis.* 2020;24(1):1-13. https://doi.org/10.1097/LGT.0000000000000494
25. Winer RL, Gonzales AA, Noonan CJ, Cherne SL, Buchwald DS, Collaborative to Improve Native Cancer O. Assessing

Acceptability of Self-Sampling Kits, Prevalence, and Risk Factors for Human Papillomavirus Infection in American Indian Women. *J Community Health*. 2016;41(5):1049-61. https://doi.org/10.1007/s10900-016-0189-3

26. Whop LJ, Smith MA, Butler TL, Adcock A, Bartholomew K, Goodman MT, et al. Achieving cervical cancer elimination among Indigenous women. *Prev Med*. 2021;144:106314. https://doi.org/10.1016/j.ypmed.2020.106314
27. Serrano B, Ibanez R, Robles C, Peremiquel-Trillas P, de Sanjose S, Bruni L. Worldwide use of HPV self-sampling for cervical cancer screening. *Prev Med*. 2022;154:106900. https://doi.org/10.1016/j.ypmed.2021.106900

Part V

Cancer Services and Cancer Care

Perspectives of a Young Diné Caretaker

43

Marc Emerson

Key Points

- As a caretaker for my father, I saw him experience structural barriers to accessing quality healthcare.
- Culturally appropriate healthcare is of the utmost importance. Access to a Navajo-speaking nurse provided my father with a sense of being cared for, acknowledged, and appreciated.
- We need more Indigenous researchers addressing Native health inequity issues to reduce negative health outcomes and help decolonize the cancer research space.

Yá'át'ééh shí eí Marc Emerson E níshyé'. I was born on Diné Bikéyah (Navajo Nation). My mother is Jemez, Ma'iideeshgiizhnii (Coyote Pass). I am born for Tsenahabgiłnii (Sleeprock people). My maternal grandparents' clan is Ma'iideeshgiizhnii (Coyote Pass), and my paternal grandparents' clan is Hoganłani (Many hogans).

This introduction identifies me with my ancestors and the natural world. Beginning with the Diné protocol is important and helps integrate my Indigenous identity with my personal and professional identity, which is a central theme to my current cancer-related work. Bringing my Native identity into my research grounds and enhances my work, which allows me to be more fully myself in an academic role. This practice, rooted relationality, and kinship are what my father taught me as I grew up on the family farm on the Navajo Nation.

My father was a brother, a son, a father, an Elder, a mentor, a relative, an observer of kinship, an artist, a writer, and a teacher. While I share these labels, I can hear him say that they are not needed for identity and permanence and that one's identity is more rooted in knowing and expressing who we are via culture, language, and heritage. My father would say that he is Diné, and there is power in that—it makes him strong. For my father to be truly known, people would have to know that he was Diné. Using the Diné introduction was one way in which he spoke true to who he was and now I do the same. This quote from him exemplifies his thinking of strength (Fig. 43.1):

> It is an act of decolonization to arrive at this place of beauty and to want to protect it. It is an act of decolonization to sense and experience the Great Mystery and the harmony, respect, and balance that ceremonial process offers. We decolonize when we embrace family members, friends, community members, and celebrate solidarity. It is an artful act of love and resistance to declare that colonialism, despite all its insidious practices of conquest, subjugation, and control, still did not or could not colonize such ancient feelings or methodologies that have a loving and compassionate propensity to restore the human soul and spirit in a very special way [Larry Emerson, my father].

I grew up on the farm, playing and learning the Diné ways of knowing. I assisted my father in ceremonies and learned how to take care of the land, the plants, and the animals we had on the farm. It was his strong opinion that the Beauty Way teachings and philosophy were the best gift that he and the older Diné generation could give to the younger, upcoming ones. I remember he would get me up in the early mornings to run to greet the sunrise and put down our tobacco on the earth as morning prayers. I remember when I would return home, we would enter the hogan to share, sing, and learn (Fig. 43.2).

During my cancer-focused epidemiology PhD program, my father was diagnosed with late-stage stomach cancer. As an only child, I moved home back to the family farm to be his caretaker until he passed. For much of the time I was his sole caretaker, it was difficult as it was also hard to care for myself. Additionally, because of our rural location, accessing care was difficult. It was only when we had a caretaking team of friends and family that the caretaking was more manageable.

During his care, we experienced many of the structural barriers to quality healthcare that exist in the Navajo Nation. The Navajo Nation is one of the largest Reservations in the United States. It consists of more than 27,000 square miles, which is roughly the land size of New Hampshire, Vermont, and Massachusetts combined. Yet despite its geographic

G. Garvey (ed.), *Indigenous and Tribal Peoples and Cancer*, https://doi.org/10.1007/978-3-031-56806-0_43

size, it has fewer than 15 grocery stores and only eight Indian Health Service units. The delivery of care via the Indian Health Service is complex, fragmented, and limited due to consistent underfunding. When my father was receiving cancer care, all of his medical consultations and cancer surgeries were at the University of New Mexico's Comprehensive Cancer Center in Albuquerque, New Mexico—210 miles from the farm. Even his subsequent chemotherapy appointments were a 28-mile drive to a border town.

Fig. 43.1 My father, Larry Emerson. (Photo: Family collection)

Other environmental exposures exist here, including over 500 abandoned uranium mines and contaminated seep water that residents and livestock can drink. Like the Navajo Nation, other Tribal nations can face similar barriers, including geographic remoteness, poor infrastructure, limited transportation, and limited healthcare provider availability.

There are pathways to providing better care and promoting health equity. Culturally appropriate care is of the utmost importance. For my father, some seemingly small things made the world of difference. For example, the hospice nurse who drove to the farmhouse to care for my father (and check in on me) spoke Navajo. Under the relationality of the Navajo clan kinship, she referred to him as a family member. This seemingly simple practice made my father feel taken care of, seen, and valued (Fig. 43.3).

The emotional impact of losing my father to cancer fueled my commitment to cancer prevention and control. Now, my professional goal is to combine my integrative knowledge of cancer epidemiology methods with Navajo epistemology to define health-related interventions that can help decolonize the cancer research space. We need more Indigenous researchers addressing Native health inequity issues to reduce negative health outcomes.

These efforts are not only an important part of how I contribute to diversifying the research community; they also are critical to my personal healing process. My father, himself an academic, was forced to suppress his Native identity at an early age when he and his siblings were forcefully removed from their family and sent to Indian boarding schools. This harmful, racist action against the Navajo Tribe was one of the many actions intended to disconnect individuals from their

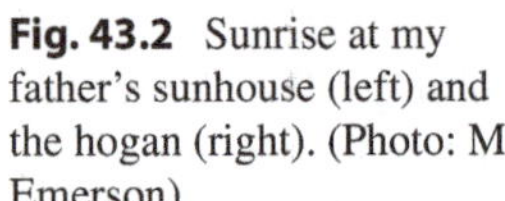

Fig. 43.2 Sunrise at my father's sunhouse (left) and the hogan (right). (Photo: M Emerson)

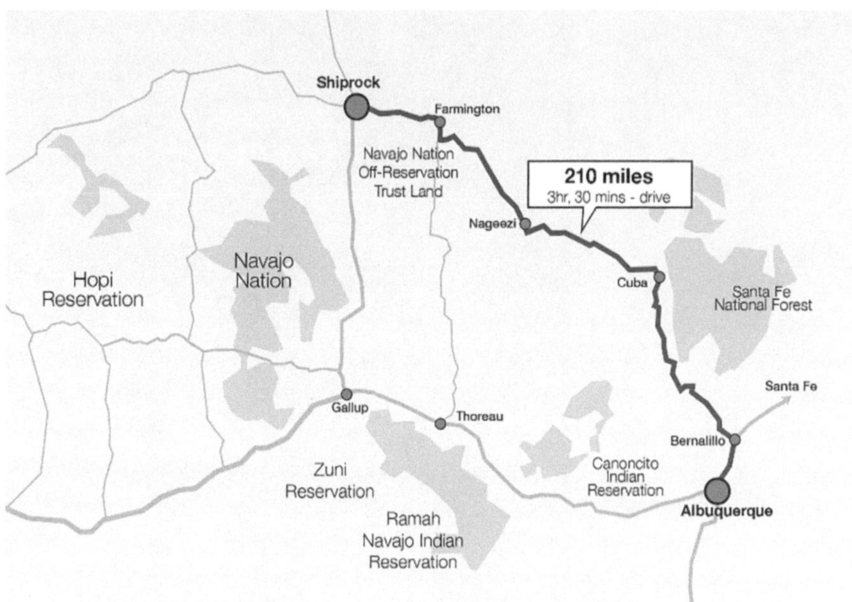

Fig. 43.3 Map showing travel distances for my father's cancer care. (Map: C Lourenco)

Native identity. I grew up seeing firsthand the lasting impacts of these traumas on my father and others. By reconnecting with his Native identity later in life, my father was able to heal and powerfully reverse these traumas by encouraging me to embrace my Native identity while remaining competitive in a modern, Western context. His encouragement was particularly meaningful since he fully understood both the context of my Native identity and the value of academic research, which is something I greatly value. I am committed to actively practicing my father's values, applying the lessons he taught me, and doing my best to live out his legacy in my life and in my work.

44 Narratives of First Nation Knowledge Holders' Experience and Perspectives of the Cancer Care System

Lea Bill, Victor Bruno, Rose Richardson,
Jeannette Nancy Starlight, and Gordon Courtoreille

Key Points

- Ancestral connections strengthen and support patients and families during life-challenging experiences.
- Traditional medicines, along with Western medical interventions, extend and save lives.
- Language considerations are important for culturally safe care.
- Compassion facilitates good relations and the best outcomes.
- Teaching cancer healthcare providers about traditional medicines is important.
- Transferring traditional medicine knowledge to youth is important.

In Canada, cancer rates have increased among First Nations, Inuit, and Métis people in the past few decades and, in some populations and for some cancers, are now at or above the incidence rates in the general Canadian population [1]. This chapter shares four cancer care stories from knowledge holders who have had direct experience with cancer and the cancer care system. Their narratives offer real-life wisdom to learn from and influence positive change for improving the direct care of Indigenous cancer patients.

The first story speaks of the prevalence of cancer in one family and their utilization of both traditional medicines and Western approaches to treating cancer.

The second story speaks of the limitations of Western biomedical approaches to dealing with cancer and, in particular, the lack of knowledge, understanding, and sensitivity present when patients and families wish to use traditional approaches to treatment, including end-of-life transition management.

The third story reflects how life history and trauma are relevant when Indigenous patients are seeking services related to cancer care, including how a diagnosis is delivered and how language can leave a patient poorly prepared to make informed choices for cancer care and treatment.

The final story is about the power of traditional medicine and the importance of ensuring that the next generations are provided with medical knowledge to apply to their lives and wellbeing.

Story 1: Family, Traditional Medicine, and Faith in the Creator

We carry on our ancestors' work. My Cree name is Kakaki Kaoskiikit (Forever-Young Man), and my English name is Victor Bruno from Samson Cree Nation. We have too many First Nations people stricken with cancer. As a Nehiyaw (Cree) family, we made a commitment to support Indigenous-led cancer research within Alberta and the work of the Alberta First Nations Information Governance Centre (AFNIGC). This story is to bring you back to what we are all here for and why we as Elders/knowledge holders are involved in this work.

My personal loss of so many sisters and brothers to cancer is part of the reason why my wife and I decided to work with AFNIGC. I had six sisters and eight brothers, and there are only five of us left now. My wife and I are thankful that we are on this journey together to work in this area. We want to connect our beliefs, our cultural ways, and our medicines to combine Western and traditional ways and to see how we can help our people who are suffering from cancer. I have learned about cancer through being involved with AFNIGC, and I was prepared when I got the shocking news in the fall of 2019 that I, too, was diagnosed with cancer.

Traditional medicine ways helped us as a family. We used both Western and traditional medicine, but I found that Western medicine did not stop the cancer. When I took our traditional medicine, it started working right away, and I continue to drink the medicine to stop the cancer.

Cancer has also affected our children. My wife, Sophie, shares our family cancer journey:

> All my five daughters had cancer. I lost my oldest daughter to cancer. Also, two granddaughters went through cancer, including our newborn granddaughter who had a growth removed in her breast area. Our other daughters were diagnosed with breast

G. Garvey (ed.), *Indigenous and Tribal Peoples and Cancer*, https://doi.org/10.1007/978-3-031-56806-0_44

> cancer and after I lost my oldest daughter, a month later my other daughter was diagnosed with stomach cancer. Two weeks after that, my granddaughter who lives in Winnipeg was diagnosed with breast cancer. We used both ways, the native with Western medicine, but prayer played a major part [Personal conversation, Sophie Bruno, 2023 August 16].

When we lost our daughter to cancer, I thought maybe I should step away from the AFNIGC project. I had a long, serious thought about it. But I thought to myself that I would be giving up on my people. I had to continue. Whatever little I can do, whatever little knowledge I can share to help with this work, I need to share. Helping my people has helped me to continue, and my grandfather always said to never give up. You have to continue; you have to stand.

We use these cultural beliefs along with Western medicine. We combine them with the hope of achieving something that is going to help our people, especially the young people. When you want to follow and include our ways, it is important to do this meticulously. My mentor showed me and passed the pipe on to me. We had four sweat lodges for me to use the pipe; the ceremony was done very, very slowly and diligently, and we followed each ceremony according to the plan for four sweats. Our mothers, grandfathers, grandmothers, and lots of mosôms (grandfathers) and kokums (grandmothers) teach us these things.

I am hoping that this story will help along the way to give you a better understanding of why we have Elders involved in this research—the cultural aspect of traditional and Western medicine.

Time is of the essence for our people.

Hiy Hiy (Give thanks).

Story 2: Land-Based Medicine, Cultural Practices, and Respect

My name is Rose Richardson. I am Indigenous and have lived most of my life in the northern village of Green Lake, Saskatchewan. Knowledge of plant use was passed on through oral tradition and other forms of knowledge through dreams, visions, and kosapachkewin (the ability to see through dreams and visions). Kosapachkewin is a form of knowledge transfer to certain people, through a different way of knowing. In most cases, it is described as a spiritual insight from other dimensions, which is sometimes conducted through ceremony, fasting, or sweat lodges. Some people are born into this realm and see vision and are able to recognize plants and their uses.

Many of our cultural practices were banned and only practiced covertly. My mother often told me, as I explained to her my dreams, visions, and experiences, "one day you will be put in jail, we can only use White man medicine now." I grew up supported and taught quietly by Elders, little people, and three beautiful, kind, and transparent ladies (spirits) who simply appeared and vanished into thin air. My mother cautioned me not to tell anyone because I would be ridiculed and maybe taken away.

The culture, lifestyles, values, language, and religious and spiritual beliefs of people must be taken into consideration in cancer care. As Indigenous Métis people, our environment has influenced our culture, lifestyle, and spirituality. For many, being Métis means appreciating and knowing how to survive in nature. Métis believe that every plant has the creator's signature, with specific plant uses. There is general knowledge of plants, and then there is specific knowledge given to some people.

Many of our people are busy struggling to survive and are held back by a colonialized system, which stifles their cultural practices. Another factor influencing our traditional use of medicine is the limitations of not allowing us to take our own land-based medicine that we used traditionally for healing and health.

Medical services are not readily available in many areas, and people have resorted to land-based medicine. Many people in the remote areas of Canada and possibly the world rely on plants that grow within their traditional lands. Today, there is an effort to combine traditional and Western medicines wherever possible. Some headway with traditional medicine use is being made, especially since hearing about issues concerning medical system shortfalls.

On June 17, 2020, I lost my husband, Ric Richardson, due to cancer. Five years earlier, he had been informed about it. The oncologist said, "you have stage 4 cancer, it's terminal and irreversible." To make sure we understood, the oncologist further added, "and you're going to die." The oncologist's language was crude and uncaring, but he said we could do chemo and radiation, which might add a couple more months.

Ric and I left the clinic and cried in each other's arms. I promised we would go back to my spirit world and get the answer. We journeyed through dreams and visions, and Ric informed the oncologist that we planned to use traditional medicine. We asked for regular follow-up, even though we were using our traditional medicine. It was a challenge to get this care, but through our persistence, we successfully received subsequent care. Then COVID-19 came along and brought more challenges as we could not do our traditional methods and I was not allowed in the hospital. I waited all day in the hospital parking area so Ric would know I was close by. During Ric's last few days, we continued to face additional challenges due to the disrespect and unkindness of the medical staff. That day, my spirit died too.

Education is very important in terms of the accessibility of food sources that are readily available in the specific areas or regions where people live. Métis people must be trained to return to their own communities and support the establishment of centers and services to offer traditional medicines. Healthcare professionals must also work alongside Métis people and acknowledge and respect our choices and traditional values.

Story 3: The Reality of Trauma and the Necessity for Trauma-Informed Care

My traditional name is Itsagha Dinisjosh (Bluebird). My English name is Jeannette Nancy Starlight. I am 74 years old, and I have two sons: my oldest son, Emil, whose wife is Kristin Starlight, and my younger son, Bernard, whose wife is Moriah Whitney Starlight. I have two grandsons, Suh Tsi'do and Nists'i Whitney Starlight. We live in the Tsuut'ina Nation in Alberta, Canada.

I am sharing my cancer journey of the last 15 years. During this journey, my daughter-in-law, Kristin Starlight, helped me understand the extent of this disease; I had stage 3 cancer. I deeply thank Kristin for her presence.

I think it is important that I share a story from my childhood for a little glimpse of context. When I was 8 years old, I had to get my tonsils removed. I remember waiting for my parents, by myself, in the examination room. The doctor walked in with several male interns (five or six), and I was lying down wearing just a hospital gown. The doctor disrobed me and said to the interns, "this is what an Indian looks like." My mind went blank, and they all left before my parents arrived. I never told my parents—I did not know how to say it.

My first diagnosis with cancer was when I was 59 years old. Returning to the medical system for care was overwhelming, but I knew I had to take care of my body, which was no longer well. My experiences with the medical system for my cancer have left me feeling unsettled, disquieted, and traumatized.

First, I could not really comprehend the extent of the disease because of the medical terms used and the way medical personnel spoke to me. I could not visualize the words when they were talking to me since the words were all new to me, and I was not familiar with the medical language.

Second, racism was present—I sensed it in the tone of the doctors and their assistants. Their communication was demanding and pressuring rather than offering kindness and informed choices. The environment lacked cultural safety or connection, and I felt so vulnerable. As I looked around, I saw blood on the floor from previous patients. Seeing this blood increased my stress; my breath stopped, and I could no longer hear clearly.

Some medical staff advocated for me and supported me to make informed decisions. They engaged with me with humility and compassion. They could sense my fear. They met me in relational ways where I could feel their presence and their kindness; the way they took and held my hand supported me to experience safety and connection.

The healthcare system must listen to First Nations patients. Our relationships with our bodies are different. Medical professionals might learn about First Nations history, and I invite them to embrace with compassion these histories because our lived experiences are relevant today. It would be more support of medical professionals to learn about us as people and not just the disease.

Before I go to the hospital, I put down tobacco. I pray for the land, the place, the path, the surgeons, and the helpers. I pray that everything will be cared for, for strength, for guidance, and for everything to go well for all of us. I know I had to go through this. I have learned to deepen my understanding of what my body is sharing with me, and now I know how to share with you. Family love has been a critical aspect of support during my journey, and I would like to deeply thank them and all the people who sent prayers for me.

Guja (Good). Siyisgaas (Thank you).

Story 4: Cancer and Traditional Medicine Use

My name is Gordon Courtoreille from Swan River, Alberta, Canada. I am a Cree Elder and holder of knowledge. I am a survivor of cancer, and I believe my survival is due to listening to my Elders about traditional medicines. The cancer was pretty bad when I started using traditional medicines, but I soon started to feel better.

When I was diagnosed with prostate cancer, my PSA was one of the highest the specialist had seen. I had an appointment scheduled to discuss my treatment options, but nothing was explained. When I came home from the doctors, we had a family meeting to let them know about my diagnosis.

My wife Doris talks about breaking the news to the family:

> I felt that all the family should know, not to keep them in the dark as to what their dad was going through. There was a lot of tears and sadness going on there and Gordon said, "don't cry, I'm still here." I remember him going downstairs and I kept trying to console the kids, not to cry. There was just no happiness in our house. After a while, Gordon came up from downstairs with this crate of medicines that he had picked over the years. Not only months or weeks, it was years, that he had gathered these things, and without saying anything or why, and he made himself a tea.
>
> So, we went back to the specialist and we were told the PSA level had significantly dropped. The doctor questioned Gordon, "what are you doing?" And Gordon told him he was taking traditional medicine. He said, "whatever you're doing, continue, and we'll make another appointment." So the discussion about chemo, radiation, or surgery treatment did not happen.
>
> Gordon continued to use the tea he was making. And when he went back for follow-up, the specialist said there was no sign of cancer, and no sign of diabetes after 30 years; and to this day still there's no sign of diabetes and the cancer is gone [Personal conversation, Doris Courtoreille, 2020 November 13].

When I was young, I always sat with the Elders, and that was where I got all the medicines. They told me what to use and to teach younger generations to gather medicines—to tell them what type of medicine to use and what kind of roots. I would sure like to have people know about our medicines to help themselves and help their children and their grandchildren. I have seen a lot of people having a hard time and not using our medicines because they do not know their power and how healing they are. I know it helps us. I know it helped me. Well, I am still here!

Thank you for hearing my story.

Reference

1. Canadian Partnership Against Cancer. *First Nations Cancer Control in Canada Baseline Report*. Toronto: Canadian Partnership Against Cancer; 2013. Available from: https://s22457.pcdn.co/wp-content/uploads/2017/12/first-nations-cancer-control-baseline-report.pdf

45 Psychosocial Aspects of Cancer Care for Indigenous Peoples

Gail Garvey, Brian Kelly, Angeline Letendre, Carole Mayer, and Joanne Shaw

Key Points

- Psycho-oncology is a subspecialty of cancer care that focuses on the personal and social impacts, psychosocial dimensions, and cultural meanings of suffering and experiences of cancer.
- Attention to the psychosocial aspects of cancer is integral to comprehensive quality cancer care, yet many of the services provided to Indigenous cancer patients fail to recognize and respond in culturally appropriate and safe ways.
- Recent work has developed culturally relevant tools, designed to appropriately assess aspects of Indigenous patients' experiences of cancer.
- Psychosocial care should ideally be integrated as a core element of cancer care for all patients, with a focus on preventing and alleviating psychosocial distress, to assist patients and families in managing the many challenges they face throughout their care.

Recent advances in cancer care have contributed to significant improvements in cancer survival. Regrettably, these gains are not evenly distributed. Disparities in cancer incidence, prevalence, and outcomes among Indigenous peoples globally are well documented [1]. The origin of such disparities is multifactorial, with potentially modifiable social, economic, cultural, and health system factors all contributing [2]. Social determinants of health (e.g., poverty, racism, and lack of culturally responsive healthcare services) are key considerations [2]. In addition, the increased prevalence of other chronic health conditions, including type 2 diabetes, chronic renal failure, and/or respiratory conditions [3], exacerbates the burden of disease, morbidity, and mortality among Indigenous peoples.

These factors provide the context for psychosocial issues relevant to cancer care among Indigenous peoples. Throughout this discussion, it is important to highlight the need to consider the whole person and their context of care and to avoid broad generalizations about any individual based on assumptions about their culture. Genuine interest, inquiry, and commitment to understanding the patient as a person in their cultural context are fundamental to comprehensive care and, in particular, the psychosocial dimensions of cancer and cancer care.

Understanding Indigenous perspectives of health and wellbeing is critical to considering the impacts of cancer and its treatment. The broader definition of health for many Indigenous cultures extends beyond the individual to incorporate social, cultural, spiritual, emotional, and physical aspects of wellbeing within the whole community. Furthermore, for many Indigenous people, the primacy of community connection and place are key considerations in shaping the experience of health and illness and in engagement with healthcare services. The influence of these factors on an individual's cancer experience, including its psychosocial impact, is a core consideration for Indigenous people. In this vein, the extent to which health services and care providers understand and respond appropriately to these contexts is key to optimizing cancer care and improving cancer outcomes.

It is widely recognized that attention to the psychosocial aspects of cancer is integral to comprehensive quality cancer care for all patients. This has been incorporated into national and international guidelines and policies relating to cancer care [4, 5]. At all stages of cancer care, people experience high levels of emotional distress and report psychosocial concerns, including the impact on family, financial and social concerns, and direct impacts of the disease on physical and emotional functioning. Regrettably, many of the services provided to Indigenous cancer patients fail to recognize and respond in culturally appropriate and safe ways [2].

The significance of this issue is highlighted in the adoption of distress as the "sixth vital sign" in international cancer care policy and the momentum to promote and implement standardized assessments of distress in cancer services, alongside the integration of psychosocial care as part of standard cancer care [5]. Driving many of these initiatives, psycho-oncology has gained international recognition as the field of research and clinical practice that focuses on the

G. Garvey (ed.), *Indigenous and Tribal Peoples and Cancer*, https://doi.org/10.1007/978-3-031-56806-0_45

psychosocial aspects of cancer, including cancer prevention, early detection, treatment, recovery, and end-of-life care, including bereavement.

This chapter discusses approaches to the psychosocial aspects of cancer care for Indigenous peoples, including considerations in both clinical care within cancer services and for related psychosocial research.

Identifying Needs and Experiences

While there have been developments in patient-reported outcomes and experience-of-care measures, few studies have addressed their application to Indigenous peoples. It is essential that any assessment of needs is inclusive of and relevant to Indigenous people. This requires a more detailed understanding of those needs across different Indigenous cultures and settings as a foundation of patient-centered care [2]. It is critical that the specific values, preferences, and expressed needs of individuals are captured, using tools that encompass culture, language, and specific concerns that may influence levels of distress and responses to cancer. The latter may include histories of adverse experiences within health services, the legacy of past trauma, the cumulative burden of illness, level of trustworthiness of healthcare services, systemic barriers to healthcare, and experiences of institutional racism. Tools must appropriately assess aspects of Indigenous patients' experiences of cancer if they are to accurately inform treatment and provide a measure of quality of care.

Recent work has developed culturally relevant tools tailored for use among Indigenous people, such as the Supportive Care Needs Assessment Tool for Indigenous People (SCNAT-IP) [6]. Such studies have identified that the most commonly reported domains of unmet need are cultural, psychological, and practical [7]. This process of screening for unmet needs is now considered a standard of quality cancer care [5, 8]. However, to ensure equitable care, distress screening needs use culturally appropriate measures and methods. The principles of partnership, sovereignty, and co-design are especially relevant to attending to the personal experiences and psychosocial impacts of cancer.

Several factors need to be considered when developing more effective psycho-oncology services and related psycho-oncology research within Indigenous communities. First, Indigenous people need to be involved at all levels of care and research development. Establishing appropriate models of governance enables Indigenous communities and community members to take leading roles in identifying key questions and designing and tailoring interventions through genuine collaboration with policymakers and care providers. This approach also enables community philosophies and values to be utilized to better understand and develop appropriate responses to psychosocial needs, thus reducing barriers to engagement in care.

To recognize the specific personal history and context of many Indigenous people, a trauma-informed approach to care can provide a helpful framework for health services and clinicians [9]. This can include the impact on health and vulnerability to illness over time due to the disruption to traditional lifestyles. Furthermore, many aspects of cancer care can reignite or exacerbate prior trauma experiences. This can include demands for separation from community and family for essential treatment, demands for hospitalization and medical procedures, and distressing cancer treatments, all of which require trust and a sense of cultural and psychological safety. For example, the sensitive and often invasive nature of cancer care, including screening, early diagnosis, and treatment, in addition to a lack of culturally informed care providers, can lead to hesitation to access care on the part of Indigenous patients. For these reasons alone, cancer care programs and providers must work to build trust and instill a sense of safety to mitigate the effects of past trauma while ensuring no harm.

Providing Care

Psychosocial care should ideally be integrated as a core element of cancer care for all patients, with a focus on preventing and alleviating psychosocial distress to assist patients and families in managing the many challenges they face throughout their care process [4]. This includes (1) steps to ensure optimal communication between patients, families, and healthcare providers; (2) assessment of patients' key concerns and needs; and (3) provision of appropriate and effective steps to support the psychosocial needs of patients and their families throughout all cancer stages.

A growing body of evidence supports the effectiveness of psychosocial interventions when appropriately tailored based on an understanding of these needs. Models of "stepped care" have been proposed that ensure both the tailoring and monitoring of psychosocial interventions, ranging from universal needs for accurate and appropriately delivered information to specialized psycho-oncology treatments specifically developed for cancer patients and families with more complex needs (e.g., psychotherapies, counseling) [10]. In keeping with a stepped-care approach, Canada has developed guidelines for the screening, assessment, and management of psychosocial distress, depression, and anxiety in adults with cancer. Once the patient completes a self-reported outcome tool, the healthcare provider is expected to review, acknowledge the report with the patient, assess the severity of the symptom(s), provide intervention within their scope of practice, and further refer the patient to the appropriate service provider for the management of symptoms [11]. This model of care was piloted with First Nations communities in northeastern Ontario. Qualitative data revealed that both healthcare providers and patients supported the model of care. There is still work to be done to adapt these tools to the needs of Indigenous patients and to provide culturally appropriate and safe psychosocial services and interventions [12]. This should include steps explaining how to support Indigenous patients and communities living in more rural and remote locations.

The specific psychosocial themes that underpin such interventions should include significant cultural aspects. However, the relevance and effectiveness of existing models and interventions have not been evaluated for Indigenous populations. This includes supportive/expressive psychotherapy or meaning-based interventions, mindfulness-based interventions, or the digital delivery of psychosocial care. Unless relevant to the experiences, values, and languages of Indigenous people, interventions are less likely to engage Indigenous participants and provide the necessary psychosocial support required to address health and well being inequities. The importance of family, kinship, community, and connection to Indigenous people is emphasized in a large body of evidence. In addition, for many Indigenous people, a connection to place, land, and Country (Tribal lands) should also be considered in the provision of care. Healthcare that isolates and disconnects from family, community, and Country can contribute to distress and disengagement from services.

Conversely, strategies that promote cultural links and acknowledge cultural identity can provide an important source of meaning, connection, and support that is well understood to promote resilience, healing, and psychological well being. For instance, the role of community and community identity can be key protective factors in supporting patients through cancer. This may work to provide insights into how care needs to be adapted to include appropriate community carers and also recognize their support needs. Critical to appropriate psycho-oncology care for Indigenous patients is the recognition of the salience of family and the primary role it plays in many cultures. Models of care are needed that recognize these important community networks and their roles in improving outcomes. This is demonstrated in innovations that have been implemented in some settings to increase outreach for cancer care in areas with few health professionals where there is reliance on key community members. Such models may include "patient navigators" or patient liaisons living and working within Indigenous communities. This kind of on-the-ground support has been found to enable the knowledge of Indigenous communities and cultures to play an important part in providing care based on trust, thereby ensuring that the needs of patients are met from within psychosocial contexts and lived realities [13, 14].

Family and kinship networks can also provide invaluable guidance on the ways cancer care can be tailored to provide necessary practical and emotional support to Indigenous people. This is particularly important for end-of-life care and bereavement care through recognizing family and kinship networks and the significant role of specific cultural practices and rituals [15]. Bereavement practices are a critically important embodiment of deeply held cultural beliefs. An understanding of the meaning of suffering and dying, and respect for these rituals and customs, is essential to culturally inclusive psychosocial care of families and communities, to reduce fear and anxiety during end-of-life care and to support appropriate bereavement care when needed. This can include understanding the meaning of death and ways of communicating about the deceased. Ensuring that the community, family networks, and cultural practices are respected and supported will also promote recovery and optimal bereavement outcomes.

Considerations for Psycho-Oncology Research Practice

Building and promoting cultural capacity and inclusiveness within research teams is essential. Of particular relevance to psycho-oncology is understanding cultural and historical influences, such as the experience and impact of past trauma, displacement, and transgenerational psychosocial consequences that may influence psychosocial needs throughout cancer care and impact engagement with healthcare providers and researchers. Building such understanding among healthcare providers and researchers is a foundational step to shaping the focus and conduct of research, ensuring it leads to improved outcomes [2, 6].

Building greater opportunities for Indigenous people to become health professionals, health policy leaders, and research leaders in psycho-oncology is essential to improving outcomes through building deeper understandings of Indigenous knowledge, empowerment, and trust. Furthermore, this ensures that the research undertaken and the resulting strategies to improve psychosocial outcomes better reflect the needs and experiences of the priority populations that health services aim to serve.

Psycho-oncology practice and research also extend to support for those caring for people with cancer, in both formal health professional roles and informal roles within communities. The emotional impact of cancer care can be substantial [16], and culturally based models of support that help promote well being, that give this work a sense of purpose and meaning, and that appropriately recognize carer roles are important in sustaining health professional teams. Similarly, attention to and respect for differences in concepts of professional boundaries and responsibilities to one's community by Indigenous healthcare providers are important.

In addition, it is important that systemic and environmental factors influencing health and health behaviors are recognized. While many research strategies to reduce cancer risk focus on individual risk behaviors and lifestyle factors, these are heavily influenced by social and environmental contexts, such as chronic adversity, poverty, marginalization, and disadvantage.

Conclusion

A key element of quality cancer care is attention to the psychosocial needs and impacts at all stages of cancer. Psychosocial needs are deeply embedded in personal values, experiences, and cultural and spiritual perspectives and are especially relevant to psycho-oncology care. By addressing these needs, patient engagement, experiences of care, and clinical outcomes can be improved. Developing a culturally informed and inclusive approach to psycho-oncology care requires culturally appropriate assessment tools to better understand and monitor patient and family needs and to evaluate the quality of care provided. Furthermore, culturally appropriate information, materials, and strategies to build an understanding of cancer and its treatment are essential and need to include an understanding of the potential psychosocial impacts of cancer and build confidence in available interventions. These issues are particularly relevant to psycho-oncology research with Indigenous peoples.

Underpinning this research is the development of trusting relationships with communities to ensure appropriate research questions and modes of inquiry, understanding Indigenous knowledge frameworks, and developing agreed-upon models of Indigenous ownership and sovereignty in research. These general principles are especially relevant to psycho-oncology research that aims to better understand personal experience, values, and needs and that seeks to address the often-complex determinants of distress among Indigenous patients and families.

Finally, psycho-oncology is a subspecialty of cancer care that focuses on the personal and social impacts, psychosocial dimensions, and cultural meanings of the suffering and experiences of cancer; therefore, cultural knowledge, respect, and compassion for differences are foundational to this field of work and essential to improving the outcomes for Indigenous peoples globally.

References

1. Sarfati D, Robson B, Garvey G, Goza T, Foliaki S, Millar E, et al. Improving the health of Indigenous people globally. *Lancet Oncol.* 2018;19(6):E276. https://doi.org/10.1016/S1470-2045(18)30336-X
2. Garvey G, Cunningham J, Mayer C, Letendre A, Shaw J, Anderson K, Kelly B. Psychosocial aspects of delivering cancer care to Indigenous people: an overview. *JCO Glob Oncol.* 2020;6:148–154. https://doi.org/10.1200/JGO.19.00130
3. Diaz A, Sverdlov AL, Kelly B, Ngo DTM, Bates N, Garvey G. Nexus of cancer and cardiovascular disease for Australia's First Peoples. *JCO Glob Oncol.* 2020;6:115–119. https://doi.org/10.1200/JGO.19.00088
4. Institute of Medicine. *Cancer Care for the Whole Patient: Meeting Psychosocial Health Needs.* Washington, DC: The National Academies Press; 2008. https://doi.org/10.17226/11993
5. Bultz BD, Watson L, Loscalzo M, Kelly B, Zabora J. From Foundation to Inspiration: Implementing Screening for Distress (6th Vital Sign) for Optimal Cancer Care- International Leadership Perspectives on Program Development. *J Psychosoc Oncol Res Pract.* 2021;3:2. https://doi.org/10.1097/OR9.0000000000000051
6. Garvey G, Beesley VL, Janda M, Jacka C, Green AC, O'Rouke P, et al. The development of a supportive care needs assessment tool for Indigenous people with cancer. *BMC Cancer.* 2012;12:300. https://doi.org/10.1186/1471-2407-12-300
7. Bernardes CM, Diaz A, Valery PC, Sabesan S, Baxi S, Aoun S, et al. Unmet supportive care needs among Indigenous cancer patients across Australia. *Rural Remote Health.* 2019 Sep;19(3):4660. https://doi.org/10.22605/RRH4660
8. Pirl WF, Greer JA, Wells-Di Gregoria S, Irwin S, Fasciano K, Wiener L, et al. Framework for planning the delivery of psychosocial oncology services: an American Psychosocial Oncology Society task force report. *Psycho-Oncology.* 2020;29:1982–87. https://doi.org/10.1002/pon.5409
9. Davidson CA, Kennedy K, Jackson KT. Trauma-informed approaches in the context of cancer care in Canada and the United States: A scoping review. *Trauma Violence Abuse.* 2022 Sep:15248380221120836. https://doi.org/10.1177/15248380221120836
10. Butow P, Price MA, Shaw JM, Turner J, Clayton JM, Grimison P, et al. Clinical pathway for the screening, assessment and management of anxiety and depression in adult cancer patients: Australian guidelines. *Psychooncology.* 2015 Sep;24(9):987–1001. https://doi.org/10.1002/pon.3920
11. Howell D, Keshavarz H, Esplen MJ, Hack T, Hamel M, Howes J, et al. *A Pan Canadian Practice Guideline: Screening, Assessment and Care of Psychosocial Distress, Depression, and Anxiety in Adults with Cancer.* Toronto: Canadian Partnership Against Cancer and the Canadian Association of Psychosocial Oncology; 2015 Jul.
12. Mayer C, Aslam U, Collins M, Maguire T, Grigull A, Williamson P, et al. *Two-Eyed Seeing – Cancer Symptom Management for First Nations Peoples: Learnings from mISAAC.* Report submitted to the Aboriginal Cancer Control Unit. Toronto: Cancer Care Ontario; 2019.
13. Cooper E, Sanguins J, Menec V, Chartrand A, Carter S, Driedger S. Culturally Responsive Supports for Metis Elders and Metis Family Caregivers. *Can J Aging.* 2020;39(2):206–219. https://doi.org/10.1017/S0714980819000321
14. Letendre A, Arrow Big Smoke, Petricone-Westwood D. *The Role of Indigenous Cancer Patient Navigation in Addressing Psychosocial Aspects of Care to Reduce Cancer Burden in Alberta Indigenous Populations.* Paper presented at: Canadian Association of Psychosocial Oncology Annual Conference; 2021; Calgary, Canada.
15. Ntizimira C, Deo MS, Dunne M, Krakauer E. Decolonizing end-of-life care: lessons and opportunities. *Ecancermedicalscience.* 2022 Apr 28;16:ed121. https://doi.org/10.3332/ecancer.2022.ed121
16. Turner J, Kelly B, Girgis A. Supporting Oncology Health Professionals: A Review. *Psychooncologie.* 2011;5:77–82. https://doi.org/10.1007/s11839-011-0320-8

46 Be Persistent in Seeking Treatment

Des McGrady

Key Points

- The diagnosis of my stage 4 nasopharyngeal carcinoma took almost 18 months, with doctors initially believing I had a sinus infection.
- I gained strength from my family, living in my home Country, and using bush medicine alongside medical treatment.
- Since being diagnosed with cancer, I have become a cancer ambassador for the Aboriginal and Torres Strait Islander community. I encourage people to be persistent about asking questions and seeking the best medical support.

I am a proud Kamilaroi man from the Darling Downs region in Queensland, Australia. I am committed to sharing my culture and supporting my community. But in March 2016, I was the one who needed support. I was diagnosed with stage 4 nasopharyngeal carcinoma—a rare type of head and neck cancer. I found support from my family, being on Kamilaroi Country, and from the medical staff who looked after me (Fig. 46.1).

I cannot remember exactly when I first started to feel unwell. It was one of those things that just slowly creeps up on you. In 2014, I was living in Alice Springs in Central Australia, working to support Aboriginal children who were in foster care. I went on holiday to Katherine, around 1000 km north of Alice Springs. While I was there, I developed what I thought was a sinus infection. At the time, I put it down to the change in climate and the humidity. But when I got home from holidays, I was sick enough to take time off work. My doctor agreed that I was suffering from a sinus infection and prescribed sinus medication. But the sinus medication did not make any difference at all, and my health slowly declined. By January 2016, I could barely breathe through my nose, I could no longer smell anything, I had persistent sinus headaches, and my sleep was disrupted. I was in a pretty bad way.

All through 2015, I saw the doctor regularly, and I accepted his diagnosis of a sinus infection. In January 2016, he organized a computed tomography (CT) scan and suggested I should have a sphenoidotomy. Thankfully, the sphenoidotomy was delayed because I had a fever. By this stage, I was increasingly concerned that the sinus diagnosis was not correct. It did not seem right that I would suddenly have such severe sinus problems when I never had it before.

I decided to leave Alice Springs and go home to be near my family and near Kamilaroi Country in the Darling Downs area. I thought that maybe I would recover if I was at home. I also knew that I would have better access to specialists in Brisbane.

I arrived in Brisbane in March 2016, almost 18 months after I first visited the doctor with sinus symptoms. Within four days, I had been diagnosed with stage 4 nasopharyngeal carcinoma and had been told about the months of treatment ahead, with 35 treatments of radiation, plus three rounds of chemotherapy. I was ready to fight! The first four weeks of treatment did not seem too bad, but then I got hit with the side effects of radiation and chemo. And on top of my cancer treatment, I was struck down with chickenpox.

In the second half of 2016, I looked fear in the face. I was in my early 30s, and I was not ready to let cancer win. I kept positive by promising myself that I would go fishing and camping with my family at Christmas.

I was lucky to be diagnosed early enough to receive treatment. And I was fortunate that the hospital in Brisbane chose the right treatments, and they worked for me. Slowly but surely, I made progress. I achieved my dream of a Christmas fishing trip, but there were many times when I struggled to remain positive. Three things kept me going—support from my family, living in my home Country (Aboriginal lands) near Rosewood, and using bush medicine alongside medical treatment to keep me as healthy as possible.

Since that treatment in 2016, I have had good days and bad days. I try hard to stay positive, and I continue to fight the cancer. But I have gained strength, courage, and confidence

G. Garvey (ed.), *Indigenous and Tribal Peoples and Cancer*, https://doi.org/10.1007/978-3-031-56806-0_46

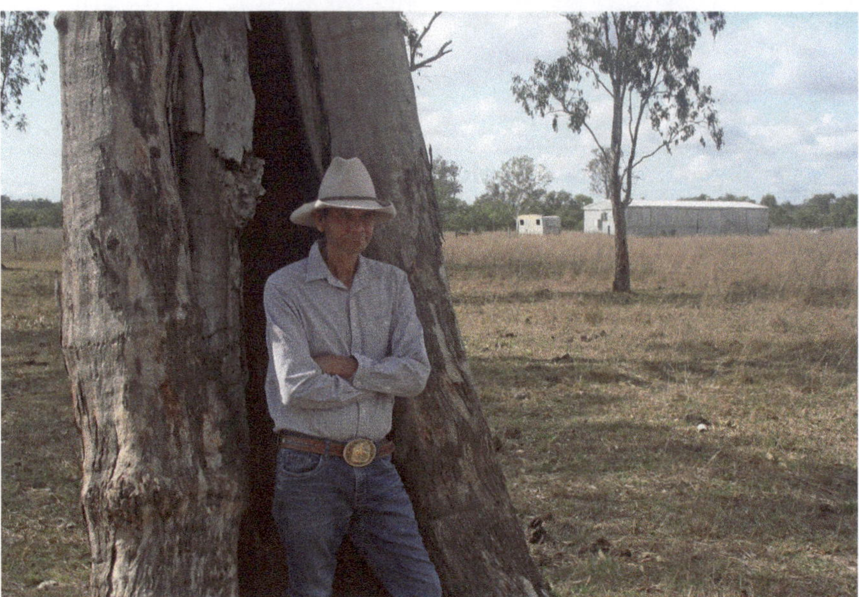

Fig. 46.1 Des McGrady, at home in the Darling Downs region of Australia. (Photo: C Carson)

through the experience. I have learned that I can do things I did not believe were possible.

Since being diagnosed with cancer, I have become a cancer ambassador for the Aboriginal and Torres Strait Islander community in Queensland. I have joined all sorts of committees and provided advice to government and researchers. I do a lot of work in the community, encouraging people to get tested and advocate for their rights. I encourage all the Aboriginal and Torres Strait Islander people I meet to be persistent about asking questions and making sure they get the right medical support.

Fear of Cancer Recurrence Among Indigenous and Tribal People

47

Ben Smith, Kate Anderson, Sophie Lebel, Verena S. Wu, Tamara Butler, and Gail Garvey

Key Points

- The limited available research on fear of cancer recurrence (FCR) in Indigenous populations indicates cultural differences in its experience and management.
- The first study to specifically focus on FCR in an Indigenous population found that clinically significant FCR appears to be more prevalent in this population.
- Aboriginal and Torres Strait Islander people's experiences of FCR are likely to be impacted and amplified by experiences of racism, inequality, and mistrust in their encounters with the healthcare system.
- Leveraging Aboriginal and Torres Strait Islander cultural strengths and providing multidisciplinary care that encourages cultural connection and supports a more holistic view of wellbeing may help mitigate FCR.
- Culturally appropriate FCR care may be enabled by increasing the presence of Aboriginal and Torres Strait Islander staff in healthcare settings and using culturally sensitive tools to screen for FCR.

Fear of cancer recurrence (FCR), defined as "fear, worry or concern relating to the possibility that cancer will come back or progress" [1, p. 3266], is common among people living with and beyond cancer. Experiences of FCR range from minimally intrusive and transient thoughts to debilitating and enduring fears that impact daily functioning and wellbeing [1]. Low levels of FCR could be considered a normal response to the possibility of recurrence that may encourage health-promoting behaviors to reduce recurrence risk. However, a meta-analysis of FCR research largely conducted on non-Indigenous people indicates that most report moderate (40%) or severe/clinical (19%) FCR [2]. Clinical FCR is characterized by persistent, high levels of preoccupation or worry and hypervigilance or hypersensitivity to bodily symptoms lasting for more than three months and impacting daily functioning [3].

This chapter includes results from the first study specifically exploring how FCR affects Indigenous people, which focuses on Australian Aboriginal and Torres Strait Islander women diagnosed with breast cancer. The chapter provides practical suggestions for supporting Indigenous people affected by FCR. We respectfully use the phrase "Indigenous people" to refer to global Indigenous and Tribal populations and "Aboriginal and Torres Strait Islander people" to refer to the Indigenous people of Australia.

Identification, Prevalence, and Severity

A 2020 systematic review of quantitative and qualitative research evaluating FCR in Indigenous and ethnic minority people affected by cancer found that the prevalence of FCR varies considerably (14–67%), potentially due to variable measurement and underlying differences between ethnic and cultural groups [4]. For example, Hispanic people in the United States appear to experience more severe FCR, while non-Hispanic Black cancer survivors experience similar or less severe FCR than non-Hispanic Whites. However, of the 19 studies reviewed, only one evaluated FCR in an Indigenous population. This single qualitative study of Native Hawaiian women affected by breast cancer briefly noted that managing FCR is a supportive care need [5]. Therefore, there is a clear need for:

- Further research exploring Indigenous people's experiences of FCR.
- Culturally relevant and specific tools to assess FCR in Indigenous populations.

Case Study: FCR Among Aboriginal and Torres Strait Islander Women with Breast Cancer

To address the paucity of evidence on FCR among Aboriginal and Torres Strait Islander people in Australia, an Aboriginal-led team partnered with Breast Cancer Network Australia (BCNA)

G. Garvey (ed.), *Indigenous and Tribal Peoples and Cancer*, https://doi.org/10.1007/978-3-031-56806-0_47

to explore (1) FCR prevalence and levels among Aboriginal and Torres Strait Islander breast cancer survivors relative to non-Indigenous counterparts, (2) FCR qualitative experiences and coping strategies (Round 1 interviews), and (3) preferred screening and support options (Round 2 interviews) [6].

Adults who identified as Aboriginal and/or Torres Strait Islander were selected from a BCNA database of people who had volunteered to be contacted regarding research. Recruitment strategies included invitation emails, videos of Elders sharing their breast cancer stories and encouraging participation, and social media posts. Interview participants were offered a $30 gift card for their time. Consenting participants completed an online survey (approximately 15–20 minutes to complete) that included demographic and clinical information and the Fear of Cancer Recurrence Inventory (FCRI) [7]—a validated 42-item multidimensional measure comprising seven subscales (triggers, severity, psychological distress, functioning impairments, insight, reassurance, and coping strategies). FCRI items are answered on Likert scales from 0 (never/not at all) to 4 (all the time/a great deal). Scores range from 0 to 168, with higher scores indicating worse FCR. The FCRI severity subscale (also known as the FCRI-Short Form), has established cut-offs for clinical FCR (≥22/36) and subclinical FCR (≥13/36) [8].

Nineteen participants completed the survey, with almost half (42%) reporting clinically significant FCR and a further third (37%) reporting subclinical FCR. These results suggest that clinical FCR is almost twice as prevalent in this population than in breast cancer survivors generally (42% vs 22%) [2].

Survey participants were invited to participate in a follow-up semi-structured telephone interview, which further explored their experiences of FCR using open-ended questions informed by the seven FCRI subscales. Ten women took part in the first round of interviews—five reported clinical FCR, three subclinical FCR, and two mild FCR. An additional six women participated in the second round of interviews, which explored participants' perspectives regarding FCR identification and support options. Five women from the second round provided survey data; all reported clinical FCR. Interviews were conducted by experienced female qualitative researchers, with thematic analysis of transcripts guided by Mertens' transformative approach [9], which privileges the voices of marginalized groups to reduce inequities. Deductive coding (using FCRI subscales) preceded inductive coding to generate new themes. The perspectives of Aboriginal researchers in the team were privileged in consensus finding. Table 47.1 outlines themes, subthemes, and illustrative quotes.

Factors Exacerbating FCR

These qualitative findings suggest that unique aspects of Aboriginal and Torres Strait Islander breast cancer survivor experiences exacerbate FCR and may contribute to a seemingly higher prevalence of clinically significant FCR in this population (see Butler et al. [6] for further details). For example:

- FCR induced by medical appointments may be exacerbated, owing to a mistrust of the medical system stemming from experiences of institutional racism [10].
- The higher prevalence of comorbid chronic illnesses in cancer survivors stemming from unequal social determinants of health may make survivors more prone to hypervigilance regarding physical symptoms, which commonly trigger FCR.
- A poorer cancer survival rate and greater likelihood of experiencing life-limiting illness within the family/community may lead to heightened concern about the inevitability and impact of recurrence.
- FCR-related distress seems strongly linked to concerns about the impact of recurrence on the family, reflecting the central role of family and community in this culture.

Factors Mitigating FCR

We found that social interaction lessens FCR by limiting rumination or providing emotional support for concerns. While the desire to protect family and friends sometimes inhibits sharing FCR with loved ones, as seen among Native Hawaiian women with breast cancer [5], sharing experiences of cancer and FCR with other cancer survivors, friends, and, in particular, family helps women validate concerns and obtain emotional support. Healthcare professionals should support Aboriginal and Torres Strait Islander people with cancer to discuss FCR with friends/family. However, if people feel uncomfortable sharing their concerns with family/friends, they may benefit from connecting with culturally safe support groups (e.g., yarning circle), where they can share stories and get support.

There is a clear need for culturally appropriate information and resources about the cancer journey and cancer recurrence. Some women find that seeking information helps reduce uncertainty; however, this is sometimes hindered by the lack of information and support that is sensitive to Aboriginal and Torres Strait Islander needs. For instance, follow-up appointments tend to focus solely on medical issues while neglecting psychosocial issues—such as the impact of FCR on social and emotional wellbeing, which are key elements of the more holistic Aboriginal view of health [11]. More holistic care may be achieved through providing multidisciplinary care teams, including psychologists and allied health workers, who can more effectively address culturally important factors, such as the impact of cancer on family, work, and lifestyle behaviors. Activities that help Aboriginal and Torres Strait Islander people connect with

Table 47.1 Themes, subthemes, and exemplar quotes: Aboriginal and Torres Strait Islander women's experiences of fear of cancer recurrence, identification, and support

Themes	Subthemes and exemplar quotes
Based on FCRI subscales	
Psychological distress, severity, and insight into FCR	*Constant source of worry* [Cancer] is … just the most annoying thing ever. It's like this monkey on your back that just is never going to go away. *Impact of worry on family and relationships* In the back of my mind, I just thought I couldn't go through this again. It was painful, the vulnerability, you know, everything and my kids seeing me go through this and everything.
Predisposition to cancer and triggers	*Family history of cancer and other major illnesses* I'm the youngest of the five children. My brother died of a heart attack last year, he was 59. And then the other second sister, the next one down, she had aneurisms a few years ago. So, it's like my turn now, hey. *Physical and mental health concerns* And I've even only got to get the slightest headache and I'm like, "Oh, it could be a brain tumor. It might've come back in my brain." *Medical appointments and treatment* I think my worst time for thinking about all of that was just before my first chemo session … you had to do your bone scan and your CT scan, and so just to check to see whether it's metastasized … I think was the worst week and a half ever … I just worked myself up into such a state about it …
Functioning impairment	*Family, relationships, and work* I'm a little bit hesitant at starting any new relationships, like, with anyone … even friendships … but part of me just says, "Oh well, I might be, you know, dead in six months from now, so what's the point?"
Reassurance and coping	*Social support* They keep my mind active, you know? I love my kids and grandkids and, yeah. So, I was there for them and now they're, sort of, here for me. … [M]y daughter … if she thinks that I'm being silly or anything, she'll tell me, "Just pull in your head in mum," or, "Don't be a pork chop," or anything. *Self-examination, screening, and medical appointments* I check every lump, bumps, everything – every single day. Every time I have my scan, I'm thinking, am I going to get it again … they found another lump in my mastectomy, so my right side, I thought, how can I, they've taken it away. So, it came clear, but you're still in the back of your mind, "Am I going to get it again?" *Trust in cancer care team, medical system, and treatment* … being able to be part of the solution with your doctors, you do what they say you have to do, and I've been very lucky where I've had really good doctors and it's worked out so far. *Outlook and self-care* … [T]hat was a whole attitude I took through the whole process … it was just, right, let's get on with it … From day one, we both just said, right, we'll do whatever treatment that's needed. It's all about living, not about dying. When I used to get it all in my head, I'd just get up and go for a walk ...
New themes	
Need for information and resources	[Information on recurrence] would have helped me a lot, because I felt like I was on my own and I was feeling this on my own.
Communication and holistic care from cancer health professionals	[Cancer care team usually asks about] how you've been going and the tablets I'm on. Usually, I'll go in with a list of questions, but as for my anxiety and stress … I've never, sort of, brought that up with them, maybe I should but, yeah … never had they asked about my actual well-being … Like, how am I coping and everything like that. Dietitians and nutritionists should be a part of aftercare as well, that would help a lot with the worry because there's just so many conflicting information on the internet about what to eat, what not to eat and all this. It's something that someone can clarify that sort of thing. Dietitian or nutritionist I think would help a lot with that, the reoccurrence, fear of recurrence.
Culture and cultural safety	I'm looking actually to try and do some painting, so my Aunty said, "It's very therapeutic." So, I've, sort of, done a few sketches, but I'm yet to go and get my paints and things like that. So, I want to draw on my culture, I'm still learning about my culture … … to be able to stop and have a bit of a yarn to someone [who is also Aboriginal and Torres Strait Islander] … it really makes a difference. I'm trying to articulate it. I think there's a different kind of a connection that you get …
FCR screening	*Cultural congruency* Mob have their own language and their own like colloquialisms and stuff. So, you can direct it towards that kind of language if you worked with the community. *Frequency* I reckon every three months or something, cause that's interesting too. When I go for my checkups … with the team at the moment … they actually could get me to fill in the questionnaire. *Follow-Up* I mean, if you've got an Indigenous liaison officer, they would be good but also a social worker or a psychologist, even the breast care nurse … I don't think it matters who does as long as they are really looking into the answers that are given. I think that's a really good thing to do.

culture and community (e.g., art groups), which were reported to help reduce FCR, should be integrated into care where possible. In the absence of multidisciplinary care, owing to limited resources in rural areas, timely referral to community-based organizations (e.g., Cancer Council in Australia) that provide informational, practical, and emotional support is needed.

Systematic screening for FCR may overcome the reported lack of discussion among healthcare professionals, which is an issue more broadly [12]. Participants in the BCNA study indicated that FCR screening needs to use culturally congruent language and be repeated during follow-up, with results actioned. The routine use of the Supportive Care Needs Assessment Tool for Indigenous People (SCNAT-IP) [13] may aid in the culturally sensitive identification of FCR. SCNAT-IP was developed to accommodate the language, customs, and cultural needs of Aboriginal and Torres Strait Islander people with cancer, and it includes the item "worrying about your illness spreading or getting worse." Study participants indicated that a brief questionnaire would be a useful prompt to discuss concerns with their healthcare team and consequently get the support needed. A follow-up assessment of those reporting FCR in initial screening with the FCRI-SF can determine the severity of FCR and inform treatment recommendations. Cultural competence training for non-Indigenous healthcare staff to increase the understanding of Aboriginal and Torres Strait Islander patients' culture and health perspectives and the recruitment and training of more Aboriginal and Torres Strait Islander healthcare staff may further enable FCR to be raised and addressed in culturally acceptable ways.

Conclusions

There is still much to learn about FCR in Indigenous people affected by cancer. The experience of FCR is likely to be impacted and amplified by experiences of racism, inequality, and mistrust in the healthcare system. FCR may be mitigated by leveraging Aboriginal and Torres Strait Islander cultural strengths and providing multidisciplinary care that encourages cultural connection and supports a more holistic view of wellbeing. Increasing the presence of Aboriginal and Torres Strait Islander staff in healthcare settings and the use of culturally sensitive tools to screen for FCR will lead to more culturally appropriate FCR care. Further research with larger samples in different Indigenous contexts is needed to better understand the prevalence and severity of FCR and implement mitigating strategies.

References

1. Lebel S, Ozakinci G, Humphris G, Mutsaers B, Thewes B, Prins J, et al. From normal response to clinical problem: definition and clinical features of fear of cancer recurrence. *Support Care Cancer*. 2016;24(8):3265–8. https://doi.org/10.1007/s00520-016-3272-5
2. Luigjes-Huizer YL, Tauber NM, Humphris G, Kasparian NA, Lam WWT, Lebel S, et al. What is the prevalence of fear of cancer recurrence in cancer survivors and patients? A systematic review and individual participant data meta-analysis. *Psychooncology*. 2022;31(6):879–92. https://doi.org/10.1002/pon.5921
3. Mutsaers B, Butow P, Dinkel A, Humphris G, Maheu C, Ozakinci G, et al. Identifying the key characteristics of clinical fear of cancer recurrence: An international Delphi study. *Psychooncology*. 2020;29(2):430–6. https://doi.org/10.1002/pon.5283
4. Anderson K, Smith AB, Diaz A, Shaw J, Butow P, Sharpe L, et al. A Systematic Review of Fear of Cancer Recurrence Among Indigenous and Minority Peoples. *Front Psychol*. 2021;12:621850. https://doi.org/10.3389/fpsyg.2021.621850
5. Braun KL, Mokuau N, Hunt GH, Kaanoi M, Gotay CC. Supports and Obstacles to Cancer Survival for Hawaii's Native People. *Cancer Pract*. 2002;10(4):192–200. https://doi.org/10.1046/j.1523-5394.2002.104001.x
6. Butler T, Smith B, Pilatti K, Brown B, Anderson K, Morris B, et al. Fear of Cancer Recurrence among Aboriginal and Torres Strait Islander Women Diagnosed with Breast Cancer. *Curr Oncol*. 2023;30(3):2900–15. https://doi.org/10.3390/curroncol30030222
7. Simard S, Savard J. Fear of Cancer Recurrence Inventory: development and initial validation of a multidimensional measure of fear of cancer recurrence. *Support Care Cancer*. 2009;17(3):241–51. https://doi.org/10.1007/s00520-008-0444-y
8. Fardell JE, Jones G, Smith AB, Lebel S, Thewes B, Costa D, et al. Exploring the screening capacity of the Fear of Cancer Recurrence Inventory-Short Form for clinical levels of fear of cancer recurrence. *Psychooncology*. 2018;27(2):492–9. https://doi.org/10.1002/pon.4516
9. Mertens DM. Transformative Mixed Methods Research. *Qual Inq*. 2010;16(6):469–74. https://doi.org/10.1177/1077800410364612
10. Henry BR, Houston S, Mooney GH. Institutional racism in Australian healthcare: a plea for decency. *Med J Aust*. 2004;180(10):517–20. https://doi.org/10.5694/j.1326-5377.2004.tb06056.x
11. Gee G, Dudgeon P, Schultz C, Hart A, Kelly K. Aboriginal and Torres Strait Islander social and emotional wellbeing. In: Dudgeon P, Milroy H, Walker R, editors. *Aboriginal and Torres Strait Islander Mental Health and Wellbeing Principles and Practice*. Barton ACT: Australian Government; 2014. p. 55–68.
12. Liu J, Butow P, Beith J. Systematic review of interventions by non-mental health specialists for managing fear of cancer recurrence in adult cancer survivors. *Support Care Cancer*. 2019;27(11):4055–67. https://doi.org/10.1007/s00520-019-04979-8
13. Garvey G, Beesley VL, Janda M, O'Rourke PK, He VYF, Hawkes AL, et al. Psychometric properties of an Australian supportive care needs assessment tool for Indigenous patients with cancer. *Cancer*. 2015;121(17):3018–26. https://doi.org/10.1002/cncr.29433

BY NC ND

48 Cancer and Comorbidity in Indigenous Populations

Mi Hye Jeon, Jason Gurney, Gail Garvey, and Abbey Diaz

Key Points

- Cancer patients commonly live with additional chronic conditions, which may affect their prognosis and outcomes.
- The international literature suggests that Indigenous peoples with cancer are more likely to have concomitant comorbidity than non-Indigenous peoples.
- Diabetes, cardiovascular disease, and respiratory disease are the most common comorbid conditions among Indigenous peoples with cancer.
- Diabetes and cancer commonly co-occur in Māori in Aotearoa New Zealand. Higher rates of co-occurrence are observed for Māori compared to non-Māori for most cancer types, particularly for gastrointestinal, endocrine, and obesity-related cancers.

People who are diagnosed with cancer commonly have additional coexisting chronic conditions, referred to as comorbidity [1]. Comorbidity has been associated with elevated excess mortality in cancer populations [2, 3]. Preexisting comorbidity may affect treatment options, decisions, and tolerance. Both existing and new comorbidities that develop during and after cancer treatment can impact opportunities to participate in clinical trials. As such, the personalization and optimization of cancer care requires a careful consideration of an individual's comorbidity burden [1, 2].

Generally, Indigenous people with cancer have a higher prevalence and increased severity of preexisting comorbidity compared to non-Indigenous people with cancer. The measured prevalence of comorbidity is likely to depend on the population, clinical features, comorbidity measures, and data sources. In Australia, the reported prevalence derived from hospital admission data of having at least one comorbidity ranges from 10% in Aboriginal and Torres Strait Islander women diagnosed with breast cancer [4] to 61% in Aboriginal and Torres Strait Islander people diagnosed with any cancer type [5]. When using medical chart data, the estimates range from 37% in Aboriginal and Torres Strait Islander people diagnosed with head and neck cancers [6] to 60% in Aboriginal and Torres Strait Islander people diagnosed with non-small cell lung cancer [7].

In Aotearoa New Zealand, the prevalence of having at least one comorbidity ranges from 10% among Māori women diagnosed with cervical cancer [8] to 63% among Māori diagnosed with stomach cancer [9]. In the United States, 52% of American Indian and Alaska Native peoples with cancer had at least one comorbidity [10].

The most prevalent coexisting comorbid conditions in Indigenous populations are respiratory disease (range: 6–74%) [11, 12], cardiovascular disease (7–52%) [12], hypertension (11–47%) [13], and diabetes (12–45%) [6]. Generally, these conditions were more prevalent in Indigenous than non-Indigenous cancer populations. Survival inequalities between Indigenous and non-Indigenous cancer patients have been shown as partly due to the underlying elevated comorbidity burden in both Australia [11] and Aotearoa New Zealand [14]. Inequalities in intermediate factors, such as time from diagnosis to treatment, may also be affected by the presence of comorbidity, as shown in the United States [10].

The Co-occurrence of Diabetes and Cancer for Indigenous Māori in Aotearoa New Zealand

Indigenous Māori in Aotearoa New Zealand (NZ) are around 20% more likely to be diagnosed with cancer but nearly twice as likely to die from cancer in comparison with non-Indigenous New Zealanders [15]. In addition to experiencing a disproportionate burden of cancer, Māori and Pacific peoples are also more likely to develop diabetes. The prevalence of diabetes mellitus is increasing in NZ by 7% per year and is approximately three times higher among Māori and Pacific people than in European New Zealanders [16].

G. Garvey (ed.), *Indigenous and Tribal Peoples and Cancer*, https://doi.org/10.1007/978-3-031-56806-0_48

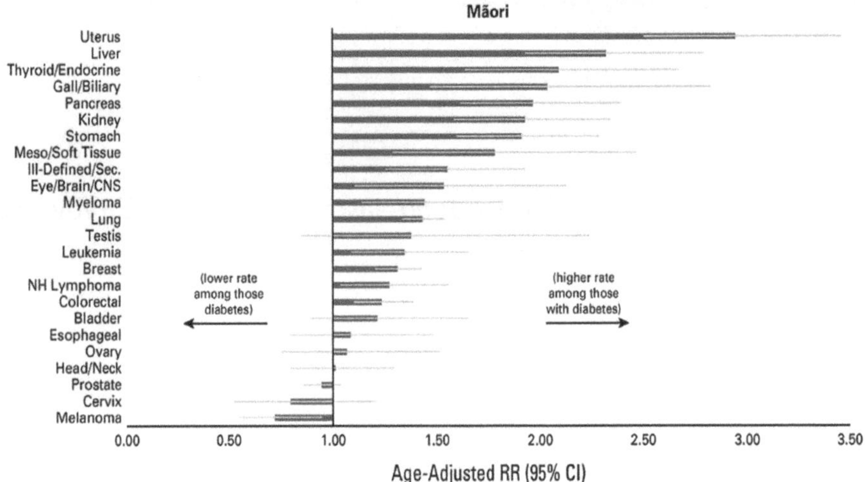

Fig. 48.1 Forest plot comparing rates of individual cancers among Māori with diabetes compared to Māori without diabetes. (Source: Gurney et al. [25])

The co-occurrence of diabetes and cancer arises from a combination of factors:

- *Shared risk factors*: obesity and physical inactivity are key risk factors for both diabetes and cancer. The majority of diabetes cases can be attributed to obesity [17], while around 25% of postmenopausal breast cancers and 20% of both uterine and colon cancers can be attributed to obesity [18].
- *People with diabetes are more likely to get some cancers*: diabetes is linked to an increased risk of multiple cancers due to a combination of shared risk factors, insulin-resistance-related cell proliferation and dysfunction in programmed cell death, and chronic inflammation [19].
- *People with some cancers are more likely to get diabetes*: in the other direction, those who develop cancer are more likely to also develop diabetes than those who do not develop cancer. For example, there is an increased risk of diabetes development among colorectal cancer patients [20].
- *Both conditions occur commonly*: aside from being directly linked, the co-occurrence of diabetes and cancer is also related to both conditions being common—wherein an individual may have both conditions, without the two being linked at all.

The co-occurrence of cancer and diabetes has important consequences for cancer outcomes. The presence of diabetes can lead to delays in cancer diagnosis [21], increased risk of developing metastases [22], and reduced likelihood of receiving aggressive curative cancer treatment [23]. An Australian study showed that Indigenous Australians with cancer and diabetes were 40% more likely to die compared with Indigenous Australians with cancer but no diabetes (adj. hazard ratio: 1.4, 95% CI 1.1–1.8)—but found little evidence for differences by diabetes status for non-Indigenous patients (adj. hazard ratio: 0.8, 95% CI 0.5–1.2) [24].

A recent study in NZ examined differences in the rate of diabetes and cancer co-occurrence, both within and between ethnic groups [25]. To do this, national-level data on diabetes prevalence were extracted from New Zealand's Virtual Diabetes Register, and national-level data on cancer registrations were extracted from the New Zealand Cancer Registry. Nearly five million individuals over 44 million person-years were used to describe the rate of diabetes and cancer co-occurrence, with an emphasis on comparing rates between Indigenous Māori and the majority European population.

The investigation found that the rate of cancer (including the majority of individual cancers) was highest for those with diabetes compared to those without diabetes—but more importantly, the rate of cancer and diabetes co-occurrence was much higher among Indigenous Māori compared to other ethnic groups (age-standardized rate (ASR): Māori 1304/100,000 person-years (PY); Europeans 1165/100,000; Pacific 949/100,000; other Asians 670/100,000; South Asians 474/100,000) [25]. When the study directly compared ethnic groups, only Māori with diabetes had a higher rate of cancer than Europeans with diabetes (rate ratio (RR): 1.12, 95% CI 1.08–1.16).

For Māori, the rate of cancer was higher for those with diabetes for the majority of cancer types (Fig. 48.1). The highest rate of cancer and diabetes co-occurrence for Māori was found for uterine (RR: 2.94, 95% CI 2.50–3.46), liver (RR 2.32, 95% CI 1.93–2.80), thyroid/endocrine (RR 2.10, 95% CI 1.64–2.68), gallbladder/biliary (RR 2.04, 95% CI 1.47–2.83), pancreatic (RR 1.97, 95% CI 1.62–2.40), kidney (RR 1.93, 95% CI 1.59–2.34), and stomach (RR 1.91, 95% CI 1.60–2.29) cancers.

As such, gastrointestinal, endocrine, and obesity-related cancers formed the bulk of those cancers that co-occurred most commonly among Māori. This finding strongly reinforces the need to prevent those risk factors that are shared between diabetes and cancer. It also reinforces the need for a multidisciplinary approach to the care of both diabetes and cancer, particularly for Indigenous populations who experience a disproportionate burden of both conditions.

Conclusion

The heightened risk of comorbidity in Indigenous peoples with cancer seems to partially explain elevated excess mortality. Diabetes, cardiovascular disease, and respiratory disease are particularly prevalent. Culturally responsive strategies for the prevention and early detection of these conditions after a cancer diagnosis may help address the persistent gaps in cancer-specific and overall survival experienced by Indigenous peoples.

References

1. Sarfati D, Koczwara B, Jackson C. The impact of comorbidity on cancer and its treatment. *CA Cancer J Clin.* 2016;66(4):337–50. https://doi.org/10.3322/caac.21342
2. Pal SK, Hurria A. Impact of age, sex, and comorbidity on cancer therapy and disease progression. *J Clin Oncol.* 2010;28(26):4086–93. https://doi.org/10.1200/JCO.2009.27.0579
3. Søgaard M, Thomsen RW, Bossen KS, Sørensen HT, Nørgaard M. The impact of comorbidity on cancer survival: a review. *Clin Epidemiol.* 2013;5(sup1):3–29. https://doi.org/10.2147/CLEP.S47150
4. Fitzadam S, Lin E, Creighton N, Currow DC. Lung, breast and bowel cancer treatment for Aboriginal people in New South Wales: a population-based cohort study. *Intern Med J.* 2021;51(6):879–90. https://doi.org/10.1111/imj.14967
5. Banham D, Roder D, Brown A. Comorbidities contribute to the risk of cancer death among Aboriginal and non-Aboriginal South Australians: Analysis of a matched cohort study. *Cancer Epidemiol.* 2018;52:75–82. https://doi.org/10.1016/j.canep.2017.12.005
6. Moore SP, Green AC, Garvey G, Coory MD, Valery PC. A study of head and neck cancer treatment and survival among indigenous and non-indigenous people in Queensland, Australia, 1998 to 2004. *BMC Cancer.* 2011;11(1):460. https://doi.org/10.1186/1471-2407-11-460
7. Whop LJ, Bernardes CM, Kondalsamy-Chennakesavan S, Darshan D, Chetty N, Moore SP, et al. Indigenous Australians with non–small cell lung cancer or cervical cancer receive suboptimal treatment. *Asia Pac J Clin Oncol.* 2017;13(5):e224–e231. https://doi.org/10.1111/ajco.12463
8. Brewer N, Borman B, Sarfati D, Jeffreys M, Fleming ST, Cheng S, et al. Does comorbidity explain the ethnic inequalities in cervical cancer survival in New Zealand? A retrospective cohort study. *BMC Cancer.* 2011;11(1):132. https://doi.org/10.1186/1471-2407-11-132
9. Signal V, Sarfati D, Cunningham R, Gurney J, Koea J, Ellison-Loschmann L. Indigenous inequities in the presentation and management of stomach cancer in New Zealand: a country with universal health care coverage. *Gastric Cancer.* 2015;18(3):571–9. https://doi.org/10.1007/s10120-014-0410-y
10. Adams SV, Bansal A, Burnett-Hartman AN, Cohen SA, Karnopp A, Warren-Mears V, et al. Cancer Treatment Delays in American Indians and Alaska Natives Enrolled in Medicare. *J Health Care Poor Underserved.* 2017;28(1):350–61. https://doi.org/10.1353/hpu.2017.0027
11. Diaz A, Baade PD, Valery PC, Whop LJ, Moore SP, Cunningham J, et al. Comorbidity and cervical cancer survival of Indigenous and non-Indigenous Australian women: A semi-national registry-based cohort study (2003-2012). *PLoS One.* 2018;13(5):e0196764. https://doi.org/10.1371/journal.pone.0196764
12. Basnayake TL, Valery PC, Carson P, De Ieso PB. Treatment and outcomes for indigenous and non-indigenous lung cancer patients in the Top End of the Northern Territory. *Intern Med J.* 2021;51(7):1081–91. https://doi.org/10.1111/imj.14961
13. Hill S, Sarfati D, Blakely T, Robson B, Purdie G, Dennett E, et al. Ethnicity and management of colon cancer in New Zealand. *Cancer.* 2010;116(13):3205–14. https://doi.org/10.1002/cncr.25127
14. Hill S, Sarfati D, Blakely T, Robson B, Purdie G, Chen J, et al. Survival disparities in Indigenous and non-Indigenous New Zealanders with colon cancer: the role of patient comorbidity, treatment and health service factors. *J Epidemiol Community Health.* 2010;64(2):117–23. https://doi.org/10.1136/jech.2008.083816
15. Robson B, Purdie G, Cormack D. *Unequal Impact II: Māori and Non-Māori Cancer Statistics by Deprivation and Rural-Urban Status, 2002-2006.* Wellington, New Zealand: Ministry of Health; 2010.
16. Health Quality and Safety Commission. *Atlas of Healthcare Variation - Diabetes.* Wellington, New Zealand: Health Quality and Safety Commission; 2020.
17. Flegal KM, Panagiotou OA, Graubard BI. Estimating population attributable fractions to quantify the health burden of obesity. *Ann Epidemiol.* 2015;25(3):201–7. https://doi.org/10.1016/j.annepidem.2014.11.010
18. International Agency for Research on Cancer. *Global Cancer Observatory: Cancer Attributable to Obesity* [Internet]. 2020 [cited 2020 Jul 17]. Available from: https://gco.iarc.fr/causes/obesity/home
19. Giovannucci E, Harlan DM, Archer MC, Bergenstal RM, Gapstur SM, Habel LA, et al. Diabetes and cancer: a consensus report. *Diabetes Care.* 2010;33(7):1674–85. https://doi.org/10.2337/dc10-0666
20. Singh S, Earle CC, Bae SJ, Fischer HD, Yun L, Austin PC, et al. Incidence of Diabetes in Colorectal Cancer Survivors. *J Natl Cancer Inst.* 2016;108(6):djv402. https://doi.org/10.1093/jnci/djv402
21. Gurney J, Sarfati D, Stanley J. The impact of patient comorbidity on cancer stage at diagnosis. *Br J Cancer.* 2015;113:1375–80. https://doi.org/10.1038/bjc.2015.355
22. Du W, Simon MS. Racial disparities in treatment and survival of women with stage I-III breast cancer at a large academic medical center in metropolitan Detroit. *Breast Cancer Res Treat.* 2005;91(3):243–8. https://doi.org/10.1007/s10549-005-0324-9
23. Renehan AG, Yeh HC, Johnson JA, Wild SH, Gale EAM, Møller H. Diabetes and cancer (2): evaluating the impact of diabetes on mortality in patients with cancer. *Diabetologia.* 2012;55(6):1619–32. https://doi.org/10.1007/s00125-012-2526-0
24. Martin JH, Coory MD, Valery PC, Green AC. Association of diabetes with survival among cohorts of Indigenous and non-Indigenous Australians with cancer. *Cancer Causes Control.* 2009;20(3):355–60. https://doi.org/10.1007/s10552-008-9249-z
25. Gurney J, Stanley J, Teng A, Robson B, Scott N, Sika-Paotonu D, et al. Equity of Cancer and Diabetes Co-Occurrence: A National Study With 44 Million Person-Years of Follow-Up. *JCO Glob Oncol.* 2023;9:e2200357. https://doi.org/10.1200/Go.22.00357

BY NC ND

49 Health Equity Through Networked Healthcare Systems Using Telehealth

Sabe Sabesan and Liela Murison

Key Points

- Innovations in system strengthening and creating formal networks can assist in bridging the health inequality gap faced by Indigenous communities.
- Telehealth-enabled models of care can provide cancer care closer to home.
- Health inequalities need to be standing agenda items at team meetings of all layers and streams of health providers and of all committees and working groups for them to be systematically addressed and improved.

Indigenous people from regional, rural, and remote (RRR) Australia live in small communities that usually lack the infrastructure critical for effective healthcare delivery. Care delivery issues are compounded by difficulties in attracting and retaining healthcare workers and providing specialist services in stand-alone centers. RRR communities rely on advocacy and support from their colleagues, government departments, and politicians. This calls for a networked approach to healthcare delivery, whereby small communities are linked with larger regional and rural towns and tertiary care facilities, allowing care delivery and workforce planning to be addressed holistically rather than relying on siloes [1].

To create this networked approach to enable equitable health systems, a culture of collaboration, purpose, and values alignment needs to occur across all layers of the system, from the political sector to the frontline workforce [2]. It also requires collective leadership and governance so that Indigenous communities do not have to rely on champions. Co-designing models of care with communities can instill a sense of ownership.

Telehealth-Enabled Cancer Care Systems

Telehealth has been established as a tangible model of care to create networked systems across the world, especially in response to the COVID-19 pandemic [3, 4]. Over the last two years, the world has seen the rapid growth of telehealth models as part of government agendas to address health inequities and keep communities safe from the pandemic. Telehealth has been used for consultations in primary and specialist care settings, shared-care models, remote supervision of chemotherapy and biotherapy administration and other medical procedures, clinical trials, preventive education for patients and their families, and remote education and mentoring of health professionals [5]. A hallmark of these models is the collaboration between health professionals and organizations that form the foundations of networked systems.

Telehealth models are welcomed by communities and health professionals for their many benefits. In a study by Mooi et al., health professionals listed professional support and networking, on-the-job learning of specialist topics, family involvement in care, and shared-care models with local health professionals as some of the key benefits [6]. While people prefer care closer to home, they expect the same quality of care as enjoyed by their metropolitan counterparts.

Clinical Consultations

Telehealth has been widely used to provide clinical consultations, including new and ongoing reviews. When a face-to-face consultation is offered to RRR patients at a larger center, they may need the help of an escort and may not be able to suddenly drop their day-to-day business for that visit. In most cases, only one escort can travel with a patient, who may or may not be familiar with the healthcare setting at a larger center. Telehealth can enable timely reviews closer to home [7].

New consultations via telehealth can be useful for triaging patients and coordinating the necessary activities when patients travel for in-person care and reviews. While physical examination has been cited as an issue, this has been addressed through shared-care models with rural GPs, junior doctors, physicians, and healthcare students in placements.

G. Garvey (ed.), *Indigenous and Tribal Peoples and Cancer*, https://doi.org/10.1007/978-3-031-56806-0_49

Examples of Telehealth Models

Several models of telehealth have been adopted by health professionals to provide care closer to home—depending on the nature of the care required, site capabilities, the type of available technology, and family and health professional support. Regardless of the availability of care they can receive closer to home, a few patients elected to travel to larger centers for privacy reasons (being from a small community) and due to the unavailability of family members for support, being away from home. For consultations, local support can be provided by nurses, health workers, medical and nursing students, and family members. Occasionally, when technology permits, consultations have been provided at home, with other family members attending in person or virtually. For chemotherapy administration and complex medical care, partnership with general practitioners and other professionals with specialized skills is necessary.

Chemotherapy and Biotherapy Administration

Multidisciplinary remote supervision models offer the opportunity to provide chemotherapy and biotherapy closer to home right across the country. For example, the Queensland Remote Chemotherapy Supervision (QReCS) model sets out governance for safety and the quality of services [8]. These models are underpinned by a collaboration between nurses and medical and pharmacy professionals through telenursing, telemedicine, and telepharmacy mechanisms. This model is adopted or adapted for remote chemotherapy and biotherapy delivery in Queensland, Northern Territory, New South Wales, South Australia, and Western Australia.

The choice of chemotherapy delivered at rural sites will be determined by site capabilities, the availability of support for complications, and the nature of the chemotherapy conducted. Usually, complex regimens that cause complex reactions are not suitable for rural sites unless support mechanisms are available. Two North Queensland studies reported patient and family satisfaction with these models and the safety of remote chemotherapy supervision. A review by Deloitte demonstrated that the models offer a good return on investment [9, 10].

Clinical Trials

The Australasian Teletrial model has leveraged telehealth and telechemotherapy experiences to transform the way clinical trials are delivered to regional, rural, and Indigenous communities [11]. Based on positive pilot results in Victoria, New South Wales, and Queensland, the Medical Research Future Fund (MRFF) set up Australian Teletrial and NSW/ACT RRR programs to roll out this model across the country [12]. The aim is to transform Australia into a networked clinical trial system so that communities can gain access to some or all aspects of clinical trials closer to home. The pilot study showed that clinical trial clusters can be developed through collaboration between health professionals, regulatory officers, and managers. This program also offers an opportunity to streamline regulatory processes so that the workforce can focus on care delivery without wasting time on unnecessary and duplicative processes. Safety and quality are ensured by documentation about the nature of the collaboration, with supervision plans and legal requirements covered by cluster subcontracts.

Prevention Initiatives

One of the key benefits of telehealth models for Indigenous communities is that family members can attend consultations together with their loved ones [6], giving them the opportunity to learn about the illness and methods to prevent recurrence. One successful example is My Family's Anti-Tobacco Education pilot, which demonstrated that the model was feasible and accepted by families and patients to manage tobacco-related head and neck cancer [13]. In this model, the specialist who is caring for a patient with a smoking-related illness becomes a mentor for the close and extended family of the patient after receiving consent. The specialist uses test results and medical images of the patient to explain the impact of smoking on their loved one. By combining a few in-person visits with virtual visits, the specialist supports family members to decide to quit. Once they have decided to quit, they are helped by primary care physicians who are a part of the group. The success of these models depends on the willingness of specialists and a stable primary care sector.

Rural Capacity Building as a Key Outcome

While providing services to patients is the key focus of telehealth on a day-to-day basis, sustainability is required to achieve long-term outcomes. Experiences in Mt Isa (Queensland) have highlighted the platform that telehealth models offer for system-building initiatives to ensure sustainability [14]. Through a networked approach between Townsville University Hospital and Mt Isa hospitals, Mt Isa acquired a new cancer center; employed more nursing, pharmacy, and medical staff dedicated to cancer care; and provided the most complex systemic therapy regimens locally. Recently, Mt Isa has become a hub for remote communities such as Cloncurry, with some cancer services (such as pump disconnection) now performed locally under remote supervision from Mt Isa. Mt Isa was also activated as a satellite site for the MONARCHE trial (comparing hormonal therapy with Abemaciclib and hormonal therapy in early breast cancer), though no recruitment occurred given the trial's short duration. Through the Teletrial model, Mt Isa has become a routine part of the Townsville cluster.

New Culture of Implementation

Current siloed approaches continue to perpetuate the disparities in outcomes, access, and resources faced by RRR communities. Staff turnover, of both managers and frontline workers, as well as the critical shortage of staff with leadership talent, compound the issues. New approaches to leadership, culture, and governance are needed, as outlined by Health Q32—the Queensland Government's 10-year health plan [1, 2]. As a minimum, these communities need to be integrated into statewide systems rather than being treated as isolated entities. This requires a mindset of integration and collaboration at all levels of the system and with primary care, regardless of the territorial status of the health services. This methodology enables a whole-of-system approach to manage workforce distribution, training, access, handovers, ward reviews, treatment, and resource allocation. This culture of collaboration and integration requires purpose-aligned teams, a culture of co-design, and workforce-enabling operational behaviors, policies, and procedures. It also requires the monitoring and enabling of these activities at local and system levels.

References

1. Queensland Health. *Health Q32: A vision for Queensland's health system* [Internet]. 2023 May 3. Available from: https://www.health.qld.gov.au/system-governance/strategic-direction/plans/healthq32
2. Sabesan S, Kirk M. Health systems run differently: flatten the pyramid and try something new. *The Health Advocate*. 2022 Nov;69:22–24. Available from: https://issuu.com/aushealthcare/docs/the_health_advocate_november_2022
3. Hazin R, Qaddoumi I. Teleoncology: current and future applications for improving cancer care globally. *Lancet Oncol.* 2010;11(2):204–10. https://doi.org/10.1016/S1470-2045(09)70288-8
4. Sabesan S, Larkins S, Evans R, Varma S, Andrews A, Beuttner P, et al. Telemedicine for cancer care in NQ: bringing cancer care home. *Aust J Rural Health.* 2012 Oct;20(5):259–64. https://doi.org/10.1111/j.1440-1584.2012.01299.x
5. Sabesan S. Medical models of teleoncology: Current status and future directions. *Asia Pac J Clin Oncol.* 2014 Jun 17. https://doi.org/10.1111/ajco.12225
6. Mooi J, Whop L, Valery P, Sabesan S. Teleoncology for Indigenous patients: The responses of patients and health workers. *Aust J Rural Health.* 2012 Oct;20(5):265–69. https://doi.org/10.1111/j.1440-1584.2012.01302.x
7. Sabesan S, Roberts L, Aiken P, Joshi A, Larkins S. Timely access to specialist medical oncology services closer to home for rural patients: Experience from the Townsville Teleoncology Model. *Aust J Rural Health.* 2014 Aug;22(4):156–59. https://doi.org/10.1111/ajr.12101
8. Queensland Health. *Queensland Remote Chemotherapy Supervision guide (QReCS).* Brisbane: Queensland Health; 2019. Available from: https://www.health.qld.gov.au/__data/assets/pdf_file/0029/818246/QReCS-Guide-2019-Compressed.pdf
9. Sabesan S, Senko C, Schmidt A, Joshi A, Pandey R, Ryan CA, et al. Enhancing Chemotherapy Capabilities in Rural Hospitals: Implementation of a Tele-chemotherapy Model (QReCS) in North Queensland, Australia. *J Oncol Pract.* 2018,14(7):e429–e437. https://doi.org/10.1200/JOP.18.00110
10. Jhaveri D, Larkins S, Kelly J, Sabesan S. Remote chemotherapy supervision model for rural cancer care: perspectives of health professionals. *Eur J Cancer Care (Engl).* 2016;25(1):93–8. https://doi.org/10.1111/ecc.12309
11. Department of Health. *National principles for Teletrials in Australia.* Canberra: Commonwealth Department of Health; 2021. Available from: https://www.health.gov.au/resources/publications/national-principles-for-teletrials-in-australia?language=en
12. Sabesan S, Malica M, Gebbie C, Scott C, Thomas D, Zalcberg J. Implementation of the Australasian Teletrial Model: Concept to implementation using implementation science frameworks. *J Telemed Telecare.* 2023 Sep;29(8):641–47. https://doi.org/10.1177/1357633X211017805
13. Sabesan S, Kelly J, Budden L, Geia LK. My Family's Anti-Tobacco Education (My-FATE) model for Aboriginal and Torres Strait Islander peoples. *Aust J Rural Health.* 2015 Jun; 23(3),189–90. https://doi.org/10.1111/ajr.12130
14. Sabesan S, Allen D, Caldwell P, Loh PK, Mozer R, Komesaroff PA, et al. Practical aspects of telehealth: Establishing telehealth in an institution. *Internal Medicine Journal.* 2014;44(2):202–5. https://doi.org/10.1111/imj.12339

50 Satellite Telechemotherapy as a Model to Overcome Geographic Access Barriers to Cancer Care in Peru

Tatiana Vidaurre, Guillermo Valencia, Patricia Rioja, Andrea Meza, Jule Vásquez, Luis Mas, Claudio Flores, Jeannie Navarro, and Stéphane Bertani

Key Points

- The geographical remoteness of Amazonian Indigenous communities in Peru limits their access to cancer care.
- Satellite telechemotherapy helps overcome geographic barriers to cancer care in remote regions.
- A telechemotherapy center was successfully implemented in the Amazonian city of Lamas, home to the Kichwa-Lamista people.
- Satellite telechemotherapy can provide significant cost savings and demonstrable improvements in the quality of life in Amazonian Indigenous communities.

Cancer is the second most common cause of death worldwide and was responsible for approximately one in six deaths (nearly ten million) in 2020. Approximately 70% of cancer deaths occur in low- and middle-income countries, and less than 30% of these countries have treatment services for cancer patients comparable to those of high-income countries [1]. According to Globocan 2020, cancer was the leading cause of death in Peru (14.8%) [2], with an estimated 34,976 incidences. The most frequent cancers were prostate (12.5%), breast (9.8%), stomach (9%), colorectal (6.6%), and cervical (6.1%) [3].

Peru's national cancer plan (Plan Esperanza) was launched by the Instituto Nacional de Enfermedades Neoplásicas (INEN) in 2012. Multiple strategies were identified and implemented, including (but not limited to) decentralization, the development of institutional clinical practice guidelines, access to new oncological drugs, and awareness campaigns [4]. However, one of the most significant barriers to accessing cancer care in Peru is its complex geography. Nearly 50% of patients have to travel long and even dangerous distances to receive adequate cancer care mainly in the capital, Lima (at INEN), with expensive out-of-pocket costs [5]. Moreover, 75% of the cases referred to Lima are in advanced stages, which require systemic treatment (mainly chemotherapy) [6]. This barrier is common in remote regions, especially in Amazonian Indigenous communities, where few services for optimal cancer management exist. However, telemedicine has been demonstrated to play an important role in medical care worldwide, being widely used in the COVID-19 pandemic, even in countries with limited internet access [7]. In this context, the present study concerns a "distance-telemedicine-enabled" strategy that has been enacted by medical oncologists through an outpatient telechemotherapy module in a Peruvian jungle hospital (Lamas Hospital, San Martín) [8].

Methods

A Satellite Telechemotherapy Centre was implemented in Lamas Hospital, Lamas, San Martín department (region) (1100 km from Lima) for II-E (second-level) care from November 2015 to March 2018 as a remote oncology service located in the Peruvian jungle with a considerable Indigenous population. Its implementation and efficacy analysis were conducted in three main stages:

1. Organization—health professionals were trained, and a central chemotherapy room was developed.
2. Definition of inclusion criteria and application of systemic treatment—the inclusion criteria were as follows: patients >18 years from the San Martín region with a histopathological diagnosis of cancer, performance status (ECOG) <3, in need of systemic chemotherapy, and first cycle of chemotherapy received in Lima (INEN) without serious adverse events. The exclusion criteria were the presence of an uncontrolled comorbid disease, contraindication of chemotherapy, pregnancy, and participation in an ongoing clinical trial.
3. Analysis and monitoring—efficacy, patient adherence to systemic treatment, adverse events, patient quality of life (QoL), and costs were evaluated.

G. Garvey (ed.), *Indigenous and Tribal Peoples and Cancer*, https://doi.org/10.1007/978-3-031-56806-0_50

Organization of Implementation

A working team was trained at INEN and included one medical officer, three medical oncologists, three nurses, and one pharmacist. A central chemotherapy module with 18 chairs for infusions, a hospitalization room, one medical office, one nursing station, and one administrative office room was established (Fig. 50.1). Consultations on complex cases or for therapeutic decisions were conducted in INEN (Lima) via satellital telemedicine.

Patients and Application of Systemic Treatment

Patient selection was initially performed exclusively at INEN with adherence to the inclusion and exclusion criteria above. A total of 121 patients were considered, and 56 were enrolled in the program. Patients received systemic treatment according to INEN policies and protocols. Chemotherapy was initiated at INEN and continued in Lamas. The procedures were supervised by medical oncologists from INEN and were reg-

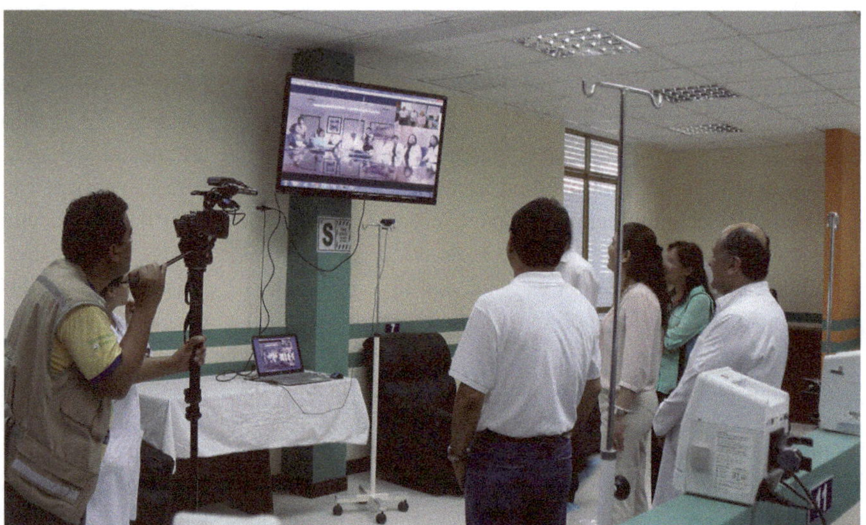

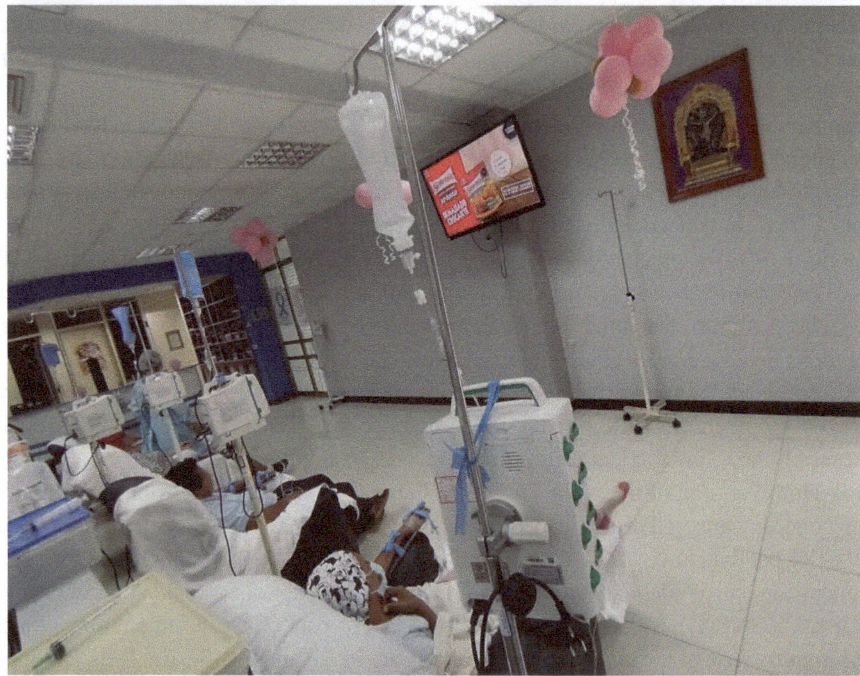

Fig. 50.1 The chemotherapy module at Lamas Hospital, Lamas, San Martín, Peru. (Photos: INEN hospital collection (top), Andrea Meza (bottom))

istered in both centers. The medical team at Lamas and INEN held medical evaluation meetings before each cycle of treatment.

First-Step Analysis

An estimated 300 new cancer cases are reported in San Martín annually. INEN receives referrals from all centers under comprehensive health insurance in Peru (SIS—a system of free or low-cost health insurance) across the country. Nearly 80 patients from San Martín were being initiated chemotherapy at INEN each year. Procedures were recorded in medical records at Lamas hospital and INEN. Epidemiological data, oncological diagnosis, types of chemotherapy and/or hormonal therapy, number of chemotherapy sessions, and description of adverse events (graded according to CTCAE version 4.0) were included. A cost survey was used to evaluate patient travel from home to Lima or Lamas, including transportation, food, and accommodation costs. Quality of Life (QoL) was assessed using a questionnaire (EORTC QLQ-C30 version 3) validated in Spanish [7], which evaluates patient perception of global health, functional status in different spheres, and symptoms related to the disease.

Implementation Results

A total of 56 patients were included for telechemotherapy; the median age was 56 (19–78), and most were women (73.2%). The most frequent cancers were breast (32.1%), cervix (18.9%), and gastric (17.0%). In terms of clinical stage, the majority had metastatic disease (73.2%). Including a median follow-up 24 months from the initiation of telechemotherapy, 501 telemedicine sessions were performed. A total of 232 cycles of chemotherapy were administered (82% intravenous, 13% oral, and the remaining 5% hormone therapy). No acute complications were reported. Late hematological complications included grade 2 neutropenia (15.7%), grade 4 neutropenia (afebrile) (5.2%), grade 1 anemia (5.2%), and grade 4 thrombocytopenia (5.2%) with ecchymosis and resolved with adequate support. Nonhematological adverse events were grade 1 neuropathy (10.5%). Complete adherence was achieved (100%); neither patients nor relatives traveled to Lima, instead receiving chemotherapy close to home. QoL was improved in the third month (global health status increased from 76.67% to 83.33%), particularly in terms of social and emotional wellbeing. Symptoms tended to decrease with time (chemotherapy effect on disease control), and patients reported a decrease in economic difficulties over the three-month treatment period. Regarding costs, there was an average saving of 500 Peruvian soles (PEN) (or 153.54 USD).

Dissemination of Oncology Services in Lamas

San Martín is the fifth most Indigenously populated department (region) of Peru with approximately 24,319 Indigenous inhabitants, representing 4% of its total population. These inhabitants come from four linguistic families and are distributed in different ethnic towns in each of the department's provinces, with the exception of Mariscal Cáceres. The provinces with the largest Indigenous populations are Lamas (7624 inhabitants), San Martín (6182 inhabitants), and El Dorado (3928 inhabitants). The Lamas Chachapoyas provinces are Mariscal Cáceres, Huallaga, El Dorado, Bellavista, Picota, and San Martín. There are districts where the vast majority of the population belongs to Indigenous communities, such as the districts of Alto Saposoa (51%), Piscoyacu (65%) in the province of Huallaga, and Shapaja (99%) in the province of San Martín. Of the total ethnic peoples, the Lamas Chachapoyas (22,513 inhabitants) are the most prominent, being located exclusively in this department and representing 93% of the total Indigenous population. The second-most prominent are the Aguaruna, with a population of 1789 inhabitants, who are found in a small area between the provinces of Moyobamba and Rioja.

At the INEN, 3724 new patients from the Department of San Martín have been registered between 2015 and 2018. Of these, the location of the primary tumor is 886 cervical, 354 breast, 297 leukemia, 295 stomach, 245 nonmelanoma skin, 146 non-Hodgkin lymphoma, 136 oral cavity, 112 thyroid, and 80 prostate, among others.

Since 2018, specialists in clinical oncology have been included in the organization at the cancer center of Lamas to ensure self-sustainability and the continuity of cancer care in the region. From its inception in November 2015 to August 2023, 600 cancer patients were treated, of which 66% (399) were female, the most frequent age range (13%) was 45 to 49 years (78), and 98% had health insurance (SIS 80% (482) and EsSalud 18% (110)). In terms of patient location, 33.67% (202) of the patients came from the city of Tarapoto, followed by the cities of Lamas, Moyobamba, and Rioja (21.33%, 11.67%, and 10.0%, respectively).

The majority of patients seen received a diagnosis of breast cancer (25.5%; 153), followed by cervical cancer (12.5%; 75) and stomach cancer (10.5%; 63). In terms of staging, there was a higher percentage of clinical stage 4 (i.e., metastatic disease (39.2%)), as well as patients with locally advanced disease (i.e., in clinical stage III (27.7%)).

A lower percentage comes to the service in an early clinical stage (i.e., clinical stage I (8.5%)). For female patients, the most frequent cancer was breast (followed by cervical cancer); the most frequent age was 50–60 (31.4%), followed by 40–50 and 60–70 years. For male patients, the most frequent cancer was prostate, and the most frequent age range was 60 years and over (96.1%).

Most cancers were treated in clinical stage IV: stomach cancer was treated at clinical stage IV in 62.7% of cases, ovary in 37.5%, prostate in 81%, lymphoma in 57.9%, head and neck in 53.3%, sarcomas in 66.7%, lung in 77.8%, and pancreas in 100%. Cervical cancer was mainly treated at stage II (44.3%). Breast cancer was mainly treated at clinical stage III (i.e., as a locally advanced disease (47.7%)) and less commonly at clinical stage II (i.e., as an early disease (33.6%)). Most patients received antineoplastic treatment such as chemotherapy with cytotoxic and monoclonal antibodies.

Conclusions

Satellite telechemotherapy was successfully implemented in a Peruvian jungle cancer center. This strategy represents an effective model by which to overcome geographic access barriers to cancer care in remote regions, and it may be adapted in other rural areas lacking oncological centers and resources, providing systemic treatment with significant cost-saving benefits and demonstrable improvements in QoL.

References

1. Ferlay J, Ervik M, Lam F, Colombet M, Mery L, Piñeros M, et al. *Global Cancer Observatory: Cancer Today*. Lyon: International Agency for Research on Cancer; 2020. Available from: https://gco.iarc.fr/today
2. Guillén-López OB, Casas JA. Mortality in Peru. Changes between the years 2010 and 2018. *Rev Med Hered*. 2022;33:221–224. https://doi.org/10.20453/rmh.v33i3.4344
3. International Agency for Research on Cancer. *Peru. Source: Globocan 2020*. Lyon: Global Cancer Observatory; 2021. Available from: https://gco.iarc.fr/today/data/factsheets/populations/604-peru-fact-sheets.pdf
4. Vidaurre T, Santos, C, Gomez H, Sarria G, Amorin E, Lopez M, et al. The Implementation of the Plan Esperanza and Response to the imPACT Review. *Lancet Oncol*. 2017;18,595–606. https://doi.org/https://doi.org/10.1016/S1470-2045(17)30598-3
5. Valencia-Mesías G, Rioja-Viera P, Morante-Cruz Z, Toledo-Morote Y, Neciosup-Delgado S, Gómez-Moreno H. The current situation regarding the availability and accessibility of anticancer drugs for breast cancer in the Peruvian public health systems. *Ecancermedicalscience*. 2021;15:1224. https://doi.org/10.3332/ecancer.2021.1224
6. Ministry of Health of Peru (MINSA). Declares of national interest the Integral Cancer Care and Improvement of Access to Oncological Services in Peru and other measures are enacted. DS N°009-2012-SA, Official Journal of the Peruvian Republic, Lima, Peru, 17.
7. Alvarez-Risco A, Del-Aguila-Arcentales S, Yanez, JA. Telemedicine in Peru as a Result of the COVID-19 pandemic: Perspective from a country with limited internet access. *Am J Trop Med Hyg*. 2021;105(1): 6–11. https://doi.org/10.4269/ajtmh.21-0255
8. Vidaurre T, Vasquez J, Valencia F, Alcarraz C, Mas L, Poma N, et al. Implementation of a Telechemotherapy Module in the Peruvian Jungle with Adequate Quality of Life: Breaking the Access Gaps to Health with Teleoncology. *J Cancer Ther*. 2019;10(8):677–89. https://doi.org/https://doi.org/10.4236/jct.2019.108056

Chamorros, Carolinians, Cancer, and Creativity in the Northern Marianas

51

Peter Brett and James Hofschneider

Key Points

- Indigenous Pacific Islander Chamorros and Carolinians had little access to local cancer care in the Northern Mariana Islands before 2019.
- In 2019, the arrival of a medical oncologist and the development of an oncology treatment team led to patients receiving more comprehensive, state-of-the-art, local cancer treatment, but with challenges requiring creative solutions.
- An important part of the cancer program is cancer prevention and screening.

The Commonwealth of the Northern Mariana Islands (CNMI) comprises 14 islands north of the US Territory of Guam in the Northwestern Pacific Ocean, approximately 1500 miles from Japan and the Philippines, and nearly 4000 miles west of Hawai'i. The largest island is Saipan. The islands in this Micronesian archipelago were settled several thousand years ago by peoples sailing from Southeast Asia who became Chamorro Indigenous Pacific Islanders. Carolinians arrived in the mid-1800s from the Caroline Islands near New Guinea. In 1987, the CNMI emerged from the Trust Territory of the Pacific Islands (TTPI), which the United States administered on behalf of the United Nations after 1947. Today, this island group is a US commonwealth territory, with over 40% of the population of 50,000 made up of Indigenous Pacific Islander Chamorros and Carolinians (the rest are largely immigrant Asians). The median household income in 2010 for a Chamorro family of four was about $30,000 and for a Carolinian family of four about $20,000. In the mainland United States, it was over $60,000.

Healthcare on the island is largely provided by the public Commonwealth Healthcare Corporation (CHCC), which runs the only hospital in the territory and administers all public health programs. Some patients are seen in outlying clinics by private providers. Financing of health services is based on the US model. Medicaid (US and locally funded medical insurance for the poor) provides healthcare for over 60% of the population. Medicare (US government insurance for the elderly, disabled, and patients with kidney failure on hemodialysis), Aetna, and other small private insurers provide coverage for the rest. Many immigrant Asians have no health insurance at all.

Challenge

Prior to 2019, no oncology physicians were available in the CNMI. When a patient developed cancer requiring treatment, they would travel off-island to a distant US jurisdiction or to the Philippines—if it was possible to travel at all. The local government has a variably funded medical referral program, a legacy of the TTPI, which arranges for off-island appointments, travel, lodging, food, and medical care. However, because of this variable funding and logistical challenges, often off-island care was not possible. For islanders, off-island care is always difficult, due to anxiety, uncertainty, fear of the unknown, an unfamiliar and intimidating medical environment, absence of supportive extended family, prolonged stays (sometimes months or years), estrangement from their community, and added financial burden. Almost no one with cancer could continue working while off-island. Furthermore, if patients died off-island, bringing them home would have incurred a high cost.

Developing a Cancer Program

In 2019, a medical oncologist began working full-time in the CNMI for the first time in its history. Many of the 200+ patients newly diagnosed with cancer each year began to receive cancer care without leaving the CNMI. A cancer care team was assembled, comprising cancer-oriented pharmacists, oncology nurses, nurse practitioners, physicians' assistants,

G. Garvey (ed.), *Indigenous and Tribal Peoples and Cancer*, https://doi.org/10.1007/978-3-031-56806-0_51

and internists with an interest in oncology. The team's mission was to provide state-of-the-art, local, and culturally sensitive oncology care to the Chamorros, Carolinians, and others in the CNMI community.

Establishing the first oncology clinic led to improvements in other on-island diagnostic services, such as the availability of an interventional radiologist for expedited tissue biopsies, upgraded mammography with 3-D tomosynthesis, a faster CT scanner, and the addition of bone density radiography for osteoporosis in patients on estrogen deprivation therapy for breast or prostate cancer.

It quickly became clear to the oncology team that many Indigenous people with cancer in the CNMI had cancers that were related to certain lifestyle and traditional cultural norms and were highly preventable. Many in the CNMI still smoke cigarettes, and this leads to smoking-related cancers like lung cancer. A large number of Chamorros and Carolinians chew betel nuts, a habit that is discouraged but remains legal. In the Marianas, betel nut is inexpensive to grow and easy to buy. Over 20 Chamorros and Carolinians each year present with oral cancers that are typically very advanced and life-threatening. Aggressive treatment of advanced oral cancers off-island typically involves extensive surgical excision, radiation, and reconstructive surgery, resulting in gross facial deformities, impaired speech, poor nutritional intake, and social isolation/self-ostracization.

The high prevalence of obesity, hypertension, and diabetes predisposes patients to endometrial cancer. In addition, many have cancers that would have been caught at much earlier stages if they had received appropriate cancer screening, such as mammograms for breast cancer, HPV testing/Pap smears for cervical cancer, and low-dose CT scans of the chest for lung cancer. Some patients with chronic hepatitis B infections are not offered treatment or liver surveillance, resulting in a late diagnosis of hepatocellular carcinoma.

Prior to 2019, many patients with significant symptoms from progressive cancer such as pain, constipation, anorexia, nausea, and anxiety also experienced a lack of comprehensive palliative care. Today, many patients with advanced cancer and serious symptoms receive a comprehensive assessment of ways to help them feel more comfortable, and they are often visited at their homes by a medical provider trained in palliative care.

After 2019, the hospital's vision of cancer control began a focus on cancer prevention, screening, and treatment, led by the newly formed oncology department. Referrals for off-island care fell dramatically, saving costs for the government and hospitals. Furthermore, patients presented with cancers at earlier stages, and hence were easier to treat. Patients now often receive their care entirely in the CNMI, without leaving their jobs, family, and friends. We believe that cancer care for Pacific Islanders can now be provided at a level that often equals or exceeds that received by mainland US residents.

Treatment Challenges: A Case Report

There are ongoing challenges in cancer control in the CNMI, including procurement of expensive anti-cancer medication (e.g., immunotherapy such as pembrolizumab), and this is where creativity in devising solutions has been necessary. The program is able to obtain certain expensive medications for patients at no cost through patient assistance programs offered by some drug companies, resulting in savings of thousands of dollars. This is illustrated in the following case study of a CNMI patient who had a large disabling oral cancer and was unable to travel.

Patient X (identifying information has been removed) is a 63-year-old man with diabetes and receiving hemodialysis for end-stage kidney disease. He's very frail and uses a wheelchair for mobility. He's completely unable to travel off-island for medical care. In 2021, he presented with a large mass covering his mouth, arising from the right inner cheek and lower lip. He'd been a lifelong betel nut chewer. The mass he had went unnoticed during his dialysis sessions as he had been wearing a mask to protect against COVID-19. Eventually, he could not get any food into his mouth, and the mass would often bleed and hurt (see Fig. 51.1).

In the mainland United States, the patient would be considered too frail for surgery but could have received six weeks of palliative radiation treatment. This would shrink the tumor, but not likely cure it. In the CNMI, he would have to travel off-island for radiation and would have to continue dialysis off-island, which he was unable to do. The creative solution was to identify medications likely to shrink the cancer for a time without causing substantial side effects (as chemotherapy can do), which the patient would be able to tolerate. The patient was given IV immunotherapy (pembro-

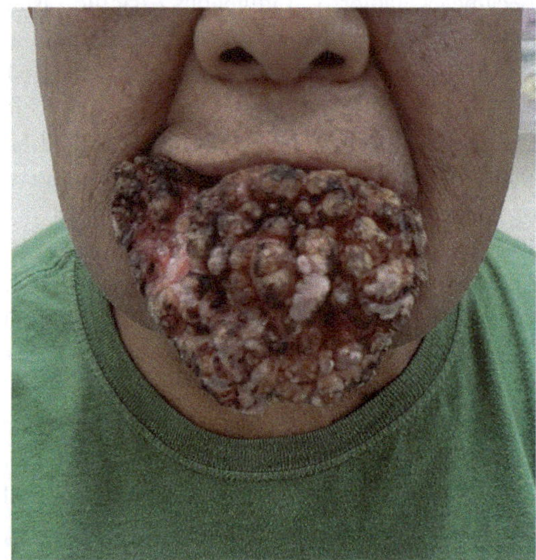

Fig. 51.1 Patient's initial presentation: Massive oral tumor arising from the lower lip. (Photo: P Brett)

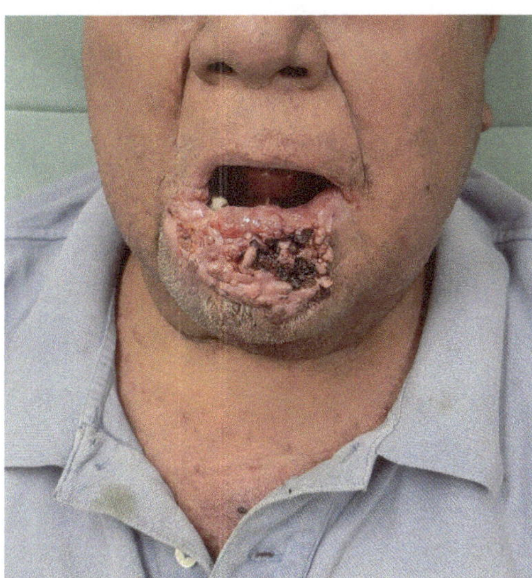

Fig. 51.2 Patient after one year of treatment: Tumor is substantially smaller. (Photo: P Brett)

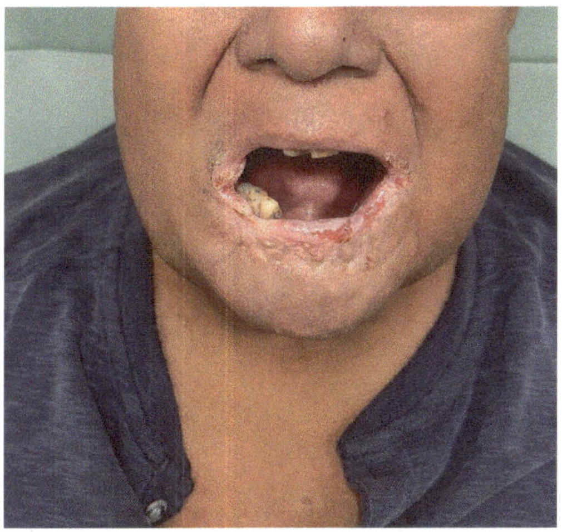

Fig. 51.3 Patient after two years of treatment: Tumor has nearly resolved. (Photo: P Brett)

lizumab) and IV anti-epidermal growth factor treatment (cetuximab), and the cancer has gradually shrunk, now for two years. The patient's quality of life has improved substantially, and he can eat, drink, and talk normally. Furthermore, he's had almost no side effects. The cancer may still grow back, but probably not for many months to years. Figure 51.2 shows the patient after one year of treatment, and Fig. 51.3 after two years of treatment.

We have learned that having medical oncology available in the CNMI allows for sophisticated, often creative treatment that sometimes obviates the need to refer off-island for radiation treatment or complex cancer surgery, which is still not available in the CNMI. Many patients are still unable or unwilling to travel. Often, systemic cancer treatment is given as the only possible treatment in the absence of viable alternatives. Patients often derive substantial benefits from such measures.

Prevention/Screening Challenges

Another complex challenge faced by Indigenous Pacific Islanders is poor access to cancer screening and prevention. If no one smoked, fewer people would develop lung cancer; if no one chewed betel nut, fewer people would develop oral cancer; if all young women received the HPV vaccine, fewer would develop cervical cancer; if people were screened regularly for lung cancer (if smokers), colon, cervical, breast, and oral cancers, treatment would be far more successful, since cancers would be detected earlier.

The oncology team set up a cancer screening and prevention program subsidized by the hospital, with the expectation that medical costs would decrease when cancer is prevented or detected early, rather than treated at advanced stages. About 500 patients have entered the screening/prevention program so far. However, to have a real impact, we believe 10,000 patients per year will need to take part. We currently think the biggest barriers are a lack of community awareness and too few healthcare workers to perform screening. Our creative solution is to have community healthcare workers do much of the program intake and community outreach, with tests reviewed by medical providers. We are also preventing maternal-to-child hepatitis B virus transmission with mandatory screening of expectant mothers and vaccination of all newborns.

Conclusion

A two-pronged approach of providing expert medical oncology care to Indigenous Pacific Islanders (as well as other Asians in the CNMI community) and no-cost screening and prevention should save many lives in the CNMI community and improve quality of life. However, this will require health promotion and education programs developed for and with Indigenous populations to support healthier habits and mitigate the risk of developing cancer, especially the cessation of betel nut chewing and tobacco use. In addition, targeted initiatives to promote cancer screening programs and support Indigenous people to participate in regular cancer screening programs, which are now available on the island, are essential.

The long-term sustainability of this on-island cancer treatment and prevention program requires stable funding and the availability of trained, interested medical practitioners. The island's medical infrastructure is fragile, and we hope that there will be enlightened creative government leadership that places healthcare services as one of its highest priorities.

BY NC ND

Culturally Appropriate Cancer Care for Community Elders in the Northern Territory

52

Michael Penniment

Key Points

- The Alan Walker Cancer Care Centre in Darwin has significantly improved cancer care in the Northern Territory, but barriers still exist for patients who live in remote locations.
- Patients are often required to travel for cancer care without a clear plan and timeline for their treatment. Events like tracheostomies cannot be planned in advance and may require big lifestyle changes.
- As a health practitioner, I need to be aware of two gaps we need to close—one about treatment outcomes, and one about mutual understanding. Health practitioners need to lose their focus on "paternalistic good" and replace it with respect and a yearning to understand.

For almost 30 years, I have provided radiation therapy treatment for cancer patients from the Northern Territory. I've learned a lot about the problems faced by Indigenous cancer patients who live long distances from a major center and who need to deal with life-threatening diseases without good support. I've also learned a lot about my attitude to life and to cancer care. In this case study, I share an example from my practice and explore some of the lessons I've learned over the years.

My Patient

My patient is a 65-year-old Elder from a community located a one-hour flight from Darwin.

He first presented with a painful mouth, having experienced two months of increasing pain while swallowing. He was seen by doctors in Darwin and diagnosed with a typical squamous cancer in the tonsil region. His cancer did not show signs of being caused by HPV and thus was diagnosed as related to a long history of smoking. Based on the tumor position, he was referred for major surgery, which would be performed in Adelaide (a four-hour flight from Darwin).

As part of the surgery, the patient needed a tracheostomy to ensure his airway was good during recovery. The surgeons were able to avoid removing his voice box, so the patient knew the tracheostomy was likely to be temporary. When he left Adelaide, he had both the tracheostomy and a feeding tube in his stomach (PEG). He knew that he may need the PEG for several months, but it was not expected to be permanent. There was no sign the tumor had extended into his lymph nodes, and extensive x-rays before surgery confirmed the tumor had not spread to other organs, in particular to his lungs.

The medical team concluded the patient had potentially curable but extensive cancer, and radiotherapy was recommended. As his lymph nodes were not involved and the tumor was removed cleanly, there was no benefit in adding chemotherapy.

Radiotherapy involved a CT scan at the Alan Walker Cancer Care Centre in Darwin to plan his treatment. While he was in Darwin for the scan, he was also checked by the dentist and saw experts about managing his PEG. At this stage, the tracheostomy was removed, as his post-op swelling had settled. Radiotherapy was planned, with six weeks of daily treatment (Monday to Friday) in Darwin. The patient was accommodated in Darwin for treatment.

The patient completed his radiotherapy without problems. He required pain relief for mucositis during the last two weeks of treatment, but this was not required when he was seen for a follow-up four weeks after treatment was completed. He had minimal skin irritation and managed his PEG well. His eating recovery was quick. He was booked for a follow-up PET/CT scan three months after treatment, plus an ENT community review one month after treatment.

The patient's PET/CT scan was slightly delayed due to transport issues in getting to Darwin from the community. When he was reviewed four months after radiotherapy, doctors found a new area of uptake on the skin over the upper jaw, which was consistent with further disease a few centimeters from his previous tumor. This uptake needed a biopsy, and the patient was aware that he may need further surgery.

G. Garvey (ed.), *Indigenous and Tribal Peoples and Cancer*, https://doi.org/10.1007/978-3-031-56806-0_52

The biopsy led to a lot of anxiety for the patient, with testing that required additional trips to Darwin. After around three weeks of delay, new disease was discounted, giving the patient a positive outcome.

Learning from This Case

The case described is not unusual in the Northern Territory, where neck cancer related to smoking is common among the Indigenous population. While still curable, the cancer carries a worse prognosis in active smokers than for similar cancers caused by viral infections. Smoking prevention to decrease cancer incidence and to help cure diagnosed cancers remains a problem.

Having the Alan Walker Cancer Care Centre in Darwin has significantly improved patients' access to first-class cancer care, but there are still barriers for patients who live in remote locations. Visiting Darwin for diagnosis and planning, treatment, and follow-up is always a challenge. Because of the distances and transport logistics, we need to coordinate as many investigations as possible during each visit to Darwin, and this requires substantial case coordination.

Complex care for patients who live in the Northern Territory may still involve a transfer to a major center such as Adelaide, as it did for the patient described above. The patient often needs to leave their home without having a clear plan and timeline for their treatment. Events like tracheostomies and PEGs, which may not be planned in advance, require big lifestyle changes and ongoing community care. Big problems like a stroke or heart attack can occur as a result of complex surgery, and this can make it impossible for the patient to return home. The patient may die away from their Country. These issues need to be considered before a patient travels for care. Our patients often have ongoing challenges, including susceptibility to infection with chemotherapy treatment, severe pain, long-term PEG dependence, and permanent tracheostomy. Fortunately, for the patient described above, treatment was reasonably straightforward, no chemotherapy was needed, and he was able to return home.

As the senior members in their communities, Elders are used to providing support to their communities. When an Elder becomes a patient, they may have a greater understanding of the health system than other community members, but they find themselves facing their own health challenges and possibly dependence on carers. As medical professionals, we need to be aware these patients may not seek the help they need.

What This Means for My Work

As a young doctor, I thought that my job was to organize treatment. Gradually, I learned about the many other factors involved. Some of these are obvious—such as patients facing time away from work and family, and treatment side effects. But cancer also has a culturally specific meaning, which may need to be explored. Patients may be thinking about why they got cancer, what effect it will have on their future, and how it will impact their time on earth in the context of family and community. I don't have any answers for these concerns, but I've learned a little more about the deep connection many Indigenous patients have with 65,000 years of culture and the powerful effect this has on how they live life. As a health practitioner, I need to be aware of two gaps we need to close—one about treatment outcomes, and one about mutual understanding. Giam Kar's reflections in this volume highlight some of the work being done at the Alan Walker Cancer Care Centre as we all try to understand these gaps.

I've noticed that medical practitioners who spend time working at the Alan Walker Cancer Care Centre learn deep lessons around mutual respect and caring. They tend to lose their focus on "paternalistic good" and replace it with respect and a yearning to understand.

Some of the significant approaches implemented in the Northern Territory, which may contribute to successful cancer care for Aboriginal people living in remote communities, include:

- Building the Alan Walker Cancer Care Centre and giving people access to high-quality treatment closer to home.
- Introducing telemedicine to help people understand their planned treatment before they leave home and to check on their post-treatment recovery.
- Upskilling community care networks.
- Sharing good stories—both back to communities and with staff (who are rightfully proud of their work).
- Considering innovative technologies—particularly whether we can offer radiotherapy in smaller population centers, with the treatment designed in the main center.

Perhaps the most important suggestion for health practitioners is to keep an open mind and try their best to help.

TRIBES and STITCH: A Sustainable Cancer Control Model for Scheduled Castes and Tribes in India

53

Rajkumar Rajamanickam and J. Anitha

Key Points

- TRIBES and STITCH are heuristics that guide a sustainable approach to cervical cancer testing in rural India.
- The TRIBES concept involves training Accredited Tribal Social Health Activists who conduct the intervention in their local communities, working from Tribal Mini Health Centers.
- The STITCH strategy is a way of approaching cancer screening in rural India.
- TRIBES and STITCH provide a framework to help address barriers such as poverty, low health literacy, cultural and religious differences, and challenges created by difficult-to-access, remote locations.

In India, the most common cancer types are breast, lung, mouth, cervix uteri, and tongue [1]. Knowledge of cancer and cancer prevention is limited in many rural communities, particularly among Scheduled Castes (SCs) and Scheduled Tribes (STs) (these terms are recognized in the Constitution of India). SCs and STs are the most socioeconomically disadvantaged groups in India, making up approximately 16.6% and 8.6% of the population, respectively [2]. People belonging to SCs are subject to untouchability, suppression, oppression, discrimination, and exploitation. ST populations typically live in isolated, remote, hilly, or forested areas and are often separated from the wider Indian population. Both the SC and ST populations largely rely on traditional medicines and local healers [3].

In this case study, we describe an approach to developing a sustainable cancer control program among SC and ST populations, defined through two heuristics: a concept called TRIBES and a strategy called STITCH.

What We Did

The demographics of our study population were 20% Tribal community, 50% SC, and 30% other castes. In this population, we implemented a randomized controlled trial with healthy women aged 30 to 59 years to develop and test an approach to cervical screening using visual inspection with 4% acetic acid [4]. Of the 114 study clusters in India's Dindigul district, 57 were randomized to one round of visual inspection by trained nurses, and 57 to a control group. Screen-positive women received colposcopy, directed biopsies, and, where appropriate, cryotherapy by nurses during the screening visit. Over five years, the study demonstrated a 25% reduction in the cervical cancer incidence rate and a 35% reduction in the mortality rate.

We developed the TRIBES concept and STITCH strategy for the study described above. We believe that, for both the Tribal and SC populations, TRIBES and STITCH played an important role in our project's success. We argue that they offer a valuable heuristic for future cancer control projects among Indigenous and Tribal populations.

The TRIBES Concept

The TRIBES concept provides a heuristic for planning a cancer control program. A central part of our approach is recruiting and training Accredited Tribal Social Health Activists, who conduct the intervention in their local communities.

T—Translational training and technology Organizations involved in cancer screening programs should select volunteers from relevant ST and SC communities and offer them

G. Garvey (ed.), *Indigenous and Tribal Peoples and Cancer*, https://doi.org/10.1007/978-3-031-56806-0_53

certified training in primary healthcare with special emphasis on cancer screening techniques and pre-cancer management. This must be supported by an effective referral system. In our cervical cancer study, we selected women as volunteers.

R—Research Research projects should include community-based interventions, with all tools evaluated for their acceptability, availability, and cost-effectiveness. Randomized controlled trials are needed to test recommendations about cancer control.

I—Indigenous Indigenous and Tribal peoples should be involved in cancer screening in their communities. This empowers communities and creates local employment. In our work, we developed the role of Accredited Tribal Social Health Activists (ATSHA), individuals who are nominated from and supported by their local communities. These health activists must complete a health center–based structured training program. Known and trusted in their local communities, they become powerful healthcare providers.

As part of this approach, we recommend opening Tribal Mini Health Centers, each built to serve a population of approximately 1000 people. These mini centers should be equipped with basic medical equipment and provide a base from which the Accredited Tribal Social Health Activists can work. These mini-centers require funding, which might be garnered from local sources, health insurance, government, or non-government organizations. Tools and tests for cervical cancer screening can be made locally.

B—Behavior change Behavior changes among local populations should be encouraged through intensive, focused, tailor-made health education models and activities, implemented and conducted by local health activists and with a focus on local activities.

E—Empowerment Accredited Tribal Social Health Activists can be empowered by the provision of simple and effective screening tools, including Pap smear kits, acetic acid, Lugols iodine, speculums, simple portable colposcopes, and cryotherapy equipment.

S—Social status and recognition Relevant government and non-government agencies should give appropriate recognition and status to Accredited Tribal Social Health Activists as they are part of the local health workforce.

The STITCH Strategy

Our proposed STITCH strategy provides a useful way to approach cancer screening in rural India. We believe that implementing the STITCH strategy can help to close the cancer care gap experienced by SC and ST populations.

S—Screening Screening should be available, applicable, acceptable, and affordable, and should give assurance of efficacy and sustainability in healthcare delivery.

T—Treatment Treatment of precancers should be standard procedure, with outcomes monitored through follow-up biopsies until a status of "cured" is achieved.

I—Immunization Immunization should be more effectively implemented in rural communities. For example, the HPV vaccine should be promoted through the health communication process of "information, motivation, and action."

T—Translational research Researchers should engage in the translation of research results in which strategies, technologies, and resources flow from high-resource to low-resource settings, offering greater benefits for Indigenous and Tribal populations.

C—Continuum of care Cancer care organizations should offer a continuum of care from screening, through treatment, and beyond. These organizations need to be trustworthy, transparent, dependable, and reliable if they are to win the confidence and mandate of local communities. Health programs should not close down or stop abruptly and without warning.

H—Health policy Health policy should be framed to prioritize primary, secondary, and tertiary prevention measures for the entire population, regardless of location.

Challenges and Opportunities

TRIBES and STITCH offer ways to think about cancer control programs for Indigenous and Tribal peoples. In rural India, these heuristics have proved helpful in developing and designing a cervical cancer control program.

Our approach has provided several opportunities, including funding and support from government and non-government organizations. The approach has also provided opportunities for health education and technical training within local communities and led to the development of a local income-generating scheme.

The TRIBES and STITCH approach provides a framework that has helped us to address barriers such as poverty, low health literacy, cultural differences, religious differences, and challenges created by difficult-to-access, remote locations.

Conclusion

TRIBES and STITCH provide heuristics that describe our approach to cervical cancer testing, with demonstrated success in rural India. We believe this approach has broad application for cancer control among Indigenous and Tribal communities in other rural locations and contexts.

References

1. Kumar C, Singh MM. Cancer vulnerability in an indigenous Himalayan population in Arunachal Pradesh. *E Cancer Medical Science.* 2022 May 30;16:1405. https://doi.org/10.3332/ecancer.2022.1405
2. Wikipedia. *Scheduled castes and scheduled tribes* [Internet]. Available from: https://en.wikipedia.org/wiki/Scheduled_Castes_and_Scheduled_Tribes
3. Maity B. Comparing health outcomes across scheduled tribes and castes in India. *World Development.* 2017;96:163–181. https://doi.org/10.1016/j.worlddev.2017.03.005
4. Sankaranarayanan R, Esmy PO, Rajkumar R, Muwonge R, Swaminathan R, Shanthakumari S, et al. Effect of visual screening on cervical cancer incidence and mortality in Tamil Nadu, India: A cluster-randomised trial. *The Lancet.* 2007 August 4;370(9585):398–406. https://doi.org/10.1016/S0140-6736(07)61195-7

Ngā Tapuwae Ki Hawaiki Nui: Sacred Footsteps Home

54

Tess Moeke-Maxwell, Ria Earp, Vanessa Eldridge, and Brianna Smith

Key Points

- Māori (Indigenous New Zealanders) draw on relationships with whānau (family, including extended family) to provide culturally appropriate end-of-life care, including spiritual care, to family members with incurable cancer.
- Aotearoa New Zealand healthcare providers and the palliative care workforce should implement palliative care cultural safety training to ensure the relational needs of whānau are supported.
- Adopting palliative care cultural safety training as outlined in the *Mauri Mate: Māori Palliative Care Framework for Hospices* could support the health sector in ensuring whānau caregiving customs are practiced no matter where care is provided.

Māori whānau (families, including extended family) optimize tikanga (cultural customs) to awhi (embrace) and tautoko (support) ill and dying loved ones who live with, and die from, cancer. Discussions about Māori living with incurable illness often position whānau within palliative care deficit narratives, highlighting difficulties accessing health and palliative care services, which are often regarded as culturally unsafe and underserving whānau needs [1]. Within this "vulnerable" positioning, mātauranga Māori (Māori knowledge), cultural aspirations, and ways of caring delivered by whānau are often occluded within palliative care conversations. Drawing from the Pae Herenga study [2, 3], this chapter shares a culturally agentic and positive narrative in which whanonga pono (ancient values) and customs inform whānau support systems and caregiving practices. Our findings support the importance of whanaungatanga (relationships/connections) and the ways in which whānau exercise their right to exercise authority, leadership, and rangatiratanga (chiefly autonomy) over how they live, and die, with cancer through these vital relationships.

Māori and Palliative Care

Palliative care is an important part of the cancer continuum. It provides physical comfort and attends to the psychosocial needs of patients and bereaved whānau [4]. Palliative care in Aotearoa New Zealand requires updated services to better meet the growing demand and needs of Māori cancer patients and their whānau [1]. Accessing palliative care is difficult for Māori whānau, particularly in rural areas where services are scarce [4]. Misinformation about palliative care services [5, 6] and experiences of discrimination when using health services are ongoing barriers for Māori [8–10]. The New Zealand Palliative Care Strategy outlines the requirements of Māori patients for specific policies, community linkages, and care coordinators to ensure cultural safety and competence in services [11]. Palliative care services, including hospice care, are informed by a mono-cultural healthcare system that prioritizes the medicalization of dying over the cultural aspirations, needs, and lived realities of whānau. However, negative perceptions of hospice care are changing as whānau share positive experiences of accessing such services.

Compared to non-Māori, Māori tend to prefer community hospice care over hospice inpatient unit (IPU) care. This is evident in death records, which show that 44.8% of Māori deaths due to cancer occur in private residences (44.8%) and only 12.2% in hospice IPUs, compared to 26.0% and 19.7%, respectively, for non-Māori [7]. Regional patterns of place of death vary substantially for cancer, based on different models of contracting, care, and resourcing. In some districts, hospices contract palliative care beds from public hospitals or residential aged care [7].

While the aggregate proportion of Māori using residential aged care at the end of life seems low (17.9% for Māori and 47.2% for non-Māori), this is partly due to cancer patients preferring to die at home. Low uptake of aged residential care can stem from the decision to remain in the whānau

G. Garvey (ed.), *Indigenous and Tribal Peoples and Cancer*, https://doi.org/10.1007/978-3-031-56806-0_54

home, from health service barriers, or due to the lower life expectancy of Māori [7]. When age at death is taken into account, there is little difference between Māori and non-Māori rates of dementia and use of residential care. As life expectancy among Māori increases, as predicted by Stats NZ, the New Zealand official data agency, the prevalence of dementia and the use of aged residential care is likely to increase [7]. To accommodate an aging Māori population, palliative care must shift at structural, systematic, and individual scales.

Māori Palliative Care Response

The right to quality palliative care has not gone unnoticed by Māori healthcare workers, allies, and researchers [4]. The *Mauri Mate: Māori Palliative Care Framework* focuses on access to palliative care for Māori adults and includes guidance on quality care, comfort, compassionate care, and support for whānau during and after the end of life, including spiritual care and grief support [4]. Another initiative, *Whenua ki te Whenua; A Taonga for your Whānau*, provides advance care planning advice to whānau to support end-of-life discussions [11]. A research-informed website, Te Ipu Aronui, provides information about caring for adults and kaumātua (Māori elders), utilizing digital stories reflecting whānau end-of-life care experiences that have been curated by the Digital Storytelling in the Pacific team [2, 3].

Methods

The research team's official cultural advisory group, Te Ārai Kāhui Kaumātua, expressed the need for a project to inform fellow whānau caregivers about traditional Māori end-of-life caregiving practices for kaumātua, leading to the inception of the Pae Herenga project [3]. We interviewed Māori health professionals, tohunga (spiritual leaders), and rongoā (natural healing practitioners) with experience providing end-of-life care and bereavement support. We explored structural and systemic barriers impacting whānau from using tikanga within palliative care services [12]. Furthermore, we aimed to produce an informational resource for whānau and health professionals.

The study applied a Kaupapa Māori research approach philosophy, ethical framework, methodology, and inductive thematic analysis guided by the Māori worldview, working with and for Māori communities, and involving participants in each phase from preparation to dissemination [12]. We conducted 61 face-to-face interviews encompassing both individuals and whānau, to include a total of 103 participants from Mid-North, Hawkes Bay, Wellington, and Whanganui [2, 3]. Of these, three of the individual interviewees were living with incurable cancer, and 41 individual interviewees and 17 whānau interviewees spoke about cancer caregiving experiences.

Findings

Whanaungatanga (Relationships)

Whanaungatanga (relationships) are the cornerstone of whānau caregiving, bolstering whānau members to provide a collective system of care. Participants value whānau relationships, and the beneficial relationships and support received from health professionals, tohunga (spiritual leaders), and rongoā (natural healing practitioners). Specifically, when traditional customs were implemented correctly, relationships that supported the dying were dependent on Tribal cultural beliefs and practices, whānau resources, and demographics (i.e., proximity to other whānau and community support). Relationships are underpinned by the depth of aroha (love, care, and compassion) felt and expressed toward the ill and dying and their whānau.

Manaakitanga (Care)

Whānau contribute their knowledge, skill, time, and resources to ensure the ill and dying are attended to at every phase of their illness trajectory. They provide practical support and comfort in times of change and crisis. While large whānau have a bigger pool of human resources to draw on, smaller whānau manage to support their loved ones by taking turns with hands-on caregiving at home or in hospital, hospice, or residential aged care settings, assuming different roles such as overseeing medical appointments, obtaining and administering medicines, providing clinical support, taking charge of financial matters, running the home and caring for others who are māuiui (sick) or dependent, planning and carrying out post-death care, and performing tangihanga (funeral rituals).

Whānau function as a team, with individuals stepping forward to provide support over different time periods and gathering when death is imminent. At least one or two whānau members remain constantly at their loved one's bedside. As a collective force, whānau function to make decisions and share the end-of-life care privilege and responsibility to support the dying person and each other during this spiritual transition. Some whānau set aside personal differences for the common goal of caring for dying loved ones. A participant, Jeff, reflects on his whānau's caregiving experiences when his wife Ripeka had cancer. Jeff and his daughter, Amber, were her main caregivers, receiving a korowai (cloak) of support from their whānau:

> It was whānau being around her to support her in one sense. But also, to meet her needs ... some of the whānau weren't [close]; there was a split, a rift, but as soon as she got sick, we just formed a circle around her ... take care of her, any of her needs and whether it be a karakia [prayers] or waiata [singing], anything.... Just trying, trying to meet her needs along the way on that journey, and making sure that I was there. And this is where, mine and Amber's role come in. We always made sure that when she was in hospital that one of us was there, or both of us.

Another participant, who had incurable cancer, encouraged her whānau to connect with and comfort her husband who was unconscious and dying of lung cancer. She asked them to talk to him and sing, but they just sat quietly, without speaking. The participant sang to her husband, and at the end of the song he reached up to her and said he loved her.

Awhi (Physical Presence, Emotional and Spiritual Support)

Quality end-of-life care occurs when whānau come together to be with, and to care for, the dying person. Having the right people, in the right roles, at the right time, helps to ensure things run smoothly. Hearing the words and upholding the requests of the dying contributes to a peaceful transition through the ārai (veil). Well-established relationships ensure practical, emotional, and spiritual support for the dying person. Whānau members are called upon to visit and sit with the māuiui person to support them and offer companionship. This allows the māuiui person to talk about their personal feelings or to reflect on things that are troubling them.

Strong connections mean the māuiui person and their whānau caregivers are comfortable having other whānau, friends and members of the community visit them at home. Together, visitors and the whānau share stories to uplift the spirit of the ill person and bring comfort to the whānau. Kaumātua (Māori elder) Arena and his wife use their cultural expertise to comfort grieving and bereaved whānau within their local community during the death and dying journey:

> We go over and over the stories. It's not frivolous but it allows those who are especially saddened to respond, and it engenders laughter and entertains them. Then you see by their faces, the spirits are uplifted. Don't allow them to sit in their sadness. Bring them out; make them laugh. These are the beautiful aspects.

Wairuatanga (Spirituality)

The whānau interviewees discussed many forms of wairuatanga (spirituality). Some individual interviewees observed diverse spiritual beliefs and practices, adhering to Tribal customs alongside Christian practices or drawing on spiritual healing modalities from other cultural traditions (e.g., crystal healing, energy healing, Eastern spiritual practices). One participant who had incurable cancer spoke about her Christian faith and her belief in rongoā Māori (natural healing). She felt that faith and belief helped to keep her well and get her through the difficult times.

Meanwhile, participant Arena, a spiritual community kaumātua, spoke about visiting and providing comfort through prayers and karakia (chants) to whānau caring for their loved ones at the end of life:

> In the homes, and if we are known to the family, there is a sense of wellbeing that pervades the family; especially when they see and feel the love and support that is present. We pray for compassion and wellbeing within; these prayers are not for me. They are for strengthening the mind and thoughts of the person who is terminally ill. To pray to the Lord, "This is your servant, help him," and the help is immediate when we die. During the gravity of the illness, the Lord will be in our midst. In my own faith and according to the instructions of my ancestors, the first initiative is to pray and seek guidance from the Lord. This will strengthen your resolve.

Together, whānau use their established relationships to support those who are ill and dying and the other members of their whānau. Whānau carry out the practical aspects of caring but, importantly, they also ensure that the emotional, social, cultural, and spiritual needs of those who live with, and die from, cancer are fulfilled.

Discussion

Whanaungatanga (relationships) are weighted as a relational system of knowledge and resource exchange where whānau aroha, manaakitanga, awhi, and wairuatanga are expressed, and tikanga are shared and actioned to assist a loved person on their sacred walk home. Loving and caring relationships are an energy life force that nurtures and sustains the spiritual, physical, practical, emotional, and cultural realms of both people with incurable cancer and their whānau.

The findings reveal the significance of delivering culturally safe palliative care and other health services that support those who are ill and their whānau [6]. From a Māori perspective, successful health interventions are informed by customs, which place the person with cancer at the heart of the whānau. Once a connection has been established with the person who is ill and with their whānau, palliative care professionals can support the whānau to support the patient when accessing services and receiving treatment, and at the most sacred of times, when the spirit leaves the body.

The development of new and local models of palliative care service delivery must be inclusive of whānau to ensure services are oriented toward relational care practice. At a systemic level, collective action is necessary to support patient and whānau wellbeing at the end of life; this may resemble the implementation of cultural safety for healthcare professionals and cancer service providers when working with and for our Māori communities. Services need to respond more effectively to the palliative care needs of an aging Māori demographic with complex health needs, co-morbidities, cancers, and social determinants leading to health inequalities. The specific needs of individuals and whānau relative to their personal histories and life experiences must be taken into account and healthcare professionals should engage with the cultural safety and education training outlined in *Mauri Mate* [4].

Conclusion

Whānau step into cancer caregiver roles when loved ones become unwell and require support, providing home palliative care support, including hospice support. In addition, whānau also provide care for other whānau members who are grieving the loss of loved ones [6]. However, without establishing good relationships with whānau, access to support that aligns with cultural customs and unique needs will remain out of reach. Māori cultural safety training supports the healthcare workforce in integrating Māori cultural norms into palliative care [1]. From a palliative care service perspective, the health system must invest in resources to support whānau. Finally, since the 2021 legalization of assisted dying in New Zealand, whānau face new palliative care possibilities and challenges as they navigate the sacred pathway of caring for loved ones who seek physician-assisted deaths. Where these pathways will lead remains to be seen.

References

1. Jones RM, Signal V, Smith M, Stairmand J, Davies C, Gurney J. Palliative care and quality of life needs and outcomes for Māori with cancer: what do we know? *AlterNative*. 2023 Apr 3;19(2):219–28. https://doi.org/10.1177/11771801231163919
2. Gott M, Wiles J, Mason K, Moeke-Maxwell T. Creating 'safe spaces': A qualitative study to explore enablers and barriers to culturally safe end-of-life care. *Palliat Med*. 2022 Nov 22;37(4):520–9. https://doi.org/10.1177/02692163221138621
3. Moeke-Maxwell T, Mason K, Williams L. Digital story-telling research methods: Supporting the reclamation and retention of indigenous end-of-life care customs in Aotearoa New Zealand. *Prog Palliat Care*. 2020 Jan 17;28(2):101–6. https://doi.org/10.1080/09699260.2019.1704370
4. Te Ohu Rata o Aotearoa. *Mauri Mate: Māori palliative care framework for hospices* [Internet]. Te Kahu Pairuri o Aotearoa, Hospice New Zealand; 2020. Available from: https://teaho.govt.nz/publications/cancer-state
5. Simpson M, Berryman K, Oetzel J, Iti T, Reddy R. A cultural analysis of New Zealand palliative care brochures. *Health Promot Int*. 2015 Jul 9;31(4):839-848. https://doi.org/10.1093/heapro/dav067
6. Slater T, Matheson A, Ellison-Loschmann L, Davies C, Earp R, Gellatly K, et al. Exploring Māori cancer patients', their families', community, and hospice views of hospice care. *Int J Palliat Nurs*. 2015 Sep 2;21(9):439–45. https://doi.org/10.12968/ijpn.2015.21.9.439
7. McLeod H. *Planning for palliative care services in Aotearoa – what our population data tells us*. Presentation prepared and recorded for Te Whatu Ora; 2023, May 23. Available from: https://www.tewhatuora.govt.nz/for-the-health-sector/specific-life-stage-health-information/palliative/hui-planning-for-palliative-care-services-in-aotearoa-what-our-population-data-tells-us/
8. Te Aho o Te Kahu, Cancer Control Agency. *He mahere ratonga mate pukupuku cancer services planning i he mahere ratonga mate pukupuku cancer services planning: A vision for cancer treatment in the reformed health system* [Internet]. Te Aho o Te Kahu, Cancer Control Agency; 2022. Available from: https://teaho.govt.nz/publications/cancer-services-planning
9. Te Aho o Te Kahu, Cancer Control Agency. *Rongohia te reo, whatua he oranga: The voices whānau Māori affected by cancer* [Internet]. Te Aho o Te Kahu, Cancer Control Agency; 2023. Available from: https://teaho.govt.nz/publications/hui-reports
10. Ministry of Health. *The New Zealand Palliative Care Strategy*. Wellington: Ministry of Health; 2001.
11. Health Quality and Safety Commission, NZ. *Whenua ki te whenua*. Wellington: Health Quality and Safety Commission, NZ; 2021.
12. Hudson M, Milne M, Reynolds P, Russell K, Smith B. *Te Ara Tika: Guidelines for Māori Research Ethics: A framework for researchers and ethics committee members*. Health Research Council of New Zealand; 2010.

Strategies for Effective Cancer and End-of-Life Communication with Indigenous Patients

55

Ian N. Olver, Kate M. Gunn, Jaklin A. Eliott, and Alwin Chong

Key Points

- Strategies to improve cancer and cancer treatment, communication, and Advance Care Directives for Indigenous patients to facilitate informed choices about the uptake of optimal care pathways were identified.
- Experienced healthcare communicators shared the importance of culturally comfortable settings for consultation, the use of visual metaphors to explain new concepts, and utilizing Aboriginal interpreters when possible.
- Effective communication relies on understanding the cultural importance of family and community, and the context in which cancer is perceived, particularly when communicating sensitive topics such as end-of-life care.

Two studies sought to identify strategies to improve communication with Indigenous Australian peoples across the cancer journey (with respect, we use the term Indigenous Australians which encompasses Aboriginal and Torres Strait Islanders as appropriate). Ensuring that information from diagnosis, through treatment, to end-of-life care is provided in a culturally appropriate manner and is understood by Indigenous patients and their families facilitates informed decision-making about care and positive interactions with the healthcare system.

In the first of the two studies, healthcare professionals, some Indigenous, who regularly communicate cancer diagnoses and treatment options to Indigenous people were interviewed to determine the most effective communication strategies and settings. In the second, ongoing study, an Indigenous student undertaking a Masters of Philosophy of Public Health engaged with Indigenous individuals and community groups in yarning circles in order to better understand the low completion rate of Advance Care Directives among Indigenous patients and to explore preferences for end-of-life care planning.

A Qualitative Study of Cancer and Cancer Treatment Communication

Improving how cancer is explained to Indigenous Australians has been identified as a way to increase uptake of optimal cancer care pathways [1].

To better understand the most effective cancer and cancer treatment communication strategies, the first study included 23 semi-structured interviews with healthcare professionals who regularly engage in such communication with Indigenous patients in urban, rural, and remote settings [2, 3]. These professionals included nurses, medical practitioners, Aboriginal health workers, a radiation therapist, and administrative and public health professionals from two Australian jurisdictions (Northern Territory and South Australia).

While we acknowledge the differences between Indigenous cultural groups and individuals, six consistent themes emerged from our interviews.

Create a Safe Environment, Engender Trust, and Build Rapport

The environment or setting in which a conversation about cancer takes place is important in helping Indigenous patients feel comfortable. Outside spaces or larger indoor space with at least a view of the outdoors may be desirable. Sitting with, rather than opposite, the patient can be helpful, and matching the gender of the patient and provider may overcome cultural sensitivities that should be considered in the context of communication.

Beginning a conversation with topics that are important to the patient, such as home and family, will help to develop rapport and build trust. It is important not to appear rushed, to use plain language, and to clearly explain medical terminology in lay terms. Observing non-verbal cues and checking that the patient understands what has been said are vital.

G. Garvey (ed.), *Indigenous and Tribal Peoples and Cancer*, https://doi.org/10.1007/978-3-031-56806-0_55

It is also essential that the healthcare professional takes the time to allow the patient and their support network to communicate their preferences for treatment options. Healthcare professionals should avoid assumptions about group behavior and instead concentrate on the individual patient, thus catering to each patient's specific needs.

Employ Specific Communication Strategies to Explain Cancer and Cancer Treatment

The healthcare professionals we interviewed strongly emphasized the use of visual examples and familiar metaphors when explaining new concepts to Indigenous patients. For example, cancer might be illustrated as a tree with roots spreading underground and branches above, with scattering seeds representing cancer metastases. Similar visual aids can be extended to explain more challenging concepts such as adjuvant radiotherapy. For example, the healthcare professional might use the metaphor of pulling up weeds but not being sure that all the roots have been pulled out; thus, radiotherapy is used to kill any remaining roots so that the weeds do not sprout again. Similarly, the metaphor of a dammed creek might serve to explain obstructive symptoms.

Other metaphors for cancer in the body might include the familiar sight in Northern Australia of cars abandoned in the desert; from a distance, they look reasonable but, on closer inspection, they are revealed to have rusted and rotted from the inside. Healthcare professionals might also characterize the body as a dot painting, with the cells of the body represented by individual dots, some of which are starting to look different. Other visual means of communication can also be effective, such as showing the patient scans of their tumors, explaining how radiotherapy equipment works using images on tablets, and using pamphlets and flipcharts to illustrate treatments and their side effects.

Repetition and reinforcement help to ground understanding. The cancer communicators in our survey agreed that it is generally better to avoid statistics and medical jargon, and to be led by what the patient wants to know so that they are empowered to make decisions about their treatment. Patients and their families should be provided with advance warning in situations in which a healthcare professional foresees a difficult discussion about sensitive issues or when they need to "break bad news." This can help avoid shock, and will ensure that the patient's supporting family or community members are included in the discussion.

Obtain Support from Those Who Can Assist in Communication

When discussing cancer and cancer treatments with patients for whom English is not a first language, it is essential that Indigenous interpreters are physically or virtually present, to ensure patient understanding. If a formal interpreter is unavailable, then Aboriginal Liaison Officers, who are very experienced in communication, or any on-site Aboriginal Health Worker may be able to assist. Aboriginal Liaison Officers usually work in hospitals to help with transitions between the community and hospitals. Aboriginal Health Workers usually provide care in community clinics.

Patients are often accompanied by patient escorts (e.g., family member, friend etc.) who may also be able to help interpret for the patient. These escorts often return home to the community with the patient, and may help to explain follow-up care to the patient's family. However, it is always preferable to use professional interpreters rather than escorts or relatives to ensure accuracy of translation. It should be noted that, in small communities, it may be difficult to find an interpreter without kinship ties to a patient, and both male and female interpreters may be needed depending on the gender of the patient and their preference for only discussing their health with someone of the same gender or not discussing these issues with someone to whom they are related.

Engagement with Indigenous interpreters (professional or otherwise) is more than a matter of linguistic translation; it also helps to ensure that cultural sensitivities are integral to the therapeutic conversation. It is also important that the patient's preferences are recognized and that they give their consent for engaging others, such as interpreters or Aboriginal Liaison workers, in their care and treatment.

Consider Culture

An Aboriginal Liaison Officer interviewed for this study provided the important insight that Indigenous peoples tend to live more collectively and are far less individualistic than non-Indigenous Australians. What is best for the community can often outweigh individual priorities. With regard to healthcare, collectivism may manifest as prioritizing a community responsibility, such as sorry business, over attending a cancer treatment appointment. For the patient, this is an appropriate prioritization, even if it leads to a poorer cancer outcome. The importance of being physically and spiritually connected to Country and to family cannot be overstated and not being in Country can, in itself, lead to poor health outcomes. Patients may reject treatment or not complete a full treatment plan if it requires long periods away from Country. Furthermore, a patient may deny a cancer diagnosis to avoid the shame of bringing cancer back to their community.

Patients may wish to incorporate traditional remedies into their treatment and should be given the opportunity to express and do this.

Awareness of the Context of Behavior

Both healthcare professionals and patients may bring to their consultations biases and attitudes based on past experiences, cultural differences, and beliefs. Identifying these requires self-reflection on the part of the healthcare professional. Historical wrongs, such as the Stolen Generation or more recent experiences of discrimination, may result in mistrust and fear [4]. Patients who present with late-stage disease and have poor outcomes reinforce negative attitudes that the Indigenous community may have towards Western medicine. A cancer diagnosis may carry a different significance for the patient and for the healthcare professional. For example, the patient may attribute their diagnosis to unresolved family disputes and may require different or additional remedies to those offered by Western medicine.

Indigenous Australians represent a great variety of languages and belief systems. Health workers must ensure that patients understand what is being communicated to them. Some patients may indicate understanding to avoid discomfort and embarrassment, or to avoid being labelled as ignorant. They may not wish to shame health professionals for poor communication or simply assume that health professionals lack the skills to communicate appropriately.

Failure to attend an appointment may be due to the culturally appropriate prioritizing of community or family responsibilities [5]. In addition, healthcare services may face difficulties following up with patients who have changed phones, live outside urban areas, are transient and of no fixed address, or have left town to avoid matters they do not wish to discuss.

Characteristics of a Good Communicator

From the Indigenous perspective, a good communicator shows respect by deep quiet listening (Dadirri – in the Ngan'gikurunggurr and Ngen'giwumirri languages in the Daly River region of the Northern Territory), being open and still, and letting a story unfold. Ganma (Yolŋu people's concept from Arnhem land in the Northern Territory) is cultural knowledge sharing in which each participant recognizes the combined and individual experiences of the other and mixes these together to form new knowledge [6]. In this context, a good communicator is generally considered to be someone who is personable, honest, person-centered, demonstrates a genuine interest in the other person, and displays genuine empathy. This requires a willingness to engage in personal reflection and self-awareness.

Drawing on the experience of health professionals who communicate about cancer and its treatment to Aboriginal Australians we developed insights into successful strategies for effective communication. These include establishing a rapport in the appropriate setting, using pictorial illustrations, and utilizing people in the health team who can help the clinician understand the language, the social context, and culture of the patient.

Indigenous People's Understanding of Advance Care Directives

The second study, which is ongoing, explores the issue of communicating end-of-life decision-making with Indigenous patients, with a focus on their understanding of Advance Care Directives. Death and dying are sensitive issues in all cultures and, as part of a larger study investigating whether current advance care planning policy and procedures in Australia meet the needs of vulnerable populations, this study investigates the needs of Indigenous peoples [7]. The study, conducted by Christine Doolan, an Aboriginal woman of Southern Arrente descent, explores the reasons why Indigenous people are less likely to complete Advance Care Directives or End-of-Life Care Plans that support their spiritual, physical, emotional, and cultural wellbeing at the end of life. The research includes interviews and focus groups with Aboriginal communities in South Australia.

The study to date reveals that strategies leading to successful engagement with Indigenous communities begin with the inclusion of Indigenous researchers from institutions respected by the community [personal oral communication, J Eliott, 2023 May]. Each aspect of the project, including recruitment materials, language, and visuals, must be culturally appropriate. Engagement takes time, so flexibility with regard to the time and place of meetings (face-to-face is easier), is essential and reimbursement for the participants' time is desirable.

A common starting point for effective communication is the observation of Indigenous protocols that establish the nature of relationships between individuals and where those individuals come from. Yarning and sharing stories were often vehicles for information-sharing [8]. The interviewer should not make assumptions, but rather ask and listen, creating space for Indigenous interviewees and participants to speak in their own time and space. This can encompass both research methodology and communication with patients about their end-of-life decisions.

Those who wish to engage in sensitive conversations must recognize that Indigenous people are resourceful and compassionate and often put their own needs last. Our own experience has shown that many Indigenous people mistrust the Western medical system and are unlikely to want to die in a hospital. They may even feel shame resulting from years of being blamed for their health issues, despite having limited choices.

To date, we know that end-of-life care involves more than physical care. It also involves healing that is inclusive of Indigenous communities and beliefs, and it may include traditional Indigenous healers (such as Ngangkari healers among the Ngaanyatjarra, Pitjantjatjarra, and Yankunytjatjara peoples of Central Australia).

Decisions about end-of-life care must include family and community members who are trusted to make decisions and to communicate the patient's wishes for their Advance Care Directive. Many Aboriginal people will want to return to Country to die. Those from the Stolen Generation may not know where they have come from, bringing profound sorrow. Christine Doolan's initial interviews highlight the importance of recognizing individual differences and not generalizing or regarding Indigenous people as a homogeneous group (e.g., the needs and preferences of those living in urban settings will likely differ from those living in remote communities).

Unsurprisingly, many of the Aboriginal people involved in this research were unfamiliar with the concept of an Advanced Care Directive or they assumed that it referred to funerals or Wills. The existing Advance Care Directive form or kit is not relatable to Aboriginal people. Therefore, Aboriginal Community Health Workers should be trained to explain advance care planning in ways that are meaningful and effective. However, one research participant summed up the biggest communication issue: "Death is something we don't talk about, our mob, because death most people don't talk about in general.... It's a touchy subject."

From the information gained from this research, Christine Doolan aims to provide evidence to policymakers on how Advance Care Directive procedures could be made relatable to Aboriginal people. The plan is expected to conclude during 2024.

Conclusions

The successful communication of cancer and cancer treatment involves careful attention to language, behavior, and setting, and an understanding of the cultural context in which that information is communicated. This requires input from Indigenous peoples. Techniques such as story-telling, the use of familiar visual metaphors, and creating comfortable and safe environments in which discussions can take place will likely contribute to more effective communication in a variety of settings. However, some communication strategies, and the design of outdoor spaces, artworks, and colors relevant to the Country of the people involved, will need to be tailored to fit with specific regions, cultural groups, and individuals. Careful consideration of cultural appropriateness is particularly important when communicating sensitive issues, such as those at the end of life.

The next step in the first project is to interview Aboriginal patients with cancer to further test the success of communication strategies. The innovative methods of using qualitative social science approaches in working with Indigenous health practitioners and patients with cancer will continue, and these projects will further the engagement with Indigenous researchers. The findings of the project will be used to develop training modules to educate health practitioners and researchers. As more Indigenous researchers are trained, they will conduct their own research into effective communication techniques for Indigenous patients.

There is a paucity of research into Advance Care Directives and Indigenous patients. The initial aim of the study is to use the information collected and possible future consultations with more broadly based Indigenous groups by Indigenous researchers to create advocacy tools so that the research findings can be translated into policies that will provide culturally appropriate opportunities for Indigenous patients to plan their end-of-life care.

The Advance Care Directives project was funded by a National Health and Medical Research Council Partnership Grant (1133407). Christine Doolan was supported both by a University of Adelaide Indigenous scholarship and a top-up scholarship from the NHMRC Grant-funded Supplementary Scholarship supported by the Northern Communities Health Foundation. The authors acknowledge that Christine Doolan's work contributed to this chapter.

References

1. Chynoweth J, McCambridge MM, Zorbas H, Elston JK, Thomas RJS, Glasson WJH, et al. Optimal cancer care for Aboriginal and Torres Strait Islander People: a shared approach to system level change. *JCO Glob Oncol.* 2020 Feb;6:108–14. https://doi.org/10.1200/JGO.19.00076
2. Braun V, Clarke V. Using thematic analysis in psychology. *Qual Res Psychol.* 2006;3:77–101. https://doi.org/10.1191/1478088706qp063oa
3. Olver I, Gunn KM, Chong A, Knot V, Spronk K, Cominos N, Cunningham J. Communicating cancer and its treatment to Australian Aboriginal and Torres Strait Islander patients with cancer: a qualitative study. *Support Care Cancer.* 2022 Jan;30(1):431–38. https://doi.org/10.1007/s00520-021-06430-3
4. Shahid S, Durey A, Bessarab B, Aoun SM, Thompson SC. Identifying barriers and improving communications between cancer service providers and Aboriginal patients and their families: the perspective of service providers. *BMC Health Serv Res.* 2013;13:460. https://doi.org/10.1186/1472-6963-13-460
5. Ristevski E. Thompson S, Koingaby S, Nightengale C, Iddawela M. Understanding Aboriginal peoples' cultural and family connections can help inform the development of culturally appropriate models of care. *JCO Glob Oncol.* 2020 Feb;6:124–32. https://doi.org/10.1200/JGO.19.00109
6. Sharmil H, Kelly J, Bowden M, Galletly C, Cairney I, Wilson C, et al. Participatory action research – Dadarri – Ganma, using yarning: methodology co-design with Aboriginal community members. *Int J Equity Health.* 2021 Jul 2;20:160. https://doi.org/10.1186/s12939-021-01493-4

7. Research Data Australia. *Investigating the inclusion of vulnerable populations in Advance Care Planning: Developing complex and sensitive public policy [2016–2021]* [Internet]. ARDC [cited 2023 July 13]. Available from: https://researchdata.edu.au/investigating-inclusion-vulnerable-public-policy/948832
8. Lin I, Green C, Bessarab D. 'Yarn with me': applying clinical yarning to improve clinician-patient communication and Aboriginal health care. *Aust J Prim Health.* 2016 Nov;22:377–82. https://doi.org/10.1071/PY16051

Aboriginal Cancer Healing Center

56

Ian N. Olver, Rosamond Gilden, and Kim Morey

Key Points

- Community consultation was used to inform the development of an Aboriginal cancer healing center in a rural Australian hospital.
- The community recommended a combination of indoor and outdoor spaces, with a non-clinical feel and the ability to encompass traditional healing and complementary therapies.
- In addition to wanting a more welcoming hospital environment, community participants requested more Aboriginal staff in the healing center and access to more information about support services.

The South Australian Aboriginal Chronic Disease Consortium (the Consortium) is a collaborative partnership of health organizations in South Australia that aims to improve the health and wellbeing of South Australia's Aboriginal people through health promotion and support for those living with chronic diseases such as cancer. The Consortium developed a Cancer Healing Model to complement medical treatment by guiding service provision and designing an environment that supports healing [1]. The model was designed to support healing processes that support Aboriginal people's spiritual, cultural, mental, and physical strengths throughout cancer treatment and recovery.

The Cancer Healing Model has three core elements:

1. Services to support the individual with cancer and their family and community.
2. A physical environment that offers culturally safe and welcoming clinical, indoor, and outdoor spaces.
3. Enablers to support the model, including careful attention to the workforce, governance, cultural safety, technology, and monitoring and evaluation.

In partnership with Nunyara Aboriginal Health Service in Whyalla (regional South Australia), the Consortium developed the Cancer Healing Model through community consultation to ensure it would meet the cultural and medical needs of Aboriginal people affected by cancer and their families and communities. In this case study, we discuss the model's development. In future work, we will evaluate what constitutes a culturally appropriate and safe setting for cancer treatment in a rural hospital.

The model was developed through interviews, surveys, and workshops with the Aboriginal community, focusing on the most appropriate way to create a cancer healing center in the hospital—such as a space with a non-clinical feel and the ability to encompass traditional healing and complementary therapies. The community recommended the hospital needed both indoor and outdoor space, with the outdoor space including a garden with bush tucker, a firepit, some shelter with tables and comfortable chairs, and a "sensory" access pathway. They preferred to be outside in the open, not closed in.

Community participants suggested modifications for the consulting rooms and chemotherapy day treatment center to make them more welcoming, which included commissioning Aboriginal artwork (with the artists' full names and language groups on display) and brighter curtains (perhaps using colors from the Aboriginal flag). Participants noted the importance of regional differences—for instance, they pointed out that dot paintings are not appropriate for the local Barngarla people in Whyalla. For the hospital entrance, participants suggested Aboriginal artwork to create a welcoming atmosphere.

Community participants were asked to prioritize their preferences and wishes beyond the hospital environment. They suggested that having Aboriginal staff in the healing center was important and requested additional information that listed support services (such as counseling, mental health, legal and financial services, traditional healers, and local yarning circles). They also requested resources to support bookings and transfers to major city hospitals and information about support services in those locations.

G. Garvey (ed.), *Indigenous and Tribal Peoples and Cancer*, https://doi.org/10.1007/978-3-031-56806-0_56

The healing spaces are currently being developed, and the project will be formally evaluated when complete. If successful, the model will be disseminated.

We acknowledge with gratitude that the Cancer Healing Center Project was funded with a grant from the Hospital Research Foundation Group in South Australia.

Reference

1. South Australian Aboriginal Chronic Disease Consortium. *Aboriginal Cancer Healing Model.* Adelaide: SAACDC; 2019 Sept. Available from https://aboriginalhealthconsortium.org/our-resources/

Surgical Options for Breast Cancer and Consent Guidelines for Indigenous Women

57

Jennifer Erdrich, Felina Cordova-Marks, and Amanda Bruegl

Key Points

- Women diagnosed with breast cancer and preparing for surgery can choose between breast-conserving therapy (BCT) and mastectomy. Breast cancer survival for BCT and mastectomy are equivalent.
- Surgical patterns show that American Indian/Alaska Native (AI/AN) women in the United States have more mastectomy and less breast-conserving therapy for early-stage breast cancer compared to non-Hispanic White (NHW) women.
- For all women, regardless of race, informed consent for lumpectomy vs. mastectomy is a complex, time-intensive process entailing comprehensive counseling. Additional historical and cultural considerations must inform consent guidelines for Indigenous women preparing for breast cancer surgery.
- We propose innovative solutions to overcome the challenges that limit Indigenous women's access to their preferred surgical choice.

Breast-conserving therapy (BCT) consists of lumpectomy followed by radiation. A lumpectomy removes the tumor and surrounding rim of normal breast tissue, leaving most of the breast volume and shape intact. A mastectomy removes the entirety of the breast tissue. Randomized trials with long-term follow-up demonstrate that, regardless of the stage of disease, *survival* is equivalent for both treatment options [1–3]. While the risk of *recurrence* with lumpectomy alone is higher, modern multidisciplinary care combining lumpectomy with radiation and various forms of systemic therapy achieves a similar low risk of recurrence, allowing clinicians to offer BCT or mastectomy as equally safe standard care options. This establishes a surgical choice that is highly personal and should be individualized to consider multiple unique factors, including age, family history, hereditary gene mutations, size of the tumor relative to total breast volume, ability to complete multimodality breast care and surveillance, future plans regarding fertility and lactation, and overall best outcome for the individual's body-image, lifestyle, and peace of mind.

BCT consistently shows decreased surgical complications, decreased pain, faster recovery, more favorable cosmetics, and better-preserved sexuality and body image [1, 4]. This is not to say that it is the best choice for every woman. BCT is contraindicated for women with inflammatory breast cancer. For some, mastectomy is preferred for personal reasons, even with a full understanding of equivalent survival following BCT. Provided the patient is well-informed and has worked with her clinical team to ensure her decisions are safe, she should be supported in her surgical choice.

Surgical Disparities and Barriers for Indigenous Women

Overall, American Indian/Alaska Native (AI/AN) women have a statistically significant lower incidence of breast cancer compared with non-Hispanic White (NHW) women for all stages (RR 0.90, 95% CI 0.87–0.93) [1]. Unfortunately, despite overall lower incidence, AI/AN women have the worst breast cancer survival outcomes of all racial groups in the United States [1, 5–8]. Our data analysis, conducted with the Centers for Disease Control and Prevention, found no differences between AI/AN and NHW women in the type of operation performed for late-stage breast cancer. However, we found a statistically significant difference in the types of operations performed for early-stage disease. Overall, AI/AN women with early-stage breast cancer undergo mastectomy at a statistically higher percentage than NHW women (41% vs. 34.4%, $p<0.001$) and undergo lumpectomy at a statistically lower percentage (59% vs. 65.6%). Regional variations show a sharper disparity, with 47–49% of AI/AN women from the Northern Plains and Alaska undergoing mastectomy compared to 33–36% of NHW women in these same regions (Fig. 57.1) [1]. While our data cannot explain this phenomenon, they point to a missed opportunity for AI/AN women in the United States, and possibly for other

G. Garvey (ed.), *Indigenous and Tribal Peoples and Cancer*, https://doi.org/10.1007/978-3-031-56806-0_57

Indigenous women (depending on global surgical patterns), to treat early-stage breast cancers with BCT, a treatment with documented benefits including reduced surgical risk and pain, faster recovery, and high patient satisfaction.

Disparities in Multidisciplinary Care: The Broader Context

Data analyses using different US national registries show that AI/AN women are less likely to receive guideline-concordant preoperative biopsy, adjuvant chemotherapy, and post-treatment surveillance for breast cancer [1, 10]. There are no published data for the completion of reconstruction following mastectomy among AI/AN women. Other studies show lower rates of reconstruction for racial minorities, and the same is suspected but unproven for AI/AN women [1]. Radiation is a cornerstone of breast conservation, and our data interestingly show no overall differences in uptake of post-lumpectomy radiation treatment between AI/AN and NHW women. It is reassuring that when BCT is implemented, it is completed effectively for AI/AN women [1].

Consent Guidelines for Indigenous Women Preparing for Breast Cancer Surgery

Counseling and consent for breast cancer surgery are exceptionally intricate and time intensive. In the early history of breast cancer care, the only option was the highly morbid and deforming radical mastectomy. Through medical advances and decades of research, modern breast cancer care has replaced radical mastectomy with customized multidisciplinary treatment pathways. Patients can now choose between lumpectomy and mastectomy and consider how their choice fits into the context of other treatment decisions regarding chemotherapy, endocrine therapy, radiation, unilateral or bilateral surgery, reconstruction, surveillance, and survivorship. This range of mutually influencing decisions places understandable pressure on the central decision between lumpectomy or mastectomy. It is a clinician's responsibility and ethical duty to ensure that the patient is well-informed about her options and free to choose without coercion. For clinicians working with Indigenous and Tribal peoples, all standard tenets of consent specific to breast cancer surgical choices must be maintained. In addition, clinicians should be aware of the complex contexts in which decisions are made.

Historical, Social, and Cultural Context

There is a history of Indigenous women receiving inadequate information about procedures, being coerced into surgery, and even undergoing procedures to which they did not consent. In the mid-twentieth century, there were AI/AN women who consented to procedures such as appendectomy and then were sterilized without disclosure [11], and between 1962 and 1976, it is estimated that 25% of AI/AN women of reproductive age were forcibly sterilized [11, 12]. The methods that facilitated this dark history included, but were not limited to, the threat of withholding medical/Tribal services or removing children if women did not comply with the procedure. The fear of child removal was a very real and effective tactic facilitated by US boarding school policy and prevalent adoption practices prior to the passing of the 1978 Indian Child Welfare Act [11, 13]. When consent was obtained, it was often during childbirth, at a time when women were exhausted, vulnerable, and not in a position to make well-informed decisions [11]. The abusive practice of forced sterilization fits into a wider legacy of colonialism that has negatively affected every dimension of Indigenous health, and inevitably informs how Indigenous patients perceive modern healthcare, the degree to which they trust healthcare providers, and their interactions with health systems, including when preparing for breast cancer surgery. In addition, the functional, sexual, and symbolic meaning of the breast, together with its intrinsic meaning to personal iden-

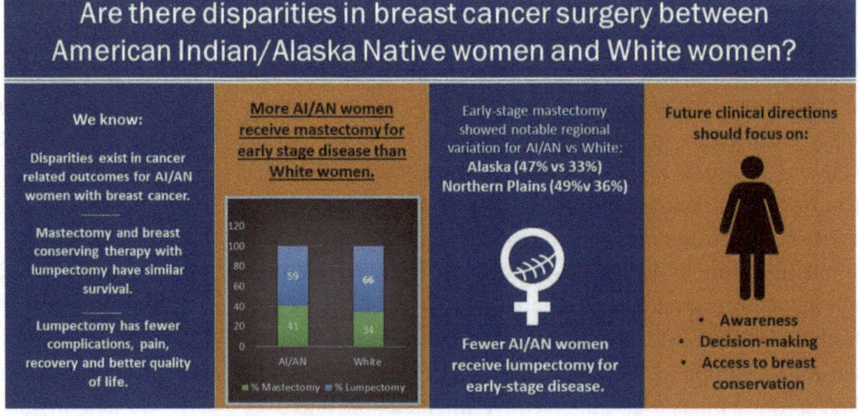

Fig. 57.1 Disparities in breast-conserving therapy for American Indian/Alaska Native women with early-stage breast cancer. (Source: Erdrich et al. [9])

tity, is rooted in highly varied cultural contexts, which contribute to a woman's choice of lumpectomy or mastectomy.

Guidelines for Informed Breast Cancer Surgery Consent Among Indigenous Women

The following suggested guidelines derive from a combination of universal ethical surgical consent practices, expansion of our previously published consent guidelines for the reproductive freedom of Indigenous women, and active clinical experience in the delivery of breast cancer care in the American Southwest [11].

1. Consent is a legal requirement and an ethical process that should respect patient autonomy and engage the patient in active, shared decision-making. To safeguard this:
   (a) Offer and provide an interpreter fluent in the patient's Indigenous language.
   (b) Use terms the patient can understand and explain new/unfamiliar terminology.
   (c) Complete the diagnostic workup prior to final surgical planning so that the patient has all available data for her decision. Although a breast cancer diagnosis might already be established, pending breast imaging and biopsies can sometimes dramatically alter recommendations and final choices.
   (d) Allow the patient ample time to ask questions and think over her options. Although some women are quick to assert their surgical choice, it more commonly takes repeated visits for a patient to arrive at a confident decision. Furthermore, depending on personal and cultural dynamics, a woman may need time to discuss her decision with her family, caregivers, or those for whom she provides care.
2. Procedures, risks, benefits, rationale, and recovery should be described as they specifically apply to lumpectomy and mastectomy to ensure accurate expectations of each pathway.
3. Patients must be assured that they will not be penalized or lose any medical or Tribal benefits by following one choice over another.
4. For women contemplating mastectomy, options for reconstruction must be clearly elucidated.
   (a) The surgical oncologist should lead the counseling, in addition to providing a dedicated consultation with Plastic surgery regarding unilateral vs. bilateral surgery, implant vs. tissue reconstruction, immediate or delayed reconstruction, and whether nipple preservation should be performed.
   (b) Reconstruction should not be over-promised if the sponsoring Tribal health facility does not have the financial budget to cover the service. This should be determined prior to mastectomy and the clinician should be familiar with the applicable regulations. In the United States, government and private insurance programs provide reconstruction, but these same protections are not guaranteed through the Indian Health Service (IHS) or Tribally run health facilities.
5. The type of treatment and surveillance following lumpectomy or mastectomy should be clearly delineated:
   (a) It should be explained that radiation follows lumpectomy and a brief overview of the anticipated treatment schedule is provided. This may impact the surgical decisions of Indigenous women faced with distance/transportation barriers.
   (b) It should be explained that, while most women who choose mastectomy do not undergo radiation, approximately 10% will have surgical pathology indication for post-mastectomy radiation.
   (c) The receptor status of the breast tumor should be described, together with the systemic therapy this will invoke (i.e., chemotherapy, targeted therapy, endocrine therapy), and the treatment sequence (i.e., preoperatively vs. postoperatively), which can vary for lumpectomy vs. mastectomy.
   (d) There may be long-term consequences for the reproductive health of younger patients. This requires transparent discussion on the effects on future fertility, on the inability to breastfeed post-mastectomy, and on possibly compromised lactation post-lumpectomy.
   (e) The frequency of health appointments and the types of imaging that will occur during survivorship should be discussed, including the cessation of mammograms post-mastectomy (a relief to some but the removal of a sense of annual security for others). For implant-based reconstruction, women may be expected to undergo breast MRI every 2–3 years.
6. Staging the axilla is a standard component of breast cancer surgery independent from the lumpectomy/mastectomy decision. While it does not carry the same nuanced choices as the breast options, it requires a thorough discussion of procedure, benefits, and risks, with particular emphasis on the risks and implications of lymphedema. For Indigenous women, an under-described secondary portion of the operation could harken historical practices of secondary coerced and unsolicited procedures (Table 57.1).

Table 57.1 Guidelines for informed breast cancer surgery consent among Indigenous women

1. Respect patient autonomy and actively engage patients in shared decision-making.	• Offer an interpreter fluent in the patient's Indigenous language. • Use language the patient understands; explain unfamiliar terms. • Ensure diagnostic workup is complete before finalizing the surgical plan. • Allow ample time to decide, providing subsequent counseling and appointments as necessary.
2. Describe the procedure steps, risks, benefits, rationale, and recovery.	• Describe these separately for lumpectomy and mastectomy.
3. Assure patients they will not lose medical or Tribal benefits by following one choice over another.	• Be sensitive that these tactics have been used to coerce Indigenous women into unwanted procedures.
4. For women contemplating mastectomy, provide education on options for reconstruction.	• Provide an introductory overview, but offer a Plastic Surgery referral for further consultation. • Do not over-promise reconstructive services; be aware of the sponsoring Tribal facility's budget and regulations for reconstruction; leverage resources from the Tribal facility and tertiary center to expand access.
5. Delineate treatment details and surveillance for lumpectomy and mastectomy.	• Explain that radiation follows lumpectomy; radiation may or may not follow mastectomy. • Describe the systemic therapy and the treatment sequence relative to the operation. • Make clear how treatment choices can affect fertility and lactation. • Delineate the frequency of visits and types of imaging conducted during survivorship for lumpectomy and mastectomy.
6. Describe axillary management and make clear it is a standard component that accompanies the breast operation.	• Be sensitive that Indigenous women have been subjected to non-consensual, surprise secondary procedures and how this has eroded Indigenous community trust in healthcare services.

Possible Solutions to Improve Indigenous Women's Access to Their Preferred Breast Cancer Operation and Treatment Pathway

Despite quality counseling and consent, barriers remain that may thwart a patient's pursuit of her preferred surgical choice. Measures can be taken to overcome some barriers, making the patient's choice more feasible. Geographic distance and limited transportation can be overcome through coordination between the multidisciplinary team to consolidate care into fewer visits. For example, Surgery, Medical Oncology, and Radiation Oncology appointments could be clustered into the same day. The team can also carefully evaluate the necessity of in-person visits. While a physical exam is indispensable for surgical planning, subsequent counseling visits can be completed via telehealth. Surveillance exams every 6–12 months can be performed by the local primary care physician. Transportation and short-term housing can often be arranged using Tribal health facility or tertiary referral center resources, community grants, or a combination thereof.

When appropriate, accelerated partial breast irradiation (APBI) can be offered, delivering radiation in courses as short as 5 days, rather than 5 weeks. This is a safe form of standard care that has become more popular among Indigenous patients. One study shows that rural AI/AN women use APBI more than twice as often as their urban counterparts [1].

Plastic surgery visits can be reduced by opting for direct implant reconstruction rather than tissue expanders. When there is limited IHS/Tribal health facility funding for reconstruction, this procedure may be delayed until discretionary funds become available. Many AI/AN women meet the criteria to enroll in Medicare/Medicaid, which authorizes reconstruction. Services for AI/AN women can be expanded by enlisting the help of social workers and nurse navigators to enroll eligible patients in Medicare/Medicaid programs.

Finally, welcoming traditional healers into the care pathway enhances trust and honors culture, thus increasing patients' confidence in their choices. While the efforts described above demand time and special attention, and do not provide guarantees, they contribute to transforming the breast cancer experience for Indigenous women, allowing them to fulfill their preferred surgical choice. Individual successes promote the institutional capacity to design system processes that beget improved care and access for future Indigenous patients. Through these measures and sensitive, culturally responsive consent, we can help narrow breast cancer surgical disparities and honor Indigenous women's surgical choices (Fig. 57.2).

Jennifer Erdrich's work reported in this publication was supported by the National Cancer Institute of the National Institutes of Health under award number K08CA276137. The content is solely the responsibility of the authors and does not necessarily represent the official view of the NIH.

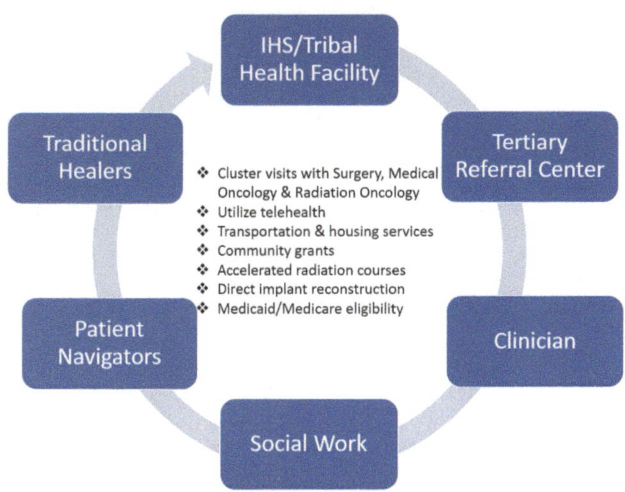

Fig. 57.2 Improving treatment choices for Indigenous women through multidirectional stakeholder coordination

References

1. Erdrich J, Cordova-Marks F, Monetathchi AR, Wu M, White A, Melkonian S. Disparities in Breast-Conserving Therapy for Non-Hispanic American Indian/Alaska Native Women Compared with Non-Hispanic White Women. *Ann Surg Oncol*. 2022;29(2):1019–30. https://doi.org/10.1245/s10434-021-10730-7
2. Anderson C, Islam JY, Elizabeth Hodgson M, Sabatino SA, Rodriguez JL, Lee CN, et al. Long-Term Satisfaction and Body Image After Contralateral Prophylactic Mastectomy. *Ann Surg Oncol*. 2017;24(6):1499–506. https://doi.org/10.1245/s10434-016-5753-7
3. Fisher B, Anderson S, Bryant J, Margolese RG, Deutsch M, Fisher ER, et al. Twenty-year follow-up of a randomized trial comparing total mastectomy, lumpectomy, and lumpectomy plus irradiation for the treatment of invasive breast cancer. *N Engl J Med*. 2002;347(16):1233–41. https://doi.org/10.1056/NEJMoa022152
4. Ng ET, Ang RZ, Tran BX, Ho CS, Zhang Z, Tan W, et al. Comparing Quality of Life in Breast Cancer Patients Who Underwent Mastectomy Versus Breast-Conserving Surgery: A Meta-Analysis. *Int J Environ Res Public Health*. 2019;16(24). https://doi.org/10.3390/ijerph16244970
5. Goodwin EA, Burhansstipanov L, Dignan M, Jones KL, Kaur JS. The experience of treatment barriers and their influence on quality of life in American Indian/Alaska Native breast cancer survivors. *Cancer*. 2017;123(5):861–8. https://doi.org/10.1002/cncr.30406
6. Javid SH, Varghese TK, Morris AM, Porter MP, He H, Buchwald D, et al. Guideline-concordant cancer care and survival among American Indian/Alaskan Native patients. *Cancer*. 2014;120(14):2183–90. https://doi.org/10.1002/cncr.28683
7. Markin A, Habermann EB, Zhu Y, Abraham A, Ahluwalia JS, Vickers SM, et al. Cancer surgery among American Indians. *JAMA Surg*. 2013;148(3):277–84. https://doi.org/10.1001/jamasurg.2013.1423
8. Simianu VV, Morris AM, Varghese TK, Jr., Porter MP, Henderson JA, Buchwald DS, et al. Evaluating disparities in inpatient surgical cancer care among American Indian/Alaska Native patients. *Am J Surg*. 2016;212(2):297–304. https://doi.org/10.1016/j.amjsurg.2015.10.030
9. Erdrich J, Cordova-Marks F, Monetatchi AR, Wu M, White A, Melkonian S. ASO Visual Abstract: Disparities in Breast-Conserving Therapy for Non-Hispanic American Indian/Alaska Native Women Compared with Non-Hispanic White Women. *Ann Surg Oncol*. 2021;28(Suppl 3):724. https://doi.org/10.1245/s10434-021-10788-3
10. Guadagnolo BA, Petereit DG, Coleman CN. Cancer Care Access and Outcomes for American Indian Populations in the United States: Challenges and Models for Progress. *Semin Radiat Oncol*. 2017;27(2):143–9. https://doi.org/10.1016/j.semradonc.2016.11.006
11. Cordova-Marks F, Fennimore N, Bruegl A, Erdrich J. What Should Physicians Consider About American Indian/Alaska Native Women's Reproductive Freedom? *AMA J Ethics*. 2020;22(10):E845–50. https://doi.org/10.1001/amajethics.2020.845
12. Theobald BA. 1970 law led to mass sterilization of Native American women. That history still matters. *Time Magazine*. 2019 November 27. Available from: https://time.com/5737080/native-american-sterilization-history/
13. Torpy S. Native American women and coerced sterilization: on the Trail of Tears in the 1970s. *Am Indian Cult Res J*. 2000;24(2):1–22. https://doi.org/10.17953/aicr.24.2.7646013460646042

Tailoring Cancer Care to Aboriginal and Torres Strait Islander People in the Northern Territory

58

Giam Kar

Key Points

- When the Alan Walker Cancer Care Centre opened in 2009, cancer mortality in the Northern Territory dropped by 15% within three years.
- We provide a community-wide, culturally welcoming approach to cancer treatment, with long consultations prior to admission, specific support for carers, training for health workers, and a strong open-door policy.
- Cancer treatment is rarely just about cancer. Most of our patients have other long-term illnesses that need to be managed alongside their cancer.

The Alan Walker Cancer Care Centre, at Royal Darwin Hospital, began operation in October 2009. Prior to 2009, most Northern Territory (NT) cancer patients traveled to Adelaide for treatment. In 2008, Royal Adelaide Hospital treated 160 cancer patients from the NT. Many patients missed out on appropriate treatment because they chose either radical surgery or complex chemotherapy. In many cases, this was because they didn't want to travel.

In our first year of operation in Darwin, we treated 260 patients. Within three years, cancer mortality in the NT had dropped by 15%. I'm convinced that's a testament to the power of local treatment.

Understanding Our Community

The NT's population is around 245,000, with roughly one-third of the population identifying as Aboriginal and/or Torres Strait Islander. Many of these people live in rural and remote areas, with English as a second or subsequent language. Statistically, we'd expect one-third of our cancer patients to be of Aboriginal and/or Torres Strait Islander heritage. But that's not how it works out—instead, the ratio is around 1 in 4.5. Over the years, I've gained a deeper understanding of the complex causes behind this disparity.

Different cancers Aboriginal and Torres Strait Islander people are more likely to be diagnosed with "younger-age cancers"—including head and neck cancers, lung cancer, and stomach cancer. Non-Indigenous people are more likely to be diagnosed with "old-age cancers" like breast and prostate cancer, which tend to have a better survival rate. That's one reason why we see more non-Indigenous people coming into the center for treatment and retreatment.

Traveling long distances Aboriginal and Torres Strait Islander patients are more likely than non-Indigenous patients to travel and stay away from home for their treatment. They often travel long distances from remote communities and spend several months in Darwin having treatment. This increases the likelihood of them being reluctant to choose to have treatment.

Cancer may not be their highest priority Many of our Aboriginal and Torres Strait Islander patients put the needs of their family and community ahead of their own need for treatment. People with caring responsibilities or family issues that need attention are likely to delay treatment for as long as possible. In addition, many people believe their symptoms are slow growing and not causing any major illness or debilitating conditions. They treat it like some of their other common health conditions, thinking it can be easily treated much later or it will heal itself. In these cases they will only seek medical help when the symptoms become unbearable.

A Community-Wide Approach to Treatment

From the day the Alan Walker Cancer Care Centre opened, we put a lot of effort into our community relationships. We wanted our patients to trust us and feel confident they'll

G. Garvey (ed.), *Indigenous and Tribal Peoples and Cancer*, https://doi.org/10.1007/978-3-031-56806-0_58

receive the best care possible in a welcoming and culturally safe environment.

Appointments prior to admission We conduct a long consultation with our Aboriginal and Torres Strait Islander patients before they begin treatment, and we schedule appointments that are twice as long as the appointments for non-Indigenous patients. We have an Aboriginal Liaison Officer involved in all consultations, plus an interpreter if needed. We make sure there's plenty of time to discuss the treatment and logistics. Our initial consultations are often conducted via teleconference and can involve anyone who needs to be consulted prior to the patient's treatment—including the patient's primary healthcare provider, family members, carers, and members of the community. Sometimes it's the community Elders or relatives who make the final decision about whether the patient can travel to Darwin for treatment, and we need to respect that process.

Supporting carers We're careful to make sure that carers understand what the patient is likely to experience and how long the treatment will last. It's very difficult for the patient if their carer leaves part-way through the treatment and the patient is left unsupported.

Training for health workers We've created links between the Alan Walker Centre and health practitioners in the community and have conducted training for health practitioners right across the NT. Our goal is to make sure they feel comfortable with us and understand the optimal care pathways we use. We now have a network of care coordinators and health practitioners who know us and trust the way we work.

Open-door policy We've implemented a strong open-door policy at the Alan Walker Centre. Any health practitioner is welcome to ring us directly and talk to our cancer care coordinators. We encourage them to call us if they have any suspicion that a patient may have cancer symptoms. Several of our staff have visited communities to understand more about primary care and disease management.

Cultural safety training We've developed our own cultural safety training, particularly focused on cancer cultural awareness. We want our staff to understand why Aboriginal and Torres Strait Islander people experience different types of cancer and different barriers to cancer treatment. We also want our staff to consider how our patients understand and view cancer.

Welcoming environment We've made the environment at the Alan Walker Centre as welcoming as possible. Even though we have a 27-room accommodation facility, most of our Aboriginal patients prefer to stay in the Aboriginal hostels. We offer a regular bus service to the hostels and make sure our patients and their carers can access whatever they need. We try to give them a home away from home because we want them to stay until their treatment is complete.

Managing comorbidities Cancer treatment is rarely just about cancer. Around 90% of our patients have other long-term illnesses that need to be managed alongside their cancer. This is a huge issue for the patients who travel to us for treatment because they don't have access to their usual health practitioners. We've developed strong relationships with local GPs and the Danila Dilba Health Service here in Darwin, and they do a lot of the heavy lifting for us in terms of chronic disease support.

Supporting the transition back home When patients finish their treatment, we support their transition back home. We contact their primary health provider to discuss ongoing care and surveillance and make sure the transition home is as easy as possible.

Part VI

Research

59 Cultural Safety Training Framework for Oncology Care Providers

Lea Bill and Barbara Frazer

Key Points

- The Indigenous-led Practice Change Implementation Model reframes cancer pathways for First Nations cancer patients and their families experiencing anti-Indigenous racism in health systems and experiencing a lack of cultural safety and acceptance of Indigenous health and healing approaches.
- The model provides an approach for standardizing culturally grounded, safe treatment in oncology care.
- Knowledge Holders/Practitioners have an essential role in Indigenous-led cancer research for practice change.

In Alberta, Canada, an Indigenous-led Practice Change Implementation Model was used to develop a culturally safe training program to increase oncologists' understanding of the need for traditional support and medicines within oncology care.

The Indigenous-led Practice Change Implementation Model is cohesive, embedding an equitable and ethical transformative process to support oncology care providers and traditional knowledge holders. The model framed specific knowledge building around cancer pathways for First Nations cancer patients and their families who experience anti-Indigenous racism in health systems, required to build oncology cultural safety training and acceptance of Indigenous health and healing approaches. The model was developed in partnership by the Alberta First Nations Information Governance Centre (AFNIGC), Alberta Health Services (AHS), and a team of Indigenous researchers, Knowledge Holders/Practitioners, and cancer care oncology champions. Supported by the cultural leadership of the Knowledge Holders/Practitioners as Right Holders, the partnership transferred four foundational concepts for practice change into the model: (1) relationships, (2) family as medicine, (3) culture as prevention, and (4) Indigenous languages as fundamental. These concepts operationalized culturally grounded training for oncology care providers and offered a cultural-grooming approach that creates awareness among oncology healthcare providers of the distinct and diverse equitable and ethical pathways unique to Indigenous cancer patients. This main focus was to create culturally safe cancer care pathways and care for/with Indigenous cancer patients and families seeking to include traditional supports for improved cancer care outcomes.

Essential Practice Change Knowledge Components

The partnership strictly adhered to First Nations philosophies of knowledge transfer and exchange, including relational processes in which respect underpins all interactions. An Indigenous lens was utilized to embed cultural approaches and community solutions into the project to address emerging Peoples-specific priorities [1].

Key concepts emerged from cultural engagement through thematic project dialogues and narrative processes with Knowledge Holders/Practitioners. They identified pivotal sites of transformation and adaptation to lead health system improvements and improve understanding of traditional supports. Key objectives of the cultural safety education modules included:

- Incorporating First Nation worldviews, language, and ceremony to guide the healing pathways of First Nation people.
- Understanding ceremony and the need to include ceremony when requested by First Nation cancer patients.
- Acknowledging and applying protocols to position culturally collaborative processes within oncology care.
- Utilizing language and oral traditions in training through stories and narratives.
- Understanding traditional principles and values associated with traditional healing.

G. Garvey (ed.), *Indigenous and Tribal Peoples and Cancer*, https://doi.org/10.1007/978-3-031-56806-0_59

- Recognizing the significance of "family as medicine" within oncology care.
- Standardizing culturally grounded safe treatment in oncology care.

Relationship Building

Relationship building is the first key concept of culturally grounded, safe oncology training and knowledge transfer/sharing. This concept places emphasis on engaging with, listening to, sustaining, and maintaining the patient-as-expert—as a rights holder defining their own pathway, and with the cultural supports required as a family. Relationship building takes time and requires mutually respectful investment, including developing awareness of historical experiences and understanding the cultural biases that may impact the relationship.

In the partnership for this project, open communication helped to establish trust between all partners and contributed to healing on both sides. Knowledge Holders/Practitioners were consistent in their messaging—such as the importance of embracing the connection to and relationship between all things in existence as part of a larger whole. Knowledge Holders/Practitioners discussed ancestral ways of "coming to know" and "being in a collective and community" as including relational kinship with the natural world. This is evidence of a strong cultural community and supports the presence of healthy family systems to support the patient. The oncology health provider is seen and included as a valued, extended family member as they enter the family circle with a specific role and function.

Family as Medicine

The second and perhaps most central cultural concept is "family as medicine." Family extends outward to include extended family, community, and kinship with the natural world. First Nation peoples have a strong sense of family and community. When one person is sick, the entire family, including extended family and community members, often gather to form a circle of support around the patient.

Developing a deeper understanding and appreciation of First Nation perspectives of the family helps oncology healthcare providers to understand the value of family as an extended resource rather than a hindrance to their cancer care role. Within the context of cancer care, family as medicine includes supportive relationships that are socially organized around health issues and challenges. Family, as the primary support structure, enhances care and fills gaps left by the healthcare system.

Culture as Prevention and Indigenous Language

Within the First Nation worldview, issues affecting the family or community are attended to, often through ceremony, through the prayerful engagement of mind, body, and spirit. The two final concepts, "culture as prevention" and "Indigenous languages," are woven into the idea of family as medicine because knowledge resides within language, and culture supports an entire knowledge system that specifies and conveys a purposeful way of life. The concept of the whole health and wellbeing of both the family and community is central to a lived knowledge base, which informs the culturally grounded training.

Practice Change Implementation Model: First Nations Knowledge Holder Transformative Processes for Knowledge Transfer and Exchange

The sharing and exchange of Indigenous and cultural knowledge is a collective activity. Knowledge Holders/Practitioners add layer onto layer, using the bodies of knowledge contained within their oral histories to create a rich living knowledge base from which to implement and align practice change. These cultural transformative processes facilitated the establishment of the aims and aspirations that informed this project. Project co-lead and Knowledge Holder/Practitioner Lea Bill developed the graphic in Fig. 59.1 that shows the embodiment of a living system of knowledge transfer and exchange where multiple levels of life principles flow, intercede, and influence within the whole being, with change as a constant that moves with living knowledge (Fig. 59.1).

Knowledge transfer and exchange are socially cohesive processes. Figure 59.1 demonstrates "group mindedness" in the decision-making processes that collaboratively organize around any issue in a dialogic, relational, and cultural way, which can be understood as embedded within collective, cultural, and collaborative processes.

First Nations Spiritual and Culturally Based Knowledge Transfer Framework

Knowledge transfer has been embedded within family systems and cultural transfer processes throughout history. However, traditional Indigenous methods and modes of transmission have been impacted by colonization. In Canada, the legacy of residential schools has interrupted knowledge transfer processes and continues to have an impact in all sec-

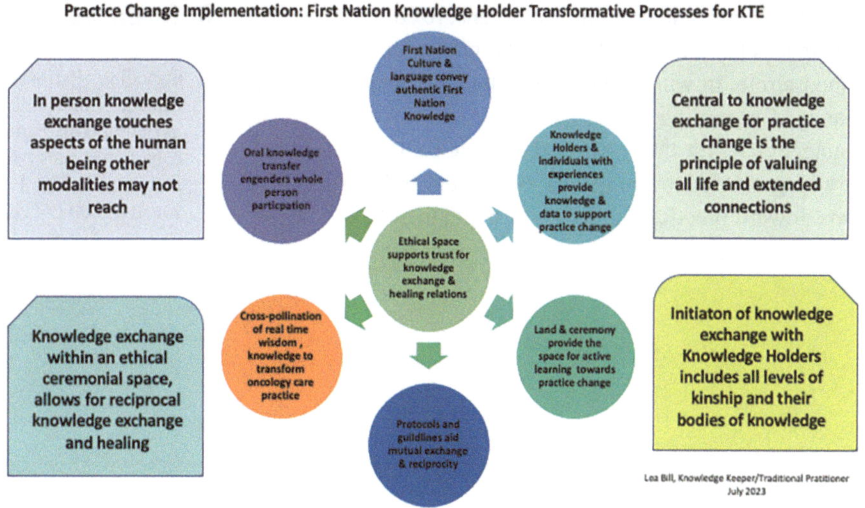

Fig. 59.1 Practice change implementation graphic developed by Lea Bill

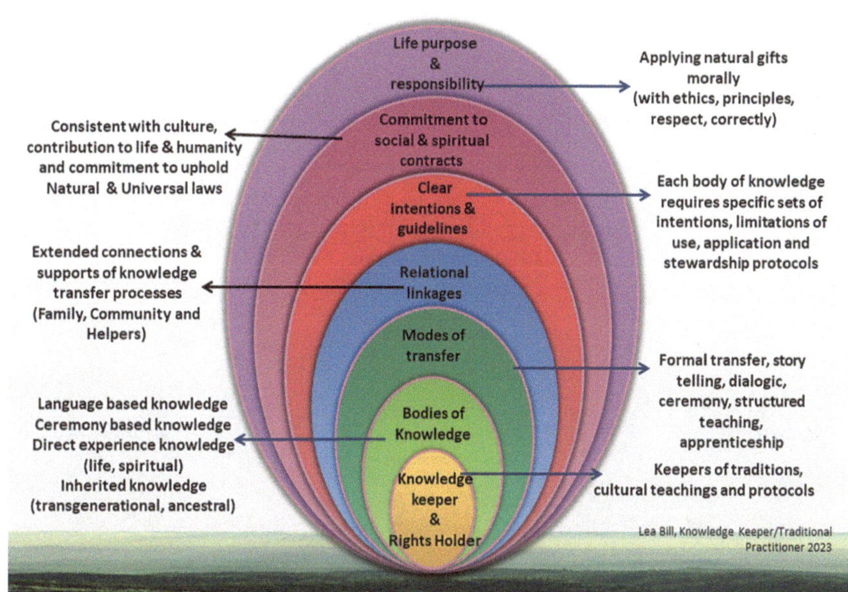

Fig. 59.2 First Nation spiritual and culturally based knowledge transfer framework

tors of education. For practice change to occur, learning about Indigenous ways and implementing new understandings linked to Indigenous practices, values, and beliefs are critical and essential.

In response to this concept, the partnership discussed a First Nations spiritual and culturally based framework, based on the values and beliefs intrinsically linked to traditional spiritual and cultural knowledge transfer methods. The framework (Fig. 59.2) comes from the direct experience and practice of First Nation Knowledge Holder/Practitioner Lea Bill. It is a high-level framework that reflects the key principles associated with and facilitating knowledge transfer.

Conclusion

The interconnected nature of family, culture, language, and community, along with ethical space and natural knowledge transfer, is positioned within a model of Indigenous-led Practice Change Implementation. This model offers an authentic transformative space that supports culturally grounded and safe training and knowledge transfer to oncology care providers. Indigenous-led cultural processes are essential for the application of intact ancestral knowledge to work toward transforming current and future oncology healthcare systems. This holistic process requires great sensitivity, respect, and commitment to ensure ethical processes and spaces [2] are upheld within the partnership. The established circle, in which knowledge, healing, and process are managed according to the pace, volition, information, and connections with the spirit of the participants, informs culturally grounded training and education and ensures that steps toward practice change place begin to occur.

References

1. Canadian Partnership Against Cancer. Canadian Strategy for Cancer Control 2019–2029. Available from: https://www.partnershipagainstcancer.ca/about-us/corporate-strategic-document/canadian-strategy-for-cancer-control/
2. Ermine W. The Ethical Space of Engagement. *Indigenous Law Journal*. 2007;6(1):193–203.

Measuring the Wellbeing of Aboriginal and Torres Strait Islander Cancer Patients

60

Rebecca Murray, Sandra Avery, and Nicole Hewlett

Key Points

- What Matters 2 Adults (WM2A)—a wellbeing measure that is culturally grounded in the values and preferences of Aboriginal and Torres Strait Islander people—is being trialed in cancer services across NSW, Australia; we present the experience of the South Western Sydney Local Health District, Cancer Services, as a case study.
- WM2A is implemented by an Aboriginal Health Worker who uses it to identify and holistically support the wellbeing needs of patients undergoing cancer treatment.
- Outcomes from the measure are used to deliver culturally responsive patient- and family-centered cancer care. Early results suggest the combined effects of the measure and a dedicated Aboriginal Health Worker are improving outcomes for Aboriginal and Torres Strait Islander patients.

South Western Sydney Local Health District, Cancer Services in Australia is one of four cancer services participating in an implementation trial of the What Matters 2 Adults (WM2A) wellbeing measure. Funded by the Medical Research Future Fund (MRFF 2007834), the trial aims to understand the contribution of Aboriginal and Torres Strait Islander culture and wellbeing to health. This collaborative project is co-led by Professor Kirsten Howard (The University of Sydney) and Professor Gail Garvey (The University of Queensland) and is conducted in partnership with The Cancer Institute New South Wales, Aboriginal Health Units, and cancer centers across four New South Wales Local Health Districts.

The WM2A measure is a new holistic wellbeing measure for First Nations adults. It is a strengths-based measure that is grounded in the values and preferences of Aboriginal and Torres Strait Islander adults and acknowledges the interconnectedness of family, community, and culture to the wellbeing of First Nations peoples. The WM2A measure consists of 32 items across 10 dimensions of wellbeing [1].

In this case study, we describe our experiences implementing the WM2A measure over the past 10 months in a large urban cancer center. At the time of writing, 26 First Nations cancer patients have participated in the trial. An Aboriginal Health Worker (Rebecca Murray) was employed to recruit trial participants, implement the measure, and work with Aboriginal and Torres Strait Islander patients to identify aspects of their wellbeing requiring attention and referral.

About Our Region and Cancer Center

South Western Sydney Local Health District serves around 820,000 people who live in seven local government areas to the southwest of Sydney, Australia. The district has six acute hospitals, 14 community health centers, and four public cancer treatment facilities. Much of the district is urban, but we also serve several regional towns and rural areas.

The district is highly multicultural, with approximately 50% of the population coming from language backgrounds other than English, with many people from Arabic, Vietnamese, and Chinese backgrounds. Approximately 1% of our population identifies as Aboriginal or Torres Strait Islander.

Our hospital employs two Aboriginal Liaison Officers who mainly support Aboriginal and Torres Strait Islander inpatients. However, most of our cancer patients are treated through outpatient services. Prior to the WM2A trial, Aboriginal cultural support for cancer patients was limited.

Factors Impacting Access to Healthcare

A history of colonization, oppression, and subjugation has translated to numerous inequities experienced by Aboriginal and Torres Strait Islander peoples today. The ongoing legacies of colonization, including systemic racism in healthcare, manifest in significant health challenges and numerous bar-

G. Garvey (ed.), *Indigenous and Tribal Peoples and Cancer*, https://doi.org/10.1007/978-3-031-56806-0_60

riers to Aboriginal and Torres Strait Islander peoples accessing healthcare. This has resulted in a deep distrust in healthcare services and is often shaped and further fueled by negative experiences when accessing care, which often leads to a reluctance to access healthcare. Many Aboriginal and Torres Strait Islander patients do not feel safe to ask questions and speak up about the issues important to them. Aboriginal and Torres Strait Islander patients in our region also face the tyranny of distance and may travel for two or three hours to receive cancer care and treatment. To assist our patients with the challenges of distance, our local Aboriginal Land Council provides an invaluable transport service. Telehealth for pre-treatment screening also helps address some of the distance and transport barriers.

Aboriginal and Torres Strait Islander patients in our region typically prioritize the needs of their families ahead of their own personal health needs. Many will not hesitate to miss a chemotherapy appointment if they have a family issue that needs their attention. Our clinicians find this difficult to understand and may conclude the patients are challenging to treat.

Implementing the WM2A Wellbeing Measure

We implement the WM2A measure alongside the other assessments we use with all cancer patients—including the Edmonton Symptom Assessment Scale and Distress Thermometer. The WM2A is only implemented with Aboriginal and Torres Strait Islander patients and is implemented by our Aboriginal Health Worker (Rebecca).

All Aboriginal and Torres Strait Islander patients are approached to participate in this trial. Rebecca provides patients with information about the measure and, if the patient agrees, they complete the consent-to-participate form. The WM2A measure is implemented through an Aboriginal way of conversing, called yarning. The measure offers a structured way of asking questions and yarning about topics that can otherwise be difficult—like racism and hope for the future. Rebecca creates a safe space, with an environment of respect and trust, then uses the measure to encourage the patient to open up about things that are important to them. She allows plenty of time for patients to complete the measure.

Benefits of Using the WM2A Wellbeing Measure

One big advantage of the WM2A measure is the structure it provides for difficult conversations. It's helpful for patients to understand that they are working through a questionnaire that will support clinicians in planning their care and treatment. It is a catalyst for establishing a trusted relationship that enables the cancer service to holistically support Aboriginal and Torres Strait Islander patients through their treatment. Anecdotally, we are observing how the WM2A is helping patients to agree and persevere with treatment.

WM2A is implemented in a conversational way by a non-clinical health worker who has a similar cultural background to the participant. We believe the non-clinical, culturally sensitive implementation and discussion about lived experiences are major elements of its success. Because of the connection and trust established, patients feel supported and do not feel judged or pressured to give a particular answer in a particular way. The cultural connection they share helps the patient to feel safe and "held." This healthcare dynamic is different from the clinical setting, and it helps to give patients the confidence to talk about the things that are important to them.

The yarn and safe space provided by Rebecca present an opportunity for patients to put aside their fear and reflect on the things that matter to them. This strengths-based approach appears to be enhancing the wellbeing of patients and opening avenues of trust in the health service. Through the WM2A measure, we can navigate the space between patients and clinicians and anecdotally we are making a difference. For example, when implementing the measure, Rebecca asked a patient if he was experiencing nausea. He said "no," then stopped and asked, "what is nausea?" In a typical clinical setting, that patient would be unlikely to ask for an explanation, and the clinician would be unlikely to notice the patient didn't understand. Our patients will ask Rebecca questions they would never feel confident or comfortable to ask a doctor or nurse.

Another patient was reluctant to accept treatment and simply wanted to go home and die. All patients are free to make that choice, but there were things influencing this patient's decision and the service could do better. Using WM2A, Rebecca uncovered many issues that were making it difficult for the patient to accept treatment. These issues were discussed, and Rebecca helped the patient to address them; the patient has since completed treatment, with a successful outcome.

Another patient was a 69-year-old woman diagnosed with stage 4 lung cancer and she wanted to complete the WM2A measure as she felt it included questions relevant to her. Given her diagnosis, this patient's survey was remarkable. She showed a strong sense of her own wellbeing and was positive about her future. She talked about her grandchildren being her greatest pleasure. She was proud of her heritage and drew great strength from her community. Although this patient passed away shortly after completing the WM2A, she remained positive to the end. Her responses underpin a central theme of Aboriginal health and a holistic approach to care: we need to treat the person, not just the disease.

Cancer care needs to systematically identify and address the cultural, social, and emotional wellbeing of Aboriginal and Torres Strait Islander patients using culturally appropriate and safe measures, like the WM2A measure.

Reference

1. Howard K, Anderson K, Cunningham J, Cass A, Ratcliffe J, Whop LJ, et al. What Matters 2 Adults: a study protocol to develop a new preference-based wellbeing measure with Aboriginal and Torres Strait Islander adults (WM2Adults). *BMC Public Health.* 2020 Nov;20:1739. https://doi.org/10.1186/s12889-020-09821-z

Communicating Cancer Survival Inequalities Among Indigenous and Tribal Peoples

61

Peter D. Baade, Jessica K. Cameron, Susanna M. Cramb, Muhammad Haroon, Jason Gurney, and Paramita Dasgupta

Key Points

- Population-level cancer survival is an important measure of the impact of cancer among Indigenous and Tribal peoples.
- Reporting survival statistics using a range of measures provides different perspectives and assists in appropriate interpretation.
- Measures of survival require accurate information on ethnicity, which is lacking in many countries.
- Absolute measures of survival, such as remaining life expectancy, crude probability of death, and avoidable cancer deaths, provide tangible estimates of the population-level impact of cancer diagnosis.
- Population-level statistics may help to inform decision-making at the individual level, although the unique circumstances of each person also need to be considered.

In the context of generally poorer health among Indigenous and Tribal peoples [1], assessing the impact of a cancer diagnosis within this population is important. Cancer survival is an important measure of this and can enable informed decision-making to improve health outcomes and reduce the burden of cancer in these populations. However, to ensure that analyses are meaningful and robust, we need to ensure we are using the most appropriate methods possible. In this chapter, we briefly summarize the concept of cancer survival, as well as contemporary methods that measure this concept.

Concept of Cancer Survival

Cancer survival refers to the probability of individuals being alive after a certain period of time following a cancer diagnosis. Often expressed as a percentage, it is designed to reflect the success of cancer treatments and overall outcomes for people diagnosed with cancer. Survival rates are usually calculated over a specific timeframe post-diagnosis, such as five years, and can vary depending on the type and stage of cancer. Cancer survival statistics provide important information for patients, doctors, and researchers to understand the effectiveness of treatments, make informed decisions about care, and assess progress in cancer management. They can also be used to assess outcomes for specific population groups, such as Indigenous and Tribal peoples, and identify inequalities compared to other population groups.

Individual-Level Versus Population-Level Survival Statistics

Individual-level survival statistics provide personalized prognosis information based on an individual's specific circumstances, including demographics (age, sex), cancer characteristics (type, how early it was diagnosed), treatment, and personal experiences. Population-level survival statistics examine groups of people to identify patterns and trends to help researchers and healthcare providers understand common risk factors, assess treatment effectiveness, and make decisions about public health strategies. Importantly, population survival statistics reflect the average over a specific population group, thus providing an important guide for planning; however, they are not necessarily relevant to an individual's own cancer journey.

Cancer Survival Versus Cancer Mortality

"Cancer mortality" and "cancer survival" focus on different groups of people to understand deaths from cancer.

Cancer mortality is an examination of the entire population to determine how many people die from cancer within a specific time period, while cancer survival focuses on the outcomes of people who have been diagnosed with cancer during that time and how many are still alive after a certain number of years post-diagnosis.

Cancer mortality is calculated as the number of cancer deaths as a rate of the total population per year. Cancer

G. Garvey (ed.), *Indigenous and Tribal Peoples and Cancer*, https://doi.org/10.1007/978-3-031-56806-0_61

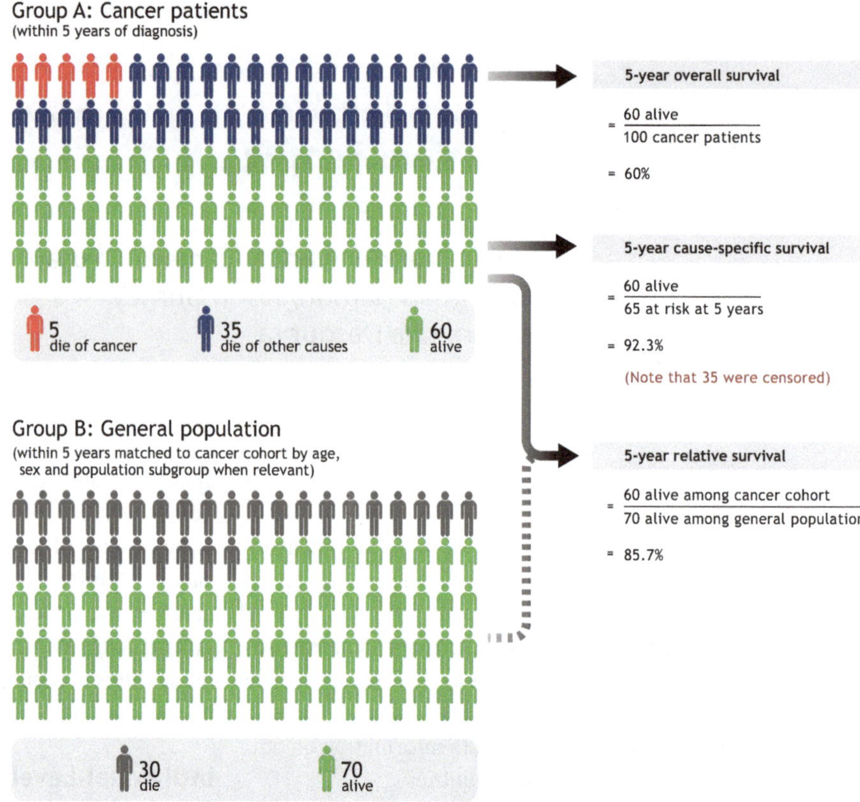

Fig. 61.1 Hypothetical scenario showing the calculation of overall, cause-specific, and relative survival for a group of people diagnosed with cancer

survival is calculated as the number of cancer deaths as a percentage of those who have been diagnosed with cancer in a given period.

All-cause survival is another useful statistic, which is measured as the number of people who die from any cause during a specific period post-cancer diagnosis.

Sources of Cancer Survival Data

Population-based cancer registries play a crucial and ongoing role in collecting and reporting cancer diagnoses within specific populations. Cancer registries link these data with national death registration records to determine the number of individuals diagnosed with cancer who have died and the time between their diagnosis and death.

Understanding cancer survival for Indigenous and Tribal peoples requires the collection of robust ethnicity data. Obtaining the necessary information to accurately establish cancer survival rates is complex, and high-quality data collection for Indigenous people is lacking in many countries [2]. For example, population survival statistics for Australian Aboriginal and Torres Strait Islander people are typically reported at the semi-national level, restricting statistics to states and territories with cancer registries known to have reliable identification data. In Aotearoa New Zealand, ethnicity data are collected through routine healthcare records and can be linked to national cancer registry and mortality data collections, enabling national-level comparisons of cancer survival outcomes between ethnic groups [3]. However, such comparisons are likely to be conservative due to the underreporting of Indigenous Māori ethnicity within these collections [4]. In the United States, American Indian or Alaska Natives are often misclassified, although data linkages to patient registration data are used to improve accuracy [5].

Methods of Reporting

Overall Survival

Arguably, overall survival is the most easily understood measure of survival. It reveals the proportion (or percentage) of people still alive after a certain number of years post-diagnosis. The example shown in Fig. 61.1 has an overall survival rate of 60%; however, this counts all deaths the same, irrespective of cause. An overall high survival rate could be due to fewer deaths from cancer, fewer deaths from other causes, or both. Overall survival, therefore, does not reveal the extent to which cancer diagnosis affects a person's life or how it differs between population groups.

Net Survival

Net survival, which accounts for other causes of death, helps to discern the impact of cancer on survival. It reflects the impact of the diagnosed cancer only, excluding other causes of death. Net survival is typically measured in one of two ways—cause-specific survival and relative survival.

Cause-specific survival uses death from cancer as the main outcome, while censoring deaths from other causes. Censoring, in this context, means that information about death from other causes is used in survival calculations only until the point at which an individual dies from another cause. For example, an individual who died from an unrelated cause six years post-cancer diagnosis will be included in calculations of five-year survival, but not of 10-year survival. In the example shown in Fig. 61.1, cause-specific survival is 92%. Since 35 people have been censored, 65 are included in the calculation, 60 of whom are still alive. However, determining the precise cause of death can be difficult, due to the disease complexity, potential treatment-related complications, incomplete medical records, and multiple health factors or comorbidities that may have contributed to the death. This is a limitation for population-based cancer registry data [6].

The second method for measuring net survival is relative survival. This compares how long a group of cancer patients lives to a similar group without cancer. It assumes that any survival difference (shown as a ratio) is because of the cancer diagnosis. The comparison group is typically the general population, using official population life tables differentiated by age and sex. In example shown in Fig. 61.1, 60% of the cancer patients have survived for five years post-diagnosis, compared with 70% expected from the matched comparison group, resulting in a relative survival rate of 86%.

Owing to the challenges in determining a single cause of death in cancer registry data, relative survival has historically been the preferred method of reporting cancer survival in population-based cancer registries [6]. However, the interpretation of relative survival statistics has a number of potential limitations.

First, valid comparisons between the cancer cohort and the general population rely on accurate population life tables [7]. This can be a particular limiting factor for Indigenous peoples, for whom ethnic identification in population mortality or cancer registry data may not be robust. Second, relative survival assumes that the only difference between the group diagnosed with cancer and the general population is the cancer diagnosis. However, other factors may be more prevalent in the cancer cohort, such as smoking. For this reason and to ensure the impact of cancer on survival is accurately conveyed, comparisons of relative survival between Indigenous and non-Indigenous populations should use population life tables specific to the subpopulation in question [7]. Third, relative survival can be difficult to interpret, as it reflects a non-realistic scenario in which a person cannot die from a non-cancer—a scenario that is not reflected in real life. A relative survival estimate is better interpreted as a ratio [8]. For example, a relative survival estimate of 70% means cancer patients are 70% as likely, or 30% less likely, to survive five years than the general population. This lacks meaning if expectations for general population survival are not also reported.

Therefore, although relative survival is the most widely used framework for calculating and reporting cancer survival estimates among populations [6], there are substantial challenges to correctly understanding and communicating the statistics to a wide audience. In addition, because it is a relative rather than an absolute measure, interpreting comparisons between populations can be difficult as differences may be due to differences in observed survival for the cancer cohort or in expected survival for the specific population. For example, while overall life expectancy in Australia is high [9], the average life expectancy among Aboriginal and Torres Strait Islander people is approximately eight years shorter than other Australians [10]. Consequently, if the overall survival of the two populations is similar, relative survival among Aboriginal and Torres Strait Islander Australians may be higher.

Absolute Measures of Survival

Absolute measures may provide more tangible estimates of the population-level impact of a cancer diagnosis on a person's life [11]. Three absolute measures are remaining life expectancy, crude probability of death, and avoidable deaths. Each is calculated within the relative survival framework, meaning that specific information about the cause of death is not required, but population-specific life tables comparable to the specific cancer cohort are required.

Remaining life expectancy, or average lifespan, post-cancer diagnosis provides another perspective on cancer survival. Remaining life expectancy is the number of years, on average, an individual can expect to live post-cancer. It quantifies the long-term impact of cancer throughout a person's remaining lifetime, rather than focusing on a specific time period following diagnosis. While this information provides an important perspective for people diagnosed with cancer, comparisons of remaining life expectancy between population groups need to first consider the differences in overall life expectancy among people not diagnosed with cancer.

Crude probability of death estimates consider other causes of death as well, making them more suitable for risk communication and clinical decision-making [12]. They describe the number of people per 100 diagnosed with a specific cancer who die from that cancer, die from other causes, or

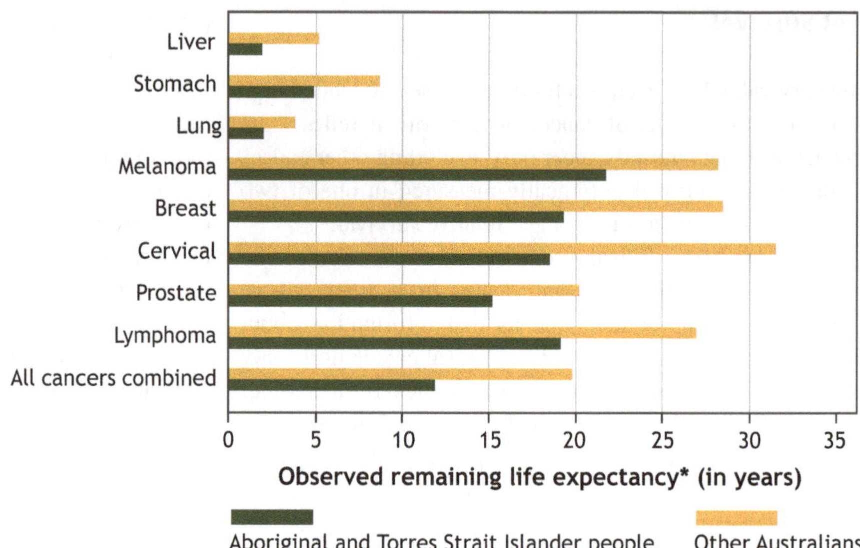

Fig. 61.2 Remaining life expectancy following a diagnosis of selected cancer types for Aboriginal and Torres Strait Islander people and other Australians, Australia, 2005–2016. (Source: Adapted from Ref. Dasgupta et al. [16])

remain alive after a certain time. Cause-of-death information is not required, as the general population mortality is used as a proxy for non-cancer causes of death. The difference between net and crude survival is small for younger people, who are less likely to die of other causes. However, for older individuals, crude probability estimates are important for accurately communicating the prognosis and the implications of a cancer diagnosis. Crude probability of death estimates must be expressed in terms of an "at-risk" period, such as the number of cancer deaths within five years of diagnosis. Crude probability of death can be very useful in understanding inequalities in cancer survival between different groups, such as Indigenous people, because it describes both the risk of death from cancer and the risk of death from other causes.

The concept of avoidable deaths conveys the impact of survival differences between two population groups by estimating the number of deaths that could be avoided if both populations have the same cancer survival probabilities [13]. Since this estimate is based on crude probability of death estimates, it must also be expressed in terms of an "at-risk" period.

Case Study

Data

To demonstrate different population-level cancer survival statistics in an Indigenous population, in collaboration with Aboriginal leader, Professor Gail Garvey, and other colleagues, we obtained cancer registry data from Australian cancer registries with sufficiently high levels of identification over the study period: Queensland, Western Australia, Northern Territory, and New South Wales [14]. These account for approximately 84% of Australian's Aboriginal and Torres Strait Islander population [15]. The study cohort consisted of over 700,000 Australians diagnosed with cancer between 2005 and 2016, including nearly 13,000 Aboriginal and Torres Strait Islander people.

Ethics approval for this study was obtained from the Aboriginal Health and Medical Research Council Ethics Committee (1256/17), the Northern Territory (NT) Department of Health, the Menzies School of Health Human Research Ethics Committee (2016–2689), and the New South Wales (NSW) Population and Health Services Research Ethics Committee (2017/HRE0204).

Relative Survival

Between 2005 and 2016, five-year relative survival for people diagnosed with cancer was 49.1% [16]. This was lower than for the rest of the Australian population over the same period (59.6%). The five-year relative survival rate varied substantially by cancer type, being substantially lower (<15%) for liver, pancreatic, and lung cancer, and higher (>70%) for prostate, uterine, and breast cancers and melanoma.

Remaining Life Expectancy

On average, Aboriginal and Torres Strait Islander people diagnosed with cancer survived for 12 years post-diagnosis. This was lower than for other Australian patients who lived, on average, for 20 years post-diagnosis (Fig. 61.2) [16]. This is after cancer type and age at diagnosis were taken into

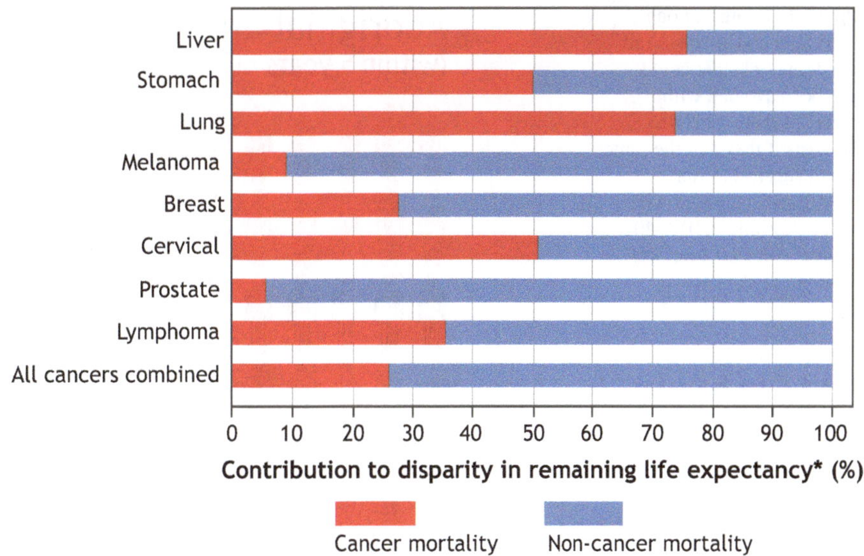

Fig. 61.3 Contributions to differences in remaining life expectancy following a diagnosis of selected cancer types between Aboriginal and Torres Strait Islander people and other Australians, Australia, 2005–2016. (Source: Adapted from Ref. Dasgupta et al. [16])

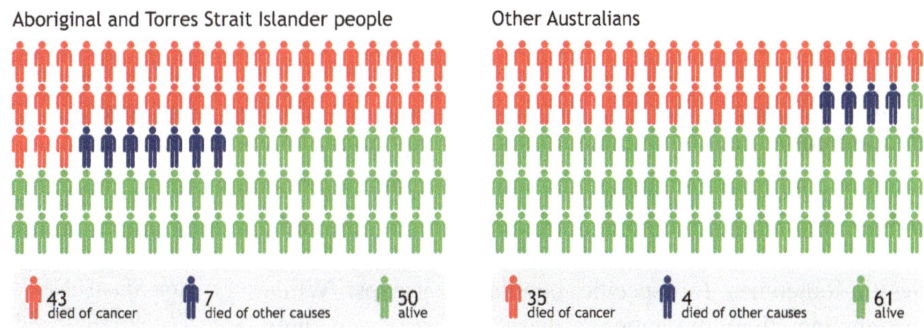

Fig. 61.4 Crude probability of death within 5 years of diagnosis for Aboriginal and Torres Strait Islander people and other Australians diagnosed with cancer, Australia, 2011–2016. (Source: Adapted from Ref. Dasgupta et al. [13])

account. The disparity was evident across all cancer types (Fig. 61.2). On average and across all cancer types, approximately one-quarter of this gap can be attributed to higher cancer-related mortality, and three-quarters to other causes of death (although it varied substantially by cancer type) (Fig. 61.3). Typically, for cancer types with high survival rates, non-cancer causes contributed more to the life expectancy gap.

Crude Probability of Death

Using the semi-national Australian cohort, out of every 100 Aboriginal and Torres Strait Islander people diagnosed with any invasive cancer between 2011 and 2016, approximately 43 would have died from their cancer within five years, and seven would have died from other causes (Fig. 61.4) [13], compared to 35 deaths from cancer and four from other causes for non-Indigenous Australians.

Avoidable Deaths

In this study, approximately 1270 Aboriginal and Torres Strait Islander people were diagnosed with cancer annually between 2012 and 2016 [13]. Of these, 646 died within five years post-diagnosis. If, however, this population group had the same survival as other Australians, 133 deaths (three-quarters of which were caused by cancer) within five years of diagnosis were potentially avoidable. In other words, for every 100 Aboriginal and Torres Strait Islander people diagnosed with cancer, approximately 11 of 50 deaths (seven due to cancer) within five years of diagnosis could be avoided if they had the same overall survival as other Australians with cancer (Fig. 61.5) [13].

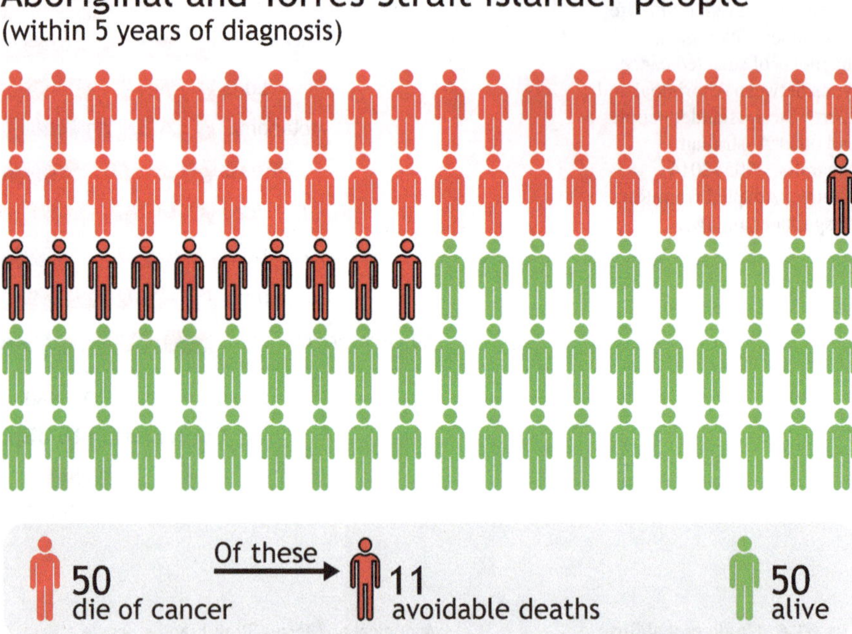

Fig. 61.5 Deaths among Aboriginal and Torres Strait Islander people that could have been avoided within 5 years of their cancer diagnosis if they had the same overall survival as other Australians diagnosed with cancer, Australia, 2012–2016. (Source: Adapted from Ref. Dasgupta et al. [13])

Conclusion

Cancer survival is multifaceted and a variety of statistics provide different perspectives, particularly regarding inequalities in outcomes for specific population groups. While recognizing their limitations, these statistics can help decision-makers and planners to appropriately focus efforts on improving outcomes and reducing avoidable deaths. The statistics can also be used to highlight where gains have been made; for example, survival among Aboriginal and Torres Strait Islander people diagnosed with cancer has improved substantially over time. However, because survival among other Australians has improved as well, the gap hasn't decreased. Effective communication of these statistics empowers people diagnosed with cancer, and those providing support, to be actively involved in the treatment decision-making process. Using different methods to explain survival rates at the population level allows for different perspectives, particularly when reporting absolute measures. Ultimately, statistics act as a guide to inform the decisions that individuals and their health professionals need to consider when taking into account each individual's unique circumstances.

References

1. Anderson I, Robson B, Connolly M, Al-Yaman F, Bjertness E, King A, et al. Indigenous and tribal peoples' health (The Lancet-Lowitja Institute Global Collaboration): a population study. *Lancet.* 2016;388(10040):131–57. https://doi.org/10.1016/S0140-6736(16)00345-7
2. Diaz A, Soerjomataram I, Moore S, Whop LJ, Bray F, Hoberg H, et al. Collection and Reporting of Indigenous Status Information in Cancer Registries Around the World. *JCO Glob Oncol.* 2020;6:133–42. https://doi.org/10.1200/JGO.19.00119
3. Gurney J, Stanley J, McLeod M, Koea J, Jackson C, Sarfati D. Disparities in Cancer-Specific Survival Between Maori and Non-Maori New Zealanders, 2007–2016. *JCO Glob Oncol.* 2020;6:766–74. https://doi.org/10.1200/GO.20.00028
4. Harris R, Paine SJ, Atkinson J, Robson B, King PT, Randle J, et al. We still don't count: the under-counting and under-representation of Maori in health and disability sector data. *N Z Med J.* 2022;135(1567):54–78.
5. Kratzer TB, Jemal A, Miller KD, Nash S, Wiggins C, Redwood D, et al. Cancer statistics for American Indian and Alaska Native individuals, 2022: Including increasing disparities in early onset colorectal cancer. *CA Cancer J Clin.* 2023;73(2):120–46. https://doi.org/10.3322/caac.21757
6. Skyrud KD, Bray F, Moller B. A comparison of relative and cause-specific survival by cancer site, age and time since diagnosis. *Int J Cancer.* 2014;135(1):196–203. https://doi.org/10.1002/ijc.28645
7. Sarfati D, Blakely T, Pearce N. Measuring cancer survival in populations: relative survival vs cancer-specific survival. *Int J Epidemiol.* 2010;39(2):598–610. https://doi.org/10.1093/ije/dyp392
8. Baade P, Cramb S, Dasgupta P, Youlden D. Estimating cancer survival – improving accuracy and relevance. *Aust N Z J Public Health.* 2016;40(5):403–4. https://doi.org/10.1111/1753-6405.12610
9. AIHW. *International health data comparisons, 2020*, Cat. no. PHE 237. Australian Institute of Health and Welfare; 2020. Available from: https://www.aihw.gov.au/reports/international-comparisons/international-health-datacomparisons/contents/overview-international-health-data-comparisons-2020
10. AIHW. *Australia's health 2020: snapshot Indigenous life expectancy and deaths.* Australian Institute of Health and Welfare; 2020. Available from: https://www.aihw.gov.au/reports/australias-health/indigenous-life-expectancy-and-deaths
11. Belot A, Ndiaye A, Luque-Fernandez MA, Kipourou DK, Maringe C, Rubio FJ, et al. Summarizing and communicating on survival data according to the audience: a tutorial on different mea-

sures illustrated with population-based cancer registry data. *Clin Epidemiol.* 2019;11:53–65. https://doi.org/10.2147/CLEP.S173523
12. Lambert PC, Dickman PW, Nelson CP, Royston P. Estimating the crude probability of death due to cancer and other causes using relative survival models. *Stat Med.* 2010;29(7–8):885–95. https://doi.org/10.1002/sim.3762
13. Dasgupta P, Garvey G, Baade PD. Quantifying the number of deaths among Aboriginal and Torres Strait Islander cancer patients that could be avoided by removing survival inequalities, Australia 2005–2016. *PLoS One.* 2022;17(8):e0273244. https://doi.org/10.1371/journal.pone.0273244
14. AIHW. *Australian Cancer Database, 2018; Quality Statement.* Australian Institute of Health and Welfare; 2022. Available from: https://meteor.aihw.gov.au/content/757686
15. ABS. *Estimates of Aboriginal and Torres Strait Islander Australians.* Australian Bureau of Statistics; 2016. Available from: https://www.abs.gov.au/statistics/people/aboriginaland-torres-strait-islander-peoples/estimates-aboriginal-and-torres-strait-islanderaustralians/jun-2016
16. Dasgupta P, Andersson TM, Garvey G, Baade PD. Quantifying Differences in Remaining Life Expectancy after Cancer Diagnosis, Aboriginal and Torres Strait Islanders, and Other Australians, 2005–2016. *Cancer Epidemiol Biomarkers Prev.* 2022;31(6):1168–75. https://doi.org/10.1158/1055-9965.EPI-21-1390

Indigenous Research Methods and Methodology

62

Tamara Butler, Kate Anderson, Elaina Elder-Robinson, Khwanruethai Ngampromwongse, Darren Garvey, and Gail Garvey

Key Points

- Decolonizing methodology and Indigenist research methods can challenge Western hegemony in research by asserting Indigenous ways of knowing, being, and doing.
- Research with Indigenous peoples should use strengths-based and decolonizing approaches to highlight cultural strengths and resilience.
- Co-designed research using one or more variations on Yarning methods is effective in empowering and privileging First Nations Australians' voices.
- Systematic use of reporting standards such as the CONSolIDated critERia for strengthening reporting of health research involving Indigenous peoples (CONSIDER statement) has the potential to increase the profile of, and enhance researcher accountability for, Indigenous research methods.

Ensuring that cancer research involving Indigenous communities fosters authentic collaboration and tangible benefit requires research methods that align with Indigenous ways of knowing, being, and doing. Given the enduring Western hegemony in research, this process must be grounded in Indigenist and decolonizing methodologies that prioritize Indigenous voices and worldviews [1]. This chapter provides a theoretical overview of Indigenist and decolonizing approaches in health research and provides some examples of research methods and reporting standards being used to prioritize Indigenous voices and paradigms.

Indigenist and Decolonizing Approaches

Indigenous communities have long been subjected to research practices that are ethically flawed, dismissive of Indigenous knowledge and expertise, and grounded in inequitable power structures [2]. This way of conducting research has historically been characterized by the acquisition of knowledge by Western researchers, the failure to compensate and/or acknowledge the community from which the knowledge was acquired, and, as such, a perpetuation of the systemic disparities and disadvantages of the very populations being researched [3]. To counter this, Indigenous researchers' resistance has given rise to decolonizing and Indigenist methodologies, grounded in Indigenous worldviews and ways of knowledge creation and sharing [4], which are central in Indigenist epistemologies [1]. These methodologies are extensions of traditional Indigenous ways of knowing, being, and doing, and they are considered "living knowledges" that are relational in nature [5].

Two significant Indigenist epistemologies have emerged from the Indigenous resistance movements of the 1990s [2, 6]. The seminal work by Professor Linda Tuihwai Smith provided the first such specific decolonizing methodology for Māori in Aotearoa New Zealand: Kaupapa Māori research [2]. Tuihwai Smith defines the aims of Kaupapa Māori research as a reclamation of space within the research world by Māori, to:

> … first, convince Māori people of the value of research for Māori; second, to convince the various, fragmented but powerful research communities of the need for greater Māori involvement in research; and third, to develop approaches and ways of carrying out research which take into account, without being limited by, the legacies of previous research, and the parameters of both previous and current approaches. [2, p. 183]

The second pioneering work, by Professor Lester-Irabinna Rigney, describes Indigenist research methodologies in Australia using three core principles: (1) notions of resistance as part of Indigenous peoples' struggle for self-determination, (2) Indigenous research leadership in representing their communities to achieve self-determination, and (3) ensuring political integrity and privileging the voices of Indigenous peoples [1]. These provisions by Tuihwai Smith and Rigney encapsulate much of the aims and principles of Indigenist and decolonizing methodologies in the Indigenous communities of colonized nations, acknowledging that the interpretation and application of such methodologies is as unique and specific as the land and communities

G. Garvey (ed.), *Indigenous and Tribal Peoples and Cancer*, https://doi.org/10.1007/978-3-031-56806-0_62

themselves. Indeed, diversity within Indigenous groups cannot be divorced from the process, acknowledging the imperative of embedding place-based approaches when using Indigenist and decolonizing methodologies.

Indigenous knowledges have been harnessed to assist understanding and provide practical tools that enable Western and Indigenous worldviews to co-exist and collaborate in practice. Two-Eyed Seeing (Etuaptmumk in Mi'kmaw) is an Indigenist and decolonizing concept originating from the Mi'kmaw First Nation in Canada [7]. As the name suggests, Two-Eyed Seeing constitutes an ability to approach circumstances with multiple perspectives, to learn:

> … to see from one eye with the strengths of Indigenous knowledges and ways of knowing, and from the other eye with the strengths of Western knowledges and ways of knowing, and to [use] both these eyes together, for the benefit of all. [7, p. 335]

This concept has been paralleled by the idea of "working at the interface"—terminology developed by Māori academic Sir Mason Durie, where Indigenous and Western knowledge systems work together in tandem, with equal standing, contributing to the co-creation of innovative knowledge [8]. Similarly, Ganma, a Yolŋu concept from Arnhem Land in the Northern Territory of Australia, references the meeting of freshwater (Yolŋu knowledge) and saltwater (Western knowledge) in the river system, creating foam. This concept depicts two-way knowledge sharing and co-creation of new knowledge, endowed with mutual respect for both [9]. In Australia, research methods have emerged as extensions of Indigenous traditional ways to bring Indigenous ways of doing into predominantly Western research spaces.

Strengths-Based Approaches

Deficit discourse is a pervasive narrative within the First Nations academic and policy arena, which focuses on problems and pathology. It frames First Nations individuals in terms of negativity and failure [10], rather than interrogating the structures, systems, and policies that create and maintain disparities in health and wellbeing. Worryingly, deficit discourse can lead to self-internalization of deficit narratives among First Nations peoples [11]. Deficit narratives can negatively frame the research questions that are asked and affect how that research is operationalized, evaluated, and transformed into policy and practice, ultimately perpetuating cycles of injustice and further entrenching notions of disadvantage [11].

Alternatively, strengths-based approaches to research highlight and integrate the strengths and cultural knowledge of First Nations people. These approaches counteract the harms of deficit narratives by disrupting and challenging their underlying assumptions of problem and pathology [12]. Importantly, they do not detract from the very real challenges facing First Nations communities, instead reframing how these issues may be addressed using community-identified strengths and assets. A growing body of research has demonstrated the benefits of incorporating strengths-based approaches in conjunction with decolonizing research methods.

Examples of Strengths-Based, Decolonizing Research Methods

There are mounting examples of research methods being used to engage Indigenous peoples in research via empowering and respectful ways. Some useful examples are detailed below.

Co-design

Culturally appropriate and effective methodological approaches are required to ensure that First Nations Australians' voices are central in directing and guiding the design and implementation of strategies to address issues affecting their communities. Co-design is one such method that is increasingly being used with both First Nations people and other marginalized groups. Co-design refers to processes and approaches whereby multiple parties, importantly including consumers or end-users, work together to find solutions to complex and persistent problems [13]. Co-design can give power to marginalized communities by prioritizing their voices and experiences, ensuring that they lead the way in finding solutions to the issues they find important. However, for co-design to work optimally, it must align with First Nations cultural values and perspectives and privilege First Nations ways of knowing, being, and doing [14, 15].

Recently, a set of key principles and best practices of co-design in health policy, practice, and research with First Nations Australians was collaboratively developed in an Australian study commissioned by Cancer Australia [14, 15]. The final set of key principles and best practices was developed through a systematic literature review [15] and rigorous stakeholder consultation [14]. Six key principles alongside numerous best practices were identified. These were First Nations leadership, culturally grounded approach, respect, benefit to community, inclusive partnerships, and transparency and evaluation [14]. Together, these principles and practices provide an essential framework for culturally safe research that favors the use of Indigenous research methods.

Social, Research, and Collaborative Yarning

Yarning is a recognized culturally appropriate style of communication among First Nations peoples in Australia and has been shown to be a powerful decolonizing research method. As a qualitative research method, Yarning centers on First Nations peoples' ways of knowing, being, and doing and respects traditional oral customs and values. Yarning builds trust and connection between researchers and participants and it is grounded in cultural connection to one another and relationality. Yarns can be conducted on a one-on-one basis or in small groups as Yarning Circles (Fig. 62.1).

Bessarab and Ng'andu describe several types of Yarning [16]. Social Yarning involves both the researcher and participant introducing themselves, their mob (e.g., family, kin, and/or language groups), and Country. The Social Yarn allows participants to situate themselves and define how they are connected to each other and the researcher, and this is key to building comfort, connection, and trust. Often refreshments are shared during the Social Yarn as an important part of cultural protocol. The Research Yarn invites participants to share their lived experiences on the topic of interest. Unlike conventional qualitative methods, Research Yarns are non-linear and may take the form of stories. The researcher's role is to listen to parts of the stories that are relevant to the research topic [17].

Collaborative Yarning Methodology is an iterative and flexible process of analysis that builds upon the concept of Collaborative Yarning identified by Bessarab and Ng'andu [16]. It brings together multiple perspectives from different First Nations individuals and groups to review, discuss, and refine data. The goal is to work collaboratively toward a shared understanding and co-analysis of data and results, ensuring that First Nations peoples are involved in all aspects and stages of the analysis and interpretation. The groups involved in Collaborative Yarning vary, depending on the specific needs and context of the project. The groups may include research participants, First Nations project advisory and working groups, First Nations researchers and investigators, and other stakeholders involved in the project. The process of Collaborative Yarning involves several recursive and iterative steps of analysis, checking, discussion, and rechecking between multiple parties and perspectives to gain feedback and guidance. An example of this process being used to develop the key principles and best practices for co-design with First Nations Australians is illustrated in Fig. 62.2 [14, 15].

Online Yarning Circles

The rapid uptake of virtual meeting platforms such as Zoom and Teams, alongside the social distancing and travel restrictions arising from the COVID-19 pandemic, has led to researchers investigating how Yarning can be conducted online. An Australian study showed that First Nations youth found Online Yarning Circles (OYCs) to be a feasible and acceptable way to both participate in and facilitate research [18]. Although there are technical and logistical challenges to overcome, OYCs can facilitate high levels of accessibility and engagement in research for First Nations peoples [18].

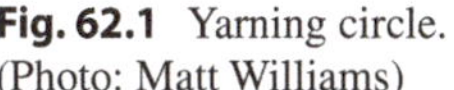

Fig. 62.1 Yarning circle. (Photo: Matt Williams)

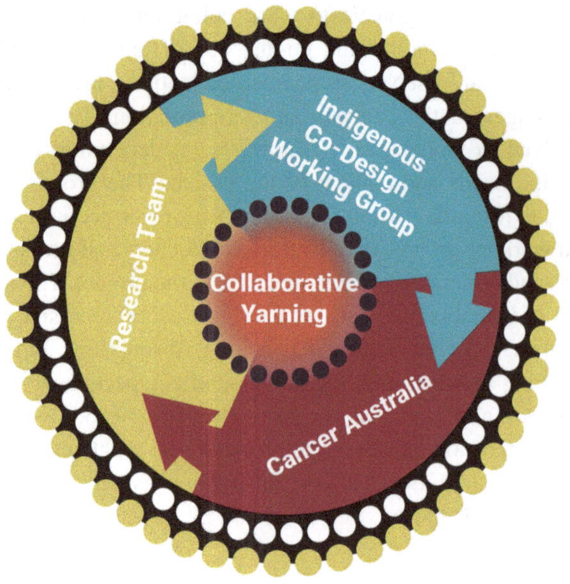

Fig. 62.2 Schematic representing collaborative yarning methodology. (Adapted from Ref. Butler et al. [15])

PhotoYarning

PhotoYarning provides another Indigenous research method that facilitates engagement and accessibility for the participant and builds on approaches based on words alone. It privileges the knowledge of community members by having them photograph their lived experience relevant to the topic of the project [19] and uses these images as the basis for Yarning about the topic. PhotoYarning acknowledges that a person possesses the expertise to Yarn about their life experiences and it facilitates that expression through photographs they have chosen to take that help describe what they see as significant themes, events, and phenomena [20]. The photographs may reveal similar or diverse images that may, in turn, be discussed with community members and researchers as part of the Research Yarn. The process moves toward a co-constructed understanding of the topic, informed by the words and images of the PhotoYarn participants. The entire process may include several stages that move the research through preparation and orientation of the task and equipment, data generation, and analyses of the photographs and Yarn transcripts.

PhotoYarning is effective as a method to explore the lived experiences of First Nations individuals and groups of people. For example, Dickson employed PhotoYarning to examine the strategies Aboriginal and Torres Strait Islander health professionals use to empower themselves within the challenging and sometimes conflicting contexts of their communities and healthcare settings [20]. Participants were able to depict and describe the challenges involved in navigating extremely complex networks of interactions at home and at work and how these challenges specifically affected the presentation of oneself seamlessly across these contexts. PhotoYarning has also recently been used to examine what young First Nations people (aged 12–17) view as important for their wellbeing. A range of images of people, places, pets, events, and objects of personal significance were shared in the context of group Yarns with peers. Researchers helped facilitate Yarns about the images, seeking input from the person who took the photo and inviting further comments from other members of the group to see if the image resonated with them and their wellbeing. Additionally, the young people participating in PhotoYarning described the process as "fun," "easy" to do, and said they "enjoyed taking the photos." Although some participants reported challenges in capturing the desired picture, they also expressed appreciation for the researchers' interest in their lives, photos, and thoughts.

PhotoYarning can be an appropriate and innovative way of gaining a visual insight into the lived realities of First Nations people, serving as a springboard for meaningful and rich yarns about complex lived experiences.

Ensuring Accountability and Transparency in the Reporting of Indigenous Research Methods

It is imperative that researchers accurately and comprehensively report on the Indigenist and decolonizing research approaches and methods used in their research projects. This will lead to greater visibility of these approaches and their value, as well as greater understanding and awareness of the diverse ways these methods can be operationalized. The CONSolIDated critERia for strengthening reporting of health research involving Indigenous peoples (CONSIDER) statement provides a systematic checklist for reporting health research involving Indigenous peoples [21]. To develop the checklist, a working group of experts in Indigenous health and health equity examined Indigenous research ethics and research guidelines globally and then conducted an iterative process of discussion, review, and consensus-finding. The final checklist includes 17 items relating to eight domains for reporting research involving Indigenous peoples. The domains are governance, prioritization, relationships, methodologies, participation, capacity, analysis and interpretation, and dissemination. The checklist is designed to apply to the reporting of any health research that includes a significant focus on Indigenous peoples [21].

Although intended as a reporting checklist, researchers should also use the CONSIDER statement to better inform research design and methodology and to prompt close consideration of the various aspects of decolonizing research. Furthermore, journals, their editorial teams, and other publication outlets should require authors to complete the checklist as part of the article submission process, including justifying statements for any criteria that are not met. Systematic use of the CONSIDER statement and similar tools will improve accountability, transparency, and integrity in reporting and using Indigenous research methods.

Conclusions

These methods provide actionable tools for Indigenous and non-Indigenous researchers to conduct research in culturally appropriate ways. The application of Indigenist and decolonizing methodologies must be grounded in an overarching Indigenist epistemology (way of understanding and interpreting the world) [4] as well as appropriate approaches to research and design [14, 15]. Doing so will ensure that First Nations people are empowered to use research as a tool for justice and health equity.

References

1. Rigney L-I. Internationalization of an Indigenous Anticolonial Cultural Critique of Research Methodologies: A Guide to Indigenist Research Methodology and Its Principles. *Wicazo Sa Review*. 1999;14(2):109–21.
2. Tuhiwai Smith L. *Decolonizing methodologies: Research and Indigenous Peoples*. Dunedin: University of Otago Press; 1999.
3. Leeuw S, Cameron ES, Greenwood ML. Participatory and community-based research, Indigenous geographies, and the spaces of friendship: A critical engagement. *Can Geogr.* 2012;56(2):180–94. https://doi.org/10.1111/j.1541-0064.2012.00434.x
4. Kovach M. *Indigenous Methodologies: Characteristics, Conversations and Contexts* Toronto: University of Toronto Press; 2021.
5. Louis RP. Can You Hear us Now? Voices from the Margin: Using Indigenous Methodologies in Geographic Research. *Geogr Res*. 2007;45(2):130–9. https://doi.org/10.1111/j.1745-5871.2007.00443.x
6. Bishop AR. *Collaborative research stories: whakawhanaungatanga*. University of Otago; 1995.
7. Bartlett C, Marshall M, Marshall A. Two-Eyed Seeing and other lessons learned within a co-learning journey of bringing together indigenous and mainstream knowledges and ways of knowing. *J Environ Stud Sci*. 2012;2(4):331–40. https://doi.org/10.1007/s13412-012-0086-8
8. Durie M. Understanding health and illness: research at the interface between science and indigenous knowledge. *Int J Epidemiol*. 2004;33(5):1138–43. https://doi.org/10.1093/ije/dyh250
9. Laycock A, Walker D, Harrison N, Brands J. *Researching Indigenous Health: A Practical Guide for Researchers*. Melbourne: The Lowitja Institute; 2011.
10. Fforde C, Bamblett L, Lovett R, Gorringe S, Fogarty B. Discourse, Deficit and Identity: Aboriginality, the Race Paradigm and the Language of Representation in Contemporary Australia. *Media Int Aust*. 2013(149):162–73. https://doi.org/10.1177/1329878X1314900117
11. Bullen J, Hill-Wall T, Anderson K, Brown A, Bracknell C, Newnham EA, et al. From Deficit to Strength-Based Aboriginal Health Research-Moving toward Flourishing. *Int J Environ Res Public Health*. 2023;20(7). https://doi.org/10.3390/ijerph20075395
12. Fogarty W, Lovell M, Langenberg J, Heron M-J. Deficit Discourse and Strengths-based Approaches: Changing the Narrative of Aboriginal and Torres Strait Islander Health and Wellbeing. Melbourne, Australia: The Lowitja Institute; 2018.
13. Slattery P, Saeri AK, Bragge P. Research co-design in health: a rapid overview of reviews. *Health Res Policy Syst*. 2020;18(1):17. https://doi.org/10.1186/s12961-020-0528-9
14. Anderson K, Gall A, Butler T, Ngampromwongse K, Hector D, Turnbull S, et al. Development of Key Principles and Best Practices for Co-Design in Health with First Nations Australians. *Int J Environ Res Public Health*. 2022;20(1). https://doi.org/10.3390/ijerph20010147
15. Butler T, Gall A, Garvey G, Ngampromwongse K, Hector D, Turnbull S, et al. A Comprehensive Review of Optimal Approaches to Co-Design in Health with First Nations Australians. *Int J Environ Res Public Health*. 2022;19(23). https://doi.org/10.3390/ijerph192316166
16. Bessarab D, Ng'andu B. Yarning About Yarning as a Legitimate Method in Indigenous Research. *IJCIS*. 2010;3(1). https://doi.org/10.5204/ijcis.v3i1.57
17. Kennedy M, Maddox R, Booth K, Maidment S, Chamberlain C, Bessarab D. Decolonising qualitative research with respectful, reciprocal, and responsible research practice: a narrative review of the application of Yarning method in qualitative Aboriginal and Torres Strait Islander health research. *Int J Equity Health*. 2022;21(1):134. https://doi.org/10.1186/s12939-022-01738-w
18. Anderson K, Gall A, Butler T, Arley B, Howard K, Cass A, et al. Using web conferencing to engage Aboriginal and Torres Strait Islander young people in research: a feasibility study. *BMC Med Res Methodol*. 2021;21(1):172. https://doi.org/10.1186/s12874-021-01366-y
19. Anderson K, Elder-Robinson E, Howard K, Garvey G. A Systematic Methods Review of Photovoice Research with Indigenous Young People. *Int J Qual Methods*. 2023;22. https://doi.org/10.1177/16094069231172076
20. Dickson M. "My work? Well, I live it and breathe it": The seamless connect between the professional and personal/community self in the Aboriginal and Torres Strait Islander health sector. *BMC Health Serv Res*. 2020;20(1):972. https://doi.org/10.1186/s12913-020-05804-3
21. Huria T, Palmer SC, Pitama S, Beckert L, Lacey C, Ewen S, et al. Consolidated criteria for strengthening reporting of health research involving indigenous peoples: the CONSIDER statement. *BMC Med Res Methodol*. 2019;19(1):173. https://doi.org/10.1186/s12874-019-0815-8

Messengers for Health

63

Alma McCormick and Suzanne Held

Key Points

- Messengers for Health is a non-profit Apsáalooke organization that addresses community health issues in a culturally appropriate way.
- Messengers for Health is guided by eight statements, all beginning with "We believe." These statements are the backbone of the program's success and community trust.
- Our community-based participatory research focuses on issues that are decided by and important to our community. We conduct research that serves our communities. Any data gathered through our research directly benefits the community.

Messengers for Health (Messengers) is a non-profit organization (NPO) located on the Apsáalooke (Crow) Reservation in Montana, USA. Our mission is growing, fostering, and supporting trusted and respected community leaders to improve the health of Apsáalooke men, women, and children using solutions that respect and honor Apsáalooke strengths, culture, stories, and language. We utilize traditional methods of knowledge transmission, harness cultural strengths, and value the guidance, knowledge, and expertise of our community members. Messengers has an Apsáalooke Executive Director, Apsáalooke Executive Board, and Apsáalooke staff.

The Apsáalooke Nation is in southeastern Montana. The reservation is rural and encompasses approximately 2.3 million acres, including the Wolf, Pryor, and Big Horn mountain ranges. As Chief Eelápuash (Chief Sore Belly) said, "The Crow Country is in exactly the right place. Everything good is to be found there. There is no country like the Crow Country." Many Tribal members speak Crow as their first language, demonstrating the strength and maintenance of the culture. Apsáalooke means "children of the large-beaked bird," referring to the raven. Apsáalooke people are known for the strength of their clan system and their strong family ties.

Messengers began as the community arm of a community-based participatory research (CBPR) project, in partnership with faculty and students from Montana State University–Bozeman (MSU), which is 200 miles from the reservation. Initially, research grants came into the university and community members were employed by the university as project staff. However, over time, Messengers established integrity, trust, and strong support in the Crow community. In 2009, to strengthen the community aspect of the partnership and with an eye toward growing and sustaining services in the community, we met with leaders of several NPOs and an NPO development professional to learn how we could become an NPO. We understand that many CBPR partnerships include NPOs. However, few NPOs are located on reservations. With a lot of assistance, we submitted paperwork to the state of Montana and received our non-profit status in 2010. We do not know of another Indigenous CBPR partner that has successfully taken these steps and we are very proud of this accomplishment.

As an Apsáalooke NPO, Messengers has the liberty to address community health issues in the most culturally appropriate way. For example, we added a men's cancer-screening program, a transportation program, and a health-promotion program to our activities. Grants can come directly to us, or we can receive a subcontract to partner with the university or other institutions. Community members who are involved in the program's administration have developed strong leadership skills and are viewed as leaders by others. In a Tribal community, people know each other well and watch each other to see their actions. The community has watched Messengers and its members evolve over time into an NPO with integrity that benefits the community.

The partnership between the community and the university grew slowly, with care and intention. Over time and from our experiences, we developed a series of statements that illustrate our partnership processes. These statements are the backbone of our success and why we are viewed with integrity and trusted in the community as a health resource. Our

G. Garvey (ed.), *Indigenous and Tribal Peoples and Cancer*, https://doi.org/10.1007/978-3-031-56806-0_63

statements begin with "We believe." We support these statements of belief with actions that match our words.

1. *We believe strengths, solutions, and expertise are in the community.* All the programs we develop use Apsáalooke cultural strengths, such as Báa nnilah (which means "the sharing of advice" and is also the name of our health-promotion program). We understand that solutions to health issues come from culture.
2. *We believe in research that is focused on issues decided by and important to the community.* We have an Executive Board that decides which topics are important. The board guides our partnership and, with their knowledge, expertise, and wisdom, ensures the CBPR process adheres respectfully to the cultural protocols of the Apsáalooke Nation. The board began informally in 1996 and was formalized in 2001. It has seven members, all of whom are enrolled members of the Apsáalooke Nation with a sincere interest in improving the health of the Apsáalooke people.
3. *We believe in research that is in service to communities.* We work to sustain programs that are effective. Instead of programs that are developed, implemented, evaluated, and discontinued through the research-grant cycle, we search for funding to continue running effective programs. An example is our recent chronic illness self-management program, which was developed, implemented, and evaluated through a randomized controlled trial funded by the National Institutes of Health. Once we saw that the program was effective in helping community members, we partnered with the Rocky Mountain Tribal Leaders Council and others for funding to continue hosting program gatherings in the community.
4. *We believe in research where any data that is gathered benefits the community directly.* When we began our work, we were told of researchers who came into the Apsáalooke community, gathered data, left, and were never heard from again. Our approach was different: we let every community member who completed a survey or interview know that what they shared would directly benefit the community. We hold community meetings to let Tribal members know how their information was used to develop programs, and we develop accessible handouts that show how community information is used to develop Apsáalooke-specific programming.
5. *We believe in research that financially benefits Tribal communities and universities, with an emphasis on community benefit.* Having community members as staff members who make fiscal decisions enables Messengers to make the best use of funds. For example, we help participants to program meetings and provide food for them. Having the funds located in Messengers instead of the university allows for greater fiscal control and strengthens our organization, leading to the management of larger grants.
6. *We believe in research where community and university researchers are partners and the community is in the driver's seat.* As mentioned above, our Executive Board decides the direction of our research projects. We continually keep in mind that university partners are engaged in service to the community, the members of which are valued as experts.
7. *We believe in research that builds everyone's capacity.* Both community and university partners grow and learn through our work. We actively seek opportunities for all partners to learn new skills and have new experiences. We want the partnership experience to support everyone to become stronger and more capable. We especially see this in our students, most of whom are Indigenous and are supported in our partnership. We have seen numerous students go on to succeed at school and in their careers.
8. *We believe in publications and presentations that are done together with community and university partners.* All of our writing is done in partnership, line by line, word by word. We jointly edit for clarity and agree on all content. Together, we make sure that the content accurately reflects our work and is accessible to the general public. Whenever possible, community and university partners present together, fully displaying our true partnership. An important outcome of this approach is that the community's voice is seen and heard clearly in our publications and presentations.

One example of our work is a program to address the low rate of cancer screening among women in the community. We adopted a lay health advisor approach and worked with the community's trusted women—those to whom others turn for support and advice, who are trusted, and who have integrity. We called these women Messengers, and their role was to visit with their family members and friends about women's health and specifically about well-women visits and cancer screening. We met with the Messengers through an annual retreat and monthly support and educational training. We conducted pre- and post-tests with random samples of community women and found statistically significant increases in cervical cancer knowledge, comfort discussing cancer issues, and awareness of cervical cancer and the Messengers for Health program. As solutions to health disparities must be sustainable, our non-profit organization continues to apply for and receive funding to provide outreach services to assist women—and now men—to receive important cancer screening.

Over time, we have been able to successfully advocate for the local community. Messengers works with businesses, government entities, individuals, and organizations to build healthy communities and lifestyles. The Legislative Branch of the Crow Tribe fully supports Messengers' work, and a Tribal Resolution (LR09–02) of approval and support is in place. We have built working relationships across multiple and diverse public and private sectors. These are strong and healthy relationships where we act as a bridge to bring people together across multiple sectors, synergistically building a healthy community. This has never existed before. We are seen as a "go-to" resource for bringing people and organizations together. For example, when there was an outbreak of Methicillin-resistant *Staphylococcus aureus* (MRSA) in the community and individuals from the Centers for Disease Control and Prevention came to address it, they turned to Messengers to help them effectively coordinate their efforts for the best chance of success. Recently, staff from the local Indian Health Service reached out to us to partner in their efforts toward diabetes prevention and service to community members with this diagnosis. They heard about our program and the trust the community has in us, and they knew that the best way to be effective in their work was to partner with us.

Co-design with Indigenous Peoples

64

Kate Anderson, Tamara Butler, Alana Gall, Elaina Elder-Robinson, and Gail Garvey

Key Points

- Co-design approaches are being increasingly used globally to find solutions to complex and persistent health issues, including cancer.
- Co-design has potential as an acceptable methodological approach to redressing the disparities facing Indigenous peoples.
- Co-design must be authentic and facilitate genuine and equitable collaboration to ensure meaningful benefits that are valued by the populations they are intended to serve.
- Co-design with Indigenous peoples must be guided by transparent, agreed, and decolonizing principles and practices.

Co-design approaches are increasingly being applied in health-related research, policy, and practice settings when seeking solutions to complex and persistent issues, including cancer research. Given the need to address the prevailing disparities in cancer experienced by Indigenous peoples, a particular focus on applying co-design approaches in this context is emerging. But what exactly is "co-design" and how should it be used with Indigenous peoples in ways that are effective, collaborative, and acceptable to community and consumer groups? This chapter presents the emergence and ubiquity of co-design, an overview of Indigenist and decolonizing methodologies, the need to embed Indigenist approaches when co-designing with Indigenous communities, and an Australian case study illustrating the development of key principles and best practices for respectful co-design with Indigenous Australians in the broader health context.

The Emergence and Ubiquity of Co-design

The term *co-design* first emerged in Scandinavian participatory research design in the 1970s; however, it took several decades for the co-design approach to be established as an accepted and valued methodology [1]. While remaining firmly grounded in its origins in participatory research, social action research, and emancipatory philosophy [2], co-design is now an umbrella term that refers to a range of approaches that facilitate collaboration between professionals and consumers to find solutions to complex and persistent health problems [3]. Currently, there is no exact consensus definition of co-design—an issue of ambiguity identified by some Indigenous researchers as fostering disingenuous research with Indigenous communities [4].

Participatory research is an umbrella term that includes a wide variety of differing research approaches, broadly defined as "systematic inquiry, with the collaboration of those affected by the issue being studied, for purposes of education and taking action or effecting change" [5, p. 327]. Participatory action research (PAR) and community-based participatory research (CBPR) are two such approaches that are more widely recognized [5, 6]. Emerging alongside co-design philosophy, participatory research principles developed from social action research and emancipatory philosophy in the Americas [2]. With the increasing adoption of participatory approaches into the late 1900s, and being concomitant with incentivized funding for increasing inclusion of research participants in research processes, participatory research was deemed a philosophical research approach rather than a methodology alone [2]. With the development of specific sub-approaches such as PAR and CBPR, participatory research has expanded to serve the needs of specific communities and ensure consultation with people having lived experience as well as research beneficiaries from the beginning of the research pipeline.

These approaches embody co-design principles with their focus on including participants as proxy researchers, and on decentralized research "expertise." This approach recognizes that knowledge from participants that the research will affect, rather than knowledge founded in Western institutions and academies, is valid and legitimate, and allows unparalleled insight into lived experiences [7, 8]. Privileging community knowledge and experience and recognizing community

G. Garvey (ed.), *Indigenous and Tribal Peoples and Cancer*, https://doi.org/10.1007/978-3-031-56806-0_64

members as valuable consultants with whom to conduct research has been a key theme emerging from Indigenous embodiments of co-design and participatory approaches. Alongside shifting understandings of knowledge legitimacy, these approaches are well-aligned with Indigenous research foci.

Over the past decade, applications of co-design have increased exponentially in health-related research, policy, and practice, and they are often considered a gold standard of collaborative approaches [9]. Co-design approaches are underpinned by ideals of empowerment, collaboration, creativity, positive societal impact, and capability building [10], which are intended to be enacted through processes such as shared decision-making, sustained community engagement, and building equitable partnerships [1, 2, 11]. In essence, co-design is intended to recognize and leverage the value of consumers' lived experiences on an equitable footing with the knowledge of professionals such as researchers, clinicians, and other experts. Co-design approaches are increasingly being used with priority and marginalized populations to address health disparities, as they offer the ability to include contextualized insights from consumers in solution-generating processes [12]. However, given the nebulous definition of co-design, real-world applications of this approach tend to vary and might not always achieve the intended ideals. In response, there are mounting calls to ensure that applications of co-design facilitate authentic and equitable collaboration and ensure benefits that are timely, meaningful, sustainable, and of value to the populations they are intended to serve [12].

Ensuring that co-design applications with Indigenous communities foster authentic collaboration and tangible benefit requires the development and implementation of co-design principles and practices that are determined with and by Indigenous communities. Given the enduring Western hegemony in research, this process must be grounded in Indigenist and decolonizing methodologies that prioritize Indigenous voices and worldviews [13]. There is a need to ensure that co-design is implemented with true participatory principles and that Indigenous control of and engagement in research is prioritized if the potential of co-design is to be realized [4].

Case Study: Development of Key Principles and Best Practices of Co-design with Indigenous Australians

To ensure that applications of co-design with Indigenous peoples are grounded in Indigenist methodologies, they must be guided by transparent, culturally safe, and decolonizing principles and practices. The development of such principles and practices is slowly beginning to happen, as the importance of research being done in the right way is increasingly recognized. Here, we describe an Australian case study that outlines the development of the key principles and best practices of co-design with Indigenous Australians within the broader health context.

In 2021, Cancer Australia, Australia's peak national cancer control agency, began evaluating the early design and feasibility of a potential national lung cancer screening program (LCSP) to detect lung cancer at an early stage and thus improve patient outcomes. Given that lung cancer disproportionally affects Indigenous Australians, Cancer Australia was cognizant that equitable co-design processes would be needed in the design of any new screening program that would meet the needs of Indigenous Australians. The lack of a clear definition and guidelines around culturally appropriate co-design with Indigenous peoples led Cancer Australia to contact our team at The University of Queensland (UQ) with the goal of developing a set of evidence-based and lived-experience-informed key co-design principles and best practices with Indigenous Australians. The initial aim was to develop the principles and practices within a broad health-care context and then embed them within the potential LCSP from its design and inception to ensure equitable uptake and benefit for Indigenous Australians. The development and content of these key co-design principles and best practices are briefly outlined below and are described in greater detail in the corresponding publications [14, 15].

Under the guidance of a leading Indigenous researcher in Indigenous cancer and wellbeing, a majority-Indigenous research team developed the key co-design principles and best practices with Indigenous Australians over two phases: a comprehensive review, followed by consultation with people having lived experience. Our UQ team conducted a comprehensive review to develop a draft set of principles and practices. Using a systematic search strategy, we searched: (1) peer-reviewed literature via academic databases, and (2) grey literature (including reports from First Nations organizations, government reports, toolkits, and guidelines) via Google, Google Scholar, and targeted searches of known key websites. Ninety-nine articles were included in the final analysis, which identified six key themes and 28 associated sub-themes relating to key principles and best practices for co-design with Indigenous Australians [15]. These findings formed the basis for consultation with people having lived experience in the second phase.

Informed by the findings of the comprehensive review, our UQ team conducted consultations with people having lived experience to refine and confirm the final key principles and best practices. Twenty-five people with lived experience from three key groups participated in online yarning circles. They included Indigenous cancer patients, carers, and family members; cancer policy experts and health care providers; and Indigenous researchers from various health disciplines with experience in co-design. They provided feedback on the draft principles and practices, identifying items that should be prioritized, restructured, or deleted, and providing input on concepts they considered to be missing.

Along with strong Indigenous leadership in the UQ research team, the First Nations Co-design Working Group and Cancer Australia's Aboriginal and Torres Strait Islander Cancer Control Leadership Group provided overarching project governance. The former included Indigenous Australians with experience in health across varying disciplines, and the latter included leaders in Indigenous health, research, and policy, as well as consumers affected by cancer. The UQ research team and governance groups engaged in Collaborative Yarning Methodology (CYM) [16] across both phases. CYM and thematic analyses were used to identify the final set of six key principles and 27 best practices for co-design in health with Indigenous Australians. The six key principles were identified as Indigenous leadership, culturally grounded approach, respect, benefit to community, inclusive partnerships, and transparency and evaluation. An outline of these key principles and their associated best practices are provided in Table 64.1.

In May 2023, Australia's Minister for Health and Aged Care formally announced that the new LCSP would be awarded. The co-design key principles and best practices identified and developed by our UQ team will be used to guide the development and implementation of the new LCSP. Furthermore, Cancer Australia has plans to develop a co-design toolkit in plain English to enable accessibility of

Table 64.1 Key principles and best practices for co-design in health with First Nations Australians

Principle	Overview	Practices
Indigenous leadership	Authentic and appropriate Indigenous leadership must be embedded within the co-design approach. The nature and function of this leadership must be determined with the community and should reflect that community's structure and interests. Indigenous leadership needs to begin during the conception stages of the project and extend beyond the completion of the project	1. Indigenous leadership directs all levels and components of the project 2. Priorities and processes are determined by Indigenous communities 3. Capabilities that support Indigenous leadership are nurtured and strengthened 4. Governance structures are determined by the community and reflect community interests 5. Appropriate cultural and community approvals are obtained

(continued)

Table 64.1 (continued)

Principle	Overview	Practices
Culturally grounded approach	The strength and diversity of Indigenous culture must be reflected in the co-design project and approach. A continuous process of striving for cultural competency and self-reflection by non-Indigenous people involved in the project is essential	6. Continuous striving for cultural competency is reflected in the processes 7. Diversity among Indigenous Australians and cultures is acknowledged and responded to by the project 8. Indigenous worldview underpins all components of the project 9. Strengths of Indigenous cultures, knowledges, and peoples are recognized and applied throughout the project 10. Continuing impacts of colonization are acknowledged and mitigated
Respect	The expertise, experience, and time of Indigenous people and organizations must be respected and recompensed to ensure equity for all involved in the co-design process. Approaches must incorporate flexibility and be familiar and engaging for Indigenous Australians to feel comfortable and welcome to lead and participate in the process	11. Expectations of Indigenous people and organizations are fair and reasonable 12. Provision of remuneration to Indigenous people and organizations equitably compensates their time and knowledge 13. Adequate time and resources are provisioned to successfully complete project objectives 14. Flexible and iterative processes are embedded and facilitated 15. Culturally appropriate language, branding, and design are used throughout the project
Benefit to community	Co-design projects must aim to serve Indigenous Australians and communities above all else. The project conception, design, processes, and outcomes must provide timely, tangible, and sustainable benefits that are valued by the community.	16. The community sets the agenda for the project 17. The outcomes of the project offer tangible and sustainable benefits that are valued by the community 18. Indigenous people and communities own the data and the knowledge resulting from the project 19. Capabilities valued and prioritized by Indigenous people are fostered and strengthened

(continued)

Table 64.1 (continued)

Principle	Overview	Practices
Inclusive partnerships	Fostering and maintaining equitable and collaborative relationships between all participants is central to driving effective co-design projects. Establishing appropriate communication channels and conflict resolution processes, formulated by and with the community, that maintain trust and support authentic partnerships is imperative	20. Sustained collaboration that fosters two-way learning is developed and maintained 21. Self-determination of Indigenous Australians is supported by the project 22. Achieving equity for Indigenous Australians is prioritized 23. Regular and sustained culturally appropriate communication channels are maintained 24. Conflict resolution protocols are formalized to manage disagreement
Transparency and evaluation	Transparency in all aspects of the co-design project is essential. Accountability to Indigenous leaders must be formalized and embedded into co-design projects	25. Transparency in decision-making and benefits to people with lived experience are ensured to enable accountability 26. Monitoring and evaluation processes are built into the project 27. Project outcomes are not pre-determined and are authentically co-designed

Source: Anderson et al. [14]

these key principles and best practices to support community members, researchers, practitioners, and policymakers in designing and implementing their own co-design projects respectfully with Indigenous peoples.

Conclusions

The use of co-design is increasing in the cancer-control sector and the field of healthcare more generally. However, the lack of a clear definition or guidance on how to enact co-design in a way that is non-tokenistic has led to concerns about its application. Clear principles and practices of co-design with Indigenous peoples are urgently needed to ensure that Indigenist and decolonizing methodologies are enacted in future efforts to improve health outcomes for Indigenous peoples. The way in which such principles and practices are operationalized must be place-based and tailored to the specific issue at hand, giving rise to exciting opportunities for the co-creation of new knowledge—Ganma—by working together in creative and dynamic ways. Importantly, while many collaborative approaches with Indigenous peoples globally share a focus on decolonizing methodologies that center on Indigenous worldviews and knowledge systems, those interested in utilizing co-design must work with local Indigenous groups to decide on appropriate local-level guiding principles. The implementation of these key principles and best practices of co-design will pave the way for culturally safe and effective co-design projects that empower Indigenous peoples globally to drive solutions and better healthcare outcomes in their communities. Doing so requires that governments, institutions, and organizations relinquish long-standing power differentials to enable truly equitable and authentic co-design approaches.

References

1. Dillon M. *Codesign in the Indigenous Policy Domain: Risks and Opportunities.* Canberra: Australian National University, Centre for Aboriginal Economic Policy Research; 2021.
2. Macaulay AC. Participatory research: What is the history? Has the purpose changed? *Family Practice.* 2016;34(3):256–8. https://doi.org/10.1093/fampra/cmw117
3. Slattery P, Saeri AK, Bragge P. Research co-design in health: a rapid overview of reviews. *Health Research Policy and Systems.* 2020;18(1):17. https://doi.org/10.1186/s12961-020-0528-9
4. King PT, Cormack D. Indigenous Peoples, Whiteness, and the Coloniality of Co-design. In: Ravulo J, Olcoń K, Dune T, Workman A, Liamputtong P, editors. Handbook of Critical Whiteness: Deconstructing Dominant Discourses Across Disciplines. Singapore: Springer Nature Singapore; 2023. p. 1–16. https://doi.org/10.1007/978-981-19-1612-0_28-1
5. Cargo M, Mercer SL. The value and challenges of participatory research: strengthening its practice. *Annual Review of Public Health.* 2008;29:325–50. https://doi.org/10.1146/annurev.publhealth.29.091307.083824
6. Baum F, MacDougall C, Smith D. Participatory action research. *Journal of Epidemiology and Community Health.* 2006;60(10):854–7. https://doi.org/10.1136/jech.2004.028662
7. Fletcher C. Community-based participatory research relationships with aboriginal communities in Canada: an overview of context and process. *Pimatisiwin.* 2002;1(1):29–61.
8. Jull J, Giles A, Graham ID. Community-based participatory research and integrated knowledge translation: advancing the co-creation of knowledge. *Implementation Science.* 2017;12(1):150. https://doi.org/10.1186/s13012-017-0696-3
9. Blomkamp E. The Promise of Co-Design for Public Policy. *Australian Journal of Public Administration.* 2018;77(4):729–43. https://doi.org/10.1111/1467-8500.12310
10. Greenhalgh T, Jackson C, Shaw S, Janamian T. Achieving Research Impact Through Co-creation in Community-Based Health Services: Literature Review and Case Study. *The Milbank Quarterly.* 2016;94(2):392–429. https://doi.org/10.1111/1468-0009.12197
11. Green LW, George A, Daniel M, Frankish J, Herbert CJ, Bowie WR, et al. *Study of Participatory Research in Health Promotion.* Ottawa: Royal Society of Canada; 1995. https://doi.org/10.1093/heapro/daac016
12. Moll S, Wyndham-West M, Mulvale G, Park S, Buettgen A, Phoenix M, et al. Are you really doing 'codesign'? Critical

reflections when working with vulnerable populations. *BMJ Open.* 2020;10(11):e038339. https://doi.org/10.1136/bmjopen-2020-038339

13. Rigney L-I. Internationalization of an Indigenous Anticolonial Cultural Critique of Research Methodologies: A Guide to Indigenist Research Methodology and Its Principles. *Wicazo Sa Review.* 1999;14(2):109–21. https://doi.org/10.2307/1409555
14. Anderson K, Gall A, Butler T, Ngampromwongse K, Hector D, Turnbull S, et al. Development of Key Principles and Best Practices for Co-Design in Health with First Nations Australians. *Int J Environ Res Public Health.* 2022;20(1). https://doi.org/10.3390/ijerph20010147
15. Butler T, Gall A, Garvey G, Ngampromwongse K, Hector D, Turnbull S, et al. A Comprehensive Review of Optimal Approaches to Co-Design in Health with First Nations Australians. *Int J Environ Res Public Health.* 2022;19(23). https://doi.org/10.3390/ijerph192316166
16. Shay M. Extending the yarning yarn: collaborative yarning methodology for ethical Indigenist education research. *The Australian Journal of Indigenous Education.* 2021;50(1):62–70. https://doi.org/10.1017/jie.2018.25

Inala Community Jury for Aboriginal and Torres Strait Islander Health Research

65

Claudette (Sissy) Tyson and Sonya Egert

Key Points

- The Inala Community Jury for Aboriginal and Torres Strait Islander Health Research reviews and approves all research conducted by the Southern Queensland Centre of Excellence in Aboriginal and Torres Strait Islander Primary Health Care.
- Researchers present their research plans to the jury for approval, explaining what the research involves, why it is needed, and how it will benefit the local Aboriginal and Torres Strait Islander community.
- The Community Jury decides whether the proposed research is responsive to local priorities and respectful of community cultural protocols and processes.

The Inala Community Jury for Aboriginal and Torres Strait Islander Health Research is Australia's first research jury. It was established in 2010 to support ethically sound, culturally appropriate, locally relevant health research. It particularly focuses on ensuring that research benefits the local Aboriginal and Torres Strait Islander community. It provides a way of ensuring that Aboriginal and Torres Strait Islander people are engaged in and benefit from the health research conducted in their community.

The Inala Community Jury is an important component of the health research conducted by the Southern Queensland Centre of Excellence in Aboriginal and Torres Strait Islander Primary Health Care (SQCoE). It is a Queensland Health service and is based within Metro South Health (a health district covering the area south of Brisbane, which provides health services to more than one million people). SQCoE is located in Inala, 18 km south-west of Brisbane, and the clinic is staffed by GPs, nurses, allied health and Aboriginal health workers, and visiting medical specialists.

The SQCoE research team is dedicated to finding and publishing evidence about how to improve the health of its patients. All research done by or through SQCoE can only proceed if it is approved by both its research committee and the Inala Community Jury.

The Inala Community Jury includes up to 14 members, who are Aboriginal and/or Torres Strait Islander people from the local community of Inala and surrounding suburbs. Four of the members are nominated by local Aboriginal and Torres Strait Islander community-controlled organizations. Other members self-nominate by submitting an expression of interest and are then purposefully selected to ensure the final jury is diverse and representative of the local community—with different backgrounds and different levels of research literacy. Jurors are remunerated for their time and expertise.

The Inala Community Jury meets three to five times each year and reviews all research undertaken by SQCoE and its partners. Researchers present their proposals to the jury, explaining what their research involves, why the research should be conducted, and how the research will benefit the community. Jury members then have an opportunity to ask questions and provide their feedback. The Community Jury decides whether the research is responsive to local priorities and respectful of local community cultural protocols and processes. The jury also provides general advice to researchers about the planning and conduct of health research in the district.

The Inala Community Jury is a way of acknowledging the wisdom of the Aboriginal and Torres Strait Islander people in the Inala community. The Jury goes beyond a simple review and approval of research proposals. The Jury process is consultative, with Jury members actively questioning researchers and contributing to research proposals. Research that does not receive Jury endorsement is not rejected; instead, it is returned to the researchers for further development in response to the Jury's feedback. When the Community Jury approves a research proposal, they provide a letter of approval for researchers to use as part of their ethics/institutional review board application. If a project does not meet the needs or priorities of the community or is not delivered in a culturally appropriate manner, the proposal will be rejected.

The Inala Community Jury emerged from the work of health economist Professor Gavin Mooney, who pioneered the concept of citizens' juries in Australia and facilitated the

G. Garvey (ed.), *Indigenous and Tribal Peoples and Cancer*, https://doi.org/10.1007/978-3-031-56806-0_65

first Community Jury conducted in Inala. The Jury processes support respectful communication and relationships between the community and researchers, which positively influence research outcomes and community engagement [1].

All research conducted through SQCoE follows relevant codes for responsible and ethical research.[1] Researchers are also expected to follow cultural and community protocols and provide in-person updates to the Community Jury. The Jury approves all research results before they are released to the public. The Jury also reviews all submissions to journals, conferences, and other forums for publication. All researchers are expected to provide an easy-to-understand report for the community.

[1]These include the NHMRC's *Road Map 3: A Strategic Framework for Improving the Health of Aboriginal and Torres Strait Islander People through Research*, the NHMRC's *Ethical Conduct in Research with Aboriginal and Torres Strait Islander Peoples and Communities*, and the NHMRC's *Keeping Research on Track II.*

Since its first meeting in March 2011, the Community Jury has approved 75 projects.

We would like to acknowledge past and present Inala Community Jury members who have dedicated their community and cultural knowledges, expertise, and time during the course of their membership. We acknowledge Professor Chelsea Watego, the founder of Inala Community Jury; Professor Noel Hayman, Clinical Director of SQCoE; previous coordinators; and researchers who have presented to the Inala Community Jury.

Reference

1. Bond C, Foley W, Askew D. "It puts a human face on the researched" – A qualitative evaluation of an Indigenous health research governance model. *Aust N Z J Public Health.* 2016 Apr;40(Suppl 1):S89–S95. https://doi.org/10.1111/1753-6405.12422

Health Literacy Research: Lessons Learned Utilizing the Lens of 'Alag'upu (Samoan Proverbs)

66

Va'atausili Tofaeono, Angela Sy, Katherine Tong, and Shawnda Schroeder

Key Points

- Low levels of health literacy may be a major contributor to poor levels of colorectal cancer screening in American Samoa.
- Our Indigenous-led public health research shows that 75.5% of American Samoans who are eligible for colorectal cancer screening have either "marginal" or "inadequate" health literacy.
- Samoan 'Alaga'upu (proverbs) help us to share our story of Indigenous-led research.

For over 20 years, the American Samoa Community Cancer Coalition (ASCCC) has been dedicated to reducing the burden of cancer in American Samoa (AS). In 2015, ASCCC received a five-year grant to build research capacity, which enabled us to partner with the University of Hawai'i Cancer Center and Vanguard University to establish the INdigenous Samoan Partnership to Initiate Research Excellence (INSPIRE). In this chapter, we use the lens of Samoan 'alaga'upu (proverbs) to share a story about ASCCC's study of functional health literacy in adults who are at risk of colorectal cancer.

Samoan proverb: O lupe sa vao ese'ese, ae ua fuifui faatasi. (We are from different parts of the forest but connected in one cause.)

Lesson learned: We may be from different cultures, but we are all connected in one cause to support our communities in achieving optimal health.

AS is situated in the heart of the South Pacific and is the only US territory located south of the equator. AS includes seven islands, with 77 square miles of land dispersed over 150 square miles of open ocean: Tutuila, Aunu'u, Ofu, Olosega, Ta'u, Swains Island, and Rose Island. Most of the population of nearly 50,000 live on the main island of Tutuila [1]. AS infrastructure operates on a hybrid of US, local, and global practices. The territory's geographic isolation, challenging political oversight and guidance, and reliance on local and regional experience complicate health interventions and widen health disparities.

A 2018 study identified that among the adult AS population, 93.5% were either overweight or obese, 78.8% consumed less than five daily servings of fruits or vegetables, 39.8% self-reported as hypertensive, and 21.5% had smoked a cigarette within the last 30 days [2]. The three leading causes of death in 2019 were heart disease, cancer, and cerebrovascular disease. The key health concerns are non-communicable diseases, including diabetes, hypertension, and cancers.

Cancer Incidence and Mortality

The American Samoa Cancer Registry (ASCR) is mandated to capture cases of cancer diagnosed both on- and off-island. From 2007 to 2018, ASCR reported 369 cases of cancer, with 90% diagnosed at stage three or higher. Breast, prostate, lung and bronchus, colon, rectum, and uterine collectively accounted for over 50% of newly diagnosed patients. Tobacco (79%) and obesity (62%) were the most common contributing risk factors in adult cancers [3].

Colorectal cancer (CRC) is the third most commonly diagnosed cancer and the top non-gender-specific cancer. It is also highly preventable through education and early detection. Several methods of CRC screening are available on the islands: fecal occult blood test (FOBT), colonoscopy, and flexible sigmoidoscopy. However, only 7% of eligible AS adults reported participating in screening, compared with 62.9% of adults in the United States [4]. Low and/or no participation in preventive health services is associated with not knowing about health promotion behaviors, low levels of health literacy, and cultural norms toward screening [5].

G. Garvey (ed.), *Indigenous and Tribal Peoples and Cancer*, https://doi.org/10.1007/978-3-031-56806-0_66

Health Literacy

The US Department of Health and Human Services has designated health literacy as a priority area and the World Health Organization included it as a key factor in health promotion [6]. For the purposes of our research, we refer to functional health literacy as "the degree to which individuals have the capacity to obtain, process, and understand basic health information and services needed to make appropriate health decisions" [6]. Patients who do not understand health information have increased hospitalization rates, disease burden, and mortality [7]. Additionally, low health literacy has been associated with poorer self-reported health status in racial/ethnic minority populations [8].

Samoan proverb: Ua o gatasi le futia ma le umele. (While the fisherman swings the rod, the others must assist by paddling hard.)

Lesson learned: We must be of one mind in the undertaking.

INdigenous Samoan Partnership to Initiate Research Excellence (INSPIRE)

The INSPIRE program was funded to build research capacity in AS and determine the effects of health literacy on low CRC screening levels. We Indigenized INSPIRE by tui/lalaga (weaving) a community-based participatory approach and known Indigenous frameworks such as the fale (traditional Samoan house) and the falefono (meeting house). Our Le Fale o So'ofa'atasiga (house for research) conceptual model, described in a previous study, led to training 14 Indigenous research assistants who contributed to various aspects of the study including cultural adaptation and participant recruitment [5].

While we understood that AS people need health interventions to reduce CRC incidence and mortality, we needed to understand more about the role of health literacy in prevention and early detection. Our goal was to assess health literacy in a sample of 780 American Samoan adults and to pilot test health promotion materials relevant to resource-poor yet tradition-rich Indigenous communities.

Sample and Methods

Participants were eligible for our health literacy and CRC screening research if they (1) were a resident of AS, (2) were 45 years or older, (3) had not been diagnosed or treated for CRC, (4) could read and speak English or Samoan, (5) could provide written informed consent, (6) had a home address and working phone, and (7) were willing to provide information on their health behaviors. We recruited participants between September and December 2018, using respondent-driven sampling. A description of the recruitment plan was detailed in a previous article [9].

Table 66.1 S-TOFHLA cutoffs

Range	Category
0–16	Inadequate
17–22	Marginal
23–36	Adequate

Table 66.2 S-TOFHLA results

	English language		Samoan language		Total	
	N	%	N	%	N	%
Health literacy (cut-offs)						
Adequate (23–26)	164	39.2	25	8.5	189	26.5
Marginal (17–22)	70	16.7	33	11.2	103	14.4
Inadequate (0–16)	184	44.0	237	80.3	421	59.1

The Short-Test of Functional Health Literacy in Adults (S-TOFHLA) is a validated tool, which includes 36 reading comprehension multiple choice questions and has a seven-minute time limit [10]. The participant score is based on the number of correct answers given, categorized depending on the cutoff ranges listed in Table 66.1. We selected the S-TOFHLA because of its use in two-thirds of published papers that measured health literacy [11] and its previous use in the Samoan population in Southern California [12].

We recruited 713 total participants (295 Samoan, 418 English). Table 66.2 shows the results of S-TOFHLA scores by language.

Results and Discussion

Our results showed that 75.5% of participants had either "marginal" or "inadequate" health literacy, meaning they would have difficulty reading and interpreting health materials. Recommended ways to address these difficulties include: having a person attend appointments to help with interpreting and reading health texts, substituting graphics or symbols when possible (for directions, information, or procedures), and rewriting health materials into simple language [13].

We found a large difference between those who had inadequate health literacy in English (44.0%) versus Samoan (80.3%). While the social determinants of health could be a reason for this, we offer an additional perspective that translation of health materials should not equate to comprehension. The written Samoan language first appeared in 1839 through translated versions of the Bible aided by missionaries [14] and could be considered "newer" than English. Additionally, Westernized concepts including health literacy are undefined in our language. We suggest, therefore, that future health literacy assessments should include listenability and oral delivery as sub-constructs and add oral comprehension assessments such as the Cancer Message Literacy Test-Listening.

A community-partnered approach from participant recruitment to data collection and interpretation resulted in a robust sample size with rich results. This has been one of the largest samples of community members who have participated in research with first-time documentation of the breadth and intensity of health literacy in the community. At the same time, English language assessments and concepts of health literacy do not accurately and adequately capture how health literacy is an issue in AS. Efforts to enhance health literacy and create culturally and linguistically congruent health messaging are critical.

Samoan proverb: A malu i fale, e malu i fafo. (If it is cold inside the house, then it is cold outside.)

Lesson: Protection for the family, protection for all.

Changing Practices for Health Prevention Messaging

We designed a randomized control trial (RCT) to assess compliance with a CRC fecal occult blood test (FOBT) home test kits using modified versus non-modified patient education materials (PEM) in both English and Samoan languages. The English PEM were found to be written at a 12th-grade level or higher using the online Simple Measure of Gobbledygook (SMOG) readability test. The study staff revised and retested the passage until a fifth-grade reading level was obtained. Unfortunately, SMOG is not reliable in non-English. Instead, we used our previous translation process and developed our own Cloze procedure test, like the S-TOFHLA. Then, we conducted 20 cognitive interviews with adults 50 years old and above to assess the contextual understanding of the Samoan messaging. None of the participants missed the same question and had a median score of 25 out of 26 points. This supported our conclusion that the reader could predict the passage contextually and it was consistent with the natural reading process.

We recruited 260 participants aged 50 and above between October and December of 2020. The final data revealed that 39 reported the results, and 30 complied with the full instructions of the test (14 experiment; 16 control). None of the 30 had scored within the inadequate range of the S-TOFHLA. Unfortunately, we were not able to make any statistically significant associations; however, we later shared our process and results with the local Department of Health's COVID-19 communication committee. This contributed to redefining vaccination concepts in the community to reduce comprehension barriers. We assisted in the development of over 250 health messages that were disseminated through social media pages, print, television, radio, and websites. These messages aided in a comprehensive effort that achieved a 91.7% vaccination rate by April of 2022 in AS, one of the highest in the United States.

Samoan proverb: Ole ala ile pule ole tautua. (The path to leadership is through service.)

Lesson: By serving others, we create a pathway to success.

Conclusion

Our story shares a unique journey where collaboratively built, Indigenous-led public health research contributed to improved health outcomes in AS. Historically, this type of research would have been performed by non-Indigenous institutions and researchers. The innovation shown is a form of tautua (service) to the AS community, creating a pathway for future Indigenous generations to lead and conduct research within their communities.

We offer fa'afetai tele lava (thank you very much) to the following people and organizations: Dr Victor Tofaeono and Mrs Luana Scanlan for their guidance as INSPIRE Multiple Principal Investigators; Drs Kevin Cassel and Lana Sue Ilima Ka'opua in designing the INSPIRE sampling and data analysis methodology; the second INSPIRE researcher cohort Magdalene Augafa, Oscar Betham, Wynona Lee, Solinu'u Savusa, and Tofoi Unutoa Mageo for their contributions to the translation and cognitive interview process; the previous and current Board of Directors of the ASCCC who have supported the efforts of the INSPIRE and ACT-AS-ONE program, staff, and co-investigators; Dr Shawnda Schroeder for her valuable feedback during the editing process; and, Lastly, the NIMHD (award number 1 U24 MD 011202), the University of Hawai'i Cancer Center (award number 5 30 CA071789), and HRSA (award number 1G32HS42576-01) in their vision to challenge structural practices to provide necessary grant funds that made these projects possible to a small community-based organization.

References

1. United States Census Bureau. *2020 Islander Areas Censuses: American Samoa* [Internet]. 2020 October. Available from: https://www.census.gov/data/tables/2020/dec/2020-american-samoa.html
2. American Samoa Government. *American Samoa Adult Hybrid Survey*. Pago Pago: Department of Human & Social Services;

2018. Available from: https://www.pihoa.org/wp-content/uploads/2022/05/American-Samoa_20Sept2019.pdf
3. Pacific Regional Central Cancer Registry. *Cancer in the U.S. Affiliated Pacific Islands 2007-2020.* Honolulu: University of Hawaii John A. Burns School of Medicine; 2023. Available from: https://pacificcancer.org/wp-content/uploads/sites/50/2023/04/PIJ-Cancer-Facts-Figures-2007-2020-Final-to-share_smallfile.pdf
4. American Samoa Department of Health. *Behavioural Risk Factors Surveillance Survey Results and Data Report.* Faga'alu: American Samoa Department of Health; 2013.
5. Tofaeono V, Ka'opua LS, Sy A, Terada T, Purcell RT, Aoelua-Fanene S, et al. Research capacity strengthening in American Samoa: Fa'avaeina le Fa'atelega o le Tomai Sa'ili'ili i Amerika Samoa. *Br J Soc Work.* 2020;50(2), 525–547. https://doi.org/10.1093/bjsw/bcz160
6. Nielsen-Bohlman L, Panzer AM, Kindig DA, editors. *Health literacy: A prescription to end confusion.* Washington: National Academies Press; 2004.
7. Aaby A, Simonsen CB, Ryom K, Maindal HT. Improving Organizational Health Literacy Responsiveness in Cardiac Rehabilitation Using A Co-Design Methodology: Results from The Heart Skills Study. *Int J Environ Res Public Health.* 2020;17(3):1015. https://doi.org/10.3390/ijerph17031015
8. Sentell T, Braun KL. Low health literacy, limited English proficiency, and health status in Asians, Latinos, and other racial/ethnic groups in California. *J Health Commun.* 2012;7(Suppl 3):82–99. https://doi.org/10.1080/10810730.2012.712621
9. Tofaeono V, Tong K, Sy A, Cassel K, Pagano I, Kaopua LSI, et al. Validation of the Short-Test of Functional Health Literacy in Adults for the Samoan Population. *Health Lit Res Pract.* 2022;6(4):e247–e256. https://doi.org/10.3928/24748307-20220920-01
10. Parker RM, Baker DW, Nurss JR.The test of functional health literacy in adults: a new instrument for measuring patients' literacy skills. *J Gen Intern Med.* 1995 Oct;10(10):537–41. https://doi.org/10.1007/BF02640361
11. Paasche-Orlow MK, Parker RM, Gazmamarian JA, Nielsen-Bohlman LD, Rudd RR. The prevalence of limited health literacy. *J Gen Intern Med.* 2005 Feb;20(2):175–84. https://doi.org/10.1111/j.1525-1497.2005.40245.x
12. Tong K. *Health literacy and health promotion behaviours among Samoans* [Doctoral dissertation]. University of San Diego: ProQuest Dissertations & Theses; 2012.
13. Baker DW, Williams MV, Parker RM, Gazmararian JA, Nurss J. Development of a brief test to measure functional health literacy. *Patient Educ Couns.* 1999;38(1):33–42. https://doi.org/10.1016/s0738-3991(98)00116-5
14. Omniglot. *Samoan (Gagana fa'a Samoa)* [Internet]. Available from: https://www.omniglot.com/writing/samoan.htm

67 Native Hawaiian Community Organization Leading Cancer Education and Research: The Story of ʻImi Hale

JoAnn ʻUmilani Tsark, May Rose Dela Cruz, and Kathryn L. Braun

Key Points

- ʻImi Hale was funded with a grant from the National Cancer Institute directly to the community-based, community-governed organization Papa Ola Lōkahi. Funds were managed and governed by Papa Ola Lōkahi, with the university subcontracted to provide assistance with research.
- ʻImi Hale demonstrated a high level of responsiveness to community-identified priorities and needs, instilling accountability to report and translate data and lessons learned to the communities served.
- ʻImi Hale invested equal time and resources in cancer education and awareness, training, service development, and research capacity building.
- ʻImi Hale developed an extensive and diverse network of local, national, and international partners to offer knowledge, resources, services, and guidance in cancer health disparities research and programming.

Native Hawaiians, Indigenous to the Hawaiian archipelago, were once a self-governed, robust, and self-sufficient group. Their advanced social, environmental, and health systems allowed them to prosper in these remote Pacific islands for over 2000 years. Colonizers brought disease, guns, and Western concepts of propriety and private property, resulting in a 90% decline in the Indigenous population within 100 years of contact, along with loss of land, livelihood, language, culture, and power [1].

Hawaiʻi began to collect race-specific cancer data in the 1970s, and the *Native Hawaiian Health Care Improvement Act* of 1988 (PL 100-579) increased attention to Hawaiian health issues. Native Hawaiians were reported to be disproportionately affected by cancer. However, fewer than five Native Hawaiians held cancer-related leadership positions in 2000. Existing research did not address Native Hawaiian priorities, was not conducted in culturally appropriate ways, and was not perceived by Hawaiians as beneficial, generating feelings of exploitation and stigmatizing Native Hawaiians as sick and uncaring about their health [2].

The ʻImi Hale Native Hawaiian Cancer Network was funded by the National Cancer Institute (NCI) from 2000 to 2017 to address cancer health disparities faced by Native Hawaiians (U01CA86105, U01CA114630, U54CA153459). The project achieved excellent outcomes, detailed in Table 67.1. Two key factors contributed to its success. First, the award was granted to a Native Hawaiian non-profit organization rather than an academic institution. Second, the project allocated equal resources to education, service, policy development, and research.

Reasons for Success

Community-Based, Community-Placed, and Community-Governed

Papa Ola Lōkahi, an organization serving Native Hawaiians and associated with five Native Hawaiian Health Care Systems (NHHCSs), was awarded funding by the NCI. While NCI typically funds universities, this arrangement provided a Native Hawaiian organization and community network a chance to promote cancer awareness and facilitate cancer research. Unencumbered by the bureaucracy and high operating costs of a university, ʻImi Hale was able to efficiently utilize resources and quickly enact subcontracts. This resulted in an infrastructure that elevated community voice and expanded Native Hawaiian capacity to engage in the research enterprise, an arena from which they were historically excluded (except as "subjects").

ʻImi Hale was conceived by Native Hawaiian healthcare providers, and 66% of staff members were Native Hawaiian with strong ties to the community. Subcontracts were established with the University of Hawaiʻi to provide research expertise. Specifically, a trusted professor with a track record in community-based participatory research was

G. Garvey (ed.), *Indigenous and Tribal Peoples and Cancer*, https://doi.org/10.1007/978-3-031-56806-0_67

contracted at 75% of full-time to provide one-on-one assistance, training, and mentorship to Native Hawaiian researchers and to assist staff in navigating the university system when needed [3]. Two more seasoned investigators provided higher-level guidance on research. The parent NCI grant solicited pilot research applications from awardees annually. 'Imi Hale gave priority to the research proposals of Native Hawaiian investigators (90% of the total), providing just-in-time training with research design, implementation, and dissemination.

Table 67.1 'Imi Hale program successes

'Imi Hale successes
Over 100 partnerships were established with local, state, national, and international groups providing funding, expertise, and connection to the community
'Imi Hale was the state's largest producer of culturally tailored cancer education materials, with 150+ field-tested brochures, posters, toolkits, and presentations
Over 15,000 individuals attended at least one cancer awareness-raising training or event
Over 150 Native Hawaiian scholars and clinicians were trained in research
Over $9 million was secured to support 50 research projects
Over 190 peer-reviewed articles were published
'Imi Hale staff edited three special peer-reviewed journal issues
Over $26 million was secured to expand cancer services in Hawai'i, including cancer patient navigation, cancer screening, cancer education, clinical trial recruitment, community-sensitive biobanking, HPV, and vaccine uptake
'Imi Hale collaborated and changed state and healthcare-level policies related to cancer patient navigation, tobacco control, HPV, and vaccine uptake
'Imi Hale collaborated to develop consent protocols for banked cancer tissue at Hawai'i's largest hospital incorporating post-op consent and patient options to be reconsented for each protocol
'Imi Hale established the only cancer patient navigation training in the state, which included 223 graduates, seven annual navigation conferences, and 50+ continuing education sessions
'Imi Hale established and managed the Native Hawaiian Institutional Review Board (IRB), Hawai'i's first community IRB

'Imi Hale was governed by predominantly Native Hawaiian working committees (Fig. 67.1). A 10-member Community Council (100% Native Hawaiian) advised on the cultural appropriateness of research, researchers, and program activities. A 10-member Scientific Council (50% Native Hawaiian) advised on the scientific merit of research projects. An 11-member Steering Committee (73% Native Hawaiian) set policy. Furthermore, 'Imi Hale established and staffed the 20-member Native Hawaiian Institutional Review Board (IRB, 78% Native Hawaiian, 40% community representatives). Council and IRB members reviewed every project, privileging Native Hawaiian priorities and views [4].

For example, Council members suggested interviewing Native Hawaiian cancer survivors to better learn about their challenges in seeking care and participating in clinical trials. On-the-ground providers helped develop interview questions, and Native Hawaiian researchers were trained to lead focus groups while following cultural protocols. The Native Hawaiian IRB mandated additional safeguards, including having counseling available for participants for a year after the study. Results were shared first with participants, then with Council members and community partners, and finally published [5].

Lacking the infrastructure of a university, 'Imi Hale sought and benefitted from the mentorship of researchers, programs, and policy experts from other institutions, including other NCI grantees, the Oregon Health Sciences University, Native American Cancer Research Corporation,

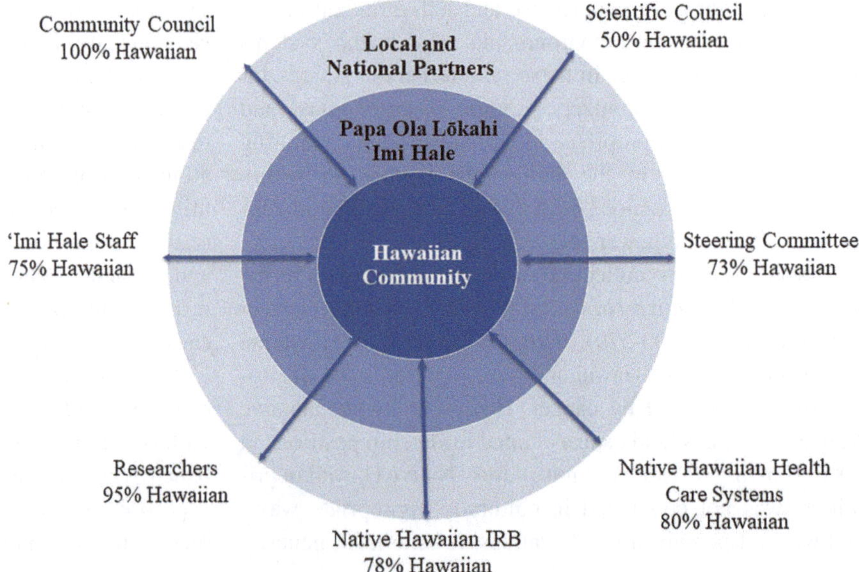

Fig. 67.1 'Imi Hale's infrastructure

the Native Hawaiian Civic Clubs, the Harold P Freeman Patient Navigation Institute, and multiple others that actively served and engaged Indigenous/minority researchers and communities.

Focus on Program and Policy, as Well as Research

Unlike traditional National Institutes of Health (NIH)–funded initiatives that focus on research, this funding mechanism required grantees to also address cancer education and awareness. 'Imi Hale invested heavily in developing culturally relevant materials to supplant national materials that had little relevance to Hawaiian communities. Using a four-step protocol that involved pretesting and feedback from consumers and providers, these products reflected Hawaiian values, language, and authentic community voices [6]. More than 150 educational products were developed, including brochures, posters, toolkits, training curricula, and presentations. For two decades, 'Imi Hale was the largest producer and distributor of cancer-education materials in the state, supplying the local health department, healthcare centers, and cancer-support groups.

In research, 'Imi Hale assisted more than 150 Native Hawaiian students, post-docs, faculty, and clinicians with research design, grant proposals, manuscripts, and presentations. Investigators applied for research funding through NCI and other sources, and more than $9 million was secured for 50 research projects. Findings from these projects appeared in over 190 peer-reviewed articles. Many investigators were supported to attend research training outside of Hawai'i, and more than 40 were assisted in pursuing graduate degrees. Today, these individuals are leading research and programs in Hawai'i.

'Imi Hale was instrumental in securing $26 million to support various cancer care initiatives, including Hawai'i's cancer patient navigation training program. Each 48-hour training involved 30 faculty who taught about cancer, clinical trials, and social services [7]. Over eight years, 16 training programs, seven annual conferences, and 50 continuing education sessions were conducted; 223 navigators, 45% from rural areas, were trained; and 13 health centers established navigation programs and positions. A rural hospital was assisted in conducting a randomized clinical trial of a screening navigation program that resulted in a significant increase in cancer screening [8]. In another initiative, Pacific Islander women were trained as lay navigators, leading to a significant increase in compliance with mammography screening [9].

In the policy arena, 'Imi Hale collaborated with state and pharmaceutical partners to expand the capabilities of pharmacies in administering HPV vaccines to adolescents and to make this a school-recommended vaccine. The team helped change state and county laws to reduce access and exposure to tobacco. These initiatives garnered support and involvement from youth and organizational partners and were reinforced by 'Imi Hale education resources [10].

In healthcare, 'Imi Hale worked with Hawai'i's largest medical center to develop cancer biobanking policies that consented patients post-op for remnant tissue, allowing them to opt out of blanket consent and choose to be reconsented when their tissue was requested for research. 'Imi Hale partnered with the same facility to increase primary care physician knowledge and willingness to refer Native Hawaiian to clinical trials [11]. 'Imi Hale trained NHHCS staff in tobacco cessation and helped the network develop and institutionalize a tobacco cessation protocol across the five clinics [12]. The program also partnered with the state's 14 Federally Qualified Health Centers (FQHCs) to provide training on updated colorectal cancer screening protocols, resulting in increased screening rates.

Conclusion

The 'Imi Hale Native Hawaiian Cancer Network serves as a compelling case study, demonstrating the effectiveness of a community-based, community-placed, community-governed, cancer-control program. Attending to Native Hawaiian self-determination, 'Imi Hale was developed and operated by Native Hawaiians for Native Hawaiians. This yielded meaningful and more equitable partnerships with the university and other providers while increasing community capacity and agency to address cancer health disparities.

References

1. Joe JR, Burhansstipanov L, Ullrich JS, Braun KL. Standing on the shoulders of our ancestors: History and contemporary health status of indigenous peoples in the US. In Burhansstipanov L, Braun, KL., editors. *Indigenous Public Health: Improvement through Community-Engaged Interventions.* Lexington, KY: University Press of Kentucky; 2022. p. 21–54.
2. Fong M, Braun KL, Tsark J. Improving Native Hawaiian health through community-based participatory research. *Calif J Health Promot.* 2003;1(1):136–48. https://doi.org/10.32398/cjhp.v1iSI.565
3. Tsark J, Braun KL. Nā Liko Noelo: A program to develop Native Hawaiian researchers. *Pac Health Dialog.* 2004;11(2):225–32.
4. Braun KL, Tsark J, Santos L, Aitaoto N, Chong C. Building Native Hawaiian capacity in cancer research and programming: The Legacy of 'Imi Hale. *Cancer.* 2006;107 (8 Suppl):2082–90. https://doi.org/10.1002/cncr.22157
5. Braun KL, Mokuau N, Hunt GH, Ka'ano'i M, Gotay C. Supports and obstacles to cancer survival for Hawai'i's native people. *Cancer Pract.* 2002;10(4):192–200. https://doi.org/10.1046/j.1523-5394.2002.104001.x

6. Kulukulualani M, Braun KL, Tsark J. Using a four-step protocol to develop and test culturally targeted cancer education brochures. *Health Promot Pract.* 2008;9:344–55. https://doi.org/10.1177/1524839907302737
7. Braun KL, Allison A, Tsark J. Using community-based research methods to design cancer patient navigation training. *Prog Community Health Partnersh.* 2008;4:329–40. https://doi.org/10.1353/cpr.0.0037
8. Braun KL, Thomas W, Domingo J, Allison A, Ponce A, Kamakana PH, Aluli NE, Tsark JU. Reducing cancer screening disparities in Medicare beneficiaries through cancer patient navigation. *J Am Geriatr Soc.* 2015;63:365–70. https://doi.org/10.1111/jgs.13192
9. Aitaoto N, Braun KL, Estrella J, Epeluk A, Tsark J. Design and Results of a Culturally Tailored Cancer Outreach Project by and for Micronesian Women. *Prev Chronic Dis.* 2012;9:100262. https://doi.org/10.5888/pcd9.100262
10. Dela Cruz MRI, Tsark, JU, Soon R, Albright C, Braun KL. Community involvement in developing a human papillomavirus (HPV) vaccine brochure made for parents in Hawai'i. *Hawaii J of Med Public Health.* 2016;75: 203–7.
11. Robinson MK, Tsark JU, Braun KL. Increasing primary-care provider support for and promotion of cancer clinical trials. *Hawaii J Med Public Health.* 2014;73(3):84–7.
12. Santos LA, Braun KL, Aea K, Shearer, L. Institutionalizing a comprehensive tobacco-cessation protocol in an indigenous health system: Lessons learned. *Prog Community Health Partnersh.* 2008;2:279–89. https://doi.org/10.1353/cpr.0.0038

68 Recruiting and Retaining Indigenous People in Research: The Indigenous Australian HPV Cohort Study

Joanne Hedges, Sneha Sethi, and Lisa Jamieson

Key Points

- The Indigenous Australian Human Papillomavirus (HPV) Cohort Study examines the prevalence of oral HPV infection among Aboriginal and Torres Strait Islander people in South Australia. To our knowledge, this is the largest Indigenous HPV cohort study in the world to track oral HPV infection and monitor the early stages of oropharyngeal squamous cell carcinoma (OPSCC).
- The study collected baseline data from 1011 participants. Follow-ups have been conducted at 12, 24, and 48 months and will also occur at 60 and 72 months.
- Strong community engagement, employing Aboriginal staff, and yarning during the data collection have resulted in excellent recruitment and retention rates in this study.

Aboriginal and Torres Strait Islander peoples in Australia have a higher incidence of, and lower five-year survival rates from, oral cancer and oropharyngeal cancer compared to the general population [1]. Information on oral and oropharyngeal cancers among Aboriginal and Torres Strait Islander peoples is lacking, creating a void in understanding these diseases and their associated complications. Persistent high-risk human papillomavirus (HPV) infection is recognized as the leading cause of oropharyngeal cancer [2].

The Indigenous Australian Human Papillomavirus Cohort Study is a prospective longitudinal cohort study developed in partnership with Aboriginal communities in South Australia and funded by Australia's National Health and Medical Research Council [3]. The primary aim of the study is to evaluate the population estimates of oncogenic genotypes of HPV in the mouth and oropharynx among Aboriginal and Torres Strait Islander communities of South Australia. The hypothesis informing the study states that the prevalence of oral HPV among Aboriginal and Torres Strait Islander Australians will be high compared with national-level estimates. The secondary aims include evaluating the rates of oropharyngeal carcinoma and the impact of HPV vaccinations, as well as evaluating the efficacy and cost-effectiveness of targeted extended HPV vaccinations among Aboriginal and Torres Strait Islander peoples.

The study is governed by an Aboriginal Reference Group, with data collected by trained Aboriginal research officers. Baseline eligibility included identifying as Aboriginal and/or Torres Strait Islander, being aged 18 years or over, and residing in South Australia. Participants were recruited from February 2018 to January 2019 across 11 South Australian sites, primarily through Aboriginal Community Controlled Health Organisations (ACCHOs).

Recruitment, Retention, and Follow-Up Strategies

Recruitment strategies were based on successful strategies utilized in the past, including (1) co-designing specific agreements with the chief ACCHOs, which were tailor-made to suit the specific needs of the communities; (2) consulting with Aboriginal community champions, some of whom were formerly involved in our research; (3) encouraging word-of-mouth spread of recruitment; (4) advertisements in local newspapers and radio shows; (5) flyers in post boxes in high-density Aboriginal locations; and (6) presentations to community groups in partnership with the community organizations. A snowballing technique was also used, with participants asked to contact any Aboriginal friends, family, and peers who may be interested in participating.

Follow-up strategies designed to ensure retention across the life of the study involved (1) retaining staff who were committed to following up participants notwithstanding challenges; (2) ensuring a regular communication link between participants and team to ensure accuracy of contact details; (3) ensuring the research officer always took the contact details of at least three key individuals (family members, friends, community members, organization managers) who would be informed about the whereabouts of participants should the current contact details (address, phone numbers) change; (4) sending birthday and Christmas cards and

G. Garvey (ed.), *Indigenous and Tribal Peoples and Cancer*, https://doi.org/10.1007/978-3-031-56806-0_68

regular newsletters to participants; and (5) encouraging a one-on-one relationship between team members and participants with a genuine attempt to ensure participants saw the same team member at each phase of follow-up.

The recruitment and follow-up strategies were employed after extensive community consultations and, to a large extent, were successful based on pre-existing working relationships and the reputation of the research team. Although these strategies can be cited as successful, the significance of pre-existing relationships based on trust, reciprocity, and faith cannot be ignored. Successful community engagement was supported by ensuring the interactions with all participants were culturally safe. Team members facilitated self-determination by encouraging participants to answer questions themselves. Team members also ensured that the project aims, expected outcomes, risks, all participant rights, and consent were thoroughly explained.

The 1011 participants recruited at baseline represented 5% of Aboriginal and/or Torres Strait Islander South Australian adults eligible during the recruitment period: 8.2% of those eligible in non-metropolitan locations, and 3% of those eligible in metropolitan locations. Participants were followed up at 12 months (March 2019 to March 2020), with data obtained from 749 (74.1%) of the original 1011 participants. This follow-up was suspended early due to COVID-19 restrictions. Follow-up at 24 months ceased in December 2021, with data obtained from 815 participants. Across baseline and 12- and 24-month follow-ups, saliva samples to test for oral human HPV infection were collected using commercially available kits, and the retrieved DNA samples were tested for HPV detection. Further funding has been granted for 48-, 60-, and 72-month follow-ups. At the time of writing, the 48-month follow-up is in the fieldwork stage.

Strong Community Engagement

Strong Aboriginal partnership, engagement, and buy-in of the first study phase were reported against the Consolidated Criteria for Strengthening Reporting of Health Research involving Indigenous Peoples (CONSIDER) statement [4]. The success of the community engagement processes can be summarized as (1) engaging with ACCHOs as equal partners from early in the research process, (2) incorporating an Aboriginal Reference Group, (3) active promotion of the study by ACCHOs, (4) having a flexible agenda responsive to broader environment demands, (5) prioritizing Aboriginal leadership and self-determination while building team capacity, and (6) shifting the narrative from a deficit discourse to a strengths-based discourse.

Specific lessons learned during the first phase included (1) the need for active and wide Aboriginal community consultation initiated early in the research process, (2) strong and sustained Aboriginal capacity building, and (3) governance from an active Aboriginal Reference Group. These lessons were incorporated into subsequent phases of the research.

The presence of Aboriginal staff as representatives in each of the field sites has additional benefits. These representatives have developed their skills and reputations in the area of oral HPV infection, an area of Aboriginal health that has not previously been recognized. The participating Australian Indigenous communities now have a local contact, with study continuation facilitating improved HPV knowledge for both the ACCHO workforce and the broader community. Future phases of the study will continue to implement and strengthen these community engagement strategies.

Empowering Communities

It is essential that this cohort study, to our knowledge the largest Indigenous HPV cohort in the world to track oral HPV infection and monitor the early stages of oropharyngeal squamous cell carcinoma (OPSCC), continues in order to yield critical information that can be added to the management armamentarium of health and wellbeing recommendations for Indigenous Australians. This is especially relevant in light of the imminent rollout of self-sampling cervical HPV testing initiatives in Australia, as it opens doors for a similar self-sampling initiative for oral and oropharyngeal cancers.

The capacity-building element of the study is an ongoing strength and includes (1) naming Aboriginal CEOs of the partnering ACCHOs as co-authors on scientific papers; (2) Aboriginal community leaders attending international conferences, such as the International Indigenous Cancer conferences, to showcase the processes and outcomes of the study's Indigenous engagement to international audiences; (3) upskilling Aboriginal organizations and staff in a new area of health knowledge aligned with oral cancer; (4) increasing the understanding of health staff/policy makers regarding fears among many Aboriginal and/or Torres Strait Islander peoples about the HPV vaccine, the general lack of awareness of the importance of regular cervical cancer screening, and the impact of HPV-related cancers for both men and women; (5) developing strong relationships with Aboriginal ethics organizations, with increased focus on cultural values when undertaking research in partnership with Aboriginal groups; (6) acknowledging the importance and value of participants' time and remunerating this appropriately; (7) disseminating dental products to both study participants and their wider households and family groups; and (8) strong advocacy by all research staff with respect to navigating dental care pathways and cancer screening pathways for communities.

Strengths of the Study Design

This project was inspired by previous community engagement during which community members identified an increase in "throat sickness" (cancer) in the community. As Aboriginal and Torres Strait Islander peoples were involved in identifying the health priority, community interest and response were strong and all decisions were culturally safe and based on self-determination. Aboriginal leadership and governance ensured the cultural appropriateness of the strategies employed. The main strength of the Indigenous Australian HPV Cohort Study has been the engagement of South Australia's Aboriginal communities. This has contributed to excellent recruitment and follow-up rates (approximately 74% at 12 months and 80.6% at 24 months), which are even more significant given the context of the research. This ongoing study is taking place over vast distances (traveling 700 km west, 400 km east, and 800 km north of the city of Adelaide) and involves highly disadvantaged participants who have, in the past, not always enjoyed positive research interactions. The fact that over 1000 participants were recruited in under 12 months demonstrates the widespread community support that exists for this research. It should also be noted that the intervention was conducted during the COVID-19 pandemic, thus limiting in-person interactions.

Strengths of the Research Team

One of the most significant aspects of research success and increased community engagement has been the research methodology employed. All members of the team were trained by an experienced Senior Aboriginal Researcher and were taught the principles of Relational Yarning, now a recognized culturally appropriate research methodology. The core values of the research team are based on prioritizing respect, relationships, advocacy, reciprocity, time, and gratitude. Aboriginal leaders continue to promote self-determination and encourage community members to trust and participate in the research. These leaders, combined with the diverse multidisciplinary skills of the research team, have played a major role in the success of the research. The members of the research team have continually recognized their own privilege, social position, and power, and situated themselves in ways that have ensured participants feel culturally safe, respected, heard, acknowledged, and appreciated at all times. They have ensured that interactions with participants are devoid of judgment or power differentials, placing the power back into the hands of the participants and communities. All research papers, presentations, and community conversations focus on a strengths-based narrative, practicing and reinforcing the principles of decolonizing research [5].

References

1. Australian Institute of Health and Welfare. *Cancer in Australia 2021*. Canberra: AIHW; 2021 Dec. Available from: https://www.aihw.gov.au/reports/cancer/cancer-in-australia-2021/summary
2. Taberna M, Mena M, Pavón MA, Alemany L, Gillison ML, Mesía R. Human papillomavirus-related oropharyngeal cancer. *Ann Oncol.* 2017;28:2386–98. https://doi.org/10.1093/annonc/mdx304
3. Hedges J, Sethi S, Garvey G, Whop LJ, Canfell K, Dodd Z, et al. The Indigenous Australian Human Papillomavirus (HPV) Cohort Study 2, Continuation for 5 to 10 Years: Protocol for a Longitudinal Study. *JMIR Res Protoc*. 2023;12:e44593. https://doi.org/10.2196/44593
4. Hedges J, Garvey G, Dodd Z, Miller W, Dunbar T, Leane C, et al. Engaging with Indigenous Australian communities for a human papilloma virus and oropharyngeal cancer project; use of the CONSIDER statement. *BMC Med Res Methodol.* 2020;20:92. https://doi.org/10.1186/s12874-020-00981-5
5. Thambinathan V, Kinsella EA. Decolonizing Methodologies in Qualitative Research: Creating Spaces for Transformative Praxis. *Int J Qual Methods.* 2021;20. https://doi.org/10.1177/16094069211014766

Strengths of the Study Design

Strengths of the Research Team

Grounding Indigenous Collaborative Processes in Research Partnerships to Maximize Outcomes

69

Lea Bill, Angeline Letendre, and Barbara Frazer

Key Points

- The Alberta First Nations Cancer Strategy and Practice Change Implementation Initiative (AFNCI) was developed to advance cancer care priorities and actions of First Nations, Inuit, and Metis peoples (FNIM) of Canada.
- AFNCI was developed through First Nations cultural social engagement methods that draw on phenomenological approaches to research.
- AFNCI was developed with guidance from Knowledge Holders/Practitioners.
- AFNCI research was developed using the OCAP® principles of ownership, control, access, and possession to assert Indigenous ownership over data and data collection.

The Alberta First Nations Cancer Strategy and Practice Change Implementation Initiative (AFNCI) is a five-year, multi-jurisdictional project developed to advance actions on the cancer care priorities of First Nations, Inuit, and Metis peoples (FNIM) of Canada. The project is supported by the Canadian Partnership Against Cancer (CPAC) and developed through collaboration with Alberta First Nations Information Governance Centre (AFNIGC), Alberta Health Services (AHS), Knowledge Holders/Practitioners, and oncology champions. To develop the AFNCI, the partners exercised First Nations cultural social engagement methods and created a collaborative framework to improve cancer pathways for First Nations cancer patients and their families. Project development included cultural processes with well-positioned, highly respected ceremonial practitioners to elaborate on how cultural and traditional practices are needed to support and benefit healing in First Nations individuals and families experiencing cancer. Through these processes, improved knowledge and awareness of Alberta First Nations families and communities have been advanced, and a culture of authentic relationships established and sustained between Knowledge Holders/Practitioners, oncology champions, and research partners.

AFNCI Partnership and Engagement Structure

The AFNCI project places emphasis on its partners, who bring their distinct strengths and visions to focus on culturally safe cancer care pathways and care. It was developed through a First Nations research methodological process. A critical juncture prior to entering the research process was to seek guidance through ceremony. Project co-leads (AFNIGC Executive Director Lea Bill, and AHS—Cancer Prevention and Screening Innovations, Indigenous Community Scientist Dr Angeline Letendre) positioned Knowledge Holders/Practitioners in a cultural leadership role, including two highly respected oncology champions from AHS. The AFNCI partnership and engagement structure (Fig. 69.1) illustrates the extent of collaboration.

The AFNIGC has emerged as a leader in Indigenous-led cancer research in Canada. In its oskâpêw (helper) role for AFNCI, the AFNIGC is mandated by Alberta First Nation leadership to oversee research and ensure researchers are informed about the principles of OCAP® [1]. These principles of ownership, control, access, and possession assert that First Nations peoples have control over data collection processes and that they own and control how collected information can be used. AFNIGC supported the AFNCI partners to develop authentic, Indigenous, informed, mixed-methods processes and chart a path toward reliable data.

The research process used for AFNCI recognizes parallel approaches where both quantitative and qualitative methods complement each other. Data gathering is a spiritual process. The sacredness of data is acknowledged in a way that is responsive to the land, people, and ancestors. AFNIGC has emerged as a leader in laying the groundwork for innovative Indigenous data governance and Indigenous-led cancer research, designing cultural data collection, and exploring and testing Indigenous research data management methodologies.

Co-lead organization, the Alberta Cancer Prevention Legacy Fund of AHS (now known as the Cancer Prevention

G. Garvey (ed.), *Indigenous and Tribal Peoples and Cancer*, https://doi.org/10.1007/978-3-031-56806-0_69

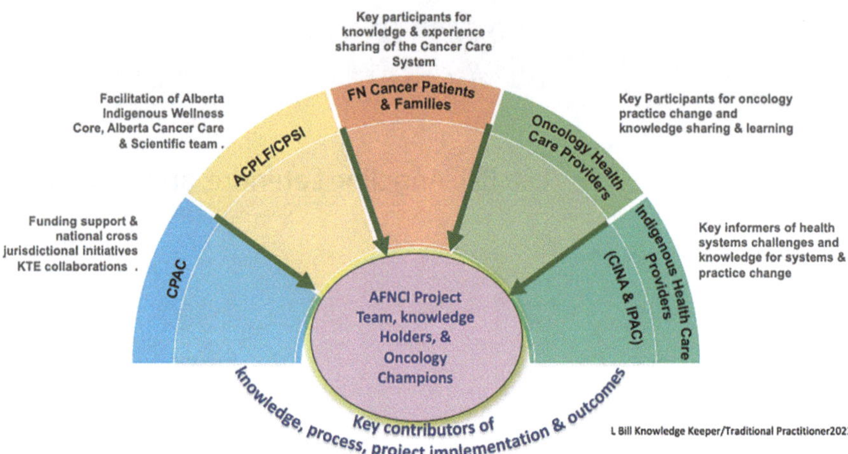

Fig. 69.1 AFNCI partnership and engagement structure

and Screening Innovations (CPSI) AHS) supported and led strategy development in cancer prevention and screening with FNIM communities in Alberta, Canada. Lead scientist of the Community Research Stream, Dr Angeline Letendre, provided Western research oversight and guidance. AHS oncology champions agreed to be project co-leads and support further collaborative engagement with Cancer Control Alberta leadership—including Dr Gregg Nelson (Tom Baker Cancer Centre, Calgary) and Dr Charles Butts (Cross Cancer Institute, Edmonton). Their positioning as champions helped to integrate research findings into strategy, services, and program delivery with a special focus on FNIM communities.

The central unifying force of the AFNCI collaboration was the contributions of Knowledge Holders/Practitioners from diverse Alberta First Nations language groups. Fluent speakers of their languages, the Knowledge Holders/Practitioners shared their knowledge and helped to shape action on pressing issues and challenges facing First Nations cancer patients. This highly specialized team of knowledge holders is recognized as ceremonial and cultural leaders within their respective communities.

All project participants acknowledged that these partners need to be involved to improve First Nations cancer pathways and care. In the true spirit of collaboration, the high-level teams engaged in dialogue that relied upon First Nations collaborative processes to identify and articulate required practice changes to improve cancer outcomes and experiences.

A First Nations Research Methodology and Cultural Approach

The AFNCI research process relied on guidance from First Nation Knowledge Holders/Practitioners. Cultural transference given by the Knowledge Holders/Practitioners was transformational and continues to inform AFNCI with an understanding of the significance of ancestral knowledge to improve cancer pathways.

AFNCI outcomes were achieved by working collaboratively from a place of trust and true partnership. Narratives and stories shared through group dialogues provided a strong culturally grounded foundation that utilized Indigenous knowledge concepts—such as Relationships, Family as Medicine, Culture as Prevention, and Use of Indigenous Languages. Key actions arising from these narratives were intended to serve Alberta First Nations peoples and preserve ancestral healing knowledge systems by supporting oral traditions and strengthening communities [2]. These narratives formed the foundational cultural collaborative framework for AFNCI, to build and establish trusting relationships where critical conversations on difficult and sensitive topics informed improvements needed across the cancer pathway. The process focused on cultural transference through oral traditions, where spoken word, narrative, and stories transmit important life histories and teachings for concepts to exist within oncology settings. Each Knowledge Holder/Practitioner accepted the protocol signifying the commencement of the sacred fire.

What emerged were research processes and methods specific to the cultures of participating Knowledge Holders/Practitioners and couched within First Nations knowledge systems. The OCAP® principles were utilized to develop Oncology Care Provider Education and Training.

AFNCI work, activities, and outcomes reflect a direct application and use of First Nations cultural collaborative processes, using a natural methodology accompanied by time-honored collaborative processes and supported by ceremonial practices. This cultural approach elicited specific knowledge, wisdom, and ways of doing for practice change. AFNCI's approach is, thereby, informed by cultural knowledge and processes.

Phenomenology: A Cultural Premise

First Nations verb-based languages provide the means to capture authentic, culturally based collaborative processes. AFNCI respected this by applying an Indigenous science methodology, underpinned by phenomenology, which valued the lived experience and cultural practices of each Knowledge Holder/Practitioner as expressed by their language.

Each engagement session created a conceptual space where storied experiences provided invaluable insight and contributed to the critical dialogic process. Speakers took turns to layer critical reflection; analyze; and communicate concepts, attitudes, and lived practice—all for the purpose of creating a shared perspective on how to improve cancer outcomes. At its root, this methodology is an inquiry of the self—of how one has been affected or impacted by the environment—in this case, the cancer care space.

Phenomenology moves narratives. It shifts language to story, becoming a vessel of knowledge as it relates to information obtained from the whole being (mind, body, feeling, and spirit) for positioning a social response. This methodology correlates to the oral transfer of knowledge, as Indigenous knowledge is housed within culture and Indigenous language. Language is a central methodological tool to construct and guide the examination of the actions required to develop understanding among the group. Knowledge Holders/Practitioners each acknowledged that they were responding from within a living process or methodology.

The phenomenological methodology connected the multitude of lived experiences and work around the sacred fire—the ethical space [3] or meeting place. The use of Cree terminology—for instance "Asapâp" (thread, the action of connecting)—offered a community approach that was understood by the group to socially organize around an issue or challenge. Asapâp was seen as a phenomenological action where symbolically and metaphorically the thread, as the connective tool of social functions, is required to support change. The thread pulls together a value system that houses built-in best practices existing within the language. Each narrative, teaching, or understanding presented by the Knowledge Holders/Practitioners represents a larger story of values to support a shift in mindset. Thread is also analogous to an implementation process, where all components integrate and merge the knowledge gathered. Asapâp helped to frame knowledgeable decisions to build the inclusive and compassionate foundation required to support cultural pathways throughout the cancer journey. Each person involved played a necessary role, as a strand of living thread creating change.

Engagement as a Strategy

Successful engagement requires strong project management and coordination, with a clear purpose, objectives, specified processes, and intended outcomes. As the primary strategy to underlay and support project outcomes, engagement for AFNCI led to multiple strategies, some occurring simultaneously to correspond with meeting project objectives and deliverables. Community-based and culturally supported engagement activities included:

- Offering protocol to Knowledge Holders, for opening and closing meetings with prayer.
- Securing commitments to creating safe spaces for trusting relationships to emerge among project participants.
- Engagement processes focused on facilitating the exchange of experiential stories linked to cancer.
- Applying First Nations languages and narratives as a basis to improve practice and communication between healthcare providers and First Nations patients and families.
- Pairing Knowledge Holders/Practitioners and oncology champions to envision a foundation for practice change and support culturally safe pathways for First Nations patients and families.

The multiple engagements undertaken to develop understandings during the AFNCI collaborative partnership process are illustrated in Fig. 69.2.

Collaborative Partnership Framework

Collaboration is essential for Indigenous communities to envision pathways that mirror their worldviews. For example, the philosophy and belief of First Nations around kinship between people, animals, land, and the spirit world supported an authentic collaborative partnership and became a necessary conceptual element. While this is a simplistic articulation of how relationality is fundamental to Indigenous ways of being and doing, it can be used to understand the sense of "naturalness" and "familiarity" that many Indigenous peoples display toward one another. From within this space, the AFNCI Collaborative Partnership Framework was realized, as captured in Fig. 69.3. The Framework starts at the center and moves outward.

Essential to the Framework is the placement and rightful role of First Nations Knowledge Holders/Practitioners, who provide guidance and directives regarding First Nations communities. These individuals possess knowledge of their

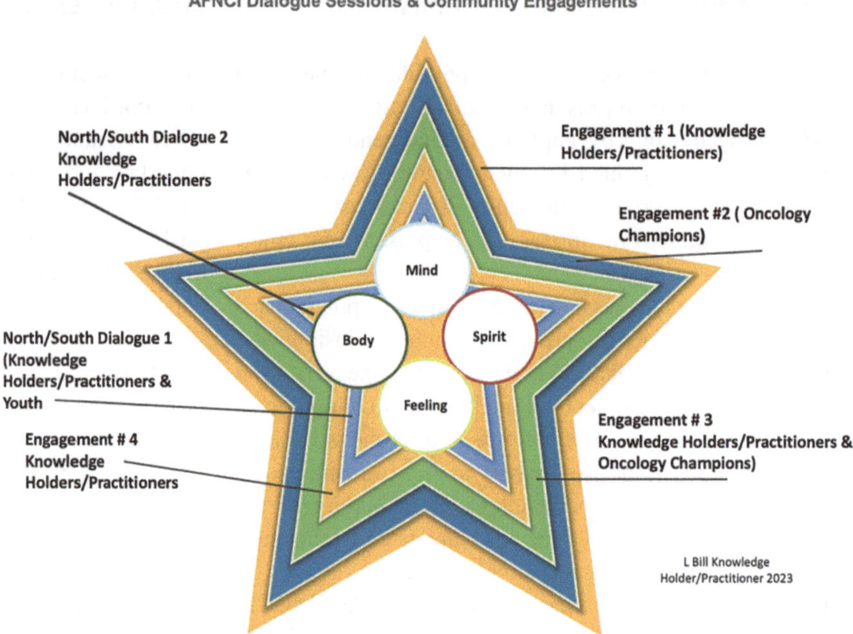

Fig. 69.2 AFNCI community engagement

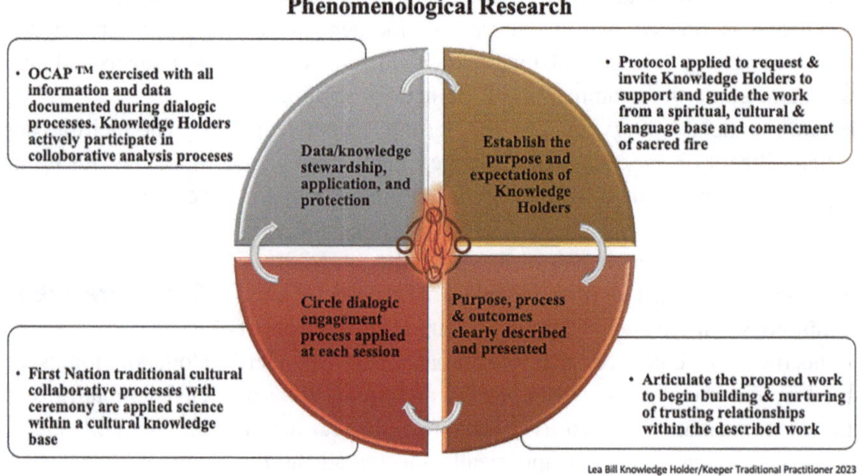

Fig. 69.3 AFNCI Collaborative Partnership Framework

histories and the trauma experienced by communities, along with the consequences of these histories on individuals, families, and communities. In addition, Knowledge Holders/Practitioners' understanding of worldviews, practices, protocols, and health and healing practices are critical to underpinning First Nations–driven solutions and were identified as a key to the Collaborative Partnership Framework.

The Framework is a strategic vehicle to implement system and practice change, and a mechanism that supports sustainability. Collaborative partnerships, with the capability to establish and maintain authentic relationships based in trust and the capability to include dialogue, need to be recognized as an essential and powerful tool for supporting systems and practice change.

Knowledge Holder/Practitioner Roles and Guidance

Each Knowledge Holder/Practitioner has observed, participated in, and led many cultural collaborative processes. Being reared within these social cohesive processes and assisted in many kinds of ancestral cultural practices, they are at ease within this collective and collaborative approach. Furthermore, they were keenly aware of their personal responsibility and roles within cultural knowledge processes.

Once the sacred fire was awakened for AFNCI, a legacy of living wisdom was placed in the center to support the concept of the whole health and wellbeing of the family and community. Truth and honesty were essential, as they identified the gaps created by intolerance and racism within healthcare settings. Knowledge Holders/Practitioners were adept at speaking their truth, through forthright stories that conveyed authentic knowledge. They committed wholeheartedly to the project, selflessly giving time and energy to the circle in their capacity as key partners with a focus on improving cancer pathways and outcomes.

The role of Knowledge Holders/Practitioners involved holding space and providing the cultural linguistic knowledge for analyzing and generating meaning from participants' narratives. They provided guidance with selecting the best approaches for participant involvement, such as directing the team to involve youth in AFNCI activities to support inter-generational knowledge transfer and including family members who had lost members from cancer. As key cultural leaders, ceremonialists, and advisors, they identified themes and subject matter for an oncology cultural safety curriculum to be piloted through an AFNIGC learning management system. Additionally, they contributed to creating the messaging for cancer prevention and screening along with teachings about traditional health and healing practices.

Knowledge Mobilization

AFNCI project leads, as Indigenous researchers, embarked on the project with prior knowledge and understanding of cultural collaborative processes. They recognized the process as a living process embedded within First Nations customs and oral traditions. Knowledge Holders/Practitioners and other project participants each contributed to knowledge transfer and exchange (knowledge mobilization) by sharing their experiences and identifying priority areas requiring change.

As a vehicle for knowledge transfer and exchange, the circle model was used during story and narrative sharing to support collaborative partner dialogue sessions. Furthermore, culturally based methods of sharing knowledge were applied to create an environment where practice change implementation could be expressed, defined, and elaborated upon within circle technology (roundtable talks) dialogue sessions, team meetings, engagement sessions, and learning events. A systematic approach of moving from one participant to the next provided an opportunity for participants to elaborate on their contributions and build upon the circles' understanding.

Cultural knowledge transference (the sharing of Indigenous and cultural knowledge) is a collective activity. Together the Knowledge Holders/Practitioners and all participants added layer upon layer, as their oral histories created a rich living knowledge base from which to implement and align practice changes and address issues around cancer care. Trust and kinship naturally formed among the group, as the Knowledge Holders/Practitioners brought a strong family approach to the project and created a sense of social responsibility within the circle. Each Knowledge Holder/Practitioner spoke of the gaps existing within oncology care and provided a platform for impactful knowledge exchange.

Conclusion

AFNCI was an iteratively developed collaborative partnership project, created with an existing core team of Knowledge Holders/Practitioners from the different Treaty regions across Alberta, all with direct lived experience with cancer. The AFNCI project demonstrates applied phenomenological research as a powerful approach to demonstrate collaborative decision-making and learning processes. It influenced "group mindedness" to collaboratively organize around an issue in a dialogic cultural way, embedded within collective cultural collaborative processes. A kinship system was formed between the Knowledge Holders/Practitioners and the research team leads, forming lifelong bonds of knowledge exchange and mutual trust.

The high-level discussions among the Knowledge Holders/Practitioners are customary ways of "coming to know" and "coming to be as a collective and community." Any issue affecting the community is attended to—through the engagement of mind, body, and spirit by the individual. It is then taken into the wider circle of influence, such as the peer group, community, and other circles. These collaborative processes, embedded within the ethos of community, provide opportunities to heal while supporting purposeful action with outcomes that meet needs and fill gaps. Much interest has been garnered throughout the provincial cancer care agencies for the oncology education and education training developed as a main output of the AFNCI work.

References

1. FNIGC/CGIPN. *The First Nations Principles of OCAP®* [Internet]. Available from: https://fnigc.ca/ocap-training/
2. Alberta First Nation Information Governance Centre. Welcome [Internet]. Available from: https://www.afnigc.ca/main/index.php?id=home
3. Ermine E. The Ethical Space of Engagement. *Indigenous Law Journal*. 2007;6(1):193–203.

International Collaborations in Indigenous Health Research

70

Gail Garvey, Sam Faulkner, Dan McAullay, Amy Budrikis, and Natalie Strobel

Key Points

- Indigenous and Tribal peoples share a wealth of knowledge and understanding of health and wellbeing, together with an imperative to lead Indigenous health research.
- Improving the health and wellbeing of Indigenous peoples in Australia, Aotearoa New Zealand, and Canada is the goal driving the continued partnership between three medical research funding agencies.
- In addition to initiatives at the international level, Australia has created many positive opportunities to accomplish the intentions of the Tripartite Agreement and to broaden the scope of international collaborations among Indigenous health researchers.

This chapter explores the benefits, challenges, and outcomes of international Indigenous and Tribal peoples' health research collaborations and the future of these collaborations in the context of the Tripartite Agreement on International Indigenous Health between Australia, Canada, and Aotearoa New Zealand. Our goal is to provide broad brushstrokes that raise awareness of the context and potential for international Indigenous health collaborations.

Conversations with three Indigenous health research leaders inform the content of this chapter.

- Gail Garvey AM, a proud Kamilaroi woman, a National Health and Medical Research Council (NHMRC) Research Leadership Fellow, and Professor of Indigenous Health Research in the Faculty of Medicine at the University of Queensland.
- Sam Faulkner, a Torres Strait Islander and Aboriginal woman from the Wuthuthi and Yadhaigana peoples, Cape York Peninsula and Badu and Moa Islands, and NHMRC Director of Aboriginal and Torres Strait Islander Health Advice.
- Dan McAullay, a Noongar man from the south-west of Western Australia, and Dean of Kurongkurl Katitjin and Director of Aboriginal Research at Edith Cowan University. He was a member of the review panel for the first International Collaborative Indigenous Health Research Partnership (ICIHRP) program.

The Tripartite Agreement

The Tripartite Agreement is a three-country international Indigenous health agreement between the Canadian Institutes of Health Research (CIHR), the Health Research Council of New Zealand (HRC NZ), and the National Health and Medical Research Council (NHRMC) Australia. Signed in 2002, the Agreement made a commitment to improving Indigenous peoples' health by supporting research activities and actions that further understanding of Indigenous cultures, health, research experiences, and approaches to health and wellness. Central to developing and undertaking activities is respecting and harnessing the expertise, culture, and values of Aboriginal and Torres Strait Islander, Māori, First Nations, Inuit, and Métis peoples. The Agreement is renewed every five years and, at the time of writing, is in the process of being renewed for another five-year period.

The four key intentions of the current Tripartite Agreement are to:

1. Strengthen the capacity and capability of Indigenous health and medical researchers.
2. Use international research initiatives and calls for research to encourage international collaboration on health and research issues of relevance to Indigenous populations.
3. Agree on research priorities of mutual and shared national priority and refresh these during each five-year term.
4. Support actions that further our understanding of Indigenous peoples' cultures, health or research experiences, and approaches to health and wellness.

G. Garvey (ed.), *Indigenous and Tribal Peoples and Cancer*, https://doi.org/10.1007/978-3-031-56806-0_70

Operationalizing the Tripartite Agreement at the International Level

While the idea of bringing together three agencies and countries with a shared goal has been positive, operationalizing the Agreement's intentions is an ongoing challenge at the funding level, given the different ways each agency operates, its maturity bases, and its resourcing and priorities.

Initially, the Agreement sought to fund international research projects between the three countries (Australia, Canada, and Aotearoa New Zealand). The International Collaborative Indigenous Health Research Partnership (ICIHRP) program was created to support international networking and linkages between Indigenous health researchers. In the first year of the program, ICIHRP focused on the theme of "resilience," with one successful project that investigated the role of resilience in Indigenous communities in response to sexually transmissible infections and blood-borne viruses.

In 2009, ICIHRP funded a limited number of research projects including (1) health literacy among cardiovascular disease patients, their families, and healthcare providers; (2) reducing chronic dental disease in early childhood; and (3) the impact of professional health education in mitigating disparities in chronic disease care.

The ICIHRP grant scheme proved difficult to administer, as projects could only be funded if they were fundable in all three countries. Owing to each country's medical research funding and assessment criteria, only a handful of project applications were successful.

The second iteration of the Tripartite Agreement (2007–2011) directed funding to short-term researcher exchanges to strengthen the Indigenous health research workforce, from early researchers and beyond. Participating Indigenous researchers found these highly valuable, providing international networking opportunities, furthering interest in their field of research, and identifying potential mentors and job opportunities in the country of exchange after the program. The exchanges were a great investment in people. The short-term exchange and financial support are available to Australian NHMRC Investigator Grant recipients who identify as Aboriginal and/or Torres Strait Islander descent to facilitate and strengthen international collaborations. The NHMRC, CIHR, and HRC NZ have also held mentoring and capacity-building workshops that provide face-to-face opportunities for networking between Indigenous health researchers.

In 2019, HRC NZ collaborated with the NHMRC and CIHR to host the International Indigenous Health Research Workshop in Auckland, which brought together 56 Indigenous health researchers to share experiences, present research, and develop collaborative activities. Early-career, mid-career, and established researchers from Māori, Aboriginal and Torres Strait Islander, First Nations, Inuit, and Métis backgrounds were overwhelmingly positive about the event [1].

Australian Initiatives and Intentions

In alignment with the Tripartite Agreement, Indigenous Australian researchers are implementing opportunities to enable international collaborations and share ideas and practical knowledge, leading to a range of health research initiatives. These encapsulate the intentions and influence of the Agreement, and represent movements beyond its operational scope, speaking to new pathways for international collaborations.

Strengthening the Capacity of Indigenous Health and Medical Researchers: Indigenous Researcher Networks

Australia has looked to CIHR's model of researcher networks to develop Indigenous capacity in health research, including Aboriginal Capacity and Developmental Research Environments (ACADRE) and the Network Environments for Aboriginal Health Research (NEAHR) [2]. The aim of building capacity has come to fruition in OCHRe (Our Collaborations in Health Research), a national network for Aboriginal and Torres Strait Islander researchers. Funded by the NHMRC and co-led by Gail Garvey AM (University of Queensland), Alex Brown (ANU), Janine Mohamed (Lowitja Institute), and Sandra Eades AO (University of Melbourne), the network is "one of the largest cohorts of Aboriginal and Torres Strait Islander researchers ever assembled in Australia" [3]. Its vision is to create a culturally resilient and all-encompassing network of Indigenous researchers spanning Australia and sovereign Indigenous Nations, and to grow the next generation of research leaders. OCHRe's early activities include professional development sessions, dissemination of information about events, employment and scholarship opportunities, and webinars about current issues of importance, such as the recent *Voice to Parliament* webinar. This network will cultivate distinctive competencies at the intersection of culture, science, and health research, ultimately leading to advancements in the health and wellbeing of Indigenous communities.

Encouraging International Collaboration: Healthy Cities Implementation Science Team Grant Scheme

Recently, the NHMRC partnered with the CIHR on the Healthy Cities Implementation Science Team Grant Scheme to support population health research studies focused on evidence-based interventions across multiple urban sites in both countries [4]. This grant opportunity builds on successful collaborations between the two countries. For example, Professor Garvey and her team, in collaboration with Ms Lea Bill and her colleagues in Canada, successfully secured funding for projects focused on supporting healthy lifestyle choices to promote the mental health and wellbeing of Indigenous youth aging out of care in urban settings. The Canadian component includes extending the Australian wellbeing measure for Indigenous youth for the Canadian context (What Matters 2 Youth) [5].

Establishing National Research Priorities: Climate Change and Health

Canada identified climate change as a health priority long before it was recognized in Australia. Between 2000 and 2018, the NHMRC invested approximately $20 million in research on the health implications of environmental change but received few grant applications [6]. This prompted the development of the Healthy Environments and Lives (HEAL) National Research Network in 2021. HEAL is an NHMRC special initiative located in Australia that aims to support environmental change and health research with AUD$10 million over five years. The NHMRC describes the funding as bringing together "Aboriginal and Torres Strait Islander wisdom, public health, epidemiology, sustainable development, and innovative data science and communication methods to address environmental change and its impacts on health across all Australian states and territories" [6].

Challenges and Opportunities: Moving Forward with International Collaboration

With any international collaborations there are challenges, which vary from the complex to the day-to-day. As discussed above, a singular complexity of international collaboration lies in research funding agency resources and funding to develop and assess grant schemes across borders. Other challenges include scheduling online meetings and phone calls between countries spanning multiple time zones. On this point, however, researchers note the significant and rapid improvements in technology, especially videoconferencing software, that emerged during the COVID-19 pandemic. International collaborations work best when there is a champion driver to provide leadership through these challenges.

The intentions of the Tripartite Agreement remain strong as the three agencies move toward signing its next iteration. Ensuring that the three key funding agencies build an intent to collaborate internationally into their own funding streams is a priority. This will make it easier to fund the international components of research studies, allow for the involvement of international investigators, and allow for the transfer of international data. While Indigenous communities share histories and health outcomes, current priorities for Indigenous communities may differ between the three countries and between other nations with Indigenous populations. Therefore, finding and negotiating topics that are of common, current interest to collaborating researchers, such as is the case with cancer research, are of great significance.

Desktop research, such as systematic reviews and meta-analyses that bring together findings from multiple countries, can help establish common interests and represent another form of international collaboration. Such reviews highlight not only similar histories and outcomes but reveal which interventions might be transferable and offer opportunities to learn from interventions that have been less successful. Building on the Tripartite Agreement, the CIHR, HRC, and NHMRC came together with the Cochrane Collaboration in 2015 to prepare a series of special collections about three important topic areas for Indigenous health, namely diabetes, fetal alcohol spectrum disorders, and suicide prevention. Sam Faulkner and Professor Davina Ghersi from NHMRC Research Policy and Translation, who co-edited the collections, note that these collections can "raise awareness of the need for better and more relevant research in these areas" by highlighting the areas that may be lacking [7]. For example, most Cochrane reviews about suicide prevention focused on pharmacological interventions and didn't evaluate non-drug interventions alone, or community interventions, or studies of Indigenous populations. Bringing reviews together in this way offers pertinent avenues for research. Another example is the Care for Child Development (CCD) program led by Dan McAullay and Natalie Strobel at Edith Cowan University. CCD aims to provide community-based interventions to enhance Indigenous mothers' capacity to engage, communicate, and meet their child's neurodevelopmental requirements during the 24 months following childbirth. It builds on a systematic review of the effectiveness of the CCD program across 19 countries.

Finally, while the Tripartite Agreement exists between Australia, Canada, and Aotearoa New Zealand, working and sharing with other Indigenous peoples around the world is essential, and there is a potential need for a much larger global research collaboration network. International agreements are a way to share knowledge and learn from other countries and researchers, which may have similar problems and be able to share solutions.

References

1. HRC NZ. *Indigenous health researchers from New Zealand, Australia and Canada convene in Auckland* [Internet]. 2019 Dec 6 [cited 2023 Nov 2]. Available from: https://www.hrc.govt.nz/news-and-events/indigenous-health-researchers-new-zealand-australia-and-canada-convene-auckland

2. Canadian Institute of Health Research. *Network Environments for Aboriginal Health Research (NEAHR)* [Internet]. 2011 Aug 31 [cited 2023 Nov 2]. Available from: https://cihr-irsc.gc.ca/e/27071.htm
3. The University of Queensland. *OCHRe (Our Collaborations in Health Research* [Internet]. [cited 2023 Nov 2]. Available from: https://public-health.uq.edu.au/project/ochre-our-collaborations-health-research
4. NHNMC. *NHMRC-CIHR Healthy Cities Implementation Science Team Grant Scheme 2021* [Internet]. [cited 2023 Nov 2]. Available from: https://www.nhmrc.gov.au/funding/find-funding/nhmrc-cihr-healthy-cities-implementation-science-team-grant-scheme-2021
5. The University of Queensland. *Health & Wellbeing of Indigenous Youth in Out-of-Home Care* [Internet]. [cited 2023 Nov 2]. Available from: https://public-health.uq.edu.au/project/health-wellbeing-indigenous-youth-out-home-care
6. NHMRC. *Environmental change* [Internet]. [cited 2023 Nov 2]. Available from: https://www.nhmrc.gov.au/research-policy/research-priorities/environmental-change
7. Ghersi D, Faulkner S. Special collection on Indigenous Health. *Med J Aust.* 2015;203(6):242. https://doi.org/10.5694/mja15.00879

Part VII

Clinical Trials and Genomics

Improving Cancer Trial Participation for Indigenous People

71

Linda U. Krebs, Linda Burhansstipanov, Brian Kelly, Nina Scott, Tina Noutsos, Joanne Shaw, Marg Lavery, Joan Torony, Julianne Rose, Te Hao Apaapa-Timu, Darren Germaine, Elizabeth Meusburger, and Gail Garvey

Key Points

- Cancer patients who participate in clinical trials typically experience better outcomes, including increased survival and improved emotional and spiritual wellbeing.
- Diverse representation in clinical trials is a matter of health equity, fairness, and public trust.
- Trial participants should reflect the population affected by the disease.
- Raising awareness, providing education, improving access, and allowing people to remain in their communities are essential for improving clinical trial diversity.
- Community visits to raise awareness and build relationships of trust and safety are important first steps in recruiting Indigenous people to clinical trials.

Cancer patients who participate in clinical trials typically experience better outcomes. They receive early access to new treatments, increased survival, and improved wellbeing. Clearly, clinical trial participants should represent the population affected by the disease being studied. In addition, people experiencing the disease should have equal access to trials, regardless of their location, culture, or socioeconomic background. However, equal access is rarely the reality. This chapter considers Indigenous peoples' access to clinical trials in Australia, the USA, and Aotearoa New Zealand.

The Australian Context

The Australian Government is committed to conducting clinical trials and ensuring that Australia remains at the forefront of cancer research, including its origins and treatment. Clinical trial participants currently do not represent the country's diverse population. While little is known about the participation of Aboriginal and Torres Strait Islander people owing to under-reporting of Indigenous status, they are thought to be under-represented in clinical trials [1].

Over 100 clinical trials in Australia are known to have focused on Aboriginal and Torres Strait Islander people. When invited, Aboriginal and Torres Strait Islander people generally participate. However, only about 1.5% of all trials in Australia focus specifically on Indigenous health, and very few of these focus on cancer. Given the disparities in cancer outcomes experienced by Aboriginal and Torres Strait Islander people, their involvement in clinical trials is critical for reasons of equity and social justice. In addition, evidence suggests that cancer patients who participate in clinical trials typically experience better survival and wellbeing outcomes. This underscores the critical importance of ensuring equity in access to critical trials.

Cancer Trial Recruitment in the Northern Territory

The Alan Walker Cancer Care Centre in Darwin (Northern Territory—NT) has a clinical trial unit, which, in 2023, had 23 ongoing clinical trials (43% of all clinical trials in the NT).

Approximately one-third of the NT population identifies as Aboriginal and/or Torres Strait Islander. However, only 15 patients (6%) in the 23 clinical trials identify as such. Clinical trial staff experience several barriers to Indigenous enrollment, including consent processes; language and literacy difficulties; communication between patients, families, and providers; and geographical remoteness.

To overcome these barriers, staff focus on improving health literacy and working with sponsors to create opportunities for local clinical trial enrollment. For example, one recent trial offered a teletrials option, designed to improve participation among the rural and remote population, including Aboriginal and Torres Strait Islander people. To help address health literacy, staff develop resources designed to create meaning in a way that makes sense within individuals' lived experiences and worldviews, often linked with local

G. Garvey (ed.), *Indigenous and Tribal Peoples and Cancer*, https://doi.org/10.1007/978-3-031-56806-0_71

analogies. For example, vines growing over a fig tree are a useful metaphor for tumor cell growth in the body, and pandanus seed falling from a tree into a creek is a metaphor for cancer metastasis.

Cancer Trial Recruitment in Northern New South Wales

The Regional, Rural and Remote (R3) Clinical Trails Enabling Program was established in 2023, with four-year funding from the Australian Government. This program is designed to increase clinical trial participation among Indigenous people in northern New South Wales. It aims to establish a strong, sustainable, local clinical trials support infrastructure and workforce; develop and implement systems and partnerships; and increase clinicians' participation in clinical trials. Its goal is to provide a virtual clinical trials support unit and deliver increased and more equitable access to clinical trials for patients in regional, rural, and remote areas.

A key focus of the program is increasing Aboriginal and Torres Strait Islander participation, primarily through a community engagement strategy. Staff engage with local communities, visit Aboriginal Medical Services, and initiate conversations about health and clinical trials. Future plans include creating a network of Aboriginal managers across New South Wales tasked with improving clinical trial recruitment and retention, opening up access in remote locations, and increasing participant diversity.

The US Context

In the USA, participation in clinical trials by American Indians and Alaska Natives (AI/AN) is an ongoing concern. Recruitment and retention are difficult, and trial findings may not be shared in ways that are relevant to participants. A key problem is that AI/AN people cannot see themselves in the data. Trials frequently report breakdowns for Caucasian, African American, and Hispanic populations, and label all remaining racial groups as "other." There are no benefits to participation for Indigenous communities who are invisible in the data.

In 1977, the US Office of Management and Budget released Statistical Policy Directive No. 15, identifying required racial groups to be included in all documents [2]. It specified that AI/AN must be included and identified as a separate population of interest. All clinical trials are required to report findings for all racial groups. To achieve this, studies often combine data from multiple years, so that results remain anonymous.

Many AI/AN people currently lack best-practice cancer treatments, and treatment may be both prolonged and require extensive travel. Most trials compare current recommended treatments with new experimental arms (perhaps adding a medication to improve patient outcomes). Therefore, a key advantage of clinical trial participation is, at a minimum, the current best-practice recommended treatment. According to Native American Cancer Education for Survivors (NACES) study data, few AI/AN patients who are not clinical trial participants receive recommended treatments [3].

Walking Forward, at Monument Health Hospital, Rapid City, South Dakota seeks to address this. Although AI/ANs have access to cancer services at Monument Health, for many this involves extensive travel, with a median distance of 140 miles. Walking Forward has had significant success recruiting and retaining Indigenous patients in clinical trials. In 2020, it recruited more than 4500 patients, with the participation of Indigenous patients equal to that of all other facilities combined [4]. It reports increased cancer treatment compliance and has recruited patients for a genetic study exploring increased incidence of side effects among American Indians receiving external beam radiation compared with non-native patients. The strategies used by Walking Forward to recruit and retain trial participants are summarized elsewhere in this volume.

The Aotearoa New Zealand Context

Aotearoa New Zealand is in the process of restructuring its approach to clinical trials. Currently, Māori experience inequitable access to clinical trials, and contemporary research tools and measures are incompatible with Māori worldviews and methodologies. The Enhancing Aotearoa New Zealand Clinical Trials report [5] proposed a model and roadmap for national clinical trials and networks for the general population. iNZight Analytics were contracted to provide a Māori analysis of the data giving insight into the unique Indigenous experience and the investments required to achieve a more equitable clinical trial ecosystem [6].

Research with 130 non-Māori researchers found that while some sought to improve their cultural research skills, others continued with inadequate consultation processes and methodologies or reverted to narrow methods of not consulting with Māori regarding the relevance and suitability of research protocols [6]. The study found that 31% used Kaupapa Māori methodology (i.e., research practices that follow Māori processes from inception to dissemination). Of note, many non-Māori researchers requested further training on topics such as Kaupapa Māori methodology, Māori data sovereignty, and data governance, indicating they want to understand the priorities of Māori researchers.

Māori workforce development continues to be a significant issue in Aotearoa New Zealand. Only 4% of the workforce is Māori. Clinical trials need qualified Māori leadership to guide and develop appropriate methodologies and research agendas. Māori communities remain under-funded and under-resourced, and racism continues to interfere with recruitment and retention in clinical trials.

The Harti Clinical Trial in New Zealand

The Harti clinical trial was designed to develop a culturally safe model of cancer care for children and their families. It included 965 participants (56% were Māori; >50% were less than one year old); half were randomized to the Harti intervention and the rest to regular hospital care.

The intervention included a Māori Model of Care, with culturally appropriate, modified internal clinic culture protocols to create a safe, culturally aligned, racism-free space. Patients and whānau (extended family) reported feeling valued, respected, and awarded dignity and gained confidence in navigating the system. Based on feedback, staff continued to revise protocols guided by expert advisors, whānau, clinical staff, and evidence reviews, and to track improvements.

Based on this success, program staff expanded the Māori Model of Care to adult and elder cancer patients through the Whānau Hauora Integrated Response Initiative (WHIRI) clinical trial. Individuals who have been referred to Waikato Hospital with a high suspicion of cancer are eligible for participation. The trial involves three phases: (1) review of clinical notes and interviews with Māori cancer patients and their whānau, (2) project co-design guided by the He Pikinga Waiora Framework (Māori implementation framework), and (3) pilot testing with Māori patients and their families.

Key Issues Relevant to Indigenous Participation in Clinical Trials

1. *Racism*: Racism in a cancer facility offering clinical trials results in few or no Indigenous participants. Racism manifests in at least three ways [7, 8]: (1) institutional racism, leading to clinical trial information not being shared with Indigenous patients; (2) interpersonal racism, which may manifest as bias about Indigenous patients' likelihood to comply with clinical trial protocols, rude or disrespectful treatment by service providers and co-workers, or service refusal; and (3) internal racism, which may involve Indigenous people accepting negative racial characterizations and demonstrating lack of respect for other Indigenous peoples [8, 9].
2. *Implicit or explicit eligibility bias*: Some physicians assume Indigenous patients will not comply with clinical trial protocols and decide not to discuss the topic. However, Indigenous cancer patients typically say they are willing to do whatever is necessary to survive the disease.
3. *Distrust of research*: A history of unethical research has created distrust among Indigenous people. For example, in the USA, members of the Havasupai Tribe consented to blood sampling to understand a genetic link to type 2 diabetes. Years later, participants learned that these blood samples had been shared, without their consent, with other researchers to study other diseases [10, 11].
4. *Lack of consideration for cultural aspects of Indigenous life*:
   (a) Indigenous people may perceive health differently from non-Indigenous people and may have different perceptions of health and wellbeing that are conceptualized through beliefs about life, land, and community.
   (b) Many Indigenous people have limited or no awareness and understanding of cancer and clinical trials.
   (c) Indigenous people within and across countries speak many Indigenous languages and dialects [12, 13]. Creating information materials in all the Indigenous languages spoken in the world is not feasible. Similarly, each Indigenous culture has its own icons and symbols, with unique connotations, and these cannot be simply dropped into materials in an attempt to be inclusive.
   (d) Communication gaps are most pronounced in remote areas, where cultural and linguistic differences are the greatest. Language and culture are closely related, amplifying these gaps [14].
5. *Trial information is often in medical language*: Trial materials, especially informed consent, are often long and complex. If information is not communicated in an understandable way, or if physicians explain options too quickly or using unfamiliar language, patients are more likely to say no.
6. *Demands or costs of participation can limit access*: Trial participants may face challenges related to costs (e.g., time off work, fees), transport difficulties (magnified by increased distance from trial sites), and support requirements (emotional or physical). Due to these factors, clinical trial participation may not be feasible even for those who want to participate.
7. *Systemic barriers*:
   (a) There are often insufficient trials for cancers common among Indigenous people.
   (b) Few Indigenous people are involved in the development, implementation, and analysis of cancer clinical trial research.
   (c) Non-Indigenous methodologies ignore Indigenous cultures and strengths, contributing to inequities and

low clinical trial participation. There often are insufficient Indigenous healthcare staff to help bridge this problem.
   (d) Large clinical trials may take 10 years or longer before findings are available. While participants are not expected to personally benefit from participation, they need to be informed of the findings.
   (e) Strict inclusion and exclusion criteria can create barriers to Indigenous participation. Indigenous peoples are over-represented in adverse health conditions and chronic diseases which may lead to clinical trial ineligibility [15].
   (f) Funding is frequently limited to specific trial activities and may not extend to activities such as hosting meetings to enable partnerships and establish trust with Indigenous communities.
   (g) Many clinical trials are based in universities and hospitals, which may not be safe spaces for Indigenous peoples.
8. *Poor recruitment and retention strategies*: Many trials recruit participants using advertisements in traditional media or social media and these rarely result in Indigenous people requesting information. Face-to-face discussions are most appropriate for recruiting Indigenous peoples to clinical trials.
9. *Language and communication barriers*: Many words integral to clinical trials can alienate and/or confuse potential clinical trial participants. Some Indigenous participants may believe they will receive the placebo and not the actual treatment. Time and effort are required to redress misconceptions. Researchers must take such communication needs seriously in order to avoid less-optimal healthcare outcomes, lack of trust and engagement with healthcare settings, and non-compliance with treatment plans [16].
10. *Insufficient participation information*: Researchers require more information concerning when, where, and how Indigenous peoples can participate in clinical trials, and why participants do not continue or are dropped from clinical trials.

Solutions and Key Components of Success

1. *Overcome and address racism*:
   (a) Treat patients with dignity, respect, and value; this will lead to further positive engagement with services.
   (b) Build trusting relationships with Indigenous communities and services.
   (c) Involve Indigenous people in leadership and decision-making roles.
   (d) Involve staff, providers, Indigenous leaders, communities, and families in identifying problems and co-designing solutions, including system-wide modifications.
2. *Improve communication* [17]:
   (a) Utilize medical and cultural interpreters.
   (b) Use diagrams and illustrations.
   (c) Demonstrate procedures first where possible.
   (d) Use plain language and avoid idioms.
   (e) Allow extra time for Indigenous patients to respond or tell their stories.
   (f) Seek culturally meaningful analogies that make sense within the patient's lived experience and worldview.
3. *Recruitment and retention*:
   (a) Re-examine recruitment and retention protocols.
   (b) Ensure inclusion of Indigenous populations.
   (c) Create programs such as Walking Forward to guide recruitment and retention.
   (d) Design trials with more time and increased resources to engage Indigenous communities.
   (e) Conduct trials in regional and remote locations. Bringing clinical trials to the community (rather than the community to the trial) will increase awareness and understanding.
4. *Navigation*: Employ trained patient navigators to work with patients and clinical trial recruiters. Indigenous navigators support in-person, one-on-one contact; can discuss clinical trials with patients and families; and support patients throughout their participation. They can help to bridge the gap between services and patients/families [18].
5. *Community engagement and partnerships*: Strong community engagement and Indigenous leadership are key components of success. Trusting partnerships need to be established and supported across countries, states, Tribal nations, and Indigenous organizations.
6. *Education, materials, and resources*: Quality resources can create meaningful local analogies that support depth of meaning and build cancer and clinical trial literacy in ways that are meaningful to patients' lived experiences. Education activities should focus on:
   (a) Improving the health literacy of individuals and their communities.
   (b) Communicating specific clinical trial recruitment resources and the value of participation.
   (c) Collaborating with others to develop specific and relevant resources.
   (d) Providing presentations for staff at health facilities and for communities, starting small and local, and expanding.
   (e) Drawing on successful programs such as Clinical Trials Education for Native Americans (designed to

help Indigenous cancer patients and their families make informed choices about clinical trial participation) [19] and materials such as those available on the Psycho-Oncology Co-operative Research Group website (https://www.pocog.org.au/).

(f) Sharing resources and services and updating them to meet patient and family needs.

Conclusion

Indigenous participation in clinical trials is important, and researchers need to implement specific strategies to ensure Indigenous peoples are represented in trials. Achieving this requires trust, engagement, commitment to genuine partnerships, and willingness to understand people and their communities. Most importantly, it requires time and commitment to work in culturally appropriate and sensitive ways and a workforce dedicated to ensuring that Indigenous peoples are fully represented in clinical trials.

References

1. Cunningham J, Garvey G. Are there systematic barriers to participation in cancer treatment trials by Aboriginal and Torres Strait Islander cancer patients in Australia? *Aust NZ J Public Health.* 2021;45(1):39–45. https://doi.org/10.1111/1753-6405.13059
2. Management and Budget Office. *Initial Proposals for Updating OMB's Race and Ethnicity Statistical Standards* [Internet]. Federal Register; 2023 Jan 27 [cited 2023 Aug 11]. Available from: https://www.federalregister.gov/documents/2023/01/27/2023-01635/initial-proposals-for-updating-ombs-race-and-ethnicity-statistical-standards
3. Goodwin EA, Burhansstipanov L, Dignan M, Jones KL, Kaur JS. The experience of treatment barriers and their influence on quality of life in American Indian/Alaska Native breast cancer survivors. *Cancer.* 2017 Mar 1;123(5):861–8. https://doi.org/10.1002/cncr.30406
4. Dignan MB, Cina K, Sargent M, O'Connor M, Tobacco R, Burhansstipanov L, et al. Increasing Lung Cancer Screening for High-Risk Smokers in a Frontier Population. *J Cancer Educ.* 2023 Sep. https://doi.org/10.1007/s13187-023-02369-7
5. Bloomfield F, Harwood M, Sharples K, Stamp L, Dalziel S, et al. *Enhancing Aotearoa New Zealand Clinical Trials.* Auckland: University of Auckland, Liggins Institute, and University of Otago; 2022 Jul.
6. Greaves L, Diamond L, Sporle A. *Māori Relevant Themes in the Enhancing Clinical Trials Project.* iNZight Analytics; 2022 Apr. Available from: https://cdn.auckland.ac.nz/assets/liggins/docs/Appendix%20A-M%C4%81ori%20Relevant%20Themes%20in%20the%20Enhancing%20Clinical%20Trials%20Project.pdf
7. Jones CP. Levels of racism: A theoretical framework and a gardener's tale. *Am J Public Health.* 2000;90(8):1212–5. https://doi.org/10.2105/ajph.90.8.1212
8. Braun KL, Harjo LD, Burhansstipanov L, Kawakami KL, Palakiko DM, McElfish PA, et al. Addressing racism in Indigenous health. In: Burhansstipanov L, Braun K, editors. *Indigenous Public Health: Improvement through Community-engaged Interventions.* Lexington, KY: University Press of Kentucky; 2022. p. 55–79.
9. Williams DR, Mohammed SA. Discrimination and racial disparities in health: evidence and needed research. *J Behav Med.* 2009;32(1):20–47. https://doi.org/10.1007/s10865-008-9185-0
10. Garrison NA. Awareness and Acceptable Practices: IRB and Researcher Reflections on the Havasupai Lawsuit. *AJOB Prim Res.* 2013 Oct;4(4):55–63. https://doi.org/10.1080/21507716.2013.770104
11. Garrison NA. Genomic Justice for Native Americans: Impact of the Havasupai Case on Genetic Research. *Sci Technol Human Values.* 2013;38(2):201–23. https://doi.org/10.1177/0162243912470009
12. AIATSIS. Languages alive [Internet]. Available from: https://aiatsis.gov.au/explore/languages-alive
13. Statistics Canada. Indigenous languages across Canada [Internet]. 2023 Mar 29. Available from: https://www12.statcan.gc.ca/census-recensement/2021/as-sa/98-200-X/2021012/98-200-X2021012-eng.cfm
14. Amery R. Recognising the communication gap in Indigenous health care. *Med J Aust.* 2017 Jul 3;207(1):13–5. https://doi.org/10.5694/mja17.00042
15. Umaefulam V, Kleissen T, Barnabe C. The representation of Indigenous peoples in chronic disease clinical trials in Australia, Canada, New Zealand, and the United States. Clin Trials. 2022 Feb;19(1):22–32. https://doi.org/10.1177/17407745211069153
16. Mitchell AG, Lowell A, Ralph AP. Report on the Patient Educator service at Royal Darwin Hospital, 2001-2009: Insights into inter-cultural communication in healthcare. Darwin: Aboriginal Resource and Development Services; 2016 [cited 2017 Mar]. Available from: https://www.researchgate.net/publication/304121921_Report_on_the_Patient_Educator_service_at_Royal_Darwin_Hospital_2001-2009_insights_into_inter-cultural_communication_in_healthcare
17. Amery R. Recognising the communication gap in Indigenous health care. *Med J Aust.* 2017 Jul 3;207(1):13–5. https://doi.org/10.5694/mja17.00042
18. Masters-Awatere B, Graham R. Whānau Māori explain how the Harti Hauora Tool assists with better access to health services. *Aust J Prim Health.* 2019;25:471–7. https://doi.org/10.1071/PY19025
19. Burhansstipanov L, Krebs L. Clinical Trials Education for Native Americans. Native American Cancer Research Organization. [cited 2023 Jul 14]. Available from: https://natamcancer.org/userfiles/2021/Repository/NACR-Curricula/RESOURCES_CURRICULA_ClinicalTrials_Educ_Nat_Am_Handout.pdf

Oncology Clinical Trials and Indigenous Native Hawaiian and Other Pacific Islander Erasure

72

Ryan Benavente, Megan Gimmen, Luke Roberto, and Kekoa Taparra

Key Points

- Clinical trials ensure that newly created medical interventions are safe and effective for general use, regardless of race, ethnicity, socioeconomic status, or social background.
- Native Hawaiian and other Pacific Islander (NHPI) patients are underrepresented in oncology clinical trials, despite cancer disparities and willingness to participate.
- Multiple geographic, systemic, and socioeconomic barriers prevent NHPI patients from enrolling in clinical trials.
- NHPI representation in oncology clinical trials can be improved with intentional cultural sensitivity, community engagement, and healthcare workforce diversification.

Clinical trials are instrumental research studies that seek to ascertain the safety, efficacy, and benefit of new pharmaceuticals, surgical procedures, or other medical interventions. Phase III clinical trials are especially important in establishing whether an intervention is consistently effective across the general population [1, 2]. Greater population sampling should lead to heterogeneity in socioeconomic status, race, ethnicity, and geographic region, with data informing the clinical application of new treatments to specific subpopulations [1, 2]. Although race is a social construct, certain ethnic groups and ancestral identifiers may share common genetic patterns, disease burdens, or social circumstances that influence their responses to tested therapies [1, 2]. Inclusivity in clinical trials, therefore, has the potential to promote generalizability for newly developed treatments.

Current Representation Issues

Despite efforts to improve racial inclusivity, clinical trial diversity in the United States remains unsatisfactory, with only 44% of clinical trials reporting participants' race/ethnicity [3]. While disparities in Black and Hispanic representation have been highlighted, Native Hawaiian and Pacific Islander (NHPI) representation is under-acknowledged and underreported (see Gimmen et al. in this volume). NHPI representation comprises only 8% of clinical trials (compared to 70% White, 59% Black, 54% Asian, and 14% American Indian/Alaska Native) [4], making NHPI among the most understudied groups in clinical trials, despite high rates of cancer incidence and mortality in this population.

Barriers to Clinical Trial Participation

Several factors influence clinical trial participation among NHPI communities (Fig. 72.1).

Perceptions of Research

Studies show that members of minoritized groups are willing to participate in research if offered the opportunity [1]. However, distrust of the medical system is common within the NHPI community, derived from a history of colonial trauma and resource and labor exploitation [5]. Many NHPI patients have had negative experiences in healthcare settings and perceive them as places of sickness and suffering, rather than of healing and comfort [5, 6]. For example, Indigenous Chuuk Pacific Islanders report cultural disconnection and discrimination when interacting with Western doctors, exacerbated by a lack of NHPI healthcare professionals [5, 7, 8]. A lack of cross-cultural humility stymies the potential to create strong foundations to build patient–physician relationships. Differences in cultural expectations and norms also create barriers [1, 6]. A study of Native Hawaiian men found that underutilization of healthcare and avoidance of discussing health topics is due in part to a desire to not appear weak or be a burden [1, 6].

Despite these negative perceptions of Western healthcare, many NHPI patients value their overall health and wellbeing [5, 6]. Native Hawaiian values, including pono (harmony/

G. Garvey (ed.), *Indigenous and Tribal Peoples and Cancer*, https://doi.org/10.1007/978-3-031-56806-0_72

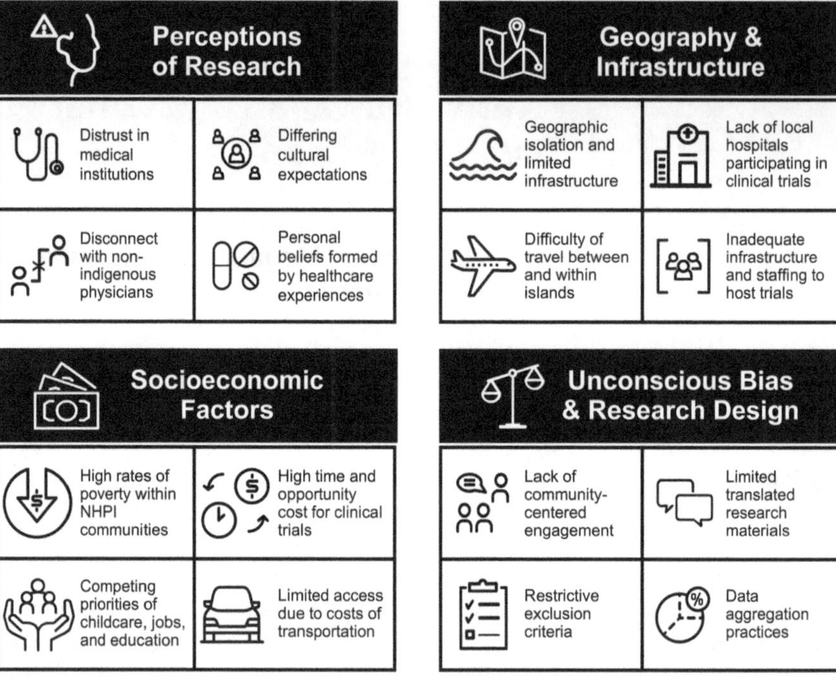

Fig. 72.1 Barriers to NHPI participation in clinical trials

righteousness), are embedded in community, evidenced by the prevalence of Indigenous healers and health teachers. Research has found that NHPI patients are willing to participate in clinical research when provided with complete information. "Unwillingness" to participate is not a limiting factor; rather, an accumulation of structural barriers, many embedded within the research process itself, make it difficult for NHPI individuals to participate in clinical trials [1].

Geographic and Structural Barriers

While there is a significant NHPI population in the continental United States, most of the population remains on remote and isolated islands across the Pacific, with some regions, such as the Federal States of Micronesia and the Commonwealth of the Northern Mariana Islands, composed of several smaller island communities, further subdividing the populations [5]. Uneven population distribution has led to disparate healthcare access across Oceania. While Hawai'i has 28 hospitals, the 28 populated areas of the Marshall Islands rely on two hospitals—in Majuro and Ebeye [5]. Access to subspecialty care is often challenging. Hawai'i—the most urbanized of the Pacific Islands—is home to only one American College of Radiology–accredited radiation oncology center that services the entire state and the United States Affiliated Pacific Islands (USAPI).

Distance and travel times to clinical sites are major barriers to recruitment, discouraging enrollment and adherence [1]. These are even more extreme for remote islands separated by vast distances of ocean. For the Indigenous people of Yap in Micronesia, the nearest major hospital, on Guåhan, is only accessible by limited boat or plane options, and patients are unlikely to travel frequently for check-ups and treatment [5]. Even in Hawai'i, with its major airports, travel duration to clinical trial sites is both substantial and financially and environmentally unsustainable. Once on island, ground transportation can be a further challenge, due to a lack of paved roads or reliable vehicles [5]. Thus, incentivizing patients to participate in clinical trials, even those with potential life-saving benefits, can be difficult throughout the Pacific.

Researchers are even less likely to conduct clinical trials outside of Hawai'i. In a study of 83 clinical trials, only 6% were conducted in the USAPI and the rest in Hawai'i or the continental United States, possibly owing to the lack of infrastructure and funding to conduct clinical trials in island hospitals [5, 9, 10]. Lack of community outreach and/or lack of general researcher interest are likely other contributing factors, as even telehealth and focus group studies are not widely conducted [1, 5, 9]. The need for oncology care remains strong throughout the Pacific Islands, particularly by healthcare professionals deeply rooted in these islands.

Socioeconomic Barriers

An estimated 50% of clinical trial participants have high socioeconomic status [1]. People from lower socioeconomic backgrounds are likely to face greater challenges, such as multiple jobs, constricting work hours, limited ability to take time off, greater travel distances to hospitals, child and family care, and education, all of which are opportunity costs that conflict with clinical trial participation.

The NHPI population is among the most impoverished in the United States, with 15% living at the poverty line and 6% unemployed [10]. Many NHPI patients are food and housing insecure, and the population experiences an extensive chronic disease burden [5, 10]. The opportunity cost of attending time-consuming clinical trials, therefore, deters eligible NHPI individuals from participating in potentially beneficial treatments.

Unconscious Bias in Research Design

Research design can be unconsciously biased, perpetuating multiple-level inaccessibility. Site selection and time expectations exclude large numbers of eligible NHPI individuals who live in rural or remote areas, lack suitable transportation, have constraining work hours, or have competing familial responsibilities [1, 5, 9].

Modern research recruitment advertising methods (mass media, the internet, television, etc.) may potentially miss eligible NHPI candidates, owing to a lack of phone and internet access in some regions. Furthermore, given the role of trust in Indigenous communities, lack of investment in word-of-mouth marketing, engagement in community norms, or meeting with community leaders further isolates eligible participants [1, 5, 9].

A further barrier is the lack of research materials in Indigenous languages or simple English. Although English is commonly spoken in Hawai'i and Guåhan, native dialects are spoken elsewhere, making understanding of consent forms difficult if they are poorly or simply not translated [1, 5, 9].

Restrictive patient inclusion and exclusion criteria, generally aimed at recruiting "healthier patients" are also a barrier. The NHPI community experiences a high comorbidity and disease burden, combined with a lack of early diagnosis (due to limited preventative services), resulting in more severe end-stage diseases, thus excluding many NHPI patients from trial participation [1, 5].

Finally, NHPI participants are often aggregated with Asian participants during data analysis (see Gimmen et al. in this volume). Historically, this helped to increase the political leverage of both groups; however, in the medical research setting, it masks disparities between them, leading to false and overgeneralized conclusions concerning the health of NHPI communities [5, 9].

Increasing NHPI Representation in Clinical Trials

NHPI individuals, community organizations, and NHPI allies have invested significant effort in improving research participation, as shown in these examples.

- The Ka-Holo trial investigating the therapeutic value of the traditional Hawaiian dance, hula, in treating hypertension, found that the intervention significantly improved blood pressure [11]. This trial should serve as a framework for future studies, demonstrating the integration of clinical science through a culturally relevant lens, led by Indigenous researchers, and aimed at creating health interventions applicable to a particular population [11].
- No Ke Ola Pono o Nā Kāne combined the traditional practice of hale mua (men's house) with cancer and hypertension prevention education to create a culturally relevant space for men to talk about health and foster holistic wellbeing [12].
- Community-based organizations such as 'Imi Hale spread awareness of Native Hawaiian health issues, educate patients about cancer and clinical trials, engage with research leaders, secure funding, and set norms on how research should be conducted within communities [13]. Notably, they have created pathway programs to train young, prospective Indigenous researchers in proper conduct and in gaining exposure to NHPI health issues.
- A Center for Pacific Islander Health has been established at the University of Arkansas to conduct research on the state's growing Marshallese population, emphasizing intercultural communication [14].

While great strides have been taken particularly for Native Hawaiian health, programs that serve other Pacific Islanders are urgently needed.

Cultural Competency and Respect

The future of NHPI-inclusive oncology clinical trials depends on the factors outlined in Fig. 72.2.

To mitigate NHPI mistrust of the medical community, researchers should recruit influential community leaders and leverage established local networks to contribute to study design and oversight, ensuring that communication methods and subject-recruitment practices are culturally informed. Full commitment to building rapport within the community by honoring cultural norms, such as employing oral tradition formats in focus groups or hosting communal events, such as meals or discussions, can nurture long-lasting relationships of trust that support research engagement [10]. Ultimately, bidirectional learning between clinical researchers and the NHPI community is essential.

Intentional research design can lower barriers to participation by offering more flexible data collection methods. Researchers can increase accessibility by collecting data in community or faith centers, offering telemedicine collection in areas with internet access, and providing free transportation to data collection sites [1, 9]. Similarly, investing in the

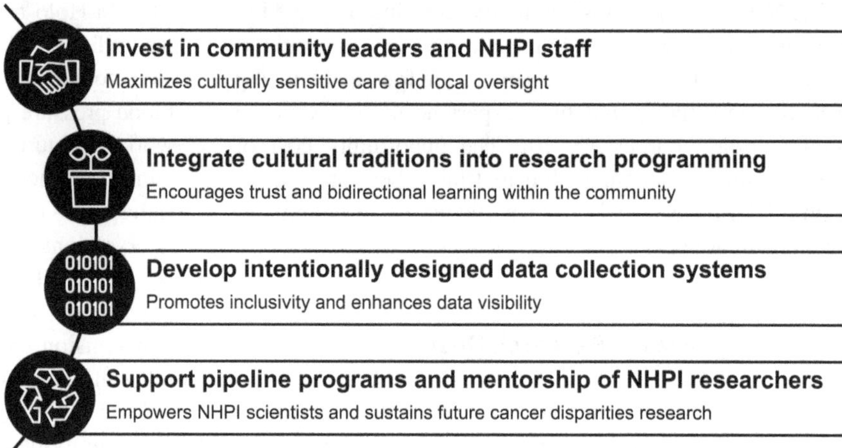

Invest in community leaders and NHPI staff
Maximizes culturally sensitive care and local oversight
Integrate cultural traditions into research programming
Encourages trust and bidirectional learning within the community
010101
010101
010101
Develop intentionally designed data collection systems
Promotes inclusivity and enhances data visibility
Support pipeline programs and mentorship of NHPI researchers
Empowers NHPI scientists and sustains future cancer disparities research

Fig. 72.2 Keys to promoting sustainable clinical research inclusive of NHPI populations

recruitment and training of local investigators empowers communities to have greater research conduct oversight and creates a more approachable presence on the ground. Local investigators, possessing the Indigenous context to retain idiomatic or nonverbal information often lost in verbatim translation, can monitor medication regimens, provide guidance, and collect data from patients at home [9].

These suggestions rely on sufficient research funding, with resources available for community investment. We propose supporting initiatives to restructure clinical trial funding that prioritizes the recruitment of diverse subject pools [1].

- Convenience sampling, which targets one population over another due to ease of access, leads to selection bias and should be avoided. We advocate for proactive engagement with Indigenous communities by financially empowering key community champions and leaders, thereby enhancing access to and awareness of available opportunities [15].
- To ensure that diversity and equity remain clinical research priorities, we support pathway programs such as ʻImi Hale that offer Indigenous youth exposure to the STEM disciplines and provide science and leadership mentorship. While the recent 2023 United States Supreme Court decision on affirmative action has overturned historical precedents in education, it serves as a reminder that the values of diversity and inclusion should not be taken for granted. In this context, allies should make every effort to advocate for the safeguarding of diversity in education and research.

Embracing cultural competency, involving community leaders, and providing flexible data collection methods can foster inclusivity. Prioritizing diverse NHPI populations and supporting NHPI researchers will pave the way for a more equitable healthcare system.

KT was supported by the Stanford Cancer Institute through the Stanford Cancer Institute's Women's Cancer Center Innovation Award and Fellowship Award and by the American Society for Clinical Oncology Dr Judith and Alan Kaur Endowed Young Investigator Award.

References

1. National Academies of Sciences, Engineering, and Medicine; Policy and Global Affairs; Committee on Women in Science, Engineering, and Medicine; Committee on Improving the Representation of Women and Underrepresented Minorities in Clinical Trials and Research, Bibbins-Domingo K, Helman A, editors. *Improving Representation in Clinical Trials and Research: Building Research Equity for Women and Underrepresented Groups*. Washington (DC): National Academies Press; 2022.
2. Varma T, Jones CP, Oladele C, Miller J. Diversity in clinical research: public health and social justice imperatives. *J Medical Ethics*. 2023;49(3): 200–3. https://doi.org/10.1136/medethics-2021-108068
3. Turner BE, Steinberg JR, Weeks BT, Rodriguez F, Cullen MR. Race/ethnicity reporting and representation in US clinical trials: a cohort study. *Lancet Reg Health Americas*. 2022;11:100252. https://doi.org/10.1016/j.lana.2022.100252
4. Taparra K, Benevente R, Shih J, Gimmen MY, Tominez P, Kekumano K, et al. Race and Ethnicity Representation in Phase 2/3 Oncology Clinical Trial Publications: A Systematic Review. *JAMA Health Forum*. 2024;5(6):e241388. https://doi.org/10.1001/jamahealthforum.2024.1388.
5. Pineda E, Benavente R, Gimmen MY, DeVille NV, Taparra K. Cancer Disparities among Pacific Islanders: A Review of Sociocultural Determinants of Health in the Micronesian Region. *Cancers*. 2023;15(5):1392. https://doi.org/10.3390/cancers15051392
6. Layi GA, Cassel K, Taualii M, Berenberg JL, Bantum EO. Understanding disparities in clinical trials for Native Hawaiian men. *J Health Dispar Res Pract*. 2021;14(3):3. Available from: https://digitalscholarship.unlv.edu/jhdrp/vol14/iss3/3
7. Inada MK, Braun KL, Mwarike P, Cassel K, Compton R, Yamada S et al. Chuukese community experiences of racial discrimination and other barriers to healthcare: Perspectives from community members and providers. *Soc Med*. 2019;12(1):3–13.
8. Taparra K, Deville C Jr. Native Hawaiian and Other Pacific Islander Representation Among US Allopathic Medical

Schools, Residency Programs, and Faculty Physicians. *JAMA Netw Open*. 2021;4(9):e2125051. https://doi.org/10.1001/jamanetworkopen.2021.25051

9. McElfish PA, Yeary K, Sinclair IA, Steelman S, Esquivel MK, Aitaoto N, et al. Best Practices for Community-Engaged Research with Pacific Islander Communities in the US and USAPI: A Scoping Review. *J Health Care Poor Underserved*. 2019;30(4):1302–30. https://doi.org/10.1353/hpu.2019.0101
10. Camacho SG, Haitsuka K, Yi K, Seia J, Huh D, Spencer MS, et al. Examining Employment Conditions During the COVID-19 Pandemic in Pasifika Communities. *Health Equity*. 2022;6(1):564–73. https://doi.org/10.1089/heq.2022.0027
11. Kaholokula JK, Look MA, Wills TA, de Silva M, Mabellos T, Seto TB, et al. Kā-HOLO Project: a protocol for a randomized controlled trial of a native cultural dance program for cardiovascular disease prevention in Native Hawaiians. *BMC Public Health*. 2017;17(1):321. https://doi.org/10.1186/s12889-017-4246-3
12. Cassel KD, Hughes C, Higuchi P, Lee P, Fagan P, Lono J, et al. No Ke Ola Pono o Nā Kāne: A Culturally Grounded Approach to Promote Health Improvement in Native Hawaiian Men. *Am J Mens Health*. 2020;14(1):1557988319893886. https://doi.org/10.1177/1557988319893886
13. Braun KL, Tsark JU, Santos L, Aitaoto N, Chong C. Building Native Hawaiian capacity in cancer research and programming. A legacy of 'Imi Hale. *Cancer.* 2006;107(8 Suppl):2082–90. https://doi.org/10.1002/cncr.22157
14. McElfish PA, Felix HC, Bursac Z, Rowland B, Yeary KHK, Long CR, et al. A Cluster Randomized Controlled Trial Comparing Diabetes Prevention Program Interventions for Overweight/Obese Marshallese Adults. *Inquiry.* 2023;60:469580231152051. https://doi.org/10.1177/00469580231152051
15. Andrade C. The Inconvenient Truth About Convenience and Purposive Samples. *Indian J Psychol Med*. 2021;43(1):86–8. https://doi.org/10.1177/0253717620977000

73 Challenges of Recruiting Indigenous Communities to Breast Cancer Clinical Trials

Anna Fitzgerald, Andrea Casey, Ali Coomber, Maria Marama, Rob McNeill, Stacey Morrison, Reena Ramsaroop, and Andrew Redfern

Key Points

- Women from Māori, Pasifika, and Indigenous Australian communities have higher breast cancer mortality rates and lower breast screening rates and are under-represented in clinical trials research compared to wider Australian and Aotearoa New Zealand populations.
- There are many challenges in recruiting these communities to clinical trials, including health systems that require an unreasonably high level of health literacy, communication barriers, socioeconomic factors, cultural literacy in the medical profession, location of trials in urban centers, the provision of culturally appropriate resources and support, cultural differences and historical trauma, clinical trial design, and complex and strained health systems.
- Inequities result in a loss of potential access to new and as yet unavailable treatments for Māori, Pasifika, and Indigenous Australian women. The quality of trial data is also reduced as it is not representative of the whole community.
- An integrated plan of activities is required to improve the diversity of participation in breast cancer clinical trials to include better engagement with and inclusion of Māori, Pasifika, and Indigenous communities and to improve health outcomes in these most disadvantaged groups.

Breast Cancer Trials (BCT) is the largest independent oncology clinical trial research group in Australia and Aotearoa New Zealand. Founded in 1978, BCT conducts a multicenter national and international clinical trials research program, involving 926 researchers in 114 institutions across both countries. To date, more than 17,000 individuals have participated in BCT clinical trials.

BCT hosts free, public events throughout the year, discussing key topics related to breast cancer and clinical trials research. On July 24, 2023, as part of the BCT 44th Annual Scientific Meeting program, BCT held a Q&A at Auckland Museum (Aotearoa New Zealand) on the topic of breast cancer in Māori, Pasifika, and Indigenous communities.

The Q&A panel was made up of women with a history of breast cancer and researchers in the field, including Ms Ali Coomber, Ms Andrea Casey, Ms Maria Marama, Associate Professor Andrew Redfern, Dr Rob McNeill, and Dr Reena Ramsaroop. The event was moderated by journalist and broadcaster, Stacey Morrison (Fig. 73.1).

Background

Breast Cancer in Māori, Pasifika, and Indigenous Australian Communities

Breast cancer is the most common cancer among women in Māori, Pasifika, and Indigenous Australian communities [1, 2].

The report *30,000 Voices: Informing a Better Future for Breast Cancer in New Zealand* found that Pasifika women are 52% more likely and Wāhine Māori (Māori women) are 33% more likely to die of breast cancer within 10 years of diagnosis, compared with Pākehā (European ancestry) women [3]. The report found that Wāhine Māori are more likely to have higher-risk HER2-positive breast cancer than Pākehā women. Pasifika women have the highest rates of life-threatening stage 3 and 4 breast cancer and HER2-positive cancers, and more fast-growing grade 3 tumors than all other ethnicities.

Aboriginal women in Australia are 0.9 times as likely to be diagnosed with breast cancer but are 1.2 times more likely to die from breast cancer than the wider population. The five-year survival rate for Aboriginal women with breast cancer is 81%, compared to 92% for the general population. Breast screening rates for Aboriginal women are 37.3%, compared to 53.2% for non-Indigenous Australians [4].

G. Garvey (ed.), *Indigenous and Tribal Peoples and Cancer*, https://doi.org/10.1007/978-3-031-56806-0_73

Fig. 73.1 The Q&A panel from L–R: Maria Marama, Andrew Redfern, Ali Coomber, Stacey Morrison (moderator), Andrea Casey, Rob McNeill, and Reena Ramsaroop. (Photo: S Ferguson)

Under-representation in Clinical Trial Participation

Research into medical oncology clinical trial participation by ethnic groups in the Auckland region of Aotearoa New Zealand from 2004 to 2010 [5] found an under-representation of Māori and Pasifika communities when compared to participation levels of people of European descent.

An analysis of Australian-based clinical trials registered on the Australian New Zealand Clinical Trials Registry or ClinicalTrials.gov from 2008 to 2018 compared trials with and without a focus on Indigenous health [6]. Of 9206 clinical trials included in the study, only 139 or 1.5% focused on Indigenous health. Among trials with an Indigenous Australian focus, those relating to cancer were significantly under-represented relative to those targeting other conditions, despite cancer being the most common broad cause of death, and breast cancer being the second most common cancer diagnosed among Aboriginal and Torres Strait Islander people [7].

In addition, a gap exists between those cancers studied in phase 3 and 4 clinical trials and those that are most common in Aboriginal and Torres Strait Islander populations [8]. Despite breast cancer accounting for 12.1% of new cancers in Aboriginal and Torres Strait Islander populations, only 7.9% of phase 3 and 4 trials are conducted in the field of breast cancer research.

The following is a summary of the Q&A panel discussion on the challenges of recruiting Māori, Pasifika, and Indigenous Australian populations to breast cancer clinical trials and potential activities that may help to overcome some of these barriers.

Breast Cancer Clinical Trial Recruitment Challenges

Socioeconomics and Geography

- Māori, Pasifika, and Indigenous Australian populations tend to be in lower socioeconomic groups, so financial costs, such as childcare, transport and travel, and time off work are barriers to participating in clinical trials.
- Trial locations frequently do not line up with where Māori, Pasifika, and Indigenous Australian people live. In Aotearoa New Zealand, for example, most cancer trials are Auckland-based, with relatively few trials available in other urban centers.

Culture and Customs

- Medical teams lack understanding of the histories of Indigenous groups and their customs, beliefs, and expectations. As a result, Indigenous communities often have difficulty trusting medical professionals with whom they are unfamiliar or with whom they lack any relationship.
- Negative experiences of the health system lead to distrust of medical professionals and of the health system in general.
- Indigenous people may be affected by historical trauma, in particular the negative hospital or health-setting experiences of past generations. This trauma can be passed down through generations, with family members continuing to share negative experiences. For example, the hospital death of a family member can leave a long-standing impression of hospitals and health settings as

places where people go to die, while the removal of children by authorities from hospital settings can create a lack of trust in the health system. Negative interactions can lead to feelings of powerlessness and vulnerability and the belief that Indigenous individuals or communities cannot impact or change the system.

- Indigenous people want to know what happens to their tissue samples or anything else that may be taken from their bodies. For example, bodily fluids and tissue contain what Māori call their whakapapa (genetic line of descent) and in the absence of information, they can be left wondering if they are part of a big experiment.

Language and Communication

- Information about clinical trials and how Māori, Pasifika, and Indigenous Australian communities can access these is lacking. Clinical trial information is often only written in English and therefore is not accessible to people for whom English is a second language.
- Despite being written for the general patient population, clinical trial materials such as patient consent information may still contain terminology that is unfamiliar and has not been created to include Indigenous trial participants. Lack of understanding of the trial rationale and expectations of specific treatments is a further barrier to participation.
- Navigating the health system is challenging and difficult at the best of times. Insufficient support personnel, including trained navigators and translators with knowledge about clinical trials and the clinical trials process, further exclude Indigenous trial participants.
- Some clinicians may not feel confident working with Indigenous individuals who are not proficient in English.
- Insufficient resources and information are available in Indigenous languages, and these are needed to enable understanding and awareness of clinical trials. For example, Aotearoa New Zealand is home to people from at least 14 Pacific nations. Current promotional campaigns do not appropriately target Indigenous audiences in their own languages.

Clinical Trial Design

- There is a lack of consultation with Māori, Pasifika, and Indigenous Australian communities in the design of clinical trials and a dearth of researchers from these cultural backgrounds.
- Exclusion criteria impact trial participation. For example, lack of English proficiency, the presence of comorbidities, or otherwise poor health status are excluding factors that are more prevalent in Indigenous communities.
- Many clinical trials are global studies and the number of trial participants required in each country may be small. Therefore, attracting meaningful numbers of Māori, Pasifika, and Indigenous Australian populations into these trials can be difficult.

Health System and Funding

- Local and international trials lack the funding to address barriers to the participation of Indigenous Australian, Aotearoa New Zealand, and Pasifika communities.
- Medical professionals recruited to and conducting trials lack cultural competency and safety training, thus diminishing trust.
- Health systems are designed on a Western/European model of healthcare and do not encompass Indigenous models of health and wellbeing.
- Individuals from European backgrounds dominate the health workforce, with an insufficient number of doctors, nurses, and health professionals from Māori, Pasifika, and Aboriginal backgrounds.
- Adequate time is required to ensure the fully informed consent of Indigenous peoples participating in clinical trials. This can be a challenge in overworked health systems where resources are already stretched.
- Bias and racism in the health system lead to lower recruitment.
- Culturally appropriate services to support Indigenous peoples through cancer treatment and post-treatment are insufficient.

Addressing Challenges

- More engagement with Māori, Pasifika, and Indigenous Australian communities and consumers is required, with greater efforts to build trusting relationships.
- Co-design and co-governance principles should be used in the design and implementation of clinical trials to ensure the integration of Indigenous communities.
- Investment and training are needed for a more diverse and culturally appropriate healthcare workforce.
- Support for Indigenous peoples and their families when navigating the health system needs to be increased.
- Health professionals need to receive more cultural competence training and cultural safety training.
- Language and communication barriers need to be reduced and people with different levels of health literacy need to be accommodated.

- Clinical trial exclusion criteria need to be reviewed and amended.
- Clinical trial reimbursement needs to cover a broader range of costs for participants, such as travel, car parking, and childcare.
- Clinicians need to be more aware of the challenges of recruiting Indigenous people to trials.
- Smaller towns and cities outside large urban areas should be included in trial recruitment and participation opportunities.
- Clinical trial campaigns should utilize languages and role models from Indigenous communities to promote the benefits of participating in clinical trials.
- Recruitment to clinical trials should be incentivized.

References

1. NZ Ministry of Health. *Health Status Indicators: Cancer* [Internet]. 2022. Available from: https://www.health.govt.nz/our-work/populations/maori-health/tatau-kahukura-maori-health-statistics/nga-mana-hauora-tutohu-health-status-indicators/cancer
2. Australian Institute of Health and Welfare. *Cancer in Aboriginal and Torres Strait Islander peoples of Australia* [Internet]. 2018. Available from: https://www.aihw.gov.au/reports/cancer/cancer-in-indigenous-australians/contents/about
3. Breast Cancer Foundation NZ. *30,000 Voices: Informing a better future for breast cancer in Aotearoa New Zealand* [Internet]. 2022. Available from: https://www.breastcancerfoundation.org.nz/what-we-do/advocacy/2022-register-report-launch
4. Australian Institute of Health and Welfare. *Cancer in Aboriginal & Torres Strait Islander people of Australia* [Internet]. 2018. Available from: https://www.aihw.gov.au/reports/can/109/cancer-in-indigenous-australians/contents/cancer-type/breast-cancer-in-females
5. Scott J, Hinder V, Ko S. *Snapshot of Ethnicity in Auckland Medical Oncology Clinical Trials. Cancer Trials New Zealand*, University of Auckland, Auckland City Hospital, Auckland District Health Board. Available from: https://www.fmhs.auckland.ac.nz/assets/fmhs/sms/ctnz/docs/NZAcres10_Poster.pdf
6. Xu G, Modi D, Hunter K, Askie L, Jamiseon L, Brown A, Seidley A. Landscape of clinical trial activity focusing on Indigenous health in Australia: an overview using clinical trial registry data from 2008-2018. *BMC Public Health.* 2022 May 14;22(1):971. https://doi.org/10.1186/s12889-022-13338-y
7. Australian Institute of Health and Welfare. *Aboriginal and Torres Strait Islander Health Performance Framework 2020 summary report.* Cat. no. IHPF 2. Canberra: AIHW.
8. Cunningham J, Garvey G. Are there systematic barriers to participation in cancer treatment trials by Aboriginal and Torres Strait Islander cancer patients in Australia? *Aust N Z J Public Health.* 2023;45(1):39–45. https://doi.org/10.1111/1753-6405.13059

Technology to Support Cancer Care Within Communities

74

Linda Fleisher, Andrea Dwyer, and Linda Burhansstipanov

Key Points

- Technology holds great promise and can be leveraged to address patient, provider, and organizational needs and goals in cancer care. It can be a powerful tool if the technology is well-integrated into the center and used to support patient care.
- As larger centers and organizations increasingly rely on technology, smaller Indigenous programs are being left behind. Many technologies are not developed based on the needs, challenges faced, or guidance from Indigenous communities and may not be accessible or appropriate. In this way, IT can contribute to health disparities by entrenching a digital divide.
- Investing in technology requires careful consideration and diligence in informed decision-making for program leaders.
- An important example of technology being integrated into healthcare practice was developed in 2016 by the Native American Cancer Research Corporation. NACI Care™ is an iPad program used for patient navigation data entry, evaluation, and tracking.

Technology and information technology (IT) breakthroughs specific to cancer and/or patient care are continually emerging. Excitement for the "shiny new tool" occasionally overshadows careful review and consideration, as well as its appropriate use. IT can be a powerful tool, but it is not the end game. In this section, the use of technology in clinic and community-based cancer care is discussed, and a short case study of NACI Care™—an iPad program used to support patient navigation—is provided.

A Snapshot of the Technology Landscape for Cancer Care

Technology is increasingly important in the continuum of cancer care, including community education, screening, diagnosis, treatment, and survivorship [1–3]. The end users of technologies can be community members and patients, providers, healthcare professionals, and healthcare organizations. In recent years, technologies have emerged to support organizations and patients across the cancer continuum, some of which are described below.

Organizational Level

- Electronic health records (EHRs): EHRs have become common in healthcare settings, allowing healthcare providers to access and share patient information easily [4].
- Mobile clinics: Mobile clinics bring cancer screening services directly to communities, particularly in remote or underserved areas. They offer mobile mammography, HPV testing, Pap smears, and other screening tests on-site, enabling easier access [5].
- Telehealth and telemedicine: Telehealth and telemedicine technologies are used to overcome the geographical and logistical barriers faced by many Indigenous communities. Through video consultations, healthcare providers can remotely guide patients on self-administered screenings or advise on the next steps based on individual risk factors [6].
- Collaborative databases and information systems: Databases and systems help bridge the gaps in healthcare data for underserved populations. By centralizing health information, researchers and healthcare providers can track cancer screening rates, identify disparities, and develop targeted interventions to improve outcomes [7, 8].
- Text message reminders: Sending text message reminders for cancer screening appointments and follow-ups can improve adherence to recommended screenings. This approach can help ensure that individuals receive appropriate cancer screenings and follow-ups in a timely manner [9].
- Artificial intelligence (AI): AI is being used to enhance cancer screening processes. For example, AI algorithms can assist in the analysis of medical images, such as

G. Garvey (ed.), *Indigenous and Tribal Peoples and Cancer*, https://doi.org/10.1007/978-3-031-56806-0_74

mammograms or CT scans, to aid in early detection and diagnosis. AI can also help streamline administrative tasks and improve patient management [10, 11].

For Patients

- Mobile applications: There are various mobile applications available that provide information on cancer screenings, appointment scheduling, and reminders. These apps often include educational content, risk assessment tools, and the ability to track personal health data [12, 13].
- Wearable devices: Wearable devices, such as smartwatches and fitness trackers, can monitor vital signs and collect health-related data. These data can be used to identify potential risk factors and encourage patients to undergo cancer screenings based on personalized recommendations [14].

Many advances in technology focus on clinical care, including imaging technologies, laboratory tests, molecular diagnostics, radiation therapy, surgical innovations, targeted chemotherapy, immunotherapy, and advanced data analytics. AI applications support clinical decision-making and enhance personalized medicine approaches.

Of course, the availability of technologies varies across organizations, regions, and health systems. Indigenous and other underserved communities have specific needs and cultural considerations that must be accounted for in developing and implementing these tools to ensure the already existing digital divide is not widened [6].

Benefits of IT

IT can be beneficial to both programs and patients. It can be used to provide patients and caregivers with timely, specific information—something which many patients feel is lacking [15, 16]. It can also be appropriate to the patient's cultural needs or health literacy level. For example, easy-to-understand videos and electronic books can explain clinical appointments and procedures. Visual demonstrations in videos can be particularly helpful, as is the ability for patients to retrieve the information as often as needed [16].

For healthcare teams, IT systems can be tailored to provide messages and reminders to patients in real time (via email or text), with automated reminders reducing the burden on healthcare staff. Systems that can be linked to the electronic medical record (EMR) can be tailored to the individual patient's issues, needs, or interests [16].

One useful example here is Cancer Advocacy and Patient Education (CAPE), a web-based patient education platform created by the Academy of Oncology Nurse and Patient Navigators (AONN+). It aims to improve patient education and enhance patient care by allowing navigators to identify resources specifically for an individual patient. The list of resources is sent from the navigator directly to patients via email or can be printed for patients who are uncomfortable with email [15]. Other technology platforms connect with the EMR and can deliver engaging patient education directly through email and text messages at the right time in the trajectory of care, such as preparing a patient for their upcoming port insertion [16].

Challenges and Limitations

IT systems bring multiple challenges, which need to be considered alongside the benefits. Many IT products are based on data sources that do not provide the detail needed for Indigenous, underserved populations. Some systems are not considered culturally appropriate by their audience [17, 18]. For example, even a well-developed and vetted tool like CAPE faced challenges because a sizable number of lung cancer patients found the materials upsetting [15].

While many technologies link to EMR data, in healthcare settings this may not be successful. Departments within the same health system may use different EMR software, with only some linking to the new IT. For example, even relatively small American Indian clinics specific to a single Tribe in the southwest use 13 different EMR programs. In this situation, the EMR programs do not interact with one another [19]. For example, a cancer patient who also has hepatitis may have data entered for the hepatitis program, but those data are not accessible to oncology program staff and vice versa. Staff must re-enter patient information, which can lead to data-entry errors and delays.

Even in centers where the same EMR system is used by all departments, the system may be used differently—with different data fields used and different criteria for inclusion. It can be challenging to have access to all data points that the program needs. No matter what system is chosen, it can only be as good as the quality of data it contains, and staff need training and support to use it appropriately [20, 21].

For small healthcare centers, there is a specific challenge. Many Indigenous healthcare centers are small and lack infrastructure. Purchasing technology that suits the location and clients can be difficult and cost prohibitive. Yet as larger centers increasingly rely on technology, smaller Indigenous programs are being left behind. In this way, IT can contribute to health disparities by entrenching a digital divide [17]. The questions for small Indigenous healthcare centers are numerous: How do Indigenous communities afford both the IT purchase and the constant upkeep? How does a small rural clinic or non-profit program connect or find resources to access and learn to use IT appropriately? How do small programs access ongoing support from people who understand the technology? [22, 23]

Currently, many IT programs do not work well together, but this may change with Health Level 7 (HL7) phrasing for programming. HL7 provides global standards for the transfer of clinical and administrative health data between applications. It enables the various systems, such as patient administration, clinical tasks, and medication management, to interface with each other [24].

Recent technology is becoming more accessible and easier to use—even for those without much technological experience. For example, tools like Microsoft Power BI can report on any device, from anywhere—creating data summaries and sharing information. Tools like this may enable communities to organize data easily and better use information to represent the community's needs [25, 26].

IT Does Not Stand Alone

Ideally, IT complements programs that are trusted in the community. These community partners can ensure that technologies are being integrated into the community setting and support the utilization of these tools, especially since most of these tools have not been developed from the community perspective. It is important that the materials, where printed or technologically generated, are designed or adapted to be culturally appropriate, easily accessible, and available in Indigenous and other languages. In addition, tools developed by and for these communities are important to explore since they are designed from the start with this perspective. It is also important to think about how these technologies support and can be used by community health workers, patient navigators, Aboriginal patient liaisons, and Aboriginal liaison officers who are often the respected and trusted sources in their community. The integration of high touch (person to person) and high tech is essential for the technologies we employ to have value in our communities and address health equity across the cancer continuum.

Case Study: NACI Care™

This case study (co-authored by Linda Krebs and Linda Burhansstipanov) illustrates how a small, minority-owned non-profit organization and its staff, the Native American Cancer Research Corporation (NACR), integrated technology with the approval of the local Indigenous community to engage Indigenous peoples in cancer research. NACR first started to incorporate technology into its work in 2003, when it adopted audience response systems (hand-held keypads) to gather real-time feedback from participants at events.

In 2016, a project titled A Tool to Improve Evaluation of Patient Navigation Services in Underserved Populations was initiated to create NACI Care™, an iPad program for patient navigation data entry, evaluation, and tracking. NACI Care™ evolved from NACR's web-based interactive evaluation program. It offered a comprehensive, portable system for staff to use when working with patients or community members. NACI Care™ (1) supports accurate and easy data input, (2) allows for real-time data entry and individual summaries, (3) allows program administrators to monitor oncology patient navigator interactions and produce activity summaries to document navigators' value, and (4) collects patient perspectives and satisfaction related to navigation services. The program provides a central data repository that uses HL7 language and has the capacity to link with EMRs. It is designed to support registered nurses, social work oncology patient navigators, administrators of navigation programs, program evaluators, and researchers.

NACI Care™ has three main components (see Fig. 74.1).

1. Patient information and healthcare visit data: Data are uploaded by the patient navigator or user, including patient identification information, demographics, general health behaviors, current health status, health history, barriers and solutions, referrals and appointments, survey results, patient program status, and an interaction summary.
2. Patient navigator information and activities: This includes data about the patient navigator, such as contact details and demographics, education and training, outreach work, and dissemination records.
3. Administrator functions and tailoring: The system administrator can add system preferences, user approvals, default reporting templates, and report filters. The program also will provide an overview of a program's return on investment.

NACI Care™ can be tailored to meet local program needs including selecting how to sort patient lists, choosing which measurement system is used (metric or imperial), selecting what topics can be accessed for data entry, and using filters to tailor reports. There are more than 5000 fields, available to be controlled by the administrator—though no program would use all of them. For example, a program focused only on outreach, education, and early detection/screening may not want the information from surveys, while another program may not want the navigator or user distracted by health behavior and status information.

NACI Care™ offers default report templates for approximately 36 navigation program metrics, which can be used to evaluate program success. These are based on nationally recognized metrics. NACI Care™ provides reports for

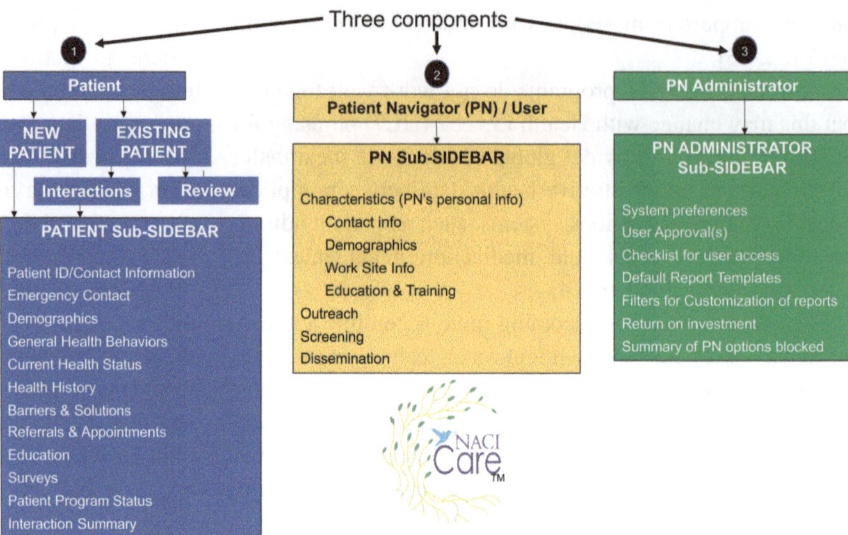

Fig. 74.1 The three components of NACI Care™

accreditation, manages patient care (in and out of clinical settings), focuses on cancer care, addresses the entire cancer continuum, and can generate tailored reports about individuals, groups, or programs.

NACI Care™ enables users to add or modify filters for all summaries and reports, including filtering for individual patient navigators, patients, or groups. A particularly useful feature is the ability to filter according to specific demographics, general health issues, cancer types, or medical issues.

NACI Care™ has received trademark protection in several countries.

References

1. Mao Y, Lin W, Wen J, Chen G. Impact and efficacy of mobile health intervention in the management of diabetes and hypertension: a systematic review and meta-analysis. *BMJ Open Diabetes Res Care*. 2020;8(1):e001223. https://doi.org/10.1136/bmjdrc-2020-001225
2. Valera P, Acuna N, Alzate-Duque L, Liang LE, Cupertino P, Merulla J. The Development and Prototype Feedback of Digital Cancer 101 Videos to Enhance Cancer Education for Marginalized Communities With Limited Health Literacy. *Cancer Control*. 2021;28:10732748211006055. https://doi.org/10.1177/10732748211006055
3. Buis L. Implementation: The Next Giant Hurdle to Clinical Transformation With Digital Health. *J Med Internet Res*. 2019;21(11):e16259. https://doi.org/10.2196/16259
4. Ambinder EP. Electronic health records. *J Oncol Pract*. 2005;1(2)57–63. https://doi.org/10.1200/JOP.2005.1.2.57
5. Degife EA, Oliveira CR, Znamierowski E, Meyer JP, Sheth SS. Uptake of Cervical Cancer Screening Among Female Patients Using a Mobile Medical Clinic. *Am J Prev Med*. 2023;65(5):835–43. https://doi.org/10.1016/j.amepre.2023.05.013
6. Calton BA, Nouri S, Davila C, Kotwal A, Zapata C, Bischoff KE. Strategies to Make Telemedicine a Friend, Not a Foe, in the Provision of Accessible and Equitable Cancer Care. *Cancers (Basel)*. 2023;15(21):5121. https://doi.org/10.3390/cancers15215121
7. Shahzad M, Upshur R, Donnelly P, Bharmal A, Wei X, Feng P, et al. A population-based approach to integrated healthcare delivery: a scoping review of clinical care and public health collaboration. *BMC Public Health*. 2019;19(1):708. https://doi.org/10.1186/s12889-019-7002-z
8. Akinfenwa CA, Allanson E, Ewongwo A, Lumley C, Bazzett-Matabele L, Msadabwe SC, et al. Mapping of radiation oncology and gynecologic oncology services available to treat the growing burden of cervical cancer in Africa. *Int J Radiat Oncol Biol Phys*. 2023 Nov 16. https://doi.org/10.1016/j.ijrobp.2023.10.036
9. Nanda AD, Reifel KR, Mann MP, Lyman-Hager MM, Overman K, Cheng AL, et al. Text-Based Intervention Increases Mammography Uptake at an Urban Safety-Net Hospital. *Ann Surg Oncol*. 2022;29(10):6199–205. https://doi.org/10.1245/s10434-022-12130-x
10. Menzies SW, Sinz C, Menzies M, Lo SN, Yolland W, Lingohr J, et al. Comparison of humans versus mobile phone-powered artificial intelligence for the diagnosis and management of pigmented skin cancer in secondary care: a multicentre, prospective, diagnostic, clinical trial. *Lancet Digit Health*. 2023;5(10):e679–e91. https://doi.org/10.1016/S2589-7500(23)00130-9
11. Spear J, Ehrenfeld JM, Miller BJ. Applications of Artificial Intelligence in Health Care Delivery. *J Med Syst*. 2023;47(1):121. https://doi.org/10.1007/s10916-023-02018-y
12. Weiss K, Abimbola O, Mueller D, Basak R, Basch E, Parisse T, et al. Feasibility, Acceptability, and Outcomes of a Mobile Health Tool for Radical Cystectomy Recovery. *J Urol*. 2023 Nov 16. https://doi.org/10.1097/JU.0000000000003787
13. Lin H, Ye M, Lin Y, Chen F, Chan S, Cai H, Zhu J. Mobile App for Gynecologic Cancer Support for Patients With Gynecologic Cancer Receiving Chemotherapy in China: Multicenter Randomized Controlled Trial. *J Med Internet Res*. 2023 Nov 13;25:e49939. https://doi.org/10.2196/49939
14. Chow R, Drkulec H, Im JHB, Tsai J, Nafees A, Kumar S, et al. The Use of Wearable Devices in Oncology Patients: A Systematic Review. *Oncologist*. 2023 Nov 16. https://doi.org/10.1093/oncolo/oyad305
15. Fleisher L, Cassidy K, Gentry KC. Cancer Advocacy & Patient Education (CAPE) Lung Pilot Study Evaluation: Findings From 4 Diverse Clinical Settings for Future Implementation and Dissemination. *J Oncol Navig Surviv*. 2023;14(8):235–46.
16. Fleisher L, Kenny C, Rusten C, Koren D, Landau Z. Right Information, Right Patient, Right Time: Utilizing the

MyCareCompass Platform to Deliver Patient Education in the Oncology Setting. *J Cancer Educ*. 2023;38(5):1420–8. https://doi.org/10.1007/s13187-023-02350-4

17. Sanders CK, Scanlon E. The Digital Divide Is a Human Rights Issue: Advancing Social Inclusion Through Social Work Advocacy. *J Hum Rights Soc Work*. 2021;6(2):130–43. https://doi.org/10.1007/s41134-020-00147-9
18. Whitehead L, Talevski J, Fatehi F, Beauchamp A. Barriers to and Facilitators of Digital Health Among Culturally and Linguistically Diverse Populations: Qualitative Systematic Review. *J Med Internet Res*. 2023;25:e42719. https://doi.org/10.2196/42719
19. Sequist TD, Cullen T, Hays H, Taualii MM, Simon SR, Bates DW. Implementation and use of an electronic health record within the Indian Health Service. *J Am Med Inform Assoc*. 2007;14(2):191–7. https://doi.org/10.1197/jamia.M2234
20. Bowman S. Impact of electronic health record systems on information integrity: quality and safety implications. *Perspect Health Inf Manag*. 2013;10(Fall):1c.
21. Wang AY, Lancaster WJ, Wyatt MC, Rasmussen LV, Fort DG, Cimino JJ. Classifying Clinical Trial Eligibility Criteria to Facilitate Phased Cohort Identification Using Clinical Data Repositories. *AMIA Annu Symp Proc*. 2018 Apr;2017:1754–1763.
22. Choukou MA, Maddahi A, Ployvyana A, Monnin C. Digital health technology for Indigenous older adults: A scoping review. *Int J Med Inform*. 2021;148:104408. https://doi.org/10.1016/j.ijmedinf.2021.104408
23. Jones LK, Jacklin K, O'Connell ME. Development and Use of Health-Related Technologies in Indigenous Communities: Critical Review. *J Med Internet Res*. 2017;19(7):e256. https://doi.org/10.2196/jmir.7520
24. Kimura M. [Outline of Health Level Seven (HL7) standard]. *Rinsho Byori*. 1999;47(12):1165–9.
25. Lall P, Rees R, Law GCY, Dunleavy G, Coltič Ž, Car J. Influences on the Implementation of Mobile Learning for Medical and Nursing Education: Qualitative Systematic Review by the Digital Health Education Collaboration. *J Med Internet Res*. 2019;21(2):e12895. https://doi.org/10.2196/12895
26. Walchshofer C, Dhanoa V, Streit M, Meyer M. Transitioning to a Commercial Dashboarding System: Socio-technical Observations and Opportunities. *IEEE Trans Vis Comput Graph*. 2023 Oct 25. https://doi.org/10.1109/TVCG.2023.3326525

75 Cancer Cell Biology Research in an Indigenous Childhood Cancer Context

Jessica Buck, Justine R. Clark, Rachel Joyce, and Alex Brown

Key Points

- There are many benefits to Indigenous Australians surrounding the use of cancer genomics and cell biology research, but also many risks.
- Indigenous leadership and governance in both precision medicine and cell biology are necessary to produce equitable outcomes.
- The ZERO Childhood Cancer program offers genomic analysis for every Australian child with cancer and has the potential to inform precision cancer treatments for Indigenous Australian children; however, the program must embed Indigenous engagement and governance into its clinical trial structure.

In Australia, cancer medicine is increasingly guided by our expanding knowledge of cancer genomics (the study of genetic information) and biology. Personalized treatments and targets are often defined by an individual's genetic profile—known as precision cancer medicine. The translation of genomics-guided precision therapeutics from bench to bedside is beginning to produce real clinical benefits for Australians living with cancer. However, Indigenous Australians are disproportionately impacted by cancer [1] and simultaneously have limited access to cancer research and specialist genetic services [2, 3], meaning that the benefits offered by precision cancer medicine are currently limited. Improving access to culturally safe cancer genetics research and genetic health services for cancer has the potential to promote effective and safe precision cancer medicine for Indigenous Australians.

A combination of novel genomics technologies and functional cell biology research has enabled the discovery of new drug targets and treatment strategies for cancer over the last two decades. However, our knowledge of the human genome that enables new discoveries fails to capture the genomic diversity of human beings, particularly that of Indigenous peoples globally [4]. Importantly, the distinct actionable genomic alterations in cancer—to which targeted cancer therapies, treatment decisions, and risk stratifications are designed—can be over or underrepresented in populations of different ethnic backgrounds [4]. This may be particularly relevant in a childhood cancer context, where genetic factors are more likely to play a role in comparison to external cancer risk factors such as tobacco and alcohol consumption and sun exposure. Furthermore, the reference genome resources that are widely used in research and to identify clinically actionable genetic alterations are predominantly European in origin. Therefore, there is a need for Indigenous genomics to inform clinical practice and ensure equitable benefits for Indigenous peoples. In response, global efforts have begun to create Indigenous variant databases [5], and ongoing projects at the National Centre for Indigenous Genomics in Australia are focusing on assembling a suitable Indigenous Australian reference genome, in consultation and collaboration with Indigenous communities [6].

In addition to clinically relevant reference genomes, effective precision cancer research currently relies upon the use of patient-derived cell lines and xenograft models of human disease. Patient-derived cell lines may be created when patients with cancer donate some of their removed cancer tissue to researchers, with the cells then grown indefinitely in a dish in the laboratory. Donated cancer cells may also be grown in other animals, for example, mice, known as patient-derived xenograft models. These models serve as laboratory-based pre-clinical tools to understand cancer biology and identify novel therapeutic targets for patients. Indigenous-led precision medicine research initiatives will require ongoing, critical conversations around dynamic models of patient consent and the potential risks and benefits associated with the creation, use, and storage of Indigenous patient-derived tissue and models. This will include governance of data derived from these models and requires collaboration between Indigenous communities, researchers, and clinical practitioners.

Precision cancer research guided by cell biology and genomics can provide opportunities to refine treatment strategies, reduce side effects, and create novel targeted ther-

G. Garvey (ed.), *Indigenous and Tribal Peoples and Cancer*, https://doi.org/10.1007/978-3-031-56806-0_75

apies that are fit-for-purpose for Indigenous Australians. Nonetheless, Indigenous Australians are largely yet to see personal benefits from these technological advances, owing to the general inaccessibility of personalized medicine services and infrastructure, perpetuated by systemic racism embedded within mainstream academic, medical research, and healthcare institutions. While there is much work to be done to ensure precision cancer medicine leads to improved health outcomes for Indigenous Australians, researchers must strike a balance between working at the pace of progress and working at the pace of trust. Exploring the opportunities for precision cancer medicine with Indigenous Australians should be Indigenous-led; centered around the priorities, needs, and interests of Indigenous communities; and ultimately maintain Indigenous governance from project planning to implementation and translation.

Risks and Ethical Considerations

Indigenous Australians have 60,000+ years of history as Australia's first peoples and first scientists. However, since colonization, Indigenous Australians have been the subjects of much research, with very little perceived benefit received by communities [7]. Indigenous peoples globally share similar experiences, and in the context of genomics, large-scale open-access genomics projects such as the Human Genome Diversity Project (HGDP) and the 1000 Genomes project have disempowered Indigenous communities [8]. Concerns of exploitation led to the rejection of the HGDP by central Australian Aboriginal communities in the 1990s [9]. Their concerns were justified; open-access genomics projects ultimately enabled the generation of profits by pharmaceutical and ancestry testing companies, with no direct benefits provided back to the Indigenous communities involved [10].

These risks of exploitation must be managed through purposeful Indigenous-led design and governance. Australian Indigenous health research codes of conduct enshrine principles of respect, reciprocity, community partnership, and Indigenous data sovereignty. However, the unique ethical and cultural implications of precision cancer and genomics research remain poorly defined within these codes in Australia. Furthermore, Indigenous Australians must be consulted on the storage, scientific use, and governance of cancer samples for the creation of patient-derived models, as these samples and their use may be of great cultural significance. Currently, the onus is placed on researchers, Aboriginal health research ethics committees, and communities to ensure that Indigenous Australians are not exploited. Best-practice guidelines, such as those existing internationally, and importantly Indigenous Australian leadership in this research are essential to avoiding the perpetuation of past exploitation and ensuring Indigenous Australian communities reap the benefits of precision cancer medicine.

The ZERO Childhood Cancer Program

The ZERO Childhood Cancer program is a clinical trial (NCT05504772) that performs detailed genomic sequencing to identify precision cancer treatments for Australian children diagnosed with cancer. This trial began by focusing on children with high-risk cancers, with great success in improving health outcomes for children within this population through the provision of precision medicine [11]. The expansion of this initial trial aims to include every Australian child, which will incidentally include Aboriginal and Torres Strait Islander children. This trial should provide a rich data source for research into new population-specific treatments and may enable real-time recommendations for precision cancer treatments for Indigenous Australian children with cancer.

In addition to performing genomic testing on patient samples, where possible, the ZERO Childhood Cancer program will also create cell lines and PDX models [12]. This allows high-throughput drug screening to be carried out, which may contribute to treatment recommendations. The ZERO Childhood Cancer program must consider the ethical and cultural implications of generating the first known Indigenous Australian cancer cell lines and the Indigenous governance structures that are to be placed over these cell lines. The program must also contend with the global history of cancer cell line generation, which is fraught with the exploitation of people of color.

The ZERO Childhood Cancer program was designed iteratively, following input from pediatric oncologists, scientists, researchers, and consumers, including parents of children diagnosed with cancer. To ensure the existing clinical trial structure is adapted to one that also benefits Indigenous Australians, the ZERO Childhood Cancer team will need to engage with Indigenous Australian researchers, healthcare providers, community members, and families. The ZERO Childhood Cancer team is cognizant that potential benefits from the ZERO Childhood Cancer trial may be limited for Indigenous children involved in the study, owing to a paucity of pre-existing, clinically relevant knowledge regarding cancer biology and genetics. A study design that is Indigenous-led, informed by current Indigenous genomics research, and in line with health systems approaches to improving equitable access to cancer care for Indigenous Australians is, therefore, needed to achieve equitable health and wellbeing outcomes. To this end, the ZERO Childhood Cancer team has established a working group that includes Aboriginal precision cancer researchers to identify the potential risks of their program and a way forward to ensure equitable benefits for Indigenous Australian children with cancer.

We acknowledge our Elders and the communities in which we live and write. We also acknowledge Indigenous people living with and passed from cancer, and their families. The authors would also like to acknowledge the contributions of the ZERO Childhood Cancer team to this chapter and to the progression of precision cancer research for Indigenous children with cancer.

References

1. Australian Institute of Health and Welfare. *Cancer in Australia 2021*. 2021. Available from: https://www.aihw.gov.au/reports/cancer/cancer-in-australia-2021/summary
2. Luke J, Dalach P, Tuer L, Savaririyan R, Ferdinand A, McGaughran J, et al. Investigating disparity in access to Australian clinical genetic health services for Aboriginal and Torres Strait Islander people. *Nature Commun*. 2022;13:4966. https://doi.org/10.1038/s41467-022-32707-0
3. Cunningham J, Garvey G. Are there systematic barriers to participation in cancer treatment trials by Aboriginal and Torres Strait Islander cancer patients? *Aust N Z J Public Health*. 2021;45(1):39–45. https://doi.org/10.1111/1753-6405.13059
4. Freedman JA, Al Abo M, Allen TA, Piwarski SA, Wegermann K, Patierno SR. Biological Aspects of Cancer Health Disparities. *Annu Rev Med*. 2021;72:229–41. https://doi.org/10.1146/annurev-med-070119-120305
5. Caron NR, Chongo M, Hudson M, Arbour L, Wasserman WW, Robertson S, et al. Indigenous Genomic Databases: Pragmatic Considerations and Cultural Contexts. *Front Public Health*. 2020 Apr;8. https://doi.org/10.3389/fpubh.2020.00111
6. National Centre for Indigenous Genomics. Long read genome assembly 2023 [Internet]. Austalian National University. Available from: https://ncig.anu.edu.au/research/projects/long-read-genome-assembly
7. National Health and Medical Research Council. Ethical conduct in research with Aboriginal and Torres Strait Islander Peoples. 2018. Available from: https://www.nhmrc.gov.au/about-us/resources/ethical-conduct-research-aboriginal-and-torres-strait-islander-peoples-and-communities
8. Fox K. The Illusion of Inclusion – The "All of Us" Research Program and Indigenous Peoples' DNA. *N Engl J Med*. 2020;383(5):411–3. https://doi.org/10.1056/NEJMp1915987
9. Dodson M, Williamson R. Indigenous peoples and the morality of the Human Genome Diversity Project. *J Med Ethics*. 1999;25(2):204–8. https://doi.org/10.1136/jme.25.2.204
10. Tsosie K, Yracheta J, Kolopenuk J, Geary J. We Have "Gifted" Enough: Indigenous Genomic Data Sovereignty in Precision Medicine. *Am J Bioeth*. 2021;21(4):72–5. https://doi.org/10.1080/15265161.2021.1891347
11. Wong M, Mayoh C, Lau LMS, Khuong-Quang D-A, Pinese M, Kumar A, et al. Whole genome, transcriptome and methylome profiling enhances actionable target discovery in high-risk pediatric cancer. *Nat Medicine*. 2020;26(11):1742–53. https://doi.org/10.1038/s41591-020-1072-4
12. Lau LMS, Mayoh C, Xie J, Barahona P, MacKenzie KL, Wong M, et al. In vitro and in vivo drug screens of tumor cells identify novel therapies for high-risk child cancer. *EMBO Mol Med*. 2022;14(4):e14608. https://doi.org/10.15252/emmm.202114608

Tracking Down the Origins of a Divergent Subtype of Liver Cancer in Indigenous Americans in Peru

76

Juan Pablo Cerapio, Eloy Ruiz, Sandro Casavilca-Zambrano, Nils Graber, Pascal Pineau, and Stéphane Bertani

Key Points

- Indigenous peoples of the Americas can develop liver cancer at an early age in the absence of cirrhosis.
- Integrative genomic analysis has uncovered peculiarities both in gene expression and epigenetic reprogramming, revealing a divergent molecular subtype of liver cancer.
- This divergent molecular subtype of liver cancer is associated with infection by an autochthonous sub-genotype of the hepatitis B virus.

The idea that ancestry modulates the molecular determinants of cancer is relatively new in genomic research and requires further study [1]. While the scientific question is fascinating, the health issue is alarming since Indigenous peoples remain starkly under-represented in cancer genomics studies, effectively excluding them from the benefits of such research [2]. Our work has shed light on this phenomenon in cancer patients with Indigenous American backgrounds. Specifically, we have identified a strong correlation between Indigenous American ancestry and the development of an early-age subtype of hepatocellular carcinoma (HCC), the main form of primary liver cancer [3].

HCC is one of the most prevalent and deadly tumor types worldwide. It usually afflicts individuals in middle and old age after protracted liver diseases, such as cirrhosis. Considerable efforts have been dedicated to elaborating a clinically relevant molecular classification of HCC [4]. However, a unifying classification that includes the whole heterogeneity of HCC will remain an ongoing concern—if not an unattainable goal—as long as some populations, such as Indigenous peoples, are under-investigated [2]. For instance, the early-age onset of non-cirrhotic HCC presented in a significant fraction of Indigenous American patients originating from Alaska and the Andes who are infected with the same autochthonous sub-genotype F1b of the hepatitis B virus (HBV) represents an illustration of this concern [3, 5].

Accordingly, our main objective has been to characterize the early-age form of non-cirrhotic HCC developed by Indigenous peoples of the Americas at the genomic level based on a cohort of Native Andean patients from Peru. It should be noted here that Peru is, with Bolivia, one of the countries in the Americas with the highest level of Indigenous genetic structure in its general population [6]. Around 80% of Peruvians self-identify as either Andean-Amazonian Indigenous or mixed-Indigenous ancestry.

Methods

An integrative analysis of gene expression and DNA methylation in non-cirrhotic HCC developed by Native Andean patients, including adolescents and young adults, was conducted to understand the molecular correlates and determinants of the disease in this population. Native Andean patients were recruited while receiving treatment for liver tumors at the National Cancer Institute of Peru (INEN) according to Institutional Research Ethics Committee Protocol 10-05.

Biobanking

One of the primary challenges we faced was accessing biological samples from cancer patients with Indigenous backgrounds. Accordingly, to promote the inclusion of individuals from under-represented Indigenous peoples in genomic studies, we developed biobanking activities, which led to the creation of the National Tumor Biobank of Peru in 2022 (Peruvian Law 31336). Hosted at INEN, this facility is firmly involved in collecting biological samples as well as sociodemographic and clinical data from cancer patients of the Andean-Amazonian Indigenous communities of Peru and their descendants, in accordance with local laws governing

G. Garvey (ed.), *Indigenous and Tribal Peoples and Cancer*, https://doi.org/10.1007/978-3-031-56806-0_76

Indigenous and personal ownership of data (Peruvian Laws 27811 and 29733, respectively).

Indigenous Ancestry, Cancer Genomics, and Virus Detection

The Indigenous American ancestry of the cancer patients was determined by their mitochondrial DNA haplotype. Human mitochondrial DNA haplotypes are used by population geneticists to trace the matrilineal inheritance of modern humans and their distribution around the globe. Most of the members of the Indigenous American communities typically carry one of the four ancestral lineages labeled haplogroups A, B, C, and D [7]. Through integrative genomics, we then evaluated gene expression, pathway analyses, and DNA methylation in the early-age HCC developed by Native Andean patients [3]. In parallel, we conducted an in-depth molecular analysis of HBV genomes and viral loads using ultra-sensitive molecular assays, as described previously [8].

Results and Discussion

According to transcriptome analysis, HCC is normally divided into two classes, i.e., proliferative and non-proliferative, based on differences in pathway activation, phenotype, and prognosis (Fig. 76.1) [4]. However, we reported that Indigenous American haplogrouping is associated with peculiarities in gene expression in Native Andean patients who develop non-cirrhotic HCC around 20 years of age [3]. While Andean HCC falls roughly into the proliferative class, it also exhibits idiosyncratic traits in additional signaling pathway activation (Fig. 76.1). From a molecular standpoint, Andean HCC features a divergent subtype between the proliferative and non-proliferative classes, usually regarded as mutually exclusive according to the molecular classification of HCC (Fig. 76.1). Additionally, Andean HCC displays high levels of DNA methylation, contrasting with the global hypomethylation pattern considered a hallmark of HCC [3]. In this regard, our findings uncover an original biological model of epigenetic reprogramming in cancer development.

As HBV is suspected to be the prominent risk factor for HCC in South America, we performed a comprehensive molecular study of HBV infection in Native Andean patients. Intriguingly, HBV infection in Native Andeans is associated with a very low viral DNA burden, disclosing a significant rate of occult infections [8]. This observation sharply contrasts with the prevailing paradigm that relates higher HBV DNA loads to the onset of HCC, considered "early," at around 40 years of age [9]. A phylogenetic analysis of the HBV genome clustered every isolate within the sub-genotype F1b, a viral clade infecting historically Indigenous American peoples [10]. Such high prevalence rates of occult infection with autochthonous HBV clades (F, G, and H) have been documented to a large extent in the Indigenous peoples of the Americas [5, 11]. It is noteworthy that Native Alaskans from the Yupik tribe with early-onset HCC associated with the same sub-genotype F1b have also been described [5]. Our assumption is that the HBV-associated carcinogenic process might differ substantially in Indigenous populations of the Americas from that generally observed in other populations. In this view, the distinctive tumor dynamics could result from an incomplete adaptation of Indigenous Americans to the autochthonous HBV sub-genotypes [12].

Our findings reveal a major role for bio-anthropology in molecular oncology, with the characterization of a clinically

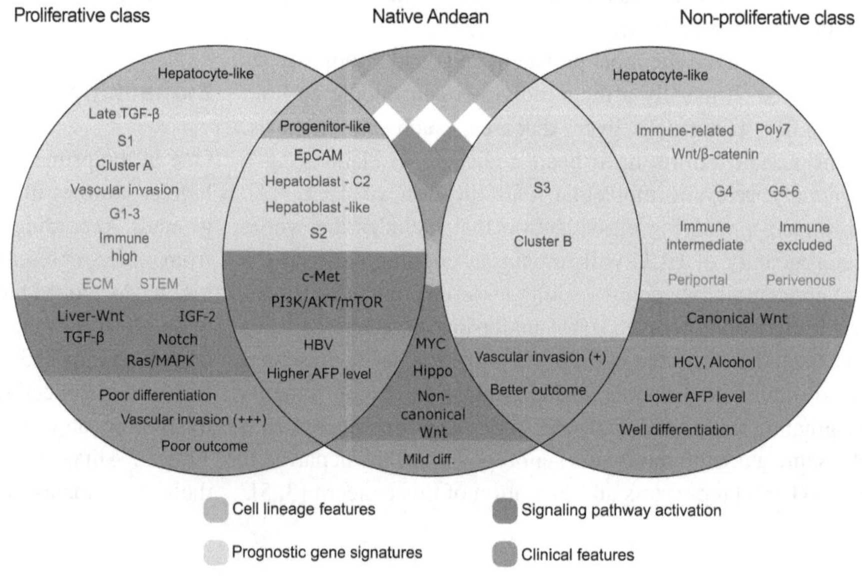

Fig. 76.1 A schematic representation of HCC molecular classification, integrating Andean liver tumors. According to prognostic gene signatures and signaling pathway activation, Andean specimens fall into a nontypical position within the classification

relevant molecular subtype of HCC in patients of Indigenous American descent. Overall, our research represents the first integrative genomic characterization of a molecular subtype of cancer that preferentially affects people of Indigenous ancestry. Our study stresses the necessity of conducting further bio-anthropological research programs with Indigenous people to meet their specific needs in cancer detection, prevention, and treatment. In this regard, we will continue to collaborate with medical anthropologists to improve our understanding of the socio-economic and cultural factors influencing access to care for Andean-Amazonian people.

We are grateful to all patients whose participation was essential to this research. This work was supported by ITMO Cancer of the French National Alliance for Life Science and Health (Aviesan) and the French National Cancer Institute (INCa) with funds administered by the French National Institute of Health and Medical Research (Inserm), grant agreement 21CD025-00. This work was also supported by ANRS | Emerging Infectious Diseases on funds administered by Inserm, grant agreement AO 2021-1 CSS12.

References

1. Carrot-Zhang J, Chambwe N, Damrauer JS, Knijnenburg TA, Robertson AG, Yau C, et al. Comprehensive analysis of genetic ancestry and its molecular correlates in cancer. *Cancer Cell*. 2020 May 11;37(5):639–54. https://doi.org/10.1016/j.ccell.2020.04.012
2. Ma L, Wang XW. Dissecting liver tumor heterogeneity to improve health equity. *Trends Cancer*. 2022 Apr 1;8(4):286–90. https://doi.org/10.1016/j.trecan.2021.12.001
3. Cerapio JP, Marchio A, Cano L, López I, Fournié JJ, Régnault B, et al. Global DNA hypermethylation pattern and unique gene expression signature in liver cancer from patients with Indigenous American ancestry. *Oncotarget*. 2021 Mar 2;12(5):475–92. https://doi.org/10.18632/oncotarget.27890
4. Llovet JM, Kelley RK, Villanueva A, Singal AG, Pikarsky E, Roayaie S, et al. Hepatocellular carcinoma. *Nat Rev Dis Primers*. 2021 Jan 21;7(1):1–28. https://doi.org/10.1038/s41572-020-00240-3
5. Hayashi S, Khan A, Simons BC, Homan C, Matsui T, Ogawa K, et al. An association between core mutations in hepatitis B virus genotype F1b and hepatocellular carcinoma in Alaskan Native people. *Hepatology*. 2019 Jan;69(1):19–33. https://doi.org/10.1002/hep.30111
6. Homburger JR, Moreno-Estrada A, Gignoux CR, Nelson D, Sanchez E, Ortiz-Tello P, et al. Genomic insights into the ancestry and demographic history of South America. *PLoS Genet*. 2015 Dec;11(12):e1005602. https://doi.org/10.1371/journal.pgen.1005602
7. Mulligan CJ, Hunley K, Cole S, Long JC. Population genetics, history, and health patterns in Native Americans. *Annu Rev Genomics Hum Genet*. 2004;5:295–315. https://doi.org/10.1146/annurev.genom.5.061903.175920
8. Marchio A, Cerapio JP, Ruiz E, Cano L, Casavilca S, Terris B, et al. Early-onset liver cancer in South America associates with low hepatitis B virus DNA burden. *Sci Rep*. 2018 Aug 13;8(1):12031. https://doi.org/10.1038/s41598-018-30229-8
9. Yang JD, Gyedu A, Afihene MY, Duduyemi BM, Micah E, Kingham TP, et al. Hepatocellular carcinoma occurs at an earlier age in Africans, particularly in association with chronic hepatitis B. *Am J Gastroenterol*. 2015 Nov;110(11):1629–31. https://doi.org/10.1038/ajg.2015.289
10. von Meltzer M, Vásquez S, Sun J, Wendt UC, May A, Gerlich WH, et al. A new clade of hepatitis B virus subgenotype F1 from Peru with unusual properties. *Virus Genes*. 2008 Oct;37(2):225–30. https://doi.org/10.1007/s11262-008-0261-x
11. Roman S, Tanaka Y, Khan A, Kurbanov F, Kato H, Mizokami M, et al. Occult hepatitis B in the genotype H-infected Nahuas and Huichol Native Mexican population. *J Med Virol*. 2010 Sep;82(9):1527–36. https://doi.org/10.1002/jmv.21846
12. Enard D, Cai L, Gwennap C, Petrov DA. Viruses are a dominant driver of protein adaptation in mammals. *eLife*. 2016 17;5:e12469. https://doi.org/10.7554/eLife.12469

The Power of Genomics

77

Kimiora Henare, Mackenzie K. Connon, Nadine R. Caron, and Alex Brown

Key Points

- The promise of genomics-guided precision oncology is highlighted by recent approvals of molecularly guided therapies coupled with companion diagnostic tests.
- A critical limitation of genomics-guided oncology is that it is unlikely to serve Indigenous cancer patients unless Indigenous rights-based approaches to genomics-guided cancer research and clinical care are prioritized.
- Relevant Indigenous datasets that can support precision oncology are needed.
- Indigenous access to and governance over key infrastructure are needed.
- We must grow and empower an Indigenous workforce with subject matter expertise and clinical acumen to ensure that genomics-guided precision oncology can sustainably benefit Indigenous cancer patients.

Due to an advanced understanding of cancer biology and the rapid development of genomic technologies,[1] cancer has shifted from 200 diseases based on pathology (i.e., what a tumor looks like under the microscope) to thousands of diseases based on molecular tumor profiles (i.e., what a tumor looks like when its altered genome[2] is interrogated) [1]. Most cancers arise from alterations to the genome, including changes in the number or structure of chromosomes and variations in a single building block of the genetic code (e.g., base pairs). Often, multiple changes need to occur, disrupting multiple checks and balances that prevent the uncontrolled proliferation and survival of abnormal, cancerous cells. While radiotherapy and surgery have focused on removing cells that have suffered irreparable damage to their DNA, and chemotherapy aims to disrupt cell growth by exploiting the subcellular machinery involved in cell proliferation, targeted therapy enabled by genomic profiling focuses on the molecular drivers and features of each condition, identifying and treating its "Achilles heel." This chapter examines the current potential impact of genomics-guided oncology for Indigenous peoples and highlights potential solutions to possible future challenges.

The Potential Impact of Genomics in Oncology

Globally, oncologists are embracing the integration of molecular tumor profiles (i.e., the unique DNA changes in a person's cancer) used in synergy with new and traditional tools, technologies, and multidisciplinary knowledge to inform clinical decision-making with patients (Fig. 77.1). This includes matching patients to the best treatment options available for their particular DNA profile. Highlighting the speed at which the field of genomics-guided precision oncology is moving, at least 20 biomarker-specific medicines or combinations received regulatory approval (including tissue-agnostic approvals)[3] for treating solid tumors based on comprehensive genomic profiling in the United States and Europe between April 2019 and April 2021 [1]. Many of these biomarker-matched medicines are also approved or marketed in Canada and Australia for the same indications, while public access in Aotearoa New Zealand lags behind.

In cases in which a test result is matched to a readily available treatment, this process can be relatively straightforward. For others, where genomic test results and treatment options are less clear-cut, physicians may be able to present their case to a molecular tumor board (MTB)[4] [2]. The MTB can provide expert guidance on the scientific and clinical sig-

[1] **Genomics**: the study of an organism's genome.

[2] **Genome**: a set of all the genetic information or DNA code that makes up an organism.

[3] **Tissue-agnostic approvals**: regulatory approval of a medicine based on its effectiveness in treating a specific genetic mutation or biomarker, rather than the location or type of cancer.

[4] **Molecular tumor board (MTB)**: a forum of experts who discuss a patient's genomic testing results to support clinical decision-making.

G. Garvey (ed.), *Indigenous and Tribal Peoples and Cancer*, https://doi.org/10.1007/978-3-031-56806-0_77

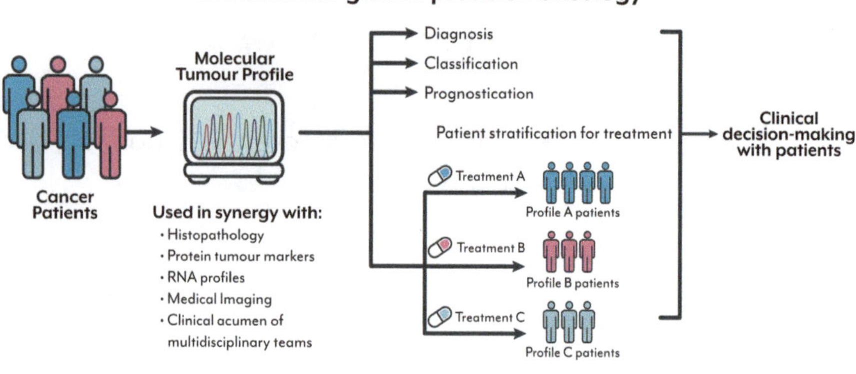

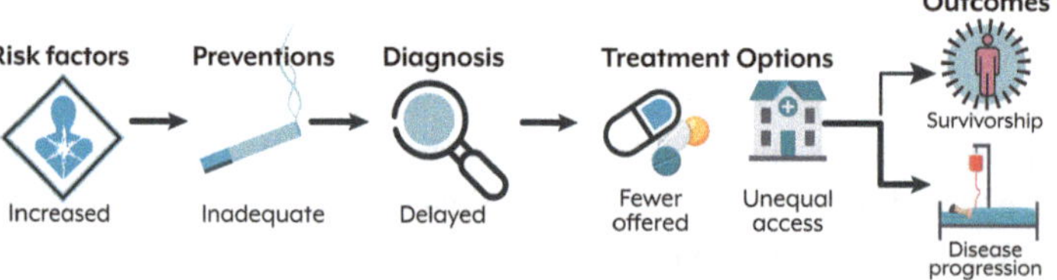

Fig. 77.1 Genomics-guided precision oncology promises to improve clinical decision-making between the patients and their attending physician (**a**). However, precision oncology widens inequities if introduced into existing health systems (**b**) without adequate attention to the needs of all populations. (Design: C Lourenco)

nificance of a gene variant[5] identified from a genomic test, and on therapeutic options, including access to clinical trials, depending on available evidence. Emerging international evidence suggests that MTBs can improve patient outcomes. One study found that patients who receive MTB-recommended treatment are better matched to therapy and achieve better outcomes compared to those who receive treatment based on the physician's choice alone [2]. In many countries, the MTB option is limited largely to academic centers with sufficient capacity, as it draws on the time and expertise of multidisciplinary teams of experts, including clinical variant curators, geneticists, bioinformaticians, and physicians [2]. Telehealth and streamlined virtual platforms [3] offer solutions that address access barriers to centers with MTB capability; however, limited research or involvement of Indigenous peoples limits our knowledge of the impact of MTBs on Indigenous populations. We are beginning to see the benefits of molecularly guided therapy in cancer patients, particularly those with tumors that have traditionally been difficult to treat. However, significant work remains to ensure this promise reaches Indigenous cancer patients [4, 5], beginning with overcoming crucial limitations.

Limitations of Genomics in Oncology

Historically, the deployment of new technological solutions has often served to widen inequalities between populations defined by socioeconomic position, ethnicity, gender, or geographical location. Simply implementing new technologies into current health systems does not achieve health equity in and of itself for several important reasons. First, our current health systems already underperform for Indigenous populations (Fig. 77.1b). Outcomes are often worse for Indigenous peoples as a result of cumulative inequities along the cancer care continuum. Second, access to medicines that target specific biomarkers is gatekept by access to relevant testing and technology. Geographically, this favors major metropolitan communities in wealthier countries, as comprehensive genomic profiling is mostly limited to well-resourced, research-capable facilities. Socioeconomically, this favors individuals/countries with the means to access testing and treatment. Moreover, Indigenous peoples around the world are disproportionately affected by inequities in the social determinants of health shaped by ongoing histories of colonization [6].

Third, Indigenous peoples remain poorly represented in genome-wide association studies (GWAS),[6] despite improvements to the overall proportion of peoples of non-European ancestry within GWAS datasets globally [4]. Lack of

[5] **DNA or gene variant**: different versions of the same gene, representing variations or alterations in the DNA sequence of a gene, which may alter the function of that gene. Variants can be harmless or pathogenic.

[6] **Genome-wide association study (GWAS)**: a study that scans entire genomes to find genetic variants associated with a particular disease, often requiring large sample populations.

Indigenous background variant databases (BVD)[7] for the interpretation of targeted gene panels[8] and genome sequencing poses problems with diagnostic accuracy for Indigenous patients, as current non-representative BVDs are used for diagnosis via clinical genomic variant analysis [4, 7].

As nations expand the use of comprehensive genomic profiling in oncology services and as new genomic research seeks to address the lack of representation in genomic databases, we must not follow the same pathway taken by previous genetic and genomic research, causing further harm to Indigenous communities [4, 7]. Indigenous peoples often choose to participate in research not for their own immediate or direct benefit, but to contribute to the health and wellbeing of future generations. However, such altruism must never come at the cost of exposure to unsafe research environments or harmful data-use practices. Genomic research involving Indigenous peoples needs to be rights-based and Indigenous-led, addressing Indigenous priorities, and with appropriate governance. What should this look like in the context of precision cancer research and clinical care?

Generating the Relevant Data to Support Precision Oncology

First, we need genomic data that serve Indigenous communities. To achieve this, relevant Indigenous BVDs need to be developed to support rapid and accurate interpretation of genomic tests, to avoid the needless pursuit of variants as potential disease candidates when those variants may simply be alternatives to currently available reference genomes. A comprehensive understanding of how genetics affects medicine safety and efficacy is essential. Pharmacogenomics focuses on gene variants involved in the metabolism of a wide range of medicines. Pharmacogenomic tests are crucial for ensuring that cancer medicines are given at doses that are safe (i.e., the medicine itself is not causing greater harm) and efficacious (i.e., the medicine achieves clinical benefit). We also need to understand the genomic profile of cancers impacting Indigenous patients in order to best inform the prioritization of cancer medications in the oncology "medicine cabinet" available to Indigenous communities. Many cancer-causing variants of key genes (e.g., *TP53*, *KRAS*, *BRAF*) have been identified across human cancers, but at the current rate, it seems unlikely that genomic research will identify any cancer-causing variants unique to Indigenous peoples at the population level. However, appropriate research platforms should also be capable of responding to variants of unknown significance (VUS)[9] as they emerge from genomic tests involving Indigenous patients. Ethical frameworks for genomics research have already been developed and published by Indigenous scholars to inform best practice [8], including specific examples in cancer genomic research [5]. Indeed, Indigenous-led or co-designed clinical genomic research platforms and clinical tools are being developed for the purpose of better diagnostics and clinical decision-making for Indigenous peoples.

The Australian Alliance for Indigenous Genomics (ALIGN) is an Indigenous-led national alliance representing a commitment from academia, industry, government, and Indigenous communities to work collectively to develop a framework, designed by and for Indigenous people, to deliver the benefit of genomic medicine to all Australians. Core activities include establishing Indigenous governance over genomics research and clinical care, developing best practice data systems and data sovereignty, outlining key genomics policy, and growing capacity in Indigenous genomics. These represent key foundations for ensuring that Indigenous Australians benefit from genomics. Flagship programs will include focusing on pharmacogenomics, precision medicine, genome biology, and rare diseases.

The Rakeiora Project is a pathfinder project that seeks to identify the best means to enable national-scale genomic precision medicine research and practice in Aotearoa New Zealand. Rakeiora consists of two pathways, one for primary care and one for secondary care, with the latter taking place in oncology settings co-led by Dr Helen Wihongi (Ngāti Porou, Ngāpuhi, Te Whānau a Āpanui, Ngāti Hine) and Professor Cristin Print. Rakeiora has established a prototype cancer genomic medicine research information technology (IT) system co-designed and co-led with/by Māori, with tikanga Māori (Māori cultural protocols or principles) at its core. While Rakeiora currently focuses on translational research, it seeks to be scalable to clinical settings.

Access to and Governance over Key Research Infrastructure

Genomic research to address the clinically focused applications described above, including Indigenous background variant databases, pharmacogenomics, and targeted therapy, requires, as one key infrastructure pillar, the development and appropriate governance of biobanks. Tissues generously donated by participants to enable research have been instrumental in driving medical science, innovation, and clinical

[7]**Background variant database (BVD)**: a database of all the DNA variants in a population of people without severe genetic conditions.

[8]**Targeted gene panel**: a genetic test consisting of a predetermined set of genes known to be associated with a disease or condition.

[9]**Variant of unknown significance (VUS)**: a variant identified through testing that does not have a well-established association with a specific disease or condition, making it unclear whether it is benign or pathogenic in nature.

care. Often tissues are collected with consent to address defined questions. However, the rapid advancement of genomic and imaging technologies, biobanks, and, more importantly, the precious tissues and data stewarded within, will enable future investigations of cancer biology and novel treatments, including questions we have not yet thought to ask. However, this powerful research requires donors to consent to future unspecified use of their tissues, causing tension among Indigenous donors, which can be understood in the context of cultural understandings of the connection of bodily substances to place and ancestors, the information contained within, the beneficence of researchers, and concepts of ownership [9]. Another critical tension that requires attention is the power imbalance between institutions and Indigenous communities or Tribal authorities. Indigenous peoples are often asked to gift their tissues and their trust to institutions that may be resistant to suggestions of Indigenous data sovereignty or Tribal authority over how these tissues will be used [10]. By extension, Indigenous peoples require reassurance of the benefits that they and their communities will derive from the sharing of these materials.

From a rights-based perspective, Indigenous governance over Indigenous genomic resources *can* be asserted through the United Nations Declaration on the Rights of Indigenous Peoples (UNDRIP), but this requires nation-states to sufficiently and sustainably resource such endeavors as redress (in part) for land alienation, cultural subjugation, and the subsequent inequities borne out of colonization. However, existing complexities within legislative approaches to the protection of traditional knowledges and Indigenous cultural and intellectual property remain significant ongoing issues to the acknowledgment and protection of Indigenous peoples' rights in genomics and biomedical research.

The Northern British Columbia (BC) First Nations Biobank is a project in development in partnership with the BC First Nations Health Authority and the 55 First Nations of Northern BC. First Nations biobank governance—founded on over 10 years of community discussions, First Nations–led consultations, and ongoing presentations to First Nations leaders—aims to create an independent First Nations biobank to enable communities to have the choice to participate in and benefit from future cancer-focused genomic research. At the core of this project are, *inter alia*, governance and Indigenous data sovereignty, and the implementation of cultural approaches to consent, stewardship, and research oversight.

Growing an Indigenous Workforce to Lead and Deliver Precision Oncology and Research

Building the infrastructure to support comprehensive genomic profiling in clinical services and research is only part of the solution. We need an Indigenous workforce to ensure that Indigenous populations benefit from benchtop to bedside, and beyond. From a healthcare delivery perspective, this includes Indigenous family physicians, surgeons, oncologists, radiation oncologists, nurses, pharmacists, geneticists, variant curators, and bioinformaticians to support the accurate interpretation of genomic data in clinical contexts. From a medical science perspective, in the delivery of relevant datasets and tools to support clinical decision-making and monitoring, this includes Indigenous researchers in key leadership roles in cancer genomic research, from basic science through to designing, steering, and running clinical trials, in addition to managing, maintaining, and governing established biobanks, cancer genome atlases, or BVDs containing Indigenous samples, DNA, or data. An increase in Indigenous capacity in clinical and research spaces would be further enhanced by an Indigenous presence on MTBs. Moreover, the sustainable inclusion of Indigenous voice and leadership within MTBs should be considered a vital addition to technical, scientific, and medical expertise when considering treatment for Indigenous patients, to ensure that the emerging benefits of MTBs [2] reach Indigenous patients.

The Summer Internship for Indigenous Peoples in Genomics (SING) Workshop is a week-long internship for Indigenous students and community members to learn the fundamental concepts of genomics and bioinformatics, as well as their cultural, ethical, legal, and social implications (CELSI) [4, 8]. SING is a "for Indigenous, by Indigenous" model of capability and leadership development that, since its inception in the United States in 2011, has expanded globally to include SING-Aotearoa (New Zealand) since 2016, SING-Canada since 2018, SING-Australia since 2019, and SING-Mexico since 2023. Given the application of genomic technologies to cancer research and treatment, Indigenous cancer clinicians and researchers contribute their expertise to SING as faculty members in their respective countries as well as reciprocally between countries, and a growing number of SING alumni are beginning careers or hold positions in cancer-related fields and careers around the world, or serve in community-based Indigenous leadership and advisory roles.

While such efforts are essential for Indigenous self-determination and must be prioritized if organizations are truly committed to achieving health equity globally, growing the Indigenous workforce is not enough. Given the demographic minority occupied by Indigenous peoples, it is critical that healthcare providers and researchers are called upon to adopt cultural safety and critical consciousness practices [11] to ensure the wellbeing of Indigenous patients and the families who accompany them on their cancer care journey, as well as the wellbeing of Indigenous students, colleagues, Elders, and communities involved in research. Healthcare systems must implement and enforce policies to demand such respect and cultural safety and have zero tolerance for the Indigenous-specific racism that has been highlighted in personal stories, media coverage, and formal inquiries [12]. The absence of cultural safety greatly impacts access to and utilization of all cancer care services and the research that can greatly impact those services. Such a task involves each one of us, with the concept of reconciliation increasingly emerging as a necessary step that we are still far from achieving.

Conclusion

Globally, oncology services embrace the power of genomics to inform precise cancer care for individual patients. Indigenous cancer patients have a right to the best standard of care, including molecularly guided therapy, while maintaining the right to self-determination about the best path forward for them. No matter how promising a new technology may be, implementation into existing health systems is not enough to achieve health equity. We must learn from the past, prioritize Indigenous-led cancer care (including genomics research infrastructure), and grow an Indigenous workforce to sustainably ensure that genomics-guided precision oncology reaches all who need it, while maintaining the Indigenous right to self-determination.

References

1. Mateo J, Steuten L, Aftimos P, André F, Davies M, Garralda E, et al. Delivering precision oncology to patients with cancer. *Nat Med.* 2022;28(4):658–65. https://doi.org/10.1038/s41591-022-01717-2
2. Kato S, Kim KH, Lim HJ, Boichard A, Nikanjam M, Weihe E, et al. Real-world data from a molecular tumor board demonstrates improved outcomes with a precision N-of-One strategy. *Nat Commun.* 2020;11(1):4965. https://doi.org/10.1038/s41467-020-18613-3
3. Tamborero D, Dienstmann R, Rachid MH, Boekel J, Lopez-Fernandez A, Jonsson M, et al. The Molecular Tumor Board Portal supports clinical decisions and automated reporting for precision oncology. *Nat Cancer.* 2022;3(2):251–61. https://doi.org/10.1038/s43018-022-00332-x
4. Garrison NA, Hudson M, Ballantyne LL, Garba I, Martinez A, Taualii M, et al. Genomic Research Through an Indigenous Lens: Understanding the Expectations. *Annu Rev Genomics Hum Genet.* 2019;20(1):495–517. https://doi.org/10.1146/annurev-genom-083118-015434
5. Henare KL, Parker KE, Wihongi H, Blenkiron C, Jansen R, Reid P, et al. Mapping a route to Indigenous engagement in cancer genomic research. *Lancet Oncol.* 2019;20(6):e327–e35. https://doi.org/10.1016/S1470-2045(19)30307-9
6. King M, Smith A, Gracey M. Indigenous health part 2: the underlying causes of the health gap. *Lancet.* 2009;374(9683):76–85. https://doi.org/10.1016/S0140-6736(09)60827-8
7. Caron NR, Chongo M, Hudson M, Arbour L, Wasserman WW, Robertson S, et al. Indigenous Genomic Databases: Pragmatic Considerations and Cultural Contexts. *Front Public Health.* 2020;8:111. https://doi.org/10.3389/fpubh.2020.00111
8. Claw KG, Anderson MZ, Begay RL, Tsosie KS, Fox K, Garrison NA. A framework for enhancing ethical genomic research with Indigenous communities. *Nat Commun.* 2018;9(1):2957. https://doi.org/10.1038/s41467-018-05188-3
9. Aramoana J, Koea J. An Integrative Review of the Barriers to Indigenous Peoples Participation in Biobanking and Genomic Research. *JCO Glob Oncol.* 2020(6):83–91. https://doi.org/10.1200/JGO.18.00156
10. Tsosie KS, Yracheta JM, Kolopenuk JA, Geary J. We Have "Gifted" Enough: Indigenous Genomic Data Sovereignty in Precision Medicine. *Am J Bioeth.* 2021;21(4):72–5. https://doi.org/10.1080/15265161.2021.1891347
11. Curtis E, Jones R, Tipene-Leach D, Walker C, Loring B, Paine S-J, et al. Why cultural safety rather than cultural competency is required to achieve health equity: a literature review and recommended definition. *Int J Equity Health.* 2019;18(1):174. https://doi.org/10.1186/s12939-019-1082-3
12. Turpel-Lafond M. *In Plain Sight: Addressing Indigenous-specific Racism and Discrimination in BC Health Care.* BC Ministry of Health; 2020. Available from: https://engage.gov.bc.ca/app/uploads/sites/613/2020/11/In-Plain-Sight-Summary-Report.pdf

Index

G. Garvey (ed.), *Indigenous and Tribal Peoples and Cancer*, https://doi.org/10.1007/978-3-031-56806-0